This Book Belongs to

BoBBY J

D0594183

THE BOSS

Militant
Scargill and the Miners
The March of Militant
Manchester United: The Betrayal of a Legend (*with David Smith*)
Jeffrey Archer: Stranger Than Fiction
The Complete Manchester United Trivia Fact Book
Michael Heseltine: A Biography

THE BOSS

The Many Sides of Alex Ferguson

This Book Belongs to Bobby Johnstone

MICHAEL CRICK

SIMON & SCHUSTER

London · New York · Sydney · Tokyo · Singapore · Toronto · Dublin

A VIACOM COMPANY

First published in Great Britain by Simon & Schuster UK Ltd in 2002
A Viacom Company

1 3 5 7 9 10 8 6 4 2

Simon & Schuster UK Ltd
Africa House
64–78 Kingsway
London WC2B 6AH

Simon & Schuster Australia
Sydney

www.simonsays.co.uk

A CIP catalogue for this book is available
from the British Library.

ISBN: 0-7432-0748-3

Typeset in Berkeley by M Rules
Printed and bound in Great Britain
by The Bath Press, Bath

Contents

Contents

Preface

What a 'marvellous achievement' said the female admirer who had just tapped Alex Ferguson on the shoulder. The elegantly dressed lady had shown a surprising interest in football for someone of her background, expressing the view that Manchester United's historic treble might never be achieved by an English club ever again. 'I have to agree with that,' replied a beaming Ferguson. Except that now he was Sir Alex, thanks to the small ceremony just performed by the elderly lady with whom he was in conversation.[1]

I wasn't present, of course, when Alex Ferguson went to Buckingham Palace to receive his knighthood from the Queen in July 1999. But I did witness every moment of the thrilling climax to Manchester United's great treble season, and those incredible eleven days in May when the club collected the Premier League title in Manchester, the FA Cup in London, and the European Cup in Barcelona. I have been following Manchester United home and away for more than thirty years – since I was twelve – which means I was fortunate enough to see the Reds lift all but one of the fourteen major trophies collected during Alex Ferguson's sixteen-year reign at Old Trafford. Indirectly, the United manager has given me hundreds of hours of entertainment, excitement and enjoyment; his teams have provided so many magical moments that I treasure. And I estimate that I have watched around three-quarters of United's games during Ferguson's time at the club, a figure which would be greater but for my working for two years in America at the end of the 1980s.

Alex Ferguson has been prolific in his own literary output, and not shy to relate his accomplishments in British football, both at United and before that at Aberdeen. The best-known volume on the shelf of Fergiana is his highly readable and best-selling autobiography, *Managing My Life*, which was published in the glorious summer of 1999, but this is only the most substantial of the seven books he has written. Sir Alex's writing career began with his 1985 account of the Aberdeen years, *A Light in the North*, and was followed by records of his early struggle at Old Trafford, *Six Years at United* (1992), and then his first English league title, *Just Champion!* (1993). Since then there have also been two volumes of diaries, *A Year in the Life* (1995) and *A Will to Win* (1997), and finally his story of the 1998–99 season, *The Unique Treble* (2000). An eighth book, provisionally entitled *The Final Furlong*, is also promised. Until now, Sir Alex has pretty much cornered the market in recounting his career, apart from Stephen F. Kelly's 1997 book *Fergie*, and Harry Harris's compilation of Ferguson stories, *The Ferguson Effect* (1999), both of which left much unexplored. There have also been several videos and television programmes, though his broadcast output has mostly been produced with his editorial control or veto.

As a curious journalist, a United fan, and also a bit-part player in some of Manchester United's more recent history, I felt that there must be much more to the Alex Ferguson story, and that it would be worth re-examining more thoroughly every episode of a fascinating and complex life, and viewing things from other angles. So it has proved. Indeed, when I started on my long biographical journey in the middle of 2001, I did not appreciate quite how fascinating, or just how many sides to Sir Alex there would turn out to be.

I have established a personal practice as a biographer of not seeking the co-operation or blessing of my subjects, as I think it is important not to become dependent on them. Ferguson was in any case unlikely to agree to co-operate, having only recently published his own autobiography, and given his reputation for insisting on an abnormal degree of control in his dealings with journalists. Nonetheless, in March 2001 I wrote to Sir Alex to tell him what I was doing. I did not receive a reply, but he never indicated directly to me that he was hostile to my work. Indeed, he appeared happy to let many of his closest friends talk to my research team or to me, though I was surprised at how little some of them had to say. I got the impression that one or two had been advised to be very guarded in their comments, and the result was that they did not do justice to his compelling personality. Sir Alex's brother Martin was a notable exception, granting two long and highly revealing interviews. The United manager's sons Mark and Jason, in contrast, were very frosty when I approached them. Manchester United's attitude was even more difficult to fathom. Officially the line from Old Trafford was 'Don't help,' an instruction which was often ignored by many senior figures within the club.

This book attempts to apply the stringent methods one expects of a political, literary or scientific biography to a field where books often seem to have more to do with merchandising and PR. Indeed, the currency of most football books is anecdote, gossip and hyperbole. That's why this is probably the first football book aimed at the mass market to contain source references. I like to think that no biography of any character in English football history has been investigated more thoroughly. My research team has conducted interviews with at least 250 people – Ferguson's friends and colleagues, associates and admirers, rivals and enemies. While it would take an unjustifiable amount of space to name them all here, I am grateful to them all for their time and insights. Most of those who spoke on the record are cited in the references; others, perhaps conscious that football can be an unforgiving business, asked not to have their comments attributed.

I must also thank certain individuals who particularly went out of their way to help. These include several historians at Scottish clubs: Hector Cook at Queen's Park; Duncan Simpson at Dunfermline; Michael White at Falkirk; Duncan Carmichael at Ayr United; and Kevin Stirling at Aberdeen. Jim Crawford at St Mirren and Richard McBrearty at the Scottish Football Museum were also a great help. Especially co-operative among newspaper people were Kevin Collins at the Express Group and Ian Watson of the *Glasgow Evening Times* over the picture research, and Ray Smith of the News International cuttings library. Sadly, as becomes clear in Chapter 26, several others in the media were too frightened of Ferguson to assist me.

Alan McKinlay of the University of St Andrews looked into Ferguson's years as an engineering toolmaker and trade unionist. Sean Magee guided me through the unfamiliar world of horseracing. Jim White and Sue Simpson both offered wise advice, and between them recommended three wonderful researchers.

Rochelle Libson did a very thorough organisational job in finding and collating everything that has ever been written or broadcast by or about Alex Ferguson, and her work will eventually be made available to future historians. Angus Dixon did the work in Scotland almost single-handed, wading through Ferguson's early years and the records of nine different clubs, and taking this ignorant Englishman through the complexities of Scottish football and culture. Alex Millar conducted most of the interviews and investigative work covering Ferguson's career at Old Trafford. Alex displayed at twenty-two all the journalistic skills and experience of someone twice his age: he is set for a successful career in the media world, whether as a reporter, writer, broadcaster or editor. Thanks also to Chris and Margaret Kirrane for being so accommodating and incredibly helpful to Alex during his work in Manchester. I also had great assistance from Chris Green, David Conn and Nick Menzies. Iain McCartney provided access to his voluminous collection of Manchester United cuttings.

Andrew Curry knocked my words into a presentable form, as usual; one day the extent of his role in rewriting my books will be exposed, to the embarrassment of both of us. Bob Davenport scoured my text for any ambiguities and inconsistencies; it's an agonising process, but good for me, and nobody does it better than Bob. My agent Bill Hamilton negotiated my contract and nobly read the resulting work despite not liking football. Andrew Gordon has been a calm and understanding editor, while my publisher and fellow United fan Ian Chapman was enthusiastic and encouraging, particularly when I needed it most.

I am also indebted to Steve Condie and Paula Davies for their work on the accompanying BBC documentary, along with the camera team, Neville Kidd, Douglas Kerr and Stephen Mochrie.

Finally, my thanks to Catherine for being so tolerant. You can now use the computer again.

Michael Crick
April 2002

The Boy Out of Govan

'When the wind's howling down the Clyde, that's what forges your character.'

ALEX FERGUSON[1]

Nothing could be clearer. Or less clear, to those who have difficulty with the Glaswegian accent. 'AHCUMFIGOVIN' declares the sign in capital letters on his office wall at the Manchester United training ground. 'I come from Govan.' Not Glasgow, he insists, but Govan.

At the start of the twentieth century Govan was one of the great workshops of the British Empire. 'Within its boundaries, it is impossible to get beyond the sound of the hammer,' wrote one observer. 'From early morning till late at night we hear the continuous hum of industry.'[2] By the middle of the century, Clydeside on the west coast of Scotland was the shipbuilding capital of the globe, and Govan boasted three famous yards – Alexander Stephen, Fairfields, and Harland & Wolff. 'You couldn't sleep at night for the noise of the riveters and cawkers on the night shift,' Alex Ferguson once said. 'It was murder, it was agony. But it embedded a spirit and a sense of community in everybody that was passed from father to son, and it also taught the meaning of hard work.'[3]

Govan was originally a quiet fishing and farming village, but its fame and prosperity were founded on shipbuilding after the first yard opened in 1840. Govanites regarded themselves as a community separate from Glasgow, and in the late nineteenth century Govan was a separate burgh, before the growing City of Glasgow finally gobbled it up in 1912. '*Nihil Sine Labore*' proclaimed the Govan coat of arms – 'Nothing Without Work'. Like all the best mottos, it can be read in different ways, and seems particularly apt for the subject of this biography.

Govan today, with its depressing blocks of council flats and neglected open spaces, has lost much of the vibrancy it enjoyed during Alex Ferguson's childhood, though its new science parks and television studios may prompt a revival in the twenty-first century. In the mid twentieth century, when its population was three times greater than today, much of Govan consisted of dense rows of tenements – the blocks of cramped flats which housed much of the working population of Glasgow. There grew the roots upon which Alex Ferguson places so much emphasis, and he often likes to repeat the local saying 'You can take a boy out of Govan but you can't take Govan out of a boy.'[4]

The Fergusons originally lived at 6 Broomloan Road, next to a bakery on one of the main streets of Govan. Not long after Alex was born, they moved round the corner to a first-floor flat above a pub, at 667 Govan Road, on the corner with Neptune Street, where the family had what was considered to be the luxury of an inside lavatory. The property was demolished years ago, to make way for a fire station, though appropriately the site next door is occupied by an all-weather football surface.

The family lived only a few hundred yards from the southern bank of the Clyde, the river which provided work for most of the local community. The shipbuilding industry dominated the town. Between the wars, members of the royal family had regularly travelled to Glasgow to launch a succession of luxury liners, and during

2

the Second World War the yards built warships for the Royal Navy.

The Ferguson family had worked in shipbuilding for generations: in official records, Sir Alex's grandfather, John Ferguson, is described as a 'ship plater's helper' and his great-grandfather, Robert Ferguson, as a 'riveter'. Alex's father started as a labourer, helping the platers to fix the great steel panels on ships.

Previous generations of Fergusons had hailed from the other side of the Clyde, about twelve miles further downstream from Glasgow. They lived first in Renton – just north of the river – and then in the nearby port of Dumbarton (where the *Cutty Sark* was launched in 1869). Living in these two Dunbartonshire towns in the last two decades of the nineteenth century, the Ferguson family was inevitably caught up in the exceptional success the area briefly enjoyed in Scottish football. In the fifteen years from 1874 to 1888 three neighbouring Dunbartonshire sides – Renton, Dumbarton and Vale of Leven – won six Scottish Cup finals, and later, in 1891 and 1892, Dumbarton won the first two Scottish championship titles, the first time jointly with Rangers. It was remarkable that such football success should be concentrated within only two or three square miles. Renton and Vale of Leven football clubs are long gone, while today Dumbarton languishes in the Scottish Third Division.

For a time, the success of Dunbartonshire football extended beyond Scotland. In the early years of the English FA Cup and the Scottish Cup it was traditional to hold a challenge match between the two winners, and in 1888, when Renton faced West Bromwich Albion at Hampden Park, this was billed as the 'Championship of the World' – with some justification, since there was still no organised club football beyond Britain's shores. One hundred and twelve years before Alex Ferguson's Manchester United team failed to attain a similar title in Brazil, Renton defeated their English challengers 4–1.

But the three neighbouring Dunbartonshire clubs were slow to turn professional. Before long, most of the best players were lured to clubs in Glasgow or England who were happily prepared to pay them – though it's said that at one point vigilante committees were formed in Dumbarton to chase predatory scouts out of town.

If shipbuilding was a Ferguson family tradition, so too was football. Sir Alex Ferguson's grandfather, John Ferguson, played at centre-half for Dumbarton before the First World War, by which time the team had fallen into the Scottish Second Division. Sir Alex's father (who was also an Alex, so I'll call him Alex Snr) was born in Renton in 1912, and also became a keen player. When his widowed mother remarried and moved to north Glasgow in the 1920s, Alex Snr won the Scottish Boys' Club Cup with Hamiltonhill. But his greatest footballing success, according to his sons, came during the 1930s, when the family moved briefly to Northern Ireland and Alex Snr worked in the famous Harland & Wolff shipyard in Belfast. 'His own football career reached its high point in Belfast,' says Sir Alex, 'when he played for Glentoran alongside the man he said was the finest player he ever saw, the great Peter Doherty.'[5] If Alex Snr did play for Glentoran it seems to have been at a pretty minor level, for the club historian can find no record of any Ferguson playing for the first team in the late 1920s or early 1930s. (His attempt to obtain further details from Sir Alex himself met with no response.)[6] 'Like me, he was a bit on the slow side,' Sir Alex's younger brother, Martin, says of their father as a player. But 'He was two-footed – he could use both feet.'[7]

Alex Ferguson Snr had been one of the brightest pupils at his secondary school, and his headmaster had pleaded in vain with his mother to let him stay on beyond the age of fourteen. 'My gran wanted him to go out and work,' Martin Ferguson explains. 'It's a shame, because his talents were wasted. He was a bright, bright fella.'[8] After Belfast, Alex Snr had a spell in Birmingham working for the engineering company BSA, before the family returned to Glasgow, where he got a job in the Govan shipyards and soon met his future wife.

Elizabeth Hardie was almost ten years younger than Alex. The daughter of a Glasgow tram conductor, she was a true Govanite, having been born and brought up in the district. Liz or Lizzie, as she was known, spent her working life in local industry. At the time of her marriage to Alex, in the summer of 1941, she was employed in a rubber factory, and she later worked in a munitions plant in Craigton, but for most of her working life she was employed at Christie's Wire Works on Broomloan Road, near the family home. Today the building houses the Govan Initiative regeneration project and is named Ferguson House in honour of the area's most distinguished son.

Liz was three months pregnant when she married Alex Ferguson at St Mary's Church of Scotland on Govan Road, where baby Alex was christened the following year. When brother Martin arrived less than twelve months later, at the end of 1942, their family was complete. It was unusually small for working-class Scots.

Sir Alex Ferguson was born not in the heart of Govan, but a mile or so to the west, at 357 Shieldhall Road in West Drumoyne – an area which he calls 'an extension' of Govan.[9] The council house, then his paternal grandparents' home, still stands – one of a nondescript terrace – though today the area is dominated by a busy dual-carriageway overpass running from the M8 motorway to the Clyde Tunnel. 'They should have a plaque up there, you know,' Ferguson joked when visiting the site for a TV documentary a few years ago, '"This beast was born here."'[10] And underneath, presumably, would be the date: 31 December 1941 – New Year's Eve, or Hogmanay.

He was christened Alexander Chapman Ferguson, taking his first name from his father, though both men would always be known as 'Alec' to family and friends. His middle name, 'Chapman', came via a great-aunt on his father's side, who had married a man called Alex Chapman. (So, by coincidence, Alex Ferguson carried as his middle name the surname of one of the greatest English club bosses of all time – Herbert Chapman, manager of Huddersfield Town in the 1920s and of Arsenal in the 1930s.)

Although he was born on the outskirts of Govan, Sir Alex Ferguson spent his childhood in the heart of the district. It was wartime, of course, but, while many bombs dropped on Clydeside, the Fergusons don't seem to have felt they were in much danger. Martin Ferguson says his father was 'desperate to join up'. He applied to both the Army and the Navy, Martin says, but they rejected him because shipbuilding was a reserved occupation. The story goes that Alex Snr was eventually accepted by the RAF, but his wife refused to let him go. 'Apparently our mother took Alec and me up in her arms and dumped us on the table and said, "If you're taking my husband you can take them as well." And that was the end of it.'[11]

Glasgow and the Clyde area had close links to Northern Ireland, and for much of the twentieth century the west of Scotland was almost as divided as Ulster (and reacting to that sectarianism was to play a crucial role in Alex Ferguson's life). Unusually, two past generations of Fergusons had mixed marriages from a religious point of view. In 1912 John Ferguson was a Catholic while his wife, Jenny, was a Protestant. In 1941 Sir Alex Ferguson's father was a Protestant and his mother a Catholic. In both cases the couples brought their children up as Protestants, probably because even after the Second World War it could still do serious harm to your job prospects to declare that you had gone to a Catholic school – and the question of your schooling was frequently asked.

In Govan the majority was Protestant, though there were also large enclaves of Irish Catholics – Neptune Street, for instance, right next to the Fergusons' home, was known as 'the Irish Channel'. Govan was in fact a bastion of the Protestant Orange Order, which held great celebrations on 12 July every summer. 'The Govan Orange Walk used to come along the Govan Road,' says Martin Ferguson, 'and sometimes you'd get a bit of bother – not often, but sometimes.

It was usually caused by people watching it rather than taking part – people drinking and that. Other than that it generally went by pretty peacefully.'[12]

Religion permeated Glasgow football to the core. Rangers were a Protestant team; Celtic, with their name and green-and-white hooped shirts, were Catholic. And the supporters of each club hated those of the other with a sectarian intensity which it would be hard for English fans to comprehend. In Govan most local bars were either Rangers haunts or frequented by Celtic fans. Sam Gilmour, a former shop-steward convener at the Fairfields ship-yard, says the strip along the Govan riverside 'was mainly Celtic pubs, but move about twenty yards inland and they were all Rangers pubs'. But it didn't always follow that the pubs' customers were Catholic or Protestant in accordance with the clubs' tradi-tional religious affiliations. 'In the street where Alex Ferguson came from,' says Gilmour, 'they called them all Roman Protestants, because they were all Celtic supporters. Even the Proddies were Celtic supporters!'[13]

The Ferguson family could never escape from the sights, the smell and the incessant sound of shipbuilding. Their tenement flat on Govan Road was overshadowed by the tall cranes of Harland & Wolff – an offshoot of the Belfast yard, whose workforce, even in Govan, was substantially of Ulster Protestant origin. Sir Alex's father now worked for a rival firm, Fairfields, half a mile downriver, which employed 4–5,000 people. (The yard still exists, though much reduced in size after numerous changes of ownership in recent times.) Alex Snr worked for Fairfields for most of his forty years on Clydeside, and Sir Alex subsequently named his Cheshire home 'Fairfields', in tribute to his father's toil.

Alex Snr eventually became an assistant timekeeper at Fairfields – not the most popular job in the yard. 'Timekeepers are normally uni-versally detested,' says Sam Gilmour. 'But he wasn't a mug. He was hard but fair. I never heard a bad word about him – which was extremely unusual. He wasn't Santa Claus, but "respect" is the way I would put it. He was straight as a die.'[14]

Sir Alex's close friend, the journalist Hugh McIlvanney, has written much about the fact that four of Britain's greatest-ever football managers – Matt Busby, Jock Stein, Bill Shankly and Alex Ferguson – were all brought up in tough working-class communities within the twenty-five-mile arc of the Clyde Valley. Unlike Ferguson, however, Busby, Stein and Shankly were all from mining stock.

But in many ways conditions in the shipyards were just as harsh as underground. Nowadays most ships are built inside huge, cavernous buildings, but in the past the work was done in the open air, which could be very unpleasant in winter. If the men wanted to be paid, they had to carry on working in wind, rain and snow. Sir Alex is a great believer in the unintended benefits of such a hard environment, though he never worked in the yards himself. 'That is exactly what formulates character – having to work on the top of a ship in the middle of winter with the wind howling down the Clyde. It's character when people have to work with rags round their hands because it's so cold the metal burns you when you touch it.'[15]

Alex Ferguson often speaks about the day he came across one of his father's wage packets. 'I was quite young at the time, about ten or eleven,' he says:

> It was for £7. Now £7 was £7, a reasonable amount in those days. But it took him about twenty hours on top of his basic week in the yards to earn it. They did forty-eight hours at the time and my dad would work a Tuesday and Thursday night, a Saturday morning and all-day Sunday on top. So that must have made about sixty-eight hours in all – for £7.[16]

Sir Alex remembers his father as a 'strict disciplinarian . . . who taught me the values of life and the values within yourself, but there was no family in our area that wasn't like that'.[17] Alex Snr, says

Ferguson, was 'the one who drove me on as a kid, who never allowed me to be satisfied'.[18]

Their father would very occasionally lose his temper, according to Martin Ferguson. 'He was a very impatient man. He was quick, he was fiery – exactly like Alec. That's where Alec gets it from,' he says. 'Alec and him had a few clashes in their day.'[19]

Ferguson seems also to have inherited his father's obsessive punctuality. 'My mother used to say that [my father] opened the gates at the yard in the mornings,' he says.[20] And Alex Snr was as demanding of his family. When he arrived home in the evening he expected his hot supper to be ready on the table, which meant his mother needed to get the timing perfect. Young Alex would be sent to spot his father coming home from the shipyard. 'To get it right,' Ferguson once explained, 'I had to watch him coming up the road. I would see all the workers teeming out of the yards, a sea of bunnets, because everyone wore caps. I could pick out my dad half a mile away by the way he walked.'[21] As he came up the street, young Alec would cry out, 'He's at Harland & Wolff, now he's at the Plaza cinema.'[22]

On Friday nights another duty was to collect his father's evening treat from the fish-and-chip shop across the road. Alex hated doing this, for the manageress never called him by his proper name, Alec or Alex, or even Alexander, but 'Sandra'.[23] It was humiliating.

Liz Ferguson ran a happy home, full of talk, laughter, fun and singing. As she did her household chores, she'd have the wireless tuned to music. Martin Ferguson recalls how their mother also loved singing to herself, just as his brother does today. 'Any music – just as long as the radio was on, she used to sing away. She was a good singer. My father wasn't a bad singer either, and all his family were singers. So when we had all the family in the house – my father's family and sisters and brothers and all that – there was always a good sing-song.'[24]

While Alex Ferguson inherited the disciplined side of his

character from his father, the genes from his mother seem to have made the decisive difference. 'People used to say I was like my father,' he observes, 'but I think people who really knew my father say I was more like my mother, because she had a fantastic determination, incredible determination.'[25] Martin Ferguson agrees. 'She never walked anywhere,' he says. 'She always ran a hundred miles an hour.'[26]

Liz Ferguson was the more dominant of the two parents, particularly at home. Despite his occasional temper, Alex Snr was generally more quiet, even reserved. It was only later that the Ferguson sons realised how respected their father was in the Govan community. People called him 'Big Fergie' – he was only 5 feet 10½ inches high, but that was quite tall at the time. Sir Alex recalls how, when he'd achieved fame as a football manager, he visited a Govan bowls club to present the annual trophies. 'Someone pointed me out to this old guy as Alex Ferguson's boy. And the old man simply turned to me and said: "You'll never be as good as your father."'[27] Similarly, Martin Ferguson recollects the day he went to see the Fairfields' personnel manager for a job: 'He asked my name and what school I went to – the usual things – and did I "have any relations that work in here"? And I said, "My dad works in here," and he said, "Who's your dad?" "Alec Ferguson." He said, "Are you Fergie's boy? Start Monday." So he was obviously well known, my dad.'[28]

Apart from poverty, Govan's biggest social problem was alcohol. It's said there were more than fifty bars along a mile of the Govan Road, and drinking was a serious occupation for many people. The Fergusons themselves lived directly above two pubs – the Victoria Bar and Dick Welsh's, which was popular with Celtic supporters. But Alex Snr wasn't tempted, say his sons. 'We were very fortunate: my father wasn't a big drinker,' Martin Ferguson recalls. 'He would have the odd drink, but I think I can only recall seeing my father drunk once.'[29] If he had any indulgence at all, it was gambling. Bookmakers' shops were then illegal, so the boys were deputed to take their father's stakes to unlicensed bookies. These took bets under a system of code names, in case they were caught by the police, and operated through networks of runners. One of them, Jimmy Shearin, ran his illegal business from the flat above the Fergusons. 'He would have people all over the place down the streets and they would bring the bets to him,' Sir Alex once recalled. 'He would honour them or pocket the money. That was the environment, the habitat, I was in. It was natural for people from that area to have a bet.'[30]

It was, of course, a deprived existence by modern standards. The Fergusons' flat was very small. The kitchen, with its cooking range, roaring coal fire and big hearth, also had to serve as living room, parents' bedroom and bathroom. Of the two proper bedrooms, one was used by the boys, while the other was rented out for a few years to an Irish couple called McKeever. The only other space was the precious inside lavatory and a long hallway – known as a lobby, but pronounced 'lobey' – where the two boys would often kick a ball about. Like many families, the Fergusons had no plumbed-in bath, but used a zinc tub in the kitchen. Nonetheless, their home was nothing like as crowded as some. A similar flat on the same landing held a family of sixteen.

In the 1920s and '30s Govan suffered badly from high unemployment as shipbuilding orders slumped. People would scavenge through dustbins for scraps of food, and many suffered malnourishment and poor health. But the war and post-war years, in contrast, were times of bulging order books, buoyant employment and relative prosperity. 'There was not a lot of money flying about, but my background was not poor,' Ferguson says.[31] 'We used to live in the kitchen, where my mum and dad also slept in a recess bed. But at least we had an inside toilet, which most people didn't have. There were a lot less well-off than us.'[32] 'In Glasgow at that time, any slum with an inside lavatory was officially designated as a non-slum,' says the journalist and former trade-union leader Jimmy Reid, who also came from Govan. 'It was a tough area. A cat with a tail was immediately recognised as a tourist. Sure, it coarsened some. Demoralised others into accepting defeat without fight. Yet the majority always refused to be brutalised or beaten. They fought back in their own different ways.'[33]

'We would consider ourselves privileged in many ways,' says Martin Ferguson. 'Always food on the table and clothes on our backs, and our mother and father went out of their way to make sure we came first.' It helped that Alex Snr did plenty of overtime and Liz Ferguson was sensible with the family budget. 'My mother was a great one for utilising her money properly,' says Martin Ferguson. 'They weren't going out and spending all their money on drink and horses and all that.'[34] One day her son Alex would take a similarly prudent approach to his transfer dealings.

In the 1950s the area saw plenty of violence and suffered local gangs such as the Bingoes, though they tended to use fisticuffs rather than the razors for which other parts of Glasgow were notorious. Martin Ferguson describes how the boys' bedroom provided a safe vantage point from which to watch as people were thrown out of the pubs below at closing time. 'Our entertainment on a Friday or a Saturday was to lift the windows up and watch the fights. You always got a good fight on a Friday or a Saturday night – no weapons or anything: just a couple of guys having a fight until it was broken up.'[35]

Govan was full of 'last-word experts' explains Alex Ferguson's lifelong friend John Donachie. 'No matter what you throw away, bang, wallop, they will always come back on it.' It was an environment in which you had to be competitive to survive, Donachie adds. 'You were always having to push yourself, and parents were pushing their kids, with a basic discipline. "Get up!" in the morning. "Get out and do this!"'[36]

'He stuck out like a sore thumb as far as I'm concerned,' says Tommy Hendry, who was in Ferguson's class at school and has known him almost all his life. 'He would start an argument. He had quite a temper on him – no question about it.'[37]

Alex Ferguson's aggression was apparent to everyone. 'Could start a fight in an empty room' is the phrase his teacher Elizabeth 'Liz' Thomson uses to describe the boy she taught in his final year at Broomloan Road Primary School. She remembers his assertive 'body language' and how he always had his 'head forward' even at the age of eleven or twelve. 'He's still got that same attitude,' she says.[38] When the class played rounders, she found it hard to 'stop him clouting [the ball] out of the yard'.[39]

Nonetheless, Liz Thomson talks of her pupil as 'a very normal, nice boy. Of course, he wasn't really interested particularly in school-work at that point,' she says. 'Little girls are inclined to want to please the teachers. Little boys really couldn't care less whether the teacher is pleased or not.'[40]

Even then Alex Ferguson displayed two sides of his complex character. Liz Thomson, he says, was 'the heroine of my child-hood . . . a stunningly attractive young woman', and, 'like nearly all of my schoolmates, I had a crush on her'.[41] In 1953, when his teacher announced that she was getting married, Alex organised a gang of boys to take a ferry across the Clyde and make a surprise entrance at her church wedding ceremony. 'I'm not quite sure how they found their way,' she says. 'It was very smart of them to manage it – it wasn't an easy journey.'[42] 'I nearly died! . . . They all arrived – as Alex says, "the wee scrubs from Govan". I think the ushers were a bit doubtful about this shamble of young men. However, Alex was the bold one . . . He says, "It's our teacher", and that was it. My cousin Arnold was quite disconcerted.'[43]

Ferguson had stayed on a year at Broomloan Road Primary School after missing much of the previous year through medical problems – two hernia operations, then kidney illness – which left him in the same class as brother Martin. 'His parents came to tell me they were worried about Alex,' says Liz Thomson.

So after that I kept an extra special eye on him . . . A few teachers had found him very awkward but I never had any problems and I can't even remember having to punish Alex. I was a very strict disciplinarian and any idea he had of stepping out of line was probably stopped on his first day at handwork lessons, when I had to belt one boy. I didn't have much trouble after that – certainly not with Alex – and although I could be hard, I was always fair.[44]

The buildings of Broomloan Road Primary School still stand, though they're boarded up and a rather forlorn sight amid the derelict open spaces of modern-day Govan. It's a sign of how important he considers his roots in the area that Alex Ferguson has kept in touch with Liz Thomson ever since his schooldays. She's been to stay at Fairfields in Cheshire; Sir Alex also drops by sometimes when he's in Glasgow, and keeps in touch by phone. More than fifty years later he still maintains friendships with several boys from primary-school days.

'People say mine was a poor upbringing,' Sir Alex once remarked. 'I don't know what they mean. It was tough, but it wasn't bloody poor. We maybe didn't have a TV. We didn't have a car. We didn't even have a phone. But I thought I had everything, and I did: I had a football.'[45]

Left Foot Forward

'The truth is Alex was a bit of a holy terror. He'd half of our school, Govan High, terrorised, because it had to be Fergie's way – or nothing.'

MARTIN FERGUSON[1]

'If ever a city had a centre spot for a heart and goalposts for bones,' said the writer Patrick Prior, 'it is Glasgow. From the nineteenth century onwards the obsession with football has ruled hearth and home, marriage, birth and death.'[2] On a par with the Clydeside shipyards in moulding the young Alex Ferguson was the proximity of Ibrox Park, the home of Glasgow Rangers, one of the most famous football teams in the world. It was merely a 'stone's throw' or a 'goal kick' away from the Ferguson home, so cliché would have it. In fact Ibrox was about a third of a mile away, straight up Broomloan Road, after which the ground's western stand is named.

By the 1940s, Rangers had become the most dominant side British football had ever seen. Scottish League champions for 16 of the 21 seasons between the two great wars, they remained top dogs through most of Alex Ferguson's childhood in the 1940s and '50s. Rangers had achieved their first league and cup double in 1928, and repeated it at regular intervals thereafter – in 1930, 1934, 1936, 1950 and 1953. But their greatest season so far was 1948–49, when they became the first team to win the treble in Scotland, adding the new Scottish League Cup to the league title and the Scottish Cup.

Ibrox was a huge stadium, second in size in northern Europe only to Hampden Park a couple of miles further south. In January 1939, 118,567 people had crammed into the Rangers ground to witness the annual New Year's game with Celtic. (The official capacity remained above 100,000 until the mid-1970s.) On three sides of the pitch stretched vast banks of terracing; on the fourth stood a magnificent red-brick grandstand, which, in total contrast to the impoverished surrounding community, was fitted out inside like a country house, with a marble entrance hall and staircase, wood-panelled corridors, art-deco lamps, and, in pride of place, a large trophy room.

Occasionally the young Alex Ferguson would sneak into games at Ibrox by climbing over a back wall, though once he was caught by club officials. 'They started chasing me and I fell down a hole,' he later related – 'a bloody big pool of water – and I got caught, and he said, "What's your address? I'm telling your mother."'[3] Ibrox also provided a steady income. Alex would climb into the gentlemen's enclosure 'to nick the enamel Bovril mugs to collect the tanner deposit on them before the police could feel my collar', and he also collected screw-top beer bottles from around the ground, which were worth a few pennies when returned to local pubs.[4]

Unusually, the Fergusons' loyalties were divided between the great Glasgow sides. In supporting Rangers, Alex was defying his father, who not only stood out by being a Protestant who followed Celtic, but was even chairman of the local Celtic supporters' branch – the Windsor Club (though only in Govan would a Celtic club carry the same name as the royal family). The club had its own premises in Epsom Street, right in the heart of Govan, and Ferguson organised buses to take the fans to Parkhead, four miles away, even though Rangers were the local favourites and Govan was predominantly Protestant. Martin Ferguson insists, however, that there was none of the traditional sectarianism of Glasgow football in the Windsor Club. 'You weren't allowed to sing any religious songs,' he says. 'You couldn't sing any Irish songs, or IRA songs or anything. He never allowed it, and I think that speaks volumes for him.'[5]

From the age of five or six, Martin and Alex started going to football matches with their father. Martin Ferguson liked to accompany his father to Celtic games: he thought the team was the more attractive footballing side, though he later joined his brother in supporting the Ibrox club. 'I was one of the Passage 12 gang in those days,' Alex said later, 'and that mentality of being a terrace follower hasn't ever left me.'[6] Alex Snr didn't seem to mind that his two sons ended up supporting his team's sworn rivals. 'As long as we didn't go to Celtic–Rangers games,' says Martin. 'He liked us to stay away from those matches, because in those days there was always trouble.'[7] In May 1953 the eleven-year-old Alex Ferguson saw Manchester United for the first time, when they beat Rangers 2–1 in the one-off Coronation Cup at Hampden Park.

Living in Glasgow also gave Alex Ferguson the chance to watch international fixtures, in an era when his country was still a formidable footballing force. The following year, for instance, he saw Scotland in a World Cup qualifying match at Hampden against the England of Billy Wright and Tom Finney. 'It was pouring with rain,' he says. 'I was lifted over the barrier next to the invalid cars. I stood there and watched the game.'[8] The Scots lost 4–2.

When Celtic, Rangers or Scotland weren't at home, most of the boys' spare time was spent playing football. Games at playtimes and in the lunch hour at school would be treated like a long series, with the scores totted up to produce a winner at the end of the week. Duncan Petersen, who has known Alex Ferguson since they were at infants' school, would join the Ferguson brothers and their father for practice in the local Pirie Park. It was here that Alex established a reputation for being strong with both feet:

His father coached him to be left-footed. He was right-footed like most people, but his father always wanted him to be two-footed. But it got to the stage where he was better with his left than his right. He's a natural right-hander, but he kicked with his left. He was always a good goalscorer. Even when he was a wee boy he always played up-front – although he'd play in goal sometimes, just for a laugh. But he'd deliberately let in a goal to get back out.[9]

Another childhood friend, Tommy Hendry, says that even at primary-school age Ferguson had a 'kind of aura':

There was something different about him. He stuck out. But the funny thing about it was, if somebody kicked him or the ball hit him in the body or something, he would pull down his trousers. He was showing off his scar. He'd just had a hernia operation, and he was showing off his scar. We were all killing ourselves laughing at this. 'Look at these scars,' he would say – 'you nearly burst my stitches.'[10]

Outside school, groups of boys would kick a ball about in the back courts, the areas between one row of tenement blocks and the next, where clothes poles became goalposts and there was always the danger of breaking windows. It was also an 'ideal' spot for head tennis, says Martin Ferguson. 'Everybody who wasn't playing was sitting it out, and then two came off and two went on. You played two against two and things like that.'[11] Performing in such a confined area made them better ball-players, Alex Ferguson has said. 'With any number of boys playing in those small spaces, on a hard, uneven surface, they developed skills and techniques which are lacking in the modern player.'[12]

At weekends and in the holidays, games would last all day, and there was strong competition to take part. Often boys gathered on a piece of wasteland known as The Works, the site of an old factory. They didn't always have a proper ball, but made do with whatever they could find. Alex's boots were hand-me-downs from a cousin. The Ferguson brothers hung around watching games involving older boys, in the hope that they'd get their chance. 'There was a lot of good, talented young players – natural footballers,' says Martin Ferguson. 'You'd hope that maybe one of them wouldn't turn up, or would get called in for his tea, and then you would get on.'[13]

Duncan Petersen remembers a trick Alex loved to perform with a pre-decimal penny: 'He would rest it on his foot, then flick it on his knee, then drop it back on his foot, and then catch it on his forehead. We'd all shout at him for being a show-off. He was only about twelve or thirteen.'[14]

Martin Ferguson agrees with others that the young Alex was a tough and highly aggressive player. 'He didn't like you to take the ball off him,' he says. 'If you did, he'd kick you.'[15] He could look after himself – and others – off the pitch as well.

> He didn't like anyone bullying his pals, didn't like people trying to pick on younger people or take the mickey. He was always the first in; he was always the first to stand up to them. It didn't matter how big they were – he would have fought Goliath off. He wouldn't go looking for it, but he'd be the first to respond to it.[16]

Martin recalls the time he heard about a big fight up on the local football pitch:

> This guy had been picking on one of Alec's pals, and Alec of course took up the challenge. And, when I got to it, there was a whole story – a big crowd of boys, a circle of schoolboys, and there was a fight in the middle of it, and I had to force my way through to get in to see what the situation was. And

19

there was Alec boxing the living daylights out of this guy. And the guy must have been a few stones heavier, and bigger, and bulkier than Alec.[17]

Yet the young Fergie also knew when to beat a retreat. At school he had found a secret hole in the school wall which was just the right size for him to squeeze through, but too tight for the bigger boys. 'That was my escape hatch,' Alex says. 'When I was getting chased or in fights, I'd get through that gap and no-one could catch me.'[18]

Alex wasn't beyond the occasional bit of bullying himself – of his younger brother at least. 'He used to batter me,' says Martin Ferguson. 'We used to fight like all brothers, like cat and dog over all sorts of things.'[19] Martin also accuses his brother of foul play at cards. 'Alec used to cheat all the time,' he says. 'He would tell you different, but once he had five pontoons in a row and he told me he wasn't cheating!'[20]

Alex Ferguson was in the swimming team at Broomloan Road Primary School, but it was always a great disappointment that the school had no proper football side which could play competitive matches. There was no teacher to act as football coach. Liz Thomson occasionally served as referee for the boys, but by her own admission she was hardly the ideal coach. 'The only reason I was a ref was because I had a whistle,' she says. 'I'm still not clear on what's onside or offside even though Alex has tried to explain it to me.'[21]

Instead, Alex and Martin Ferguson helped organise unofficial fixtures against other junior schools in the vicinity, and especially the nearby local Catholic school, St Saviour's. 'They were probably the best, or one of the best, in Glasgow primary schools,' says Martin Ferguson. 'We used to go round there and beat the life out of them regularly, but we didn't have a teacher who would take us, which was a bit sad.'[22]

From the age of nine, however, Alex and Martin also played in a team organised by the Life Boys, the junior section of the 129th Company of the local Boys' Brigade in Govan. Founded in Glasgow in 1883, the Boys' Brigade describes itself as the 'oldest voluntary uniformed youth group in the world'; broadly speaking, it's similar to the Boy Scouts, but more regimented and religious. The Brigade, which is particularly strong in Scotland and Northern Ireland, is an overwhelmingly Protestant institution, with an ethos summed up in its motto of more than a century: 'The advancement of Christ's Kingdom among Boys and the promotion of habits of Obedience, Reverence, Discipline, Self-respect and all that tends towards a true Christian manliness.'[23] It's not far off the Ferguson philosophy, in fact.

It was clear to the local Boys' Brigade leader, John Boreland, that football was the real reason Alex joined. The Ferguson family were never great churchgoers, but Alex dutifully attended the Life Boys' Sunday schools, Bible classes and weekly Wednesday meetings. 'Despite the drill and the parades, through it all Alec had one thought, and that was football,' says Boreland, who'd endured a long spell as a prisoner of war, and became a Christian after finding loose pages of the Bible in a field while waiting to be picked up by the Germans. He says of the nine-year-old Ferguson, 'His first question whenever he arrived at a meeting was, "Sir, is there a game on Saturday?" And I would tell him, "Well, it depends on how you get on tonight, Alec." And he would go and do his work.'[24]

One Wednesday evening, Boreland was puzzled as to why Ferguson hadn't turned up, until he discovered he'd been to see a game at Ibrox. 'I challenged him,' says Boreland, 'but he was honest, and that was the main point – he admitted where he'd been straight away. He didn't lie like other boys might have, and so he didn't get dropped. I always admired his honesty.'[25]

Ferguson was also 'a very modest lad', Boreland recalls. 'I never at any time had any trouble from him, except trying to get through to him that there were another ten men on the team and not just himself, and he should keep passing the ball to all.' At one match, when the team were 4–0 up at half-time and Ferguson had scored most if not all of the goals, Boreland told him to give his teammates more of the ball. Ferguson ignored his coach and scored again as his side won 7–0. 'I had told him he'd scored already, and to give the other boys a chance, and it was his opportunity to get them all involved – but not Alec.'[26]

Occasionally Ferguson would get the chance to play schoolboy football on the Ibrox pitch. He assumed that the legendary Bill Struth, who'd been manager of Rangers since 1920 (and the most successful boss in British history), would be watching from his office window. 'Often I made sure I was playing outside-left one half and outside-right in the other half so that he had every chance of seeing me, so convinced was I that he had to sign me immediately – at ten years of age!'[27]

It was with the Life Boys that Alex won the first of his many honours in football. Boreland remembers both Ferguson brothers playing in a team which won a five-a-side trophy. 'That was his first success, his first taste, and I'm not sure but I think it was a pencil case they won that day.'[28] Ferguson himself recalls his team beating Polmadie Company to win the Boys' Brigade's Glasgow and District Cup. 'What we felt was more than pleasure. It was joy,' he writes in his memoirs. 'Johnny Boreland bought us all ice creams with double nougat wafers and eating them walking down the Polmadie Road, with our boots tied at the laces and dangling round our necks, was the most exhilarating experience of my young life.'[29]

A player with 'outstanding ability, out to win at all times', and who 'wasn't afraid of anything' is how Boreland sums up his young goalscorer. 'He could look after himself OK, Alec, especially on the football park. He took many a dunt and many a tackle, and he never complained once, never – not like some boys, who'd say, "I'm no' playing." Alec was always there.' During one game his knee was so badly bruised that Boreland had to take him to the local hospital. 'He was treated that night and I took him home, and sure enough he was playing the next weekend. Despite it being a serious injury, he had a never-say-die attitude.'[30]

Alex Ferguson had just celebrated his thirteenth birthday when he arrived at secondary school in January 1955. He arrived about eighteen months later than his contemporaries because his medical problems in primary school meant that the first time round he failed the 'qually' – Scotland's equivalent of the eleven-plus examination. The fact that his schoolmates were now all a year younger dented his confidence. 'Being pitched into a much younger group had a traumatic effect on me,' he wrote in his autobiography. 'The embarrassment I felt, especially in relation to the girls, was so deep that I never overcame it and the rest of my time at school was torture, at least as far as lessons were concerned.'[31]

It was a pity, for Ferguson had gained excellent marks the second time he took the 'qually', which put him in the top stream. 'He was very, very clever,' says Bill Dobie, his form teacher at Govan High, 'and if he'd been born into a different background he could have gone on to university.'[32] Ferguson sometimes admits he regrets not trying harder at school, and that football provided a fortunate release from concentrating on academic work.

Dobie hardly ever used the traditional leather belt against his pupils, but Ferguson was a notable exception. It was just 'to show him who was boss', he says, when Ferguson was being cheeky and refusing to address his teacher as 'sir'. 'I said, "Just come out here," and I hammered him. I said to him, "You'll have to call me 'sir'," and after I finished I said, "Right, the war is over. You can't win. How about we call it a draw?" "Yes, sir," and that was it.'[33]

In 2001 Dobie sold his leather belt – known in Scotland as a Lochgelly – to an antique dealer for £55, writing an accompanying letter to certify that it had been used to chastise Sir Alex Ferguson.

Unlike Ferguson's primary school, Govan High did have proper football teams, and a good reputation for producing footballers.

(Other alumni included the Rangers and Scotland centre-half Ron McKinnon.) Ferguson quickly became one of the school's star players, and the school reached the final of the Scottish Shield at Hampden Park, only to be thrashed by their opponents.

Alex Snr would watch wherever the boys were playing on Saturdays, cajoling and criticising as the games were in full flow. But Bill Dobie noticed how he addressed his two sons very formally as he stood on the touchline. 'He would always say "Ferguson this" and "Ferguson that". You'd hear him during the match: "Ferguson, pass the ball"; "Hey, Ferguson." The odd thing was that as a father he never once referred to "my Alec" or "my Martin".'[34]

Frequently, Alex Snr would remind his oldest son not to let things go to his head, no matter how successful he was on the pitch, nor to come home as if he owned the place. Ferguson recalls, 'My father would say, "Don't get bloody carried away." I would come in after a game at school in the morning, and I'd scored about four goals and my mother would say, "You've done really well, son." Then my dad would say, "Bloody terrible player. Never passes a ball." He is saying that every minute I'm having my lunch.'[35]

Alex Ferguson describes his father as 'the one who drove me on as a kid, who never allowed me to be satisfied. Without him I would never have made it into football.'[36] Indeed, one suspects the persistent refusal by his late father, fifty years ago, to show he was impressed by anything he did may still help fuel Ferguson's famous hunger for greater success and public acclaim. Alex Snr 'was never off our back about weaknesses', according to Martin Ferguson:

> He was never one for praising you much. In fact I used to ask
> my mother how I'd played, because my father would never
> say 'Well played' – never. He'd always get on at you about
> something – 'You're too slow. You'll need to work on your
> sprinting. You need to work on your left foot. You don't shoot
> often enough. You'll need to shoot more. Shoot from outside

the box – goalkeepers don't expect it' – all that kind of stuff. It was always constructive criticism: it wasnae as though he was saying things for the sake of saying them. What he was saying was true. He knew his football, there's no doubt about that.[37]

From playing for the Life Boys' side, Ferguson moved to Harmony Row, a boys' club which took its name from a Govan street just round the corner from the Fergusons' home, and which is now well known throughout Scotland for the quality of the footballers it has produced. Run by a man called Bob Innes, Harmony Row was a way of keeping young lads occupied. For the half-crown annual subscription, teenagers could take part in a wide range of activities in the evenings and weekends, including snooker. Ferguson was an 'absolutely brilliant' snooker player, according to Tommy Hendry. 'He was the top player in the club. He could beat all the grown men in the place, and that was him at fifteen or sixteen.'[38]

On Saturday night the Harmony Row club held dances, and both sexes dolled themselves up and brought their records along to play over the sound system, while the lights were kept low to save lads embarrassment if they trod on their partners' toes. Ferguson had 'no hang-ups with women', Tommy Hendry says: 'I think he could get a bird now and again, no question about that. Having said that, as far as sexual conquests go, I think the two of us were wet behind the ears.'[39]

Once again, however, the prime reason for joining the Harmony Row club was football. 'It was exciting just getting there,' says Ferguson. 'We used to play soccer all the time but we had to behave. Much of my values, my success, comes from what they instilled in me there.'[40]

Ferguson's age group at Harmony Row were coached by Mick McGowan, though his methods were fairly basic, says Duncan Petersen. 'He had no tactics or whatever. He would just pick the boys he thought were good enough to play. It was once we played a team a few times that we would say, "Watch out for the winger," or "Watch out for the centre."' McGowan would occasionally hire a van, put all the boys in the back – even though there were no seats – and then drive off to far-flung places like Bradford to play games. 'And they'd come up to Glasgow to play us. It was quite an experience going all the way down to Bradford.'[41]

After winning a cup final, Ferguson's team from Harmony Row made the local papers not because of their triumph on the field, but because the Bingoes gang attacked them on their way home. 'We were wearing our colours, and they didn't take too kindly to us celebrating,' says Tommy Hendry:

> We ran for our lives that day, and we all ran back to the club.
> We had to sit in the club petrified. We were only fifteen- or
> sixteen-year-old boys, with this gang of hooligans outside
> baying for blood. Where the police were I don't know. All I
> remember is that me and Alex had to scarper down to Govan
> Road and jump in a tramcar – and it's a good job a tram was
> coming, because they were right behind us and we were on a
> hiding to nothing.[42]

The next major influences on Alex Ferguson's career were the Drumchapel Amateurs team and the man who organised it (and still runs it today), Douglas Smith. Drumchapel itself had once been a small town to the north-west of Glasgow, but gradually it became an overspill suburb as families were rehoused from the city slums after the war. For Ferguson, the trip from Govan would have involved a long trek across the Clyde and almost an hour's journey by bus, train or tram.

Nowadays the Drumchapel club – The Drum – is based in Duntocher, a couple of miles west of Drumchapel itself. The entrance to the clubhouse holds a trophy cabinet and pennants from Barcelona, Inter Milan, Manchester United and other leading clubs around the world, while a selection of cuttings details the latest exploits of Drumchapel alumni. But it's not until you enter the dressing room that you appreciate the extraordinary success that this amateur club has enjoyed in grooming football talent during the last half-century. Around the wall are edifying slogans such as 'Hard work can beat talent when talent doesn't work hard.' Then, beneath each of the clothes hooks on the walls, numbered for each team player, is a brass plate listing all the former Drumchapel footballers who wore that particular number and later played professional football. There are almost 300 in all, including 29 who won international caps. The roll of honour includes Mo Johnston, Andy Gray, Eddie McCreadie, Asa Hartford, Iain Munro, Archie Gemmill, David Moyes, Tommy Craig and John Robertson. And second on the list for the number-10 plate, beneath John Wark, is Alex Ferguson.

In 2000 Ferguson returned to Glasgow to play in a special match to celebrate Drumchapel's fiftieth anniversary – an Old Boys XI against the present side. Drumchapel was in its infancy in his time, and it wasn't really until the 1960s that its production line became prolific, but he identifies the club as the place where he learned to think big.

Drumchapel's founder, guiding spirit and chief talent spotter, Douglas Smith, had an unlikely background for a Glasgow football scout. He came from a wealthy middle-class home, and had gone to Cambridge University before returning to Scotland to run the family business, the shipbreaker's Arnott Young. Until he retired from the firm in 1980, nurturing young soccer talent was simply a hobby, and he always insisted he was only a football scout, not a coach. 'In the very early days, yes, I ran the team. But we tended to put eleven very good players together, and because they were good players they tended to be able to improvise and do things themselves.'[43]

Drumchapel was a well-organised club, even though Smith ran

things almost on his own in Ferguson's day, aided by one or two parents. The general pattern was for each of the Drumchapel teams to be selected at the start of the season, and Smith then tried to stick to that eleven. If a boy lost form, he would be kept in the side while his teammates made up for him. Then each team would move up a grade to the next age level, thereby maintaining continuity year after year.

Every week, team members would learn by post whether they were playing, and when and where to report on Saturday. 'There they were in this back close in Glasgow,' says Smith, 'and they got this letter every Thursday and it made them feel like somebody.'[44] On match days Smith would also treat his team members to lunch at Reid's tea room in Glasgow, where they would often spot the Queen's Park side eating at adjacent tables before their Scottish League match that afternoon.

'We had heard about this young player out in Govan called Ferguson,' says Smith, and I went across to Govan and I went up to his close.'[45] Alex didn't say 'Yes' immediately, but eventually he signed for the club – at the age of fourteen, in September 1956. He stayed for two years.

'One trait was very noticeable,' says Smith: 'he had a very good pair of elbows.'

> He wasn't a brilliant silky player, but he was a very good player. I remember that as an under-eighteen, he made the Scotland team, so those that talk disparagingly about his ability as a player are out of order: he made all the schools' teams and got all the schools' caps that were going, and he also made the full SFA [Scottish Football Association] youth team. He wasn't a brilliant on-the-ball player, but he was hard-working, with a bit of dirt in his play.[46]

His brother, Martin, says that as a boy Alex was a much more skilful player than people might imagine from the reputation he subsequently acquired as a professional:

> People put him down as being a hustler bustler, but when he was a youngster he could play football. In fact often he would score goals for the school team where he would beat three or four players – that was a regular thing for Alec. We used to call him a greedy bastard. As a young player he was more of an individualist. He was a dribbler – he was always good at beating players and scoring goals. Alec scoring four goals in a school game wasn't unusual.[47]

Ferguson had no shortage of outlets for his talents, playing for both Harmony Row and Drumchapel Amateurs at the same time, and also turning out regularly for Govan High School. And by the time he was fifteen he was chosen for the Scottish schoolboys' team. One game, in April 1958, involved a train trip down to London to play at Dulwich Hamlet's ground, where the Scots lost 4–3 to England, though Ferguson was only substitute. A member of the side was another future Scotland manager, Craig Brown. 'Fergie was what you would euphemistically call a hard player,' Brown says. 'He didn't want to lose, and would always go in with his feet high and his elbows in your side.'[48]

'Ferguson's craft, flair for a shot and expert use of the ball are astonishing for a sixteen-year-old,' one newspaper report said,[49] but he wasn't always praised. One of Ferguson's last games as a schoolboy, a few weeks before he left Govan High in June 1958, was for the Glasgow Schoolboys' team against their London counterparts at Hampden Park. Local reporter Malcolm Munroe lamented the Glaswegian boys' complacency as they lost 3–1:

> These young Scots seem to think they've made it already.
> Alex Ferguson was a classic example. With the score at 1–1

he was awarded a penalty kick for a foul on himself. He placed the heavy ball, took a step forward and glided it with the side of his foot. The brilliant young English goalie J. L. Barr saved it easily – I could have got down from the press box and stopped it before it reached the goal line. Young Ferguson then stood with his hands on his hips and shook his head at Barr's goal-saving. Am I being hard on a sixteen-year-old? Nope – if I don't pick out his faults, he may grow up with them. Ferguson shows promise, but he'll have to buckle to. Right now he's too casual.[50]

With a touch of humility which would astonish his modern-day critics, Alex Ferguson wrote back to the paper. Courageously, he thanked Munroe for 'the piece of criticism you dealt out to me'.

You were absolutely correct. You could have caught the penalty-kick, and, now that I have seen daylight, I hope you will come back and see me again, for I am sure I will play a lot better. On Saturday I was really disappointed with myself as I was making my departure from school football and am really sorry I had to leave it with such a morbid display.[51]

Munroe was impressed by this act of contrition. 'Alex, my boy,' he replied, 'I felt after I wrote it that I'd perhaps been too hard on you. But from your letter I can see you're a man – even at sixteen.'[52] The editor was so impressed that Ferguson's letter was awarded a guinea.

'I was on the crest at school,' Ferguson would admit in an interview with Malcolm Munroe six years later, 'getting all the caps, getting big-headed with them. I needed somebody to sort me out. You did it. I'm much obliged.'[53]

Apprentice Striker

*'Oh, aye, I was carrying the banner all right. It was a
great feeling for a young lad, you know, a kind of adventure.'*

ALEX FERGUSON[1]

For a man who was to scale the heights of the world game, Alex
Ferguson's first experience of league football could hardly have
been more modest. In November 1958 he travelled with his teammates by train from Glasgow down to Stranraer, the ferry port on the
south-west tip of Scotland. Stranraer have always been one of those
clubs that make up the numbers in Scottish football. They have
never played in the top division, nor boasted a single player who
played for his national side.

Ferguson's team, Queen's Park, had a pedigree very different from
Stranraer's, though by 1958 they were aristocrats who had long
fallen on hard times but still occupied a large, if run-down, stately
home. Queen's Park is the oldest football club in Scotland, responsible for introducing many basic features of the modern game such
as crossbars, free kicks and half-time, and even turnstiles and crush
barriers. In the early years of organised football in Scotland – well
before Rangers or Celtic, the so-called Old Firm, were established –
Queen's Park were the top club in Glasgow, and in the twenty

seasons between 1874 and 1893 they won the Scottish Cup ten times. They'd also been allowed to compete in the early years of the English FA Cup, and in 1884 and 1885 they became the only Scottish team ever to reach the final, losing both times to Blackburn Rovers. Queen's Park players also dominated the Scottish national team in the late nineteenth century, and the club provided all eleven players for the very first international against England, in 1872.

By the late 1950s, however, Queen's Park were swimming with the minnows of the Scottish game. The spring before Alex Ferguson made his debut at Stranraer, the club was relegated from the Scottish First Division, having finished bottom with just four wins in thirty-four games. Never again would the distinctive black-and-white hooped shirts of Queen's Park return to the top flight.

Ever since the foundation of the club, Queen's Park had also provided a home for the Scotland team and the Scottish Football Association, and in Hampden Park they boasted for many years the largest soccer stadium in the world. For much of the twentieth century, Hampden's terraces, built of wooden beams and crushed ash, could hold 150,000 people. So it was a grossly inappropriate venue for a club which could only attract a few thousand spectators.

Alex Ferguson was seven weeks short of his seventeenth birthday that Saturday at Stranraer – extremely young for a debutant into league football, even at a small club like Queen's Park. He had initially been picked for the club's fourth team – the youth side – when he joined in the summer of 1958, but he climbed rapidly through the third team and reserves in the space of just three months. He had 'made such rapid progress', said the *Glasgow Evening Times*, 'that he just had to be given his big chance today'.[2]

Ferguson talks of his debut for Queen's Park as being close to a 'nightmare'.[3] First, he says, he wasn't used to playing at outside right, though all reports have him at inside forward. Then, astonishingly, the opposing full-back bit him while they were both lying on the ground, and at half-time he got a rollicking from the team coach. The second half degenerated into a battle, with a player from each side being sent off. Stranraer won 2–1 in front of 1,650 people, but at least Ferguson marked his debut with a late goal, having 'ended a great solo run with a flashing drive'.[4] Strangely he omits this from his autobiography (which is surprising when throughout his career he kept detailed records of every goal he scored or assisted). He scored again, with a header, on his home debut at Hampden Park the following week against Alloa. This time Queen's Park won 4–2. 'Ferguson's craft, flair for a shot, and expert use of the ball was astonishing for a sixteen-year-old,' reported the *Scottish Sunday Express*.[5]

'He was a battling centre forward,' Malcolm Mackay, a former Queen's Park director, told a previous Ferguson biographer, Stephen Kelly:

> A bit like a Mark Hughes rather than a Gary Lineker, always a handful in the penalty area . . . He was still a young lad, though even as a youngster he was having to fight his own corner. That took character. He was playing for a side in the Scottish League, at a much higher level than he had ever played in before, and he had to battle to claim and then keep his place. He didn't like losing.[6]

He may have hated being beaten, but at Queen's Park Ferguson had to get used to it. After a reasonable start to the season, the team lost fifteen of their remaining twenty-one matches following the Alloa victory. They finished second from last in the Scottish Second Division, equalling the worst placing in the club's history. Alex Ferguson was one of forty-three players the club used in that campaign. He had certainly started from the bottom.

In his two years with Queen's Park, Alex Ferguson usually played in one of the inside-forward shirts, but he never quite secured a permanent place in the line-up. His best run was thirteen matches.

He missed both Queen's Park's worst-ever home league defeat – an 8–1 drubbing by Dundee United in September 1959 – and their best-ever league victory – a startling 9–1 win at Cowdenbeath the following February. Nonetheless, Ferguson claimed fifteen goals in his 31 league games – a rate of one every two matches. He was soon being noticed. 'The leggy Ferguson was a finer type, who excelled in his ball skill and passing. At times he was well out of position because of his urge to go forward,' wrote the future Rangers manager Willie Waddell.[7]

The move to Queen's Park had caused a fierce row with his father, who was worried that, by signing for a Scottish League club, Alex would disqualify himself from playing in non-league football after-wards. While at Queen's Park, Ferguson also graduated from the Scotland schoolboys' side to the national youth team, playing five games in 1959 and 1960. One of the fixtures, against England on Tyneside, led to an approach from Newcastle United, though noth-ing came of it. Even at that age he wasn't afraid to tell the SFA coach, Roy Small, what he thought about being played on the wing instead of at inside- or centre-forward, according to a teammate, Hugh McDonald. 'He would say, "Look, I'm wasting my bloody time here. What are you doing to me? You know I want to play here." That's the way Alec spoke. Roy Small accepted it, and played him where he wanted to play.'[8]

Queen's Park may not have won very often, but they provided a good grounding in many ways. The club boasted several other play-ers who were to have distinguished careers. Goalkeeper Jim Cruickshank – another Drumchapel graduate – went on to play for Hearts and Scotland, while Willie Bell, who also won a couple of caps, moved to Leeds United and played an early part in the great Don Revie side of the 1960s. Although Ferguson was the youngest member of the first-team squad, he was a bit 'headstrong' and 'not short of opinion' says Willie 'Junior' Omand, the Queen's Park cap-tain, who acted as a kind of father-figure to him. Ferguson certainly wasn't afraid to tell his colleagues what was wrong with their performance and what they should be doing instead. 'It was necessary to quieten him down and tell him some home truths,' says Omand. 'And that he could talk when he started shaving.'[9]

Pre-season training sessions with Queen's Park often involved four circuits of the stadium, pounding up and down every step of the forty-two stairways of Hampden's massive bowl of terracing, 'with my lungs protesting against the scale of the place'.[10] Calmer, more enjoyable, moments came for Ferguson when the ground was truly deserted and he took a ball out on to the grass on his own, imagining he was wearing the dark-blue shirt of Scotland. He then fired the ball into the net and fantasised that 150,000 fans had gone delirious all around him.

'It was great to play there,' says his childhood friend Duncan Petersen, who joined the club around the same time as Ferguson and also made the first team. 'You felt a bit special, but it was wide open and you could hear anyone shouting if you made a mistake – "Away back to school, ya dumpling" and all that. You heard everything, because it was so empty.'[11]

Alex Ferguson remembers the 'wonderful spirit' at Queen's Park – 'a camaraderie that extended from the senior players right down to the rawest teenagers'.[12] Part of that spirit arose from the club's unique distinction of being still strictly an amateur club – the only one in either the English or the Scottish League. This meant Queen's Park was a more gentlemanly institution than the professional Scottish League sides. The team was picked by a committee rather than a manager, and the club still had an old-fashioned Corinthian ethos. 'We were concerned about giving people a future and showing them the best way to behave in society,' says the Queen's Park defender Bert Cromar. 'That may sound arrogant, but that's the way it was.'[13] And if players didn't behave, they weren't selected.

Unlike Ferguson, many Queen's Park players came from middle-class backgrounds. 'A lot of their parents were professional people –

teachers, doctors, people like that,' says Duncan Petersen. 'We were ordinary, simple people, and our parents worked in the shipyards or were joiners or whatever, and I think it was a bit of a new trend for Queen's Park.'[14]

The two lads would wear their old school ties when they went for the traditional pre-match meal. 'Maybe they were used to it,' says Petersen, 'but it made you feel good because you had a jacket and tie and all that.'[15] But, as a working-class Govan teenager, Alex Ferguson plainly found it difficult to fit into this different social milieu. 'He was a firebrand,' says one colleague, 'and he was hyped up, and he didn't have the social graces when he was sitting in the stand.' Bert Cromar remembers Ferguson turning up as a 'mild tearaway' who lacked maturity and manners:

> I could have cuffed his ear sometimes, without any
> compunction – and should have! He did not greatly
> appreciate discipline, and over the period of time he was with
> us he gradually accepted and understood the rule of being
> diplomatic and not firing off words, or actions. He was
> immature, and matured through the assistance of the more
> senior players. Alex Ferguson left a more rounded individual
> than when he came.[16]

None of the Queen's Park team members was paid: the club also insisted on not making profits and never buying or selling players. So Ferguson didn't receive any remuneration. He worked full-time, and travelled by bus to evening training stints after work. No wonder he tried to lie in as late as he could on Saturday mornings. Alex Willoughby, who also played for Drumchapel and the Scotland Youth team, remembers how Ferguson would urge his mother to bring him a fry-up in bed.[17] Sometimes she agreed.

Alex hadn't done well enough at school to stay on beyond sixteen and take his Higher Leaving Certificate (the Scottish equivalent of

A-levels). There's no question he was bright enough, but he just hadn't applied himself. However, he had plenty of opportunities for work in what was an era of almost full employment. His wisest decision was not to follow his father into the shipyards. Shipbuilding work was insecure and unpleasant, and the industry's future was already uncertain. While the Clydeside yards had enjoyed a post-war boom, as the world struggled to replace the huge tonnage destroyed during hostilities, they were also afflicted with absurd inefficiencies and waste, terrible labour relations and absenteeism, poor investment, and complacent management. Before long, British shipbuilders would face serious decline and stiff competition from the more modern yards of Japan, Germany and Korea.

At one point Alex Ferguson toyed with the idea of becoming a full-time Customs & Excise official, but that would have involved work on Saturdays. Instead, he approached several of the engineering firms in the area and joined a company on the Hillington Industrial Estate, about three miles west of Govan. Wickman Lang's was a machine-toolmaking company which was known for the quality of its precision engineering and its carbide-tipped tools. He signed up for a five-year apprenticeship as a toolmaker. It meant learning the necessary skills – working on lathes, grinding, milling, and electrical work – and also involved a day a week studying at a local college. The toolroom is traditionally the heart of an engineering factory; toolmakers are generally better paid and regarded as the aristocrats of the shop floor – rather like faceworkers in a coal mine. But Wickman's future was precarious; several workers had already been made redundant, and, as a junior employee, Ferguson was more at risk than most. The general manager mentioned the possibility of moving to Wickman's parent plant in Coventry, but Ferguson's football commitments made that unattractive.

Instead the manager arranged to transfer Alex's apprenticeship to Remington Rand, an American firm which was famous for its typewriters and electric shavers, and employed about 2,500 people locally. Remington's factory was also located on the Hillington estate, and its toolmaking work was more sophisticated and challenging than that at other firms. 'I can see why Alex would have picked Remington Rand,' says a former shop steward, Gavin Keown. 'You were making tools straight from a drawing – some very complicated tools at that.'[18]

It was at Remington that Ferguson first became active in his trade union, the Amalgamated Engineering Union, or AEU.[19] The company had agreed to recognise unions only a few years before, and the AEU's convener at Remington, an active Communist Party member called Calum Mackay, explained before his death in 2001 how he tried to encourage promising new apprentices like Ferguson to get involved in the union. 'Alex used to come to meetings. He was on the shop stewards' committee and was also on the district committee of the junior workers. They'd meet every Saturday morning at the AEU headquarters in Renfrew Road. He was nearly always there, always involved,' according to Mackay. 'He was a committed trade unionist. I wouldn't say he was a leader, but he was well-liked.'[20] Mackay may have overemphasised Ferguson's role at young workers' meetings, however, for his name appears nowhere in the minute-books, and Saturday meetings were difficult for Ferguson, of course, because of football fixtures in the afternoon, often miles from Glasgow.[21]

Like many American firms in Scotland, Remington Rand had a reputation as a 'really hard-nosed employer', according to Alan McKinlay, a specialist in Scottish industry at St Andrews University. 'In the middle of the 1950s, when they were facing demands for union recognition, they tried to stop them by building a wall across the factory. They would recognise the skilled workers in the toolroom as AEU, but the other areas, where all the assembly took place, they wouldn't recognise them there.'[22]

During his six years at Remington, Ferguson became involved in two famous labour disputes. The first was in the winter and spring of 1960, when engineering apprentices across the UK were becoming increasingly agitated about their poor rates of pay, which had improved little during the previous six years. Yet most British workers – including those in engineering – were enjoying growing prosperity during the 'Never Had It So Good' years of the late 1950s. The apprentices thought they were being exploited by management as cheap labour, especially when many were earning less than friends of their own age who did unskilled jobs elsewhere. At the same time the young men felt badly let down by their representatives in the Confederation of Shipbuilding and Engineering Unions – the Confed. A national apprentices' pay claim had first been tabled in March 1959, but almost a year later it had yet to be resolved with the Engineering Employers' Association. Some apprentices felt that their older workmates, who were qualified at their trades, were no longer interested in the welfare of junior colleagues.

Ferguson says he had no great quarrel with Remington Rand itself, and he acknowledges that its wages 'were better than most'. What's more, being in the toolroom, he would also have been more highly paid than workers in other parts of the plant.[23]

The unofficial action, which eventually affected the whole of Britain, started on Clydeside in February 1960, when boys from just five firms, including Remington Rand, approached their managers seeking a significant pay rise for apprentices, and warned of a one-day protest strike. Clydeside had a reputation for agitation by apprentices. Indeed, the area was known as 'Boys' Town' because of the large numbers of young men involved in shipbuilding, and employed at lower rates of pay than adult workers. Previous Clydeside apprentices' strikes had become legendary within the Labour movement – in 1911, 1937 and 1941, and then in 1952, when action was led by the young Communist shipyard worker Jimmy Reid.

The leaders of the 1960 action adopted the same name as the previous protests – the Clydeside Apprentices' Campaign Committee –

and their offices were a few hundred yards down the Govan Road from the Fergusons' home. In rough terms, their demands would have entailed an average pay rise of £2 12s. 6d. (£2.62½) a week. This would have doubled the earnings of fifteen-year-olds, while twenty-year-olds would have gained increases of more than 50 per cent.

More than half the apprentices on Clydeside joined the first one-day stoppage – about 6,000 in all. The picture was confused, with lads walking out from different plants at different times of the day. At first the main support for the action came from shipyards lower down the Clyde, in Port Glasgow and Greenock. Lads at yards and factories in the Govan area were initially reluctant to join in, and strike leaders picketed workplaces and urged apprentices to show solidarity. The ringleaders included Gus Macdonald, a young Trotskyist who worked at Alexander Stephen. 'We used to go marching to each of the yards trying to get them to come out and support the fight,' says Macdonald, who later achieved fame, wealth and power in successive jobs as a TV presenter, chairman of Scottish Television and a Labour minister. 'I remember that we also went up to Remington Rand's at Hillington and put our case to them.'[24] Another of the Alexander Stephen strikers was the future comedian and actor Billy Connolly. The only document that seems to survive from that initial protest is a scrawled handwritten note delivered to the Employers' Association after that day's demonstration. It contains the signatures of seven apprentices' leaders. Alex Ferguson wasn't one of them.[25]

'I felt I had to do something in support,' says Ferguson, who may have met Macdonald and his delegation that day, though Macdonald himself has no memory of him. As acting shop steward for the Remington apprentices, Ferguson summoned a meeting of his dozen or so colleagues in the men's lavatory. 'There were eleven of us there and I told them there could be no question about it, we had to support the other striking apprentices in Britain.' When it came to a vote, the lads were equally divided, and so Ferguson says he thrust his hand in the air and cried, 'Casting vote – we're out!' though he now admits the decision was something of a fiddle.[26]

> Little did they know it needs a two-third majority to go on strike, but I pushed it through that way, you see – casting vote. So I went up to the superintendent, Jimmy Cameron . . . and he said, 'You can't go on strike. You're indentured apprentices.' 'We're not indentured apprentices –' 'You're committed until you're –' I said, 'I'm sorry, but we have to go. The whole of bloody Scotland is waiting on us.'[27]

At first, national union officials had been upset with the apprentices for taking unofficial action, and insisted that the claim should be handled through the normal negotiating procedures. It was different locally. When Ferguson went to see Calum Mackay, the shop-steward convener at Remington, he got a sympathetic hearing. Mackay, who also worked in the toolroom, lent the apprentices the AEU's branch banner. 'A great big colourful thing it was,' says Ferguson, 'and we went marching out of the factory that day with all the other lads banging on the machinery with their spanners and hammers, saying, "Well done, lads."'[28]

Employers wrote to parents asking them to ensure their sons stayed at work, and some companies suspended lads for taking part in one-day protests. But, on the whole, firms responded cautiously, fearing that the dispute might spread to adult workers if these were made to carry out tasks normally done by boys. There were also the usual accusations that the action was organised by Communists, and the Party undoubtedly did its best to encourage the dispute.

In March the Clydeside lads called on their fellow apprentices in London and Manchester to join their next one-day protests, which were both planned for the end of April. 'Must we Scots do all the work,' they pleaded in an open letter, 'must the boys of Clydeside lead the English apprentices by the hand?'[29] Thousands in Manchester, Merseyside, Tyneside and Belfast joined the April 1960 strikes, and employers reported a response of around 90 per cent on Clydeside.

Eventually, AEU national officials were obliged to back the boys' claim. Thanks partly to contributions from older workers, the apprentices' leaders were even able to offer limited strike pay. At some Scottish sites, including Remington, striking apprentices were joined by their qualified journeymen colleagues (despite the potential erosion of differentials). At one point 1,000 Remington workers came out in support of Ferguson and his dozen workmates. Nonetheless, some apprentices in the Glasgow area ignored every strike and stayed at work.

After three weeks the protests were called off, when employers and national AEU leaders agreed to negotiations on the pay claim. These resulted in a substantial increase in apprentices' wages.

Alex Ferguson seems to have been liked by most of his work colleagues. 'He was quite protective of the other apprentices, and he made sure they were not messed about,' says Stephen Shanahan, a fellow shop steward. 'He had an enthusiasm for what he was doing, and he spent quite a bit of time going round other apprentices and making sure there wasn't anything wrong.'[30] Jimmy Wilson, who worked in Remington's automatic machine shop next to the toolroom, and often ate lunch with Ferguson in the canteen, recalls him as 'a very forceful speaker and a good organiser. Alex was one of the lads and always having a joke and a laugh. He never boasted about his football.'[31] 'There is no doubt he was very popular,' said Calum Mackay, who thought Ferguson's penny trick was a 'miracle'.[32]

Four years later, in March 1964, Ferguson was involved in another famous dispute when Remington decided to sack Mackay, who had acted as the firm's union convener for the past twelve years. Claims of victimisation against effective union officials were fairly common in the 1950s and '60s, but then Remington had suffered numerous strikes – seventy, for instance, in just a few months of 1961. Remington managers had secretly measured Mackay's output against that of five other toolmakers who were also doing general repairs at that time – including Alex Ferguson. They concluded that Mackay was 'the most inefficient toolmaker in the department', spending twice the average length of time on his tasks.[33] Surprisingly, given his well-known work rate nowadays, the Remington analysis also suggested that Ferguson was almost as slow as Mackay. Ferguson's repairs took him fourteen and a half hours on average, compared with just over seven hours for the others.[34] Perhaps Ferguson, too, was spending a lot of time on union duties.

Mackay's colleagues accused Remington of 'a brutal use of economic power' and 'an obvious and blatant act of victimisation' in sacking him.[35] Mackay was a popular figure, despite being a Communist, and toolmakers always carried considerable clout in engineering factories because they played such a vital role in the production process. In many cases firms found it preferable to keep them quiet with extra money rather than face disruption (and at times the union hierarchy found the toolroom men just as difficult to handle as management did). 'Being an American company they were keen to crack down on union activity,' says Jimmy Wilson. 'At that time you couldn't do that like you can now.'[36] The other shop stewards claimed that the management were flouting agreements with the union by dismissing Mackay without consultation and without first raising any problems with him. Remington replied that if it had really wanted to sack Mackay because of his union work it would have done so the previous year, when it had cut the workforce from 2,500 to 800.

Ferguson was twenty-two at the time, and had only just completed his apprenticeship and qualified as a journeyman toolmaker. In his autobiography he describes how he assumed leadership of the unofficial dispute which followed. Even though, as a Communist, Mackay was well to the left politically, Ferguson felt the sacking was unjust and a matter of principle. 'Nobody else was stepping forward to organise the protest against what had been done to Calum,' he says, 'so there was no option but for me to accept the job and get the troops out on strike.'[37] Yet Ferguson's memories seem somewhat at odds with other people's, and he may have exaggerated his role in what followed. 'He was involved when Calum was sacked,' says Jimmy Wilson, 'and he would have been part of the strike committee, but he wasn't the one to suggest it.' Calum Mackay's widow says Ferguson took over from her husband as the toolmakers' shop steward, but she doesn't think he led the protest strike.[38] Nor, in interviews he gave before his death, did Mackay himself mention that Ferguson took a leading role in organising the action.[39]

As with the 1960 apprentices' strike, Alex Ferguson clearly played a part, but one must be careful not to overstate his significance. This was an era when engineering firms kept detailed files and blacklisted employees they perceived as troublemakers, and many of their archives still survive. Ferguson's name does not seem to feature anywhere as a strike leader, but the names of plenty of other people do. 'If he had been a spokesman his name would certainly have cropped up in the files,' says Alan McKinlay.[40]

In March 1964, 650 workers at Remington held a two-day strike and then struck indefinitely, with strong support from the local Paisley district committee of the AEU and financial assistance from other engineering plants around Clydeside. At one point 7,000 workers from other factories staged a one-day strike in solidarity. After almost five weeks, Mackay himself recommended they should go back to work and await the outcome of negotiations. By August, however, Mackay still hadn't been reinstated. The district committee, which was dominated by a few Communist activists, now urged the Remington men to mount a third strike over Mackay. This advice didn't go down well on the Remington shop floor, and Mackay was doomed once it became clear that not even his former colleagues in the toolroom were willing to stop work again.

'We've had enough, Calum!' declared the front page of the *Daily
Record* after an unofficial gathering of 300 men unanimously rejected
the strike call.[41] The fight was lost. 'The fact that Calum himself was
not present gave a few of them the heart to oppose the motion,'
writes Ferguson, who apparently wanted to maintain the struggle. 'I
could never agree with anyone declining to fight against the kind of
injustice done to our shop steward.'[42]

The dispute was not just a straight case of management versus
unions: it also exposed serious political divisions within the AEU,
which had also strong religious undertones – the Catholic Action
group within the union was fiercely anti-Communist. There's good
evidence that AEU right-wingers, at loggerheads with the strongly
left-wing Paisley branch, secretly plotted with the Remington management to engineer Mackay's downfall.

Alex Ferguson probably knew little of such machinations. He
believes, however, that his experiences as a shop steward helped
him greatly when he later went into football management. 'I think
that gave me some organisational skills. It gave me some responsibility to people.' In particular, he says, he acquired the prerequisite
for any person in management – the ability to make a decision.[43]

Today, Alex Ferguson insists his activity in the engineering union
was never a question of being 'anti-Establishment'. His mother had
worried that he'd become a Communist – though unnecessarily, for
he too was anxious about the increasing influence of the Communist
Party within the AEU, and felt that trade unions in the engineering
industry sometimes went too far.

> Any proper trade union background is about the fairness of
> how the worker is treated and that was uppermost in my
> mind. There were many things that I disliked about trade
> unionism in my time . . . The continual strikes, which were
> for no benefit and had no rhyme or reason and which helped
> to destroy the union, were totally counterproductive. It was

the fight for the fairness of things that always got to me. I was prepared to stand up against the unfairness of things.[44]

By the time of the 1964 dispute over Calum Mackay, Alex Ferguson was better off financially than most of his work colleagues, since he was also being paid for a second job – playing football. In the summer of 1960 he'd left Queen's Park for a much bigger club, St Johnstone, which had just been promoted as Scottish Second Division champions. Perhaps the Perth club's greatest distinction was its old ground, Muirton Park, which was one of the most impressive stadiums outside Glasgow, and boasted the biggest pitch in Scotland.

Ferguson remained an amateur at first. The plan was to work at Remington during the day and then train in Perth, sixty miles away, two evenings a week. This entailed expensive and complicated round trips involving combinations of buses, trains and taxis which meant he didn't get home until one o'clock in the morning. He had trouble getting reimbursed by the club. Later on, when it was decided the travelling was too tiring, he arranged instead to train with the players of the now defunct Glasgow side Third Lanark, and later with Airdrie, two clubs much closer to home. The arrangement was not ideal. 'The only time I'm in touch with Saints is when I'm playing on a Saturday,' he explained at the time.[45]

His four years at St Johnstone were not happy. They were punctuated by regular transfer requests, regular refusals, and repeated failed deals. Ferguson describes his joining the club as 'a blunder that led to a nightmare'.[46] The Saints were always short of money, and the club philosophy was to pick up young players cheaply and then develop them in the hope that they might later be sold for big fees. It was never going to be a place where Ferguson might win serious honours. 'It was a journeyman's club,' says his colleague Doug Newlands, 'and if you did well it could be a stepping stone to moving on, as was the case with Ally McCoist many years later. If you played well, the serious clubs would come in for you.'[47] The trouble was that Ferguson was never in the first team enough to make use of the stepping stone, even though he'd gone professional after a year (while remaining a toolmaker). In his first season he scored just twice in only five appearances, though he did at least help win a trophy – the Scottish Reserve Cup. And over his four years in Perth, between 1960 and 1964, and despite the barren spells, Ferguson kept up his scoring rate of a goal every two games – with 23 strikes in 47 appearances.

He was 'useful' but never 'brilliant', is the verdict of his boss at Muirton Park, Bobby Brown, who later became manager of Scotland. 'He had a very good eye for the goal, and he was awkward to play against. He was always good for scrapings in the penalty box. Anything that was loose in the box, Alex would be on to it and find the net.'[48] The former St Johnstone full-back Willie Coburn agrees: 'He could hold his own, and he could sniff out chances. Like the majority of players at that time, he would argue his case with the ref. He was a union boy, so he was used to it.'[49] 'He played hard,' says Doug Newlands, 'but there wasn't much of him. He was a slim guy.'[50] A report of one game spoke of Ferguson moving round the 'goal area with the merciless menace of a spider stalking his prey. Nobody need shout "Use your head!" to this youngster. He does just that – to great advantage. One of these days he'll stop hitting them against the crossbar and his goals total will catapult upwards.'[51]

But the games were too infrequent for that. Between September 1960 and February 1962 he went seventeen months without a goal, and appeared in just seven first-team games. The eleven months between April 1962 and March 1963 also saw no Ferguson goals, and only four appearances. As with Queen's Park, he never became a regular in the St Johnstone team. Hence the frequent attempts to escape.

Bobby Brown also remembers Ferguson as 'a bit of a barrack-room lawyer' who spoke up on behalf of his colleagues, even though he was only in his late teens and early twenties while at St Johnstone. 'Alec had good leadership qualities,' says Brown. 'He certainly said his piece, and whenever it was wages and bonuses he was always in the forefront wanting to know what they were. He was always the spokesman for the rest, and, if there was anything to be said, Alex Ferguson always stuck his neck out.'[52]

When it came to any money the players might be due, Ferguson took a particularly close interest. 'Alec was always the one who queried it,' says Brown. 'He always struck me as being a bit money-orientated, I've got to say that. He used to accuse me of being niggardly with the expenses. I think he was maybe overgenerous to himself, in that he had to be curbed a little bit. But he was a young player, and they try to get away with as much as they can.'[53]

These were typical yo-yo years for the Perth club. St Johnstone were relegated in 1962, and Ferguson appeared in the game that confirmed their demise against the new league champions, Dundee, though they went down only on goal average (under the old system whereby teams on equal points were ranked by dividing the goals they'd scored by the number they'd let in). But they bounced back as Second Division champions twelve months later, when Ferguson got nine goals in fifteen matches – his best tally for the Saints.

Ferguson refused to re-sign his contract at the start of the 1963–64 season in the hope of finally getting the move he wanted. The result was that he spent much of the first half of the season stagnating in St Johnstone's reserves (and was also off for six weeks with various broken facial bones, as well as ligament problems). In November 1963 Bobby Brown at last agreed to transfer him to the Second Division side Raith Rovers. But Ferguson rejected the deal, and Raith went for another Saints player instead. The following month another move was mooted – to Third Lanark, the First Division side with whom Ferguson had once trained. The Glasgow club decided to watch him play in a St Johnstone reserve game, but

Ferguson was switched to wing-half, because of a selection crisis, so Third Lanark couldn't assess his abilities as a striker.

Towards the end of 1963 Ferguson's spirits were so low that he seriously thought of giving up football and emigrating to Canada, where toolmakers were in heavy demand. (Interestingly, Ferguson's great predecessor as Manchester United manager, Sir Matt Busby, almost took a similar decision as a young man.) The week before Christmas, Ferguson was so fed up with the thought of playing for St Johnstone reserves again that he arranged for Martin's girlfriend to ring Bobby Brown, pretending to be his mother and claiming he had flu. His parents were furious when they found out. Then a telegram arrived from Brown asking Ferguson to phone him urgently.

Although Brown hadn't fallen for the flu trick, he wanted not to reprimand Ferguson, but to summon him back to the first eleven. Brown had spent the week trying to buy a new goalscoring inside-forward; having failed with three different targets, Ferguson was his last resort. But a return to first-team football was a daunting prospect. St Johnstone were playing at Ibrox, against a Rangers side which was top of the League and still indisputably the greatest force in Scottish football. Rangers had won the double the previous season, and would go on to complete the treble that year. It was a difficult first half, and St Johnstone were losing 1–0 at the interval. 'The pace was a lot faster than I've been used to for a while,' said the rusty toolmaker. 'I just couldn't get in the game.' So at half-time Bobby Brown told Ferguson to 'lie further upfield'.[54]

It worked. St Johnstone produced the 'shock result of the season', winning 3–2.[55] It was all thanks to a Fergie frenzy in the second half, when he scored a hat-trick within the space of twenty-three minutes, all with his favoured left foot. He also hit the bar twice, in a match which took place in freezing conditions. It was only the second time the Saints had won at Ibrox in their history – the previous time was in 1925 – and to this day it also remains the only occasion a St

Johnstone player has ever scored three times against Rangers. Remarkably, it wasn't just Ferguson's first hat-trick in top-class football, it was also the first senior game he'd played for more than seven months. Sadly, not many witnessed his achievement: the 14,000 crowd was one of Rangers' lowest for years.

Coming against his local club, of course, and the team he'd supported as a boy, his Christmas hat-trick was even more special. He felt it was almost supernatural. 'Since then,' says Ferguson, 'I have never been sceptical about the existence of influences beyond ourselves.'[56]

Yet even in this, his son's greatest hour as a player, Alex Ferguson Snr refused to be impressed. When the Saints' hero took the short walk home down Broomloan Road that night he says his father merely told him the game had been 'OK', before reminding him once again that if he didn't shoot he wouldn't score.[57] The All Saints branch of the Celtic Supporters' Club, near to the Fergusons' family home, was rather more enthusiastic about the St Johnstone goal-poacher. So jubilant were they, in fact, that they made Alex a patron 'saint' of the club. More important, Ferguson's achievement had made the rest of Scottish football sit up and take notice.

'The Man Who Shook Rangers,' said the headline in Scotland's *Sunday Mail*.[58] Ferguson was later photographed clutching a folded copy of the paper, and several newspapers ran features on the unknown star. 'He's an ordinary sort of bloke,' said the *Glasgow Evening Citizen*, 'lives in Govan Road, is a toolmaker by trade, likes the Beatles.' The interview was accompanied by a picture of a very young and slightly shy-looking Ferguson smiling enthusiastically while working at a lathe, dressed in overalls and with a ruler poking out of his pocket. The interview had been conducted by Malcolm Munroe, the reporter who'd been so critical of Ferguson's lackadaisical penalty miss for Glasgow Schoolboys six years before. 'What'll happen now Alex?' asked Munroe, 'now that you've scored three against Rangers – you'll be very closely marked by the opposition. You won't get room to move . . .' 'In that case,' Ferguson replied, 'I'll just have to play harder!'[59]

The *Scottish Daily Express* photographed him outside the gates of Ibrox, crouching next to the L-plate on his car (having failed his driving test the previous week); the picture appeared under the headline 'Alex Passes Test'.[60] 'A transfer for Ferguson?' his manager, Bobby Brown, was reported as saying. 'Definitely not after this game!'[61] His feat had now made it even more difficult for him to get away from St Johnstone, as was explained by an article in a Perth paper headed 'The Crazy World of Alec Ferguson'. 'From "just another player" seeking a transfer,' it said, 'the Govan boy . . . is suddenly in the goldfish bowl. Now it's all eyes on Alec . . . Before the "hat-trick", a reasonable offer would have been taken [by] Perth. Now? Saints would not be unreasonable in thinking he is worth a substantial fee.' While St Johnstone claimed Ferguson was no longer for sale, he reiterated his requests to leave, and appealed against the £3,000 fee the club had put on his head. 'A happy solution,' the paper suggested, 'would be a transfer to Rangers, the club at the root of the problem. Before you scoff, consider this. The Gers are often slow to act, but lads who turn on the humdinger stuff against Rangers are seldom forgotten.'[62] The article would prove to be very prescient.

Six weeks later, in February 1964, Alex Ferguson was asked to come to St Johnstone's rescue again, though this time in a very different role, and one he'd no doubt prefer to forget. The Saints were drawing 1–1 at home to Hearts when in the sixty-fifth minute their goalkeeper, Harry Fallon, was injured and carried off to hospital. This was the era before teams had any substitutes, let alone a replacement keeper, so Ferguson left the forward line to wear Fallon's yellow jersey instead. 'He played a wonderful stop-gap role and cut out some menacing crosses,' according to one report.[63] The statistics, however, tell a sorrier story of Ferguson the goalie. He conceded his first goal after only a few seconds, and two more in the last five minutes, as Hearts won 4–1.

Despite two jobs, and his union activity, Alex Ferguson had enough spare time, and the money, to enjoy life. Like his father, he loved betting, and this became easier once betting shops became legal in 1961. To outsmart the bookies, Alex kept 'meticulous' records of horses' past form, says Duncan Petersen. 'I think he did it as much for the challenge as the money. He knew which horses had done well, in which conditions, and he'd have flutters on them.'[64]

Friends say Alex was never a great drinker, but he loved music, and was always singing himself. 'Alec's a hopeless singer, tuneless, but loves music,' says his friend John Donachie, who also became a professional footballer. 'I mean *loves* music, and we sang Neil Sedaka numbers with him. Alec's song was "I Go Ape", and I don't even know if Sedaka knows the words to it, but Alec always had a go at it and made his own words up.'[65] Together on Sunday nights the lads went dancing at the Locarno ballroom in Sauchiehall Street in the centre of Glasgow. The evening would start with the girls at one end and all the boys at the other before they started mixing, and would always end with 'Smoke Gets In Your Eyes'. 'Alec had a Crombie jacket and he had the winklepicker shoes and a Perry Como hair-style,' according to brother Martin.[66]

His friend Hugh McDonald says that, after an evening out, the boys would often stop off to buy chips, and then the natural temp-tation was to screw the wrapping paper – what they called the poke – into a ball and kick it along the pavement until it was aban-doned in a gutter or a dark doorway. 'But Ferguson would hold that poke until he got to a bin. He never, ever threw paper down. He'd say, "It goes in the bin where it should go, and you should be pick-ing that stuff up. You left it there, you know."' McDonald says Ferguson might even pull his friends up for the lazy way they ambled along. '"Why do you walk that way, slouching there? Get your shoulders back!" That's the kind of thing he would say to you.'[67]

Alex Ferguson had had two or three girlfriends by now, and then one night at the Locarno he spotted Cathy Holding, a girl from Remington Rand whom he'd been eyeing up for several weeks. 'Of course, I thought it was just another girlfriend,' says Martin Ferguson, who wondered how long she would last.[68]

Cathy was more than three years older than Alex and came from Govanhill, on the south side of Glasgow. But her first impressions of Alex Ferguson weren't favourable, and he certainly didn't come across as a tidy, litter-conscious young man. A friend even suggested to her that he might be a boxer, judging from his appearance. 'He had two black eyes,' Cathy recalls, 'and a broken nose, and I thought he was a thug. But he had broken his nose in the football, which I didn't know, because I didn't know he was a footballer.'[69] She gave him the benefit of the doubt. It helped, says Cathy, that Ferguson was better off than other Remington workers, because of his extra income from football. He was smitten, says John Donachie. 'I remember Alec: "*Phwoar*, this is it." I mean, from being a Jack the Lad and girlfriends here and there . . . that was him. He was game, set and match. He had found the girl of his dreams.'[70]

4

Razor Elbows

*'I was three years at the club and still hold the scoring
record . . . That was in a Scottish First Division where
men were men. In the Kingdom of Fife!'*

ALEX FERGUSON[1]

To followers of modern-day football, Alex Ferguson's move from
St Johnstone to Dunfermline Athletic in the summer of 1964
may not look like a step up. But the 1960s were a golden age for
Dunfermline, in which the club was a leading challenger to Celtic
and Rangers. The emergence of the so-called Pars (from 'paralytic',
the way they once played) was almost entirely due to a man whose
career would become entwined with that of Alex Ferguson. The
former Celtic captain Jock Stein had taken over as manager at East
End Park in the spring of 1960, helped Dunfermline avoid relegation, and then won the Scottish Cup the following year with a 2–0
win over his former club. It was the first of twenty-six major trophies
Stein would win during the next fifteen years – a record unsurpassed by any other post-war British manager. (At the start of 2002
Ferguson was next, with twenty-three.)

The 1961 Scottish Cup triumph had established the small club
from Fife as a contender north of the border, and Dunfermline began
to broaden their horizons. Throughout the 1960s they participated

almost every year in the fledgling European competitions, the Cup-Winners' Cup and the Inter-Cities Fairs' Cup, and enjoyed considerable success.

Alex Ferguson often claims that at 'every club I was with I was always the top goalscorer'.[2] This isn't accurate. At neither Queen's Park nor St Johnstone was he ever the leading scorer, partly because he didn't play enough games. But he more than made up for his previous disappointment, by finishing as Dunfermline's leading goalscorer in each of his three seasons at East End Park. The Dunfermline years, from 1964 to 1967, represent the peak of Ferguson's career as a player.

It was Jock Stein's idea to sign Ferguson for Dunfermline, in a straight swap for the Dunfermline player Dan McLindon. When Stein suddenly left for Hibs in April 1964 the plan seemed to have fallen through. Then that summer, after Ferguson rejected another exchange deal with Airdrie, the McLindon swap was resurrected by Stein's Northern Irish successor, Willie Cunningham. Ferguson soon gave up his engineering job and turned professional full-time. It was just as well, for by the end of the decade Remington Rand had closed its Glasgow plant and moved its operations to Sweden, citing poor industrial relations among other reasons.

Until now, Ferguson felt he was going nowhere very fast in football. Indeed, he acknowledges that his brother, Martin, who was playing for a very successful Partick Thistle side, had enjoyed a more fruitful career until that point. Martin actually played in Europe before Alex did: after coming third in the Scottish League in 1963, Thistle played in the Inter-Cities Fairs' Cup. But Alex was used to being considered second fiddle – because Martin was bigger, Alex was often assumed to be the younger of the two brothers; others mistook them for twins.

At Dunfermline, however, Alex Ferguson's career quickly picked up. 'He was a goal-poacher,' remembers the club historian, Duncan Simpson – 'always there to poke out a foot at the vital moment.'[3]

'He had these skinny legs, and he didn't have the timing that other players had,' says Harry Melrose, who was also a Dunfermline forward. 'But anything that came back off the keeper he was well in there. And he was very good in the air.'[4] 'He had the sharpest elbows I've ever seen,' says another colleague, Alex Totten. 'He wasn't a big burly type, so he had to look after himself in other ways. He was a great eighteen-yard-box player.'[5]

Indeed, Ferguson had a reputation for rarely scoring goals from outside the penalty area. Totten and his colleague Bert Paton both vividly remember one particular Ferguson strike from twenty-two yards out, in a cup-tie, because it was so unusual. 'I think we all fell over with shock,' says Paton. 'He was the sort of player defenders hate . . . He was always moaning, complaining if he didn't get the ball. But he was an inspiration with his goals.'[6] One report described him as 'a rampaging raider, a one-man commando force in a highly organised side'.[7]

'It's the fifty-fifty balls that make me a striker,' he told one paper in his third year at Dunfermline, explaining the Ferguson philosophy of playing up front. 'You get them, others don't. So you can't let defenders muscle you around. You make your position near goal – and you keep it!' But Ferguson revealed that ideally he wanted to play further back, to be the withdrawn striker, or the inside-forward rather than the centre-forward: 'I like to be in the game all the time . . . If there's action, then I want to be part of it. But the boss keeps chasing me up the park – and he's dead right. It's a tremendously demanding job, especially if you get a bit of a reputation. The marking becomes tighter and tighter.'[8]

Ferguson's hero and role model was the Scotland and Manchester United striker Denis Law, who had just been crowned European Footballer of the Year and was only a couple of years older than him. 'Sometimes I would hold on to my cuffs in the way Denis did,' he wrote later, and, like Law, Ferguson was always ready to pounce if the ball rebounded off the goalkeeper. 'These were little things that you picked up off your heroes – and everybody's got heroes.'[9]

The former Scotland manager Craig Brown has vivid memories of playing for Falkirk against Alex Ferguson. One day a Falkirk full-back passed the ball back to his goalkeeper, Willie Whigham, who rested his hand on it – as the rules then permitted – and started grumbling at his defender about the back-pass. 'Fergie came in on his blind side,' says Brown, 'knocked the ball out from under Willie's hand and tapped it into the net.' Whigham protested, but the referee allowed the goal to stand:

> It was a bit of pure cheek, and the reason I remember it was that when Willie Whigham came into the Falkirk dressing-room at half-time, our manager Willie Ormond started giving him stick about the goal. Big Willie took his jersey off and said, 'Right – get somebody else to go in goal, then!' and went off to the bath.[10]

Whigham was eventually persuaded to play the second half, but it wasn't his day: Ferguson got four goals, as Falkirk lost 6–1.

The abiding memory of former colleagues is Ferguson's spirit, and his constant determination to win. 'Nobody likes to lose but when we'd all get in the bath afterwards you could see he took it hardest,' says Harry Melrose:[11]

> He was a born winner and a bad loser. It did not matter what he was doing – playing golf or whatever – he wanted to win badly. Whatever he was doing at that time he did 100 per cent. If there was a game to be won, it didn't matter if you were his best pal or not, he would have to win it by fair means or foul . . . There were quite a few sore eyes and bloody noses when Fergie was playing. 'Razor Elbows' they called him.[12]

'He wasn't sturdy, but wiry,' Melrose adds, 'and his elbows always seemed to be stuck down the centre-half's throat.'[13]

Whenever former colleagues recollect Fergie's playing style, his legendary elbows get far more mentions than his feet. 'We used to say that he sharpened his elbows before he went on the pitch,' says Bert Paton.[14] 'He was very difficult as an opponent,' says the former Rangers captain John Greig, 'not because of his ability, but because of the way he played. He played with elbows out, and we used to always say that he wore his boots on his elbows. He probably could have controlled the ball better with his elbows.'[15] Yet years later, as a manager, Ferguson described the use of elbows as 'mean' and 'extremely dangerous'. He wrote in 1994, 'I think we have reached the stage where it would be better to err on the side of even penalising people wrongly so that everyone keeps their elbows and arms to themselves. And don't give me this stuff about needing to use your arms to propel you into the air. It's a feeble excuse.'[16]

'I was never a really dirty player,' Alex Ferguson often claims, 'but I do still believe a front player has to be hard. I don't think strikers should ever let defenders mess them about.'[17] 'Strikers have to be able to take it,' he admits, 'but I could give it back.'[18]

Sometimes his victims were his own colleagues. Bert Paton remembers how Ferguson got into five or six serious skirmishes in training sessions, 'actually coming to blows with his teammates'.[19] On one occasion, in a European tie, Paton even had to step in and prevent a fight between Ferguson and one of his colleagues on the pitch. Typically, Ferguson had given his teammates a rollicking, only to have one of them answer back.

One Dunfermline player, George Miller, has memories of Ferguson as a 'determined' player, 'full of confidence', and who 'obviously knew the game inside out'.[20] 'Alec always had something to say about working conditions,' says Alex Smith, another colleague. Smith recalls how Ferguson had a phenomenal knowledge of other sides and players, not just in Scotland but throughout Europe.

Acquiring such information was much more difficult in the days before videotapes, the Internet, regular football on TV, or even extensive coverage in newspapers and magazines, but Smith remembers Ferguson reading *World Soccer*, one of the few serious football publications at that time. 'He had a vast knowledge of the players. The rest of the lads were more interested in the women. He knew all the opponents. It was quite unusual, as everybody wasn't as enlightened as they are now.'[21] Bert Paton, who later became Dunfermline manager, feels that, of all the club players of that era, Ferguson was one of the least likely to become a manager, however. He was so 'harum-scarum', he says, a 'Jack the Lad' who was always 'the last out of the dressing room'.[22]

Most of his colleagues disagree, and say that Ferguson's managerial qualities were apparent even then. Sometimes, for convenience, Ferguson would train with his brother's club, Partick Thistle, based just across the Clyde from Govan (though in 1965 Martin was transferred to Barnsley in England). The Partick manager, Willie Thornton, knew Ferguson had management potential from his constant questioning during training sessions. 'He wanted to learn, he was always asking, "Why are you doing this?" and "Why are you doing that?" That made an impression because coaching in the modern game was only in its early stages in Scotland. People played it by ear.'[23]

It was at Dunfermline that Ferguson showed the earliest signs of wanting to stay in the game after playing, and in the summer of 1965 he attended his first coaching course at the SFA centre at Largs on the Ayrshire coast. He got his coaching 'badge' the following year, and attended refresher courses for several summers thereafter.

'Even then, he knew the game,' says Alex Totten, who has since gone into management himself, most recently with Falkirk. 'He was effectively a coach even when he was only a player. He was always telling players what to do and what not to do.' Ferguson was still only in his early twenties, but 'he was a leader in the dressing room', says Totten. 'He was always the spokesman. He seemed to have been around . . . He was very serious as regards football, but he liked a laugh as well.'[24]

After training, the players would sometimes work together practising corners or free kicks, which again was unusual in those days. Then they'd go off to the Regal building in the town, which boasted a restaurant, cinema and snooker room. Lunch at the Regal was 'a highlight of my time at Dunfermline', says Ferguson. After the meal the more thoughtful players would spend much of the afternoon plotting tactics on the table, using napkins, salt cellars and sauce bottles as props. 'It was probably there that the seeds of my managerial career were planted,' he says.[25] The gatherings were partly a result of the influence of Jock Stein, who had accustomed the players to thinking and talking about their football, which was quite revolutionary for the British game.

The other factor, of course, was the novelty of playing in Europe. 'You went abroad and saw these things and then you thought, "I'll try those for myself,"' says Harry Melrose. 'That would be the start of Fergie thinking on a higher plane and seeing other styles of play.'[26] It was similar to the so-called 'academy' of thinking players which came together under Ron Greenwood at West Ham in the late 1950s. Ferguson was just one of the Dunfermline group who went on to successful careers in football management.

Despite being a full-time professional, Ferguson didn't spend all his time on discussions about the game. As well as snooker and golf, the Dunfermline squad enjoyed a bet. Although he'd played for east-coast clubs since 1960, Ferguson still lived on Clydeside, and a Dunfermline minibus, with the club's name printed along the side, would collect the Glasgow contingent every morning and take them to training. To the annoyance of their manager, Willie Cunningham, Ferguson and his colleagues would regularly stop the minibus and drop into a Dunfermline betting shop before arriving at the training ground. Why did they have to park right outside the bookie's and embarrass the club? Cunningham asked. Why couldn't they use the car park round the corner?

Bert Paton and Harry Melrose both noticed how Ferguson always seemed to try hardest in the big fixtures. 'He always pulled out that extra bit when he was playing Celtic,' says Melrose.[27] In December 1964, for instance, almost exactly a year after his famous hat-trick at Ibrox, he got the winning goal as Dunfermline won at Celtic for the first time in their history. Ferguson 'scored a lot of important goals in important games', confirms the Dunfermline historian Duncan Simpson, 'and lots of hat-tricks too' – seven of them in three years.[28]

His first hat-trick for Dunfermline came early in his first season, in a 7–2 win over Clyde, at the start of what was to become the most successful campaign in the club's history. Ferguson scored twenty-two times, with fifteen goals in the League and seven more in cup competitions. By mid-April 1965 the Pars were in the running for an improbable league and cup double. The League involved a three-way tussle with Kilmarnock and Hearts – the only time in Scottish football history that the Old Firm would both finish outside the top three. In the Scottish Cup, Dunfermline faced Celtic in the final. It was then that Alex Ferguson's season began to unravel.

Dunfermline's penultimate league game was at home to his old club, St Johnstone. It looked an easy prospect, but the Pars dropped a valuable point as it ended 1–1. Ferguson scored his side's only goal, but he also missed numerous other chances. Willie Cunningham detected a sudden drop in form.

The press began speculating whether Ferguson would play in the final. On the Friday before, the *Daily Record*, for instance, explained that he would have to 'sweat it out' until just before kick-off. The paper listed the probable Dunfermline line-up, with his fellow forward John McLaughlin as the alternative to Ferguson. 'He doesn't mind,' said the paper. 'He knows that everyone at Dunfermline has played their part, and if he is chosen he'll be just one of the team.'[29]

The 1965 Scottish Cup final would etch itself in Alex Ferguson's memory, though not because of anything that happened on the pitch. The Dunfermline players gathered that morning at East End Park, ate lunch, then left by coach for Glasgow without knowing which of them was actually going to play. Even as they walked into the Hampden Park dressing room there was still no news of the team from Willie Cunningham. 'The tension was tearing at my insides,' says Ferguson.[30] 'I could see it was a problem for him. I could tell because I could see him faffing around the place.'[31]

Cunningham left the dramatic announcement until well after two o'clock, and then listed his eleven in front of all the players, with the club chairman and secretary standing at his side. When the manager finally announced McLaughlin at centre-forward and confirmed the number 11, Jackie Sinclair, Ferguson knew he was out. 'You bastard!' he shouted at Cunningham, and carried on protesting. In the era before substitutes, there was no point in even putting on his kit. What particularly upset him was that the manager had given him no warning. 'I lambasted him in front of everyone, and he had no answer because he knew he should have spoken to me.'[32] A colleague had to intervene before Ferguson stormed out to watch the game from the stand.

Alex Ferguson had been the Pars' leading goalscorer that season. 'I'd played in all the rounds up to then. I'd scored most of the goals. I'll never forget that.'[33] But John McLaughlin was in better form than Ferguson. 'My thinking on it was like any other manager,' says Cunningham. 'He hadn't been hitting the high spots, so there was no way he was going to be in, and he just had to accept that – which of course he didn't do. He never did. It wasn't worrying to me in the least. I was quite willing to take his bluster.'[34]

Being dropped was bad enough. What made it worse for Ferguson was that he believed Cunningham had been unprofessional in his handling of the matter. The manager had clearly been nervous about how his striker might react, had postponed telling him until the last moment, and then, when he did, had embarrassed him in front of his teammates. Cunningham's behaviour that day would remain for Ferguson a searing memory in the years ahead when he himself repeatedly wrestled with the problems and diplomacy of choosing and announcing cup-final teams.

Yet he had surely overreacted. Cunningham's decision can't have been a surprise, nor the lateness of his announcement, for the press had been suggesting as much all week. Ferguson had had plenty of time to consider his response if the decision went against him.

Alex Ferguson must have had mixed feelings as Dunfermline went on to lose the final 3–2, with McLaughlin one of the losing side's two scorers. The Celtic defender Billy McNeill, an infrequent goalscorer at that time, won the Cup with a header from a corner – a formula Ferguson would experience again. It was Celtic's first honour in seven years – ending their worst-ever silverware drought – and marked the beginning of the most successful period in the Glasgow club's history.

In the end, Dunfermline also failed to win the championship. Although they took revenge on Celtic with a 5–1 win in their final league match – and a restored Ferguson struck one of the goals – the point dropped against St Johnstone proved decisive. In the tightest three-way finish in Scottish League history, Dunfermline finished third, a point behind champions Kilmarnock and runners-up Hearts. It was the highest place in their history; had they beaten St Johnstone they'd have won the title because of their far superior goal average. Ferguson said later that 'some of the lads were very nervous' towards the end of the season. 'We found ourselves holding back, trying to play it carefully instead of playing our normal game.'[35]

Ferguson asked for a transfer after the cup final, but Cunningham refused. (By now Ferguson's transfer requests had become annual events, whatever his club.) Yet the following season, 1965–66, was undoubtedly, in personal terms, the best of Ferguson's playing career, perhaps because of his sense of injustice after the disappointment of

Hampden. The only slight blemish was being sent off for fighting with an opposing player in a 6–1 win over Motherwell in January 1966. The opponent was John McLaughlin – the man who'd taken his place in the cup-final side, but was subsequently transferred to Motherwell. Ferguson was suspended for a fortnight by the SFA at what happened to be a historic hearing – the first time he and several other players were allowed representation by their union, the Scottish Professional Footballers' Association (SPFA).

Ferguson's 31 goals in 31 league games in 1965–66 remains a Dunfermline record for the top division – easily beating the previous best of 25. The Pars scored 94 league goals in all – another club record, and the second highest total for any club in Britain that season. But again Dunfermline had no honours to show for their toil. Ferguson was also joint top scorer in the Scottish League with Celtic's Joe McBride (who, coincidentally, came from the street next to Ferguson in Govan). Adding cup and European games, his total of 45 goals in 52 appearances outstripped McBride's overall tally to make Ferguson the most prolific striker in Scotland. All in all, 1966 was a good year for Alex Ferguson – despite England's famous victory in the World Cup.

In fact Ferguson was barely able to take a break from football for his wedding. On the second Saturday in March he married Cathy Holding in the morning, before going to Dunfermline to play his part in a 1–0 win over Hamilton. The wedding was a very simple affair, conducted at the Martha Street Register Office in the centre of Glasgow, rather than in a church, because, like his parents' and grandparents' marriages, it was religiously mixed. 'Nobody wanted to give,' says Cathy, who is a Catholic, and in those days such issues were taken very seriously in the west of Scotland.[36] The Fergusons moved into a new semi-detached house in Simshill on the south side of Glasgow. There wasn't time for a honeymoon, since Dunfermline had to travel out to Zaragoza the following week for a Fairs' Cup match. From the very start, Cathy Ferguson learned the sacrifices she was expected to make as a 'football widow', in the cause of a game she has never enjoyed very much and considers rather trivial.

Dunfermline had provided Ferguson with an excellent introduction to top-class Continental football. At the time, playing in Europe was still an adventure: the European competitions had been going only a few years. Football under floodlights was fairly novel in itself, and playing against overseas teams with strange names, odd-looking kits and different styles of play generated an extra buzz of excitement and interest, especially for an unfashionable side like Dunfermline. (Ferguson had already experienced some of that buzz as a Rangers fan, travelling to watch European ties at Wolves and Spurs while he was a St Johnstone player, and even following the team to a game in Sweden.)

Ferguson's European debut had been in 1964, in a goalless draw against Örgryte of Sweden in the Inter-Cities Fairs' Cup. It occurred in the Ullevi stadium in Gothenburg – a venue which would later play a sparkling role in Ferguson's career. Although the Pars never came close to winning any of the three major European trophies, Ferguson faced several top Continental sides of the 1960s, including Stuttgart, Athletic Bilbao and Dynamo Zagreb. In home legs Dunfermline seemed invincible, winning all eight games at East End Park during Ferguson's days at the club.

Ferguson again tried to leave Dunfermline in the summer of 1966, insisting on a substantial pay rise to stay. He got his increase, on the understanding he'd be able to leave twelve months later, but 1966–67 was almost bound to be disappointing compared with the previous season. That he scored twenty-nine times (twenty in the League; nine in cup fixtures) is all the more remarkable given a spell of fourteen matches when he went without a goal. He was also laid off for five weeks with a knee injury.

The *Daily Record* called Ferguson 'the prince of goal-snatchers', spoke of his 'dazzling ability to score goals', and highlighted a personal £1 bet with Alex Smith (who'd left Dunfermline for Rangers the previous summer) over who would score more goals.[37] Ferguson won by six goals, which may not have gone unnoticed at Ibrox.

The 1966–67 season also saw Ferguson's first brief recognition at international level. In March 1967 he played for the Scottish League against the Football League, an old-fashioned annual fixture which used to rank just below a full international. 'He has become a prolific scorer,' said the Hampden Park programme:

> his opportunism and cuteness off the ball making him an elusive, menacing forager difficult to counter. He can outwit the most compact defence by his alacrity and acceleration, particularly over the first ten yards, and split-second timing of his delivery. Many defences have set out to box him in and siphon him of his menace, but he has generally emerged the winner. The English League defenders, who know little of him, have been warned of what he may do if not closely policed.[38]

The Scottish team included Billy McNeill, John Greig, Tommy Gemmell and Willie Henderson, while Bobby Moore, Jimmy Greaves and Geoff Hurst played for the English eleven. Scotland lost 3–0, with a Ferguson strike ruled offside. 'He was hardly in the game,' says the English centre-half Brian Labone, who marked him.[39]

That spring, Ferguson was on the fringes of the full Scotland team, which was now managed by Bobby Brown, his former boss at St Johnstone. He claims to have been picked for the squad for the Scots' historic 3–2 win at Wembley – England's first defeat since winning the World Cup – though there was little chance of his displacing the great Denis Law. Brown also chose Ferguson for the SFA's five-week summer round-the-world tour, taking in Israel, Hong Kong, Australia, New Zealand and Canada. The man described in programme notes as 'probably the best snapper-up of goals in Scotland today' managed to score ten times in seven appearances for the touring eleven, though the opposition was feeble.[40] Events were more noteworthy off the field than on it. The Six Day War broke out in the Middle East while the Scots were in Israel, and in Hong Kong they found themselves in the midst of violent demonstrations by Maoist students.

The touring team was far from the full Scotland side, since Celtic, Rangers, Leeds and Manchester United had all withdrawn their players – the majority of a typical national line-up. Instead the squad included prospects such as the Burnley (and future Manchester United) winger Willie Morgan and the prolific striker Joe Harper, then at Huddersfield, and with whom Ferguson seems to have conducted something of a duel to finish as top scorer. To Ferguson's everlasting disappointment the games weren't deemed to be full internationals by the SFA, so no caps were awarded.

Ferguson always mentions the 1967 tour if he's questioned about playing for his country, and he devotes a whole chapter to it in his autobiography, but he knows the fixtures weren't the real thing. Bobby Brown says Ferguson never really came near to a place in the full Scotland side. 'I don't think he was ever really considered for a full cap.'[41] His only other senior representative outing was another Scottish League fixture that autumn, when he scored in a 2–0 win in Belfast against the Irish League, though he reportedly 'had a poor match'.[42]

Alex Ferguson was a victim of his times. Today the SFA might be more relaxed and award caps for the world tour. And in the mid to late 1960s the competition among Scottish forwards for a place in the national side was far more formidable: Denis Law, Alan Gilzean, Steve Chalmers and Willie Johnston were all playing regularly for Scotland. These days the national side plays far more fixtures than it did then (the full Scotland side played only four times in 1967), and players' chances are far greater now because teams can deploy several substitutes. If Ferguson had been born thirty years later he almost certainly would have earned several international caps.

5

Lone Ranger

'No other experience in nearly forty years as a professional player and manager has created a scar comparable with that left by the treatment I received at Rangers.'

ALEX FERGUSON[1]

One Saturday afternoon in July 1967, Alex Ferguson was watching athletics on television when a young man knocked at the door of his home. He announced himself as the son of Scot Symon, who'd been the manager of Rangers for the past thirteen years. The visitor said he didn't want to be spotted, handed over his father's address, and said that Symon wanted Ferguson to go and see him that evening. By Monday, Ferguson had signed for his lifelong idols, proclaiming to the *Daily Record*, 'I'm ready to play my heart out for Rangers.'[2]

If the transfer seemed sudden, the encounter had been carefully prepared. The foreplay had involved false names and phone calls to a neighbour's home. Jim 'Jolly' Rodger, a football reporter on the *Daily Mirror*, had played a clandestine role in orchestrating the transfer, as he did in several other important moves of Alex Ferguson's career.

Ferguson's spell at Rangers was to be a defining experience in his development, but not in the way that he hoped when he joined. He was twenty-five, and reaching his peak as a player. He should have had the world at his feet, with the prospect of fame, wealth, trophies and international recognition. 'This is it, I'll get forty caps and loads of medals,' he thought to himself.[3]

As he emerged from Ibrox, the club's new star striker was mobbed by small boys demanding autographs. And he himself had now realised a childhood dream, becoming one of the few Govan boys actually to play for the local side. He'd often done well against Rangers. Apart from his 1963 hat-trick, he'd scored twice more in Dunfermline's 3–2 win over the Ibrox club in December 1966. 'Now I've achieved my ambition,' he proclaimed. 'I was very conscious I was playing for a transfer last season, and the harder I tried to score the more difficult it became. Now, the pressure is off.'[4]

The truth was the complete opposite, of course. Now Alex Ferguson really was in the spotlight. His every success and failure were about to be scrutinised many times over by Rangers' fanatical fans and in the media. At Dunfermline 'you weren't in the public eye and you could go out and about without anybody looking at you', Cathy Ferguson once observed. 'When you were with Rangers, the pressures were on.'[5]

To say things never worked out is an understatement. Alex Ferguson's failure at Rangers contributed enormously to his subsequent hunger to succeed as a manager. Without the twenty-nine months at Ibrox the Ferguson story might have been very different. More than a decade later, when he had already emerged as a successful club manager, he gave a glimpse of the hurt he felt when he told an interviewer how he hated being called 'Alex Ferguson, the former Rangers player'.[6]

Perhaps he should have known things might not go well at Rangers. The hierarchical, highly disciplined and conservative club was hardly likely to accommodate an opinionated trade unionist who had a habit of complaining about the slightest grievance. Two years before, a former Ibrox player, Ralph Brand, had written a series of newspaper articles condemning the club for a 'feudal attitude' towards players and an 'antiquated training routine'.[7] It was often observed that, compared with the more free-spirited Celtic, there was no sense of enjoyment about playing for Rangers. It hardly sounded like the kind of environment in which Alex Ferguson would thrive. Ibrox was no place for troublemaking mavericks.

Rangers were the toffs of British football, the richest club in Scotland, and used to thinking of themselves as the very best. They had dominated the Scottish League and Cup competitions for more than half a century. Their only long-term rivals were Celtic – a rivalry which extended beyond the football pitch. But in the summer of 1967 Rangers were a club in transition. They had been getting used to coming second.

Ferguson joined Rangers during one of the darkest spells in the club's history. Six months earlier they'd been knocked out of the Scottish Cup by tiny Berwick Rangers. Even today this is still regarded as the greatest act of giant-killing in the long history of the Scottish Cup. (Such upsets are much rarer than in English cup football.) Rangers had responded ruthlessly to the defeat. George McLean and Jim Forrest, their two strikers against Berwick, never played for the club again. Perhaps ominously, both were graduates of Drumchapel Amateurs, like Ferguson.

In other respects, Rangers' 1966–67 season hadn't gone too badly: they'd reached the final of the Scottish League Cup, and put up a strong fight for the league title. They lost just three league games all season – two to Ferguson's Dunfermline – only to falter in the closing matches and finish second. What's more, Rangers had also reached the final of a major European competition, the Cup-Winners' Cup, where they met Bayern Munich. They gave a creditable performance against the emerging Bayern side of Maier, Beckenbauer and Müller, who had the great advantage of playing on German soil. The game went to extra time before Rangers lost 1–0.

The big problem wasn't really Rangers' record that season, but that of their arch-rivals. For Celtic won every competition they entered in 1966–67. At home they collected the Glasgow Cup, the League Cup, the Scottish Cup and the Scottish League. More humiliating still for Rangers' fans, Celtic not only had got to the final of the European Cup, but had gone on to defeat Inter Milan 2–1 in Lisbon to become the first British side to lift the top European club trophy. Local rivalry was ratcheted up a notch or two by the fact that all eleven of the Lisbon Lions, as the European Cup team became known, had been born within forty miles of Glasgow (and eight were home-grown). And, to top it all, their excellence extended beyond the football field: a Celtic team also won the BBC's football-based TV general-knowledge contest, *Quizball*.

Rangers' greatest handicap, especially now Forrest and McLean were banished, was the lack of a natural goalscorer – indeed, on the day of the Cup-Winners' Cup final their chairman rather tactlessly said they needed several new forwards. Rangers fans were also in desperate need of something to console them for Celtic's success. It was Alex Ferguson's job to satisfy both needs. His fee of £65,000 was a record between two Scottish clubs – £10,000 more than the previous highest, and the equivalent, Ferguson once claimed, of £6.5 million today (which is reasonably accurate, based on the hundred-fold inflation in transfer fees).[8] This was, of course, in an age when Scottish clubs rarely bought players from England or the Continent. 'When he joined Rangers we were delighted,' says John Greig, the Ibrox captain. 'We thought he would solve our problems up front and at the time he was the best player in Scotland in that position. He was also very Rangers-orientated. His heart was at Ibrox.'[9]

Ferguson wasn't just attracted to Rangers as a lifelong fan. He was also a huge admirer of Scot Symon, who'd won fifteen trophies in his thirteen years as manager. To this day Ferguson identifies Symon as one of his managerial heroes; at the time he saw him as an almost supernatural figure. 'The term magic is often misused,' Ferguson once said. 'But I would say that it did apply to Scot Symon.

He had that something special about him and I held him in very high regard.' When Symon entered the dressing room, Ferguson said in 1978, 'everybody stopped talking or even tying their laces. We all just sat there waiting for the OK to start talking again. I have been around a bit in my career, but have never come across an atmosphere to equal that at Ibrox at that particular time.'[10]

Yet Scot Symon is a rather unlikely hero for Alex Ferguson, whose management approach has always involved the most up-to-date techniques. Symon, in contrast, was a very old-fashioned type of boss – sometimes described as the last of the Homburg managers. 'He never got involved in training,' Ferguson says, 'always came in his soft hat, wearing his waistcoat, immaculately dressed.'[11] Sir Alex freely admits that Rangers' training sessions were 'mired in . . . outdated methods' and were 'an archaic mixture of track work and uninspired physical exercises'.[12] More surprising still for Ferguson the socialist, the trade unionist and the enemy of sectarianism, Scot Symon had for thirteen years sustained Rangers' notorious failure to hire Catholic players. Ferguson's continuing admiration for the Ibrox boss may have more to do with his record of achievement and other aspects of his style.

First, Symon was a stern disciplinarian, who wouldn't even let players stand with their hands in their pockets. In part this was an inheritance from Symon's immediate predecessor, Bill Struth, another Ferguson hero, who had ruled at Ibrox from 1920 to 1954. Struth insisted his players had ironed creases in their shorts and came to training sessions in jackets and ties, and banned travelling on the Glasgow subway system. Ferguson was also impressed by the way Scot Symon never said anything against members of his team beyond the walls of Ibrox. 'He'd never criticise his players publicly. He'd defend them to the hilt.'[13] Ferguson once said, 'You could see the strength in his eyes, so nobody messed with him too much.'[14]

Alex Ferguson's career at Rangers got off to a slow start. While he produced a hat-trick in his first home appearance – a friendly against

Eintracht Frankfurt – and 'might have had five' said one report, by the end of October he had managed only six goals in sixteen competitive games.[15] This didn't seem to matter that much, since Rangers were top of the table and undefeated in the League. But then, on 1 November 1967, Scot Symon was dismissed without warning. Worried about the success of Celtic, who'd recently eliminated Rangers from the League Cup, the Ibrox directors clearly sought a more modern figure like Jock Stein, who was often seen out in a tracksuit on the training pitch and loved talking tactics with his men. 'Top of the League, we hadn't lost a game, and they sacked this wonderful manager,' says Ferguson. 'But Celtic were doing well and there was this great cry in Scotland for the track-suit manager.'[16] 'The minute Scot Symon left Rangers, they seemed to lose their greatness,' he said later, and he considered Symon's dismissal 'the worst thing that ever happened to that club'.[17]

The man they chose in Symon's place was David (or Davie) White, whom Symon had appointed as his assistant just that summer. The managerial change was a huge shock, not least to Alex Ferguson, whose immediate reaction was to tell White he wanted to leave Ibrox, and formally to request a transfer. 'I never saw eye to eye with him,' he says, 'and I don't think he was strong with his board. He didn't fancy me and I suppose I should have left then but I tried to fight it and it became confrontation all the time with the manager.'[18] Ferguson clearly perceived White as a weak character. Although White's previous club, Clyde, had done exceptionally well (coming third in the First Division), he was not used to handling big-name players. 'Fergie always spoke up for himself,' says the former Rangers sweeper Dave Smith. 'So it might have been that Davie just didn't take to him in the first place.'[19]

Ferguson believes his Rangers career was doomed from the moment that White took over. That wasn't immediately apparent, however, for his goalscoring picked up. He scored twice against Cologne in the Fairs' Cup, got a hat-trick against Raith, and then earned a degree of forgiveness from Rangers fans for the famous 1963 hat-trick he'd scored against their team for St Johnstone. Now playing against the Saints, he went one better and scored four, including a penalty. Less glorious was Rangers' exit from the Fairs' Cup, courtesy of a 2–0 defeat by Leeds United, whose first goal at Elland Road was a penalty awarded when Ferguson handled on the line. He finished the season as Rangers' top scorer, with 19 in the League, and 24 in all competitions – four more than his colleague Willie Johnston.

But Ferguson still had no medals to show for his effort. He was desperately unlucky. Rangers had topped the league table for much of the season, having dropped a mere seven points and lost only once – their final game at home to Aberdeen. Their 61 points from 34 games (under the old two-points-for-a-win system) were almost 90 per cent of those available. In almost any other season Rangers would easily have been crowned champions. Indeed, only three times in the whole of the twentieth century did any Scottish team take a higher percentage of points – Rangers themselves in 1921, Hearts in 1958, and, in that very season, their Old Firm enemies Celtic. The Jock Stein side of 1967–68 was at the peak of its powers and managed two points more than the Ibrox team. As the Rangers historian David Mason observes, 'It all gets down to comparisons with what goes on on the other side of the city.'[20] The Glasgow Rangers of Alex Ferguson's day were undoubtedly a very good side; it's just that Celtic, the champions of Europe, were a great one.

In contrast to Davie White, Celtic boasted one of the greatest club managers of all time. Ferguson himself dates his side's late-season stumble from the moment Jock Stein publicly announced that Rangers were so far ahead that the title was theirs, and that Celtic could win only if their rivals threw it away. It put huge pressure on the Ibrox men, of course. Many years later Ferguson would try the same psychological ploy, though without the same result.

Though people talk about Rangers losing their last game, the fact is they would have lost the title race even if they'd beaten Aberdeen 10–0 in that match, simply because Celtic had a far superior goal average. But losing to Aberdeen had a traumatic effect on the Rangers fans, some of whom began to blame Ferguson, even though he'd been the club's top scorer.

If failing in such a tight league race wasn't bad enough, it must have been even more frustrating for Ferguson to observe events at his former club, Dunfermline Athletic. After the three years he spent at East End Park just missing out on honours, the Pars finally collected the Scottish Cup in 1968.

Things got worse for Ferguson himself during the Glasgow club's end-of-season trip to Denmark. In a reception at the British Embassy, the elderly and forgetful Rangers chairman, John Lawrence, went along the line introducing his players to the ambassador, but when he got to Ferguson he couldn't remember his name. According to his teammate Dave Smith, 'Lawrence said, "This is, um, this is, oh, I just can't remember." It was very embarrassing and Fergie was furious, but that wasn't the end of it.' Later the ambassador was heard asking Lawrence, 'Now, what's this I hear about you getting a new centre-forward?'[21]

If the less-than-diplomatic embassy reception wasn't bad enough, during the same trip Cathy Ferguson rang her husband to tell him of a spate of newspaper reports which all effectively said that he was finished at Rangers. Ferguson concluded that the press stories bore the fingerprints of the Rangers public-relations man, Willie Allison, whom he suspected of briefing journalists against him.

That afternoon Ferguson spent several hours in a bar with his teammates – 'more than long enough for me to be well gone', he admits.[22] He returned to the team hotel that afternoon determined to find Allison to let him know what he thought. Fortunately John Greig managed to bundle Ferguson off to his room before he could do too much damage. The Rangers captain put him to bed before he and the other players went back out to sample the delights of Copenhagen.

But Ferguson wasn't finished. He got up and went downstairs to have another go at Allison. John Greig came back to the hotel and found Ferguson – wearing bright red pyjamas – wandering round in a highly distressed state. 'He was drunk, which was very, very surprising because he didn't drink,' says Greig,

> and he was shouting and bawling about Willie Allison . . .
> I took him up to his room and stuck him in a cold bath and
> a cold shower. He was freezing cold, and we got him to
> calm down a bit and then got room service to send up steak
> and chips and a pint of milk. You can understand his
> disappointment. This was the club he'd always wanted to
> play for, that he lived next door to. He was getting told from
> his wife over the phone that he wasn't going to play again. He
> was very, very angry to say the least, and we got him sobered
> up and he calmed down.[23]

Greig says he and his colleagues got Ferguson dressed again, and then took him out to get drunk once more, simply to help him forget his problems and to show they were all still friends.

Today, Ferguson is forthright in expressing his views on the late Willie Allison, whom he accuses of 'poisonous hostility' fuelled by sectarian prejudice. 'Allison was a religious bigot of the deepest dye,' he says, blaming the Rangers official for whispers which had started to circulate about Cathy being a Catholic. 'Such facts were sure to count for much in the twisted mind of Allison and, as an intriguer behind the scenes at Ibrox, he was as dangerous as he was despicable.'[24] Ferguson's teammate Davie Provan agrees: 'The only guy who was chasing that kind of story was Willie Allison, who hounded him as far as the players were concerned. The players wouldn't bother their arse.'[25] A sign of how strongly Ferguson felt about Allison came a year later, when the Rangers official privately told him he had cancer. 'I know it is a terrible thing to say,' admits Ferguson, 'but I did not have a crumb of pity for him.'[26]

The depth of the religious fanaticism which surrounded Glasgow Rangers Football Club in the 1960s is hard to comprehend today. Rangers hadn't knowingly had a Catholic player since the First World War. This was an uncomfortable fact which Ferguson had chosen to overlook in his eagerness to join his boyhood idols. A sign of how adamant they were in their refusal to countenance Catholics was that they refused even to consider signing the outstanding defender Danny McGrain when he was a teenager, simply because his name suggested he *might* be Catholic. He was Protestant, in fact, and proved to be a huge loss to Rangers.

The effective religious bar hadn't always been so strong: Rangers employed several Catholics in the early years of the twentieth century. It's thought the sectarianism may have increased with the opening in 1926 of the nearby Harland & Wolff shipyard, a firm which was notorious for discriminating in favour of Protestants. Rangers' management always denied any prejudice or that Catholics were banned: it was merely, they claimed, that fans would never accept a player who was not committed to wearing the blue shirt of Rangers. If anything, the sectarianism between the Glasgow clubs intensified in the 1970s, reflecting the violent conflict in Northern Ireland. It was not until 1989, and the signing of Mo Johnston, that Rangers finally abandoned their bar on Catholics – and even then not without much controversy. (The change was implemented by Rangers' young new owner, David Murray, and his manager, Graeme Souness, though the more telling factors were probably growing concerns by potential sponsors, along with pressure from the European football union, UEFA, and the danger that Rangers might be banned from Europe for breaching European law.)

Accounts of Rangers' trip to Denmark in 1968 are interesting in illustrating not only the internal tensions at the club, but also the lack of control by the manager, Davie White, who often joined his players' drinking sessions. Ferguson insists that he himself was 'not a drinker', but there is some evidence to the contrary.[27] He tells of a night in Yugoslavia when he and several Rangers colleagues dropped in on a nightclub and ended up on stage singing with the band and donning their fancy costumes. Several colleagues say he happily drank as much, if not more, than they did, though he had the advantage – usually – of being able to sleep it off before training the next day. Denmark provided a notable exception, however – a really throbbing hangover which, according to Dave Smith, did little for Ferguson's career prospects. The problem arose when the players had to do heading practice. 'Mostly he was missing by five feet,' says Smith, 'because he was probably seeing two balls and trying to head the wrong one, but again this was noted by the directors who were standing at the side of the pitch.'[28]

The following season, 1968–69, proved even more frustrating, for both the man and his club. Ferguson lost his place in the first team after a double defeat by Celtic in the League Cup, after which Rangers broke the Scottish transfer record again by spending £100,000 on the Hibernian striker Colin Stein (with whom Ferguson had been sent off after a brawl the season before). Things had not looked good for Ferguson when Rangers had earlier tried to persuade him to move to Hibs in part exchange for Stein; his prospects were even less rosy after he refused, and for a spell he was banished to training with the reserves. At least this gave him some time to spend with Cathy and their new baby boy, Mark, who was born in September 1968 (prompting questions at Ibrox about whether he was baptised a Catholic).

Despite a few first-team games in cup competitions, Ferguson didn't start a league fixture until February. Nonetheless he managed a respectable 12 goals from 22 matches that season, and by March his prospects and popularity were looking up again, especially after scoring in a 6–0 win over St Mirren. This match proved there was 'no more popular player among the Ibrox support' than Ferguson, said the *Glasgow Herald*:

This man of many clubs may not have the natural ball-playing talent of Henderson, the speed of Johnston, nor the delicate touches of [Alex] Penman, but one thing is indisputable – the majority opinion on Saturday at Ibrox was that Ferguson should make more regular appearances in the side . . .

Whatever else Ferguson may be, he is certainly a trier. He came on for the second half as substitute for the injured Johnston and his aerial acrobatics, boundless energy, and sheer zest for the game, instantly transformed a fluent but somewhat punchless Rangers attack into a deadly striking force, which long before the end was to leave St Mirren's defence in complete disorder.

The upsetting effect Ferguson had on his opponents was plainly visible from the moment he first came in contact with the ball. He scarcely lost a duel in the air, and in consequence a good deal of the weight was shifted from the worker, Stein, and St Mirren's defence became more and more uncertain. It is small wonder, then, that the predominant sound in the second half was the appreciatory terracing chant of 'Fergie'.[29]

'The eager Ferguson worked non-stop,' said the *Daily Record* after a lacklustre 0–0 draw at Aberdeen a month later. 'He created several openings but his out-of-touch partners were never able to capitalise on them.'[30]

As Rangers flagged in the League, all hopes rested on beating Celtic in the Scottish Cup final. Players were rested from league fix-tures as the whole of Ibrox got itself into a state of nervous excitement about the game. Colin Stein, however, was suspended from playing at Hampden because of a previous sending-off. As a result, Ferguson was prime candidate to wear the number-9 shirt in the final, though he preferred to play at inside-forward.

The respected *Daily Record* reporter Ken Gallacher suggested that Ferguson's anxiety about making the final 'has made his play nervous and jerky'.[31] Ferguson was of course desperate to make up for what had happened when Dunfermline reached the same final four years before. 'I've never won a medal in senior football,' he reminded people, 'and this is my chance to get one if I'm picked.'[32] In 1965 he'd missed the final despite playing in every previous round; this time he made the team sheet at Hampden even though he had missed every other Scottish Cup game that season. But again it ended in humiliation – witnessed by 130,000 spectators and millions more on television.

The *Glasgow Herald* described the match as a 'bitter, spiteful battle', 'a disgrace to football' and an 'orgy of crudeness'.[33] Rangers were thrashed 4–0 – their worst ever loss in a Scottish Cup final, and their first defeat in the match for forty years. Worse still, the victors were Celtic.

In the years to come, Alex Ferguson would often be blamed for Celtic's winning goal after just two minutes. Just as in Celtic's Scottish Cup triumph in 1965, it came when a corner was headed in by Billy McNeill. The Celtic captain didn't score often, but was always a menace at corners because of his height. And he had a habit of scoring on big occasions. Ferguson had been ordered to mark him at set pieces, though he was several inches shorter.

'When the ball came across I couldn't believe it,' says McNeill, who reckons it was one of the easiest goals he ever scored. 'I was on my own and I could see a big space at the near post . . . I always remember saying to myself, "How in the name of hell did I get so free?"'[34] Ferguson claims the defender Ron McKinnon should have attacked the ball. Pictures show that the far post was unguarded; protecting it had been the job of Kai Johansen, the Rangers right-back.

'The man supposed to be marking Billy wasn't doing his job,' says Bobby Lennox, who took the corner. 'He should have picked him up, but it was very early in the match, the noise was deafening as usual and I suppose he was just settling into the game.' Lennox adds mischievously: 'You can just imagine what Fergie would do to one of his players who made that mistake now.'[35] Billy McNeill himself thinks it's wrong to blame a centre-forward for losing a goal, and that if anyone was the culprit it was the Rangers manager. 'I would always have backed myself to beat Fergie,' he says. 'I would say to Davie White, "You made the mistake – Fergie wasn't capable of marking me."'[36]

At half-time White duly admonished his centre-forward. But by then it was all over, since Celtic had scored twice more at the very end of the first half. The McNeill goal had upset the team's rhythm and careful pre-match planning. Ferguson might have redeemed himself had he not squandered two excellent chances, including one when he fell over as he raced in to meet the rebound from a powerful shot by Greig. In Ferguson's defence, a goal in the second minute had left his side with the remaining eighty-eight minutes in which to recover, and Ferguson wasn't held responsible for any of the other three goals they let in. 'I can't say anything because I gave away a howler of a goal as well,' says John Greig, who dropped the ball to an opposing player at a throw-in, which led to Celtic scoring.[37]

Today, when every match is analysed in minute detail by television and the press, especially big games such as cup finals, Alex Ferguson would be crucified by the commentators. The *Glasgow Evening Citizen* did suggest that if he and Willie Johnston had concentrated on scoring 'and not on starting feuds with opponents of great physical qualities things might have been different', but he received virtually no immediate criticism over McNeill's goal.[38] It took several days, in fact, for it even to become known that Ferguson had been told to mark the Celtic skipper. He was soon made a scapegoat, however, by the same Rangers fans who'd been worshipping him only a few weeks before with their chants of 'Fergie, Fergie'.

Davie White also accused Ferguson of bad-mouthing him to the press. Dropped for the four remaining games that season, he never played for the Rangers first team again.

Ferguson remained at Ibrox into the following season, 1969–70, but was excluded from practice sessions and made to train with the reserves or even the apprentices, and sometimes on his own. He was also required to play for the Rangers junior side against opponents such as Glasgow University and the Corporation Transport team. Although, in that era, this was quite a common fate for players who were out of favour, it was a dreadful period for Ferguson personally. He was trapped on the books of the club he'd adored since childhood, at a time when he should have been at the pinnacle of his abilities. The seventeen-year-old Alfie Conn, a future star with Rangers, Celtic and Spurs, was among the youngsters training with him. 'It would have been a slap in the face to be sent to play with the fifteen- and sixteen-year-olds, but Fergie never let slip why he was there,' Conn says. 'He never moaned about being there, and was very encouraging. In the few games that I played with him in the reserves he was always demanding that extra 2 per cent. He was a motivator and he never stood back – he always gave 100 per cent.'[39] The future Scotland goalkeeper Alan Rough recalls that, after a game he'd played against Rangers reserves, Ferguson encouraged him, saying he 'would go on to do well in football'.[40] Another reserves opponent was the promising young Celtic forward Kenny Dalglish, to whom Ferguson occasionally gave lifts in his car (having now passed his test). 'He never thought I would become a footballer,' says Dalglish, who remembers Ferguson saying, 'That wee fat boy won't make a player.'[41]

Ferguson may have hated it, but at least training with the junior sides gave him the opportunity to pass on some of the tips he'd picked up on coaching courses, and to give fatherly advice to the younger players. Tom Donnelly, who was then a young Rangers reserve player while also at university, says Ferguson was one of the few senior players at Ibrox who ever took any notice of the members of the junior teams. 'Fergie was always the one who would trundle along the corridor – the youngsters were in the away dressing room – and he always knew your name and he was always asking how were you getting on – "How's the studies going?" He always had a word to say, and never ignored you.'[42]

Ferguson would later acknowledge that in the long term his treatment by Rangers helped him become a better manager:

> I was left out in the cold really . . . the end period of that last
> six months was disappointing for me because I was then
> having to play with the third team and things like that, and it
> was a bit humiliating. But, nonetheless, it did give me a
> certain drive, and also a good learning curve in terms of
> management about how to treat players, how to treat people,
> how to deal with situations where you maybe don't get on
> with a particular player, and that was important for me.[43]

In October 1969 Rangers arranged to sell Ferguson to Nottingham Forest in the English First Division for £20,000 – less than a third of what they had paid for him two years before. But Ferguson went along with the deal only on condition he received 10 per cent of the fee – £2,000 – which Rangers grudgingly agreed. He admits to making a commitment to the Forest manager, Matt Gillies, but Cathy Ferguson then made it clear she was not keen on leaving Scotland.[44] So, when a last-minute bid came in from Falkirk, Ferguson grabbed this alternative, even though they were a much smaller club and in the Scottish Second Division. And he still got his £2,000.

Perhaps Ferguson should have taken more notice of the signs that Davie White's reign was drawing to a close, and held on at Rangers for a little longer. White had never found life easy at Ibrox: many never liked him because he'd never been a Rangers player

83

himself; he looked uncomfortable dealing with the press; and he clearly faced interference from a board who were themselves under intense pressure. 'He was the right man at the wrong time,' says the Rangers forward Alex Willoughby, who is sympathetic to White and says he was a 'players' man through and through'. He finds the clash with Ferguson hard to understand. 'I never knew anybody that would fall out with Davie White if they went and spoke to him . . . If you couldn't talk to Davie White, there's something wrong with you.'[45]

A few days after Ferguson had left, White was sacked. His replacement was Willie Waddell, a former Rangers player and past manager of Kilmarnock, who'd spent the past few months attacking White in his newspaper column. Waddell was an admirer of Ferguson, and had been extolling his abilities in print since his days at Queen's Park. Ferguson also admired Waddell's qualities, and had he stayed at Ibrox there is no doubt he would at least have been given another chance to prove himself.

Statistically, Alex Ferguson's two years at Glasgow Rangers were perfectly respectable. He scored 36 times in 68 games – a good rate for a striker, and well in line with his career average of a goal every two appearances. Yet, having arrived at Ibrox with the expectation of being showered with honours and caps, he left with no more than a losers' medal from the dreadful 1969 Scottish Cup final. Martin Ferguson says his brother took that experience so badly that he threw the medal away.[46]

The 1969 final combined with religious bigotry – that's the Ferguson version of why everything went wrong at Rangers. It seems absurd that a man should suffer because of his wife's religion, but a more blatant example occurred at Ibrox four years later, when a director, David Hope, was blocked from becoming chairman because he too had married a Catholic. Hope's case was even more ridiculous, in that the wedding had taken place in 1937 and his wife had been dead for more than a decade. In 1978 another former Rangers player, Graham Fyfe, claimed that he had also suffered discrimination for marrying a Catholic.[47]

Many of Alex Ferguson's Rangers contemporaries, however, feel he's been unfair in his criticisms of the club, and of Davie White and Willie Allison in particular. Few of them believe that Cathy Ferguson's religion played a major part in the matter.

Like many of his colleagues, Willie Johnston believes Ferguson's experience was typical of what dozens of footballers face every season when they are displaced by superior players and argue with their managers. He disagrees strongly with Ferguson's account:

> To be honest, Fergie was a good striker but Steiney was
> better. That's the whole crux of it: Stein was a better all-round
> player. If Fergie and Steiney were in the same team and the
> team was playing well, Fergie would still score goals, but
> Steiney could hold up the ball, bring other players into the
> game. Fergie was more of a box player: he'd work hard and
> everything, but he wasn't the best at bringing the players into
> the game.[48]

Willie Johnston has vivid memories of how, just as at Dunfermline, Ferguson would sit around with senior players such as John Greig, Willie Henderson and Ronnie McKinnon debating football issues and what had gone wrong in the latest match. 'Even then he was saying, "We should have done this, we should have done that." He always thought about who he was playing against and how he could get the best against them.' On one occasion, after a match in Germany, an exasperated Henderson, who had played for Scotland at the age of eighteen, turned to the upstart Ferguson and said, 'What the fuck do you know about football?' Nowadays Willie Johnston takes great delight in teasing Henderson about the story. 'Every time I see him I say, "That boy Ferguson – done not bad, eh?"'[49]

Observing the scene around him at Ibrox, and contrasting the set-up with that of Rangers' highly successful rivals Celtic on the other side of Glasgow, had taught Ferguson several valuable lessons. Ever since then he seems to have thought of Davie White as an example of how *not* to be a manager. Ferguson noted the lack of collective team spirit, and the way two of the best players, Willie Henderson and Ronnie McKinnon, were constantly arguing about how much they were paid and making disparaging remarks about each other's wives. There were heavy drinking sessions, of course, and serious gambling, which Davie White seemed unable to stop, perhaps because he himself often socialised with some of the players. It wasn't unusual, Ferguson says, for a player 'to win £2,000 or £3,000 in one session'.[50] White himself refuses to comment.

'My best years as a striker were between twenty-five and twenty-nine,' Alex Ferguson once said.[51] He had spent half that time at Rangers, and had next to nothing to show for it. It's interesting to speculate how his subsequent career might have developed had he enjoyed a reasonably successful time there, with the haul of medals that a typical Ibrox player can expect. In any other era, that Rangers side would have done much better, especially with a stronger manager. Certainly there's a persuasive case for saying that, had he done better, Ferguson would not have displayed the insatiable desire for success for which he became famous during the next three decades. 'The feeling of rejection and failure when I was discarded by Rangers was a real bad one,' he says. 'Yet, out of that adversity, I found a sense of determination that has shaped my life. I made up my mind then that I would never give in.'[52]

Fighting on All Fronts

'I was more afraid of getting a tongue lashing from him than the boss.'

GREGOR ABEL, former Falkirk player[1]

British football clubs traditionally arrange their annual photo shoot on a quiet morning during pre-season training. It's an opportunity to pose for the latest group picture, often in a new kit, and for photographers then to wander round the ground snapping reel after reel of stock shots. Their pictures of players crouching on the grass, juggling with a ball, or simply grinning into the lens will decorate the nation's sports pages for the next twelve months – and in that era the annual sets of schoolboy bubblegum cards too. As the Falkirk squad assembled at their Brockville Park ground in July 1970, clad in their latest blue-and-white strip, two players were missing. One was recovering in hospital from an operation; the other, Alex Ferguson, had actually turned up earlier, but had disappeared when he spotted one of the photographers. According to the local paper, it was a cameraman 'with whom he had exchanged words a season or two back when he was a Rangers player'.[2]

Not only did the out-of-favour cameraman not get any pictures of Ferguson: nor did the three other photographers who turned up that day. And Falkirk's 1970 team picture, celebrating their promotion from the Second Division, lacked the famous features of the club's star striker. It's hard to believe Sir Alex Ferguson would ever allow David Beckham to boycott the Manchester United annual photo because of a personal spat.

Ferguson's four-year career at Falkirk would see no break in his habit of getting into arguments. If anything he became more belligerent. He had taken a considerable demotion in leaving Ibrox for Falkirk the year before. If they weren't one of the minnows of Scottish football, Falkirk were one of many medium-sized fish. Their cramped Brockville ground had the smallest pitch in the entire Scottish League, and crowds in those days were tiny compared with those of Rangers – barely 4,000 for home games. Falkirk had spent most of their history in the top flight, and had even won the Scottish Cup a couple of times, but in 1969 they'd just been relegated from the Scottish First Division. Their nickname was 'The Bairns', after the town motto, 'Better meddle wi' the De'il than the Bairns o' Falkirk'.

In December 1969 Ferguson had few doubts about meddling with the Bairns, though it seemed uncertain that they would make an immediate return to the top division. What clinched the move for him was that Falkirk was run by Willie Cunningham, his former manager at Dunfermline, who had made 'an offer that was quite incredible'. Although it had been Cunningham, of course, who had dropped him at the last moment before the 1965 Scottish Cup final, Ferguson broadly respected his abilities. He admits it was a 'volatile' relationship: there would again be frequent quarrels, and Ferguson says they almost came to blows on one occasion.[3]

Willie Cunningham needed a new goalscorer. Ferguson immediately delivered, quickly forging an effective partnership with his fellow striker Andy Roxburgh. Ferguson scored on his league debut, in front of 1,650 fans at Berwick, then Roxburgh got a hat-trick at Queen's Park, before Ferguson himself got three goals and Roxburgh another in a 6–1 drubbing of East Stirlingshire, Falkirk's local-town rivals. Two more Ferguson strikes on goal that day were disallowed.

'Our manager's scoop in bringing Alex Ferguson from Rangers has infused the urgency that was previously lacking,' declared the programme for Falkirk's next home fixture. 'Our striking twins, Fergie and Andy Roxburgh, once again turned on an irrepressible attacking display,' it said of the East Stirling victory, adding that Ferguson was 'already a big favourite with the fans'.[4] 'Andy was a very cultured player,' says Willie Cunningham, who's always been amused by having had two future Scotland managers as his strike force. 'He was a great foil for Fergie, and did all the digging for him. I could always see them going on to great things. Andy was always keen on coaching, and so was Fergie.'[5]

Ferguson and Roxburgh had first known each other at Queen's Park, and later met on the SFA summer coaching courses. At Falkirk they also took part in *Quizball*, the BBC TV contest between four-man sides provided by various British football clubs. (Teams were offered four different 'routes' to goal, ranging from one hard question to four easy questions – hence the phrase, coined by the show, 'route-one football'.) Ferguson was a natural choice: he loves general knowledge, has a superb memory for trivia, and takes part in quizzes with almost the same fervour as he brings to his football. Falkirk beat Huddersfield 1–0 in the first round and then faced Everton in a semi-final which was recorded at the BBC studios in Birmingham. Falkirk were losing, and for the final question Andy Roxburgh was asked which jockey had won the previous year's Grand National. Roxburgh knew nothing about horse racing. Ferguson tried to whisper the answer to his fellow panellist, but nervously Roxburgh blurted out, 'Lester Piggott.' Ferguson's disgust was audible. He was astonished that anyone could think the world's best-known flat jockey could have won the greatest steeplechase. 'He was incandescent with rage,' says the Falkirk historian, Michael White, who was sitting in the audience. 'It was embarrassing how angry Fergie was.'[6]

As Roxburgh came on to the field before the following home game, Falkirk fans chanted, 'Lest-er Pigg-ott! Lest-er Pigg-ott!' So forceful was the chant that Roxburgh reckoned Ferguson must have gone out with a loudhailer beforehand to rehearse them. The *Quizball* incident has gone down in Falkirk folklore.

By the end of that season Ferguson had scored 18 times in 24 league and cup matches. 'He seemed to always buy a lot of time near the goal before he shot,' says the Falkirk midfielder Jim Shirra. 'His shoulders and arms were always all over the place. He seemed to take for ever to put his shot in, but he always seemed to find time and space.'[7] The Bairns were duly promoted, and Ferguson won a Second Division championship medal for the second time in his career.

Falkirk fans recently voted the 1970 squad as their 'team of the millennium', though presumably there wasn't much competition from medieval sides. In the First Division in the 1970–71 season, encouraged by a bonus system which paid the players £40 for each week they were in the top ten, the team ended in seventh spot. It was Falkirk's highest league placing for more than twenty years, and Ferguson finished as leading scorer for the season at his third successive club, scoring 14 times in 28 matches.

'Alex Ferguson was Alex Ferguson,' declared one match report. 'Fergie argued with the referee, took his usual swallow dives looking for penalties, became involved in skirmishes with opponents – but still found time to head against the bar, shoot against the post and bring out the save of the day with the shot of the day.'[8] At the same time, Falkirk's star goal-poacher was increasingly displaying an aggressive, sometimes violent, side to his game. In less than four years at Brockville he was sent off three times. (This added to his three dismissals at previous clubs, starting with a reserve game for St Johnstone in 1964). Today, of course, it's relatively common for a player to be dismissed, for instance after receiving two yellow cards for less serious misdemeanours. In the late 1960s and early '70s it was still quite rare for players to be ordered off. In Ferguson's case it was always for acts of violence.

His first sending-off with Falkirk had an air of inevitability about it. It came in September 1970, on the first time he returned to Ibrox, ten months after his transfer. Falkirk went down 2–0. When Ferguson elbowed aside John Greig, the Rangers captain aimed a kick at him in retaliation, though he claims to have missed. Both were sent off. The referee concluded that both were at fault, though Greig seems to have been the main culprit. 'Quite frankly,' wrote the possibly partisan *Falkirk Herald* reporter,

> Fergie, who is no lamb, didn't even deserve to be spoken to
> for what was no more than his usual bustling, niggling
> tactics. But John Greig, who ran two yards after Ferguson and
> deliberately kicked him on the leg, deserved every bit of the
> treatment he received . . . It was there for all who wanted to
> see it, crude and intentional. I believe that Fergie was sent off
> after him to appease the baying Ibrox legions.[9]

For John Greig, a player with a similarly tough approach to his football, it was the first time he had ever been dismissed, but he was surprised that Ferguson should have been sent off too. 'He actually did nothing,' he says, adding generously that Ferguson was really punished for protesting on Greig's behalf. Both offenders were suspended for seven days and fined £25 each. 'I tried to plead in his defence,' says Greig, but Ferguson's previous form can't have impressed the SFA.[10]

Only seventeen months later, Ferguson was suspended for two weeks for kicking the full-back Eric Schaedler in a game against Hibernian. The loyal *Falkirk Herald* again felt the sentence had been unjust, as the referee had ignored serious offences by Hibs players. 'How the indulgent, inconsistent Mr MacDonald permitted goal-keeper Jim Herriot to remain unpunished after he *twice* attempted to bounce the ball in Ferguson's face is beyond understanding.'[11]

The Falkirk team manager, Willie Cunningham, was rather more critical of his player than the local paper was. 'I must say that any early bath he got under my managership was entirely deserved,' he says. 'He could have an irritating way with him on occasion with his fellow professionals.'[12]

Alex Ferguson strongly denies he 'was ever a dirty player', but the notoriously aggressive use of his elbows suggests otherwise.[13] In his defence Ferguson notes that, despite his high number of dismissals, he was booked relatively few times in his sixteen-year career. The official figures say he had fifteen cautions – not quite one a year, which is indeed a low tally for such a physical player.

By the early 1970s Ferguson was waging football battles off the pitch too. In 1970 he was elected chairman of the Scottish Professional Footballers' Association, and he held the post for the next three years. For most Falkirk players the SPFA meant little more than Ferguson collecting their subscriptions. "It was a case of persuading us we should put money in to make sure we've got a future,' says Gregor Abel, who is now a youth coach with Rangers. 'He emphasised the togetherness: that if we stayed together we wouldn't get walked all over by the bosses.'[14]

In 1972 Ferguson assumed a leading role in a famous dispute at Falkirk, when the players very nearly went on strike. The row was triggered by a 6–1 League Cup defeat at his former club St Johnstone, in which Falkirk's play was described as being 'without one redeeming feature'.[15] Fortunately, perhaps, Ferguson wasn't fit enough to play that night and had been away on a scouting mission for Willie Cunningham. The manager announced he was punishing the players for their dreadful performance by withdrawing their expense allowances for lunch and travel to and from home. The players decided to walk out just before an extra training session, and also threatened to go on strike for the upcoming Saturday game against Montrose. 'We realise we are professional footballers with contracts to honour but when men are treated like children, it's high time something was done about it!' said an unidentified players' spokesman (who, if not Alex Ferguson, was certainly doing a good impression).[16] What incensed the players was the unfairness of Cunningham's punishment, since it hurt some people more than others, and particularly one young player who travelled a long distance from Ayrshire every day. The dispute was resolved, only two hours before kick-off, when the board met the team, overruled Cunningham, and reinstated the allowances. It left the Falkirk manager in a difficult position, and his authority never recovered.

In his autobiography, Alex Ferguson says the players' action was 'hasty', and that he 'wasn't entirely happy' with it. But his misgivings were not apparent at the time. Colleagues agree that he was effectively the strike leader and, as he admits, the 'spokesman for his mutinous crew'. Looking back, he wonders whether 'perhaps I should have been stronger in arguing against the strike but I would not ever have wanted to be known as a boss's man. To someone with my upbringing that would have been a heinous crime.'[17]

Yet, in his own managerial career, it's easy to see Alex Ferguson acting in a similar manner to Cunningham. Perhaps his ambivalence about the protest results from respect for Cunningham's position as a manager, maybe even a sense of shame about the part he played in undermining him, for he accepts that the players contributed to the manager's unhappy departure later in the season. Only a year earlier, Cunningham had turned down the job of Scotland boss (an unusual offer, given he was Irish) to stay at Falkirk. But his career never recovered from being faced down by his players, and he never fulfilled the expectations that he was destined to manage one of Scotland's big clubs. In an age when there was far less money in professional football than there is now, and players and managers were not able simply to retire when they left the game, he ended up running a sports shop.

One of the mysteries of the 1972 Falkirk dispute was that part of the secret of Cunningham's success had been that he was close to his players, and made sure that they were rewarded when they did well. Indeed, they were extremely well paid in comparison with those at other middle-ranking clubs. 'The pay was brilliant,' says Jim Shirra, 'and it was Cunningham that got it for us as well. He actually had a meeting with us once and said, "Don't go home and tell your wives what you're getting paid," because he was paying us big, big bonuses at that time, because we were doing so well. He was a great players' manager.'[18] Cathy Ferguson would certainly have been pleased with the money, and the family needed it. On 9 February 1972 she delivered twin boys, Darren and Jason. Ferguson says he fainted during the delivery, though he recovered in time for that evening, when he returned to Ibrox for a Scottish Cup replay. But he failed to score, and Falkirk lost 2–0. The 43,000 attendance was Ferguson's biggest audience since the 1969 Hampden final, and the last big crowd of his playing career.

After the dispute Cunningham was surprisingly forgiving of Ferguson, and seemed to bear no grudges. 'Somebody had to lead them,' he says. 'No, I never held that against him.'[19] Five months later Cunningham appointed the strike leader as player/coach – his deputy – and gave him responsibility for preparing the team for matches, though perhaps he was following Lyndon Johnson's dictum that it's always better to have someone pissing out of the tent rather than in. The promotion arose from an altercation earlier in the season, when Ferguson wanted to accept a transfer bid from Hibernian. When Cunningham refused to let him go, the argument got so heated that the club physiotherapist had to prevent a fight. Ferguson was persuaded to stay at Falkirk only with the promise of a better contract, but Cunningham also offered to help him find a career in management after he'd stopped playing – a promise which he kept.

Of course, Ferguson had already played something of a leadership role in his first three years at the club, partly because of his seniority and experience, and partly because of his natural assertiveness. It's a curious fact, however, that, despite his obvious leadership qualities, none of the six clubs for whom he played ever made Alex Ferguson team captain.

The position of player/coach was really a junior management role, which meant he had to resign as chairman of the SPFA. Ferguson loved his new job. He worked his teammates hard, brought in new ideas, and rejigged the training schedule to include afternoon sessions, especially with the younger players. 'I've never seen anyone with such enthusiasm,' says Cunningham. 'He was very astute – a bugger, but very astute – and I thoroughly enjoyed my time with him.'[20]

Ferguson's memory is that results slowly improved once he took charge on the training pitch. The records suggest otherwise: Falkirk gradually slipped further down the table. They won only seven league games all season, and were lucky to avoid relegation.

Any hopes of consolation in the Scottish Cup were extinguished when they lost 3–1 at Aberdeen. They might not have fared so badly had their coach of just four weeks' standing not disgraced himself early in the game with an attack on the tough Aberdeen defender Willie Young (later of Spurs, Arsenal and Nottingham Forest). The incident arose only a minute after Falkirk had had a goal disallowed, and it seems to have borne similarities to the offence for which David Beckham was dismissed against Argentina in the 1998 World Cup. Ferguson fell over as his team won a corner and, while lying on the ground, aimed what the Falkirk paper called a 'needless' and 'half-hearted' kick at Young. 'The referee had a clear view of the incident,' said its report, 'and no doubt recalling an earlier warning for a similar needless foul had no hesitation in sending Ferguson to the pavilion.'[21] This time the SFA suspended Ferguson for fifty-three days – almost eight weeks – split between the end of the 1972–73 season and the start of the next one. 'It would appear,' wrote the *Falkirk Herald* reporter,

Ferguson has been punished severely not so much for the offence – it was relatively minor – or even his record, which is not exactly spotless, but for the militant views he expressed as former boss of the players' union. Ferguson has never been slow to express his opinions and I feel he has had a raw deal from the beaks.[22]

Though Ferguson insists that Willie Young kicked him first, he acknowledges that he had a duty to behave, having only recently been promoted to a position of responsibility. But the incident wasn't just embarrassing in terms of the faith placed in him by Willie Cunningham. The Aberdeen manager, Jimmy Bonthrone, later revealed that before the game he'd been about to offer Ferguson a job as his assistant at Pittodrie. The Young incident changed his mind, and Aberdeen had to wait.

Nor did Alex Ferguson contribute much as a player in the 1972–73 season, his last at Brockville. He was out for ten weeks in the autumn because of an injury to the ligament behind his left knee: it was so serious that it sparked fears that his playing days might be over. His scoring rate had already started to decline, and when he returned to the side his goals almost dried up altogether while his club was perilously close to relegation. Ferguson managed just one goal in twenty-two league and cup appearances.

Once the season was over, the Falkirk manager was forced to resign and Ferguson was given temporary command of the playing squad. Cunningham urged him to apply for the permanent post, but he was unlikely to get it given the trouble of the previous twelve months. He was too much of a rebel for the directors' liking. Quite apart from his SPFA role and the threatened strike, the sendings-off and the barneys with Willie Cunningham, there was also his boycott of the team photo.

The new Falkirk boss was the former Scotland manager John Prentice. It was not good news. He immediately demoted Ferguson to being an ordinary player again, after his six months of coaching responsibilities, and compounded the insult by replacing him with the Falkirk trainer, who'd previously been third in command and therefore his junior. 'He will be just like everybody else at Brockville,' Prentice said of Ferguson. 'He will have to buckle down and prove he is worth his place in the team.'[23]

Prentice must have known that Ferguson would find the situation humiliating and, on his past record, would ask for a transfer. When he did, Prentice let him go for free. Ferguson couldn't find another coaching post, but in the summer of 1973 he was given a two-year playing contract by Ayr United, who were then being managed by another future Scotland boss, the ebullient Ally MacLeod. Although only a part-time club, Ayr were going through the best spell in their history. They were certainly better than Falkirk at the time, having finished the previous season in sixth place in the top division. As so often with footballers nearing the end of their careers, the move to a new club gave Ferguson a new injection of form. He soon forged a successful partnership with one of the strikers he'd replaced at Rangers, George 'Dandy' McLean – 'Fergie' and 'Dandy' the fans dubbed them.

'He had an outstanding debut,' reported the Ayr United match programme, 'and was unlucky not to score. He set up the first goal for George McLean and was brought down in the box to give United a penalty . . . for the second goal.'[24] The barren patch was over, as he struck seven times in his first eight league games, including twice at Dumbarton and twice at his old club Dunfermline. For a week in October, after Ferguson's winning goal at Motherwell, Ayr stood second in the table.

Ally MacLeod had assembled a strong squad, many of whom, like Ferguson, were seasoned pros nearing the ends of their playing careers. There was a good team spirit, and plenty of time to enjoy drink and horses. Ferguson often placed bets with George McLean, who was involved in a bookmaking business. 'He was livid one time,' says the Ayr captain Johnny Graham, 'because George wouldn't pay him out until he got to the bookmaker on Monday. Fergie said, "But I gave you the money today."' Ferguson was as combative as ever. On another occasion he was found rolling about the floor of the team coach with his teammate Johnny Doyle after a dispute over a game of cards. 'We had to separate them. It was probably over a 10p bet or something,' says Graham.[25] Ferguson's main rival for the number-9 shirt, Alec Ingram, remembers how they once clashed and both got sent off in a practice match.[26]

'I think he got a surprise when he came to Ayr,' Johnny Graham explains. 'I think he thought he was coming to play out the rest of his career and coming into a team that was less than what he'd had before.' Graham was impressed at how, after training, Ferguson would do an extra fifteen minutes working on his stomach – an unusual routine for the early 1970s. 'He felt that was where the strength of footballers came from. Now it's common practice.' But on the pitch, says the Ayr captain,

> He talked all the time, shouted all the time, got on at you all
> the time. We just ignored him. It was his way. During a match
> there was always something that would be annoying him. If
> he missed a goal, you could always hear him shouting at
> himself. There was an old left-back – John Murphy, an Ayr
> stalwart – who had a vicious temper. The two would be
> screaming at each other. He'd tell Murphy what to do, and he
> wouldn't take it. They'd be arguing while the game was going
> on, and I'd be saying, 'Let's get on with it.'[27]

Ferguson's sweetest moment must have been his revenge on the club which had just discarded him. He came on as a late substitute against Falkirk and, Solskjaer-like, scored with what was virtually his only touch of the game. 'The other Brockville defenders seemed to have short memories of their former team-mate's deadliness in the box,' said the *Sunday Post*. 'They didn't move in on him. So he stuck it into the net for safe-keeping.'[28]

'He used to score from two yards,' says Johnny Graham. 'He wasn't fast at that time, and he had the most ungainly run I've ever seen. He was never a great footballer, just a journeyman. As George McLean used to say to him, "There's labourers and tradesmen, and you're the labourer."'[29]

On 2 February 1974 Alex Ferguson scored his last senior goal in football, in a 1–1 draw in front of 1,900 people at another of his former clubs, St Johnstone. The promise of September had fizzled out, and he was increasingly wearing the Ayr substitute's shirt, and then found himself out of the side altogether. He notched up ten goals in twenty-four league and cup games in his final season. As ever, Ferguson claims to have been Ayr's top scorer, which is true only if one goes through the contortion of counting only league games and excluding penalties. That spring he decided to give up playing after a doctor warned that his arteries were enlarged, though they never caused Ferguson any subsequent difficulties.

His last appearance – again appropriately – was at Falkirk in April 1974. He'd played 432 senior games in Scottish club football, and scored 222 times. He'd appeared in senior matches on every Scottish League ground (except that of Meadowbank, who'd only just joined the League), and had scored against every club except, curiously enough, the first side he'd played for, Queen's Park.

His move to Ayr United had meant that, for the first time since 1964, Ferguson was again playing football part-time. Training at Somerset Park took place on Tuesday and Thursday evenings, and Ferguson took it in turns with colleagues to drive down from his home in the new town of East Kilbride (where he'd moved from Simshill). Johnny Graham remembers driving with him one night through torrential rain. 'We were not looking forward to training at all,' he says. 'Then he asked, "Were you at the game last night?" I was wracking my brain to think of what game. It was Brechin versus

Stenhousemuir, or something like that. He was such a fanatic that whenever there was a game he would go. He talked football constantly – you'd get fed up listening.'[30]

But Alex Ferguson had never found football challenging enough to absorb all his energy. While at Rangers he'd acted as an afternoon sales rep for Matt Thomson, a former Motherwell player and SPFA activist, who'd just set up his own printing business in East Kilbride. Thomson subsequently built the firm into a multi-million-pound operation which today employs 700 people, and he often employed players on his sales team, knowing that potential customers were unlikely to snub a football star. In many ways, of course, learning the skills of salesmanship was excellent training for football management.

And, like many professional footballers, Ferguson toyed with the idea of opening a pub, though his real ambition was to run a restaurant. Any account of Ferguson's life should acknowledge the role played by the Beechwood, a large restaurant-cum-bar which was located right next to Hampden Park. The Beechwood was effectively Ferguson's local eating place and drinking spot, in an era when the Glasgow licensing laws were especially strict and large parts of the city were deemed 'dry'. It was a strong football establishment, but Ferguson was an unusual customer in being a Rangers man. The manager, Pat Harkins, had previously done most of the catering work for Celtic, and his restaurant had become a favourite haunt for Parkhead players and management. (His daughter Marina eventually married one of Celtic's greatest stars, Kenny Dalglish.) It was while dining at the Beechwood on Saturday nights with Cathy that Ferguson really got to know the Celtic manager Jock Stein, who often went there with his wife.

Quite apart from helping to establish an important personal friendship, the Beechwood also helped tutor Alex Ferguson in the catering and licensing trades. Pat Harkins was delighted to give him on-the-job training, and the pupil would spend a couple of weeks on each different aspect of the business, from waiting on customers to cooking in the kitchens. Billy McNeill has fond memories of finding Ferguson in a chef's hat being taught by Harkins how to fry fish. Ferguson particularly loved Italian cuisine, and worked with the Beechwood's Italian chef, Guiseppe. He wasn't paid, says Harkins, but at least he ate well. 'He's a big eater,' he says. 'Although Ferguson was very thin, he really enjoyed his food. I asked him one day how he was getting on in the kitchen and he said, "Good, but I don't think I'd make much money in there. I'd eat the whole lot."'[31]

Harkins particularly noticed how well Ferguson got on with members of his business luncheon club, going out of his way to learn their names and what they all did. 'I'd known the chaps for years,' says Harkins, 'and I couldn't even tell you what line of business they were in. Fergie had a fantastic memory for faces. He could fit names to faces, which is a real gift.'[32]

It was through Pat Harkins that Ferguson met Sam Falconer, who owned a pub called The Matelot in East Kilbride and gave him further on-the-job experience of the licensing business. Ferguson helped out behind the bar, learned the techniques of storing beer, and acquired the diplomacy needed to handle drunk customers. The authorities wouldn't grant a licence to anyone in Glasgow who wasn't adequately trained in the skills needed to run a pub.

When he was sufficiently qualified, Ferguson acquired his own premises, Burns Cottage in Govan. It had previously been a kind of Robert Burns theme bar, though Ferguson renamed it 'Fergie's', in the hope of exploiting his fame as a Rangers player, discarding the Burns ephemera. It was located at the junction of Govan Road and Paisley Road West – at the point where the old toll between Glasgow and Govan was once sited, and in the heart of what was then still a populous area around the old docks. It was almost opposite another pub, Baxter's, owned by the Scotland star Jim Baxter, who'd returned to play for Rangers just before Ferguson left. Fergie's pub still exists, though it's now called The Angel and serves a very different community. Much of the local housing has disappeared, and the area is now dominated by modern business parks, along with an American-style leisure park complete with a bowling alley and a McDonald's.

Owning a pub is a common occupation for ex-footballers, of course, but they are usually content to let others manage the business while they entertain their friends – especially after hours – mulling over old times, and drinking the stock. Ferguson was unusual for the extraordinary amount of work, effort and imagination he put into his business, at a time when he was still a First Division footballer and also busy in the players' union.

Among several attractions for Fergie's regulars was the popular annual outing, when Ferguson would hire a coach and take a day trip to destinations such as Troon on the Ayrshire coast or Cardenden in Fife. His customers would spend the afternoon taking part in games and competitions he organised, or in old-fashioned sing-songs. 'Alec liked a good laugh with the punters,' says John Telfer, who often drank in Fergie's. 'When we went on bus runs we would always arrange a football match, and he would always play in it.'[33] Back in Govan, Ferguson would hire bands and singers to perform in the downstairs lounge – renamed the 'Elbow Room' in acknowledgement of his style as a player.

Ferguson encouraged customers to play dominoes and cribbage, and established two darts teams which he managed as competitively as any football side which has ever appeared under his command. One team captain, John Stewart, says Ferguson wasn't very good at darts himself but was 'beside himself with joy' the year they won the Govan Darts League. 'He was so pleased that he went out and bought every one of the sixteen-strong team jumpers with our names on it. It must have cost him nearly £500.'[34]

Fergie's was a far from genteel establishment, however, and it brought Alex Ferguson into contact with some of the nastier aspects of Glasgow's infamous underworld. He himself has described the night a huge fight broke out when one of his waitresses tried to stop a woman leaving the premises with cocktail glasses in her bag. As friends came to the waitress's aid, one of Ferguson's tougher customers grabbed a docker's hook from behind the bar. The end result was a man lying out in the street 'with blood gushing out of his face and neck; his wife was bending over him, screaming wildly. At first I thought he was dead and it was a tremendous relief to discover he was not.'[35] The police warned Ferguson that he would lose his licence if the hook-wielder was ever spotted in his pub again.

On another occasion the pub was the centre of gang warfare over a £40,000 whisky robbery, and his manager rang Ferguson to say a man was in the bar brandishing a shotgun. Afterwards the police told him that the gunman was one of Glasgow's most notorious criminals. Ferguson's manager promptly disappeared, terrified that he might be required to give evidence against the gangster in court.

Ferguson also admits in his autobiography that his pub became a marketplace where people sold goods pilfered from the nearby docks. He was fully aware of what was going on, even though handling stolen goods is a serious offence of dishonesty. 'I must confess that I fell prey to many of the wheeler-dealers,' he writes, 'and Cathy used to go off her head when I brought home clothes, binoculars, lengths of silk, china, cutlery and sorts.' He even describes how there was a sophisticated service for buying wedding presents, which could be stolen on request. 'All you had to do was put in an order for cutlery or china or crystal and the next week, without fail, there it was all gift-wrapped and ready to be conveyed to the happy couple.'[36] Davie Provan, a former Rangers teammate, who often worked in Fergie's, argues there was nothing unusual in stolen goods being on sale: it was typical of many pubs in Glasgow, especially in the vicinity of the docks.[37]

Later, in 1975, Ferguson went into partnership with Sam Falconer and acquired a second pub, Shaw's, near Bridgeton Cross in the East End of the city. It was named after the previous owner, Hughie Shaw, who was said to have played for Rangers. (He always denied it, though the reputation of having done so did his business no harm.) The two men put up £2,000 each, and a further £18,000 came from the brewer's, Drybrough's, to buy what was an odd-looking one-storey building located between two tenement blocks. 'A lot of people used to call Shaw's a pokey wee hole,' says John Telfer, whose wife worked there. 'It was just a typical man's pub. You wouldn't take your wife in there.'[38] If women came in they'd generally sit in the 'snug', a small enclosed booth at the end of the bar where people often sang, including an Italian who came in and delivered operatic extracts. Ferguson himself would often join some of his older customers for dominoes, playing 'knockout' for 10p a hand. The pub boasted two darts teams, one of which was called The Carpetbaggers after a nearby carpet factory. Shaw's was also popular with members of the Territorial Army, who often came round from the local TA drill hall, and it attracted supporters of Clyde football club, being close to their old Shawfield ground.

Shawfield also boasted dog racing, which Alex and his brother would sometimes attend on Fridays, after which they would drop into Shaw's and buy everyone a round. 'He was famous for it on Friday nights,' says Jim Martin, who worked in the pub. 'Some freeloaders would come and try and get a double or an expensive drink.' Martin describes Ferguson as ' a gentleman' who never argued with customers or staff, but he feels he was too 'kind-hearted' to run a pub. He was too ready to give customers 'tick', says Martin, and too busy to notice that one of his staff was stealing a large part of the stock.[39]

In the 1920s and '30s the Bridgeton area was home to a notorious Protestant gang, the Billy Boys, and some of this legacy remained. Ferguson says he was obliged to open early in the morning on the day of traditional Orange marches, 12 July, and felt he had no option but to join in the singing of Orange songs. John Telfer remembers offering to bring about 'forty punters' over early on 12 July. 'It ended

up getting a bit noisy and the police came. Nine o'clock in the morning and they were battering at the door – "You're done, Ferguson"
and what have you – and they took us all out. But he told me he
never ended up getting done. It was well outside hours – the pub
didn't open until eleven.'[40]

Ferguson's real ambition – to open a restaurant – never came to
fruition, however. He did set up a company, Alexander Ferguson
Restaurants Ltd, and by 1973 he had identified an appropriate site in
Christie Street in the centre of Paisley, just west of Glasgow. But
permission was required from the local council, and by the time it
was granted, in 1975, Ferguson seemed to have lost interest.

By then he would have more pressing commitments in Paisley.

'A Big Job on My Hands'

*'I was only there four months but we had some hilarious
times. The foundations of managership can be traced to
those days.'*

ALEX FERGUSON[1]

As you get off the train at Falkirk Grahamston station, it's hard to
believe you are within a few minutes' walk of two Scottish
League grounds. But then it is one of the mysteries of Scottish football that a small town like Falkirk has two senior clubs in the first
place, especially when a third side, Stenhousemuir, lives barely three
miles to the north.

One of Falkirk's two football stadiums, Brockville Park, is located
beyond the western end of the station. It's just about visible from the
platform, in fact, if you know where to look. Yet modest Brockville,
which was deemed unfit for the Scottish Premier League in 2000, is
truly a Nou Camp or a Maracaña compared with Falkirk's other
Scottish League venue. East Stirlingshire FC is only about 600 yards
down George Street, but finding it requires the detective skills of the
most seasoned football-ground-hopper. With no towering floodlight
pylons to mark the site, only a Comet guides you. Firs Park lies
unnoticed these days at the back entrance of Falkirk's modern retail
park, overshadowed by the more enticing attractions of Homebase,

Curry's and the Comet electrical store. Even at three o'clock on a Saturday when East Stirling are playing at home, most shoppers probably don't even notice it is there.

'Stadium' is far too grand a term for this location; 'ground' just about sums it up. East Stirling's home isn't just a prime candidate for the most concealed league venue in Britain, it's also among the least well endowed, with facilities which would even embarrass sides in England's lowly Diadora or Dr Marten's leagues. 'Firs Park is an anachronism which no amount of emotion can deny,' writes Simon Inglis in his bible of British football grounds.[2]

Today, the main entrance consists simply of a heavy-duty metal door over a hole cut into a concrete wall. One end of the ground has no terracing or seats, just the same concrete wall a few feet behind the goal line, so any shots off target are liable to rebound back on to the pitch. The main stand – indeed, the only stand – stretches barely twenty-five yards along the edge of the pitch and holds just 297 seats. On the other side of Firs Park, at the end of a quiet back street, are East Stirling's six dilapidated turnstiles, one of which doubles as a letterbox. Yet in 1969 a record 11,500 people packed into this ground for a Scottish Cup tie against Hibs. At the start of 2002, however, with crowds down to a mere 70 paying customers, East Stirlingshire finally acknowledged reality and sought permission to move to the athletics stadium in Grangemouth, three miles away.

Just as he had begun as a young player, in 1974 Alex Ferguson was starting his managerial career on one of the lowest rungs of the profession (and, coincidentally, East Stirling's black-and-white hooped colours were copied from those of Queen's Park). Yet Queen's Park boasted a famous ground, a distinguished history, and proud traditions. East Stirlingshire – better known as 'East Stirling', but nicknamed 'The Shire' or simply 'Shire' – can display nothing more than a couple of lower-division titles on its honours board, though the club joined the Scottish League in 1900, a couple of years before its neighbours Falkirk. Perhaps the most exciting moment in Shire's history was a geographically bizarre marriage in 1964 with Clydebank, twenty-five miles away, to create ES Clydebank. They divorced after just twelve months. Professional football doesn't get much lower than this.

The thirty-two-year-old Ferguson had been proposed for the manager's job by Ally MacLeod, his boss at Ayr, who had been singing his praises to anyone who would listen. MacLeod had, in fact, previously recommended him to Queen's Park, but the interview at Hampden was a 'disaster', Ferguson says. This was partly because several members of the selection panel knew him from his days as a young player. 'I surrendered to nerves and failed to offer a shred of justification for employing me.'[3]

Credit for getting Alex Ferguson on to the first rung of management partly belongs to Bob Shaw, a director and secretary of East Stirling, who'd stood in as the club's caretaker manager the previous season and was now looking for a permanent replacement. While flying out to the 1974 World Cup in West Germany, Shaw bumped into Ally MacLeod and took the opportunity to ask whether Ferguson might be available. 'Knowing that he had been at Falkirk and was a wee bit of a hothead, that was maybe what tempted me to him,' Shaw says. 'You would think he would be all right because he wouldn't take any nonsense.'[4]

MacLeod confirmed that Ferguson was keen to go into management, though he still had hopes of holding on to him as a player at Ayr. Says Bob Shaw, 'I can always remember Ally saying, "He's my twelfth man, what am I going to do?"'[5] Ferguson then agreed to see the East Stirling chairman, Willie Muirhead – though largely out of courtesy – and in late June the two men met in a Falkirk hotel, accompanied by their wives. By now Muirhead was getting desperate, as the new season was only a few weeks away. More than twenty people had applied for the job, but none was considered suitable. But Ferguson's 'manner and confidence, sincerity and knowledge' immediately impressed. 'He was a family man, a trustworthy person,'

Muirhead said later. 'I knew straightaway I had got myself a manager far superior to anyone I had interviewed.'[6]

The budding boss needed some persuading, however. 'You could describe Bill as a real third-degree man,' Ferguson later explained. 'He kept pestering me and every time I bumped into him he would say: "Come on, son, take it."'[7]

The job was part-time; the pay a mere £40 a week. With a few players having left over the summer, East Stirling had only a tiny squad when Ferguson took over at the end of June 1974. Worse still, the budget to buy new talent was just £2,000. 'I have a big job on my hands,' he admitted to the local paper, the weekly *Falkirk Herald*. 'Shire has been in the doldrums for some time and it will be a long and gradual process to change the image of the team.'[8]

His first priority was find some new players. 'I can hear him almost begging this player to come out of retirement and play for East Stirling,' says Mel Henderson, a *Falkirk Herald* reporter who turned up at Firs Park one day to find Ferguson busy on the phone. 'Alex was looking at this booklet that the Scottish League brought out with all the free transfers on it – all the players that were available – but because he came in late in the close season he was obviously getting rejections. Players had already decided to go to other clubs.'[9]

'When I took over,' Ferguson loves to relate, 'the new season was just three weeks away and we had just eight players and no goalie.' The story, which has become part of Ferguson mythology, then goes that he jokingly reminded his chairman, 'You need eleven to start a game of football.'[10] The facts suggest some harmless embellishment. Of the sixteen men who played for Ferguson at East Stirlingshire, twelve had in fact been playing for the team the season before. This squares with his own comment the week he arrived that 'We have twelve signed players at the moment.'[11]

Still, the bit about having no goalkeeper was true. Alex Ferguson's first signing as manager was Tom Gourlay from Partick Thistle, who arrived on a free transfer, but cost a £750 signing-on fee. The problem was that Gourlay wasn't fit: he'd spent the previous season in the Thistle reserves as understudy goalkeeper to Alan Rough, and apparently weighed almost fifteen stone. 'We're fattening him up for Christmas!' Ferguson joked to one reporter.[12]

Willie Muirhead had gone away on holiday, and asked Ferguson to contact him if he signed any new players. Within days Ferguson had rung again to say he was buying Billy Hulston, an old favourite who was returning to East Stirling after spending the best years of his career in the top division with Clyde and Airdrie. The only problem was the price, £2,000 – Ferguson's entire transfer kitty (and he had already spent £750 on Gourlay). Hulston had originally been tempted to sign for nearby Stenhousemuir, but agreed to meet Ferguson after a last-minute telegram. 'After speaking for half-an-hour I knew I wanted to sign,' Hulston says,

> but I asked to be allowed to phone Alex Smith, the
> Stenhousemuir manager, to tell him our deal was off . . .
> Fergie was having none of that. He said he wanted my
> signature right then and added, 'If it's more money you want,
> I'll give you £50 out of my own pocket.' He took out his
> wallet and put the notes on the table. He was such a strong
> character, so positive. He decided what he wanted and got
> it.[13]

Alex Ferguson was fortunate in that East Stirling had an excellent physiotherapist, Ricky McFarlane, who knew about a lot more than just treating injuries. He was effectively Ferguson's assistant, and an experienced mentor. 'Ricky and Alec were a great team,' says player Jim Mullin. 'Ricky had been involved in football for some time and knew a fair bit about it, so, apart from injury things, Ricky used to do warm-ups and gave Alex Ferguson some good help.'[14]

Ferguson would serve as East Stirling's manager for just 117 days.

But during that short spell he quickly displayed many of the features for which he would make himself world-famous during the next three decades. It was East Stirling fans who first experienced his emphasis on attacking football; the investment in youth; confrontations with his chairman; intolerance of the slightest dissent; psychological manoeuvres against opponents; brilliant handling of players; and a refusal to accept defeat.

The last two traits were illustrated in his very first competitive fixture with the club – a Scottish League Cup match watched by just 700 souls at Forfar Athletic, sixteen miles north of Dundee. After forty-five minutes East Stirling were seemingly dead and buried, losing 3–0. Winger Bobby McCulley went in at half-time expecting the greatest of roastings. 'Already he terrified us,' says McCulley, 'I'd never been afraid of anyone before but he was a frightening bastard from the start.' To the team's astonishment, though, the manager told them they'd played well in the first half. 'And another thing – you can win the game,' Ferguson reportedly said. 'He was right in that we had been unlucky, but we thought he was mad,' says McCulley.[15] Reinvigorated, East Stirling stormed back in the second half to snatch a 3–3 draw.

It wasn't long, however, before Alex Ferguson was demonstrating the motivational powers of household crockery during his mid-game or post-match talks. 'He was so wound up,' says forward Jim Meakin. 'He'd come in and kick the half-time tea tray all over the place because we weren't playing.'[16] Yet Ferguson often thought carefully about what affect he wanted his words to have on his players. On one occasion he was found rehearsing one of his outbursts in advance, enquiring of a listener, 'Does that sound OK?'[17]

Jim Meakin adds, 'Even if we won he could come in ranting and raving, telling us not to get cocky just because we had won and then telling us where we had gone wrong.' One can't help thinking Ferguson had been influenced by his father in this, remembering the days when Alex Snr refused to praise his schoolboy son even when he'd scored four goals, fearing he might get too big-headed. 'To be fair, he was usually right,' says Meakin. 'Even then his use of substitutes was brilliant. He knew how to change a game and how to motivate us. When he was talking, nobody dared open their mouths.'[18] Meakin, who recalls having previously been involved in 'one or two skirmishes' with Ferguson as a player, was successfully converted from midfield to centre-forward by his new manager. He immediately noticed how Ferguson cleverly exploited people's different attitudes to their new boss, either one way or the other. 'If you loved him, you played for him. If you loathed him, you tried to prove him wrong.' He also experienced at first hand the risks of stepping out of line. Already on the transfer list, Meakin sought permission to miss a Monday-evening training session because he wanted to take a quick family break in Blackpool. Ferguson said 'No', because he expected Meakin to play an essential part in that Wednesday's match. Meakin ignored him, went away as planned, and then turned up as usual for the midweek game. 'He caught me, and suspended me indefinitely,' says Meakin. 'It was his way or no way. You had to succumb to his methods.'[19] Ferguson put no time limit on Meakin's suspension, though the directors eventually persuaded him to lift it after three games.

Ferguson's action was perhaps understandable for a young manager who needed to stamp his authority on his players. What made his decision more courageous was that Meakin was son-in-law of the director Bob Shaw, who tried to intervene on Meakin's behalf. It was just a small sign of the way Ferguson wanted to make the club more professional. Another was his demand that players train on Saturday mornings before games – which was unheard of before – and then turn up for matches in collars and ties. But Ferguson's attempt to replace East Stirling's traditional black-and-white hooped colours, with white shirts, black shorts and red socks, was vetoed by the board.

In the brief time he was in charge, East Stirling's results were a distinct improvement on the previous season's. The club finished second in its six-team group in the Scottish League Cup, and in twelve league games the Shire won seven, drew two and lost three. This was with many of the same players who had ended the previous season fourth from bottom of the League.

It was behind the scenes where Alex Ferguson made the greatest impact. 'Everything was focused towards his goals,' says Bob McCulley. 'Time didn't matter to him, he never wore a watch. If he wanted something done, he'd stay as late as it took, or come in early.'[20] And his dedication is all the more remarkable given that Ferguson was working part-time, and still running Fergie's.

Frustrated by the lack of money to buy players, he took the first steps to starting a youth programme. A junior side called Glasgow United agreed to come and play East Stirling's young prospects in a friendly, and Ferguson offered to pay the visitors £40 for the cost of hiring a team bus. He then found himself summoned to an emergency meeting of the East Stirling board in a room at the supporters' club, to discuss a serious matter regarding the club finances. 'I was petrified wondering what I'd done wrong,' he later said. 'I wondered whether somebody had stolen money and I was getting the blame.'[21] When the directors complained he hadn't sought permission for the £40 for the Glasgow United bus, Ferguson was amazed. 'I remember just standing up, reaching in my back pocket, pulling out £40, throwing it on the table, saying "Here's your money – you can keep your job!"'[22] Later that evening Willie Muirhead, who'd missed the board meeting, rang Ferguson and persuaded him to withdraw his resignation.

On another occasion, when East Stirling were losing, Ferguson says Muirhead suddenly appeared beside him in the dugout and asked, 'What are you going to do, Alex?' The manager told him: 'For starters I'm going to turf you out of here.'[23] Muirhead remembered entering the dugout for rather different reasons on another occasion. He said that during one game he 'had to jump out of the directors' box to pull him [Ferguson] back from squaring up to a referee . . . and ended up sitting next to him in the dugout for the rest of the match, just to make sure'.[24]

Though confronting the East Stirling board over what he could spend, Ferguson was himself strict with players' expenses. As at most clubs, players were compensated for the cost of attending evening training sessions, but when he found out that a group from Glasgow were sharing a car but each claiming the allowance, he insisted that only the driver would be paid in future. 'The Glasgow boys weren't happy about that,' says Tom Donnelly (the former Rangers reserve), who was usually the driver. 'He was always looking for money to buy players. We were only getting £2 or £3 or whatever it was.'[25] And yet only two years before, in the very same town, Ferguson had almost led a players' strike over an attempted cut in similar travel allowances, though in Willie Cunningham's case it had been imposed for disciplinary reasons.

Still only thirty-two, Ferguson took part in training sessions, eager to show his men what a good player he was himself. 'Training was always sharp and enjoyable. He was always right in the middle of things,' says Billy Hulston, 'unlike many bosses back then, who just sat in their office.'[26]

'He always joined in and would have us playing in the dark until his team won. He was ferocious, elbowing and kicking,' says Bob McCulley. 'We'd say to each other, "Just let him score and we can all go home," but it didn't work because if we weren't trying, he knew.'[27] Tom Donnelly says Ferguson would often entertain the younger players with accounts of heroic deeds on the turf of Hampden and Parkhead, and how he'd made monkeys of great Scottish defenders such as Billy McNeill. Donnelly remembers him practising corner kicks one day:

He said, 'I used to get Big Billy rattled all the time, elbows out, and in his face when the ref wasn't looking, and then the ball came across and somebody else would header it in while Big Billy was looking at me.' He had a lot of good patter like that for the young boys, because he played at Ibrox and the boys were never going to get to that high level of play.[28]

No one dared mention the 1969 final, one imagines.

Ferguson finished at East Stirlingshire with a flourish. On the first Saturday in October 1974 they faced Falkirk at Firs Park. Not only was it a derby match against their close neighbours, who'd been relegated from the First Division the previous May, but Falkirk, of course, had only recently ignored Ferguson's potential as a manager. This time Willie Muirhead agreed that Ferguson could take the team to a local hotel for lunch beforehand, and later recalled how his manager then revealed 'brilliant' skills as a psychologist:

Little did we know he had chosen the Claddens Hotel, the same place where Falkirk always chose to go before a game. Well, as we passed by a large window which looked into where they were dining, Alex ordered everyone to begin laughing and joking. So we walked past and the Falkirk lads looked out and saw a team in great spirits before a game.[29]

Ferguson knew most of the Falkirk players, of course, and could discuss them with authority, having been their coach only eighteen months before. Says Bob McCulley, 'Fergie stood pointing, "Look at him, he's never a player. And him, he doesn't know how lucky he is to be eating there for free."'[30] 'I know all the players from my own days at Brockville,' Ferguson told the *Falkirk Herald*, 'how they play and what their strengths and weaknesses are. In fact, I probably know some of them better than they know themselves.'[31]

In his team talk, Ferguson told his men they were up against it, and that even the local paper was biased in favour of the town's bigger club. And he went through their opponents, highlighting every flaw. 'He spent an hour identifying all their weaknesses,' says the captain and central defender Gordon Simpson. 'So and so lacked pace, that guy's only got one foot, this player is weak in the tackle. We went out there believing we were by far the better team.' Gordon Simpson was an early example of the Ferguson sort of captain – the Willie Miller/Bryan Robson/Steve Bruce/Roy Keane type who strains every sinew and never gives up. He supposedly had a cartilage which had a habit of popping out of his knee during games. When it did, so the story went, Simpson simply gritted his teeth and pushed it back in again. 'I led by example and complained a lot to referees, both of which he liked,' says Simpson. 'If we differed, I said so, but calling a spade a spade was always OK with him.'[32]

The strikers were also told what to do if they were ever one-on-one with the Falkirk goalkeeper. 'He said, "Don't let him take you on because he'll take the ball off you," ' Jim Meakin recalls. 'He said, "Pick your corner and hit it." '[33] Which is exactly what happened.

In front of a crowd of 4,650 – huge by East Stirling standards – the home side won 2–0, and deservedly so. That was followed by a 4–3 win at Hamilton and a 4–0 victory at home to Alloa, lifting Shire to fourth place. Ferguson spoke of winning the Second Division title. And the Falkirk public had quickly responded: 1,250 saw the Alloa match, compared with around 400 for each of the three opening home fixtures.

The win over Alloa in mid-October proved to be Alex Ferguson's last game in charge of East Stirlingshire. A few days earlier he'd been phoned by his former boss Willie Cunningham, who was now running St Mirren after his unfortunate departure from Falkirk. They agreed to meet at Love Street, St Mirren's ground in Paisley. Ferguson assumed it was merely a chance to catch up on old times, and was therefore shocked when Cunningham announced he was giving up football. Would Alex be interested in taking his place? Ferguson was doubtful. After what he'd already achieved for East Stirling, St Mirren were starting to look like an inferior prospect. At that moment the Paisley club sat a couple of places below Ferguson's team in the Second Division, and their crowds were now barely any better.

Ferguson agreed, however, to meet the St Mirren chairman, Harold Currie, at his office in Glasgow. Again it was mainly out of courtesy, for he already felt some loyalty to Shire, and was worried that St Mirren seemed to have some inherent problem, having gone through a new manager roughly every year for the previous decade.

Currie says the conversation lasted three hours. 'I realised then that Alex Ferguson was somebody of exception,' he says. 'He knew what he wanted in life.' But did he really believe East Stirlingshire could become a big club? Currie reportedly asked him. 'I said, "Don't make up your mind now, only come to St Mirren if you feel your future, or your immediate future, is here. Don't join us if you're not entirely happy about it."'[34]

It took several days to reach a decision, and Ferguson's initial inclination was to say 'No'. The press was full of rumours that he might go to St Mirren, though he lied that 'no approaches have been made to me'.[35]

To resolve his dilemma, Alex Ferguson phoned his hero and friend Jock Stein. The oracle duly delivered, but not with a straight answer. Ferguson should go and sit in the highest point in the stand at St Mirren and look out over the ground, the Celtic boss advised, and then repeat the exercise at his current home, Firs Park. The answer, Stein said, would be obvious.

Ferguson's last act for East Stirling was to recommend as his successor Ian Ure, the former Scotland centre-half, who had been Sir Matt Busby's last signing for Manchester United. It was 'one of the few mistakes [Ferguson] made as a Shire employee', says the club history.[36] Ure lasted barely a year – though that's almost par for the course for lower-division Scottish managers. His fifteen successors would include Alex Ferguson's brother, Martin.

'He [Alex Ferguson] was only three months at the club, but by

God he did a lot for us,' says Bob Shaw. 'We knew it would only be a stepping stone for him but I'm proud we gave him his first chance. The man is a winner, through and through.'[37] Ferguson's departure was 'a bloody tragedy for East Stirlingshire', Willie Muirhead would repeatedly say before his death in 2001. 'He was the best thing that ever happened to the club.'[38]

And there was always a certain cachet for Muirhead in being able to boast of being the first to employ Alex Ferguson as a football manager.

The Paisley Pattern

'When I was at St Mirren, it was a desolate place. Even the birds woke up coughing.'

ALEX FERGUSON[1]

Alex Ferguson's time in charge of St Mirren – or rather the way it ended – remains the blackspot of his long managerial career. In his 500-page autobiography, for instance, he devotes just fourteen pages to his four years at the club, rushing through events as quickly as he decently can to move forward to happier memories. And in the acknowledgements, where he generously recognises his debt to colleagues at both Aberdeen and Manchester United, the Paisley club is forgotten.[2]

Yet the St Mirren years are fascinating, in that – like his brief spell at East Stirlingshire – they illustrate many of the qualities which explain Alex Ferguson's success. They were also the only time in Ferguson's career when he experienced that traditional fate of football managers – the sack. What caused the scars, and his evident wish to forget, is that Ferguson compounded the understandable pain of his sudden dismissal by disputing it, and doing so very publicly. Yet he wasn't sacked for want of football success.

For the fourth time he was with a team who played in black and white – this time, vertical stripes. Their name, 'St Mirren', comes from a local sixth-century saint, St Mirin, who is supposedly buried near the site of Paisley Abbey. The 'Saints' or the 'Buddies', as they're nicknamed, were in the doldrums when Ferguson arrived in the autumn of 1974, but historically they were a far bigger outfit than East Stirlingshire. They'd won the Scottish Cup in 1926 and 1959, been beaten finalists three times – most recently in 1962 – and spent most of their time in the top division. Alex Ferguson understood the potential that Paisley offered, for Govan was only four miles down the road, and the Hillington Industrial Estate where he'd once worked was even closer. Yet Paisley has always considered itself independent of Glasgow. Officially it's one of the largest towns in Scotland, and in 2000 it applied, unsuccessfully, for city status. What's more, unlike Falkirk, St Mirren had no rival league clubs in the town. 'There is only so much you can do with a club like East Stirling,' Ferguson announced as he arrived in Paisley. 'St Mirren was a club comparable with Rangers and Celtic only a few years ago. This has got to happen again.'[3]

Ferguson faced two immediate problems at Love Street. The first was that the Scottish League was due to be reorganised at the end of the 1974–75 season. The existing two divisions of eighteen and twenty teams would be carved into three new sections: a new Premier Division for the top ten sides, then two leagues of fourteen clubs each below them, which were confusingly to be called Division One and Division Two. Under the scheme, the six teams at the top of the old Second Division would join the eight sides at the bottom of the former First Division to form a new Division One which, despite its name, would actually be the middle tier of the new League. It was essential that St Mirren finished the season in the top six to qualify for this middle division. The club lay in sixth place when Ferguson arrived – just on course to make it into the new Division One.

Ferguson's second problem was that St Mirren's crowds had

dwindled away. Officially, Love Street had a capacity of 53,000, but the club didn't attract that number of customers for all its nineteen home league games added together. Indeed, attendances averaged 1,200 for the three home games before Ferguson took over. The new manager would have to increase attendances fivefold if St Mirren was to have the financial clout to sustain his long-term goal – a place in the new Premier Division. The trouble was that Glasgow was right next door: Ibrox and Parkhead were only a few minutes' drive down the M8, and every Saturday coaches would take Paisleyites from the centre of the town to watch the Old Firm. Nor did the size of St Mirren's ground help, since what little noise the fans made tended to get lost on the large, open terraces.

But the relationship between Paisley and Glasgow was always strained, as so often happens when towns are overshadowed by powerful, assertive neighbours. Alex Ferguson reckoned that, if he could create a new local pride in the St Mirren team, he then could use Paisley's resentment of Glasgow to good effect. 'Paisley is in the shadow of Glasgow and the people there have a chip on their shoulder about Glaswegians,' he once said.

> They lost their cotton industry and then their car industry and were hit by a depression left by the lack of employment. They were the type of people who needed to be lifted. I set about trying to give them some optimism through their football club. Because they were a one-team town I felt I had the chance to create an identity. I did it by making the people feel they were involved, by infecting them with my own desire.[4]

Yet Ferguson had very little to work with at first. Just as at East Stirling, he began at St Mirren on a part-time basis, and continued running his pub during the rest of the day (and two pubs from 1975). Indeed, he was so involved in his licensed premises that on one occasion he nearly lost an eye when a canister exploded in his face in the cellar at Fergie's. Yet his position as manager of St Mirren Football Club was just that. He wasn't just running the football team: he was also in charge of all the club's affairs (to the extent that he was also called 'secretary' at one point). He was as likely to be ordering toilet rolls, or interviewing cleaners, as arranging player transfers. Ferguson himself tells the tale of what happened just before a big game against Celtic. 'I was in the middle of my team talk, about ten minutes before the kick off . . . when one of the stewards poked his head through the door and said: "Excuse me, boss – the toilets in the stand are blocked."'[5]

He also set out to reduce petty fraud at Love Street. All unsold programmes had to be accounted for in future, along with the cash takings, which suddenly made the programmes profitable. And the Love Street turnstiles were modified to put an end to the practice whereby many fans jumped through them, having bribed the turnstile operators.

If it snowed – not unknown in Scotland – Ferguson would be out helping to clear the pitch. On one occasion he persuaded local farmers to supply bales of straw to keep the ground covered. Late on another night, the St Mirren electrician, Fred Douglas, was sitting at home when it began snowing heavily. He rushed down to Love Street, turned on a floodlight, and began clearing off the snow, in the hope of preserving the pitch for a vital cup match the following day. Around 1.30 a.m., Douglas got the shock of his life when he felt a hand on the back of his shoulder. It was Ferguson. 'He'd seen the snow as well,' says Douglas, 'so he'd belted down 'cos we wanted this game on, and I nearly died of fright. No sound or anything – I never even heard him coming up.'[6] Together they cleared and covered the goalmouths, though it wasn't enough to prevent the game being frozen off.

'He was running everything, right down to the cleaners,' Cathy Ferguson once said.

He was here, there, everywhere, days, nights, Sundays,
building up the team. Clubs asked him here and there, and
he had to go himself. He is that type. He likes to be in the
thick of things. He would be out from nine in the morning
till after midnight. Apart from the football, there were our
two pubs in Glasgow to supervise . . . The kids hardly saw
him at all. And I did find it difficult not having a man about,
especially with boys. They got too wild and ran rings round
me.[7]

At times the boys were taunted about football at their school in
East Kilbride, so much so that the eldest son, Mark, refused to go to
school at times. Ferguson would later admit he 'rarely saw' his sons
'during the week, and only at weekends did I manage to resume the
role of father'.[8] Even at home he found it hard to switch off and deal
with the boys. 'Are you going to talk to these weans or not?' Cathy
would ask.[9] Ferguson seemed driven by his work. At Christmas 1976,
for instance, for three nights running he had to make the dinners at
Fergie's himself, because the chef had resigned. On Christmas Day he
barely saw his family: after travelling with St Mirren to a match at
Clydebank, he then went to the pub to cook the evening meals.

'He used to come into the club early in the morning, before
anyone else,' says his chairman, Harold Currie, 'and he'd be there
until eight or nine.' Currie – an Englishman who ran the Chivas
Regal whisky company – even recalls lying in bed at night getting
calls from his manager, who was still at Fergie's. 'Day or night he'd be
totally running St Mirren. And with that attitude, all the players
and all the people at the club could see that example to follow, and
this is where you get the leadership.'[10] 'He was building a club, not
just a team,' says his former captain Tony Fitzpatrick, who later had
a couple of spells managing St Mirren himself. 'There's managers
who'll go out and build a team short-term, but Fergie built a club
wherever he went.'[11]

There was little money for transfers. The only option, as at East Stirling, was to concentrate on grooming the club's own young players. A myth has developed over the years that Alex Ferguson established the youth policy at St Mirren. In fact the club already had a youth programme in place when he arrived, and young players were starting to graduate to the first team. Two of the most promising youngsters, Tony Fitzpatrick and Bobby Reid, had both signed for St Mirren before the new manager turned up. However, Ferguson undoubtedly put much more emphasis on the youth side of the club, appointing two club scouts and setting up four youth teams at different age levels. He also raised standards, so that the club didn't waste too much time assessing mediocre prospects. Two of his greatest finds were Billy Stark and Frank McGarvey. McGarvey, who later played for Liverpool and Scotland, was also a Rangers reject of sorts. Ferguson heard about him through a tip-off from one of the Glasgow club's coaches, and learned that Rangers themselves weren't interested in the player because he was a Catholic. But Ferguson allowed a far greater prospect to slip through his hands. Ally McCoist was one of three teenagers to whom Ferguson gave regular lifts from East Kilbride to youth training sessions at St Mirren. He went on to score well over 300 goals for Rangers, won the Golden Boot as Europe's top scorer two years running, and gained sixty-one caps for Scotland. But in the mid-1970s Ferguson thought McCoist was too small, and so didn't sign him.

Ferguson could introduce the club's youngsters only gradually, and in his first season he had to blend them with older players acquired from other sides. At the same time large numbers of players were thrown out – eighteen, Ferguson recalls, at the end of his first season. It was perhaps a sign of the state of the squad he inherited that few of those he axed found themselves another senior club. It was an agonising procedure to have players come to his office one by one to hear the bad news, so the next year he decided to tell eight players in one collective announcement. 'What a mess that was. Disaster,' he says. 'And they were all young lads – maybe one or two older ones who knew they needed a change anyway. But that was hopeless.'[12]

It was some months before his team began to gel on the pitch. St Mirren took only two points from Ferguson's first five games, and slipped down the table. Then suddenly in the new year, after a 6–1 thrashing of Brechin City, results picked up. To emphasise the importance of new blood, Ferguson appointed Tony Fitzpatrick as his team captain, even though at eighteen he was one of the youngest skippers ever seen in Scottish football. Ferguson told Fitzpatrick he was going to rebuild the side round him and one or two of the other young players. 'He'd probably seen something in me,' says Fitzpatrick,

> and that's what I needed to get the best out of me – to give me that responsibility. And, to be fair to him, he treated me like a captain although I was young. He said, 'I've watched you in training and the way you play your game. I'm going to bring this club into the Premier League. We're going to build a club that's going to overtake Celtic and Rangers' – that was his ambition.[13]

Eight wins in a row hoisted the side back up again, and St Mirren secured their place in the top six with a couple of games to spare.

Perhaps the worst moments that season came when East Stirling exacted revenge on the man who had left them. Ferguson boasted of knowing his old players' weaknesses, but East Stirling knocked St Mirren out of the Scottish Cup, winning 2–1. Worse followed when Shire hammered Ferguson's men 5–0 in a meaningless end-of-season league game. Ferguson had decided to test the quality of his beefed-up youth programme by fielding seven teenagers. The teams shared the same dressing room at Firs Park, and Ferguson was taunted by the home players about whether it had been a good idea to leave. The setback didn't deter him.

Ferguson's emphasis was on attacking football, to keep the fans entertained. 'He was very keen on wide players', says Harold Currie, 'and he had some very good ones. They were so fast they'd get behind defences and take them by surprise.'[14]

Ferguson always tried to ensure he knew everything about his squad. In some cases this would mean being informed about any personal problems. He'd want to know, for instance, if a player was having marital difficulties, so he could then have a quiet word with him. But Ferguson also wanted to know if anybody was misbehaving off the pitch. Fred Douglas, who often went drinking with the players, recalls how one day Ferguson asked him to report back on any excesses. 'Alec said, "Tell me who drinks", and I said, "Well look, if it's going to come to that, I'll just not go out with the players." I said, "They're my friends. You're my friend. I don't really want to be taking sides." He said, "That's fair comment. OK, better get somebody else to do it."' Instead, Douglas says, Ferguson got reports from one of his old Govan pals, John Donachie, who proved to be more effective, because most players didn't know who he was.[15]

One of the victims was Frank McGarvey, whom Donachie spotted in a Glasgow bar the night before a big game. When McGarvey later confessed, Ferguson reacted in characteristic fashion. 'I told him that he would be withdrawn from the Scotland Under-21 game, that he was finished with football and I never wanted to see him again.'[16] After pleadings from players, apologies from McGarvey, and even a sympathetic word from Cathy Ferguson, the manager finally forgave the young player.

The former St Mirren striker Jimmy Bone tells of the time Ferguson rang McGarvey's home one Friday night to check he wasn't out drinking. His mother said he'd just nipped out on an errand and she'd ask him to phone Ferguson when he got back a few minutes later. Ferguson's suspicions were aroused when the player duly rang back and Ferguson heard the pips which in those days indicated the call came from a phone-box. Suspecting the player had rung from some bar, Ferguson immediately drove round to McGarvey's house to check up. He was at home, though – and so was the call-box. 'They had a phone-box in the house,' Jimmy Bone explains. 'It was that big a family, to save on the bills, they had a box put in.'[17]

Ferguson was rather tolerant of gambling, however – though certainly not on the scale he had witnessed among the players at Ibrox. Players and manager would regularly have a flutter on the horses, or run internal sweeps on goalscorers.

Alex Ferguson still had many rough edges, and still tended to speak before he thought. 'I'd make some comment after the match and read it the following morning and think, "now why the hell did I say that?"' His old friend Willie Waddell would ring to bring him 'back to earth with a right bump', reminding Ferguson he was only managing 'a bloody wee club like St Mirren' rather than a World Cup side.[18] On another occasion, after St Mirren had won five games in a row, Ferguson cockily claimed they wouldn't just secure promotion but would win the League 'no bother', only to lose the next four games. 'The lesson was sorely learned. Don't open your mouth unless you can fulfil every word.'[19]

Even as a player, Ferguson had established good relations with journalists – or at least those he liked, such as Jim Rodger of the *Daily Mirror*. He began a weekly column called 'Fergie on Friday' for the *Paisley Daily Express*, though in reality it was ghost-written after an interview by the reporter Stan Park. 'Alex Ferguson even at that time had an eye for publicity,' says Harold Currie. 'Journalists liked the idea they could approach him and get a story, and Alex Ferguson was always willing to let them know what was going on.'[20] When Currie organised an improbable St Mirren tour to the Caribbean in the summer of 1976, reporters were flattered to get calls from Ferguson on some exotic island conveying the latest news. Only they weren't told quite everything.

Take an incident in Guyana. During a game against the national team, Ferguson was furious about the way the Guyanan centre-half kept clattering St Mirren's teenage striker Robert Torrance, yet escaped unpunished by the referee. So, to effect retribution, Ferguson put himself on as substitute. 'In the first contest for a cross, I exacted a bit of revenge on the centre-half, whose squeals caused the referee to point at me ominously. The competition became fierce until I nailed Torrance's abuser perfectly. As he rolled about like a dying man, the referee sent me off.' The St Mirren players were ordered not to tell anyone about the dismissal – the seventh of Ferguson's career. By his own admission it was the only time he 'took the field with the intention of damaging an opponent'.[21]

The abusive, bellicose and sometimes violent Alex Ferguson was always simmering not far beneath the surface. 'The quickness of my temper and depth of my anger often worried me,' he openly admits, and he himself tells of the time when his brother Martin came across several St Mirren players in the Waterloo bar in Glasgow the night before a game, boasting about their bonuses. In the dressing room after the match – which they won – Ferguson flew off the handle about the incident. 'My anger intensified with each decibel until I lost control, lifted a bottle of Coca-Cola and smashed it against the wall above their heads. Not one of them moved as the Coke ran down the wall and the glass dropped on to their strips.'[22] Ferguson said they'd have to train all night unless every player signed a statement he'd typed guaranteeing that they'd never visit the Waterloo bar again. And sign it they did.

When the team won, 'He'd cuddle you and be all over the top of you,' says Jimmy Bone.[23] Sometimes, however, even when his team were victorious, Ferguson was quite capable of flying into a rage. Tony Fitzpatrick recalls an example:

Personally I thought we'd played well, but he felt our passing was awful and he let us know it. I was silly enough to say,

'What the fuck are you looking for? We won 5–0. Are you not happy?' He came over and gave me a 'Fergie special'. He told me in no uncertain terms that he was the manager and it was his standards that counted . . . He was right . . . The passing wasn't sharp, the crossing wasn't that good. It makes you look at it – although you won 5–0, there is room for improvement.[24]

If his players were one Fergie target, referees were another. In January 1974 he was fined £10 by the SFA for 'using foul language' at the end of a 1–0 defeat at home to Raith Rovers.[25] A year later he stormed out of an SFA hearing accusing the Association of being 'the laughing stock of British football'. He refused to pay a £50 fine they'd levied for 'foul and abusive language towards the linesman' at the end of a home draw with Airdrie the previous November. In a portent of what would come two years later, he threatened the SFA with legal action for not giving him a fair hearing or allowing legal representation. 'I cannot afford to give the SFA £50,' he said, 'but I can afford to spend £10,000 to take them all the way in a courtroom.'[26] Ferguson admitted he'd been 'a bit over-enthusiastic and let off steam', but was particularly upset that the SFA should have brought up his poor disciplinary record as a player. 'They could keep on referring to it for another 40 years,' he complained. 'They would not have treated Jock Stein or Willie Waddell the way they treated me. They had a complete disregard for me.' Harold Currie and the St Mirren vice-chairman, Willie Todd, offered their 'full support' to Ferguson's threatened action, but he quietly backed down.[27]

If anything, the SFA Referee Committee seem to have been remarkably lenient, for at the same meeting – largely unreported by the press – they also condemned Ferguson for forging the signature of a St Mirren player on a letter in which the player purportedly said he wanted to appeal against a booking. Ferguson escaped punishment for this offence.[28] Three months later he was again in trouble with the SFA after bursting into the referee's room and making 'ungentlemanly remarks' after a Scottish Cup tie at Motherwell. Ferguson thought the official hadn't done enough to protect his players. He was fined £25 and forced to sign an assurance that during the next two seasons he would never talk to referees or linesmen on match days.[29]

Each season at St Mirren saw steady improvement. The team finished sixth in the new Division One in 1975–76 with perfectly balanced figures – 26 points from 26 games, 37 goals for, and 37 against. In the following season, however, they earned a place among the elite of Scottish football after lifting the Division One championship by a four-point margin. They'd lost only twice all season, and had gone undefeated for twenty-eight matches. It was Alex Ferguson's first trophy in football management.

Earlier that season, as St Mirren sat on top of the Division One table, it was clear that Scottish football was starting to notice Ferguson's attributes as a manager. A 4–1 win over Dundee United in the Scottish Cup was especially impressive. 'They play with infectious enthusiasm,' the *Daily Record* said of his side. 'They play with rare skill. They play to a pattern of devastating attack.' Christening them 'Fergie's Furies', and with a touch of hyperbole, the paper even claimed his St Mirren could rank alongside the Busby Babes, Stein's Stunners, and the Wembley Wizards of 1928.[30]

There were rumours at the start of 1977 that Ferguson might soon replace the Rangers manager Jock Wallace. 'Rubbish' was his reaction, as he described being manager at Love Street as 'the biggest job in the country and I would be foolish to think of anything else'.[31] At this time Ferguson seems genuinely to have thought that St Mirren could one day challenge the Glasgow giants. 'There is only one way for me – or anybody associated with me,' he wrote – 'and that's winning. I'm not in this game to be a middle of the road manager, or a "nearly" manager. I'm in it to win everything – and the players are bred that way.'[32] His formula for success was emerging –

assembling a squad of players who would follow the Ferguson philosophy.

A manager can be the greatest of tacticians, but he is doomed if he cannot motivate players. Ferguson possessed this skill in abundance – though in his case it was generally based on fear more than inspiration. Says team captain Tony Fitzpatrick, 'He would say at half-time, as we were going out, "I'll tell you now – if you are beat, don't come in that dressing room, don't come near here." So there was no way we were going to get beat and face Fergie.'[33]

Surprisingly, perhaps, he could be a very nervous, inarticulate speaker in his team talks, though he gradually improved with practice. For the big matches, particularly against Rangers and Celtic, he always had extra psychological ploys up his sleeve. 'He was very good at taking the pressure off players before a big game by taking it on himself,' says the future Scotland player Iain Munro. 'Before games against the Old Firm he would invariably make some inflammatory statement that not only got the punters along but turned the spotlight on him and away from the players.'[34]

Ferguson realised, that to achieve his ambitions, St Mirren would have to carry out a complete overhaul of their operations, and to think big. 'Our organisation must be bang on,' he insisted, though today it seems ludicrous to cite Carlisle United as the model of a well-run small provincial club, as he did.[35]

First, Ferguson knew he had to make the playing squad more professional – partly to attract better players. Until now, just like Ferguson himself at St Johnstone, St Mirren players worked during the day at full-time jobs – the side contained a millworker, a welder, a computer programmer and a car mechanic. Although they were also paid to play football, they had to train in their spare time, which usually meant a couple of evenings a week. The first step towards a full-time, professional squad would be for players to replace their existing day jobs with part-time morning work, leaving every afternoon free to concentrate on football. In a new development in

131

Scottish football, Ferguson publicly urged Paisley employers to come up with part-time positions for his players – not an easy request at a time when unemployment was climbing rapidly. A job he found for one player was as an undertaker's assistant, nailing down coffin lids. Tony Fitzpatrick became a part-time painter and decorator, Frank McGarvey a joiner.

This was the era when football clubs first began to appreciate the possibilities of commercial activities that would generate significant extra income beyond simple turnstile revenue. St Mirren were pioneers. They set up a lottery which was soon bringing in about £4,000 a week – a huge sum by the then standards of Scottish football. Ferguson himself also pushed through plans to install more powerful floodlights, both to prepare the Love Street ground for future European football and to enable TV companies to film evening fixtures. The lights hadn't previously been strong enough for colour cameras. More TV games would in turn boost revenue from the pitch-side advertising hoardings. The need to pay for the new lights led to the formation of the St Mirren Centenary Committee (later the Development Committee). Ferguson would attend their meetings to offer encouragement.

Before St Mirren were in a position to qualify for Europe, they announced their ambitions for the future by taking part in the old Anglo-Scottish Cup. They won 6–4 over two legs against Fulham – for whom George Best was a scorer – then beat Notts County 2–1. In the final, however, they succumbed 3–2 to Bristol City, then in the English First Division.

The French champions, Saint-Étienne, agreed to visit Love Street for a friendly, though the arrangement eventually fell through. To celebrate St Mirren's centenary in 1977, Ferguson also persuaded Liverpool to come to Paisley, and the Buddies lost the match only on penalties. This was the Liverpool side at the peak of its powers – the champions of both England and Europe. Ferguson had gone to Anfield for their European Cup quarter-final win over Saint-

Étienne, and couldn't conceal his admiration for the 'incredible' Merseyside club and its fans. 'I didn't walk away from the ground after the game, I floated out,' he wrote. 'It was as if I had been given an injection of one of those stimulant drugs. Instead, all that happened was I had been caught up in the most exciting football atmosphere I have ever experienced . . . these Liverpool fans support with PASSION . . . that visit to Anfield made me realise exactly what we must all strive for at Love Street.'[36] As for Manchester United, then experiencing a renaissance under Tommy Docherty, Ferguson said very little.

Then there was public relations. Ferguson wanted St Mirren to employ a full-time PR officer – a post which was rare even at leading British clubs in those days. His reasoning was it might take some of the pressure off him (though later he would resist such an appointment at Manchester United, where the media spotlight is many times greater.) He also started a weekly club newspaper to communicate with the fans. *The Saint* was professionally produced, and no mean achievement for a club of St Mirren's size, especially at a time when only a handful of other British sides had regular publications.

His rapport with the fans paid off in more ways than one. When Ferguson bought an experienced centre-half, Jackie Copland from Dundee United, for £17,000, most of the fee came from funds lent by the St Mirren Supporters' Club, which had even come up with the idea of signing Copland.

Much of Ferguson's time at Love Street involved working with the fans, and trying to drum up more support. Locals, he said, should 'get off their backsides and come and see for themselves what they are missing. It is an era for St Mirren FC which I'm sure will be compared with any period in St Mirren's past . . . The tragedy of it all is that an awful lot of Paisley folk are missing out on it.'[37] There is a famous picture of Ferguson touring local housing estates in a loudspeaker car exhorting Paisley folk to come to the home game that afternoon, looking like a political candidate trawling for votes. In fact, according to several club sources, Ferguson did this only once or twice. 'He was never there,' says one of them. Most of the time the car played a recording of a taped message from Ferguson, or the club electrician, Fred Douglas, drove round working the loudspeaker himself. Douglas was told that, if anyone asked, he was to say it was Ferguson speaking.

Two Thursdays a month, however, after evening training, Ferguson would be found with the punters in the St Mirren Social Club under the main stand. 'Fergie would be in there ticking his numbers off and shouting "Bingo!" with the rest of them,' according to Tony Fitzpatrick. 'It's impossible not to be carried along by his enthusiasm.'[38] 'He has an infectious personality,' agrees his physiotherapist and trainer at St Mirren, Ricky McFarlane, who'd followed him from East Stirling, 'and he mixes easily with people from all walks of life.'[39]

But generating passionate support from Paisley citizens would prove to be a frustrating battle throughout Ferguson's four years at Love Street. 'When we saw that crowd of only 4,300 against Aberdeen, it really took the wind out of our sails,' he wrote in one club programme. 'If the people of Paisley don't support us how can we possibly match the ambitions of the Fitzpatricks and McGarveys?'[40]

Ferguson's final year at Love Street was a struggle simply to survive in the Premier Division. He would later admit he should have dipped into the transfer market to insure against injuries, and he particularly regretted not offering enough money for Morton's high-scoring striker, Mark McGhee. The Saints finished third from bottom, but with a comfortable six-point gap between them and the two relegated clubs, Clydebank and Ayr. As the season ended, there was new speculation about Ferguson moving to Rangers, following the resignation of Jock Wallace.

St Mirren's outward success on the pitch, certainly compared with what went before, hid growing tensions behind the scenes which would eventually lead to Alex Ferguson's departure. The chairman who had appointed Ferguson, Harold Currie, had been succeeded by Willie Todd, who ran a local decorating business and was also the Conservative leader on Paisley council. Todd was a very different character – 'not a lot of fun to be with' and 'very strait-laced' says Fred Douglas. 'You never got a lot out of him.'[41]

The club may have been called the Buddies and the Saints; it may have played at Love Street, but the St Mirren boardroom was a snake-pit in the 1970s and '80s. The directors were split into opposing cliques who spent much of their time pushing each other on and off the board like schoolchildren playing King of the Castle. Many involved with the club feel that some directors were involved merely for the local prestige and influence that came from being a director or, better still, chairman. 'It was just to have some power,' says one board member, Tom Moran. 'A lot of them were involved in politics at that time, and I think that maybe had something to do with it.'[42] Nor can it have helped that it was Conservative politics they were involved in, whereas their manager had always been a committed socialist.

Ferguson found it increasingly difficult to get on with Todd and his deputy, John Corson, whom he thought knew nothing about football. In his autobiography, Ferguson claims Corson asked him to identify Tony Fitzpatrick even though Fitzpatrick had been team captain for the previous two years.[43]

Ferguson admits that Willie Todd 'was a genuine fan. But from the moment of my arrival, when he was all over me, I suspected that his ego might easily run wild. If there was a hint of glory, nobody could beat him at basking.'[44] Campbell Scouler, a former director, felt Todd 'was a bit of a dictator'.[45] Another ex-director describes him as an 'autocratic' type who 'saw himself in competition with Alex Ferguson over who would be seen as Mr St Mirren'. According to Tom Moran, 'Bill Todd was one of those guys that once you got on the wrong side of him, that was it, there was no dealing with him, and from then on he and Fergie were at each other's throats.'[46] Ferguson himself accuses Todd of a 'growing hunger for power' and of being a 'megalomaniac', but this was clearly the mirror image of what the St Mirren chairman thought about his manager.[47] Todd himself clearly felt much the same about Ferguson, whom he accuses of wanting everything his own way. Ferguson was less than delighted when Todd announced that he was going to work for St Mirren full-time.

The Ferguson era at St Mirren was to end in acrimony after less than four years (see Chapter 9). But they were years of huge progress. Ferguson had 'made himself into Mr Love Street', said the *Glasgow Herald* in its tribute when he left. 'He did the lot. Alex Ferguson took likely lads and made them into players for the most exciting team the Mirren has ever had. Besides that, he gave at least twenty-six hours of every day to the organisation of the club.'[48]

Some people have exaggerated the increase in crowds at Love Street. There's little need, since the true figures are impressive enough. St Mirren had an average home gate of 1,908 the year before Ferguson arrived, compared with 11,230 in his final season – almost a sixfold increase. Another sign of how much the club grew under Alex Ferguson comes in St Mirren's annual financial reports. Income had risen from £83,840 in 1974–75 to £286,826 in 1978–79. Allowing for the high inflation of the time, this means the club almost doubled in size financially.

The greatest testimony to Ferguson's time in Paisley is the club's subsequent record. Having survived one season in the top tier, the players went full-time the following season, as Ferguson had always planned. In the next decade St Mirren always managed at least a respectable mid-table position in the Premier Division, and often qualified for Europe. The peak was 1980, when St Mirren came third – their highest-ever placing – qualified for the UEFA Cup (formerly the Fairs' Cup), and also became the first Scots side to win the Anglo-Scottish Cup in its ten-year existence. Tony Fitzpatrick remembers the incredible enthusiasm Ferguson generated around the club. Like others, he cites the night an estimated 10,000 travelled to a Scottish Cup tie at Motherwell in 1977. 'There was just a great atmosphere,' he says of Fergie's time, having been involved with the club on and off ever since. 'That era just seemed to be something special.'[49]

'In the Alex Ferguson era there was almost a magic,' says former St Mirren director Bill Waters. 'The improvement in the club and the sudden appearance of crowds were absolutely astonishing. It only lasted a few years, but I'll never forget it. Who knows what we could have done if he'd stayed.'[50] 'He started a whole generation of St Mirren supporters in Paisley,' says Jim Crawford, the former lottery manager, 'and when you go to away games you can see the faces from that era that are still going. There were kids going at that time who are still going, and they have now got the family going too. It's that kind of club.'[51]

Iain Munro, who appeared for him only briefly at St Mirren, feels that Ferguson is wrong to play down his period at the club. The manager's achievements at Love Street, Munro believes, rank along-side his later success at Aberdeen and Manchester United. 'I think he does himself a great disservice not mentioning these things, because I think the job he did there equals anything he's done anywhere else. Maybe if he'd stayed as manager instead of going, St Mirren might have won the League in 1980 instead of Aberdeen.'[52]

The subsequent continuity was provided by Ferguson's physio-therapist and trainer Ricky McFarlane, who upset Ferguson by declining to go with him when he left. McFarlane became St Mirren manager in 1980 after a short reign by Ferguson's immediate suc-cessor, Jim Clunie (a favourite son who'd returned to Paisley after being Lawrie McMenemy's assistant at Southampton). Clunie had taken St Mirren to third position in 1980, and under McFarlane they finished fourth, fifth and fifth in the next three years – a remarkable run for such a poorly endowed club, and undoubtedly the best period in its history. 'If St Mirren had lost Fergie and Ricky

McFarlane,' says Iain Munro, 'it would have been a massive blow. But Ricky was right in there with Fergie, every inch of the way.'[53] 'Ricky's contribution to St Mirren was incredible,' agrees Jimmy Bone, who subsequently managed the club himself.[54]

Yet many people associated with St Mirren are shocked and upset that Ricky McFarlane is not mentioned once in Ferguson's auto-biography. The two men had worked closely together for almost four years, first at East Stirling, and then, after a short gap, for three whole seasons at St Mirren. Davie Provan, on the other hand, is credited several times. Although Provan was officially Ferguson's second in command at Love Street, and held the title 'assistant man-ager', he ran the St Mirren reserves and, unlike McFarlane, didn't work full-time. As Provan himself says, 'Because he [Ferguson] was the first team and I was the second team, I didn't see him that much. Ricky McFarlane and him were the only two who went with the first team.'[55]

McFarlane's abilities as a manager would subsequently be recog-nised by the SFA, who put him in charge of the Scotland Under-21 team. For almost 200 games he and Ferguson had sat side-by-side watching St Mirren in draughty dugouts all over Scotland. They also travelled together to watch many other fixtures which didn't involve St Mirren, sharing the journeys from their homes, which were close to each other in East Kilbride. But readers of the Ferguson memoirs would not know any of this. It's as if McFarlane has been airbrushed from history.

'The fact that Ricky McFarlane is not mentioned is a significant thing,' says Jimmy Bone. 'Very Fergie. There's no doubt: once you cross him, that's it.'[56]

When Fergie Was Fired

*'I learned a big lesson from that part of my career . . .
because I didn't believe I could get the sack.'*

ALEX FERGUSON[1]

'SAINTS SHOCKER' cried the front page of the *Paisley Daily Express.*[2] Outsiders were astonished by the news; those in the know had seen it coming for months. On the last day of May 1978 Alex Ferguson was summoned to Love Street for what he was told was an emergency board meeting. When he got to the ground, the proceedings were brief. Willie Todd told Ferguson that the five directors had met the night before and had unanimously decided to sack him. He then read out thirteen offences from a typewritten numbered list. Ferguson's reaction was to laugh, and say the only reason for sacking someone was if he was 'not good enough at his job'.[3] Later that morning St Mirren issued a forty-nine-word statement blaming Ferguson's departure on 'the serious rift which had occurred between the board and the manager and the breaches of contract on the manager's part'.[4]

In fact four of the St Mirren directors had decided to sack Ferguson two weeks earlier, in a secret meeting held in the Excelsior Hotel at Glasgow Airport, just north of Paisley. The announcement was delayed until the end of the month, however, to allow the fifth board member to return from abroad.

Most St Mirren fans were puzzled, and furious. As far as they were concerned, Alex Ferguson was the best thing that had ever happened to their club. Indeed, the reason why St Mirren sacked Ferguson remains cloudy almost a quarter of a century later. Nobody disputes that in playing terms the board was delighted with the success that Ferguson had created. The football rumour-mill offered several colourful explanations for his departure – among them that he was involved in illegal payments and tax fiddles. The more plausible reason – broadly endorsed by both sides – is that Ferguson had a serious personality clash with the St Mirren chairman, Willie Todd. A wealth of background material supporting this explanation surfaced six months later, when Ferguson took St Mirren to an industrial tribunal, claiming he had been dismissed unfairly. Earlier his lawyers had asked the club for £50,000 compensation to cover the three remaining years on his contract, which was due to expire in 1981.

It was then unprecedented for a football manager to dispute his dismissal through the formal processes of employment law. Even today such cases are rare, and industrial tribunals would have little time for any other hearings if soccer managers marched through their doors every time they were sacked. Ferguson's attitude stemmed partly from his background as a trade unionist and an active member of the SPFA – indeed, he even consulted an SPFA solicitor, who advised him the case wasn't worth fighting. The chairman of the club where by now he was working, Aberdeen, gave similar advice. 'But I felt degraded by being sacked,' Ferguson later explained, though he recognised the risks of challenging this in terms of publicity and possible embarrassment. 'After all I'd done for them, I was obsessed with getting back at them. I wanted to humiliate them the way they had me.'[5]

Cathy Ferguson may have tipped the balance in persuading her husband to go to law. 'Alex said it was up to me whether he should go to the tribunal,' she later revealed. 'He said they were going to drag everything out. But I felt he should clear his name.'[6]

The hearing took place in Glasgow on four separate days in November and December 1978. The then chairman of the Scottish industrial-tribunal system, William Courtney – a former professional cricketer – chose to preside over the case himself, as he knew it would receive considerable attention. He was joined on the three-man panel, as is customary, by a representative of management, Sir Peter Thomas, and a trade unionist, Ralph Auchincloss. The public benches were packed with reporters, and at the end of every day Ferguson gave an impromptu press conference.

St Mirren's case consisted of two very different strands. The first was to go on the offensive and argue that Alex Ferguson had engineered his dismissal in order to win compensation. St Mirren pointed out that he had found a new post, as manager of Aberdeen, within less than forty-eight hours. They claimed that Ferguson had lined up the job long before he was dismissed, and that he hoped to squeeze recompense out of St Mirren even though he intended to leave the club anyway.

Ferguson's lawyer, James Fraser, responded that the timing of the new appointment was pure coincidence. Ferguson himself insisted that he had received no approaches from Aberdeen before he was sacked. When St Mirren's solicitor, Raymond Williamson, asked him when he was first contacted by his new club, he replied, 'The night I was sacked.' Williamson persisted and asked again whether he'd been approached by Aberdeen before his dismissal. 'Definitely not,' Ferguson said. So, Williamson suggested, 'the moves which took place at that time were just a happy coincidence then?'[7] Ferguson responded that he had 'no inkling' that Aberdeen were about to offer him a job.[8] He had no contact with Aberdeen, he said, until their chairman, Dick Donald, rang him on the day he was sacked and invited him to come north for an interview.[9]

141

Williamson's questions were based on evidence the board had obtained that both Ferguson and his assistant, Ricky McFarlane, had indeed been 'tapped' by Aberdeen *before* his sacking. McFarlane had rejected the approach: according to Jimmy Bone, it was because he had a large and young family, and didn't want the upheaval.[10] His relations with Ferguson were never the same again. Ferguson seems to have regarded McFarlane's refusal to join him in Aberdeen as a snub (magnified in his eyes, perhaps, because it came during a period of personal crisis).

One St Mirren director, Tom Moran, says he perceived an abrupt change in Ferguson's attitude in the spring of 1978, and believes this was part of a plan to get himself sacked before going to Aberdeen. First he demanded that the club give him a Jaguar, because the manager of Motherwell also had a Jag. 'It just came out of the blue,' says Moran. 'He was making a lot of demands about salaries and other things, and it ended up quite acrimonious.' Things boiled over at a board meeting on 4 May 1978. Afterwards Moran invited Ferguson to lunch:

> I tried to smooth things over and ask if there was any way we
> could sort things out, and I told him there was no way the
> board would give him what he was looking for – they didn't
> have that kind of money. He just seemed disinterested, and
> it ended up costing me a lunch and I never achieved
> anything.[11]

Ferguson's consistent denials at the 1978 tribunal that he was 'tapped' were starkly contradicted twenty-one years later by himself. In his autobiography, first published in 1999, Ferguson recounts in detail two approaches made by Aberdeen well before he was dismissed. The first move came after St Mirren were promoted in the spring of 1977, when the Aberdeen manager, Ally MacLeod (Ferguson's former boss at Ayr), announced he was leaving the club to take charge of the Scotland team in the run-up to the 1978 World Cup. MacLeod himself rang Ferguson on Aberdeen's behalf to ask whether he'd like to be his successor. 'Like an idiot,' Ferguson writes, 'I replied that I wanted to build St Mirren into an Aberdeen and therefore must turn down the offer with sincere thanks.'[12]

A year later Aberdeen contacted him again. Ferguson does not date this second approach in his book, but it is obvious that it must have been weeks, if not days, *before* he was sacked. In an earlier book Ferguson revealed that this 'contact was made with me' through the late Jim Rodger, the *Daily Mirror* reporter who had also helped fix his move to Rangers. 'Jim is a man of the utmost integrity,' he added, 'and one you can trust with your life, so when he approached me I knew it was for real.'[13] This time, 'there could be only one reaction', Ferguson says, suggesting that he immediately decided to leave Paisley to go north. 'My position was complicated by the fear that St Mirren might have enough of a contractual hold on me to encourage them to sue. So I foolishly delayed announcing my decision to leave and thus gave Todd a chance to implement his plans to get rid of me.'[14]

These two Ferguson accounts cannot be reconciled. If his 1999 memoirs are accurate, then he must have lied to the 1978 tribunal about having 'no inkling' of the Aberdeen job. Indeed, his tribunal testimony would have been perjury, for, like courts of law, industrial tribunals require all witnesses to swear their evidence on oath. Had the panel members known the details which later appeared in Ferguson's book, they wouldn't have taken very seriously his demand for compensation. Twenty-four years on, however, St Mirren are hardly likely to demand a police investigation, especially since the club won the tribunal case.

Today, the industrial-tribunal report makes particularly interesting reading in the light of Sir Alex Ferguson's current exalted reputation as a football manager. It provides a rare insight both into the chaotic workings of a middle-ranking football club and also into Ferguson's complex character. The tribunal chairman, William Courtney, wrote the document with considerable style. 'The honeymoon' between Ferguson and St Mirren 'was a long one', he says, as if presiding over a divorce case:

> The parties held each other in high mutual esteem. When the deterioration in relations did come, it was rapid, and so far as the club was concerned, terminal. On [St Mirren's] evidence the first rift occurred only about the middle of March 1978. The applicant [Ferguson] himself considered the relationship to be a harmonious one until about the middle of April 1978.'[15]

The second strand of St Mirren's case was the list of allegations which Willie Todd had presented to Ferguson when he dismissed him, and later submitted to the tribunal. These were evidence, the club argued, that the manager had 'by his conduct destroyed the trust and confidence which must exist' between an employer and a senior employee. Most of the thirteen charges related to St Mirren's claim that Ferguson 'was unwilling to work under the supervision and direction of the board'. But the club weakened its case by including several minor misdemeanours alongside more serious charges. This would open St Mirren up to ridicule in the years ahead, and helped Ferguson claim the moral high ground. Among the more petty accusations, which he answered, were that, without consulting the directors:

1. Ferguson had paid the players an extra £60 bonus – £780 in all – after winning a crucial end-of-season relegation game against Ayr. The tribunal heard, however, that when the board rebuked Ferguson he accepted this admonishment 'with uncharacteristic meekness'.[16]
2. He had offered Alan McCulloch, a goalkeeper on loan from

Kilmarnock, a £500 tax-free bonus if St Mirren stayed in the Premier Division. The tribunal decided there simply wasn't enough evidence to assess this.

3. He had allowed the Love Street ground to be used for a Scottish Junior Cup semi-final free of charge, thus losing a possible fee of up to £1,000.

4. He had attended the 1978 European Cup final in London.

Another of St Mirren's accusations was that Ferguson had allowed friends and other club staff to drive his club car when they weren't covered by the insurance policy. He had been asked to complete a new insurance form to cover the extra drivers, but had failed to do so. Ferguson willingly admitted he'd been negligent on this.

If these had been the only reasons given for Ferguson's sacking, then St Mirren's case would have collapsed. But the club also presented several charges of a more serious nature.

The first of these was that Ferguson had been taking £25 cash from the club every week, nominally to cover expenses. He'd done this without the directors' knowledge, St Mirren said, and then carried on taking the money even when they found out and told him to stop. Indeed, it even got to the point where they had to block his access to the club's petty cash. The St Mirren vice-chairman, John Corson, described how he'd warned Ferguson at the board meeting on 4 May 1978 that for tax reasons he simply couldn't condone the expenses payments. 'I told him I was not going to jail for him,' Corson told the hearing. Ferguson insisted the payments should continue, the vice-chairman alleged, and then stormed out of the meeting shouting, 'Just sack me and I'll sue you.' Corson said this wasn't the only occasion when Ferguson seemed to ignore tax obligations. 'I was tearing my hair out at this. You would think there was no taxman in this country. Everything was being done behind your back.'[17]

In response, Ferguson produced a letter from 1977 which stated that, on top of reimbursement of expenses for which he could produce receipts, he was also entitled to claim up to £25 a week for unreceipted expenses, provided he produced his own note explaining what the money was for. Ferguson told the tribunal that he understood that this letter gave him licence to draw £25 a week in cash, whether he had incurred the 'expenses' or not. He also claimed that the money was used to pay the expenses of St Mirren schoolboy players, though the club said it was another employee's responsibility to draw cash for this purpose.

The tribunal concluded that the terms of the 1977 letter simply did 'not bear the interpretation he seeks to put on them'. They also asked why, if he was perfectly entitled to the £25 payment every week, did Ferguson 'ascribe the payment to fictitious expenses' for schoolboy players? At best, the tribunal concluded, Ferguson had 'adopted a method whereby he evaded payment of tax on these sums', and St Mirren 'would share the criminal consequences of any such evasion'. At worst, they declared:

> he took sums of money belonging to [St Mirren] to which he ought to have known he had no right. We do not consider that [Ferguson] deliberately set out to defraud [St Mirren] of £25 per week, but we do say that he acted with a reckless disregard of his rights if any to the money. A belief by [Ferguson] of his right to these expenses is a comment on his ability to manage. It would have been at least arguable from [St Mirren's] point-of-view, that [Ferguson's] action in regard to these alleged expenses was in itself sufficient to justify dismissal. It was in any event a matter which would well entitle [St Mirren] to consider the extent to which they could place financial trust in [Ferguson], either then or in the future.[18]

St Mirren's second serious charge was what the tribunal called the 'bookie allegation'. The editor of the *Paisley Daily Express*, James Neil, testified that he'd invited the St Mirren manager to a press lunch in Glasgow and that they drove there together in Ferguson's car. En route, Neil said, Ferguson stopped to give a couple of match tickets to a bookmaker called David McAllister. Neil said that, when they resumed the journey, Ferguson revealed that McAllister was a long-standing friend who often consulted him for advice on the outcome of games. In particular, Neil alleged, Ferguson revealed that he'd recently advised McAllister that St Mirren would probably win their crucial relegation game against Ayr (which they did). Coupled with two other results, McAllister had won £3,900 in bets. 'And [Ferguson] said with a smile,' Neil testified, 'that on Monday after the game a case of champagne from the bookmaker was delivered to Love Street.'[19]

The editor said he had been shocked by this revelation. He thought it 'strange that a bookmaker should ask [Ferguson] for advice on the result of a football match, in which the applicant was himself involved'.[20] Even though he was a journalist, Neil had done nothing about it until a few weeks later, when he learned that Ferguson was at loggerheads with the St Mirren board. On hearing about the dispute over the unauthorised bonus Ferguson had paid his players for beating Ayr, Neil told the St Mirren chairman, Willie Todd, what his manager had said about the dealings with the bookmaker. Neil then claims to have visited Paisley police station on Todd's advice to repeat what Ferguson had said, as he was worried that 'there might have been something devious involved'.[21] Neil said the chief superintendent took a statement from him, but neither the superintendent mentioned nor his deputy has any recollection of this, even though it would have been quite a memorable event. The police never contacted Ferguson, and don't appear to have taken matters further.

Alex Ferguson admitted to the tribunal that he and McAllister had been friends for twenty years, since their days together in schoolboy football, but he denied that he'd ever advised McAllister – 'or any other bookmaker'. Such advice wouldn't have been worth having, he added, since he was too involved to be objective.[22] A team could not 'be corrupted to win', and 'he found the idea repugnant that any manager would ask his team or any members of it to lose'. Ferguson agreed he'd stopped briefly to deliver some tickets to McAllister, but denied 'in its entirety' the conversation related by Neil. He also denied receiving any champagne from McAllister – 'not even one bottle'.[23]

Yet it's hard to believe that James Neil would have fabricated his story and all its detail, especially when he went to the police with his concerns. But it is equally hard to believe that if Alex Ferguson was up to no good, and colluding with a bookmaker to fix matches – as Neil clearly feared – he would have talked so openly, especially when, on his own evidence, he had never met the editor before.

What now seems clear is that Ferguson was again less than frank with the tribunal. His autobiography two decades later seemed to accept that much of what James Neil said was indeed true. In contrast to what he told the hearing about not advising McAllister, Ferguson admits he had, in fact, often discussed future matches with the bookmaker and their likely outcomes, including the Ayr fixture. 'We socialised quite a bit', he writes, 'and regularly exchanged views about what we thought were the good bets on the coupon. I always fancied St Mirren, so my comment about the Ayr match was hardly precious inside information, and to define it as a breach of contract was, I thought, absolutely ludicrous.'[24]

In the end, the tribunal dismissed the 'bookie allegation'. While they felt that James Neil had no reason to lie about the conversation in Ferguson's car, they agreed with the manager that the association Neil had described would be 'worthless' to any bookmaker. As they put it, 'Managers' punditry in greater depth than this about the prospect of their side the following day, can be read any Friday for the price of a newspaper.'[25]

Another of the board's allegations – broadly upheld by the

1. The victorious Govan High School football team. Alex Ferguson is sitting on the right of the middle row.

2. The twenty-one-year-old Ferguson in 1963 working in the toolroom at Remington Rand, where he served his apprenticeship and played a leading role in two major strikes.

18. The Fergusons, Cathy, Mark, Alex, Darren and Jason, with the European Cup-Winners' Cup and Scottish Cup in 1983. It was only the second time in the twentieth century that any Scottish team outside the Old Firm had won two major trophies.

19. With Jim Leighton after the 1984 Scottish Cup final, as Aberdeen won the cup for a third successive year. Things were less happy when Ferguson dropped Leighton for the 1990 FA Cup final replay, and their relationship never recovered.

tribunal – illustrates the skills that Alex Ferguson was already acquiring in manipulating and intimidating the media. Indeed, the tribunal concluded that 'his relationship with the press was never far from his thoughts', and that he 'was anxious that no one and in particular the press should think him for a minute, to be a directors' manager'. St Mirren claimed that when they held their board meeting on 4 May to discuss the growing problems with Ferguson he 'dangled the carrot of newsworthy events' to reporters and advised them to come to Love Street around the time of the meeting. A Paisley journalist, Stan Park, revealed that Ferguson had emerged halfway through the proceedings to announce that he had effectively got what he wanted from the board. Because of this apparent settlement, Ferguson claimed he would reject an 'unbelievable offer' from an American club. The St Mirren manager also told the two journalists waiting outside that there would in future be no interference from the board in the running of the team, or on general team policy.[26]

Park decided, however, that 'it would be politic to soften the abrasive quality of some of [Ferguson's] observations' and to get the views of the chairman, Willie Todd. Later that night, Park said, an angry Ferguson rang to ask him what he'd told Todd, claiming that the material he'd provided outside the board meeting had been off the record. As a result, Park's article was toned down, to the extent that it erroneously described the meeting as 'amicable'. The tribunal decided Ferguson had been wrong to make strong critical comments about the club to outside journalists, and said the 'episode was indicative of [Ferguson's] virtual obsession of showing his independence of the board of directors'.[27]

Perhaps the most damaging allegation against Ferguson concerned his behaviour towards his office secretary, June Sullivan. In subsequent years Ferguson has tried to play down this charge, saying, 'One of the more serious accusations was that I had sworn at a female secretary.'[28] The charge was actually much more substantial (and Ferguson swears all the time, by the way, at most people).

The problems arose when Ferguson asked June Sullivan to pay one player his travelling expenses free of tax, but she said she couldn't do so because she had to certify that tax had been paid on the money. Ferguson reacted badly and, as the tribunal reported, 'He swore at her, though not in the most spine-chilling terms.'[29]

Ferguson's account is that this outburst occurred after the tax matter had been taken to Willie Todd, who took the same view as Sullivan. He had clearly begun to suspect that Todd and June Sullivan were colluding against him. Says Ferguson, 'She said, in front of us, "Well, I think the chairman's right," and when he'd gone, I just told her: "Don't you bloody do that again."'[30]

June Sullivan's response was that she was employed by the club, not by him personally. At one point Ferguson tried to get Todd to sack Sullivan for 'not carrying out her duties properly', but the chairman refused. 'This dispute reached its ultimate absurdity', the report says, when Ferguson refused to speak to Sullivan for the remaining six weeks he was at St Mirren. He confiscated her keys, and henceforth all communications between the two of them had to be channelled through the only other person in the office, a seventeen-year-old secretarial assistant. Ferguson's explanation was that, while he had almost immediately regretted the row with her, 'he considered he was due an apology from Mrs Sullivan, and that until such time as it was forthcoming, he was not prepared to speak to her'.[31]

This incident portrayed Ferguson 'in a particularly petty, immature light', was the tribunal's verdict. Then they said of the man who would become one of the greatest managers in the history of British football, 'It shows him as one possessing neither by experience nor talent, any managerial ability at all . . . When he was the author of a particularly absurd situation, it was more than ever his duty to resolve it. His reaction was a childish one, and one likely to stultify and cripple the day-to-day office activities.' St Mirren were right, the tribunal said, 'to regard it as casting reasonable doubt on his ability to conduct an important part of his function as manager adequately in the future'.[32]

Alex Ferguson made several counter-allegations against St Mirren. First, he said matters had began to deteriorate when he learned that three of the club's star players, Bobby Reid, Tony Fitzpatrick and Frank McGarvey, had all been offered contracts with rates of pay which were better than his own salary. (This was £10,000, plus a £5,000 bonus if St Mirren retained their Premier Division status.) 'I felt that was unfair,' he told the tribunal. 'The manager surely cannot get less than the players. The players could have got around £15,000 a year, and all I wanted was to make sure that the players were not getting more than me.'[33] When Willie Todd pointed out that the Dutch superstar Johan Cruyff earned more than his manager at Barcelona, Ferguson replied that the three St Mirren men weren't in Cruyff's class. Ferguson also objected that some players had signed new contracts directly with club directors, without he himself being present. Then there was his demand for a new Jaguar car on the grounds that the Motherwell manager already had one.

The tribunal decided that Ferguson's fears were exaggerated. For the players to earn more than their manager would require 'an unprecedented success in League, Scottish Cup, League Cup, and Anglo-Scottish Cup. While the possibility of the club winning all three [*sic*] was remote, he [Ferguson] regarded it as an important point of principle that a player should never be paid more than the manager. This grievance helped to promote a dissatisfaction with his own salary.'[34] The question of differentials between Ferguson and his players would be a running grievance during his next quarter-century in football. It may stem from his background as an active member of the AEU, a union which has long been keen on maintaining hierarchical differentials in pay.

What had worsened the rift with Willie Todd and his directors, according to Ferguson, was the manager's decision to retain a young winger, Ricky Sharp. He was 'shattered' that Todd had questioned his judgement. 'That was the first indication that things were going wrong,' he told the tribunal. At a board meeting, John Corson

151

backed Todd in arguing that Sharp should be released, but then Corson confessed that he knew nothing about football. Ferguson admitted he had quickly retorted, 'If you know nothing about football you should shut up.'[35] 'This', the tribunal report observes, 'was not a remark calculated to endear him to Mr Corson, and it is certainly the type of remark which made the board of directors sit up and take notice.'[36]

Ferguson's case, advanced by his solicitor James Fraser, was that the thirteen allegations were not the true reasons for the dismissal but were 'absolute and contrived trivia'.[37] The real explanation, he suggested, 'was that Mr Todd had decided for unknown considerations' to get rid of him. It might be, Fraser added, that 'This was because the applicant had the temerity to disagree with Mr Todd on matters important or unimportant.'[38]

Todd was 'the dominant figure on the board', Fraser claimed, 'who rode roughshod over the views of the other directors'. As evidence, the solicitor cited the testimony of two St Mirren staff who said that June Sullivan had hinted in April that Todd planned to get rid of Ferguson. This idea could only have been planted in her mind by Todd himself, said Fraser. Where Ferguson 'had been at fault', his lawyer argued, 'the events complained of were trivial and did not justify dismissal'.[39]

Fraser also attacked St Mirren for having disclosed publicly, in the 'sundry debtors' section of St Mirren's annual accounts, that his client still owed the club £3,503 – a fact which was then drawn to the attention of local reporters. 'It was a way for Mr Todd to get back at Mr Ferguson,' he said, accusing the St Mirren chairman of a 'vicious and underhand approach' and 'sheer nastiness'.[40]

It's clear from evidence submitted to the tribunal, however, that the problem wasn't simply a clash between two men: the chairman and the manager. The St Mirren vice-chairman, John Corson, also described Ferguson as being 'impossible to live with'.[41]

The industrial tribunal recognised that football management was rather different to other jobs. 'Managers and clubs take part in a "Paul Jones",' the inquiry concluded, again being unable to resist a sexual analogy. 'When the music stops from time to time they pair off. Sometimes the result is a lasting love affair, but more often it is a brief but casual coupling.' The three-man panel knew of no previous case where a football manager had gone to an industrial tribunal. There were 'no comparative standards of fairness to be applied', and 'the fairness of the dismissal can only be viewed against what is known of the practices in the football world, and on a general concept of fairness'.[42]

Having said all that, the tribunal then came down heavily in favour of St Mirren. Relations between Ferguson and his directors had got so bad, they concluded, that the club had no option but to dismiss him. The acrimonious board meeting in early May had revealed that Ferguson 'had drifted away from his board of directors'.

> [St Mirren] were entitled to wonder what would come next. They were entitled to think that the deterioration in relations was likely to be irreversible. In this event it was only a short, logical step for [St Mirren] to decide they had no choice but to dismiss [Ferguson], and in the Tribunal's view this was a conclusion reasonably arrived at.

'Ironical as it may appear,' William Courtney's report concluded, 'it was the very characteristics of impatient energy and single-mindedness which so contributed to [Ferguson's] success as a team manager, which led to his dismissal.'[43]

The verdict was delivered four days before Christmas 1978. It was a 'hammer blow', Ferguson says. 'I couldn't take it in.'[44] 'I know within myself that I was right to go ahead with this action,' he said at the time. 'I would not risk everything if I had not thought so. I don't regret having gone to the tribunal but obviously I do regret having lost.'[45] 'I was shattered,' said Cathy Ferguson, 'more for Alex, for the way he'd been treated. I couldn't understand how he lost.'[46]

Yet the tribunal's verdict had been unanimous. Even the trade unionist, Ralph Auchincloss, had agreed that St Mirren were right, although as a shop steward he sympathised with Ferguson and suspected he had been 'set up'. Looking back, more than two decades later, Auchincloss says that, while Todd wasn't very credible, he had a good solicitor and strong evidence to back his case. Ferguson, in contrast, had a weaker lawyer and didn't perform well himself. 'He had a sort of a nervous disposition, and hesitated when he was talking,' he says.[47]

But, despite the robust nature of the tribunal report, the press gave Ferguson pretty benign treatment over the outcome. The *Glasgow Herald,* for example, omitted any mention of tax evasion, dishonesty, or fictitious expenses, and overlooked the strongest line of all: about Ferguson's lack of managerial ability. In spite of the relentless scrutiny of his affairs ever since then, it seems that no journalist has ever bothered to look up the report and publish extracts.

Willie Todd, now in his early eighties, clearly feels sheepish about the whole affair. It cannot be easy walking round Paisley and being identified, even mocked, as the only football chairman who ever sacked Sir Alex Ferguson. 'It's water under the bridge as far as I'm concerned,' Todd says. 'I certainly regret it, and I am quite sure Alec wishes it hadn't happened either.'[48]

Ferguson's lawyer apparently told him he'd probably win 'hands down' if he appealed to a higher court. Ferguson quickly realised, however, that the whole tribunal business had been a grave error.[49] 'How stupid I had been to bother trying to equal the score with St Mirren,' he would admit. 'I took a good look at myself and saw what an idiot I had been. If I had anything to prove to St Mirren or anyone else, the best way to do it was by bringing success to Aberdeen.'[50] The irony was that Ferguson would have received little financial compensation anyway, even if he'd won, and certainly nothing like the £50,000 he'd originally demanded, which was way above the then limit on industrial-tribunal awards. Compensation is partly linked to loss of earnings: in Ferguson's case this would have been negligible, since he'd immediately found a new job that, if anything, was better paid. Going to the tribunal was all about saving face, and coping with the sense of humiliation which had been a recurring theme of his career so far.

The tribunal hearings had received substantial coverage in the Scottish press – particularly the 'bookie allegation'. They had revealed the huge gulf between the accepted standards of behaviour in football and the much stricter norms in other walks of life. More telling, the case exposed many of the less attractive sides of Alex Ferguson's character – the bullying, the desire for total control, the obsession with money, the dishonesty, and the pettiness. Above all, it exposed the immature arrogance that made Ferguson think that his achievements at St Mirren allowed him to do almost as he pleased, and had made him unsackable. As the wounds healed, and with quiet reflection, he seemed to acknowledge that hubris. 'I was thirty-four or thirty-five and that made me vulnerable to my own success,' he confessed two decades later.[51]

In the years since then Ferguson has often linked the tribunal defeat with the death of his father. Just before the verdict, his father went into the Southern General Hospital in Glasgow and his health deteriorated rapidly. 'My father was desperately ill. He faded badly after hearing the news,' Ferguson writes in his memoirs.[52] He died two months later.

Sadly, the tribunal's verdict indicated that one of Alex Snr's most important lessons, the need for humility, had yet to be learned.

Aberdeen Fairy Tale

'He had come from the shipyards of Govan and he
wasn't going back there without a fight. And fight he
did. With anyone, any authority, anything that stood
between him and success.'

ANDY MELVIN, former Aberdeen journalist[1]

A beach is perhaps the last place you would expect to find Alex
Ferguson in the middle of a football season. But if you had
taken a stroll along Aberdeen's north shore on a midwinter morning
in the early 1980s you might well have spotted him, in tracksuit and
bobble-hat, kicking a ball about with players from the local football
club. Between the wooden groynes, a pitch would be marked out on
the sand with plastic cones. For long periods in winter in this part of
Scotland, ordinary grass surfaces can be frozen, and dangerous to the
players. The open sands were the best area available.

Aberdeen's exposed Pittodrie stadium, just a few hundred yards
from the beach, is a ground where fans carry Thermos flasks, wrap
themselves in scarves and woolly hats, and even take rugs and blan-
kets in the depths of winter. It's not just cold, but remote too –
nearer to Denmark and Norway than to London, 125 miles from
Edinburgh, and almost 150 from Glasgow.

Alex Ferguson's arrival to manage the 'Dons' in June 1978 got little attention from the Scottish media. The sports pages were dominated instead by Ally MacLeod talking up Scottish hopes for the forthcoming World Cup in Argentina – sadly dashed, of course. The other big back-page stories were the recent changes in command at the Old Firm clubs. John Greig had just replaced Jock Wallace at Rangers, but bigger news still were the latest developments at Celtic. Indeed, Alex Ferguson was the unintended beneficiary of some of the musical chairs involving the two Celtic giants who'd already played leading parts in his life story.

By the spring of 1978 the Parkhead directors had decided that Jock Stein was no longer an effective manager. Just as Scot Symon's fate at Rangers a decade earlier was largely determined by Celtic's success, so in turn Stein was now partly the victim of Rangers' revival in the mid-1970s. Rangers had just won the treble for the second time in three years, while Celtic had suffered their worst-ever season under Stein, who seemed unable to recreate the green-and-white glory days in which the club had won nine league titles in a row. Stein was too much of a legend to sack, so the directors promoted him to the board, and then gave him the job of running their pools operation. In the face of this clear insult Stein eventually left to manage Leeds United (albeit only for forty-four days). The obvious candidate for the Celtic job was Billy McNeill, who had been in charge at Aberdeen since Ally MacLeod had taken on the Scotland managership twelve months before. Alex Ferguson believes Stein was treated 'disgracefully' by the Celtic board. 'I think if I were as badly used as Jock was at the end by Celtic,' he later wrote, 'I would find it hard to be as philosophical or as generous as he was.'[2] But whatever his personal views, these developments paved the way for his own next step.

There was an element of destiny about Billy McNeill's move back to Celtic, though he was still inexperienced and felt it was too early: 'I probably knew that it wasn't right from a practical point of view,' he says. 'But I had no option. I couldn't say "No" to it with my background. I couldn't take the chance – the job might not be there when I thought it was the right time to go.'[3]

Alex Ferguson's basic starting salary as McNeill's successor at Aberdeen was £12,000 a year. But he also got a £7,500 Rover car and a £18,000 interest-free loan to buy a house (a considerable benefit in a period of high interest rates). There was also a generous bonus scheme. He was promised £6,000 if Aberdeen won the Premier Division, £4,000 for coming second, and £2,000 third, as well as bonuses for winning the main knockout competitions and success in Europe. Nonetheless, as at St Mirren, he was still aggrieved at being paid less than some of his players. The Aberdeen captain Willie Miller, for one, would earn more than Ferguson in the years ahead.

It's tempting to assume that Alex Ferguson inherited a club which was in a mess. In fact, unlike either East Stirling or St Mirren (and, later, Manchester United), Aberdeen were in pretty good shape by the summer of 1978. While the north-east side had not won the League since 1955, recent years had seen a gradual revival, sparked by a 3–1 victory over Celtic in the 1970 Scottish Cup final. The next lift came with the two-year reign of the showman Ally MacLeod, who brought Aberdeen the League Cup in 1976–77. Ferguson credits MacLeod with bringing such 'hope and optimism' to the club 'that everyone believed the team could climb Everest with their slippers on'.[4] Ferguson also acknowledges the 'sound foundations' then laid by MacLeod's successor, Billy McNeill.[5] McNeill stayed only a year, but took the club to second in the League – two points behind Rangers – and again to the Scottish Cup final. Ferguson took over a team which hadn't lost a league match since the previous December.

He also knew he was unlikely to experience the same boardroom troubles he had encountered at St Mirren. It must have been unusual – if not unique – for a football-club board to consist entirely of ex-players. All three directors – Dick Donald, Chris Anderson and Charlie Forbes – had worn Aberdeen's colours in their youth, and Ferguson later said it was 'a manager's dream to have a board like ours'.[6]

The vice-chairman, Chris Anderson, was untypical of football directors in being not a businessman, but an academic administrator, working as secretary of the local Robert Gordon Institute of Technology (now a university). He was also vice-chairman of the Scottish Sports Council. While the chairman, Dick Donald, clearly had the money and financial acumen, Anderson was widely regarded as the progressive force at Pittodrie, an ideas man whose background in higher education helped him get on with young people. Anderson had been a leading advocate of the new Premier Division consisting of just ten clubs who played each other four times a season instead of twice. Anderson was also the brains behind Aberdeen's scheme – unveiled just after Ferguson's arrival – to abolish the standing areas and turn Pittodrie into Britain's first all-seated, all-covered ground. The club also installed glass-fronted executive boxes – a novelty in Scotland. Whereas Donald felt uncomfortable with the press and microphones, Anderson was articulate and usually acted as club spokesman.

Not long before his death in 1986, Anderson explained the rationale behind Alex Ferguson's appointment. In the mid-1970s the club had decided it needed to make dramatic changes in response to the new challenges posed by the Premier Division, and also by the fact that Aberdeen was rapidly changing from a rural farming and fishing community into the wealthy 'oil capital of Europe'. Although it's sometimes said that Ferguson and Aberdeen were greatly boosted by the local oil boom, the club got very little *direct* commercial benefit from it, and the multinational oil companies were reluctant to sponsor the team. Nonetheless, the sense of prosperity in the local community must have assisted both gate revenues and the income from the new boxes and executive seats.

It sounds like rationalisation after the event, but Anderson claimed that the appointment of each Aberdeen manager had been part of a careful strategy, starting in 1975 with Ally MacLeod. 'His whole attitude was magical. He breathed new life into us and the city and everybody was dancing on air.' Billy McNeill was then chosen as 'somebody with a track record as a player', Anderson explained, 'and although we didn't win any honours with Billy it was clear that we were becoming steadily more substantial as a club'. Having lost two managers in quick succession to higher things, Anderson and his colleagues wanted someone who could change the club so much that he would 'think twice about leaving'. Aberdeen decided Ferguson best fitted the bill, though, says Anderson:

> Many people . . . thought we were daft and crazy to appoint Alex Ferguson. But we didn't need someone with a great record as a player; we needed a manager with an abundant and wide knowledge of the game – a top coach . . . That man, the one with all the warts about him at that time, was Alex Ferguson. We had watched his progress with St Mirren, observed his huge vitality and realised that although he had ended up fighting a messy industrial tribunal with the club after he was sacked, in fact, his energy and commitment had overwhelmed them.[7]

Almost immediately he arrived at Pittodrie, Anderson whisked Ferguson off on a three-week trip to the United States to study how American sports teams were organised. It was also a chance to get to know the new man. Surprisingly perhaps, he found Ferguson chastened by the experiences which led to his sacking by St Mirren. 'He came here very humble,' Anderson said later, 'because we had rescued him from a rough time he was going through.' Indeed, Ferguson might have found it hard to get a suitable managerial job anywhere else in Scotland, and might have joined a lower-division side in England, had Aberdeen not wanted him. But the American trip apparently 'energised' him, and he was 'bubbling over with ideas' by the time he came home.[8]

The fact that the Aberdeen board contained only three directors – again unusual in football – also made decision-making a lot easier, in theory at least. They rarely held formal board meetings: instead, most important matters were discussed when Dick Donald came into Pittodrie every day at twelve o'clock. Decisions would be taken in a quick huddle in the corridor, during a brisk walk round the pitch, or in the canteen at lunchtime, when Donald often sat down with Alex Ferguson for a bowl of soup.

Most people say it worked well that so few were involved in decision-making, but Gordon Strachan, a pivotal member of Ferguson's Aberdeen team, paints a different picture. 'Re-signing talks seemed to go on for ever because Alex handled them,' he says.

> But, obviously, before finalising anything, the chairman Dick Donald had to be consulted. So Alex would approach a player with an offer and the player would ask for something else. That meant Alex had to go back to the chairman to clear that point and then another little point would arise which had to be sorted out too. Naturally other things would come up between times and the re-signing talks would be shelved for a week or two and then be picked up once more. You would eventually find yourself arguing over a fiver a week.[9]

Ferguson's relationship with Dick Donald was undoubtedly the best he has enjoyed with a club chairman. Donald, then in his sixties, would often be whistling, and always wore a brown trilby. Ferguson says one could predict his mood by whether the hat was 'planted firmly on the back of his skull' (worried) or 'jauntily on one side' (contented).[10] For away games Donald would usually be picked up by the team coach from outside his home, clutching a bag of sweets as he cheerfully clambered on board. He had made his money through the family chain of twenty-one cinemas in north-east Scotland (later converted into bingo halls) and in property; Aberdeen was something of a hobby for him. While he took a great interest in the state of the pitch, he also kept a firm grip on the club's finances.

'His humility is the pervading factor at Pittodrie and the club operates from that base,' Ferguson wrote in 1985, towards the end of his time at the club.[11] Donald's 'main strength', he said, was 'that he didn't care what people thought of him'.[12] The Aberdeen chairman clearly sandpapered some of his young manager's rougher edges; Donald's son Ian says Ferguson 'was very headstrong' when he first arrived, but mellowed under the 'calming influence' of his father. 'Once or twice he came with all guns blazing, and Dad would have said, "Wait a minute, Alec, let's have a cup of tea."'[13]

In the early days Donald and his colleagues had to be clear with Ferguson about which areas were and were not his responsibility, though gradually he was allowed more autonomy. Player bonuses, for example – a contentious area at St Mirren – were eventually left to Ferguson. Donald also advised him how to be more businesslike, teaching him, for example, how to negotiate and how to draw up contracts. He clearly saw Ferguson as a long-term proposition who needed time. 'He had a wonderful way,' Ferguson told the Aberdeen team's historian. 'He would say, before a cup final perhaps, "It won't be the end of the world if we lose this one. The players are getting a bit carried away." It was his way of saying to me, "Don't worry if you lose. Your job is safe."'[14]

Modern observers may find it hard to believe, but Ferguson often lacked confidence, especially after the trauma of leaving St Mirren. Donald did much to restore his self-belief, and Ferguson was always grateful for the way the Aberdeen board supported him during his industrial tribunal, which took place six months after arriving at Pittodrie. Donald had been 'like a father to me', Ferguson once said, and of course he lost his real father within a year of moving to Aberdeen.[15] Not everyone noticed, but he claimed to have 'learned humility' from Donald (and, interestingly, 'humility' is often a word Ferguson uses when talking about Alex Snr).[16]

If Donald was generous with his support, he did little to improve Aberdonians' reputation for being tight-fisted. Whereas most football chairmen will allow their clubs to go into debt and make a loss if they think it will develop the club, Donald was keen for Aberdeen to stay profitable. It meant that when Ferguson first arrived the team travelled to away games in an old-fashioned public-transport bus, suffering the hard-backed seats and no radio. Gordon Strachan felt Ferguson was too keen to help the board stay in the black, at the expense of his players. 'It was always as if Alex saw himself as the guardian of the club's finances and it made negotiations very, very difficult.'[17]

Ferguson's routine was to come in promptly at 8.30 every day to deal with paperwork. Teddy Scott, the reserve-team manager, recalls that the manager insisted on having the newspapers at his desk every morning and 'would go through them one by one very carefully'.[18] Aberdeen staff remember his phenomenal memory. He amazed colleagues by the way he remembered phone numbers without writing them down. A couple of hours later he could still dial them from memory. His secretary, Barbara Cook, says that when checking letters Ferguson never missed a spelling mistake.

Aberdeen may have been among the half-dozen biggest clubs in Scotland, but it was nonetheless a homely place, with a family atmosphere. The defender Willie Garner says that when he was with Celtic, players left straight after training, whereas at Aberdeen 'people would stay behind for a game of table tennis or a game of snooker. We'd be at the club all day.'[19] Pensioner volunteers came in every day to look after the players' boots and kit, and to tidy up the ground. Apart from players and training staff, the club employed only about a dozen people. Nobody epitomised the family spirit better than Teddy Scott, a warm, gentle man, who has worked for fifteen different managers in almost fifty years at Pittodrie, and still works as Aberdeen's kit manager, even though he's now in his early seventies. Scott's 'den' in the heart of the main stand is stuffed with football strips and memorabilia. In Ferguson's time Scott would scour the Highlands for young players, and would think nothing of driving off with a junior team on what were called his 'mystery tours', friendly fixtures arranged at a moment's notice.[20] Having returned, the priority was to put the kit into soak, and if Scott missed the last bus home, he'd sleep overnight on the snooker table. In 1999 Ferguson returned to Pittodrie with the Manchester United first team, in the midst of the busy 'treble' season, to participate in Scott's testimonial.

The club may have prided itself on being progressive, but it lacked basic facilities. There was no training ground, for one thing. Instead, the players might be found running up and down the sand dunes in the few hundred yards between the Pittodrie stadium and the North Sea. In winter they used the beach itself – having checked the tide tables – though the cones denoting the pitch had constantly to be moved in or out with the sea. Occasionally injured players took quick dips in the freezing-cold sea, having been persuaded that salt water has excellent healing qualities. On other occasions they practised at the university or on the club's all-weather surface opposite the entrance to the ground, or at the Gordon Highlanders' barracks just north of Aberdeen. The most frequent location was beneath the tall trees of Seaton Park beside St Machar's cathedral, which must be one of the most delightful training areas in British professional football. But, as Seaton is a public park, there was nothing to stop the media or the public watching – or, when Aberdeen had a home European fixture, spies from the visiting team.

By his own account Alex Ferguson had a 'troubled time' with the Dons at first. He was burdened by too many outside worries. The 'emotional battering' of the industrial tribunal and then the illness and death of his father overshadowed his first year.[21] There were also the pubs, which Ferguson decided were a commitment too many: he'd sold Fergie's just before leaving St Mirren, but he wasn't able to get rid of Shaw's until 1980 (by which time it was losing money and he'd fallen out with his partner, Sam Falconer). Nor was it an easy time for his wife and their three young boys. Cathy Ferguson had been worried about the idea of moving to Aberdeen, away from her family and friends in the Glasgow area, though the boys were quite excited by the prospect. The family remained in East Kilbride for several months while Alex shared a flat in the centre of Aberdeen with his assistant, Pat Stanton, and returned home on Saturday evening after matches. When his family eventually joined him, towards the end of 1978, Cathy disliked their new flat as it over-looked an undertaker's and she found it depressing to watch the hearses coming and going all day. Early in 1979 the family moved into a large bungalow on a new estate in Cults, a village just west of Aberdeen, where the boys had plenty of open space.

Pat Stanton wasn't Ferguson's first choice as assistant manager, which explains why he didn't join Aberdeen until after the start of the 1978–79 season. After failing to persuade Ricky McFarlane to come with him from St Mirren, Ferguson says he opted for Walter Smith, who was then a Dundee United player (and later manager of Rangers and Everton). But Smith was still only thirty, and his man-ager, Jim McLean, refused to release him.

So Stanton, once a star with Hibs and Celtic, was third choice at best. After Aberdeen games, he and Ferguson would go for a drink and mull over what had gone right or wrong. 'He could talk football all night,' says Stanton. 'He could be great fun with his little quirks. He was also one for coming out with the strangest of things. A couple of Fergieisms were: "Have you ever seen a Pakistani funeral?" or "Have you ever seen an Italian with a cold?" He would just come out with them and that would be it. You would be left to ponder what he meant.'[22]

Ferguson's many assistants over the years fall into two categories: those who reflect his own character, and those who act as 'good cop' to Fergie's 'bad cop'. Stanton was the latter. 'They complemented each other magnificently,' says the then Aberdeen player Alex McLeish. 'Pat was the calm, thoughtful character who frequently came along to mend relationships with a quiet word of explanation to the player whose feelings had been ruffled in a brush with the manager.'[23] Says the star striker Joe Harper, 'When Fergie would come in growling, "You're not working hard enough", Pat would simply say, "Just keep on doing what you're doing. The chances will come." And inevitably the chances would come.'[24]

If the Ferguson family expected to see more of Alex once they moved to Aberdeen, they were to be disappointed. East Stirling and St Mirren had been located within Scotland's central belt, well within an hour's drive of most other league grounds. Aberdeen, in contrast, was the most isolated of Scotland's senior clubs, and most away matches involved substantial excursions. Glasgow, for example, was three hours by road. 'My assistant and myself would drive six hours to watch 1½ hours football and then be up for training in the morning. There wasn't time for anything else,' Ferguson remembers.[25] Ferguson is a notoriously fast driver, to the extent that he terrifies many of his passengers: Pat Stanton called trips with his boss 'white knuckle jobs'.[26] It was surprising that Ferguson never had a serious accident. 'Sometimes he wore glasses when driving and sometimes he didn't,' says the youth coach Len Taylor. 'I was a quivering wreck as I sat beside him.'[27]

Ferguson had inherited some excellent players from Billy McNeill, including many who would find fame and glory under his own stewardship. The squad he took over included Stuart Kennedy, Willie Miller and Joe Harper, who had all played for Scotland, along with Alex McLeish, Gordon Strachan, John McMaster, Drew Jarvie, Doug Rougvie, Steve Archibald and Ian Scanlon. It also included the long-standing former Scotland goalkeeper Bobby Clark, and also the young Jim Leighton, who made his debut in senior football in Ferguson's first league match, a 4–1 win at Hearts. 'He could have a great future in the game,' his manager predicted.[28]

Some in Aberdeen were initially suspicious of Ferguson. Aberdonians are generally reserved, undemonstrative people, and their new manager came with a passionate, troublemaking reputation. Many at the club still remembered the 1973 Scottish Cup tie, when Ferguson was sent off for kicking Willie Young. His first season would prove to be one of the most difficult periods of his career. 'It was a shattering experience,' he later confessed. 'For the first time in my life I couldn't wait for the season to end. The players resented the way I wanted to change certain ideas. They were suspicious of my intentions.'[29] But Ferguson also admitted that he himself was partly to blame. 'I can honestly say that my contribution that season was less than it should have been. I did not make the right decisions, nor did I make them early enough.'[30]

'He came fairly quietly among us at first,' says Gordon Strachan, who points out that Ferguson – still only thirty-six – wasn't much older than some of his players. 'It seemed at times as if some of our older lads were trying to run the training sessions, dictating how free kicks should be taken and so on. He listened and took it all in. Maybe he listened too much at first. But there came a time when he seemed to say to himself, "Enough is enough."'[31] 'There were players who had played against him,' says Pat Stanton, 'and there was maybe a bit of resentment with Alec being seen as a firebrand and he was in the players' union and all that.'[32]

'His first year was pretty traumatic,' says the former Aberdeen club secretary Ian Taggart. 'A lot of pros didn't take kindly to the way he worked, and didn't take kindly to the way he talked.'[33] A major row occurred after a 3–0 defeat in a European match in Düsseldorf. Ferguson reluctantly agreed to let the players go out and enjoy the German nightlife, only to regret his decision when they lost again the following Saturday, 2–1 at home to Hearts. Never again, he insisted in the dressing room, picking on one of the younger players, Alex McLeish. 'Why don't you get on to the older ones?' the captain, Willie Miller, butted in – sparking a heated exchange.[34] Rumours reached the local press of 'mass transfer requests and even physical confrontation between Alex Ferguson and a player'.[35]

Early on, manager and captain had had what Ferguson calls an 'eyeball-to-eyeball' in which neither would budge. The manager felt that Miller and his fellow defenders were staying back in the penalty area too much. 'It was almost like OK Corral with guns blazing, but it was the best thing that happened,' he later recalled.[36] The captain apologised afterwards, and the relationship prospered. 'I may have had ambition,' Miller says, 'but I needed to be convinced to go that final mile.'[37] Three years later he rejected a lucrative offer from Sunderland, having decided, he says, that Aberdeen had huge potential with Ferguson at the helm.[38] In time, Ferguson would describe Miller as 'the best player to emerge in Scotland in the fifteen years from the early 1970s to the late 1980s'.[39]

Weekend commuting from Glasgow didn't help his relationships with the players in the early months. After away matches, Ferguson would go home to East Kilbride, leaving his senior players to grumble to each other at the back of the coach on the long journeys back to Aberdeen. The ringleaders were the midfielder Dom Sullivan and the strikers Ian Fleming and Joe Harper. 'To be perfectly honest with you,' says Harper, 'I wasn't going to put up with this rubbish from him, thinking because he was a manager he could do this and do that.'[40]

Harper says Ferguson's temper 'could get so totally out of control', and he recalls how the manager 'stormed into the dressing room at half-time like a madman' when Aberdeen were drawing 0–0 in one game in his first season. 'He smashed his fist into the table. Cups went flying and he kicked a boot straight at Doug Rougvie, who just managed to get out of the way in time. He would scream, shout and throw things around if anybody stood up to him or if things weren't totally going his way.'[41]

After a spate of bookings and what he regarded as silly sendings-off, Ferguson warned he would henceforth impose heavy fines for such offences. 'I'm not talking about fines of £10 or £20,' said the man who had been dismissed seven times in his own playing career, and was still banned from talking to referees. 'They will be fined heavily, and I mean heavily . . . Bookings for talking back to the referee, not standing ten yards away at free kicks and for kicking the ball away will just not be tolerated. And they will be punished severely by the club . . . I want to see our "crime rate" become the lowest in Scotland.'[42]

Ferguson was speaking after a particularly ill-tempered game at St Mirren – only his second visit to his old club since they'd sacked him. He had been unhappy with the referee's decision to go ahead with the game, given the poor state of the pitch. At half-time, when Aberdeen were 2–0 up, he went into the referee's dressing room to query some of his decisions, whereupon the official warned Ferguson that he would report him to the SFA. In the second half the referee sent off both Willie Miller and Ian Scanlon and, Ferguson claims, 'awarded St Mirren enough peculiar decisions to let them salvage a 2–2 draw'.[43]

The SFA's official minutes merely say the Aberdeen manager 'passed remarks to [the referee] in an aggressive manner' at half-time, though apparently the referee also wrote of Ferguson 'lunging' at him, which Ferguson vehemently denied.[44] This was all in breach of the SFA ban, imposed while he was at St Mirren, on his talking to officials. There's also confusion as to whether Ferguson approached the referee again once the game was over. In a book written in 1985, Ferguson denied that he 'at any time attempted to speak to the referee or even go near him after the game'.[45] Yet in his autobiography, published in 1999, Ferguson says that 'At time-up I went wild at the referee, who announced that he was reporting me to the SFA.'[46]

It was only a few minutes later that Ferguson was told that his father had passed away. He'd died at the very moment when all the trouble was erupting on the pitch. The St Mirren electrician Fred Douglas recalls how after the game he tried to attract Ferguson's attention to tell him the bad news, but his former boss insisted on hammering away on the referee's door. 'He was blazing,' says Douglas. 'He said, "I want to see this cunt."'[47]

The SFA were not sympathetic, especially since there were several weeks to go before the expiry of Ferguson's undertaking not to contact match officials during or after matches. The SFA were also annoyed about an earlier game against Hearts, when Ferguson had refused to carry out a linesman's request. He was now banned from appearing on the touchline or in the dugout until the end of 1979. He was also fined £100 for the two offences, though even then he failed to pay on time.

Willie Miller says Ferguson's first eighteen months were 'turbulent'. Miller had been appointed Aberdeen captain by Ally MacLeod at the age of twenty, and he kept the job under both McNeill and Ferguson. The new manager's problem was that, while McNeill had been a physically imposing character with a formidable playing record, Ferguson had to earn the team's respect. He adopted an irritating habit of comparing the Aberdeen squad with the players he'd left behind at St Mirren. 'Every time we had a practice game,' says Willie Miller, who went on to win sixty-five caps for Scotland, 'the manager would at some point remark: "Jackie Copland would have cleared that ball" or "Jackie would have done it this way." Much as I respected Jackie as an excellent player, frankly, I thought that my method of doing things was just as effective and I did not appreciate the constant comparison.'[48]

Joe Harper, in turn, would be compared unfavourably with Frank McGarvey, and Gordon Strachan with Tony Fitzpatrick. But, as Harper says of the St Mirren men, 'Those three guys were never in the same class as me, Strachan and Miller.'[49] Ferguson would later admit it had been unwise to make the comparisons.

Inside the club the dissidents were known as the Westhill Mafia, after the village outside Aberdeen where they all lived. 'They were gunning for him,' says Ian Taggart. 'They wanted him out – that's how serious it was.'[50]

Joe Harper, in particular, posed a huge challenge for the manager. In retrospect, he is an early example of Ferguson's ruthless attitude to players who, despite their talents, don't fit in with his ethos. Harper was a colourful, mischievous character who was hugely popular with the fans. They called him 'King Joey', and accorded him godlike status after he had been involved in all three goals in the club's celebrated 1970 Scottish Cup-final triumph. (Even today he's sufficiently revered to write a weekly column for the local paper.) Harper was also a great goalscorer – the most prolific in Aberdeen's history, with 199 goals in just 308 games. That he scored 32 in Fergie's first season was not exceptional, but typical. Harper was easily the top scorer in Scotland, and was understandably furious when Ferguson dropped him for several of Aberdeen's final matches. He responded by scoring five goals in a reserve game. Yet Harper was never a great team player. When he played for Hibs in the early 1970s it's widely thought he was disruptive and caused the break-up of a promising side.

However, the incident which especially provoked Harper was not about team selection. Ferguson had switched from Aberdeen's traditional 4–4–2 to a 4–5–1 formation. With noticeable parallels with what he did at Manchester United in the autumn of 2001, Ferguson had Joe Harper working as the lone forward, with his usual striking partner, Steve Archibald, pulled back into midfield. It didn't work. Harper says that the following Monday Ferguson asked the team to explain what had gone wrong. Nobody wanted to say anything, so the manager asked Harper directly. The striker criticised the new formation, only to find himself summoned to Ferguson's office.

> He started pointing his finger in my face and said, 'Don't you ever fucking bring my tactics down in front of anybody. Who the fuck do you think you are?' And at that point I grabbed his finger and I said, 'None of that. First of all,' I said, 'if you don't want me to give an opinion – and I don't get paid to

give opinions at this club, I get paid to do a job – then do not ask me to give one.' From that moment on there was a problem.[51]

Harper's verdict on Ferguson is that he was a 'bully who intimidates people'.[52] They had never got on, he admits, since being rivals for the striking roles on the SFA's 1967 summer world tour, when Harper upstaged Ferguson by scoring eight times in the only two games he started. 'I ended up getting all the headlines back home,' says Harper, 'and I don't think Fergie appreciated that.'[53]

'I thought he was a marvellous player,' Ferguson said later, 'a magnificent finisher and had an excellent football brain'. But he also felt Harper 'was a bit of a luxury at times', suspected 'he was an artful dodger', and thought he 'wasn't a hard trainer'.[54] Ferguson was not impressed to find himself lapping Harper on a pre-season run. He felt the star goalscorer didn't seem to accept that the forwards had to play their part in defence if the whole Aberdeen team was to develop a more attacking style. Ferguson also reckoned that not enough of Harper's goals were scored away from home (just about true, statistically). There were also problems with Harper drink-driving.

Steve Archibald was a headache too – though, unlike Harper, he was always forgiven. Trouble arose after Archibald scored a hat-trick for Aberdeen against Celtic, and claimed the ball as a memento (which was then much less common than nowadays). Ferguson insisted he should return it. Aberdeen didn't want any 'big-headed superstars', he said: football was 'a team game'. The next morning the office door flew open and Archibald punted the ball inside, shouting, 'Here's your bloody stupid ball, man!' as it rebounded around the walls.[55] 'We picked fights with each other just for the sake of it,' Archibald once claimed, 'but I enjoyed our battles because they helped keep me sharp and aggressive.'[56] Although they were often in conflict, Ferguson seemed to have a soft spot for the forward, and gave him more leeway than other players. He admits he saw Archibald as a kindred spirit, the same kind of stubborn striker he had once been.

Ferguson says he hadn't yet realised that it was 'usually unnecessary to seek direct confrontation' with players, and that he was 'too impetuous' in trying to discipline them.[57] 'He could be a frightening character,' says Gordon Strachan. 'It was almost a test of character when he had a go at you. He wanted to know if you had enough bottle to stand up to him – and that would prove that you had the same bottle to help you succeed on the park.'[58]

Aberdeen finished fourth in Ferguson's first season, reached the semi-finals of the Scottish Cup, and lost 2–1 to Rangers in a bad-tempered Scottish League Cup final. In the latter, goalkeeper Bobby Clark was awaiting treatment for injury when Rangers scored their first goal, and then defender Doug Rougvie was sent off after clashing with Derek Johnstone – the first time since the war that a player had been dismissed in a Hampden final, though the players felt that Johnstone had feigned injury and Rougvie was innocent. Ferguson's opening campaign had been disappointing, given the high expectations generated by Billy McNeill's brief stewardship.

The 1979–80 season also started unsatisfactorily, with five league defeats by November. Consolation came in the League Cup, where Aberdeen eliminated both Rangers and Celtic before facing Dundee United in a December final. A goalless draw at Hampden led to a Wednesday-night replay at Dens Park, the home of Dundee United's neighbours, Dundee. Aberdeen had dominated the first game, and Ferguson knew that the Dundee United manager, his friend and rival Jim McLean, would reshuffle the United side for the replay. Ferguson's initial impulse was to counter McLean's expected changes by rejigging his own eleven. He was distracted, however, because an Aberdeen youth player had a serious medical problem that week which required an immediate operation. Mindful too, no doubt, of his own disappointment when left out of the Dunfermline side at the last minute in 1965, Ferguson announced early on that the line-up would remain the same. 'I decided to go the easy way, telling them they should have done it in the first game and that the team was good enough to do it in the second.'[59]

Aberdeen crumbled 3–0. 'We were simply torn apart,' says Willie Miller.[60] While it didn't help that Ferguson had been confined to the stand because of his touchline ban, he later confessed that his failure to make changes against Dundee United 'was a really bad mistake. It cost us the Cup.'[61] He realised he should have followed his convictions and not been frightened to upset players by reshaping the team. 'That experience,' he said later, 'probably more than a lot of happier occasions, helped to forge my character in management terms.'[62] Ferguson would clearly remember the lessons on the only other occasion he faced a cup-final replay.

Harold Wilson, who often compared himself with a football manager, once observed that conducting Cabinet reshuffles and telling ministers they were sacked was the worst aspect of being Prime Minister. 'To tell a player that he's dropped is still the most difficult part of my job,' Alex Ferguson has said. 'From the players' room to my office is just a few yards, but when I call someone in the walk seems to take an eternity . . . You're giving a player reasons why he's not included, but he doesn't want to know. He's not listening to what you're saying.'[63]

It was Aberdeen's third final defeat in three years, and one of the truly black moments of Alex Ferguson's career. 'I couldn't sleep a wink. In the morning I just felt like packing everything in because the season had promised so much.' Instead he went into the ground early and greeted each player as they arrived, commending them for their efforts. 'I stressed it was a time to go on, it was a time to look forward.'[64] It was a clever psychological ploy, since most of the side would have been expecting a typical Fergie bombardment.

Aberdeen's form improved considerably in the New Year. After Joe Harper was injured, Steve Archibald teamed up with either Drew Jarvie or Mark McGhee, whom Ferguson had signed in the previous season from Newcastle United for £80,000. The other main acquisition was Doug Bell, from St Mirren on a free transfer. Yet by early March Aberdeen were nine points behind Celtic (when it was still only two points for a win). The Glasgow side seemed to be sauntering to the title, but a run of winter postponements meant Aberdeen had five games in hand with which to close the gap. Gradually Ferguson's team crept up on Billy McNeill's men with a run of fifteen games undefeated, including two victories over Celtic at Parkhead – 2–1 and 3–1 – before the Glasgow side suffered an astonishing 5–1 defeat by Dundee, who were later relegated. The championship hung on the last Saturday of the season.

Ferguson's side scored five without reply at Hibernian, but had to wait until after the final whistle for confirmation that they were champions. A signal from the press box indicated that Celtic had been held to a 0–0 draw with Ferguson's former club St Mirren, who finished third.

The Old Firm had been denied the Scottish League title for the first time in fifteen years. Gordon Strachan was the Scottish Player of the Year, and was also picked for the national side for the first time. After winning Aberdeen's first championship in a quarter of a century, Ferguson felt his position with the club and the players was now firmly cemented. 'That was the achievement which united us,' he said later. 'I finally had the players believing in me.'[65]

He jigged across the Edinburgh pitch, dressed in his usual camel-hair coat. As the fans chanted his name – 'Fer-gie, Fer-gie, Fer-gie' – he went into the announcer's box to thank them for their support. He loved them all, he told them. Then, rather rashly, he added that they were welcome to come round to his home that evening to continue the celebrations there. 'So, halfway through the night,' he relates, 'the bell goes at the house and here are two supporters: "Can we come in for a drink?" I said, "Certainly you can, in you come."' Cathy, fortunately, had gone to bed, but Ferguson and his brother were still drinking and replayed the video of the game to their two visitors. 'I don't know to this day who they were. They introduced themselves certainly, but that just completed the night.'[66] It was a small glimpse of the personable side of the Aberdeen manager – the charming and gregarious Fergie that had been seen in his pubs, but less frequently at his football clubs.

Another such glimpse came a few days later as the Aberdeen squad prepared to board an open-top bus for a triumphal tour of the city. The goalkeeper Jim Leighton was reluctant to join the party, as he'd played only once all season, and then in a home defeat. Ferguson insisted Leighton should come on board, whatever his contribution, and it had an important psychological effect on the young keeper. 'When I looked out over streets filled with our celebrating fans,' Leighton says, 'I promised myself I would be back for more.'[67]

After twenty-two years in top-class football without a major trophy to his name, Ferguson too now wanted more. During the remaining years of his career, winning honours would become an increasingly addictive drug. 'It gave us the smell of success,' he wrote of the 1980 title. 'It whetted our appetite. The more success you achieve, the hungrier you get.'[68]

Furious Fergie

'He could be murder to work with. He wouldn't settle for anything less than perfection. But you got caught up with his own ambitions. I wouldn't have had such a good career without him.'

WILLIE MILLER, Aberdeen captain[1]

A lex Ferguson suggests, very bluntly, that one of the turning points of his first championship season was when Joe Harper was injured in November 1979. Indeed, he goes further: 'Personally, I don't think we would have won the League Championship with Joe in the side.'[2] The two men had been involved in numerous bust-ups, and Harper loves relating the stories. One involved a party given by a mutual friend in Aberdeen, the day after they had beaten Rangers. Harper helped himself to a plate of the traditional Scottish dish of haggis and neeps (turnips).

Fergie bursts in and his words were 'What the fuck are you doing, Harper?' And I said, 'I don't get your point, boss. What do you mean?' And he grabbed the plate of haggis and neeps off me and threw it in the sink – which was very ignorant of him, because he was in someone else's house anyway. He says, 'You've got a weight problem, you're not fucking allowed to eat that.' So me, being a shy, unassuming person,

went over and got a plate and put double the amount on it
and started to eat it, and my wife was staring at me and
saying, 'Joe, don't', and I could see her praying.[3]

Harper's punishment was to train with the reserves. Although he
recovered from the injury sustained during the championship
season, the striker would play only once more for Aberdeen.

There's considerable evidence, however, that many of Alex
Ferguson's famous outbursts were not spontaneous, but premeditated. Ferguson's youth coach, Len Taylor, relates how on one
occasion he overheard the manager agreeing his tirade in advance
with a seasoned Scottish international:

He said to him, 'I'm gonna give you the biggest row you ever
had in your life, and you're gonna say nothing. You're gonna
sit there and just take it.' The young ones thought that if he
could do that to international players, 'What's he gonna do to
us?' He would show the young kids this is the standard, even
if they are international level. 'Never, never allow anyone to
fall beneath that,' he would say.[4]

Gordon Strachan says Ferguson 'put the fear of death in players',
and used it 'as a motivation'. But if you weren't the victim, he adds,
'He might give you a crafty wink as he left the dressing room.'[5] The
trouble was that it wasn't always easy to work out when Ferguson
was angry, when he was putting it on for effect, or when he was
simply joking. 'He could switch from high good humour to apparent
fury and back again in the space of a few minutes,' says Alex
McLeish. 'I use the word "apparent" because there was often a suspicion that the anger wasn't real, although it was convincing
enough.'[6] 'He'd motivate every player in a different way,' Willie Miller
once said. 'Some he'd leave alone, some he'd make play by making
them dislike him.'[7]

Privately, some players would mutter about leaving as soon as they could. They couldn't help noticing the nervous cough their manager seemed to develop just before big matches. 'Ten or fifteen minutes before we went out,' says John Hewitt, 'the boys could always hear him out in the toilets at the back coughing heavily, as if he were going to be sick. The tension was building up prior to a game. He was never sick, but it sounded as though he would be sick.'[8] 'It was like that clock that got stuck in the crocodile's throat,' says Willie Garner. 'You thought, "Here he's coming", and you'd scarper.'[9] Then there was Ferguson's slight speech impediment: instead of 'bloody' he'd say 'bwoody'. Before long, around Pittodrie he had acquired the nickname of 'Furious'. 'I used to get calls saying, "Is Furious there?"' says the Aberdeen club secretary Ian Taggart. It all started, he says, when a player emerged one day to warn people that the manager was 'furious'. 'So they dubbed him "Furious Fergie", then dropped the "Fergie" bit.'[10]

One of the most cherished examples of Furious Fergie occurred when the squad were driving back from training. Alex McLeish and a couple of colleagues had got a lift from Ferguson, and pointed out that he'd just been overtaken by John Hewitt, who was driving a smart new car. When they got back to Pittodrie, Ferguson tracked Hewitt down to the treatment room and exploded. Both McLeish and the striker Eric Black see it as an example of how Ferguson could turn his anger on and off. 'If the manager hadn't winked at me before going in to the treatment room, I would have been utterly convinced that his anger was real,' says McLeish.[11] 'I'm sure he hadn't noticed until we started winding him up about it. He was just humming away to his Frank Sinatra tapes.'[12] Joke or not, McLeish remembers that Hewitt had to pay a hefty fine merely for overtaking his manager on a public road.

Some examples of Ferguson's famous 'teacups' incidents were probably not so premeditated. The most celebrated occurred in 1981, when Aberdeen were losing 2–0 at half-time during a UEFA

Cup tie in Romania against a side called Argeş Piteşti. Ferguson had again tried to play a 4–5–1 formation instead of the customary 4–4–2, with Mark McGhee as the single striker and Gordon Strachan playing wide on the right. Strachan had his own ideas about what he and the team should be doing, and Ferguson lambasted him from the dugout for much of the first half.

'Away and shut your face!' Strachan says he shouted back to his manager on the touchline, though one suspects the actual words were stronger.

> That did it. I heard no more of him 'til half-time but I knew
> that was a bad sign . . . As soon as we reached the dressing
> room I could see him making a beeline for me. There was
> trouble in store. What happened next could have looked like
> comedy to a bystander but laughter was totally out of order
> in my position. As he swung one hand away to the left, he
> swept a row of teacups in the direction of Willie Miller and
> Alex McLeish.[13]

Ferguson himself recalls how he then whacked an old-fashioned tea urn standing in the middle of the room. 'I just booted the whole thing up in the air, and of course the tea and everything was all over the place, cups everywhere. And wee Strachan – the tea's dripping down the wall behind him – sat there and didn't say a word.'[14]

'It was a spur of the moment thing,' Ferguson later explained, 'and fortunately none of the cups hit him [Strachan] – I still don't know how I missed him!'[15] Perhaps it worked. The match ended 2–2. 'I've done things I'm not proud of,' Ferguson says of the event, 'but the temper is exaggerated. It's good to let the pressure out of your system. I don't believe in this English thing of not complaining.'[16]

Such explosions were not reserved just for big occasions. Mark McGhee remembers a similar one during a reserve match at Forfar Athletic:

In his anger he kicked the laundry basket and these pants flew through the air and landed on another guy's head like a hat. He didn't move. Just sat there rigid. Fergie didn't even notice until he had finished raging. Then he looked up at the boy and said, 'And you can take those fucking pants off your head. What the hell do you think you're playing at?'[17]

McGhee has subsequently become a reasonably successful manager himself, at Reading, Leicester, Wolves and now Millwall. He argues that these outbursts could be effective with young members of the squad, who 'were easily influenced by that sort of thing', but they didn't work with older players.[18] Gordon Strachan says that Ferguson hated it if people didn't respond. 'Go sulking in a corner, and take the huff in training for three weeks, he hates that. He would rather have a stand-up fight with somebody and have done with it.'[19]

Alex McLeish recalls with great amusement the colourful phrases Ferguson would use to drive his points home. 'I've seen more life in a dead slug,' he might tell a player. When another tried to explain that he'd been tackled because he didn't think 'there was anyone near me', Ferguson might respond testily, 'Where did you think you were – the bloody Sahara desert?'[20] His tirades were liberally punctuated with the strongest possible swear words.

The Scotland full-back Stewart McKimmie says players would try not to catch the manager's eye as they entered the dressing room at half-time. 'If you did, then he'd remember one little instance of something during the game.' But the day after he would behave as if nothing had happened. 'The next morning he'd be your pal. He'd forget about it – he'd expect you to be on speaking terms with him.' What upset many players, McKimmie says, was that Ferguson was often very personal in his criticisms, bringing up matters in the heat of the moment that had nothing to do with football, but were related to the players' private lives. 'Aberdeen is a village, and he knew everything that everybody was doing. He had a habit of biding his time and waiting for the right moment to throw something in.' McKimmie says, for example, that Ferguson criticised him for driving his wife to work every morning, feeling he should spend more time getting valuable sleep instead. He also taunted Frank McDougall, a maverick striker who had all sorts of personal problems, about the time he 'wasted' travelling to the west coast to see his children and ex-wife.[21]

If Aberdeen had played badly in an away fixture, Ferguson could spend the coach trip home in stony silence. 'You'd be frightened to put on a video,' says the midfield player Neale Cooper.

> We used to watch all the best films on the trip down – just in case! Players were not allowed out after a certain day in the week and you wouldn't dare take liberties. He'd always find you out because he had spies everywhere. And if you lost on a Saturday you'd almost feel guilty about going out that night – that's the effect he had on you.[22]

Gordon Strachan even claims to have spotted Ferguson in his car outside his house one night, checking that he was at home and not out on the town. 'What a sad man – on a Friday night, sneaking about in his car to see if I was in.'[23] Ideally, Ferguson liked his players to be married. 'It was a plus mark,' says Stewart McKimmie, 'so the days of clubbing would be over.'[24]

Pubs and clubs were out, but it was fine to spend the evening making love. 'Eat your greens and enjoy sex,' Ferguson famously told his players at one point, and even a drink after the game was acceptable. 'I don't expect them to be goody-goody monks,' he said. 'A pint after a match or a little loving beforehand doesn't do any harm.'[25]

If they didn't meet his standards in training, however, players would be threatened with a trip to the Govan shipyards, or he'd talk of sending them to work in a friend's fish factory down on Aberdeen docks. Ferguson liked to compare their well-paid jobs with his own harsh background. For pre-season fitness sessions he took the players off for a week to Gordonstoun, the public school on the Moray Firth which is notorious for its spartan conditions and has educated several members of the royal family. It had been Ally MacLeod's idea originally to take just a few players, but Ferguson expanded the trips to include the whole playing squad. Gordon Strachan dubbed the experience 'Colditz', but the week would involve an element of relaxation as well as hard training. The players would swim and play tennis; Highland League sides might be invited along for practice matches; and in the light summer evenings a Ferguson cricket XI would take on a team managed by his assistant. The Gordonstoun PT instructor George Welsh says Ferguson 'always chuckled' when he told him he'd arranged for him to stay in Prince Charles's or Prince Andrew's former house. 'He loved knowing he was staying in a house once used by a royal.'[26]

Ricky McFarlane, his former colleague at St Mirren, credits Ferguson with not panicking when things went badly at first, nor succumbing to the temptation to buy new players. 'That was quite a brave thing because he had a tough first year,' he says. 'It would have been easy to have gone out and bought. Instead he kept his nerve.'[27] There wouldn't have been that much money for transfers, anyway. Company accounts show that Aberdeen was profitable for most of Ferguson's years there, but Dick Donald's concern to remain in the black, and his hawkeyed attitude to spending, limited Ferguson's ability to compete with the Old Firm on wages or transfers. Indeed, Aberdeen tended to sell a top player every couple of years to balance the books. But then Ferguson has never found money easy to obtain at any club he has managed – not even Manchester United.

So it was back to relying on young recruits. The first thing was to ensure that Aberdeen got the pick of the local schoolboys. It sounds obvious, but it hadn't always happened. Pittodrie was still rather ashamed that the Dons had let Ferguson's old idol Denis Law get away in the 1950s. The wiry, bespectacled teenager had been lured to Huddersfield Town and the first anybody at Aberdeen Football Club knew about him, it's said, was when Law was picked for Scotland at the age of eighteen.

Aberdeen's youth-development programme had improved in the 1960s and '70s, thanks largely to the chief scout, Bobby Calder, but too many good boys were still slipping away. 'If we were to lose a Denis Law again,' Ferguson warned, 'the man responsible would be sacked.'[28] He now took an even greater interest in youth development than he had at East Stirling or St Mirren. 'Pace', 'attitude' and 'skill' were the watchwords of what scouts should look for – but especially 'pace'.

Ferguson approved each recruit himself. 'If anyone was going to be signed,' says Pat Stanton, 'he was going to see them, so that we weren't wasting the laddie's time or our time. We were trying to set a standard at Aberdeen, and keep a player for a time, not just one season.'[29] Len Taylor remembers that Ferguson felt it wasn't enough to watch a young player perform in the sunshine or when his team were on top. 'He would say, "I want to come back when it's raining, when it's teeming down, and see if he's got the character then. I want to see how he plays when they're being beaten, when they're not playing well."' [30]

And Ferguson insisted that the recruitment criteria were about more than ability or potential. Recruits had to be well-behaved too: 'He would never, ever take the boy when they didn't have the discipline,' says Taylor. 'So if there was so much as a bad report from school he would reject them because he knew one bad apple could make the difference.'[31]

Ferguson was always keen to the meet the boy's parents, even if it involved a long trek across the country. In part this was to reassure them that their son would be well looked after, but it was also, Taylor says, to assess the family background. 'He said, "What does the father do for a job? Is he of reasonable character?" You also knew by the demeanour of a boy, by the way he walked about, if he'd got the necessary character.'[32] Ferguson wanted to see for himself the size of the parents, to predict how the player might develop physically. The mother, he found, was a better pointer to future growth than the father.

Players from the east coast, Ferguson felt, often lacked the necessary 'nastiness' one found in the Glasgow area. So Aberdeen set up a subsidiary coaching school on Clydeside – the first time any Scottish club had set up such a course outside its own area. Cheekily, Aberdeen borrowed an all-weather surface within sight of Celtic's ground at Parkhead.

Ferguson maintained a close interest in his recruits. He knew all their names, and after a morning working with the first team he'd often be out with the youngsters in Aberdeen after lunch. 'He made them feel welcome,' says Eric Black. 'He had a wee bit of humour, and liked to joke around with the kids.'[33] The young players were flattered that the manager took so much interest. Ian Donald remembers how it was a point of honour to get a ticking-off from the boss: 'Alec told me off today,' he remembers young recruits saying with pride.[34] Once a month Ferguson and his assistant, Archie Knox (who replaced Pat Stanton in 1980), even drove down to Glasgow to run the Aberdeen coaching school there. 'A lot of people could have been lazy in a job like that, and let the Glasgow coaches teach the boys there,' says Alex McLeish, who reckons the kids benefited from having better coaches teach them. 'Boys would have remembered that for the rest of their football life, and can look back and say, "I remember Alex Ferguson telling me that when I was twelve. Still do that; it's still in my game."'[35]

Nonetheless, youth players also faced a tough regime. 'From the very first minute,' said Ferguson, 'we teach them self-discipline to prepare them for public exposure. This can be hard on some of the youngsters for, naturally enough, when they reach a stage of public adulation there is a danger of vanity taking over.'[36] Every Friday one poor boy would be summoned to act as referee in the highly competitive games of head tennis and one-touch football – called 'tips' – which Ferguson played with Archie Knox. It was a thankless task, carrying no reward and huge risks. 'They were terrified in case they gave a wrong decision,' says Ferguson's secretary Barbara Cook.[37] On one occasion Ferguson recruited the Pittodrie pensioner volunteers to stand at the side and cheer him on, so in retaliation Knox press-ganged a group of youth players into becoming his 'supporters'.

Knox would make the lads wash his car, and summon them back to Pittodrie to do it again if they'd not done the job properly. It was also the boys' responsibility to pack the big hampers every day with the players' bibs and boots which went by minibus to whichever training pitch the club was using. 'If they forgot anything,' says Len Taylor, 'they had to jog four miles back to Pittodrie and get it.'[38]

'His [Ferguson's] very aggressive Govan manner intimidated the kids quite a lot,' says Alex McLeish, 'and on occasion him and Archie would produce this baseball bat, and torment the boys with that. But it was all good-hearted fun.'[39] Neale Cooper, who came up through the youth ranks and is now manager of Ross County, remembers him as 'very scary. I think a lot of us were in awe when he was around. He had this sort of fear factor. You never knew when he would pop up.'[40] Willie Garner, who later became Ferguson's assistant at Aberdeen, and believes he was a 'genius', explains that it was a case of 'if you could handle the monster, you could handle anything that was flung at you in stadiums. He had this great ability to turn from being this lunatic to saying, "This is why this has gone wrong", and sorting it.'[41]

At one point, Ferguson even came into conflict with the SPFA, the players' union, which he'd chaired in the early 1970s. The dispute occurred when he punished reserve players for a particularly bad defeat. 'He withdrew their wages,' says the SPFA's former full-time secretary Harry Laurie, 'and that was quite unusual for an ex-chairman.' Laurie rang Ferguson and challenged him. 'I'll never forget his words. He said, "You're not telling me how to run Aberdeen Football Club."' Laurie replied that he had no desire to interfere in the workings of Aberdeen, but the club was contractually obliged – Ferguson couldn't simply withhold money that was owed to the players. 'He put the phone down on me,' says Laurie. 'He was bloody adamant he wasn't going to pay up.' The SPFA official resolved the issue with Dick Donald instead, bypassing Ferguson. 'He's always the boss man,' Laurie adds. 'He can be quite brutal with some people. He's got to be the gaffer.'[42]

Early on, Ferguson was worried that the teenagers weren't getting proper lunches. 'They were staying in digs,' says Ian Donald, 'and got a good meal in the evening, but at lunchtime they were eating ham-burgers and hotdogs.'[43] Ferguson persuaded the club to establish a small canteen at Pittodrie, and insisted they ate a cooked meal. It also helped build team spirit for the whole squad, says Pat Stanton. 'Instead of all going their different ways, they'd sit and have a blether, and Alec and the staff would go and sit at another table. All these wee things that people don't attach much significance to are actually vital.'[44]

Most of the young recruits came from beyond Aberdeen, and had to be accommodated in club digs. Ferguson would occasionally visit the landlords or landladies to see how things were. Jack Sim, who had the teenage Eoin Jess among the lodgers at his home just outside Aberdeen, says Ferguson was the only Aberdeen manager, among the two or three he dealt with, ever to drop by:

> He pulled no punches, and said to us that 'If any of the boys who are staying with you get out of hand, or they're doing anything they shouldn't be doing, then I want to know. And if you cover up for them I'll come and take the boys away, and

you won't get any more. If they misbehave,' he said, 'you tell us, and we'll deal with them.'[45]

The boys had to abide by the family rules, and girls weren't allowed to visit, but Sim recalls how on one occasion his Aberdeen lodgers went out and drank far too much at a club celebration party. 'They came back smashed out of their tiny minds; they came in and vomited all over the vestibule. But in the morning they were begging us not to tell "Mr Ferguson", because they knew they'd be shown the front door.'[46]

One of the punishments for misbehaving apprentices went down in Fergie folklore. One landlady complained that several boys had damaged her storage heater while playing hide-and-seek. 'If they act like children,' Ferguson said, 'I treat them like children.'[47] And he and Archie Knox made each of the teenagers learn a nursery rhyme and recite it in front of his teammates the next day. 'Ach, they loved it,' said Ferguson later, relating the incident with great amusement.[48] 'You'd be embarrassed at the time,' says Eric Black, 'but it's not going to psychologically scar you for the rest of your life. It's all part of team-building, and getting people together and getting a laugh. I don't think it's necessarily a bad thing.'[49] Another young player was punished for the then male fashion of having his hair permed. He was told to wear a balaclava, and was ordered never to turn up for training with his hair in such a state again.

Archie Knox had become Ferguson's assistant when Pat Stanton left to pursue his own career as a manager. The problem of assistants leaving to further their ambitions has been a continual irritation to Ferguson during his managerial career, and Stanton's departure seems to have been less than entirely amicable. (Stanton doesn't like to discuss the matter, but it seems strange that he should leave Aberdeen without having first secured the managerial job he wanted.) Knox had previously been the manager of tiny Forfar Athletic, and, whereas Ferguson and Stanton were opposites,

Ferguson and Knox were similar aggressive, highly committed, disciplinarian types who, says Alex McLeish, 'kept up a steady barrage of banter' and used to 'strike sparks off each other'. McLeish believes Ferguson found in Knox 'a soul-mate, someone who, like himself, lived and breathed football twenty-four hours a day, seven days a week. They would go anywhere to watch a football match, and it didn't matter too much what the standard of the teams was.'[50]

Although Ferguson would sometimes join in on the practice pitch, he increasingly delegated the running of the training, fitness and coaching sessions to his deputy. 'It was Archie who got his hands dirty,' says Eric Black. 'Archie was the coach on the field, and Ferguson, with Archie, did tactics. Although Fergie did take coaching sessions, it was mainly Archie that coached.'[51]

If Ferguson underlined the importance of discipline to his youngsters, it seemed to be a case of 'Do as I say, not as I do', for his appearances before the SFA disciplinary committee were just as regular as during his playing days. Even in May 1980, when Aberdeen were winning 5–0 at Hibernian to clinch the Scottish League title, Ferguson was accused of 'foul and abusive language' towards the referee at half-time. That time he was fined £250, and a new touchline ban was imposed, for a year.

Winning a championship for the first time inevitably raises doubts about whether it was merited or simply good fortune. Such suspicions were all the greater because Aberdeen's 1980 points total – 48 – was exceedingly low by historic standards. And, since most of his side had been inherited from Billy McNeill and Ally MacLeod, some people wondered if Ferguson had just happened to be in the right place at the right time.

The sceptics said that Aberdeen had won the League only because both Celtic and Rangers were in periods of 'transition'. This explained why two east-coast clubs had suddenly emerged as a so-called New Firm – for Dundee United had won the League Cup that year. But the New Firm would be a temporary phenomenon, according to the doubters, since the Glasgow clubs would regain their inevitable supremacy.

The prospects didn't look good when Steve Archibald left for Tottenham Hotspur within days of the championship being lifted, for a fee of £800,000. Ferguson would later admit it was a grave mistake to let him go without having found a replacement. The subsequent 1980–81 season never recovered after Aberdeen's embarrassing 5–0 thrashing by Liverpool in the second round of the European Cup and a plague of injuries which affected almost half the team. It merely fuelled the suspicion that the Dons were one-season wonders.

The long-term challenge, of course, was for Aberdeen to emulate Celtic and Rangers and become consistent contenders for every Scottish honour. No team had managed this since the start of the twentieth century. Sides such as Hearts, Hibernian, Kilmarnock and Aberdeen themselves had occasionally taken the league title, but their success was never sustained. The Edinburgh club Hibs, which won the League three times between 1948 and 1952, had come closest to upsetting the Glasgow hegemony, but its challenge fizzled out. Celtic and Rangers were too rich, too powerful and too popular. Before Ferguson arrived at Aberdeen, there had only been eleven occasions since 1900 when the league title hadn't gone to one of the Old Firm. He now saw himself as 'the man from the Monopolies Commission', charged with breaking their duopoly of Scottish football.[52]

Every time the Glasgow clubs visited Pittodrie they brought thousands of travelling supporters. 'Rangers and Celtic each have a cause,' Ferguson observed. 'Some say it is religion but I think it is their tremendous tradition.'[53] Aberdeen supporters, in contrast, lacked the fervour of west of Scotland fans. They rarely travelled in great numbers, which meant that at less popular clubs, such as Motherwell, Kilmarnock or Airdrie, matches were played before crowds of only 2–3,000 compared with gates of 10,000 or more which the Old Firm would almost always attract to such venues. The people of north-east Scotland simply weren't the type to be passionate about their football. On one occasion, when someone suggested the Aberdeen crowd had been a little noisier than normal, Ferguson famously replied, 'Aye, you could hear them rustling their sweetie papers.'[54]

Just as at St Mirren, he used the spectre of Glasgow's footballing might to squeeze better performances out of his players. Too often, he felt, leading Scottish sides had an inferiority complex when playing Celtic and Rangers, and were content to get away with a draw or even a modest defeat. He despaired one day in the dressing room before an Old Firm fixture when he heard his players planning to slow the game down. That wasn't the aggressive, go-out-to-win Ferguson style at all.

Pat Stanton, who had previously played for Celtic, believes Ferguson learned from Jock Stein the trick of creating a 'siege mentality'. 'Everyone is against us, the authorities are against us, the referees are against us – big Stein created that.'[55] It meant, of course, that every setback, misfortune or slight could be turned to the team's advantage. If Aberdeen didn't have a traditional cause, Ferguson would have to manufacture one. Recasting the formula that had worked so well at East Stirling and St Mirren, he banged on incessantly about the 'west-coast bias' in the Scottish press and how they always favoured the Old Firm. If the smallest criticism appeared in the Saturday-morning papers, Ferguson would pin the offending article on the dressing-room wall to spur the players. 'He gave us a persecution complex about Celtic and Rangers, the Scottish FA and the Glasgow media, the whole west of Scotland thing,' says Mark McGhee, 'and it worked a treat.'[56] 'You remind yourself of the number of people who don't want you to win,' said Ferguson. 'It fires you up, it gets you going, so we use it to our own advantage.'[57]

Ferguson would say that nothing gave him greater pleasure than attending a press conference after Aberdeen had beaten one of the

Old Firm clubs. Gordon Strachan recalls the kind of things Ferguson would tell his players. '"The press don't want to come to Aberdeen to see you playing top games"; "They don't like you"; "Because they come from Glasgow, they think they're a superior people." And we bought it. I fell for it. And there used to be like eleven Tasmanian Devils running about there.'[58] Ferguson even kept a log of how often each Glasgow-based journalist came to watch Aberdeen. Too many of them travelled to Pittodrie only if Celtic or Rangers were the visitors, he taunted. 'You've not been here for four or five weeks, have you?' the reporter Ian Paul remembers him saying. 'He'd ask why we weren't there when they were top of the table, and that was a totally valid point.'[59]

Of course, Ferguson had never needed a cause to fire himself up against Celtic or Rangers. As a player, he'd often reserved his best performances for Old Firm games. Now there was the personal spur of having failed in his two years at Rangers. With Celtic it helped that their manager was the former centre-half and Aberdeen boss Billy McNeill, with whom Ferguson had enjoyed a traditional centre-forward's rivalry throughout their playing days. Not only was there the haunting memory of the 1969 Scottish Cup final, but McNeill had done everything as a player that Ferguson hadn't – picking up 29 caps for Scotland and 23 major medals to become the most decorated player in British history. Ferguson wanted some of that for himself. It's generally agreed that the breakthrough was when Aberdeen beat Celtic 3–1 at Parkhead in the run-in to the 1980 league title. 'I just said, "Be *arrogant*. Get at their bloody *throats*!"' he once recalled.[60]

Gordon Strachan says that before Old Firm matches Ferguson encouraged his players to question any decisions by referees that might be 'dodgy', just as Rangers and Celtic players always did – or so he claimed.

Alex Ferguson had drummed into us that the two Glasgow giants were favoured by referees, that because of the support they carried with them to every game, officials were intimidated . . . he claimed he was speaking from knowledge, having played as a striker for Rangers himself. His argument was that these two clubs pressured referees and that we had to do the same. We had to fight fire with fire if you like.[61]

In the Ferguson years, Aberdeen approached games against Celtic and Rangers with an intensity that could be deeply unpleasant. Sometimes, says the former Ibrox player Alex Miller, he wouldn't allow his men to talk to Rangers players before the game, to make them more single-minded. There were frequent confrontations on the pitch, scores of bookings, and several dismissals in Old Firm fixtures. These sometimes led to crowd trouble, and frequently the bitterness continued with arguing and fights in the players' tunnel after the final whistle. (When trouble occurred at a Aberdeen–Rangers game early in 2002 it was blamed on rivalry dating back to the Ferguson era.)

'He used to wind us up something rotten. He had us believing that everyone in Glasgow hated us,' says Gordon Strachan, 'and so we would take to the field expecting injustice. If it came then that would fire us up still further.'[62] Aberdeen's tough young midfielder Neale Cooper says Ferguson once called him into the office early in the week to tell him he would be marking Charlie Nicholas against Celtic that Saturday. 'He wanted me to think about it all week in the build-up,' says Cooper. 'The boys had a bit of a laugh about it. They kept asking if I was thinking about Charlie. So by the time of the game, I was quite keyed up. [After] two or three seconds on the clock, Frank McGarvey passed the ball to Charlie and I went flying in. Charlie was lying there, holding his knee. At the time, I thought, you know, maybe I was a bit brainwashed.'[63] But Ferguson would have known that such a ploy would only work with tough-minded players – others might have spent the week trembling at the prospect and been washed out by Saturday afternoon.

Charlie Nicholas was so angry with Ferguson's instructions to Neale Cooper (which became something of a habit) that he called a chapter of his autobiography 'The Time I Hated Fergie!' 'There was an arrogance about them,' Nicholas said of the Aberdeen of the early 1980s, the opponents he most detested:

> And there was also the fact that at Celtic we found it hard to beat them. That wasn't easy for us to accept, and our resentment boiled up into a real dislike and brought several grudge games between us.
>
> But there were other reasons too. Particularly the tactics used to stop me. That's why I hated Alex Ferguson . . . When suddenly you're kicked just after you take the kick-off in a game, you say to yourself, 'What's going on here?'[64]

Aberdeen finally established themselves as the equals of the Old Firm, if not better, in the 1982 Scottish Cup. Alex McLeish says Ferguson built up the final against Rangers as the players' big test, a 'mental barrier' to surmount after the failures of three previous Hampden finals. 'The boss said, "You've come here many times in the past and you've been accused of bottling it, but at this stage you are in charge of your own destiny. You win this game and that's the start of many cup triumphs at Hampden."'[65] Aberdeen didn't 'bottle' it, and Ferguson's personal nightmares of 1965 and 1969 were also laid to rest, as the Dons won 4–1 after extra time. As if to emphasise their superiority over the two Glasgow giants, they had also defeated Celtic in the fourth round of the Cup that year.

The story might have been different. Just before the third-round tie at Motherwell, Ferguson had been contacted by the chairman of the distinguished English club Wolverhampton Wanderers, who were struggling near the bottom of the First Division and deep in debt. On the day their manager John Barnwell resigned, Wolves offered Ferguson £50,000 a year to succeed him.

This wasn't his first approach from England: the previous summer Third Division Sheffield United had dangled a £40,000 salary. However, this new approach was worth considering. In Ferguson's childhood, when they were managed by Stan Cullis, Wolves had been one of the great English clubs, champions three times in the 1950s, FA Cup winners in 1949 and 1960, and famous for their pioneering fixtures against top European sides such as Honvéd of Hungary. Ferguson met the Wolves chairman, Harry Marshall, and his directors, but 'was totally disillusioned by what I saw at Molineux', he wrote later. 'The stadium was in a state of disrepair and there was a general air of defeat. The most amazing thing is there was not a soul in the ground that afternoon. To me there was apathy and lack of ambition, or maybe just laziness.'[66] The set-up at Wolves seemed much worse than Aberdeen's, and, sure enough, that summer the club was relegated and went into liquidation, before being bailed out by new owners.

What really put Ferguson off was his lunch with the Molineux board. They asked numerous questions about how he managed, but seemed to know little about his record. He found the questions irritating, as he had travelled down expecting the Wolves directors to elaborate on their offer. Harry Marshall did eventually confirm their proposal, and Ferguson said he'd consider it. But he returned to Scotland knowing he couldn't accept.

'The potential of the players at Aberdeen is limitless,' he declared shortly afterwards. 'There is no telling what we can achieve.' Ferguson delivered his employers a warning for the future, however, explaining that, while he'd rejected Wolves, he ought to talk to English clubs to show that he wasn't scared of the challenge of managing south of the border. 'It's just that the time isn't right,' he added. 'My ambitions at Aberdeen are not even half fulfilled.'[67]

Glory in Gothenburg

'I had heard Aberdeen were good but I didn't realise they were that good. They are one of the best sides I have seen in Europe.'

JUPP DERWALL, Bayern Munich manager[1]

On the evening of 11 May 1983 a small group of working-class men gathered in a terraced house in a pit village in County Durham. As they sat watching television, beers in hand, they heard a knock at the door. It was opened to reveal a smartly dressed professional gentleman. He was aged thirty, fresh-faced and keen, but also slightly nervous. The young man, who'd been expected, was invited into the living room. He'd have to sit down and pour himself a drink, they told him, while they finished watching the big match. No problem, he said. Anyway, he assured them, he loved football.

Tony Blair had to wait rather longer than he might have expected. First, the European Cup-Winners' Cup final went to extra time. Then came the celebrations. Only when Willie Miller had lifted the cup and the Aberdeen players had completed their lap of honour could the Labour Party members get down to business and begin questioning their visitor. It must have been around midnight by the time they agreed among themselves that Blair would make an excellent Labour candidate for their constituency. Officially the Sedgefield shortlist was closed, but they agreed to seek dispensation and nominate Blair as a last-minute addition.

Who knows? Had Aberdeen lost that night the Labour activists might not have been in such a good mood, less well disposed to this enthusiastic barrister from down south poking his nose in at the last moment. If Alex Ferguson and his team had failed in Gothenburg, recent British history might have taken a different course.

Aberdeen competed in Europe in each of the nine seasons in which Alex Ferguson ran the club. The 1980 league title paved the way for their first shot at the European Cup (Hibernian having taken Aberdeen's place as champions back in 1955, when the trophy was first contested and not confined to championship winners). After disposing of Austria Memphis in the first round, Aberdeen were taught a lesson by the great Liverpool side of that era, who went on to win the champions' cup in 1980–81 for the third time in five years. After losing 1–0 at Pittodrie, the Dons went down 4–0 at Anfield, though the damage could have been greater. It was a traumatic result for Ferguson, indicating that Aberdeen still had much to learn about playing in Europe – particularly about discipline and the importance of keeping possession.

Ironically, given the way Ferguson used press coverage to motivate his own players, the Liverpool team had been spurred by articles in the Aberdeen papers predicting that the Dons would easily win. 'It meant a lot to me to ram those comments back down the throats of people who made them,' says the Liverpool defender Alan Hansen, who was competing with Willie Miller and Alex McLeish for a place in the Scotland side. 'I never performed with as much fire and aggression as I did in that game.'[2] The performance of Hansen and the other Liverpool Scots only heightened the tensions between Scotsmen playing in England and those still at home – an issue which would haunt Ferguson when he became Scotland manager five years later. And, from having admired the Liverpool team in the past, Ferguson now came to hate them and want revenge.

But Ferguson also learned from such experiences. He and his colleagues put a huge effort into every European fixture. The manager and his assistant would try to watch every Continental opponent personally, and would prepare several detailed pages for the squad to read, with information on each of the opposing players and the team's likely tactics, pinpointing every strength and weakness. 'I thought we were going to be tested about it the next day!' says Stewart McKimmie. 'It's the first and only time I've ever had that.'[3] The preparations didn't always go to plan. On one north-European spying mission Ferguson and Pat Stanton thought they'd kill time by sampling local culture. They spent the afternoon in a local pornographic cinema. Only later did they learn, to their horror, that the game they'd come to see was an afternoon kick-off and they'd missed it. On another occasion Stanton remembers that Ferguson brought back some souvenirs. 'We stole the coat hangers out of the hotel. I mean, you can't take the lad out of Govan. We'd had a couple of beers, but we weren't drunk or anything. You know how it is in most hotels – they're made of plastic. Well, these were solid "Clyde-built", and he just took a fancy to them.'[4]

Ferguson also learned some of the tricks of European competition. He employed extra ballboys for all home games, having noticed that Brian Clough did the same thing at Nottingham Forest to keep up the momentum. And he frequently rested players from Aberdeen's domestic fixtures, hoping both to give them a break and to keep them on their toes. It might sound commonplace today, but this was an era when most British clubs still fielded the same eleven players week after week, and long before the large playing squad he would enjoy at Manchester United. And Ferguson, ever the student, loved grilling foreign managers about what certain football terms were in their various languages.

Consolation for the Liverpool humiliation came the following season in the UEFA Cup, when Aberdeen resoundingly defeated the English holders of the trophy, Ipswich Town, 4–2 on aggregate. It was the first sign that Aberdeen might do well in Europe, since the Ipswich of Bobby Robson were widely considered to be second only to Liverpool among the English teams of that time. The tie was followed by a couple of friendlies between the two east-coast sides. Aberdeen saw Ipswich as an inspirational example of how a well-run, friendly club from a small, isolated town could be successful (and Ipswich even considered Ferguson as a possible successor to Robson).

After the exhilaration of beating Ipswich, however, the team were quickly brought down to earth when they lost 5–4 to Hamburg. By the time they embarked on their famous 1982–83 Cup-Winners' Cup campaign, Aberdeen had failed, in eleven previous attempts since 1967, to reach even the quarter-finals of a European competition.

Officially, the European Cup-Winners' Cup (which was abolished in 1999) used to be ranked second of the three main UEFA contests. In reality in most seasons it was probably the easiest to win, since domestic knockout cups are taken less seriously in many Continental countries and are often won by weaker sides. The UEFA Cup, in contrast, had one more round and also contained teams who had come close to winning their leagues. In 1982, however, the Cup-Winners' Cup entry looked unusually strong, with Bayern Munich, Barcelona, Real Madrid, Inter Milan and Spurs among the participants. Aberdeen disposed of Sion of Switzerland, the Albanian club Dinamo Tirana, and Lech Poznań of Poland with ease. For the first time, Aberdeen's European commitments stretched beyond Christmas, though the prospects after that didn't look too good, for they were drawn against Bayern Munich. The club had fared badly against German sides in recent years, and Bayern, who had been crowned European champions three times in the previous decade, had reached the European Cup final only the season before. Ferguson prepared more thoroughly than ever; he and Archie Knox took it in turn to watch Bayern several times, and distributed to the players a collection of videos of the German club's latest games.

Aberdeen's contests with Bayern Munich are seen as the pinnacle of that year's historic European success – indeed, two of the greatest games in the Scottish club's history. A 0–0 draw in the first leg, in the Olympic Stadium in Munich, involved supreme discipline and concentration, and was especially commendable since Spurs had lost 4–1 in Munich in the previous round. But Ferguson didn't want to be complacent, and he fined several players who went out to celebrate without his permission.

Afterwards, Bayern's general manager, Uli Hoeness, described Aberdeen as 'better than Barcelona, Inter Milan or Real Madrid'.[5] But not Munich, it must have seemed a fortnight later, as the Dons fell behind 2–1 at Pittodrie with less than half an hour to go. Aberdeen now needed to score twice to survive, for a 2–2 draw would see the Germans go through, having scored more away goals. Ferguson radically rejigged the team after bringing on substitutes John McMaster and John Hewitt (a striker to whom he'd given a league debut at the age of only sixteen four years before). Then, with a free kick awarded and thirteen minutes to play, Gordon Strachan performed a trick he'd practised many times on the training pitch, but which the SFA had banned at corners a couple of years earlier. Strachan and McMaster pretended to bump into each other in an apparent mix-up over who was taking the kick. While the bemused Germans were still off guard, Strachan quickly floated the ball over for Alex McLeish to score with his head. A minute later John Hewitt made it 3–2, and Pittodrie was then plunged into celebration as Aberdeen held on for the apparent eternity of the remaining twelve minutes. 'The genius of Fergie's substitutions stood out as the main factor,' said Gordon Strachan, 'and there he was skipping like a five-year-old and into the dressing room where pandemonium was breaking loose.'[6] 'We didn't play well,' Alex Ferguson later admitted. 'Nerves were evident in a lot of the players.'[7] What did it matter? Aberdeen were the only British side left in any European competition that year, and through to the semi-finals. It wouldn't be the last time a Ferguson team foiled the German club with substitutions and two late goals within two minutes.

'Winning against Bayern Munich gave us the belief that we could win the tournament,' says Willie Miller.[8] Waterschei of Belgium were relatively easy opponents in the semi-finals, and were beaten 5–2 on aggregate. This set up a final in Gothenburg against the mighty Real Madrid – though the Spaniards were far from the great team whom the teenage Ferguson had witnessed at Hampden Park in 1960, when they famously beat Eintracht Frankfurt 7–3 in what is still regarded as one of the greatest games of club football of all time.

The 1983 Cup-Winners' Cup final was held at the Ullevi stadium in Gothenburg in Sweden, the ground at which Ferguson had made his European debut with Dunfermline back in 1964. Around 12,000 Scots made the trip across the North Sea from Aberdeen. 'The whole city was buzzing,' Cathy Ferguson would recall years later. 'There was a lot of people in Aberdeen who never got a holiday that year – women – because all the men were saving up to go to Gothenburg. So you could hear them in shops, "I'm getting no holiday this year 'cause he's going to the match." And they were taking the kids with them.'[9]

Aberdeen's airport reported record sales of duty-free drinks – the equivalent of a month's takings in just three days. Many people chose to sail, and Alex Ferguson went down to the quayside to wave 493 supporters off on an overnight ferry, the *St Clair*. He promised to meet them with the cup when they returned.

Among the guests in the official Aberdeen party was Jock Stein – partly as a talismanic reminder of Celtic's European success in 1967, and partly for fatherly advice. Stein suggested Ferguson should present the Madrid manager with a bottle of whisky, to make him think Aberdeen were in awe of the Spanish side and happy just to have reached the final. Ferguson also gathered all the players' wives and girlfriends for a meeting before going out to Sweden, teasing them that they'd be living in chalets, and would have to bring along sleeping bags, cutlery and camping equipment. Some of them fell for it!

'Normally before big games,' Willie Miller noted, 'Fergie was like a cat on hot bricks and the nervous cough – a sure sign of inward stress – would make its appearance.' But this time Ferguson was relaxed, behaving as if his side was about to play a friendly, and even the dreaded cough disappeared. He made the preparations as low-key as possible, and the squad stayed in a quiet hamlet well outside Gothenburg. 'It was so unlike his customary approach,' says Miller. 'It was a performance worthy of an Oscar and it certainly helped keep the players on an even keel.'[10] To keep the squad's minds off the game, Ferguson organised a quiz in the team hotel, and a game of Scrabble which ended, according to Miller, in heated arguments over words which Ferguson claimed didn't exist.[11] There was also a three-mile race between the manager and Archie Knox round a nearby castle. 'The players swore we were off our heads,' Ferguson says, 'but it was all done just to keep things in the squad active.'[12] As a sentimental gesture, he also named Stuart Kennedy as one of his five substitutes, even though the experienced Aberdeen full-back had picked up a serious injury against Bayern and would never have been able to play. It was an extra boost to morale, and 'one of my best-ever decisions in management', says Ferguson.[13]

It seemed to rain for most of the evening, but the crowd – the vast majority of whom were Dons supporters – didn't care. Aberdeen took an early lead through Eric Black, but Madrid equalised with a penalty when Leighton pulled down Santillana following a poor back-pass by McLeish. (Fortunately for Leighton, this was before such fouls were punished automatically with dismissal.) With only eight minutes of extra time left, it looked as if the Cup might be decided on penalties. The prospect was not appealing: British sides seem to fare badly in penalty shoot-outs, and the Spaniards had been seen practising their spot kicks. Just as against Bayern, John

Hewitt had been brought on as substitute, but this time he was playing so badly that Ferguson actually thought about substituting his substitute. Fortunately he didn't.

All of a sudden the Ullevi stadium erupted, along with Tony Blair and his new-found friends in their sitting room in County Durham. Forget penalties: John Hewitt had done it again, stabbing home a cross from Mark McGhee with a diving header, and thereby branding himself for ever with the label 'Super Sub'. Ten minutes later, as the final whistle sounded, the Cup belonged to Aberdeen. 'The boss came out of the dugout like a man possessed,' says Gordon Strachan, 'fell into a puddle and Archie Knox ran right over him on his way to the players.'[14]

The following morning, schools in the north-east of Scotland were given a day's holiday. 'The Don's are the Greatest', read the ungrammatical sign on the front of the open-top bus which collected the team from the airport. It took two hours to make its way through thousands of fans lining Union Street in the city centre, and then to Pittodrie, where 20,000 more were waiting to catch sight of the trophy. Later that evening, as he'd promised, Ferguson went down to the docks and reportedly shook the hand of every one of the 493 fans disembarking from the homecoming *St Clair*.

Ferguson said the win in Gothenburg made him feel that he'd done something worthwhile with his life. Aberdeen had become only the third Scottish side to win a European trophy, after Celtic in 1967 and Rangers' Cup-Winners' Cup success in 1972. Almost twenty years later Aberdeen remain the last Scottish side to collect any honour in Europe – a record that may last for many years now that the European competitions are loaded in favour of bigger countries and big clubs. Aberdeen can also boast of being one of the last teams to win a European competition with a team composed entirely of players from its own country, a distinction that may well last for ever. 'Aberdeen have what money can't buy,' acknowledged the losing manager, Alfredo di Stefano, 'a soul; a team spirit built in the family tradition.'[15] Six of the side – Leighton, Rougvie, McMaster, McLeish, Miller and Strachan – had been inherited by Ferguson when he arrived at Aberdeen. The other six were his own men. Neale Cooper, Neil Simpson, Eric Black and John Hewitt had all graduated from the Aberdeen youth sides, while Ferguson had bought both Mark McGhee and Peter Weir – the latter from St Mirren for £300,000.

Tony Blair was picked as Labour candidate for Sedgefield ten days later, on the same day that the Dons beat Rangers 1–0 in the Scottish Cup final to become the first Scottish side from outside Glasgow in almost a quarter of a century to win two trophies in the same season. (Indeed, it had nearly been a treble, as Aberdeen came close to winning the League too.) But Alex Ferguson was not a happy man during the Scottish Cup triumph. It was the same eleven as in Gothenburg, but they looked stale. 'You're Rangers' best player,' he'd taunted Jim Leighton just before extra time.[16] When Dick Donald tried to bring the customary champagne into the winning dressing room, Ferguson told him not to uncork it.

The players didn't know it at the time, but he also denounced them in a post-match TV interview on the pitch as 'the luckiest team in the world. They were a disgraceful performance.' With echoes of his own father's refusal ever to be satisfied, he insisted he wasn't 'going to accept that from any Aberdeen team'.[17] Only Willie Miller and Alex McLeish had played well, he declared. Such comments would look odd even after winning an ordinary league match against Rangers, but the Scottish Cup final? They seemed both bizarre and mean-spirited, especially since it was only ten days after the glory of Gothenburg. Ferguson had now reached the stage where he needed not just to win, but to win in style.

Never can a cup-winning team have been so miserable. The coach journey back north was almost silent, 'broken occasionally', says Gordon Strachan, 'by somebody trying to make a joke about Willie and Alec having won the game on their own. One joker said they would only need a tandem to cycle down Union Street to salute the public!'[18] 'Some of the players were so disgusted with the manager's reaction,' says Jim Leighton, 'that they stayed away from what was supposed to be a celebratory party. There was a dreadful feeling of anti-climax within our ranks.'[19] 'Celebration?' says Gordon Strachan. 'It was more like a wake!'[20] He and his wife walked out of the party in protest at Ferguson's behaviour.

The following day the Aberdeen manager realised that he'd over-reacted, and called the squad in to apologise. 'I am not proud of myself,' he admitted, explaining that he'd not had a good night's sleep since the European final. 'Criticising them after they had won two cups and being narrowly beaten for the League was out of order . . . Next season I think I will keep my mouth shut immediately after games. I'll cool down in future before I start talking.'[21] 'The damage was done,' says Leighton, 'and we did not feel like forgiving him.'[22] Alex McLeish, in contrast, felt that the apology 'raised him in the players' estimation. They admired the bigness of a man who could admit his mistake so readily.'[23]

Jock Stein, who was now the Scotland manager, was rather more appreciative. Aberdeen men were regularly filling four or five places in his national side, including the defensive triangle of Leighton, Miller and McLeish. A record six Dons played against Northern Ireland in December 1983 – Leighton, Rougvie, McLeish, Strachan, McGhee and Weir – and it might have been seven had Willie Miller not been injured.

Alex Ferguson was awarded an OBE in the 1984 New Year honours list in recognition of Aberdeen's success in Europe. But the team had made a disappointing start to the 1983–84 season, and he threatened to bring in 'new talent' in response to the 'inadequate displays of some players'.[24] It was an autumn blip, and by the spring Aberdeen were again going for a treble. Ferguson wanted the lot, and they came very close. The League was collected this time – with a record points total, scoring 78 goals and conceding only 21. Then

Aberdeen became only the third side (after Ferguson's old clubs Queen's Park and Rangers) to win a Scottish Cup final three years running. The big disappointment was losing 2–0 on aggregate to Porto in the semi-finals of the Cup-Winners' Cup. The Portuguese were the better team, though twelve years later it would be alleged that the Romanian referee had been bribed to ensure they prevailed. Nonetheless, the Dons' first domestic double wasn't bad going.

Aberdeen's successes meant that Ferguson's players were being noticed south of the border and on the Continent. They were easy targets for English or foreign clubs, both because of their relatively low salaries and because of the new freedom-of-movement rules brought into football at the end of the 1970s. Graeme Souness, who was captain of Liverpool and Scotland at that time, says Ferguson discouraged his players in the national squad from mixing with colleagues who played for English clubs. 'I can imagine only that it was because he didn't want us to tell them what we were earning.'[25] Ferguson also seems to have kept wages low through the force of his own personality, doubtless coupled with the negotiating skills he had acquired both from his union activities and from Dick Donald's instruction. Alex McLeish says he used to 'dread' contract negotiations with him. 'I knew that no matter how well I prepared my arguments beforehand, I would go in there and he would have me signed before I knew what had hit me. It would probably be the next day before you realised that you had re-signed, when you read it in the newspapers.'[26] Interestingly, former Manchester United players say Sir Matt Busby displayed the same ability to get players to sign for less than they knew they were worth.

Nonetheless, Ferguson lost three important men in the summer of 1984. Mark McGhee's move to Hamburg was the most amicable of the departures. Ferguson seems to have respected his decision, even though he said McGhee could have been 'more honest' over the way he left, having promised to negotiate with the manager without letting on that he planned to fly to Germany the following day.[27]

Hamburg had won the European Cup in 1983, and for McGhee this was undoubtedly a move to a bigger club, even though Aberdeen had beaten the German side 2–0 on aggregate to win the 1983 European Super Cup (which is played between the winners of the two main European trophies).

Ferguson responded very differently to the decisions by Gordon Strachan and Doug Rougvie to leave. Strachan caused the greatest problems. Ferguson felt he'd done a lot to improve Strachan as a player, especially considering how, early on, Dick Donald had suggested it might be a good idea to sell him. Money was undoubtedly a factor in his leaving, but Strachan was also bored by the 'monotony of the premier league' and the prospect of facing the same teams four times a season, and leading sides more often if one included cup-ties. The intense feuding of games against the Old Firm, much encouraged by Ferguson, also depressed him. The seven fixtures against Celtic that season, for instance, had produced thirty-two yellow cards and two sendings-off, including the Celtic captain, Roy Aitken, in the Scottish Cup final:

> The whole scene became poisonous. You would be going off
> the field after a game and a player would be saying to you,
> 'Just you wait, I'll get you the next time.' . . . In the premier
> league the 'next time' could be three weeks off, maybe even
> less, so you had these troubles lying in wait for you at just
> about very game.[28]

Strachan's relations with Ferguson had grown steadily worse, especially after Ferguson spent £70,000 in the summer of 1983 to buy Billy Stark from St Mirren – an obvious replacement for Strachan on the right of midfield. Ferguson's explanation is that he bought Stark in the knowledge that Strachan was likely to leave: he wanted to get his replacement first, to avoid the problem he faced when Steve Archibald left in 1980. Indeed, he credits Strachan with giving him 'plenty of warning beforehand so that I could prepare for his certain departure'.[29]

In part, their falling-out merely reflected the natural strains between strong-willed characters of very similar temperament. Strachan irritated his manager with his constant jokes, yet he was at that time a huge admirer of Ferguson. He acknowledged that Ferguson's appointment as Aberdeen manager was 'possibly the best thing that has ever happened to my career. I wouldn't have reached international level without him.'[30] But Ferguson had already turned down his request for a move in 1982, after Strachan had attracted the attention of English clubs with his performances in the World Cup in Spain. With his contract due to run out in the summer of 1984, he signalled his wish to leave well before the end of the previous season. Indeed, there were rumours that Strachan had already signed for a Continental side. When Ferguson confronted him about these reports, Strachan denied it.

At one point towards the end of the 1983–84 season Ferguson dropped Strachan. He felt 'that a slight shock would do him no harm', though he didn't tell journalists why the player was out of the side. 'I never explain to the press whether I have dropped players,' Ferguson later revealed.[31] Strachan's response was to criticise the decision in his weekly column in the *Daily Express*. So Ferguson put a stop to the column. Strachan would later confess that there was 'too much bickering' between him and his manager 'to look at anything logically', and that Ferguson was right to drop him. 'I'll own up now,' he added. 'I did not give enough mentally to the team in those last few months of that season.'[32]

The backbiting and shouting between the two men soon turned into periods of complete silence, to the discomfort of those around them. What infuriated Alex Ferguson was that, when Aberdeen finally arranged to sell Strachan to Manchester United that spring, it suddenly emerged that there had been some truth to the rumours. Strachan had already made a commitment to join Cologne by

signing a letter of intent with the German club. (To add to the confusion, he had also signed a less binding agreement with Verona of
Italy.) 'I could have killed him!' said Ferguson, who was astonished.[33] Cologne were so angry about Strachan's reneging on their
deal that they complained to UEFA, and threatened to sue him for
breach of contract (which would have prevented him from playing
anywhere until the case was resolved). His transfer to Manchester
United for £600,000 eventually went through, but only after several
meetings in France which left the lawyers involved many thousands
of pounds better off. 'I can't believe how stupid I was,' Strachan later
admitted. 'I have to carry the can for the biggest mistake I have ever
made.'[34]

Doug Rougvie's departure was quicker, though equally acrimonious. Like Strachan, the popular full-back had also reached the
end of his contract, and now asked for the same pay as Willie Miller.
His hand was strengthened when Chelsea offered him around £720
a week – almost twice what he was paid at Pittodrie. Rougvie asked
Ferguson if Aberdeen would match Chelsea's money. Ferguson's
account is that he promised to consult the directors that afternoon,
reminding Rougvie that Aberdeen had already made a good offer,
and that better pay wasn't the only thing to consider. 'That was the
last time I saw Doug Rougvie,' he said. 'He jumped on a plane at
lunchtime that day and the next thing I heard he was in London and
had signed for Chelsea.'[35]

Rougvie's version is more colourful. Ferguson ignored his twelve
years' service, he complains, and accused him of playing off one
club against the other, using Chelsea as 'a lever'. When they met, he
says, Ferguson told him to 'Fuck off!' The player adds:

> He kicked me out of his office and, on the following week,
> wouldn't let me inside the Pittodrie door . . . He slaughtered
> me in the press but I didn't respond. I must admit I was hurt,
> though. My heart was at Pittodrie and I didn't want to leave. I

have every respect for Mr Ferguson as a football manager but not for the way he managed people.[36]

'Money', said Ferguson, was 'the sole reason why McGhee and Rougvie left . . . We have become a big club in terms of recognition, but not in terms of finance so we cannot possibly pay players £2,500 a week.'[37] Fifteen years later Ferguson took a more considered view. Aberdeen should have acceded to the demands for more pay, he felt, and hadn't really understood the impact of their success in Europe. They were 'ill-prepared for the sudden elevation and the way the rising profile of the players had altered their earning capacity'.[38]

Ferguson's relations with Doug Rougvie and Gordon Strachan were never the same again, and he seemed surprisingly unapprecia-tive about their contributions to his success. 'Those who have gone are not my players now,' he told the Aberdeen historian, Jack Webster. 'They are out from under my skin and I don't have any feel-ings about them at all.'[39] It was another glimpse of one of Ferguson's less attractive characteristics. As he'd shown with Ricky McFarlane at St Mirren, if a former colleague shows signs of disloyalty he may completely ignore him thereafter. But Rougvie, Strachan and McGhee had only behaved in the same way that Ferguson had as a player – constantly haggling for more money, threatening to leave, and looking for bigger clubs to further their ambitions.

13

Restless Ambition

'What he did at Aberdeen was almost miraculous.'

HUGH MCILVANNEY, journalist, friend
and ghost-writer[1]

As the 1980s unfolded, Alex Ferguson was increasingly approached by other clubs. Despite his insistence on loyalty from his players, he himself toyed with several job offers. Immediately after Aberdeen won the Cup-Winners' Cup in 1983, Ferguson says he was contacted by a director of Rangers about the possibility of taking over as manager there. But 'I was reluctant to even consider a move then because John Greig was still managing Glasgow Rangers and he was a good friend of mine. There was no way I was going to pull the carpet from under John's feet.'[2]

The following October John Greig resigned, having failed to win the League in his five years at the club. Ferguson was now contacted again, this time by the Rangers vice-chairman, John Paton. Ferguson was tempted. What attracted him most was the thought that, while several boys from Govan had played for the Ibrox side – including himself – 'no-one from Govan had ever actually managed the club'.[3] For ten days Ferguson fended off calls both from Rangers and from inquisitive reporters. Many friends urged him to accept. Even the former manager Scot Symon urged him to say 'Yes', though he himself had been shabbily dismissed by the club shortly after Ferguson's arrival at Ibrox in 1967. But Symon also warned him about divisions on the board, and Ferguson was concerned about the disruption to his sons' education which moving back to Glasgow would entail.

Before a European Cup-Winners' Cup match at Pittodrie, Ferguson announced that he had turned down the Ibrox job. It was a trick he had picked up from Willie Cunningham, who had once delighted Falkirk supporters just before an important home cup-tie by announcing over the loudspeaker that he wouldn't take the Scotland job. Aberdeen went on to win 4–1 that night, and the directors agreed a new contract with Ferguson worth £60,000 a year. 'I have made up my mind to commit myself to the club for the next five years,' he said.[4]

Several newspapers had suggested it was time for Rangers to take a radically new approach. 'The club has for too long been a bastion of arrogance, insensitivity and sectarian intransigence,' declared an editorial in the *Glasgow Herald*. 'The club has, in short, been presented with a momentous opportunity; it must seize it. No explicit statement has yet been issued that Catholics can be signed by the new manager, whoever he is. That statement must be issued by the board, immediately and unequivocally.'[5]

The Scottish media had been full of talk about Ferguson returning to Rangers, and there had also been intense speculation that he was the man who would end the infamous religious discrimination. 'Some of them who don't even know my beliefs were forecasting the signing of Roman Catholics,' Ferguson wrote in his book *A Light in the North*, which was published only two years later. Of the many hundreds of thousands of words Alex Ferguson has written over the years in his seven books, this passage is the most puzzling. It is worth quoting at length:

One particular news item on Radio 2 made me absolutely livid. The journalist boomed out some stuff like, 'The corridors of power at Ibrox are about to be shaken to their very roots. Alex Ferguson will be manager of Rangers Football Club tomorrow and his first signing will be a Roman Catholic.' That really angered me as, for one, the man doesn't know me and secondly, I have never spoken to him on any subject far less football. Although I did discuss the religious subject with John Paton it was not an issue with me. As far as I am concerned managing footballers is all that matters and I have never had interference of any kind from my directors at Aberdeen Football Club and would expect that policy to rule no matter where I managed.[6]

To some extent, Ferguson was probably annoyed by the idea that he could be told whom to buy or not to buy, and by the thought of making an empty gesture for the sake of it, but this does not fully explain why he should have been 'absolutely livid' rather than simply irritated. Any manager experiences inaccurate stories about possible transfer purchases, and, while it also proved to be specula-tion, this report portrayed Ferguson in a progressive and tolerant light. On the face of it, it does not seem offensive to suggest that he'd act decisively to end religious discrimination.

The passage in his 1985 book surely casts doubt on whether Ferguson would have lifted the effective ban on Catholics, as Graeme Souness did six years later after he became Rangers' manager. Ferguson's attitude seems to have been one of resignation. He appears to have assumed that if he went to Ibrox he would have to accept the religious bar, even though he personally found it abhorrent. 'How could I go back and not sign Catholics?' he reportedly asked the Scottish football journalist Archie MacPherson. 'What would I tell my friends who are Catholics – you lot aren't good enough for us? I just couldn't do that.'[7] Similarly, one of Ferguson's closest friends in

Aberdeen, George Ramsay, remembers him saying, 'I'm not going to watch twenty-two schoolkids and know that I can only sign half of them.'[8] Yet, to judge by the claim in his 1985 book that 'the religious subject . . . was not an issue' when he spoke to John Paton, Ferguson doesn't seem to have considered that he could require the ban to be ended as a condition of his taking the Rangers job.

It's also worth remembering that Bill Struth, Scot Symon, Willie Waddell and John Greig – heroes and friends of Ferguson's – had all perpetuated the discrimination against Catholics during their spells as Ibrox manager. Nor had the SPFA done anything about the problem during Ferguson's three years as chairman in the early 1970s. Alex Ferguson would also have well understood the role that religious sectarianism played in elevating Celtic and Rangers into 'causes' for their fanatical supporters and players. Throughout his managerial career he has always understood the importance of causes – generating false ones if necessary. Just as he'd tolerated and even joined in with the Orange songs in his pub, he might simply have preferred to let sleeping dogs lie.

Ferguson's assertion in *A Light in the North* that 'the religious subject . . . was not an issue with me' contrasts with his 1999 autobiography, where he cites the religious problem as the *main reason* he rejected Rangers – not because of the discrimination against players, but because of his wife's Catholicism. 'The truth', he wrote in 1999, 'is that I was already reluctant to entertain exposing my family to the risk of a recurrence of the bigotry I had encountered at Ibrox in my playing days . . . Cathy's religion would probably have been enough in itself to convince me that returning to Rangers was not a good idea.'[9]

It's easier to reconcile these conflicting strands of evidence from Ferguson if the huge change in attitudes which occurred between the early 1980s and 1999 is considered. By 1999 Britain was a much more liberal and tolerant society, where it was hard to believe that, only a decade before, the UK's wealthiest football club had been allowed to practice employment policies which many people would regard as being almost as bad as racism. In 1983, however, religious discrimination was still widely accepted in Scottish football. If Alex Ferguson had tried to stop it he could have alienated some of his Rangers friends, which may explain why he was 'absolutely livid' when the idea of his signing a Catholic was mooted on the radio. No matter what he said, he risked upsetting friends if he took the job. Far better to avoid the issue altogether by staying at Aberdeen.

A few weeks later, in December 1983, Ferguson announced that he wasn't interested in moving to Arsenal either, following the sacking of Terry Neill. It would have been hard to take that job so soon after committing himself so publicly to Aberdeen. Ferguson was familiar with Highbury, having played friendly games there for both Dunfermline and Rangers in 1967, and he admired the club. 'I think that Arsenal are the most glamorous team,' he said, 'and I include Manchester United when I say that.'[10] Arsenal appointed Don Howe, but the Highbury board approached Ferguson again when Howe stepped down in March 1986. This time he went to see the Arsenal directors. 'We never really struck it off during the interview,' Ferguson revealed later, and so George Graham got the job instead. 'They had this idea that I was all set on joining Manchester United. It was genuinely the first I'd heard of it.'[11]

The closest Alex Ferguson came to leaving Aberdeen was a few months after the first Arsenal approach, in the spring of 1984. The Tottenham Hotspur manager, Keith Burkinshaw, had given notice that he was disillusioned and intended to leave White Hart Lane. It was a strange decision, since Spurs went on to win the UEFA Cup that year. Burkinshaw had also won the FA Cup in 1981 and 1982, but he had fallen out with the board – particularly over the former Aberdeen player Steve Archibald, whom he wanted to sell. Ferguson says he liked the way Spurs was run, 'in the sense that they admired pure football and that to me was a big incentive'.[12] The Tottenham chairman Irving Scholar was similarly impressed by Aberdeen's entertaining style. Several phone calls between Ferguson and Scholar early in 1984 were followed by two meetings – held secretly in Paris, where they hoped not to be recognised. Scholar later recalled:

I spent a day listening to his thoughts and aspirations relating purely to football. He was an interesting character and clearly very hungry to succeed . . . He gave me the distinct impression he was a very clear thinker who knew what he wanted and how he would go about getting it; he had the ability to fill you with confidence. You just knew that wherever he went, he would succeed in the future.[13]

It was admiration at first sight. Ferguson liked Scholar's 'ideas and infectious enthusiasm', and he also enjoyed the way the Spurs chairman bombarded him with tricky questions of football trivia.[14] Equally, Scholar thought Ferguson 'totally dedicated, something I found very appealing'. For once, Ferguson was also happy with the pay and conditions he was being offered. At the second meeting, says Scholar, 'Alex Ferguson and I finally shook hands on the agreement that he would become our next Spurs manager . . . During all our discussions we both made it clear that once we'd shaken hands there would be no going back.'[15] It was understood that Ferguson would then prepare Dick Donald and his colleagues for the likely shock, before Scholar made a formal approach to Aberdeen. But the new recruit got cold feet. 'Unfortunately,' Scholar relates, 'Alex Ferguson finally advised me in May that he couldn't go ahead with it because he felt he would be letting his chairman down.'[16]

Ferguson undoubtedly had strong feelings of loyalty towards Dick Donald, but the journalist Mihir Bose, who co-wrote Scholar's book, offers the alternative explanation that Cathy didn't want to move to London. Fifteen years later, just after Alex Ferguson had won the European Cup with Manchester United, Scholar bumped into Cathy and her husband at Nice airport. 'Ah, you are the woman who stopped him coming to Tottenham,' Scholar reportedly said to Cathy Ferguson. She didn't reply.[17]

Publicly, Ferguson said it would have been wrong to go to Spurs when he had just signed a five-year contract with Aberdeen. 'As I am always preaching loyalty to players then I have got to set an example myself.'[18] Subsequently he said the sticking point was the length of the proposed deal. Spurs offered two years, later increased to three, but he wanted enough time 'to create that essential feeling of stability that a club needs if it is to succeed . . . Five years, I insisted. So that was the end of my Spurs story.'[19]

At that time Tottenham were regarded as one of the 'Big Five' clubs in English football, along with Arsenal, Liverpool, Everton and Manchester United, and in financial terms they were considerably bigger than United. In the eighteen years since, Spurs have won just two trophies – the FA Cup in 1991 and the League Cup in 1999 – under nine managers. How very different things might have been had Ferguson stuck to his agreement in Paris.

The other major approach during this time was from Barcelona, though it was less definite than the Spurs offer. It occurred during the 1985–86 season, when the Barcelona president, Josep Nuñez, thought he might soon lose Terry Venables, who had taken charge of the Catalan team in 1984. Nuñez and three Barça colleagues camped themselves in the Connaught Hotel in London and held informal discussions with three leading British managers of that time – Howard Kendall, who had just won the League and the Cup-Winners' Cup with Everton; Bobby Robson, the England manager; and Ferguson. It was Venables himself who actually made the approach, Ferguson says.[20]

Ferguson would later say he turned the Barcelona job down, but according to one of those present at the Connaught, quoted in Jimmy Burns' excellent history of the Barcelona club, the Aberdeen manager was not offered the post on that occasion.[21] (Ferguson may be referring to a separate approach.) In fact it was Robson who most impressed the Barcelona officials, though they eventually retained Terry Venables for another year, and Robson had to wait for his chance at the Nou Camp.

One of the main attractions of staying put was that Dick Donald allowed him a degree of autonomy at Pittodrie which Ferguson would certainly never have enjoyed in Spain or Italy (where Inter Milan were also interested in hiring him), nor indeed at some of the British clubs who courted him. 'I have the best job in the world here,' he once boasted. 'I control everything. I am the manager here not just in name only, and I would want similar working conditions wherever I should choose to go.'[22] It was in sharp contrast to the situation at St Mirren, of course, though Ferguson didn't always get his way at Aberdeen.

In the 1984–85 season Aberdeen had retained their league title despite the team having to be rebuilt after the departure of Strachan, Rougvie and McGhee. The club also won the Scottish Youth Cup, though it isn't the winning that people remember, but the way in which the trophy was secured. At half-time in the final at Pittodrie, the Aberdeen teenagers were losing 2–0 to Celtic. Ferguson walked into the dressing room and told them the club expected more from them. 'If they froze on a big occasion as youth team players then what chance had they as first team players performing in front of a crowd of 60,000 in a Cup Final against the likes of Celtic?' he asked.[23] They were being watched by the entire first-team squad – here was their chance to show what a threat they posed. 'He slaughtered them,' remembers Teddy Scott. 'Some of them were crying.'[24]

It was hard, but effective. After the Aberdeen youths let in a third goal, Ferguson made one of his inspired substitutions, bringing on two fifteen-year-olds, and the deficit was soon clawed back. Aberdeen won the Cup 5–3 in extra time, and Willie Miller and the club's other star names congratulated each teenager individually.

The following season, 1985–86, was rougher sailing, as Aberdeen went five months without an away win and finished fourth.

Nonetheless, they still won both domestic cups. It was the first time Ferguson had won the Scottish League Cup – a trophy he never considered especially important (a view he would also take of its English counterpart). Aberdeen became the first club to win the trophy without conceding a goal (a feat which Celtic emulated in both 1998 and 2000). Ferguson is always conscious of such records, and fielded three centre-backs in the final to ensure it was achieved. Aberdeen beat Hibs 3–0.

With the Scottish Cup, in contrast, it was his fourth win in five years. Here Ferguson showed his ruthless streak, dropping Eric Black after the striker announced he'd secretly agreed to join the French club Metz. Ferguson felt slighted, having nurtured the player's career since he was a teenager. 'If Eric imagined that by telling me two weeks before the Cup final he was setting up a grand exit,' he writes, 'he had a rude awakening. After training that day, I called him in to tell him there was no need for him to come back.'[25] Like Ferguson in 1965, Black had appeared in every previous round of the Scottish Cup; he had also scored important goals in all four previous cup finals he'd played for Aberdeen, including Gothenburg. No matter – the Dons beat Hearts with another 3–0 scoreline.

There was a growing sense, however, that Alex Ferguson's time at Pittodrie was drawing to a close. At the end of 1985 he published his first book, *A Light in the North: Seven Years With Aberdeen*, explaining that he 'felt compelled and totally motivated to record a period of my life which has given me enormous satisfaction and sense of accomplishment, a belief that I've done something really worthwhile'.[26] Unlike most books by football managers and players, which are 'ghosted' by a sympathetic journalist, Ferguson largely composed it himself (though an Aberdeen reporter helped with facts and statistics).

It was a refreshingly candid account for its time. 'He was one of the first people to talk frankly in a non-patronising way to his readers,' says his publisher, Bill Campbell, who used it as a springboard to bring out a series of other sports books. Over a number of 'enjoyable lunches', Ferguson and Campbell had agreed an agenda of topics. Then, whenever Ferguson began a long car journey, he simply switched on a tape and began discussing the next subject. 'He spent half his life in cars,' says Campbell. 'Afterwards we typed up a transcript and worked from that.'[27]

The book sold about 27,000 copies – a huge number given Aberdeen's modest support. When Ferguson attended a signing session at the John Menzies shop in the city centre, mounted police were needed to control the queue of fans on the pavement. 'The great thing about Alec was his enthusiasm,' says Campbell, who recalls how Ferguson would happily do signing sessions even if no one from the publisher was able to accompany him.[28]

Indeed, it's surprising that Ferguson didn't include 'enthusiasm' among the 'vital ingredients of management' which he listed in the book. These were the 'ability to assess, to judge and to act without hesitation', as well as 'being able to weigh up a player, balance a team through the selection of the right players, and, not least of all, to be able to assess yourself, critically if necessary'.[29]

In April 1986, after a comfortable win in the Scottish Cup semifinal, Ferguson broke the news to Dick Donald that he intended to leave Pittodrie that summer. He needed a new challenge. Life had become too easy; there wasn't enough to do in the afternoons. He'd realised that, no matter what he did, there was a limit to how big the club could become. Just as East Stirling could never be as big as St Mirren, and St Mirren could never compare with Aberdeen, so Aberdeen could not be as big as Celtic or Rangers, or the great English and European sides. Aberdeen had too small a population to sustain the size of the support of the Old Firm. Ferguson cites a crowd of 17,000 for the 1986 European Cup quarter-final against Gothenburg (which the Dons lost on away goals) as evidence of this.[30] The official gate was 22,000, in fact, but crowds had certainly been poor for earlier matches. Nevertheless, Dick Donald persuaded his manager not to make a rash decision, but to wait until the summer finally to make up his mind.

While Ferguson made no secret of his long-term ambition to run a really big club, friends say it's unlikely that Cathy would ever have agreed to live abroad. There were only two clubs, they say, that could have lured him even to England – Liverpool and Manchester United. He acknowledged that Liverpool was unlikely, because at that time they tended to promote their managers from within. That left United.

There had already been speculation, early in 1986, that Ferguson would soon replace Ron Atkinson at Old Trafford. The likelihood of Ferguson leaving Pittodrie increased in May that year when his greatest champion there, Chris Anderson, died of motor neurone disease at the age of sixty. But, cleverly, Dick Donald used this moment to tie Ferguson more closely to the club by nominating him as Anderson's replacement on Aberdeen's three-man board of directors. (The other member was now Donald's son Ian, who had played a handful of games as a Manchester United full-back in the early 1970s.) It was unusual at that time for a British manager to be elevated to his club's board, though it has become more common nowadays. 'The Dons are my life now,' he assured Aberdeen fans in a late-August match programme.[31] Ferguson was also given 200 shares in the company, which he has retained ever since.

Nonetheless, it looked unlikely that the next few years at Aberdeen, if he stayed, could be as successful as the last seven. In an effort to shore things up, in the summer of 1986 Ferguson brought back Archie Knox, who'd spent two and a half years managing Dundee with respectable though not spectacular results. In an act of diplomacy, Knox was made 'co-manager', though in fact he continued in the same assistant role as before. Willie Garner, who'd been Ferguson's assistant while Knox was at Dundee, was quickly dismissed. Ferguson had concluded that Garner, who'd been a player in the manager's early days at Aberdeen, was 'far too easy-going to suit my ideas about management' and too close to the players, many of whom had been his teammates.[32] He also thought Garner had been an inadequate stand-in after October 1985, when Ferguson also took responsibility for the Scotland team, and had long spells away from Pittodrie (see Chapter 14). It was a pretty brutal sacking, particularly when Aberdeen had a reputation as a family club. 'I was flabbergasted,' Garner says. 'I'd just bought a new house; I'd just moved to Aberdeen. I really detested the guy at the time, because I had a young family and all of a sudden I had no job.'[33] Because Garner had never signed a contract with Aberdeen, he received neither severance pay nor compensation. It was Garner's last job in football management. Once he'd left Pittodrie the calls dried up, and he now works for a bank.

The 1986–87 season saw the most disappointing start of any of Ferguson's nine at Pittodrie. Two of the famous youth quartet from his early days at Pittodrie had gone – Neale Cooper to Aston Villa as well as Eric Black to Metz. Aberdeen soon went out of the League Cup, and lost in the first round of the European Cup-Winners' Cup to the Swiss club Sion, whom they'd hammered 11–1 on aggregate en route to Gothenburg only four years before. This time they lost the away leg 3–0 after winning 2–1 at home. It was no better in the League, with the Dons already ten points behind Celtic by early November, when the fateful call came through from Old Trafford.

Alex Ferguson had done what nobody else had achieved in twentieth-century Scottish football – upset the natural assumption that the Old Firm must prevail, and that outsiders should count themselves lucky to collect the occasional scrap. Of the twenty-five domestic trophies contested during Ferguson's eight and a half years at Pittodrie, Aberdeen won eight, Celtic and Rangers both seven each, and Dundee United three. On top of that, Aberdeen had also won the European Cup-Winners' Cup (and the less significant European Super Cup). In three seasons Ferguson won three doubles of different varieties: 1982–83 (Cup and Cup-Winners' Cup);

1983–84 (League and Cup); 1985–86 (both domestic cups). Only once in the twentieth century had any team outside the Old Firm – Hearts in 1960 – ever won any kind of double.

The 431 league points that Aberdeen collected under Ferguson between 1978 and 1986 were bettered only by Celtic's 449 over the same period, but easily surpassed Dundee United's 396 and Rangers' 352. Ferguson's complete record in games against his main rivals was:

Opponent	*League*						*Cup*					
	P	W	D	L	F	A	P	W	D	L	F	A
Celtic	33	13	9	11	49	38	10	6	3	1	12	7
Rangers	33	17	11	5	51	25	8	5	0	3	14	7
Dundee U.	34	14	9	11	53	42	12	4	3	5	6	12

Ferguson had unquestionably bettered all three sides in their league encounters, and the only blemish was the way Dundee United had outwitted Aberdeen in the cups.

In more than a decade with East Stirling, St Mirren and now Aberdeen, Alex Ferguson had honed, developed and started to perfect a formula for success. It was based on creating a group of players who saw things his way, wouldn't argue too much, and adopted the Ferguson philosophy of playing entertaining football, constant effort, and never accepting defeat. 'Money counts for less,' he said, 'than finding and nurturing your own lads and teaching them the virtues of discipline, self-control, punctuality; those kind of things.'[34] A 'family unit' is how he described his group of players. Young men, all roughly the same age, they'd grown up and matured together in the same small city, and had developed a powerful *esprit de corps*. For many of the younger players, Ferguson became a father figure. Alex McLeish, for instance, says that when his own father died

223

unexpectedly in his early forties Ferguson stepped in and 'assured me that he would take my dad's place as much as he could in keeping me up to scratch'.[35]

At Aberdeen the stars groomed by Alex Ferguson included John Hewitt, Neale Simpson, Eric Black and Neale Cooper. But in the years to come he would conclude that he had pushed these promising stars too quickly, too hard and too early. 'He wanted to get the maximum out of his young players without any regard to the consequences,' said Mark McGhee, who describes Ferguson's attitude as 'mercenary'.[36] 'There were players shattered at twenty-five and you had to ask yourself why,' Ferguson later observed, with obvious pangs of conscience. 'Maybe they had too much first-team football with all the pressure that brings.'[37] 'No-one was to blame but we did not realise what damage was being done to our bodies,' says Eric Black, who retired early because of a back injury. 'Maybe I was asked too much too soon.'[38]

In an early analysis, in 1983, of why he had become so successful, Ferguson admitted that he'd once felt 'twinges of bitterness' after finishing his playing career without winning anything, but said they were now 'evaporating'. He also made the candid and revealing confession that 'I'm not a confident person at all. I worry like hell about all sorts of things. Team talks, for instance.'[39]

Outwardly there was little sign of any self-doubt. Indeed, perhaps the most common characteristic of Ferguson's Aberdeen teams was their mental strength. Players such as Willie Miller, Stuart Kennedy, Alex McLeish, Gordon Strachan, Doug Rougvie, Neale Cooper and Mark McGhee were the type never to break down, either from outside forces or under the incessant pressure from their manager. Playing for Alex Ferguson required stamina and resilience. Not everyone had it; nor could they always keep it up. 'Some players could maybe do it for a wee while,' says Alex McLeish,

and then it just became too tiring for them mentally –

'I cannot keep doing this. I cannot keep up this win, win, win mentality.' That's when he distinguished the quality from the guys who didn't want to do it for him. The heavy-handed style, the rule by fear and aggression, it worked in that era. If you buckled under it, if you didn't have the mentality for it, you would have been an ex-Aberdeen player. But there was a lot of character in that team, to do it week in, week out, to live up to his demands.[40]

And Ferguson could boast of a superb record when it came to buying the right players who would comply with his way of doing things. As with his young recruits, he spent a lot of time investigating potential buys before he made bids – looking into their histories, family, habits and private lives, and working out whether they'd fit into his regime on and off the park. In *A Light in the North* he cites the buying of Andy Harrow from Luton for £65,000 as 'my only real failure in my dealings in the transfer market'.[41] Others might add Davie Dodds, whom he signed for £200,000 after his book was published and who was never a great success at Pittodrie.

Twelve of Ferguson's men played for Scotland. Willie Miller and Alex McLeish both captained their country, while Miller, McLeish and Jim Leighton are among the six most capped Scotland players of all time (with 233 caps between them). Billy McNeill, his predecessor at Pittodrie, identifies the Leighton–Miller–McLeish defensive triangle as the backbone of Ferguson's successful sides. 'The importance is that if you've got a good defence it takes the pressure off your forwards, because one goal is often enough to secure victory. In Gordon Strachan he had probably one of the few genuine world-class players we've produced in modern times.'[42] Modestly, McNeill plays down his own contribution to the Aberdeen success story, though all four players were there in his day. Where Ferguson made the difference was in shaping those players – all strong characters and great competitors – into one unit playing his brand of football.

Great sides tend to spawn future managers. At least seventeen players who served under Alex Ferguson at Pittodrie tried the managerial path – Archibald, Black, Neale Cooper, Neil Cooper, Dornan, Fleming, Garner, Harper, Harrow, Hewitt, McGhee, McLeish, Miller, Rougvie, Stark, Strachan and Sullivan. So far, however, only three have really made a name for themselves: Gordon Strachan, who managed Coventry before moving to Southampton; Mark McGhee, now at Millwall; and Alex McLeish, who took over Rangers in 2001 after doing a good job at Hibs.

Eric Black, now manager of Motherwell, believes that Ferguson's success stemmed in part from his not having been a brilliant footballer himself. 'If you ask a lot of the top players to analyse "Why did you run into that position when the ball was there?" a lot of them probably wouldn't know what to tell you. They do it instinctively.' For Alex Ferguson, playing football came less naturally. He had to consider what he was doing on the field, and was intelligent enough to do so. 'It maybe forces you to think about the game a bit more,' Black suggests.[43]

The Aberdeen director Ian Donald admired Ferguson's extraordinary ability to get to the heart of any problem, situation or person. After matches, says Donald, Ferguson would go into the boardroom and analyse games 'perfectly' – and, unlike at St Mirren, he was addressing directors who knew their football. He had the same knack in assessing individuals. 'He seems to be able to sum up someone. "To speak to this guy, and handle this guy, I need to speak to him in such and such a way," he would say.'[44] 'He knew the players he could trust,' says Willie Miller, who was rarely the victim of Ferguson's tongue. 'He knew the players he had to stamp on, and he knew the times that he had to get effect. He knew the times he could take the pedal off. Judging the personalities and atmosphere is one of his strengths.'[45]

Yet, despite the efforts of Dick Donald and Chris Anderson to smooth off his rougher edges, Ferguson still displayed some of the flaws which had got him sacked from Love Street. A local sports reporter, Frank Gilfeather, remembers Chris Anderson confiding that Ferguson behaved like a 'megalomaniac', but adding that the board put up with his desire to control everything because he was so successful.[46] Anderson was particularly concerned about the abrasive way his manager handled the press (see Chapter 26).

On a personal level, Cathy Ferguson, despite her misgivings about moving north, had come to enjoy living in Aberdeen; she found the lack of religious bigotry particularly refreshing after spending all her previous life in Glasgow. The boys were at a good local school, Cults Academy, and the Fergusons had made many friends in the area. These included their solicitor, Les Delgarno; a local builder, Gordon Campbell; Alan McRae, who runs a joinery business; and George Ramsay, who owns the Aberdeen fish factory with which Ferguson sometimes threatened his players.

The Ramsays paid for the Fergusons to go with them on a cruise holiday. But, while these new Aberdeen friendships may have reinforced his marriage, they didn't make Alex Ferguson a more full-time father. 'Alex's kids never saw him when they were young,' says George Ramsay. 'He was never at home. We were out every Saturday after the game, going for meals.'[47] Even when he took his family on holiday, Ferguson found it hard to get away from football. Their trip to Spain in the summer of 1982, for example, was combined with watching that summer's World Cup.

Alex Ferguson is still in touch with this Aberdeen entourage. They are good examples of how, over the years, he has gathered round him a group of genuinely close friends who are usually not football professionals, but fans who have been successful in other walks of life – often business. The Aberdeen friends frequently come to stay at Fairfields, and, although they are all primarily Dons' supporters, they often travel with Ferguson when Manchester United play in Europe, reliving the great times they had beneath the northern lights.

With hindsight, it's clear that Ferguson chose to leave Aberdeen at an opportune moment. The great Cup-Winners' Cup side had gradually broken up; Ferguson's ally and adviser Chris Anderson was dead; and even the local economy faltered around the time he left, when the oil industry went into recession. Above all, Ferguson would have faced competition from a rejuvenated Rangers. Under the managership of the former Liverpool and Scotland player Graeme Souness, with money injected by the club's new owner, David Murray, and a totally rebuilt, all-seat Ibrox, Rangers spent the next decade as the wealthiest, best-supported and most successful club in Britain. The Glasgow side took advantage of the English clubs' ban from Europe (following the 1985 Heysel Stadium disaster) to attract from south of the border several top players who wanted to play in Continental competition. In 1988 Rangers won the first of what would turn out to be nine successive Scottish League titles, equalling the historic feat of Jock Stein's Celtic.

Aberdeen, in contrast, went into a steady decline. Ferguson thought the board mad to appoint the laid-back Ian Porterfield as his successor, and neither Porterfield nor any of the six subsequent managers lasted long. Even though Aberdeen were league runners-up five times between 1987 and 1994, they never threatened Rangers' new hegemony. The Dons also won both cups in 1990, and the League Cup again in 1996, but these successes only disguised their deterioration. In 2000 Aberdeen finished bottom of the Scottish Premier League and escaped relegation only by luck – a combination of the expansion of the League from ten clubs to twelve and the fact that Falkirk's stadium was declared inadequate for the top tier. As the club prepares to celebrate its centenary in 2003, Aberdeen fans know that more than half the major trophies in their history (nine out of seventeen) were won during the reign of Alexander Chapman Ferguson.

Today, many people in the Granite City look back on Alex Ferguson's eight and a half years in the north as a golden age. 'We just seemed to spend our lives having civic receptions and dinner dances,' says Chris Anderson's widow, Christine. 'They were wonderful evenings, those European ties.'[48] Alex Ferguson's friend Hugh McIlvanney, who also helped write his autobiography, would describe the manager's time at Pittodrie as 'nothing less than one of the most remarkable feats of management in the history of the British game'.[49]

In the spring of 1999 Ferguson returned to Aberdeen to be awarded the freedom of the city (which gave him the right to herd his sheep along Union Street). In a ceremony at the city's Music Hall, wearing a strange hat to which a scroll was then attached, he reminisced about his side's successes in Europe. 'I'm not sure anything could surpass it,' he said, abandoning any pretence to the kind of humility his father espoused. 'It was quite an emphatic time, wonderfully successful. It elevated the city and the team to a level no one could understand. In essence it was a fairy tale.'[50]

Keeping Scotland's Dignity

'Quite frankly, I wouldn't take Jock Stein's job for a million pounds! Being manager of our national side is a thankless and difficult job . . . If I were in Jock's shoes . . . then I would definitely go for a team comprising totally of home Scots.'

Alex Ferguson, 1980[1]

'Whatever the result,' Jock Stein advised his assistant, 'we must keep our dignity.'[2] The Scotland manager was talking to Alex Ferguson as they watched their team struggle with Wales in a decisive World Cup qualifying match in Cardiff in September 1985. Wales needed to win, Scotland to draw, for one or the other to go through to a play-off against the winners of the Oceania/Israel group. But the Welsh team of Ian Rush, Mark Hughes and Neville Southall were no pushover, and had already beaten the Scots in Glasgow the previous spring.

After thirteen minutes Hughes put the home side 1–0 ahead. Throughout the first half Jim Leighton seemed to be in trouble in the Scotland goal, frequently misjudging the flight of the ball. What was wrong? an angry Ferguson demanded at half-time. Leighton admitted that he'd lost a contact lens out on the pitch; worse still, he'd forgotten to bring his spare pair with him. Ferguson was annoyed and embarrassed. Annoyed that, in seven years together at Aberdeen, Leighton had never told him he wore lenses, and embarrassed because Jock Stein clearly found it hard to believe that Ferguson didn't know this. For a few moments there was a sense of panic in the Scotland camp, and Stein had no choice but to substitute Leighton with Alan Rough.

Salvation came just nine minutes from the end of the game, when David Speedie drove the ball against a Welsh defender's arm. Penalty! Davie Cooper stroked the ball past Southall, and the Scots went wild. But Jock Stein didn't say a word. While everyone else leaped to their feet, he sat motionless on the trainers' bench. Ferguson patted him on the head, not realising there was anything wrong. A few minutes later the whistle went. The Scotland manager thought the match was over, though the referee was actually blowing for a free kick. As Jock Stein rose, he stumbled. He was quickly carried away by the Scottish doctor and a policeman, who propped him up on their shoulders.

A 1–1 draw left the Welsh downcast and the Scots triumphant. As the delighted players came off the Ninian Park pitch that summer evening, a sombre-looking Alex Ferguson barred their way. He told them that Stein had collapsed, but said they should stay on the pitch and do a lap of honour for the travelling Scottish fans. When they eventually returned to the dressing room the players heard that Stein had suffered a heart attack and was receiving emergency treatment in the medical room next door.

At first Ferguson thought Stein would pull through. It was about an hour before he and the players learned the worst. According to Alex McLeish:

> Most of us had showered and dressed when Fergie entered
> the dressing room and slumped into a chair near the door
> without uttering a word.
>   'Any news, boss?' I asked, and it was as if my voice had
> aroused him from a private reverie. He started, looked up and
> said simply: 'Jock's dead.'[3]

Later Alex Ferguson had to break the news to Stein's family. In subsequent years he often wondered whether he should have paid more attention to the fact that Stein had seemed poorly earlier in the evening. Indeed, Gordon Strachan says that when he was substituted during the game he wanted to argue with Stein, but Ferguson told him, 'Leave it alone. He's not well. Just leave it.'[4] Stein's son George says Ferguson wouldn't have got far even if he had tried to check on his father's health.[5]

Jock Stein's death hit Alex Ferguson almost as hard as that of his own father six years earlier. And, just as with Alex Snr (and Dick Donald), the thing Ferguson almost invariably recalls about Stein is his modesty, and how it was difficult to get him to talk about his achievements. 'He had the kind of humility that only really great men possess,' says Ferguson. 'Not well-known men, genuinely great men. He was one of them.'[6]

Although they'd never worked together at club level, it was Stein who had first suggested Ferguson's transfer to Dunfermline in 1964, and, while Stein had moved on before Ferguson arrived, his influence was still felt at the club. Alex and Cathy Ferguson would often bump into Stein and his wife when eating at the Beechwood, the restaurant where Pat Harkins once taught Ferguson basic catering skills. 'We would sit and talk about the game for hours,' Ferguson says.[7] Stein had effectively advised Ferguson to take the St Mirren job; he'd accompanied the Aberdeen side on their great night in Gothenburg. And in the summer of 1984, when Stein needed a part-time assistant to succeed Jim McLean in working with the national side in the run-up to the 1986 World Cup, Ferguson was both the obvious choice and keen to accept the post.

He agreed despite his commitments with Aberdeen, but with conditions. He wanted to be called 'coach' rather than 'assistant' – on the grounds, he said, that 'people would start talking about me being a possible successor for the Scotland manager's job. I don't want that.

It isn't fair to anyone.'[8] On the other hand, he wanted Stein to consult him about team selection. Stein did sometimes.

In part, Ferguson wanted the job in order to learn as much as he could by working with a great manager, and he thinks Stein must at times have got fed up with his persistent questions. Ferguson's main role was to supervise the training sessions and to monitor prospective players in Scottish football. Stein concentrated on the 'Anglos' – Scots playing in England – though he had to be careful not to exert himself too much after his car crash and heart attack in the 1970s.

It helped their relationship that the two men came from similar working-class backgrounds. 'Politically, we were soul-mates,' says Ferguson, who joined the Scotland camp during the high drama of the 1984–85 coal strike. Stein, an ex-miner, would wave his fist at strike-breaking coal lorries which passed them on the road, and Ferguson tells of an occasion when the Scotland manager admonished him for neglecting to help miners who were collecting money for their strike fund outside a football ground. 'I'm surprised at you of all people forgetting these lads,' Stein reportedly told him, demanding £5 from Ferguson to add to the £10 he contributed himself.[9] The irony was that, despite their socialism, they were both 'boss'-style managers who had reputations for bullying players.

Following Stein's sudden death, Alex Ferguson was now the SFA's obvious choice to succeed him. Scotland needed a manager for the two play-off games that autumn; if they won, there was the World Cup tournament itself in Mexico the following summer. Ferguson had serious reservations. He felt that, at forty-three, he was too young to be running the national team. There was also the question of how much control the SFA would give him. He would take the job permanently, he said, only if he could run the whole set-up: not just the full national eleven, but all the younger representative teams as well – the Under-21s, Under-18s and so on. The SFA refused to accept this, so Ferguson took the Scotland post on a temporary basis, and combined it with his responsibilities at Pittodrie. It was agreed to review the situation after the World Cup.

There was one other difficulty. Ferguson was at that time again in trouble with the SFA for belligerent behaviour on the touchline as Aberdeen manager. Given his long list of punishments for previous offences, the SFA were under pressure to take a firm line with the man they were hoping would bring them glory in Mexico. Ferguson defused the issue by announcing that he would withdraw voluntarily from the side of the pitch for all future club games.

Ferguson had another concern: the obvious conflict of interest. Several Aberdeen players were either in the Scotland side or on the fringe of selection. Then there was the problem which afflicts all national team managers: of spending so little time with their players. Ferguson found it embarrassing to leave major stars like Alan Hansen out of the side, for example, 'when I don't have time to build a relationship, when the players don't know me and it's all "hello" and "cheerio".'[10]

Alex Ferguson also knew that looking after a national team was a very different proposition from being manager of a club. Unlike at St Mirren or Aberdeen, he couldn't simply mould his kind of team from his breed of men, discarding those who wouldn't go along with the Ferguson philosophy. There wasn't time to spend years nurturing young Ferguson-type footballers through reserve and junior sides.

What's more, Ferguson couldn't treat members of the Scotland team in the aggressive, overbearing way he handled club players. Many were experienced professionals with dozens of international caps, whereas Ferguson had none. The two biggest names in the squad were also managers themselves – of the most successful club in England and of the wealthiest club in Scotland. Kenny Dalglish was not only one of the most decorated players of all time, he had just won the English double at the end of his first season as player/manager of Liverpool – only the third time the feat had been performed in the twentieth century. (He'd even clinched the League personally by scoring the winning goal in his club's final game at Chelsea.)

Similarly, by the time of the World Cup, the Scottish captain, Graeme Souness (a former Liverpool colleague of Dalglish's), had become player/manager of Rangers. These were men, not boys, with football records at least as impressive as Ferguson's. Willie Miller says 'bawling at Souness or having an eyeball with Kenny Dalglish' wouldn't have worked, 'because these guys wouldn't have experienced that sort of approach. Certainly not the Liverpool team, because everything was laid-back at Liverpool. It was the boot-room scenario, wasn't it? – all pals, all having a cup of tea and a digestive biscuit in the boot room, and a chat.'[11]

It's interesting that, during his brief spell as Scotland manager, Ferguson had major problems with all three of the main Liverpool personalities – Kenny Dalglish, Graeme Souness and Alan Hansen, who was then captain of the club. All three had played for the Merseyside team on the night in 1980 when they beat Aberdeen 4–0 in the European Cup – Ferguson's worst result during his time at Pittodrie. Liverpool's victory was so comprehensive that Kenny Dalglish believes it may have left Ferguson with a permanent 'scar'.[12]

Ferguson says Jock Stein had reservations about the attitude of the Liverpool contingent, and he himself first encountered problems while Stein was still manager, during preparations for the first qualifying game against Wales. When Ferguson asked for advice on how to counter the threat of their Liverpool teammate Ian Rush, neither Kenny Dalglish nor Alan Hansen nor the midfielder Steve Nicol would say anything very helpful. This was in complete contrast to Arthur Albiston, who was happy to advise his fellow Scots on how to handle his Manchester United colleague Mark Hughes. When Stein and Ferguson raised the matter later with Graeme Souness, Souness explained it was 'the Liverpool version of *omerta* – say nothing about anything'.[13]

Alex Ferguson's first task, of course, was to confirm Scotland's place in the finals with a two-legged play-off against Australia. The Aussies were hardly giants of world football, but Scotland had a habit of stumbling against supposedly easy opponents – one only had to remember the dreadful 1–1 draw with Iran in the 1978 World Cup finals. Spurred by the thought of winning for their dead manager, Scotland followed a 2–0 victory at Hampden with a 0–0 draw in the second leg at the Melbourne Cricket Ground. But the away game involved a nine-day 22,000-mile round trip, with six days' preparation in Australia to get used to temperature and time changes. It had been difficult to get players released, particularly from English clubs. Kenny Dalglish, for instance, stayed behind because of his commitments as Liverpool manager.

Following the side's qualification, Ferguson had just four friendly games to prepare his squad for Mexico. That winter the Scots beat Israel 1–0 at Hampden, and then Romania 3–0. They lost 2–1 to England at Wembley in April, and then had a scoreless draw in Holland. The most promising sign for Mexico was the defence – five clean sheets in six games under Ferguson (including an earlier 0–0 draw in a friendly with East Germany). Indeed, only England had breached the Scottish goal.

Ferguson had far better players at his disposal than his modern counterparts. At that time dozens of Scots held regular places in the English First Division. World Cup managers always face disputes over whom they leave out of the twenty-two-man squads they are allowed to take to the finals, but Ferguson faced bigger arguments than most.

One problem was the surplus of good Scottish forwards. Heading the list was Kenny Dalglish, who had just become the top Scotland goalscorer of all time (jointly with Denis Law) on top of his 100 caps. Behind him were Charlie Nicholas, Frank McAvennie, Graeme Sharp, David Speedie, Paul Sturrock, Steve Archibald, Andy Gray, Ally McCoist, Brian McClair and Mo Johnston. Apart from Dalglish, however, none had really established himself as an international striker, nor was there any obvious pairing. McCoist, McClair and Johnston, who played for the Old Firm clubs, were given early notice of their exclusion when Ferguson announced a twenty-nine-man World Cup shortlist in March 1986. While McCoist and McClair can hardly have been surprised, since they'd never played for Scotland in the past, Mo Johnston felt 'nothing but bitterness'. He boasted a reasonable strike rate – four goals in eight Scotland appearances – and said he would never forgive Ferguson. His is 'the name I hate most in the world', he said in his autobiography two years later.[14]

Johnston felt he'd been left out because of his lifestyle, having been discovered, he admits, with a girl in his room when the squad was in Australia. Johnston also suspected there was a whispering campaign against him after police raided his home at 4 a.m. one night on suspicion of drug offences. There were never any charges, and Johnston denied ever taking illegal drugs, though he confessed to high living in other respects. 'Some people were actually capable of dovetailing nightlife with goalscoring,' he claimed. 'I could wine, dine and win.'[15]

It was not an attitude likely to impress Alex Ferguson, who felt Johnston's behaviour off the pitch made him a liability, particularly when the team would be away together for several weeks. Nor was it just a matter of having a woman in his room, for the SFA chief executive, Ernie Walker, had apparently seen Johnston cavorting naked with the girl in a hotel corridor. On another evening Johnston and Frank McAvennie had brought three women into the bar and started buying drinks for everyone.

While Johnston believed Ferguson changed for the worse 'when he became the big chief', most Scotland players thought the opposite, and noticed how relaxed he seemed to be, compared with the tyrannical Aberdeen manager of reputation.[16] Charlie Nicholas, for instance, who detested the way Ferguson's players had roughed him up whenever Celtic met Aberdeen, now 'found it impossible not to like Fergie'. In particular, he was grateful for the advice that

Ferguson had given when Nicholas was going through a poor spell with his new club, Arsenal. 'He went out of his way to encourage me, to give me the boost that perhaps I needed at that time. It was important to me and underlined, again, just how much the personal touch can mean between a player and a manager.'[17] Nicholas made the World Cup squad at Johnston's expense.

The biggest controversy came over the omission of Alan Hansen. Although the Liverpool captain was one of the most effective defenders in the world, he had long found it hard to squeeze into the Scotland side when Willie Miller and Alex McLeish of Aberdeen were such an effective partnership for both club and country. But the decision to leave Hansen behind only fuelled a suspicion that Ferguson favoured Aberdeen players.

Ferguson claims that Jock Stein had warned him that Hansen often withdrew from the squad, and that Stein had also confided before his death that he himself didn't plan to take the Liverpool defender to Mexico. Hansen had pulled out a few days before the decisive encounter in Cardiff, for example, and Ferguson finally lost patience with him just before the Scots met England in a friendly at Wembley in April 1986 – their last game but one before the World Cup finals. Ferguson had planned to pick the Liverpool man, but Hansen suffered a recurrence of a knee injury while the Scots were training in Luton, and announced he was going home to Merseyside. 'That really, to me, decided Alan Hansen's fate,' says Ferguson.[18]

Hansen has claimed that, after he withdrew from the England game, Ferguson 'blanked' him a few days later at Kenny Dalglish's testimonial. He also accused his manager of being behind a spate of newspaper articles saying he wouldn't be going to Mexico. 'One of the surest signs is when a manager stops speaking to you,' Hansen wrote later. 'I realised that the stories in the Sunday newspapers had been leaked.' He now knew he wouldn't be picked for the World Cup squad, and later described this as 'possibly . . . the biggest blow in my entire career'.[19] Yet Ferguson must have noticed that

Hansen had missed only one game in fifty-eight for his club that season.

Years later, in his 1999 autobiography, Ferguson was particularly critical of the Liverpool defender. 'His tendency to pull out of Scotland matches had raised a question in my mind about his reliability and perhaps his attitude.' Hansen was never as 'remarkable' a player for Scotland, Ferguson added, as he was for Liverpool.[20] Hansen quickly disputed these claims, accusing his former boss of failing to be straight with him at the time. 'I find it strange', Hansen wrote in response, 'that Ferguson did not appreciate my position, given that he openly campaigns for friendly internationals to be abolished and often withdraws Manchester United players from international duty if they are carrying a slight injury.'[21]

But Ferguson was worried about how Hansen's club manager and friend Kenny Dalglish might react to the Liverpool defender's omission from the World Cup party. Ferguson phoned him a couple of times beforehand to discuss Hansen and to warn Dalglish that he would probably leave the defender out. A more adaptable player was needed, said Ferguson – one who could play in two or three positions. Dalglish warned him it was a great mistake. The night the squad was announced, the Liverpool player/manager went round to Hansen's home with a bottle of champagne to console him.

Ten days later Kenny Dalglish rang Ferguson to deliver the bad news that he himself was withdrawing from the squad. A surgeon had told him not to play, he explained, as the ligament was detached from his knee. Many people naturally suspected that this was a deliberate snub by Dalglish, since Hansen is one of his closest friends. But it's hard to believe the Liverpool player/manager would have turned his back on the World Cup for such a petty reason, and given up the chance of becoming the first British footballer (and only the eighth worldwide) to appear in four finals tournaments. There would also have been the opportunity to overtake Denis Law and become Scotland's leading goalscorer outright. Dalglish had been grateful to Ferguson for making him national captain when he won his hundredth cap early in 1986, and also for managing a team in his Scottish testimonial game. Nonetheless, with hindsight, the withdrawal has inevitably been seen as the first episode in an intense rivalry between the two men. Despite their regular protestations to the contrary, and public tokens of respect and affection for each other, there's undoubtedly an underlying distrust between them, and this is partly fuelled by what happened before the 1986 World Cup.

One can understand Ferguson's frustrations. Unlike Hansen, Dalglish hadn't been a regular in the Liverpool side but had saved himself for the final six weeks of the season, when he played in every game up to the FA Cup final – only to pull out of the Scotland squad just two days later. Ferguson was so annoyed he had to go out and drive round in his car to cool down. In his autobiography he says several times that Dalglish's announcement was a disappointment, and he writes of the huge difference that Dalglish might have made to Scotland's performance. He acknowledges that Dalglish was 'a truly world-class player in the later years of his playing career and that he was in his prime at the time of the qualifying campaign for Mexico'.[22] He doesn't express scepticism about Dalglish's injury, but nor does he express any sympathy. Quite apart from the '*omerta*' incident that led him to question Dalglish's commitment, he also criticises the Liverpool man for earlier threatening to boycott a sponsored Scotland team photograph (shades of Ferguson and Falkirk) because he didn't think the £5,000 fee was good enough. Reading between the lines of the book, it's clear that Ferguson suspected that Dalglish's withdrawal was linked to Hansen's omission. 'I'd flicked half my knee ligament!' counters Dalglish. 'The specialist said that there was no way I could play, and he was the expert and Alex wasn't. What motive would I have had to deliberately miss the World Cup finals? It's every player's dream. If Alan Hansen had been on that plane, I would have still been at home injured.'[23]

Even if he had lost his star player, Ferguson had gathered a coaching team of the highest calibre. It included the two men who succeeded him as Scotland manager: his old Falkirk striking partner Andy Roxburgh and Craig Brown, who was then manager of First Division Clyde and rather surprised to be picked. The backroom staff also included Walter Smith, whom he'd failed to recruit as his assistant at Aberdeen; Archie Knox, who later filled that job; and even Teddy Scott, the Aberdeen trainer. Craig Brown remembers Ferguson's 'photographic memory' for what had happened during matches. 'I discovered that at half-time he could recollect every move, every pass in the first half. Never mind a video camera, he can recount exactly how a game went.'[24]

The Scots were drawn in Group E, which was probably the toughest of the six World Cup groupings in 1986 and acquired the 'Group of Death' label. Their opponents included both West Germany and Uruguay, who'd won the World Cup four times between them, and also a strong Denmark team. There was no point in repeating the hype of 1978, when Ally MacLeod had encouraged Scots to think they might win the trophy. In all their five previous World Cup finals tournaments Scotland had never got beyond the first group stage, and Ferguson knew it would be hard to do better this time. Perhaps because everyone's expectations were so low, the atmosphere in the Scotland party was surprisingly relaxed, both in the pre-tournament preparation in the United States and then in Mexico itself.

However complete their preparations had been on the pitch, the Scotland team had been somewhat compromised by Ferguson's part-time status. Although he had promised to 'cut down dramatically on what one might call extra-curricular activities', not even a man of his energy could devote the same attention to the job as a full-time national manager.[25] He did squeeze in a trip to Ipswich, seeking advice from the former England boss Sir Alf Ramsey about conditions in Mexico, but he inevitably had to cut corners elsewhere. A lot of preparatory work had to be left to SFA officials, and Ferguson didn't have time, for instance, to go and inspect the Scottish team's accommodation in Mexico City. 'Not to put too fine a point on it, the hotel was a disaster,' says Gordon Strachan.[26] The rooms were small and had no telephones; the food was bad; there was little to keep the squad entertained; there were guards everywhere; and the hotel was well inside the range of Mexico City's notorious pollution.

Ferguson seemed less concerned than he would have been at Aberdeen about his players occasionally going out and enjoying themselves. In the training camp in Santa Fe in New Mexico, for example, they were allowed to eat out at night, to visit the local race-track, and to have a beer and a bet during 'video racenights'. 'The manager was very much one of the boys,' said Roy Aitken. 'There wasn't a 'them' and 'us' attitude between players, staff and officials.'[27] To prevent cliques developing, players were allocated different seating places for each meal.

At one point, it's said, Ferguson even deliberately disappeared from the team hotel so that his players could let their hair down. Another evening Ferguson took the entire coaching staff out to dinner at a smart hotel where there was a baby grand piano in the lounge. Towards the end of the meal he offered to play for his colleagues, adding that it was some time since he'd last performed. His offer was met with disbelief: nobody was aware that Fergie was a pianist. 'During his time with us, he has told me everything,' said Teddy Scott, 'described in detail every daft goal he ever scored and all the easy chances he ever missed. He never keeps quiet, but I never knew he could play the piano.'[28] Little did they know that the instrument could be programmed to play automatically.

'Even the Aberdeen players were surprised by the way the manager handled the squad,' said the goalkeeper Alan Rough. 'He treated us like adults.'[29] Craig Brown says Ferguson taught him during that period that you shouldn't 'belittle' experienced professionals but should listen to what they say. 'It may be different at club level, but at international level you can't really bully players. Fergie was excellent with the players. He would sit them all round, have a blade of grass between his teeth and say, "Right, what about free kicks on the edge of the box?"' The squad made suggestions; Ferguson considered what they said, and then carefully explained what they should do. 'Whenever he talked, the players listened,' Brown says. 'They all realised how bright he was, and they wanted to learn.'[30]

Scotland got off to a disappointing start in Mexico. They lost 1–0 to Denmark, though they'd played reasonably well, and what appeared to be a perfectly good goal by Roy Aitken was disallowed for offside. Next came Franz Beckenbauer's West Germany in the scorching midday heat. Gordon Strachan raised Scots' hopes with an early strike, but they succumbed 2–1. It was two defeats from two games, yet, because of other results and the strange way the tournament was structured, Scotland could still qualify for the next stage if they beat Uruguay in the last group game. The South Americans had just lost 6–1 to Denmark.

The game could not have begun better for Scotland. After only forty seconds Uruguay were down to ten men, when José Batista was sent off for a terrible foul on Gordon Strachan. But Scotland never capitalised on their numerical advantage, and the Uruguayans were allowed to get away with many subsequent offences unpunished. The South Americans spat at the Scots, punched them when the referee wasn't looking, and pulled them up by the hair after they had hacked them down. It's even said that, during a corner, Graeme Sharp was distracted when a Uruguayan finger was pushed up his back passage. Steve Nicol missed an easy chance, and the game ended 0–0. The Uruguayans also wasted time, of course, by pretending to go down injured. The SFA chief executive, Ernie Walker, later called them the 'scum of the earth', while FIFA fined Uruguay for misbehaviour and threatened to expel them from the competition.[31]

Both Craig Brown and Alan Rough feel that Ferguson should have gambled with what the goalkeeper calls 'the kind of inspired substitution for which he had become noted' at Aberdeen and should have replaced the striker Paul Sturrock much sooner. 'There was nothing to lose and a lot to gain with a bold throw of the dice.'[32] Had Scotland played nearly as well as they had against Denmark and West Germany, however, they would have won.

The big talking point was Ferguson's decision, made public only minutes before kick-off, to drop his captain, Graeme Souness. The Rangers player/manager was thirty-three, and it was thought he might not have enough energy for a third match in Mexico's intense heat. He was losing up to twelve pounds a game through dehydration, and Ferguson and the coaching team felt he had looked tired towards the end of the fixture against Germany. Gordon Strachan says Souness looked 'as if he was playing his last game of the season. He looked really drained.'[33] Walter Smith argued that Souness should play against Uruguay; Craig Brown and the other coaches sided with the manager. It was a courageous decision, a typical Ferguson gamble. Only this time it failed.

'I made a mess of that,' Ferguson says now, admitting that Souness should have played.[34] Willie Miller feels that, after Batista's sending-off, Souness would have had the ideal experience to exploit the Scots' advantage in numbers. But Ferguson couldn't even bring him on as a substitute, having decided it would be humiliating to put Souness on the subs' bench – a view endorsed by the player himself.

Ferguson's decision not to play Steve Archibald may also have been critical, though in a different respect. Archibald 'took it badly and there was a row', the manager explained afterwards, confessing he should then have settled down and marshalled his thoughts before going on to give the team their pre-match talk. 'It was a mistake. I should have stepped back for an hour and prepared myself. We'd lost that game before it kicked off.'[35] Instead of thinking carefully through the important points to make, his talk was 'distinctly poor', and degenerated into rhetoric about how good his players all were compared with their opponents. 'That was all right when I was manager of St Mirren but was out of place with Scotland,' he wrote.[36]

Alex McLeish was also left out against Uruguay following a recent bout of flu. His place went to David Narey, though it's possible the switch might never have happened had McLeish not been an Aberdeen player. McLeish remained upset with Ferguson for several days, and this incident was another illustration of the problems of a club manager needing to avoid seeming to favour his own players when also taking charge of the national team. Steve Archibald, too, might have played from the start of the tournament had it not been for 'the nagging embarrassment about the Aberdeen connection'.[37] Yet nobody could deny that Jim Leighton, Willie Miller and Gordon Strachan all played exceedingly well over the course of Scotland's three games.

The Scots finished bottom of Group E with a single point. For the first time since 1958 they were returning from a World Cup without having won a game. And, despite the surplus of great forwards, they'd scored just once – from Gordon Strachan, a midfielder. But Scotland hadn't disgraced themselves, either on the field or off. There were no humiliating results. With more luck they might have snatched a draw against Denmark or beaten Uruguay, and reached the next round. It's highly unlikely, however, that they would have gone any further, since they then would have encountered the great Argentina side of Diego Maradona, which eventually won the World Cup that year.

'It pained me deeply that I had been unable to improve upon a depressingly familiar script,' said Ferguson later.[38] For the sixth time in six World Cup finals tournaments Scotland had failed to progress beyond the first stage. That dismal record would continue in 1990 and 1998, and Scotland remain the only country from the British Isles never to reach a World Cup quarter-final. Alan Rough felt Ferguson had been 'overawed by the Scotland job and probably did not do himself justice . . . I had the feeling that he was shocked at the pressure from the media.' [39] It came as a surprise to Ferguson to have to address press conferences packed with journalists and TV cameras, when at home in Aberdeen the usual complaint was the absence of reporters. Overall, however, Ferguson's record in charge of the national side was respectable: of ten games, they'd won three, drawn four and lost three, with eight goals scored and five conceded. The team had kept clean sheets in seven of the ten fixtures (though with four goalless draws).

Alex Ferguson delights in proclaiming his Scottishness, particularly when he's in the company of Englishmen. He proudly wears kilts to collect his royal honours, often jokes about Scots being the 'master race', and at one time his mobile phone rang to the tune of 'Scotland the Brave'.[40] Yet he was never comfortable as Scotland manager, and didn't enjoy his ten months in the job, even though the SFA were very happy with his work. There was no question of wanting to continue after the World Cup. His future remained in club football, where he became surprisingly unsympathetic to the problems faced by managers of national teams.

The wider stage of Mexico had also convinced him, as he returned to Aberdeen that June, that it was time to seek a bigger stage to display his talents.

15

Manchester Mission

'No manager is prepared for the job at Old Trafford . . .
The legend is huge.'

ALEX FERGUSON[1]

For Manchester United fans, it was one of the most depressing defeats of modern times. It involved a long trek to Southampton on a freezing Tuesday night in November, for a League Cup replay that wouldn't have been needed had United shown the slightest spark in the first game at Old Trafford, their home ground. The Reds dominated the first twenty minutes, but lost 4–1, having been destroyed by two goals from Southampton's eighteen-year-old substitute, Matt Le Tissier.

Enough was enough: it was time for a fresh face. But even Alex Ferguson would have huge problems at first, clearing up the mess he found and restoring Manchester United to their former glories.

Only a year before the Southampton defeat, in the autumn of 1985, buoyed with winning the FA Cup, United had gone ten points clear at the top of the old First Division, after a run of ten straight wins. Ron Atkinson's side – which included entertainers such as Jesper Olsen, Gordon Strachan, Norman Whiteside, Mark Hughes, Peter Barnes and Bryan Robson, the team's captain – had produced some thrilling football and netfuls of goals. Now they were fourth from bottom. In twelve months everything had fallen apart. Average crowds at Old Trafford had slipped below 40,000. Key players such as Robson and Strachan had suffered long-term injuries; Mark Hughes's form had fallen off amid the secrecy and intense speculation which preceded his reluctant move to Barcelona in the summer of 1986; and the strikers bought to replace him – Peter Davenport and Terry Gibson – had both flopped. There were serious discipline problems: seven players were fined after a drinking spree on a pre-season trip to Holland. A few weeks later Jesper Olsen had a skirmish with his teammate Remi Moses at United's training ground, The Cliff. The Dane suffered a gash above his eye which required eleven stitches, and he missed the next match. Atkinson described the incident as 'purely a training accident' where 'the two lads clashed heads', which only undermined his credibility when the truth emerged.[2]

After the expectations of 1985, Manchester United now seemed to be years from winning the league championship, which hadn't graced the Old Trafford trophy cabinet since 1967, when Sir Matt Busby was still in charge. Five subsequent managers – Wilf McGuinness, Frank O'Farrell, Tommy Docherty, Dave Sexton and Ron Atkinson – had all failed to win the title; three FA Cups (in 1977, 1983 and 1985) were the only serious silverware that the club had lifted in almost two decades.

Yet Manchester United remained one of the most famous teams in the world. They may not have won the League or European Cup since the halcyon days of Bobby Charlton, George Best and Denis Law in the 1960s, but they were still arguably the biggest club in English football, and certainly the most glamorous. Liverpool might have won the League nine times since United had last been great, and the European Cup four times, but Old Trafford still boasted bigger crowds even when the Merseyside club was winning several trophies a season. The team's support stretched round the globe, with huge supporters-club branches in Ireland, Scandinavia, Malta and even the Far East. United's aura had partly been created by the Munich air crash in 1958, when eight of the famous 'Busby Babes' team were killed on the way home from a European game in Belgrade. The outpouring of public sympathy helped turn Manchester United into the second-favourite club of many fans of other sides. But the United magic was also linked to the club's reputation for entertaining, swashbuckling football. In November 1986 Alex Ferguson was not just moving to another club, but taking on an institution with a huge tradition and history. His job was to translate United's reputation, worldwide support and huge financial turnover into trophies – and especially the league championship.

The official Manchester United version of how Alex Ferguson came to replace Ron Atkinson has gradually changed over the years. What is undisputed is that as two members of the United board – Martin Edwards, the chairman (and majority shareholder), and Michael Edelson – flew back from Southampton that night in a small chartered plane, they agreed that Atkinson had to go. The next morning, Wednesday 5 November, Edwards consulted the other two directors, Maurice Watkins and Bobby Charlton, and a formal board meeting confirmed the decision. But they waited until the following day to tell Atkinson himself, and then the press.

Within hours of the official announcement on the Thursday, Martin Edwards had unveiled Alex Ferguson as the new manager of Manchester United. Ferguson had first come to Edwards's attention when Aberdeen won the European Cup-Winners' Cup in 1983, and he had further impressed the United chairman with his handling of the tricky negotiations to transfer Gordon Strachan a year later.

For many years the official story was that United hadn't approached Aberdeen or spoken to Ferguson until *after* Atkinson had been told of his sacking on the Thursday morning. In 1986 any suggestion that United had 'tapped' the Aberdeen manager would have been particularly sensitive, since Football League clubs had only recently agreed not to poach each other's managers during the season. In the official United history, published in 1988, Alex Ferguson himself went along with this account, and the idea that everybody had acted honourably. This was his own story of that Thursday:

> It was a beautiful sunny morning and I drove back to
> Pittodrie from a training session and I saw the chairman's car
> there. And I thought to myself 'the old yen's here early
> today' – it was about a quarter to twelve . . . I said hello to
> him and told him he was in early, and he threw me a piece of
> paper. 'I've been asked to 'phone this gentleman,' he said. On
> the paper was Martin Edwards' name and phone number.
> He said, 'Do you want me to 'phone him?' and I said that I
> did, and I went out of the room because I didn't want to be
> there . . .
> I went back after going down to the dressing rooms and he
> said that he had spoken to Mr Edwards and that he was flying
> up straight away and would go to my house. He said that his
> son would collect the United chairman from the airport and
> take him there. I said it was quick, and he said
> 'If you want the job there's nothing we can do to stop you.'[3]

This 1988 account by Ferguson is interesting for several reasons. First, it seems to contradict what Dick Donald said only the day after Ferguson left for Old Trafford. The Aberdeen chairman complained publicly that he'd had no communication from Martin Edwards until the United chairman flew into Aberdeen on the Thursday afternoon.[4] What's more, we now know from Ferguson's 1999 autobiography that he had in fact met the *whole* Manchester United board in Scotland the night before – in other words, before Atkinson knew he'd been sacked.

According to this more recent Ferguson account, he was phoned the day after the Southampton match by the Manchester United director Michael Edelson, who got past the Aberdeen switchboard by putting on a Scottish accent and pretending to be Gordon Strachan's accountant. Edelson put Ferguson on to Edwards, who then gave the Aberdeen manager his number so he could ring back to assure himself that the call was genuine. As in all the best football conspiracies, they agreed to meet at a motorway service station that night – in this case on the M74 just south of Glasgow. Once they'd met up, and to avoid being spotted by anyone, Ferguson and the four United directors then drove to the home of Cathy Ferguson's sister in Bishopbriggs, on the other side of the city, where the deal was struck.

This secret rendezvous the day before Ron Atkinson was sacked may have been improper, but it was for understandable reasons. The United directors wanted to be sure that Alex Ferguson would come to Old Trafford if they got rid of Atkinson. It would be highly embarrassing to sack the manager and not find a suitable replacement – the problem they had had in 1981, when Dave Sexton was dismissed and three possible replacements (Lawrie McMenemy, Bobby Robson and Ron Saunders) declined the job very publicly before Atkinson finally said 'Yes'.

Ron Atkinson himself believes that Alex Ferguson had effectively been approached about his job many months before the M74 meeting, and that Bobby Charlton had played a central role in the plot. Charlton, who joined the Manchester United board in 1984, has subsequently claimed credit for persuading his fellow directors to talk to Ferguson.[5] Bryan Robson says Charlton told him the board had had Ferguson 'in mind for some time'.[6]

It's likely that the United board had been thinking about who should succeed Ron Atkinson since at least the spring of that year. In his autobiography, *Big Ron*, Atkinson reveals that in March of the previous season, long after United had squandered their ten-point lead in the championship, and following a depressing 1–0 reverse at

Queen's Park Rangers, he suggested to the chairman that he ought to resign:

> I turned to Martin Edwards and saw his jaw drop as I said:
> 'I'm just wondering whether this might just be the time for
> me to stand down. To get out of town for everybody's sake.'
> Quietly we discussed the implications. It remained a secret
> between us. Just a nod and a wink, that we would wait until
> the summer was over and the troops were back in camp.

When the United squad returned for pre-season training, however, Atkinson told Edwards he was willing to give it another shot. To this day, the former United manager wonders 'whether I planted the seeds of my own downfall in that late-season confessional with Martin Edwards'.[7]

Over the summer, while acting as a TV pundit for the World Cup in Mexico, Atkinson says he was told by Lawrie McMenemy, then manager of Sunderland, that Ferguson had been approached for his job at United. Atkinson suspected that, if this was so, Charlton could be the connection, since he was also working as a television analyst in Mexico, where Ferguson, of course, was managing the Scotland team.

On his return from the World Cup, Atkinson was puzzled when the United board rejected his request to buy Terry Butcher, despite his having identified the Ipswich and England centre-back as his 'no. 1 priority' for several months. Charlton, he says, was particularly vehement in insisting that Butcher was no better than United's existing defenders. 'I have never ceased to be surprised at Bobby Charlton's seemingly deliberate and obstructive stand,' he writes. 'I have pondered whether it was made as a genuine football judgement, which is the entitlement of any individual, or whether there was an ulterior motive.'[8]

In fact Ron Atkinson had always got on well with Alex Ferguson.

'If there was any manager in Scotland in that period that I regarded as a pal, it was Fergie,' he claims. Yet, like Alan Hansen a few months earlier, Atkinson found the Aberdeen manager strangely frosty when he bumped into him on a trip to Glasgow that autumn to see Celtic play Dynamo Kiev. 'He could barely force himself to say hello. He was very sheepish, more distant than I had ever known him, and really didn't want to look me in the eye. Gordon Strachan was with me at the time and couldn't understand the stand-off I got from Fergie.'[9] Two weeks later Ferguson replaced Atkinson.

Another fragment of evidence of some long-term understanding comes from an entry in Martin Edwards's desk diary for the Wednesday evening after the Southampton game – the night before Atkinson's dismissal. This notes a meeting between Edwards and his fellow director Maurice Watkins in the Post House hotel at Glasgow airport, and it does not have the air of an impromptu arrangement. If the meeting with Ferguson was agreed only that morning, then why put it in the desk diary? And, had the details been entered in the diary after the event, one imagines they would have recorded the real location of the meeting, which was not at Glasgow airport, and the fact that the United attendees included Charlton and Edelson as well as Edwards and Watkins.

In his autobiography, Alex Ferguson himself suggests that the true story of how United approached him is murkier than he admitted before. 'If I avoided specifics in the past,' he writes, 'it was out of consideration for the feelings of other people, not least Dick Donald.'[10] He then relates the M74 and Bishopbriggs story. Yet, had it been made public while Dick Donald was still alive, it is hard to believe this would have hurt the Aberdeen chairman's feelings. More offensive to Donald would have been the notion of some long-term secret agreement between Ferguson and United that his manager would go to Old Trafford when Atkinson eventually left.

In his book, Ferguson tries to deny Atkinson's charge that he was tapped by Bobby Charlton during the Mexico World Cup, but in fact he inadvertently supports such suspicions. 'Although Bobby did speak to me at the side of the pitch before Scotland's fiasco of a game with Uruguay, the furthest he went was to ask that if I ever decided to move to England I should let him know,' Ferguson writes. 'I don't think that can be considered an offer.'[11] Yet many people would take it as precisely that. Bobby Charlton wasn't just a former Manchester United star, but one of only four directors at Old Trafford. He would hardly be offering to advise on how Ferguson might get a job as coach with Stockport County.

Two other intriguing pieces of evidence also suggest that Alex Ferguson had been lined up for the job long in advance. He relates in his book what happened when he told Dick Donald the previous spring that he wanted to leave Aberdeen at the end of the season for a new challenge. 'He shook me slightly when he said categorically that there was only one job I should consider preferable to the one I held at Aberdeen. Asked to name the club, he [Donald] said, "Manchester United".'[12] But why does Ferguson say this 'shook me slightly'? It was surely no more than a statement of the obvious by Donald. Possibly Ferguson had twinges of guilt about contacts which he had already made with Old Trafford.

The strongest evidence of all comes from the late Aberdeen vice-chairman Chris Anderson. Not long before his death, Anderson wrote an account of Ferguson's time at Aberdeen which was eventually published twelve years later in a book about the United manager by the journalist Harry Harris. In his concluding paragraph, Anderson explained how suited Ferguson was to be manager of United, talking as if he had already gone to Old Trafford:

> When Manchester United recognised what he had achieved here and what he could achieve for them, the time was right for him to move . . . Alex Ferguson only had to sniff that promise in the air at Old Trafford and he realised he was the man who could do something to change it.[13]

To most readers of Harris's book, the paragraph will seem innocuous. Yet the strange thing was that Anderson died of motor neurone disease in May 1986, almost six months *before* Ferguson moved to United. According to Anderson's relatives, after March of that year he was too ill to write anything, which suggests that as early as March 1986 – or even earlier – the Aberdeen vice-chairman knew Ferguson would join Manchester United. Had perhaps Ferguson confided in Anderson about a long-term arrangement to go to Old Trafford, but kept the fact from Dick Donald?

Archie Knox, who had returned to help Ferguson at Aberdeen after the 1986 World Cup, insists he knew nothing of any understanding to join United. 'I think the Manchester United thing came out of the blue,' he says.[14] Knox was offered the Aberdeen manager's job in succession to Ferguson, but chose instead to follow his boss to Old Trafford. United paid Aberdeen £60,000 compensation for taking both men.

Ferguson himself says that, before he left Aberdeen in November 1986, Dick Donald begged him to stay, even proposing to give him the club. What's more, the Old Trafford board were offering him less money than he could earn at Aberdeen in a good year (allowing for likely bonuses based on success). Martin Edwards and his colleagues were not generous; nor would they pay off Ferguson's £40,000 loan from the Scottish club. As so often with players and staff over the years, United exploited their prestige, using people's desire to join the club to get them for less than they'd command elsewhere. Ferguson would again be earning much less than some of his leading players, including Bryan Robson (known as 'Robbo'), Gordon Strachan and Jesper Olsen. He was also worse paid than Martin Edwards, who received around £80,000 a year as chairman and chief executive. In the years to come, disputes between Ferguson and the board about money would grow increasingly acrimonious. Ferguson made a mistake in not stating more firmly from the very start his claim to be well rewarded.

It would have been difficult to stop Alex Ferguson going to Manchester United: it was simply the biggest job in football, something he thought was his destiny. Fifteen years before, in another clandestine service-station rendezvous – off the M6 near Haydock Park – the Celtic manager Jock Stein had agreed with Sir Matt Busby to become his successor at Old Trafford. A few days later, under pressure from his family, who wanted to stay in Scotland, Stein went back on the deal (rather like Ferguson himself when he changed his mind about joining Spurs). Jock Stein once told Alex Ferguson how he deeply regretted having turned down that 1971 offer from United. It made a deep impression on his young protégé.

Despite United's enthusiasm to recruit Ferguson, at that time no successful manager of a Scottish club had ever moved south and repeated his triumphs in England. Several Scots had excellent records with English clubs, of course – most notably Sir Matt Busby and Bill Shankly – but none had managed successfully in Scotland beforehand. It seemed as if the two countries required different approaches and a different character. Seven years after rejecting the Manchester United job, Stein took over at Leeds United, but stayed just ten games and forty-four days before becoming Scotland manager instead. Stein's great captain at Celtic, Billy McNeill, and the former Rangers manager Jock Wallace also achieved little in their stints in England, at Manchester City and Leicester City respectively. (More recently Martin O'Neill has been successful in both countries, though he moved in the reverse direction.)

In contemplating the United job, Alex Ferguson must have faced similar personal pressures to Jock Stein. Neither Cathy nor the boys were keen on moving to Manchester, though Mark Ferguson, then eighteen, was already a United supporter. They eventually came round to the idea, but, because of problems over moving home and the twins changing school, it was another nine months before they joined Alex in England. In the meantime he lived with Archie Knox. They stayed in hotels at first, but then for two or three months shared a semi-detached house in Timperley in south Manchester: Ferguson had the main bedroom and Knox a smaller room. On Sunday mornings they took it in turns to make breakfast or go and buy the papers. 'It was a bit of a *Fawlty Towers* experience,' says Knox, who remembers one particular Sunday when his manager did the breakfast stint. 'I heard an almighty explosion in the kitchen, and I thought, "What the hell's happened here?"' In a moment of absent-mindedness Ferguson had placed a large box of matches on top of the grill above the gas cooker.[15]

As with Ferguson's previous managerial move, it wasn't an easy time for his family. His father had died shortly after Ferguson arrived at Aberdeen, and now his mother, Elizabeth, died of cancer only four weeks after he joined United. Ferguson consoled himself with knowing that, unlike his father, she had at least seen his great successes in Scotland.

His mother's death also revived some of his political instincts. Ferguson had been shocked by the conditions in the Southern General Hospital in Glasgow, where his mother spent her final days, which he felt showed an appalling decline in NHS standards after seven years of Conservative rule under Margaret Thatcher. During the next decade he would often cite his experience of the environment in which his mother died as having stiffened his resolve to help the return of a Labour government. In memory of his mother he also established a cancer charity, the Elizabeth Hardie Ferguson Charitable Trust.

Several United players had been even more anxious than Cathy Ferguson about the idea of Alex Ferguson going to Old Trafford. They'd heard about Fergie's fearsome reputation from Gordon Strachan, who half-jokingly went round the United dressing room shaking his teammates' hands and announcing that he was off. Yet Strachan clearly had an ambivalent relationship with his new boss. While they were together on Scotland duty, his apparent misgivings hadn't stopped him telling Ferguson – before he arrived at United –

that Atkinson didn't seem to care about the corrosive effects of the drinking culture at Old Trafford. The United training regime, Strachan reportedly told Ferguson, was a 'shambles', and it wasn't until Atkinson had enjoyed his daily session on the sunbed that the squad got down to anything even as onerous as a practice match.[16] Strachan says his first day under Atkinson at The Cliff in the summer of 1984, had been 'like a day at Butlin's' in comparison with Ferguson's sessions at Aberdeen.[17]

Alex Ferguson immediately acknowledged that his first priority at Old Trafford was 'to bring back the League championship after twenty years'.[18] Initially he was anxious about whether he would be accepted by United's star names, and particularly the older players – no doubt recalling his early experiences at Pittodrie with a less distinguished squad. He had good reason to worry, for, as Mark Hughes later confirmed, 'the majority of the senior first team squad were very upset and angry' about Atkinson's dismissal.[19] 'No question at all, I was nervous,' Ferguson said later. 'I didn't know anything about this club, really. Didn't have a clue what the team was going to be. Didn't even know the make-up of the side in the Southampton cup defeat that had brought Ron Atkinson the sack forty-eight hours earlier.'[20] And his nervousness showed. The striker Peter Davenport says Ferguson was 'like a kitten' the first time he announced a team, listing 'Nigel' in the forward line. 'There was a moment's pause,' says Davenport, 'then Robbo said, "Nigel? Who's Nigel?" and Fergie points at me and goes: "Him, Nigel Davenport."'[21]

His first match as manager was away to Oxford United, who were then enjoying a four-year spell in the top flight, thanks in part to money invested by the publishing tycoon Robert Maxwell. The team Ferguson had named showed no great change from recent Atkinson line-ups: Chris Turner, Mike Duxbury, Arthur Albiston, Kevin Moran, Paul McGrath, Graeme Hogg, Clayton Blackmore, Remi Moses, Frank Stapleton, Peter Davenport and Peter Barnes, with

Jesper Olsen as substitute. But only one of them – the versatile Clayton Blackmore – survived Ferguson's surgery over the next four years.

Oxford won 2–0 in a game which showed Ferguson just how unfit his new players were, though he later regretted telling the press this. The result pushed United down to third from bottom – into the relegation zone – while a 0–0 draw at Norwich the following week left them one place lower still. It wasn't until his first match at Old Trafford that Ferguson picked up his first win, beating QPR 1–0 with a single goal from Johnny Sivebaek (though this wasn't enough to salvage the Danish full-back's career at United). Slowly the new manager hauled his team up the table, though it was perhaps foolish to say, as he had on the day he arrived, that the 'League can still be won'.[22]

In its playing style, Ferguson's team in his first season was similar to Ron Atkinson's, operating with two wingers, with the emphasis on attack, entertainment and goals. Particularly impressive was a 1–0 win at the double-winners, Liverpool, on Boxing Day, though it was typical of the Manchester United of that era that this was followed the very next day with a home defeat by Norwich City. FA Cup form was just as inconsistent: a cheering third-round victory over neighbours Manchester City was followed by a home knockout by the eventual winners, Coventry City. The cup defeat was attributed to a frozen pitch after ground staff had been caught out by an unexpected frost. They had failed to activate the hot-air inflatable covering, the replacement for an undersoil heating system which had corroded and quickly broken down. After working at Pittodrie, a stadium which copes with far more severe weather than Old Trafford, Ferguson couldn't hide his shock that his new set-up was so bad: 'the club . . . has everything with all the trappings', he said, 'except a heating blanket that works'.[23] Worse still, he found that the pitch had too little grass for the kind of football produced by players of United's skill. This was just the start of a long, frustrating battle over the poor state of the Old Trafford playing surface that has dogged Ferguson for most of his time as Manchester United manager.

The Reds finished that first season in eleventh place, just above halfway. But, within days of the final game, Ferguson faced more personal problems with revelations in the *Star* newspaper. The paper claimed that, in the year before leaving Scotland, Ferguson had enjoyed an affair with a young Aberdeen waitress called Deirdrie McHardy (though it didn't say how he found time with his two jobs, managing Aberdeen and Scotland). McHardy alleged that they'd met at a pub charity evening, and that only two nights later Ferguson unexpectedly walked into the restaurant where she worked in the city centre. 'I felt like crawling behind the counter with embarrassment. I knew he'd only come to see me.' A few nights afterwards he rang to say he was coming round. A grinning Ferguson turned up on her doorstep, she claims, leaving his distinctive Mercedes parked outside, and clutching a bottle of vodka. 'Everyone knew he was married,' McHardy said. 'It was enough to set the neighbours' tongues wagging for years. I rushed out and said, "You're mad. We can't meet here. The gossips will have a field day."'[24]

Considering what a small community it was, Ferguson seemed remarkably relaxed about the possibility of getting caught, according to McHardy. From then on, once or twice a week, Ferguson would ring her up and arrange to meet in a flat a few minutes' walk away from Pittodrie:

Sometimes I worried that he was being too carefree about our affair. He didn't think twice about pulling into a petrol station with me sitting in the Merc . . . There was no deep, burning passionate love affair between us . . . There was affection between us – intimate affection. And of course, that involved sex . . . We made love once or twice a week in the flat. But

sex was only part of our relationship. We enjoyed each
other's company. Alex talked about his wife. He said she was
a lovely lady.[25]

After previous revelations about Tommy Docherty and Ron
Atkinson, Ferguson had become the third Old Trafford manager in
ten years to have allegations about his sex life presented on the front
pages of a tabloid newspaper. Unlike Docherty, who was famously
sacked in 1977 over his affair with Mary Brown, the wife of the
United physiotherapist, there was no question of this exposé endan-
gering Ferguson's job. 'I have spoken to Alex and he categorically
denies it,' said Martin Edwards. 'And that is good enough for me,'
added the United chairman, whom the tabloids would later accuse of
having a string of extramarital affairs himself.[26]

Edwards could hardly have dismissed Ferguson after only six
months in the job. If any axe was to be wielded, it would be upon his
players. Ferguson had decided that only five or six of his squad
were good enough; the rest were dead wood. Publicly he spoke of
needing another 'four new players to make us into a team capable of
challenging for the championship'; privately he told the shocked
directors that the real figure was nine – almost an entire new team.[27]
What surprised and frustrated Ferguson even more was to be told
there was little money to pay for transfers after several expensive
purchases by Ron Atkinson, since he had always been under the
impression that United were a rich club. But, the day he arrived,
Ferguson had been warned by Martin Edwards that 'If we go on
buying players we will be forever in the financial mire.'[28]

In fact Atkinson had a transfer deficit of only £2.2 million in his
five and half years with the club, thanks largely to the lucrative sales
overseas of Ray Wilkins and Mark Hughes. The real problem was
that some of Atkinson's buys had been unwise. In particular he'd
spent almost £2 million on forwards who found it hard to score –
Alan Brazil (£700,000), Terry Gibson (£630,000) and Peter

Davenport (£600,000). Gibson and Davenport, bought earlier in 1986, appeared to be panic buys after it became known that Mark Hughes was going to Barcelona, but their dismal scoring records left the United directors in no mood to give further funds to Alex Ferguson, despite his excellent transfer record at Aberdeen. A more serious constraint was the ban on English clubs playing in Europe following the Heysel Stadium disaster. This had deprived United of the extra TV money and turnstile revenue from big games against Continental sides.

Atkinson's failures in the transfer market taught Ferguson a useful early lesson: that not all players have the character to flourish at Old Trafford. Certain footballers could be stars on the smaller stages of English football, then fall to pieces under the spotlight of United. Ferguson says Terry Gibson came and told him that 'the great expectations and fierce demands of the place, were all a bit too much for him. He just couldn't cope with it.'[29] Anyone he himself signed must be more than just a good player at another club, he announced: 'He must possess a special kind of presence, arrogance and stature.'[30]

The United manager was in a tricky position, for, if he wanted to buy in any substantial way, he first had to sell. It wasn't easy. Most Manchester United players were on long contracts and good wages; many were happy to stay at Old Trafford even if it meant reserve football and little success on the pitch. Time and again transfers would be lined up for people to leave the club, only for the players to refuse. They went along with the view that it is always downhill after Old Trafford (though Johnny Giles, Brian Kidd, Jimmy Rimmer, Peter Beardsley, David Platt and Dion Dublin might all suggest otherwise).

'I felt I was left with trying to make a silk purse out of a sow's ear,' Ferguson said later.[31] There were some obvious replacements he might have brought down from Aberdeen – the central defenders Willie Miller and Alex McLeish could have been prime Ferguson targets, along with the striker Joe Miller – but he'd promised Dick Donald he would 'not be going back for any players'.[32] However, the understanding was that Aberdeen would tip Ferguson off if any players became available.

Ferguson's initial feeling about United had been that there was 'not a lot wrong with this club'.[33] It took time to realise how bad things really were. Observing from 350 miles away, he'd been beguiled by United's reputation as a wealthy, well-supported team, with a constellation of stars. 'I had no real inkling about the demands,' he would say six years later. 'No manager is prepared for the job at Old Trafford . . . it took me three or four years to understand fully the politics and requirements, the demands and pressures.'[34] At one stage he tried analysing things by drawing charts of the club structure, listing 'the weaknesses on one side, the positive things on the other. Then after a few days I scrapped all that; it didn't work. The situation changed every day.'[35]

Norman Whiteside says Ferguson didn't seem to appreciate the scale of what he had taken on. 'He was in awe of the place. I mean, it was massive. And he would come up in training and say to me and Robbo, "Big place this, isn't it? Big club this."'[36]

Just as at Aberdeen, he trod on people's toes at first, telling United's existing coaches, Brian Whitehouse and Eric Harrison, to step aside to let him and Archie Knox take mass training sessions involving both the senior players and the apprentices. This lasted only a few weeks, however. Ferguson and Knox were primarily going through the obvious process of assessing the state of the playing staff. Almost overnight Ferguson introduced radical new training routines – tougher and more disciplined – insisting that no opposing team should ever be fitter than United.

'We needed it,' was the frank reaction of Bryan Robson to the new regime at the time. It was a remarkable admission from a player who was probably Atkinson's closest ally in the squad. The former manager had been 'far too easy-going', Robson felt:

There were one or two big stars who had faded under Ron
Atkinson and were not doing the business. They were just
taking the money – and were allowed to get away with it. It's
different now. Alex has no favourites. No players are allowed
to hide and leave it to their team-mates to pull the job round.
Ron should have had the culprits in his office. Kicked a few
backsides. Or even sent them on their way. But they got away
with it. And then they got out of the habit of even trying.[37]

'Probably we had got a little slack and needed to be given a jolt or
two,' agreed goalkeeper Chris Turner. 'We probably needed a bit
more discipline.'[38]

Colin Gibson, a defender who'd joined United from Aston Villa
the year before (and no relation to Terry), had noticed how, when the
squad were out running, he always ended up in front, alongside
Bryan Robson. At Villa he'd been around the middle of the pack.

They were so unfit I found it unbelievable. Villa were much
fitter. Ron's teams at United had talent, but they just weren't
playing to their maximum potential under him because of
this slack attitude that hung around the place. Training under
Ron was easy, a piece of piss. It was a few five-a-sides, a bit of
running, then time to go home.[39]

Ron Atkinson was in the habit of arriving at The Cliff at around
10.30 a.m. Ferguson established a radically different pattern on
his very first day, by taking an early-morning flight from Aberdeen
and turning up for training well before his new players. The playing squad was told to arrive at 9.30 a.m. from now on, instead of
10.30. Then they had to change and drive round to the nearby
Littleton Road training pitch by ten o'clock. 'Ron often used
to roll up late, whereas Fergie would always be there when you
got there, ready and waiting,' says Frank Stapleton. 'Making it

9.30 a.m. was clever. It gave us the sense that we were going to a proper job – we had to get up early and crawl through the traffic like everybody else.'[40]

Archie Knox instituted a system of punishments for any player who didn't arrive at Littleton Road on time. 'You used to hear them screeching into the car park,' says Knox, 'and the rule was they had to get their foot on the grass by ten o'clock.'[41] It became quite a battle every morning as Knox and his squad all got themselves synchronised watches, and players began telling on any colleagues they spotted arriving late. The punishment was an extra lap or two running round the practice pitch.

Ferguson suspected that the squad's repeated ham-string injuries before he arrived reflected a lack of fitness. So there was four weeks of intensive work to make everyone fitter. Players were made to run backwards to exercise their muscles in a different way. He began gruelling back-to-back fifty-yard sprints, separated by ten seconds' rest, then more sprints building up to longer and longer ones. But the work had to be done at each player's own pace. Anyone who felt any pulls or muscle tightness was told to stop and go for a massage. 'Alex has also beefed up our enjoyment,' said Bryan Robson, 'because he mixes the sessions – set pieces, tactical moves, eight-a-sides, ball work and running and stretching.'[42] Under Atkinson, according to Norman Whiteside, 'the main emphasis' had simply been 'on crossing the ball and sharpening up the shooting'.[43]

Although Frank Stapleton didn't last long under the new manager, he felt the Atkinson approach had been 'a bit unprofessional':

It was all too relaxed. If we were winning, everything was fine – there was no detailed analysis of how we were playing and where we're gonna get caught out if we don't watch it. Which is, of course, where Ferguson was great: details, details and more details . . . With Ron, we had some good players – really good players – and his attitude was always

'Let's just concentrate on our game, let them worry about us.'
But you can't just do that.[44]

Colin Gibson remembers that Ferguson spent a lot of time out
with his players 'practising positional play and marking. There was
a lot of sessions based on defending as a team.' Unlike Atkinson,
Ferguson didn't want all his defenders piling forward together at
once. If a full-back went on to the attack, other players had to stay
back in support of the centre-backs. And the new manager was con-
tinually giving his players little tips on the opposition. 'Fergie would
come up and say to you, "Their right-winger, he always goes this
way", or "He always does this trick – watch out for it." You went out
there quite often that little bit more in the know and confident.'[45]

Atkinson, in contrast, seemed too optimistic to think much about
the other side, or to have considered what to do if United's opponents took the lead. The real contrast, says Gibson, was in the
dressing room before games: 'Fergie would go on in detail – often too
much detail, actually – about what the opposition are specifically
dangerous at. Whereas Ron, he used to get the opposition team
sheet and go, "Right, that's their load of crap!" and screw it up and
chuck it away. Then he'd say, "Right, let's stuff 'em, we're much
better than that lot!"'[46]

Under Alex Ferguson, days off were suspended. Players had to
spruce up their appearance and be clean-shaven; several were sent to
the barber's, and Graeme Hogg got rid of his blond streaks. In a
throwback to the 1950s and '60s, the whole squad was supplied
with club blazers and flannels, which they were expected to wear on
match days and official trips. Peter Davenport said it reminded him
of his time under Brian Clough at Nottingham Forest. 'Cloughie
was always on to us about being smart and the two managers have
similar ideas on discipline,' he said. 'There were so many short hair-
cuts around when we went out the other day that I thought I was
back playing for the youth team.'[47]

Ferguson thought the United dressing rooms were so untidy that he insisted they be excluded from public tours of Old Trafford until they'd been cleaned up. A strict rota was started for players to entertain corporate guests at home games, and they were told to run, not walk, off the pitch at half-time. The manager was shocked at the easy lifestyles team members enjoyed: not having to pay for phone calls made from their hotel rooms on away trips, for instance. He also downgraded their accommodation – for example, giving up the Royal Lancaster Hotel near Hyde Park where United had normally stayed in London, for somewhere less expensive.

Lighter meals were instituted on match days, and steaks were banned. A cooked breakfast in the canteen at The Cliff was henceforth compulsory for all apprentices and young players who were single. 'We used to sit down and make them eat porridge,' says Archie Knox. 'They used to hate it.'[48] And they had to have plenty of vegetables with their lunch. But the younger players were also invited to join the senior ones in the daily warm-up sessions – a deliberate effort to make them all feel part of one club. And, unlike some of his predecessors, Ferguson made an effort to meet everyone at United, though with 172 staff this was much harder than with the few dozen employees at Pittodrie. When he went for tea and a chat with the two women who ran the United laundry (nicknamed 'Daz' and 'Omo'), it was reminiscent of the days of Sir Matt Busby, when everybody at Old Trafford knew everyone else and thought of themselves as one big family.

Nor did Ferguson consider the presence of Sir Matt himself, who was now in his late seventies, to be a problem. Previous United managers – notably Wilf McGuinness, Frank O'Farrell and Tommy Docherty – had decried what they saw as Busby's continuing interference. As club president when Ferguson arrived, Busby still had a small office at Old Trafford, and tried to visit the ground every day; but he was no longer a United director, and none of the players had known him as manager. Ferguson regarded Busby's record as a challenge, and Sir Matt himself as a bonus – an experienced sage to be consulted, rather than the malign influence that O'Farrell and Docherty had perceived. 'People have said that some previous managers have been afraid of the Matt Busby thing,' he claimed. 'I love it. I love to sit down with Matt and hear all about it.'[49]

He also immersed himself in reading club histories, absorbing the statistics, the players, the great games, the folklore – trying to understand what made Manchester United tick, and seeking clues as to why the club had gone so long without success. To the latter question he never really found a satisfactory answer.

Perhaps the biggest problem Alex Ferguson found at Old Trafford was the drinking culture. More than once he has famously described the United he found as a 'drinking club' not a football club.[50] Things did not look good from the start, on the night Atkinson lost his job, when part of the squad had met for what appeared to be a celebration drink. Meanwhile a second group went round to Atkinson's house for a farewell party.

No matter how bad things at Manchester United showed themselves to be, Ferguson knew that he couldn't change things overnight. 'You can't go into a club,' he said, 'and tell people their fitness is terrible, they're bevvying, they're playing too much golf and their ground is filthy. You simply have to improve things, bit by bit, and keep coming back to those which do not show the improvement you're looking for.'[51] He later admitted to working 'instinctively' in his early months, 'calling the shots I believed to be right, but . . . up to seven or eight moves I made in that period proved later to be ill-advised'.[52]

Given the financial constraints, he had little option but to give each of the players he inherited the chance to prove himself. On reflection, he believes he may have given them too long. Later Ferguson would say, 'there were too many players on the wrong side of twenty-eight or thereabouts. They were too old to go for the challenges I had in mind.'[53] In fact the basic twenty-man squad which he inherited in November 1986 had an average age of just twenty-six years and nine months – very respectable by football standards, and indeed almost two years *younger* than the 2001–02 United squad. Only Frank Stapleton and Kevin Moran were over thirty, and not by much.

Alex Ferguson's problem was more one of attitude than of age. Some players seemed incapable of adopting the Ferguson will to win. Peter Barnes was the first to go, rejoining Manchester City after just four games for his new boss in two months. Barnes was 'really no use to me at all', Ferguson said later. 'I just couldn't see how he might contrive to produce a real threat . . . he wasn't a good team player.'[54] But his biggest disappointment was Frank Stapleton. After notching up more than 200 goals for Arsenal, United and Ireland, and gaining three FA Cup-winners' medals, Stapleton was now 'a shadow of his former self', morose and quiet in the dressing room. 'His reputation was as long as your arm, but he had lost his mobility and he just didn't look as if he would ever score a goal.'[55] Stapleton actually preferred the new manager to Atkinson, but Ferguson has always found it difficult to make an impact on older, experienced players. 'The manager would lose his temper and roar and scream until he went red in the face,' says Stapleton. 'At the start the players used to dread it but after a while it didn't have the slightest impact.'[56]

Others fell victim to injury. The midfield terrier Remi Moses retired because of a persistent ankle problem; goalkeeper Gary Bailey left through a knee injury which had been aggravated during the 1986 World Cup.

During his first summer, Ferguson had mixed fortunes in the transfer market. Striker Brian McClair agreed to join from Celtic after a series of clandestine meetings held the previous season. On one occasion the new Scotland manager, Andy Roxburgh, even had to complain about Ferguson and Martin Edwards conducting negotiations in the Scots' team hotel. The £850,000 fee, set by an independent tribunal, was remarkably good value for a player who had scored 99 goals in 145 league games for Celtic. Ferguson hoped that McClair would demolish United's much-mentioned record of not having had a player since George Best in 1968 who had scored more than twenty league goals in a season. Another catch was the Arsenal defender Viv Anderson, and Ferguson was quick to point out his qualities as a teetotaller as much as an England full-back. But Ferguson failed to buy an experienced goalkeeper, while his bid for Peter Beardsley (who'd briefly been on United's books four years earlier) collapsed when the Newcastle United manager, Willie McFaul, demanded £3 million. Ferguson was furious when only days later Newcastle accepted a £1.9 million bid from Liverpool for the England star.

His frustration with the financial constraints at Old Trafford must have been all the greater when he observed how that summer Liverpool were able to replace the great striker Ian Rush – who'd gone to Juventus – by spending £4 million on three formidable newcomers: Beardsley, John Barnes and John Aldridge. 'They seem to have bought up just about every great player in the land,' Ferguson lamented.[57] The United manager could have bought Barnes himself, but rejected the idea because of mixed reports from scouts and because the club had just signed a new four-year contract with Jesper Olsen. Ferguson admits he 'boobed' over Barnes, whom he says 'might have made us better, quicker'.[58] But he also never forgave United's chief scout, Tony Collins, whom he accuses of being 'too cautious'.[59] Collins's version is that he'd been keen on Barnes, but Ferguson 'turned sour on him when a southern scout told him Barnes has a low body temperature and wears green gloves in the winter'.[60] Collins boasted an impressive scouting record, having served under Don Revie, Brian Clough and Ron Atkinson, but was subsequently eased out by Ferguson and replaced by Les Kershaw, who doubled up as a part-time chemistry lecturer at Manchester Polytechnic.

Ferguson had to confront a sudden explosion in transfer fees, with little money to spend. What made his job harder was that potential sellers upped their prices when he came on the phone, thinking – just as he had – that Manchester United was always flush with funds. 'We just don't have the money to go and buy the way we should,' he complained. 'So often I have spoken to managers about players and told them I haven't really got any big money . . . They think of United and just burst out laughing. I feel like jumping down the phone and belting them one. It's that frustrating.'[61] He warned Martin Edwards very publicly that he was 'facing two very tough choices between having a very good team and balancing the books. It is impossible to have both at present. All I can say is that at Aberdeen I bought twelve players and had just one failure, and I felt that badly. I have a respect for money.'[62]

As he prepared for his first full season in charge, 1987–88, Ferguson warned his players that he wouldn't be off their backs. 'I won't be bloody happy unless we win the League.'[63] They didn't, of course.

By January 1988, after fourteen months of Ferguson, United were hovering at around fourth or fifth in the table. That might have been satisfactory to most football supporters, perhaps, but not at Old Trafford. When the Reds lost 2–0 at home to Southampton, a substantial part of the meagre 35,716 crowd left long before the final whistle; many who stayed to the end then booed the players off the pitch. Ferguson had noticed that United often eased off against such unfashionable teams – a persistent failing of the Atkinson era – and made too many slack starts. Were these traits 'something inherent at the club' he wondered?[64] But he also criticised fans for giving up too early.

Ominously, home gates had regularly slipped below 40,000 – the level at the end of Atkinson's era – amid the first signs of dissent in that traditional medium of Mancunian insurrection, the letters page of the Saturday-night *Football Pink*. The criticism of Alex Ferguson wasn't just about bad results and absent trophies, but also about the loss of United's traditional buccaneering style. The team were boring to watch. 'He should not blame the crowd,' wrote one fan, 'but concentrate on blending a team capable of winning with flair – or get out.' 'Brian Clough,' said another, 'is the only man who can bring the Championship to Old Trafford. The sooner he arrives the sooner United can get down to business.'[65]

Privately, Ferguson was even more scathing with the players themselves. After a 1–0 defeat at Norwich in early March 1988, he ordered the team on to the coach within thirty-five minutes of the final whistle. No banter in the bath, no drinks in the players' lounge: they had to get dressed and crawl through the traffic just like the travelling fans they'd let down. The next day they were summoned to Old Trafford for a Sunday inquest into what had gone wrong.

It seemed to work. United were unbeaten in their ten remaining fixtures, including an exciting 3–3 draw at Anfield on Easter Monday. Early in the second half the Reds looked to be heading for only their second defeat against Liverpool in eighteen league games. United were losing 3–1, and then – worse still – Colin Gibson was sent off. Against the odds, however, the team clawed the game back to 3–3, and Gordon Strachan celebrated his dramatic late equaliser by cupping his ear and pretending to smoke a cigar in front of the Kop. But events that day off the pitch were just as memorable as on.

In a radio interview in a corridor afterwards, Ferguson launched an astonishing attack on the way he felt referees at Anfield were intimidated by the crowd into punishing opposing players and giving wrong decisions:

I can now understand why a lot of managers have to leave here choking on their own sick, afraid to tell the truth because they've been beaten. We've got a draw today and so I can speak the truth . . . To win here you have to surmount a lot of pressure, a lot of obstacles and if you want to blame the referee, you can't say so. The provocation and intimidation he is under are incredible. To win here is a miracle. That's the biggest handicap coming to this ground . . . Every manager who comes here knows about them but has to leave the ground biting his tongue, afraid to say anything because his team have been beaten.[66]

The Liverpool manager, Kenny Dalglish, walked past Ferguson while he was doing the interview, and was carrying his six-week-old baby, Lauren. 'You might as well talk to my daughter,' he remarked – 'you'll get more sense out of her.'[67]

The outburst came as no surprise to anyone who knew the Alex Ferguson of Aberdeen and St Mirren. Then the grouse had been that it was impossible to get fair decisions when playing in Glasgow against Celtic or Rangers. And, with United at Anfield, Ferguson's claim wasn't really supported by past history. The Reds had an undefeated league record at Liverpool's ground over the previous seven years, with four wins and three draws. Years later, of course, opposing managers would make similar claims about the handicaps of playing at Old Trafford.

After winning their final five games, United finished 1987–88 a creditable second, nine points behind Liverpool and eight ahead of third-placed Nottingham Forest. They'd lost only five league matches – the fewest by a United side since 1906 – and Brian McClair had more than fulfilled his duty, with twenty-four league goals and seven more in the cups. And during the season Ferguson acquired defender Steve Bruce in mid-season from Norwich and a seventeen-year-old winger, Lee Sharpe, from Fourth Division Torquay United, after a tip-off from a United-supporting journalist who had gone to live in Devon. Bruce cost £825,000, and Sharpe £60,000 (plus another £125,000 depending on appearances). Both players would repay those fees many times over.

Yet home crowds had become a serious concern again. The official attendances for the late-season games against Luton and Wimbledon were barely 28,000 (and the real figures would have been lower, since United count season-ticket holders whether or not they turn up).

United's position as runners-up proved to be a false dawn. Bryan Robson later admitted that the team, which still mainly comprised Ron Atkinson's players, was 'not good enough to win the League', and Ferguson confided the same thing to Martin Edwards.[68]

Manchester United was where he 'desperately' wanted his career to end, Ferguson declared during the summer of 1988. 'I am not kidding. This isn't just a job to me. It's a mission. I am deadly serious about it – some people would reckon too serious . . . We will get there. Believe me. And when it happens life will change for Liverpool and everybody else – dramatically.'[69]

Chucking-Out Time

'All this stuff about being a drinking club had to be addressed . . . I could never agree with those managers who think drinking is good for team spirit.'

ALEX FERGUSON[1]

Manchester United players soon got accustomed to Alex Ferguson's notorious outbursts. 'More rollickings have been dished than ever before,' said Norman Whiteside of Fergie's first three months at the club. 'Do something wrong and you can get both barrels.'[2] 'He has shaken us up,' said Paul McGrath, 'bawled out people if he felt it necessary, made it clear there are no stars, no favourites, and has set standards. I believe anyone who fails to maintain them will not survive here.'[3] Both men were shortly to discover the accuracy of McGrath's prediction, as Ferguson started radical surgery on Manchester United.

By the spring of 1988 Whiteside thought his career at United had 'gone stale and come to a halt. For some reason I haven't been able to get myself wound up for matches. I just haven't the enthusiasm.'[4] McGrath felt the same way. 'I'm in a rut,' he said. 'I've got to get out. My mind is made up.'[5] Both players asked separately to be put on the transfer list, and Ferguson consented. 'I need men who are desperate to play for this club,' he said, arguing that both might benefit from a change of scene.[6] 'Really there is no point having players whose heart is not in playing for you.'[7]

More than a decade later, it's hard to appreciate how shocking the transfer-listings were to supporters. Whiteside and McGrath were two of United's biggest stars, outshone only by Bryan Robson. They were also extremely popular with the fans – rare successes of the United scouting system in the Sexton–Atkinson era. One star leaving was a common hazard of football life, but two? Supporters deluged Ferguson with hostile letters, and questioned his sanity.

Like Ferguson himself, Norman Whiteside had made his league debut at sixteen (one of only five men to have played for United before their seventeenth birthday). His early career was blessed as he collected record after record. Within weeks of his debut he had become the youngest ever cap for Northern Ireland, the youngest for any British Isles country, and the youngest player in the World Cup finals. The following season he became both the youngest goalscorer in a League Cup final and then the youngest in an FA Cup final. In 1985 he helped win the FA Cup again with a fine opportunist goal against Everton in extra time after United had been reduced to ten men when Kevin Moran was sent off. Yet he also suffered periods of despair from learning around the age of twenty that, because of damage to his knees, his career might not last much beyond twenty-seven. Ferguson said later that with an extra yard of pace Whiteside would have been 'one of the greatest players ever produced in English football', and but for his injuries 'a truly world-class star'.[8] But now he sought pastures new. 'I want to play abroad,' he said. 'I would not consider playing for another English club.'[9]

Ferguson believed that McGrath, too, was a great player, with richer natural talent than any he'd ever worked with. Things had started badly between them, however, when he pulled the Irishman off at half-time during his opening game at Oxford, where McGrath played poorly as a midfield replacement for the absent Bryan Robson. McGrath immediately suspected that Ferguson might not be to his taste. 'I was just thinking that I didn't want to be under this fellow for the next six or seven years.' McGrath was fined several times for turning up late for training, and was upset towards the end of Ferguson's first season when an earlier transfer request was rejected. The United manager claims to have enlisted both a local priest and even Sir Matt Busby to explain to McGrath the error of his ways. 'What a load of rubbish,' counters McGrath, who recalls no such conversations and is not a practising Catholic.[10]

Both McGrath and Whiteside suffered from a combination of poor discipline and persistent injuries. McGrath had had eight operations on his knees, while Whiteside had problems both with his knees and with his Achilles tendon. But the biggest issue with both players was alcohol. While the links between drinking and football are close at the best of times, at Manchester United in the 1980s stars seemed to take sponsorship by the drink industry to extremes: Bryan Robson, Mark Hughes, Kevin Moran, Paul McGrath and Norman Whiteside all had reputations in and around Manchester for the amount they were able to consume. Ferguson addressed the players and insisted that if anyone could 'explain to me how drink makes you a better player, and prove it' he'd go along with it, but until then they'd have to change.[11] He then scrapped United's rule that players could drink as much as they liked so long as it wasn't within the forty-eight hours before a game. From now on there was to be no drinking at all while they were 'in training'.[12] In effect, the new rule made most players adhere more conscientiously to the old one – but not Norman Whiteside and Paul McGrath.

Both had been fined heavily in May 1987 after they'd gone out together on an all-night drinking session on a club trip to Malta. McGrath had also been banned from driving for two years after crashing his car into a front garden near his home and being found to be three times over the alcohol limit. Ferguson was also convinced that their long periods of injury gave them more time to drink – and they often drank together – and that recovery was delayed by their intake of alcohol. He had regularly lectured both men about the dangers to sportsmen of drink; he even made Whiteside stand-in captain occasionally, in the hope that the responsibility would change his habits. Each player responded to the manager in his own way, says Whiteside:

> I admit to having a few beers, but when I was in the wrong I would go straight into his office and suffer the consequences. I remember Fergie saying to me that, after someone had phoned him up to tell him about me and Paul being seen in a pub, he used to lay awake all night worrying about what he was going to say to me. And then I made it easy for him by going straight in in the morning and saying, 'Sorry Boss, I was out last night.' Big Paul wouldn't go in, he had a different relationship . . . I got on with Fergie because I was so open.[13]

The two players did not believe that drinking affected their performance on the field. Whiteside cites in his defence the time a Football League XI beat the Rest of the World at Wembley in 1987. Bryan Robson scored twice in the League's 3–0 win; Whiteside got the other goal, and Paul McGrath was widely praised for containing the great Diego Maradona.

But nobody seemed interested in buying the two wayward Irishmen – at least not at the prices United wanted: £1.5 million for Whiteside and £900,000 for McGrath. Both were still at Old Trafford when the 1988–89 season started; their names were taken off the transfer list, and they were given another chance. Ferguson would live to regret his patience.

Yet, at the same time, he tolerated Bryan Robson's drinking, which was at least as prodigious as that of Whiteside and McGrath. But drink did not seem to affect Robson in the same way: next day he would train harder than anyone, work off the alcohol, and end up fitter than most other players (at least when he wasn't injured).

'Captain Marvel' in Alex Ferguson's eyes was a hero who could turn games single-handedly. 'The difference with him was that he was still doing it on the pitch,' says Colin Gibson, who reckons the amount of alcohol consumed at United was worse than anything he'd seen at Aston Villa:

> I'm sure Fergie didn't like the way he carried on drinking despite the gaffer trying to stamp it out, but at the end of the day a match-fit Bryan Robson was always going to be in the team, especially if you're a manager struggling for results. Robson was definitely the players' leader and I'm not sure Fergie would have ever risked totally falling out with him. He was near untouchable, just so important on the pitch and so respected by the other players.[14]

Nonetheless, Ferguson once told the United directors he'd be willing to part with Robson if the right offer came along, possibly in an exchange deal. But, despite his persistent injuries, Robson, who was also England captain, proved too indispensable as the all-round player – a tackler, passer, runner, midfield engine, and inspirational team leader of great stamina and vision, superb with his timing, and a regular scorer of goals – often vital ones. Ferguson even tried him as a defensive sweeper on several occasions, fearing his days as a midfielder might be numbered, but the team never got used to it and the player hated it. The drawback to all this was that Robson was frequently injured, suffering long absences with shoulder and hamstring problems.

The other major difficulty for Alex Ferguson was Gordon Strachan, the team member with whom he was most familiar. Strachan says he felt once Ferguson was appointed that 'it would not work again', but decided to give it a try. It didn't work. 'I knew too much about his style of management and he knew too much about me. So with both of us that bit older it was never going to be a situation where the glory days of Pittodrie would be resurrected.'[15] When Ferguson tried to upbraid the redhead for something on the pitch, Strachan would be inclined to shout back, 'Hey gaffer, come on with something original. You tried that on with me on a windy night in Morton ten years ago.'[16] Strachan was especially unhappy about being played wide on the right, and knew that Ferguson was looking at other players who would be better in that position, such as Trevor Steven of Everton (who joined Rangers instead).

Ferguson was naturally wary of Strachan. Relations had deteriorated badly during their final few months at Aberdeen, and Ferguson had been disgusted by Strachan's behaviour in secretly agreeing to join Cologne. But Strachan had played well for Scotland in Mexico, and, rather disloyally to Ron Atkinson, had kept Ferguson in touch with developments during the dying days of the old regime. After eighteen months, however, it was clear that he needed a fresh challenge. 'It seemed that Alex had given up on me. He thought that I had nothing left to give and that I was not going to be able to help him get the kind of success he wanted at Old Trafford.'[17]

Ferguson finally lost patience with Strachan in the spring of 1988, when the player announced he was joining the French club Lens, even though he'd settled a new contract with Martin Edwards the previous day. Ferguson says Strachan denied he'd agreed a deal with Edwards, though the United chairman confirmed it was true. 'I decided that this man could not be trusted an inch,' says Ferguson, whose memories of the Cologne fiasco were still vivid. 'I knew in that moment that I wouldn't want to expose my back to him in a hurry.'[18] Strachan stayed on when the Lens deal fell through, but his form worsened and the goals dried up. The player says he lost confidence in his own ability, 'because the manager no longer believed in me . . . Psychologically it was hard for me to handle.'[19] In March 1989 he joined Leeds United, who were then in the middle of the Second Division.

Gordon Strachan's career was rejuvenated after Old Trafford. He won the Footballer of the Year award in 1991, and then took Leeds to the league title a year later as an inspirational captain. He continued as a top-division footballer for almost a decade, and was forty when he played his last match for Coventry City in 1997.

Another member of Scotland's 1986 World Cup squad, full-back Arthur Albiston, was also released, on a free transfer, in 1988, and in the same year Kevin Moran left for Sporting Gijon in Spain, though Ferguson later said it was possibly 'a mistake' to let him go so early. (Moran carried on playing for Ireland until 1994.) The years 1987 and 1988 saw a rapid contraction of the playing staff – although Ferguson later admitted he should not have trimmed the numbers so extensively. 'As I was to discover the hard way, I had cut us to the bone and ambitious clubs need big squads if they are to challenge on more than one front.'[20]

In some cases there was a backlash. Defender Graeme Hogg was sold to Portsmouth, and promptly attacked his former manager in the *News of the World* for treating him like a 'second-class citizen' and making him train and play with the junior teams 'at places like Rochdale' when his face no longer fitted. 'Even when I left,' Hogg said, 'Ferguson couldn't even be bothered to say "Good luck".' When United formally protested to the FA about the article, Hogg was fined several thousand pounds for the favourite catch-all offence of bringing the game into disrepute. The defender had also accused the United manager of failing to get rid of the clique of star players; nor did Ferguson help team spirit, Hogg said, 'with his rantings and ravings in the dressing room when things are going wrong . . . When he gets launched into one of his blasts, he will bawl and scream at a player with his face inches away from the lad's.'[21]

Hogg was describing what became known as the 'hair-drier' treatment, when, according to Mark Hughes, Ferguson 'would stand nose to nose to you and just shout and bawl, and you would end up with your hair behind your head'.[22] While some players dubbed the manager 'Taggart', because of his resemblance to the TV detective

281

both in his facial features and expressions and in his dour Glaswegian character, Colin Gibson says he was also known as 'the spitting cobra'. Gibson, who is now a football agent, says that, while he's a great admirer of Ferguson, he was never 'that impressed' with the way he handled players, and 'in some cases I thought it was shocking'. By the spring of 1987, Gibson recalls, he was playing so well that Ferguson suggested he might soon be picked for the England squad. 'I felt really proud. It was a side of his man-management: he will build you up when he thinks the time is right. But then he will knock you back down without hesitating. He wouldn't think twice. Blow me, was he ruthless!'[23]

Gibson experienced that ruthless side when United lost 4–0 at Spurs, with Gibson being tormented down the wing all afternoon by Chris Waddle.

> I knew I'd get all the blame. And I knew how cruel he could be when he'd lost it. 'Where the fuck is Gibson? Where is that little cunt?' That's the welcome I got when I got into the dressing room. Then he just fixed his eyes on me and started saying, 'You think you can play for England do you? You wouldn't get picked to play for England's women's hockey team!' What drove me mad is that he was deliberately trying to hurt me by mocking me over the England thing, which he'd helped put in my mind in the first place. He was trying to humiliate me in front of my team-mates. I don't think that is very good man-management or anything clever – I think that's just a guy who cannot take losing and has to bully someone to get rid of his anger.[24]

Gibson says that, when he complained that Ferguson never shouted at Gordon Strachan or Bryan Robson, the United manager tried to fine him three weeks' wages. Gibson pointed out that two weeks was the maximum allowed under clubs' agreement with the

PFA. 'That drove him mad,' says Gibson. 'He was so annoyed that his bully-boy shit wasn't working, that I was standing up to him. He shouted, "You fuckin' cunt!" and went to grab my throat, and then all the players jumped in and stopped it. I would have decked him, honestly, if he had actually laid a finger on me.'[25]

Meanwhile, problems continued with Paul McGrath and Norman Whiteside's regular injuries and persistent drinking. Ferguson had hoped they might still have a role at Old Trafford, but events of the first week in January 1989 convinced him otherwise. The two players spent much of Monday and Tuesday on a tour of south-Manchester and Cheshire pubs, while Ferguson charted their progress through reports phoned in by worried supporters. 'I can just imagine him now,' McGrath taunted later, 'sitting at his desk with a map of the Greater Manchester area plotting our drinking route, putting down pins wherever we'd been spotted. I'm glad he was keeping note of where we were – usually by the end of the night we wouldn't have a clue if we were in Hale or Altrincham – and we'd care even less.'[26] On the Wednesday, Ferguson fined both men the maximum amount he could, only to find they'd resumed their pub crawl hours later.

This was just before a third-round FA Cup tie against QPR, and Ferguson was depending on the Cup to salvage his season. Whiteside was still injured, but McGrath had just returned to the United side after a series of operations. Ferguson's patience finally ran out the night before the match, when McGrath did an interview with Whiteside for the local ITV station, Granada, and was obviously drunk.

McGrath's account is that his knee had started to cause problems again by the middle of the week, and that he reported this to the United coaching staff. So, when Ferguson told players his line-up for the QPR game late on the Friday morning (as was his usual practice), McGrath says he wasn't named even as a possible substitute, let alone in the starting eleven. The Irishman insists he was therefore exempt from the club regulation that players should not drink for forty-eight hours before a game. (He was, however, in breach of the new 'in training' rule.)

> I was injured and free to do what I wanted with my time . . .
> I was a free man, as was my great drinking partner Norman Whiteside, a long-term injury victim and a player with no chance of playing for at least another two months. McGrath and Whiteside, bosom buddies, great mates, partners in crime, were free to spend their Friday as they wished.[27]

McGrath admits that the drinking began before their Granada interview – apparently to calm their nerves – and he says they treated the questions in a light-hearted manner. However, the following day, when Lee Sharpe got flu, Ferguson tried to pick McGrath as a late replacement. The Irishman insisted he wasn't fit enough to play. The two men had what McGrath calls 'the mother and father of all rows' in the United dressing room, before the physiotherapist Jim McGregor intervened to say he didn't think the player's knees were up to it. At the last moment Ferguson had to pick as one of his two substitutes an untried youth player, Deiniol Graham, who'd already appeared for the club third team at Preston that morning. 'I just thought Fergie was being ridiculous,' McGrath said later. 'If he had said on the Friday morning that I was on standby, part and parcel of the first-team squad for that game, I would have prepared properly for the match . . . Then I was expected to make a miraculous recovery and play just because Lee Sharpe had picked up flu.'[28]

Ferguson ordered McGrath to see him on Monday morning. The player expected another routine telling-off, and was stunned to find instead that Gordon Taylor, the chief executive of the Professional Footballers' Association, had been invited to speak on his behalf in a full-scale disciplinary hearing. This astonishing occasion, which is not reported in any of Ferguson's highly detailed books, was also attended by Martin Edwards and the Manchester United secretary, Ken Merrett.

McGrath says the United officials tried to persuade him simply to retire from football, and accept an injury-insurance pay-out of £100,000 (the equivalent of about two years' pay). They also offered to provide the team for a testimonial game in Dublin. 'This was my career they were ending, as coldly and as ruthlessly as breaking a turkey's neck at Christmas,' he says. 'Fergie took the witness stand. He said one or two obvious things about my knees and my discipline, quoted from a dossier prepared for the trial. He wouldn't have any more of my indiscretions. I was out and that was the end of it.'[29] McGrath says Norman Whiteside went in next – though he got off relatively lightly, with a fine and a month's community work at Lilleshall, the FA training college.

Paul McGrath declined United's suggestion. He was insulted by the club's offer, and particularly offended that they would help with a testimonial match only in Dublin, not at Old Trafford. The player says Ferguson was 'visibly devastated' when he announced he wasn't giving up:

> He told me in no uncertain terms that I had made a mistake
> of the highest order, that there was no guarantee that I would
> ever play in his first team again. Life in the reserves, that was
> the prospective price for being a rebel. I asked for a transfer.
> That was turned down. They were prepared to let me quit but
> not to let me move to another club. Bitchy to say the least.[30]

Unlike Alex Ferguson in his final months at Ibrox, McGrath's banishment to the reserves lasted only a few days, and he was back with the senior squad within two weeks of the post-QPR showdown. Six weeks later he even played for the Republic of Ireland in a World Cup qualification game in Hungary. It was an astounding comeback, given that Ferguson had just urged him to give up football on medical grounds, and that the club had considered lodging an insurance claim which undoubtedly would have involved a large pay-out for United on top of the £100,000 they had promised McGrath.

But, though he returned to form, Paul McGrath's relationship with Ferguson never recovered. In the summer of 1989 he went to Aston Villa, two days after Whiteside joined Everton. In each case the fee was around half United's original asking prices. Ferguson would later admit he should have been quicker in selling the two men: the delay meant it took much longer to rebuild the team. Ultimately, getting rid of these players was an important matter of principle, he felt, if United was to shed its image as a drinking club.

In both cases their injuries continued to dog them. After a promising start, Norman Whiteside played just thirty-seven games for Everton before he was forced to give up football a few days after his twenty-sixth birthday. Paul McGrath, however, became a better player than ever at Villa Park, though for long spells playing matches was almost all he did. In an extraordinary arrangement, McGrath was excluded from normal training sessions for fear of aggravating his knee injuries, and was limited to work in the gym. Yet he was PFA Player of the Year in 1993, played in two World Cup finals tournaments, won a then record eighty-three caps, and played his last game for Ireland at the age of thirty-seven.

McGrath's immediate response on leaving United was to sell his story to the *News of the World* (which did a brisk trade with ex-United players at that time). He told readers that the job of manager was 'too big for Ferguson to handle', expressed astonishment that the Old Trafford board had been so patient with the manager, and said that all Ferguson seemed to know about motivation was 'the iron fist'.[31] As with Graeme Hogg, Manchester United protested to the FA about his remarks, and McGrath was fined a record £8,500 for bringing the game into disrepute. McGrath even claims that United threatened to sue him for defamation unless the FA took action, although his article was fairly mild, particularly when measured against some of Ferguson's own comments. (Indeed, years later the PFA secretary Gordon Taylor almost came to blows with Ferguson when pointing out his inconsistency after the United manager had attacked Alan Shearer.) When the United manager then attacked McGrath in his 1992 book, *Six Years at United*, the defender threatened to sue, and he gained revenge with further revelations in his autobiography two years later, though relations have been fairly cordial in recent times, and he was even invited to Ferguson's 1999 testimonial dinner.

Norman Whiteside, in contrast, claims to have turned down an offer of £50,000 to reveal all, and subsequently has kept fairly quiet about his dealings with Ferguson (declining, for example, to be interviewed for this book). The United manager admits he always had more sympathy for Whiteside – partly because he was younger – and he allowed Manchester United to host a testimonial game for him in 1992.

One can sympathise with Alex Ferguson's determination to get rid of heavy drinkers such as Whiteside and McGrath. Where his conduct is questionable, however, is in urging Paul McGrath to retire early on the grounds of injury. Nor was this a one-off incident, prompted by pessimistic medical diagnoses, for Colin Gibson tells a similar story. Gibson, too, was out of the United side for long periods (because of a cruciate injury), and he says Ferguson also tried to get him to give up football:

> I was offered £125,000 by him to retire – I think the club thought they could get £250,000 insurance money and could get a profit. I told him, 'No, I'm not gonna do it. I'm gonna play on.' It's funny: even though I was defying him, he seemed to admire that spirit, that fighting spirit. Without my injury problems, I think I could have been a 'Fergie player' – I'm his type, a fighter, and he liked that.[32]

Colin Gibson was eventually transferred to Leicester City in 1990, and again continued in league football for many years (until he was nearly thirty-five). The allegations he and McGrath make about United's attempts to get them to retire carry serious implications, especially since the suggestions were a shock to both players. The Manchester United Football Club of the 1980s did not always adhere to the higher standards of behaviour it was forced to adopt when it became a public company in 1991. Three other United stars from the 1980s did decide to give up football – Steve Coppell (in 1983, before Ferguson arrived), Gary Bailey (1987) and Remi Moses (1988). The McGrath/Gibson revelations may raise slight doubts as to whether these players, too, could have carried on in the game if they'd tried.

It was ironic that, while grappling with these two highly talented drinkers, Alex Ferguson was making strenuous efforts to sign a young player whose lifestyle would have proved as much of a challenge. Ferguson decided to go for Paul Gascoigne on Boxing Day 1987, after the young Newcastle player had humiliated a formidable United midfield of Robson, Whiteside and Moses in a 1–0 defeat at St James's Park. Gascoigne capped his performance by patting Moses patronisingly on the head. Ferguson says he approached Gascoigne's advisers in the following summer, though in truth discussions started within a few weeks of the Newcastle game. Gascoigne's financial advisers, Mel Stein and Len Lazarus, agreed to go to Old Trafford to meet Ferguson and a couple of United directors. The manager said he'd be happy to do a deal involving an exchange with any existing player at Old Trafford with the exception of Bryan Robson. According to Stein, Ferguson envisaged 'Paul and Bryan forming a partnership in midfield, with Robson as Gazza's mentor . . . and clearly saw him as the last part in the jigsaw of the all-conquering club he was trying to create'.[33]

The difficulty, however, was the personal terms sought by Gascoigne's men: a £100,000 signing-on fee for their player; a £125,000 salary (or £2,400 a week), and £5,000 for every England cap – trivial sums by the standards of today, but huge in the days before Sky was spending hundreds of millions on TV football rights. In real terms it was probably the most expensive package yet demanded by an English footballer, and this for a player who was still only twenty and had yet to play for his country. The wages sought were far greater than those earned by Bryan Robson or Gordon Strachan, both of whom were seasoned internationals. The United board could not accept these financial demands without wrecking the club's pay structure.

Ferguson told Stein and Lazarus that he wanted to talk to Gascoigne face to face, in the hope that his personal touch might persuade him that Manchester United was his best future, even if the deal offered was less rewarding than he wanted. A meeting was arranged at Stein's house in north London in March 1988, before United were due to meet Spurs in an evening testimonial match.

When Gascoigne finally arrived from Tyneside, he and Ferguson shut themselves away in the tiny office which Stein used at home. 'Paul merely listened,' Stein wrote later. 'He felt tired and confused; it had been a long drive down and all he really wanted was a meal and a drink. It was unfortunate for Ferguson that, although he'd got his meeting with his man, it was the wrong time and the wrong place.' Afterwards, when Stein asked how it had gone, Ferguson replied, 'It went well, I thought. He's a nice lad. He'll do fine with us.'[34] The United manager had greatly warmed to the player, and felt he had an appealing vulnerability about him – the air of someone who needed a good cuddle. Stein reckons Ferguson left feeling confident that he'd got his man, but Stein knew he was mistaken.

Apart from United's unwillingness to meet the financial terms being demanded by Gascoigne's advisers, there were two other reasons why Manchester United would have been lucky to get the player. First, Gascoigne himself was very keen to join Liverpool, but the 1988 league champions were still short of cash after spending heavily in 1987, and their manager, Kenny Dalglish, had asked him to wait another year. Second, the Newcastle United chairman had reached a private understanding with Irving Scholar, his opposite number at Tottenham Hotspur, that the London club would have first option if Gascoigne became available.

Alex Ferguson knew little of this. That summer he flew off to Malta for a family holiday after an anxious time personally. Cathy had recovered after a serious illness which had seen her spend a week in intensive care. Just as the family were about to go abroad, he says, Gascoigne rang to tell him, 'Mr Ferguson, you go and enjoy your holiday . . . I am signing for Manchester United when you come back.' Ferguson told the player he'd never regret his decision, and began his Maltese break dreaming of having Gascoigne in the same line-up as Bryan Robson and Mark Hughes, whom he also planned to bring back to United.[35] It was a cocktail which Manchester pub and bar owners might have found just as pleasing as that of Robson, McGrath and Whiteside.

Alex Ferguson expected Martin Edwards and fellow director Maurice Watkins to sort out the final details of the Gascoigne deal while he was away. But the Spurs manager, Terry Venables, proved far more persuasive when he met Gascoigne. The player 'recognised something in the Cockney that he'd not seen in Ferguson', says Mel Stein. 'The two of them got on incredibly well, and when Venables explained his football philosophy Paul understood exactly what he was saying.'[36] More convincing still, it appears, was the England winger Chris Waddle, who had himself moved from Newcastle to Spurs the summer before. Venables asked Waddle to speak to Gascoigne, and they met in a Tyneside pub. 'At first he told me he was going to Man. United. I gave him the spiel about Spurs and within three pints of lager he told me he had to go,' says Waddle. 'His parting words were, "Right, tomorrow I'll sign for Spurs."'[37]

Mel Stein says that when they tried to contact Ferguson on holiday, to alert him to developments, his mobile phone was dead because of a flat battery. United had eventually agreed to Gascoigne's terms, but by then the player 'felt morally committed to Spurs'. Maurice Watkins pleaded that United were now happy to pay the money. 'Yes, but Spurs gave it first,' Stein replied.[38]

Martin Edwards phoned Ferguson at his hotel in Malta to deliver the bad news. A clinching detail, apparently, had been the London club's promise to buy a house for Gascoigne's parents. 'Somebody had to lose out,' Stein concludes. 'It was just that not many players said no to Manchester United.'[39]

'The fact that he never wore the red shirt was his mistake, not ours,' Ferguson wrote in his memoirs. 'As far as I am concerned, I had a solid promise that he would sign for me and I think that his change of mind hurt both of us.'[40] But Ferguson can hardly complain. Nobody knew better than he and the Tottenham chairman Irving Scholar that promises aren't worth much in football. Indeed, Paul Gascoigne had only behaved in the same way that Ferguson himself had treated the Nottingham Forest manager, Matt Gillies, back in 1970, when, on his own admission, he changed his mind about joining Forest and went to Falkirk instead.

It's intriguing to speculate what might have happened had Paul Gascoigne gone to Old Trafford in 1988. Despite his outstanding performances for England in the 1990 World Cup, the player never fulfilled his great promise, being burdened by injuries and a private life that included regular binge drinking and beating up his wife. Ferguson was probably better suited than any manager to have got the most of Gascoigne's huge talent, though he would hardly have been reassured by Bryan Robson's subsequent pledge that 'we would have kept a friendly eye on him'.[41]

There were other disappointments on the transfer front. In 1987 Ferguson flew to Sweden to sign Glenn Hysen, only for Fiorentina to make the defender a better offer. And he tried twice to buy the Nottingham Forest left-back Stuart Pearce, who'd recently won his first cap for England. Pearce was a typical Ferguson player, whose snarling, indomitable approach would be exemplified by the famous

TV pictures during a tense England penalty shoot-out in the 1996 European Championship. The Forest manager, Brian Clough, simply wouldn't answer United's calls about the player, so in the winter of 1988 Ferguson decided to drive to Nottingham with the United chairman and call on Clough unannounced. 'It was the only option left,' he says. 'No calling card. No appointment. No nothing.'[42] And no chance either. The Forest receptionist kept Ferguson and Martin Edwards waiting ten minutes before she returned to say that Clough wasn't there, even though his Mercedes was parked outside. The two men decided to hang around for an hour or two, in the hope that Clough might appear. 'What do you do next?' asks Ferguson. 'Get an arrest warrant? No, just climb in the car and go home . . . But if they had let me get to [Pearce], just for a few minutes of talks, I think I could have sold United to him. He would . . . have been a sensation with us. This is a club built for heroes like him.'[43]

At times, Ferguson and Edwards operated like spies in a Len Deighton thriller. They went on the road again to secure the services of the Aberdeen goalkeeper Jim Leighton. Despite his promise to Dick Donald not to poach his players, Ferguson felt he was under 'no obligation' after Aberdeen sold Joe Miller to Celtic without first alerting United, as he thought they'd agreed.[44] So Ferguson went behind Dick Donald's back to 'tap' Leighton, whom he considered 'the best goalkeeper in Britain'.[45] After several phone calls, when the deal almost collapsed over Leighton's pay demands, the player had a secret appointment with Ferguson and Edwards in Glasgow early in 1988.

'It was, of course, a cloak and dagger meeting,' says Leighton, who'd borrowed a friend's car so as not to be noticed. 'Ferguson and Edwards couldn't afford to be seen talking to me or they would have been in serious trouble with the footballing authorities': approaching players without their club's permission had long been forbidden (and is also liable to action under civil law for encouraging someone to break a contract). The conspirators met just off the M73 near

Cumbernauld; Leighton joined Edwards in his car, and they followed Ferguson's vehicle to the home of one of his relatives (quite likely his sister-in-law again). But they couldn't all turn up at the same time, according to Leighton. 'He was to indicate the house at which we were to stop and where the back door would be left open for us. Ferguson would drive past the house but return later. Car telephones ensured that the manoeuvre was completed without a hitch.'[46] Manchester United paid Aberdeen £450,000, though the figure was announced as £750,000 – possibly to help Dick Donald save face with Aberdeen fans over the loss of one of his best players.

Ferguson also persuaded Mark Hughes to return to Old Trafford from Barcelona in 1988. It had long been obvious that Hughes had never really wanted to go to Spain; fans suspected the move was encouraged by his agent and the United board, who found the £1.8 million fee too good to resist (especially Martin Edwards, who got 1 per cent of all transfer profits at that time). Hughes failed to settle in Barcelona, where he was playing and competing with Gary Lineker, and ended up in the reserves before Terry Venables was sacked in the summer of 1987 (before moving to Spurs). That November, Ferguson and Edwards went on another secret mission, with the United manager telling Hughes – presumably when Edwards was out of the room – that he would never have agreed to sell him had he himself been at Old Trafford. 'He could sell ice-cubes to the Eskimos!' said Hughes. 'His sales pitch was brilliant and he meant every word. It was that deep conviction to United that swayed me.'[47] There was a hitch, however. Hughes's tax situation made an immediate return to England too expensive for him. To resolve this, he went on loan to Bayern Munich for a period, which proved rather more successful than his time in Catalonia. In the meantime Barcelona's price climbed from £1 million to £1.6 million.

Bringing Hughes back to United was a risk, since he too had been a heavy drinker during his first spell with the club – especially in his final six months, when he says he didn't want to leave Old Trafford and 'spent virtually every night drowning my sorrows'.[48] Moreover, Hughes's last exchange with Ferguson had been a row on the touch-line at the important World Cup qualifying game in Cardiff in 1985. The young striker – then only twenty-one – bravely blew his top with the assistant Scotland manager for telling the referee to book his Welsh colleague Peter Nicholas.

Hughes was a reformed character on his return; the drinking stopped, and he was now an even better player. Shortly afterwards Barcelona also approached United about selling Gary Lineker for £2.5 million. Their offer was declined, partly because there wasn't the money, and partly because forwards were no longer the priority.

Mark Hughes was always a great favourite with the United crowd, and so too was Ralph Milne, though for different reasons. It remains a mystery why Ferguson signed the Scottish winger from Bristol City, since he was never a footballer of true United calibre. 'Old Trafford was simply too much for him and he faded into the shadows,' says Ferguson.[49] Today he's cited as one of the manager's few bad buys, yet Milne also remains a cult figure among supporters, who still occasionally sing his name. Indeed, in a recent poll of fans to pick the 100 greatest United players of all time he picked up the ironic vote and squeezed into the list in last place.

Even with Mark Hughes and Jim Leighton in the side, Manchester United took a step backwards in the 1988–89 season. From runners-up in 1988 they fell to eleventh in the table. Mark Hughes was United's top scorer and picked up the PFA Player of the Year award, but his return seemed to stifle Brian McClair, who scored at barely half his rate of the season before (though he partly played in mid-field). The autumn of 1988 had seen a defeat by Wimbledon in the League Cup and a run of nine games without a win (eight of them draws). And in eight of those games United had been ahead at one point. Squandering the advantage had become something of a habit, prompting one wag to suggest that you should never let a United player take your dog for a walk, since he couldn't hold on to a lead.

Liverpool meanwhile came close to their second league and cup double in four years.

Gates at Old Trafford fell for the third year running, to an average of 36,500 – the lowest since 1962, and almost 8,000 less than in Ron Atkinson's last full season. The official attendance for the home game against Wimbledon in May 1989 was just 23,268 – the smallest Old Trafford league crowd for twenty-three years (and even this figure was inflated by including all season-ticket holders). The supporters were getting restless. An early edition of *Red Issue*, one of the fanzines which had just sprung to life at United (somewhat later than at most clubs) asked, 'When is Mr Ferguson going to realise that he doesn't know what he is doing and return to that quiet backwater Aberdeen?'[50]

The final straw for Ferguson, however, was the FA Cup quarterfinal, when United lost 1–0 to Nottingham Forest at Old Trafford. When people cite a Forest FA Cup game as being crucial in Alex Ferguson's fortunes, they usually mean the tie played the following year, but the March 1989 fixture has a better claim to be the turning point. Ferguson now realised it was time for a proper clear-out: 'I resolved that I had to change everything round and gather a squad around me capable of winning the League.'[51] If he was to succeed in England, he had to outwit two fellow Scots: the Liverpool manager, Kenny Dalglish, and George Graham, whose Arsenal side eventually pipped the Merseyside club to the league title that season with a lastminute goal in a dramatic final game at Anfield. Ferguson knew that, even after two and a half years, the Manchester United team still wasn't really his. When he surveyed the dressing room he couldn't say 'hand on heart, that the team mirrored me in any shape or form'.[52]

Orange-Juice Heroes

'I have always considered that the player you produce is better than the one you buy.'

ALEX FERGUSON[1]

W hat had shocked Alex Ferguson most when he arrived at Manchester United was the poor state of the reserve and youth teams. 'What youth policy?' he exclaimed when a friend asked him about the youth programme inherited from Ron Atkinson. 'He's left me a shower of shit.' Although United had reached the final of the 1986 FA Youth Cup, losing 3–1 over two legs to Manchester City, the team contained few promising players. (Only four – Walsh, Gill, Martin and Wilson – ever played in the first team, and none for very long.) Yet Manchester United had pioneered the practice of developing successful youth players. What had happened to the organisation and spirit which in Matt Busby's heyday had nurtured legendary stars such as Duncan Edwards, Bobby Charlton, Nobby Stiles and George Best?

In the 1950s the so-called 'Busby Babes' had been to the FA's new Youth Cup what Real Madrid were to the early European Cup, winning the trophy in each of the first five years it was contested. They had attracted crowds of 20,000 and 30,000 to Old Trafford, went unbeaten in their first forty-three matches in the competition, and regularly clocked up scores in double figures (most notably a record 23–0 win over Nantwich in 1952). As a result, in the five years before the Munich air crash in 1958 Matt Busby needed to buy only two players from outside.

But by the time Ferguson arrived, in 1986, Manchester City seemed to have stolen United's clothes. The Maine Road club had been especially successful in attracting young talent from the Manchester area, including Earl Barrett, David White, Paul Moulden, Paul Lake, Andy Hinchcliffe and the Beckford brothers, Darren and Jason, though the group looked more exciting in prospect than they do in hindsight. (None became regular internationals.) It was also notable that many of City's best young prospects were black, whereas United had very few black players in their youth teams, and none had made the first team at Old Trafford since Dennis Walker in 1963.

Ferguson was astonished that United had only four scouts working in Manchester and the North-West, whereas at Aberdeen, despite its limited resources, he had the services of thirteen to cover the central belt of Scotland – an area with a similar population. Manchester City also seemed to have much better relations with schools and local junior teams. 'I think they maybe didn't see Manchester United as a club where they were going to get a chance,' says Ferguson.[2] He admitted there was a 'sourness and bitterness in the area that we don't do enough locally'.[3] 'Even Oldham and Crewe were doing better than us,' he lamented.[4]

Since his beginnings in management at East Stirlingshire, Ferguson had always placed great emphasis on youth recruitment. The advantages were many. It was easier to indoctrinate young players rather than to eradicate bad or unwelcome habits which older recruits might have picked up elsewhere. Aberdeen had shown that youngsters who grew up together developed a sense of team spirit and loyalty, especially 'local boys because they supply a special ingredient of commitment to the club'.[5] And it was more satisfying than gambling on the transfer market – and cheaper, of course.

Ferguson had quickly identified that the main problem lay not in the way young players were being coached and nurtured at United, but in the quality of the teenage recruits in the first place. The youth-team coach, Eric Harrison, says he was upset when Ferguson called him into his office and complained that the quality wasn't good enough. How could he say that, Harrison asked, when both Norman Whiteside and Mark Hughes had come through the youth sides? Ferguson was adamant that he expected better. '"OK then," I said, "you bring some more players to the club, some good material, and I'll get some players in the first team for you."'[6] Ferguson promised to find Harrison the very best.

Within days Ferguson had gathered together the Manchester United scouting and youth-development staff to insist that things had to improve. United were the great under-achievers, he said, and the current standard just wasn't good enough. He no longer wanted any bad players. 'I think they were hurt and shocked,' he said later, 'but it had to be done. I said they must not just bring me the best boy in the street but the best in the country.'[7]

Ferguson held meetings with local soccer clubs to explain that Manchester United were back in the youth business. He admits that United then went out and signed four young Manchester players who were probably below the standard required, but it was an important gesture to show the club's new commitment. 'What we had to do,' says Ferguson, 'was to show that there was an intent: that we'd arrived, and we were going to do something about it.'[8]

United soon established a nursery team in Glasgow, and also two more elaborate youth-recruitment centres – or 'schools of excellence' – one in Belfast and another in Houghton-le-Spring in County Durham (chosen because the north-east produced more footballers than any other area. The Durham centre was run by the former striker Bryan 'Pop' Robson – not to be confused with the United team captain.) Four new scouts were recruited in Manchester, and two in the Midlands. Significantly, Ferguson appointed Brian Kidd, who had been doing community work for the Professional Footballers' Association in Salford, to run the main United school of excellence at Old Trafford. Kidd was one of the most popular of United's ex-players, having marked his nineteenth birthday by scoring one of the goals in the 1968 European Cup final. He was himself a product of the Manchester United youth system, and he knew his local geography: he'd been brought up in Collyhurst in east Manchester, where he attended the same school as Nobby Stiles (though not at the same time), and had also played for both Manchester City and Bolton. His CV also included brief, unsuccessful, spells as manager of Preston North End and non-League Barrow.

Kidd's mission was to sew up Manchester for United, and having a former Busby Babe doing the job could only impress prospective parents. 'I didn't want to hear any more about Manchester City getting the best kids,' said Ferguson.[9] As to the claim that young players got a better chance at Maine Road, he harked back to his days as a toolmaker: 'If a father is choosing an apprenticeship for his son, he's always going to take Rolls-Royce – isn't he? – over the local engineering shop.'[10]

Alex Ferguson also claimed, however, that United's youth policy had been undermined by improper practices by rival clubs. He spoke of payments of as much as £20,000 plus a new car being made to parents of young recruits, and of the players themselves getting pocket money of £100 a week. 'We refuse to be involved in illegal payments,' he insisted. 'It's illegal with obvious tax evasion, and it's against all the football rules.'[11]

Yet in the past, in Matt Busby's day, Manchester United had been quite willing to offer inducements to young players. In 1980 Granada TV's *World in Action* had exposed how throughout the 1950s and '60s Busby's scouts would regularly pay money to parents to get their sons to join United. Two notable examples were future internationals Brian Greenhoff and Peter Lorimer (though Lorimer eventually joined Leeds, and United scouts had to travel to Dundee to retrieve their £2,500).[12] Ferguson believed such payments fuelled 'jealousies' and 'squabbling', though he later hinted that the practice was still prevalent before he came to Old Trafford:

> We tackled this issue head on when I arrived at the club . . . I was well aware of the trouble that can develop if young kids are being offered money or whatever. At that age they should be playing for love, not money, and anything that sets players against each other is bad for them, bad for the team, and bad for the club. So we just said right from the start: 'If a boy wants to come to the club, he'll get the same deal as everyone else.'[13]

Nonetheless, in the years ahead Alex Ferguson's club would be punished more than once for breaking the FA rules about poaching young players from other clubs.

One of Brian Kidd's first tasks was to go and watch a thirteen-year-old Salford schoolboy who'd been recommended to Ferguson not by a United scout, but by a ground steward at Old Trafford called Harold Wood. Kidd reported back that, while the dazzling youngster was a United fan, he was training with Manchester City. Fergie ordered his staff to take a closer look. The boy's name was Ryan Wilson – he was the son of Danny Wilson, a Rugby League star – though he would later adopt his mother's surname, Giggs. He also changed his country: having been captain of England schoolboys, he later opted to play for Wales at a senior level.

Giggs took part in a United trial, but continued training with City. In November 1987, on his fourteenth birthday, the doorbell rang at Giggs's home in Swinton. It was Alex Ferguson himself. Would the lad sign schoolboy forms for United? 'If the manager of Manchester United comes round to your house,' Giggs said later, 'you tend to be a bit flattered. It's a rather nice feeling and not the kind of offer you turn down. I thought: *yes*. But my mum said she'd let him know.' Giggs explains that his mother, 'being the honourable woman she is, wanted to do the decent thing by City, because they'd been good to me. So she went to see Ken Barnes, their chief scout, to give them first refusal. She asked him if he was going to sign me and he said no, he wasn't. Not interested.'[14] So Ryan Giggs signed for Manchester United instead.

Ken Barnes admits he made a mistake; he was too slow to appreciate Giggs's talent. In contrast, both Alex Ferguson and Archie Knox say that Giggs was the only player whom they've ever seen at the age of thirteen who they could guarantee would one day make the first team. Giggs was soon training with the senior players, and making a name for himself by the way he tormented the England full-back Viv Anderson in front of his colleagues.

Before long the youth players were looking so promising that Bobby Charlton began to ask when they were next playing, and would then take time off work to go and watch them. By such things was Ferguson's long-term future assured.

Eric Harrison says that, without Alex Ferguson's involvement, Manchester United 'would definitely not have signed all our superb youngsters'.[15] As at St Mirren and Aberdeen, Ferguson himself would often intervene personally to clinch a young player's signature and persuade parents that United would look after their sons. He travelled long distances, popped up on doorsteps, and showed hesitant parents round Old Trafford. 'Trust me,' he would say, assuring them their boys would be looked after.

Winger Ben Thornley was another local boy who'd been training with Manchester City, only to be lured away by Fergie's personal touch. 'I think I must have been one of the very few privileged lads who had Alex Ferguson round here with Brian Kidd to the house, to talk to myself and my parents. And obviously, when I knew that he was interested, it swayed my decision and I went with my heart and went there.'[16] But Giggs and Thornley weren't the only ones to get personal visits from the boss. Simon Davies, too, was expected – and expecting – to sign for Manchester City on his fourteenth birthday. At the last moment a United scout suggested he take part in a trial match.

> I played half-decent in that, and Alex Ferguson and the youth-development officer, Joe Brown, came to my house the following night and signed me up. So within three days I'd gone from Manchester City to Man. United! I think my mum got the posh cups out, because I think my sister actually said: 'Mum, why have we got the cups out?'[17]

Davies (who later ended up at Rochdale) says Ferguson spent nearly an hour 'just chatting' with his parents. 'He was very relaxed and saying, "It won't be easy, it will be a lot of hard work. But we'll take care of him. And he'll have the best treatment." It's reassuring, isn't it?'[18]

Whenever he could, Ferguson would watch the United youth teams on Saturday mornings, even though the first team would usually have a match only a few hours later. He'd often spectate from his office overlooking the pitch at The Cliff, where United's A and B teams – the third and fourth sides – played home fixtures. 'He was there all the time,' says another youth player, Deiniol Graham. 'We just knew he'd be there. And if he wasn't there, we'd think he was there.'[19] If the first team was away that day, Ferguson would phone just before one o'clock to ask how the teams had done, and who had played well.

As at Aberdeen, Ferguson made an effort to get to know each teenager by name. 'I had six months under Ron,' says the former youth player Russell Beardsmore, 'and he spoke to me or said "Hello" or something once in six months. I spoke to Alex more in his first three or four days than I did to Ron in that whole six months.'[20] 'The gaffer used to watch so many games, it was incredible,' says goalkeeper Kevin Pilkington. 'He didn't get too involved; he was just there – a presence in the background. You knew he was gonna give youth a chance.'[21]

Sometimes Ferguson would stop players and ask them a general-knowledge question – for instance, how heavy is a football? – and if they got it right he'd ask them something else. At other times he and his coaches conducted quizzes for the youth players in his crammed office. 'Some of the answers they gave were absolutely hilarious,' says Eric Harrison. 'This was serving an important role. The players realised they could relax in the company of the Boss.' Yet the fun and games were combined with strict discipline, as the boys still had to do the traditional chores of football apprentices, including keeping all areas of The Cliff clean and tidy. Ferguson 'would inspect all the rooms on Friday afternoons and the apprentice professionals could not go home until everything was spick and span'.[22] Says Kevin Pilkington, 'Not a day went past when he didn't shout at Robbie Savage, "Get your fuckin' hair cut, Savage!"'[23]

Yet some felt Ferguson could be too harsh with the apprentices at times. 'I've been sickened when he's laid into the kids at reserve matches,' said the first-team defender Graeme Hogg, who was himself a past product of the United youth team. 'It was right out of order. Kids need building up not knocking down. Some would go out visibly shaken.'[24]

A sprinkling of players from the youth sides had made brief appearances for the first team in Fergie's first two seasons. They included goalkeeper Gary Walsh, defenders Lee Martin and Tony Gill, midfield players David Wilson and Russell Beardsmore, and forwards Deiniol Graham, Mark Robins and Jules Maiorana (who gave up work in the family boutique in Cambridge to sign for United). Only Gary Walsh had enjoyed a reasonable run in the senior side, but the first of the group to make an impact was the small but terrier-like twenty-year-old midfielder Russell Beardsmore. He put in a particularly effective performance in only his second full league game, United's 3–1 win over Liverpool on New Year's Day 1989, when they fielded three other young players – Lee Martin (aged twenty), Lee Sharpe (seventeen) and Mark Robins (nineteen). Ten days later, the team for the FA Cup replay at Queen's Park Rangers included six players who were twenty or under – Martin, Beardsmore and Sharpe, plus Tony Gill (twenty) and David Wilson and Deiniol Graham (both nineteen). United's first goal came from Tony Gill, and then in extra time Deiniol Graham put the Reds ahead from a David Wilson cross, only for QPR to force a 2–2 draw.

As journalists began making comparisons with the Busby Babes, the youngsters were inevitably dubbed 'Fergie's Fledglings'. They quickly caught the public imagination, and – in the days when cup-ties could go to three games or more – the second replay against QPR, back again at Old Trafford, attracted 10,000 more people than went to the original game.

The United manager had been forced to play what he pointedly called 'our orange-juice heroes' (in contrast to the drinking prefer-ences of some of his senior players) because of a spate of injuries to senior players such as Robson, Strachan and Whiteside, and the dis-pute over Paul McGrath's drinking.[25] Three of his Fledglings – Martin, Beardsmore and Sharpe – were picked for the England Under-21 team, with Sharpe the youngest man ever to play at Under-21 level. Ferguson had spoken of the possibility of 'as many as half a dozen new names featuring quite regularly on the First Division team sheet'. The two Lees, Sharpe and Martin, caused him particu-lar excitement, along with Russell Beardsmore. 'I predict all three will play for England,' he said. 'Martin and Sharpe might well make it as a rare club and country full-back pairing.'[26]

Inevitably, however, most of the youngsters lost their places when the senior players returned. Fergie's Fledglings were also unlucky with injuries. Gary Walsh was a regular victim; Deiniol Graham broke an arm; Tony Gill broke his leg and had ankle trouble; while

Jules Maiorana suffered a knee injury which for more than three years prevented him from playing football. Beardsmore enjoyed a longer spell in the first team, while Robins, Martin and Sharpe would all play significant roles in the Alex Ferguson story. But none of Fergie's Fledglings lived up to the hyperbole of 1989 and went on to fulfil people's hopes.

Gill and Maiorana eventually retired through injury, as did the defender Billy Garton (from a slightly earlier generation of young players), who suffered from ME. Some of them now believe that they were victims of the pressure on Alex Ferguson to succeed quickly. Later in 1989, when Ferguson bought five new £1-million-plus players, their opportunities to break through were again curtailed. The fact is that the Fledglings were never quite good enough to take United to the highest honours, and certainly none has come back to haunt Ferguson by forging an outstanding career somewhere else. Wilson, Graham, Beardsmore and Martin all had spells with lower-division clubs; Sharpe, Robins and Walsh are all still playing, though no longer at the top level. 'Although they weren't bad, they weren't top class,' Ferguson admitted later, 'but putting them in the team at that time gave credence to our youth system.'[27] They had helped Alex Ferguson play for time, giving United fans and directors a taste of what was to come.

In due course, a generation of Manchester United youth players *would* break into the first team. They would also go on to play together for England. And two of them would make a club and country full-back pairing. But not just yet.

18

'Fergie, Fergie, on the Dole!'

'Sometimes you have to be cold, clinical and make judgements without compassion, even to a man you know like your own brother.'

ALEX FERGUSON, 1990[1]

Michael Knighton has gone down as one of the great comic figures in Old Trafford history. The enduring image is of the moustachioed businessman, dressed in United training kit, juggling the ball from knee to knee before the club's opening game of the season in August 1989. As he blew kisses to the Stretford End and pumped the ball into an empty goal, fans acclaimed him as the new owner of Manchester United, in succession to Martin Edwards, who was unpopular with the Reds' supporters for the way he ran the club.

Edwards had told Alex Ferguson earlier that summer that he was looking for someone to buy his majority shareholding in the club for £10 million, so long as the purchaser invested another £10 million in rebuilding the Stretford End of the ground. The United manager had even put out feelers among Scottish business friends to find a suitable owner, with little response. It was only the day before the season began that Edwards let Ferguson know that the buyer would be a property speculator called Michael Knighton, who had promised to retain Ferguson as manager.

The deal eventually fell through, as Knighton had trouble raising the money (and with hindsight Martin Edwards must be hugely relieved, for the takeover would have greatly undervalued the club). Knighton subsequently scaled down his ambitions and bought Carlisle United instead. Today he remains the butt of jokes throughout football, from boardrooms to fanzines – and especially, of course, among Manchester United followers.

Yet there's a strong case for saying that Michael Knighton had a more influential role in the recent history of Manchester United than many of the club's managers, directors or footballers. He talked a very good game. United, he said, had a 'major pulling power that has not been exploited', and he predicted that the club would become a £150 million business within fifteen years.[2] (In fact this happened much more quickly, and for a few months in 2000 United was valued at over £1 billion.) Knighton commissioned a report from the accountants Robson Rhodes which identified several areas for commercial development at Old Trafford, such as TV rights, merchandise, a magazine and even a hotel, and United ruthlessly exploited such ideas in the decade ahead in a way they'd never managed in the past.

Knighton's short-term impact proved equally important. For almost three years Alex Ferguson had been constrained by Martin Edwards's tight hold on the Old Trafford purse strings. More than once the United manager had publicly voiced his frustration at being unable to match clubs like Liverpool or Spurs when it came to buying top-class talent. In the summer of 1989, however, just as the Knighton deal was being negotiated, money suddenly became available for team-building. Some of this was the proceeds from the sale of Whiteside, McGrath, Strachan, Olsen and Davenport (who raised £2.5 million in all). More important was that Edwards seemed to relax his financial stringency once the sale had apparently been secured with the putative multimillionaire, and it looked as if the club would be flush with funds under its new owner.

'Knighton coming and putting a value on the club made it easy to spend an extra couple of million,' says the director Michael Edelson.[3]

In just two months Manchester United spent close to £7 million on almost half a new team. During the close season the England midfielder Neil Webb came from Nottingham Forest for a fee fixed by a tribunal at £1.5 million. Ferguson had originally pursued Webb a couple of years earlier, but, as with Stuart Pearce, he had been rebuffed by Brian Clough. He saw the midfield playmaker as a long-term replacement for Bryan Robson and a reliable supplier of goals. Mike Phelan, who came from Norwich for £750,000, was another midfielder, but he could also help out in defence. The spending continued even after the season had started: centre-back Gary Pallister cost £2.3 million from Middlesbrough, Paul Ince £800,000 from West Ham, and the winger Danny Wallace moved from Southampton for £1.2 million. Ince's transfer dragged on for weeks, with queries about his medical record, but Ferguson kept ringing the player to assure him that the deal would eventually go through. It was resolved when United agreed to pay £5,000 a game on top of the basic fee.

In a few months Ferguson had spent almost as much as Ron Atkinson had in all his supposedly profligate five years. 'No manager on earth can have a grievance if he gets the sack for not delivering the silverware after spending that little lot,' Atkinson remarked unhelpfully.[4]

The sudden freedom to spend was best illustrated with the acquisition of Gary Pallister, who was an alternative choice after United failed for a second time to sign Glenn Hysen. Earlier in 1989 the Swede had promised Ferguson he would leave Fiorentina for United: he visited Old Trafford, and even went to see Bryan Robson at his home, but the talks stalled over money. In the end Hysen gave up waiting, and both he and the Italian club accepted better offers from Liverpool. It was intensely irritating at the time, but Ferguson was lucky not to sign him, for Hysen was a great disappointment at Anfield and stayed only a couple of seasons.

Having been trumped by Liverpool once again, United were determined to get Pallister instead. Again it was Ferguson's second try. He'd approached Middlesbrough two years earlier, after seeing the defender in a minor cup-tie at Rochdale, but the player was not pursued. United's chief scout, Tony Collins, had doubts. It was an expensive misjudgement, since Ferguson reckons the Teesside club would have been willing to take little more than £500,000 for Pallister in 1987. 'That was the price of Tony's caution,' he said later. 'He was a man who always wanted to make sure.'[5] (But perhaps such caution was understandable after the costly blunders of the Atkinson era.) Collins was not the only one to be uncertain. Many people thought £2.3 million was grossly excessive for a defender whose credentials were not proven. The Middlesbrough directors refused to reduce their valuation of Pallister, however, and at one point during the talks Ferguson was again tempted to give up. But the United director Maurice Watkins urged him to keep trying, and eventually the deal was struck. It is hard to imagine that United would have been so persistent at that price in previous seasons.

Alex Ferguson acknowledged that his future was 'at stake' that season, and within weeks many fans and observers were questioning the wisdom of his purchases.[6] United had beaten the champions Arsenal 4–1 after Michael Knighton's opening-day juggling act (which Ferguson had warned against), but the result was untypical, and the five newcomers seemed to make no difference to United's continuing mediocrity on the pitch. After scoring against Arsenal, Neil Webb injured himself playing for England and was out for most of the season. The others didn't mesh with the existing squad, and Pallister in particular got off to a poor start. The autumn saw some of the grimmest moments of Ferguson's managerial career.

The first came at Maine Road in late September, when United were walloped 5–1 by Manchester City, despite the inclusion of

Phelan, Ince, Pallister and Wallace in their side. Any defeat by their Manchester neighbours was bad news, but 5–1 was humiliation. 'What a waste of money!' the City fans had taunted. 'Fergie Out!' went up the cry from many United supporters, doubtless aided by plenty of City voices (though the more cynical among the home crowd probably prayed that Ferguson would stay).

'I'm not sure I've ever seen anyone look so unhappy with life,' said the Manchester City coach John Deehan.[7] 'You get one of these once in a lifetime and I got mine at Maine Road,' Ferguson commented afterwards, adding that it was his 'biggest ever defeat in management'. (This was not strictly true: he'd twice lost 5–0 at St Mirren, albeit in insignificant end-of-season games.) 'It hurts,' he said. 'Badly. Suicide is the only way to describe our defeat.'[8]

It could be described as a freak result. Even neutrals would agree that City scored with almost the only chances they had; Leighton had few saves to make, and United won twelve corners to City's four. Such details weren't much consolation. When Ferguson arrived home with his son Darren that afternoon, Cathy asked what the score had been. 'That's brilliant!' she exclaimed when Darren muttered that it was 5–1, before he'd had time to add 'for Manchester City'. Her husband went to bed early in the evening and hid his head under the pillow 'hoping I wouldn't wake up'.[9] When Cathy came in to ask what had happened, he says he was still so shocked he could hardly answer. 'I was as close to putting my head in the oven as I have ever been, and I think there would have been plenty of volunteers to turn on the gas had I done so.'[10]

The papers were quickly predicting that Ferguson would soon be axed, or suggesting that he should be. 'It's becoming obvious he's not the man for United,' said his former Aberdeen striker Joe Harper. 'The club and the job are too big for him.'[11] Brian Clough said that he himself should have been made United's manager years ago, while the former Liverpool captain Emlyn Hughes had already awarded Ferguson the 'OBE' – 'Out Before Easter'.[12] No wonder that after the

Manchester City debacle Ferguson quickly signed a new three-year contract which had been waiting on his desk for several months. It increased his pay to £100,000 a year.

In the face of such speculation, Ferguson says he became 'something of a hermit . . . driven into a self-imposed hiding by the failure I hate. I shut the world outside my door and just felt miserable.'[13] He couldn't face going to social events, and turned down suggestions by Archie Knox that they go out for a drink. 'I went through my training programmes, my team selections, my team talks, everything, and couldn't find anything wrong.'[14]

What Ferguson found most difficult was the feeling that he had let down Manchester United's fans. 'Every time somebody looks at me I feel I have betrayed that man,' he said. 'You feel as if you have to sneak round corners, feel as if you are some kind of criminal.'[15] One friend remembers that after Saturday games Ferguson would often go to Glasgow for the rest of the weekend to avoid meeting United supporters.

Until he came to Old Trafford he had never appreciated the scale of United's worldwide following and the intensity of its commitment to the club. He went out of his way to identify with the fans, and to meet and listen to them in a way neither Ron Atkinson nor the club chairman, Martin Edwards, had ever thought was worthwhile. For example, he wore a gold ring with the club's Red Devil logo. At the club's 1988 annual general meeting Ferguson had been approached by three shareholder fans who invited him to lunch on the spur of the moment, not expecting him to accept. 'Hold on lads, I'll join you in a minute,' he replied.[16] They spent two hours in the United restaurant discussing their passion for the club and the manager's hopes for the future, before someone came to remind Ferguson that an Australian couple called Bosnich were waiting in his office, along with their goalkeeper son.

By the autumn of 1989 most fans were rather less impressed; many of them were very angry. 'Resign now. Do the decent thing for

Manchester United Football Club,' wrote one well-known supporter, Teresa McDonald, in a 'crisis' issue of the fanzine *Red News*. 'What really hurts, Alex,' she added, 'is that under you we've had shit football, shit atmosphere, shit boardroom shenanigans, our support is drifting away.'[17]

The team were booed off the field after a 3–0 home defeat by Spurs in the League Cup in October, and part of the crowd began singing 'Bryan Robson's red and white army' as a way of indicating that Ferguson should step down as manager in favour of the United captain. 'Bye-bye Fergie,' others chanted more bluntly.[18] One fan, Pete Molyneux, created a banner from a bed sheet, with the stark message: '3 YEARS OF EXCUSES AND IT'S STILL CRAP . . . TA-RA FERGIE.'[19]

The goalkeeper Jim Leighton became another target, partly as a kind of surrogate for Ferguson himself – in rather the same way that, in politics, attacking Peter Mandelson has been a way of getting at Tony Blair. On his own admission, Leighton was having a poor season, and this seemed to fuel long-standing English prejudice against Scottish goalkeepers. After his experience of almost continuous success at Aberdeen, and the luxury of Willie Miller and Alex McLeish as his central defenders, Leighton was not accustomed to the pressure of regular defeat. The constant worry gave him a stomach ulcer and regular migraines. The fanzine *Red Issue* even ran a spoof ad cruelly depicting the United keeper promoting 'The Leighton Condom' – 'guaranteed to catch nothing! . . . easily slips through your fingers . . . clean sheets cannot be guaranteed . . . the ideal defence, Leighton condoms ensure you score comfortably and successfully.'[20]

Leighton was disappointed that Ferguson would not give him 'a public show of support' during that difficult time, even though he frequently had to speak in the manager's defence against his many critics among the United players. 'He had lost the dressing room,' Leighton says, 'but I always stood up for him. Apart from chairman

Martin Edwards, I was probably his staunchest supporter. What a pity he did not return the compliment when I most needed it.'[21] Ferguson denies this, and says he tried to boost Leighton's confidence by telling him he was the best goalkeeper to play for Scotland in thirty years.

In contrast, both Steve Bruce and Brian McClair recall that throughout this ordeal Alex Ferguson never tried to deflect the criticism of himself on to the players. 'His philosophy,' says Bruce, 'was "You go out and enjoy yourself. Don't worry about me, or don't worry yourself" . . . He never let it affect him. He never let it get through to the players.'[22]

An important ally at that time was Sir Matt Busby, who advised the United board to keep their nerve. One day Ferguson went to see Sir Matt, who puffed away on his pipe and asked how things were. Ferguson explained that he was having a hard time from the newspapers. 'And he said, "Why are you reading them?" and that is the simplest advice anyone could possibly imagine and I couldn't even think of it myself.'[23] Yet it wasn't advice Ferguson would always heed in the years ahead.

It had been widely suggested that an obvious replacement for Ferguson would have been Howard Kendall, who had revived Everton in the mid-1980s and was now nearing the end of his three-year contract with the Spanish club Athletic Bilbao. Kendall did return to Manchester that autumn – to replace Mel Machin, who was sacked by Manchester City only a few weeks after their 5–1 win in the derby game. Ferguson showed the compassionate side of his character by being one of the first managers to phone Machin to offer his sympathy. 'Even though he clearly has problems of his own, he took time to keep in touch,' said Machin, who was invited to spend the day with Ferguson, attending a junior game, having lunch, and then watching the first team play Liverpool. 'Alex confirmed he was someone I could count on.'[24]

At the end of 1989, in what Ferguson calls 'black December', he reached 'the lowest, most desperate point ever in all my years in management'.[25] On the second Saturday, Manchester United faced Crystal Palace at home, in what looked like an easy fixture against a team which had been thrashed 9–0 by Liverpool three months earlier. The game attracted just 33,514 people – a sign of the growing discontent – and Ferguson left out an off-form Mark Hughes. United started well and Beardsmore scored, only for Palace to come back in the second half to finish 2–1 winners. The crowd vented their feelings against the manager and chanted their support for Hughes. Ferguson was hugely depressed as he drove home that night through what he calls 'a horrible Manchester day, black, pouring down with rain'.[26] His seventeen-year-old son Darren, who was in the passenger seat, remembers suggesting it might be time for his dad to pack it in. 'He said, "No, don't worry, I'll win the League, it'll just take a bit longer than I thought."'[27]

On top of the defeat came further depressing news in that evening's draw for the third round of the FA Cup. It's a curious feature of Alex Ferguson's years at Old Trafford how little luck he's enjoyed in the annual December draw. Only once in the last fifteen attempts have Manchester United been pitted against a side from outside the top two divisions (Bury in 1993), and it's almost half a century since United met a non-League side in the Cup. In contrast, Ferguson has been drawn against another team from the top tier ten times (by probability it should have been about five). And so it was in 1989–90, when out of the FA's bag came the ball for Nottingham Forest. In the late 1980s Brian Clough's side had earned a reputation as formidable cup fighters, and had beaten United at Old Trafford in the quarter-finals only the previous March. Worse, the tie was away from home. 'Pass the rope' was Ferguson's immediate thought.[28]

Press speculation about the prospect of Ferguson's dismissal grew increasingly intense, with a torrent of criticism from football rivals. More hurtful was the sniping from former Old Trafford stars. 'As a fan now I don't want to watch United again for a very long time, because there is nothing worth watching any more,' said Willie Morgan, the former winger who'd accompanied Ferguson on the 1967 Scottish world tour.[29] United had been 'crazy' to sell Whiteside and McGrath for 'next to nothing', Morgan added, and to pay so much for the inexperienced Gary Pallister.[30] George Best was even more damning. 'I wouldn't walk round the corner to watch them play', he said, claiming that Pallister was the 'biggest mistake that United have made'.[31] Best said he wouldn't be interested in seeing United until they replaced Ferguson with someone like Terry Venables. Even the United star of the 1960s Pat Crerand, a fellow Glaswegian socialist, joined the criticism.

With one bookmaker offering odds of 5–2 that Ferguson would be sacked, the *Manchester Evening News* reporter David Meek, who later collaborated with him on several books, compared the manager to a prisoner on death row in America. 'The man has been condemned in so many quarters, and is being kept alive by a succession of appeals. None of them is strong enough to give him a full reprieve, but there is enough evidence to keep alive the thought that next time the judges will grant a pardon.'[32] Even more sympathetic were remarks by the journalist Rob Shepherd, who, the day before the Forest game in early January, suggested in *Today* that the directors would 'refuse to bow to the inevitable calls for the manager's head'. And, with words he's entitled to frame and put on his wall, Shepherd added, 'If his team can get a draw or pull off a win it could prove the catalyst for a complete change in the club's fortunes.'[33]

Ferguson was greatly encouraged by a letter he suddenly received from Willie Muirhead, his old chairman at East Stirling. Roughly it said, 'You show 'em son. Is this the same Alex Ferguson that I knew as a young lad, that I presented with his first chance in management? The one that I saw running full-pelt down the track towards a linesman in a rage, the one I had to haul back from any trouble? Is this the same man who is going to give in easy now at Manchester United?'[34]

315

As the 1990s began, Ferguson promised United fans 'a decade of success', but it was hard to believe.[35] The team's performances over Christmas were dismal as they lost 1–0 at home to Spurs and 3–0 at Aston Villa, then drew 0–0 at home to QPR. Many newspaper commentators predicted that Ferguson would go if United failed to win the cup-tie against Forest; he himself talked of the game as having been 'set up as my trial'.[36] The pressure was increased when the BBC chose the encounter for their live broadcast on the Sunday afternoon. Martin Edwards says he told Ferguson beforehand not to worry, though he explained that it would be counterproductive to back him publicly: 'Whatever happens on Saturday, Alec, your career does not rest on that with Manchester United. I can assure you that, whatever the result on Saturday, we will be retaining you.'[37] It was a generous gesture – though football chairmen aren't completely reliable when it comes to reassuring managers.

Alex Ferguson would always be grateful for Edwards's support during these difficult early years. 'Not once did the chairman question me. Martin Edwards was marvellous. He stuck by me.'[38] Privately, when asked about Ferguson's disappointing record, the United chairman would mention the long-term work the manager was doing behind the scenes, particularly on youth development. Nor was it just a matter of having faith in the manager: Edwards was sometimes a lightning conductor for fans' dissatisfaction with the team. Often they preferred to lambast him, not Ferguson – most notably after the League Cup defeat by Spurs in October 1989, when angry supporters burst into the directors' box and tried to assault Edwards.

As the United players took the field at Nottingham Forest, the TV pundit Jimmy Hill famously declared that they looked beaten even in the pre-match warm-up. 'Fergie, Fergie, on the dole!' chanted Forest supporters in derision.[39] The outcome is well known to any football follower. With United fans in full voice, the team defied Hill and the other experts, winning 1–0 with a header from twenty-year-old Mark

Robins, who'd been a regular substitute in the past but had started only three games in the past. 'I think we did it that day with defiance,' Ferguson later claimed – 'defiance from the supporters – and the players responded to the supporters' promptings that day. Right from the word go they were on song, our support. They were not going to lose that game.'[40]

The team looked less sure of themselves in the next round, at Fourth Division Hereford. Much of the area around Edgar Street was flooded; the pitch was like a ploughed field, and United could easily have suffered an embarrassing giant-killing which would have been almost as historic as Hereford's famous 1972 victory, as a non-League side, over Newcastle United. Hereford were well organised, and several times came close to scoring. The game was settled, however, by a goal from Clayton Blackmore with five minutes to go.

Round five saw Robins score again in a see-saw 3–2 win at Newcastle United (who were then in the Second Division), where Mark McGhee scored a penalty for the home side. An easy 1–0 victory at Sheffield United then put the Reds into the last four, where they were paired with neighbours Oldham Athletic.

'I'm sorry to say this semi-final is the highlight of my career here,' said Ferguson before the game.[41] Oldham were a Second Division club, but had already knocked Arsenal, Everton, Aston Villa and Southampton out of the domestic cups that season, and had reached the final of the League Cup. Manchester United made a habit of falling behind in FA Cup semi-finals, and 1990 was no exception. (It happened in seven successive semi-finals between 1979 and 1996.) The goals really started to flow in a ding-dong game at Maine Road in which the Reds were 1–0 down after five minutes, at full-time it was 2–2, and after extra time the match ended at 3–3. Like a dog with a meaty bone, Oldham simply wouldn't let go.

Three days later the former United player Andy Ritchie cancelled out McClair's opening goal in the replay, before Mark Robins turned up in extra time to secure a 2–1 win and Ferguson's first club trip to

Wembley. He described the replay as the most draining match he'd ever endured. 'I've never felt such pressure, so much strain in a game,' he said the following day. 'At Aberdeen, I was on top of every-thing, I controlled everything at the club. But this club, this club,' he said, shaking his head in exasperation.[42]

All was set for a Wembley encounter with Crystal Palace. The London club had struggled all season, but even so United had fin-ished only two places above Palace in the League, with the same number of points. Palace had a reputation for being as tenacious as Oldham, having beaten Liverpool 4–3 in the other semi-final. Everyone remembered, too, that Second Division Southampton had beaten United in the 1976 final, and the late 1980s had seen the underdogs triumph at Wembley more often than the favourites.

It was another 3–3 epic. Palace went ahead in the first half, and Robson equalised. Then it was United's turn to go in front, with a goal from Hughes, before the Palace manager brought on Ian Wright to partner Mark Bright. Wright made it 2–2 and scored again two minutes into extra time. There were only seven minutes to go before Mark Hughes got his second goal and the 3–3 draw consigned the teams to a replay five nights later.

The second encounter was a very different game. After a season in which United had spent more money than ever, and were parading a team that had cost £12 million, it was ironic that the team's cup-winning goal came from the only player who was home-grown. Meeting a pass from Neil Webb, young Lee Martin ran through the penalty area and unleashed his shot. It was only his second goal for the club, and the first time a left-back had scored the winner in the final.

United had won the FA Cup for a record seventh occasion, while Bryan Robson became the only captain ever to collect the cup three times. More important, Alex Ferguson had finally won his first trophy in English football, and had become the first manager to win both the Scottish Cup and the FA Cup. United were also the first side to win the FA Cup without ever being drawn at home. Yet in truth the pairings had been fairly lenient: Forest were the strongest team United faced, while Hereford, Sheffield United, Newcastle and Oldham were all from the Second Division or lower.

Unlike the first game, the Thursday-night replay was no spectacle, and Palace were widely criticised for their violent approach. But the 1990 replay will be most remembered not for the play but for Alex Ferguson's controversial decision to replace his goalkeeper, Jim Leighton.

Ferguson had considered dropping Leighton for the first game, in fact, but decided against it. However, the keeper was widely regarded as being at fault over the first and third of the Crystal Palace goals in the 3–3 draw. Ferguson felt his fellow Scot looked 'a beaten man' as he came off the pitch and then sat with 'his head between his knees' in the dressing room afterwards.[43] On the Tuesday, the manager signalled his intentions by extending the loan period on Les Sealey, who'd recently been borrowed from Luton Town as a back-up goalkeeper, but had played only twice for the first team so far.

In the five days between the two games Alex Ferguson must surely have looked back to his past cup finals. He understood from 1965, of course, the huge disappointment of being dropped publicly from the starting line-up, especially when, like Leighton in 1990, he had appeared in every previous cup-tie that season. But there was the lesson, too, of December 1979, and the only other occasion in Ferguson's career that a cup final hadn't been resolved at the first attempt. Aberdeen had lost the replay of the Scottish League Cup final 3–0 to Dundee United, and he deeply regretted not making changes to his team for the second match.

If that was the history, there must have been other considerations too. The relationship with Leighton stretched back to the manager's very first match at Aberdeen; and not even Gordon Strachan, Willie Miller or Alex McLeish had played more times for Alex Ferguson. They'd shared the highs of Gothenburg and qualifying for Mexico, and had won eight trophies together – involving six cup finals in which Leighton had conceded only three goals. Ferguson knew that if he dropped Leighton for the replay it would have a devastating effect on the player, and probably ruin their relationship. There was also Scotland to think about. Despite his poor form with United, Jim Leighton was still Scotland's first-choice goalkeeper, and the World Cup in Italy was less than four weeks away. Few understood better than Alex Ferguson the problems of preparing players for a World Cup tournament.

Ferguson lay awake much of the Tuesday night agonising over his choice. 'The easy decision was to play him again,' he'd explain later. 'The hard decision won us the trophy.'[44] The evening before, as the United squad were relaxing at their hotel, he tugged Leighton away from his colleagues and delivered the news. The goalkeeper says he was 'numbed' by 'the cruellest blow of my life', and was in tears as he then rang to tell his wife.[45] 'I know that the most critical decision of my management career will probably make me the most hated man in Scotland,' Ferguson told a newspaper two days after the game.

> It was an animal instinct. Nothing else . . . You smell danger –
> and that depth of feeling burns inside and tells you precisely
> the next move. I had to discard poor old Jim – the man I gave
> a debut to way back in 1978 – for the sake of Manchester
> United. Believe me it really hurt . . . My conscience is
> absolutely clear. I have never done anything like it before.
> And I don't want to do anything like it again – ever . . . He
> was absolutely sick – sick to the soles of his boots. The reality
> of missing out was bound to be like a knife thrust . . . But Jim
> hasn't got the rhino hide. When it is conflict like this,
> agonising over the position of a player you know so well, the
> loyalty has got to go down on the side of the club.[46]

'He wasn't a Wembley scapegoat,' Ferguson wrote three years later, 'but a sacrifice that had to be made, the head that had to roll to safe-guard the whole future of a new team.'[47]

Les Sealey duly performed well in the replay, made a good early save, kept a clean sheet, and spread confidence throughout the defence, though Palace had far fewer chances than they'd enjoyed when Jim Leighton was playing.

Alex Ferguson says that immediately after the replay Leighton's wife gave him a V-sign, though the goalkeeper denies this. Les Sealey presented his winners' medal to Leighton, though the Scot slipped it back into his colleague's pocket when he wasn't looking. And several weeks later, when the FA sent a medal to Old Trafford in recognition of his appearance in the first game, Jim Leighton refused to accept it – much to Ferguson's annoyance (though he himself had report-edly thrown his own 1969 losers' medal away).

The long-term effect on Jim Leighton was probably even greater than Alex Ferguson had feared. The United boss turned Les Sealey's loan into a purchase, and Sealey remained Ferguson's first-choice keeper throughout the following season. Before the FA Cup final Leighton had considered asking for a transfer, but he was now determined to revive his career at United. It was difficult, however, since he was no longer even second choice, but demoted to third or fourth in the Old Trafford goalkeeping roster. (Gary Walsh and a young Mark Bosnich filled in when Sealey wasn't available.) Leighton was entrusted with just one first-team game in his remain-ing twenty-one months at Old Trafford – a League Cup match the following September at Halifax Town, who then occupied bottom place in the entire Football League and hadn't scored in their open-ing six league games. Not surprisingly, he eventually lost his Scotland place too, after being blamed for one of Brazil's goals in another disappointing World Cup for the Scots. After loan spells at Arsenal (as cover) and Reading, he finally left United in 1992 to join Dundee for a knock-down £150,000. It didn't work out, and he again went on loan – to Sheffield United, again as cover – before he regained his confidence with a move to Hibernian. He won back his Scotland place in 1994.

Leighton's career took at least four years to recover. He played in the 1998 France World Cup, and eventually took his number of caps to ninety-one – second only to Kenny Dalglish among Scotland players. But for his 'wilderness' period between 1990 and 1994 he would probably have become the most capped Scot of all time. He played in three more finals in Scotland – the last for Aberdeen in the 2000 Scottish Cup, which proved almost as haunting an event as 1990. In his last senior game, at the age of forty-one, Leighton was carried off after only two minutes with a broken jaw, and Aberdeen lost 4–0 to Rangers.

Today Jim Leighton is goalkeeping coach at Aberdeen, and is reluctant to talk about his Old Trafford 'nightmare'. He claims to have removed any United mementoes from display at his home – 'even a solitary trace of my days with Manchester United, because recalling what happened still hurts'. Alex Ferguson ceased being a friend long ago. 'So strongly do I feel,' Leighton says, 'that there is not a hope in hell of that friendship ever being revived. Indeed, I have promised myself that I will never again speak to him . . . I cannot find it in my heart to forgive him.'[48]

Jim Leighton, like many goalkeepers, is a reflective, sensitive character. If his account is to be believed – and it certainly chimes with other episodes from Alex Ferguson's managerial career – then the United manager's treatment of the player after May 1990 was unnecessarily callous. What Leighton particularly holds against Ferguson is his failure to support and encourage him both before and after the key decision.

> He distanced himself from me when I was trying to pick
> up the broken pieces of my life and never offered any
> encouragement. In fact, the only time we talked during the
> rest of my stay at Old Trafford – a year and nine months of

absolute purgatory – was when I was summoned to his office, where we had several arguments. I felt like an outcast.[49]

Alex Ferguson says he tried to persuade journalists to take a sympathetic line during the 1990 World Cup. He also urged other managers to buy Leighton, but he says that nobody understood that the player's only problem was lack of confidence. Ferguson subsequently acknowledged the devastating effect that the demotion had on the player, and has sometimes suggested that he had made the wrong decision. In 1992, for instance, he wrote, 'If I could have my time over again I would not have dropped Jim Leighton, not because it was wrong from the football point of view but because it wrecked his career and cost him two years of his footballing life.'[50]

Seven years later, however, Ferguson the Govan street-fighter took a much less defensive line in his autobiography. Confronting head-on both critics of the decision and Leighton himself, he accused the goalkeeper of being 'selfish' in not acknowledging any blame. Ferguson now claimed to have 'no remorse', and resented the fact that Leighton had been 'glorified' over the years, while he himself had been accused of 'betraying' him.

> I have something to ask those who see Jim as a victim and me as a villain: if we had lost the Cup final and I had lost my job, would Jim Leighton have felt guilty? Would he have apologised? I think the answer in both instances is no . . . No, it was all Alex Ferguson's fault. It is all part of the self-protecting mentality common to goalkeepers.[51]

The passage illustrates Ferguson's odd feelings towards the goalkeeping fraternity, which would show themselves again in the years ahead. He once spoke of 'the old goalkeeper's union' – an odd jibe for a former trade unionist, though perhaps one should not expect him to have much sympathy with those whose job it is to frustrate goal-poaching strikers such as his former self.[52]

Ferguson's decision to drop Jim Leighton required a large streak of ruthlessness. It was taken against the advice of his assistant, Archie Knox, who thought it was 'a bit harsh' and would not go down well with the other players.[53] But, in purely football terms, it's hard to dispute that it was the right choice. Leighton might well have been even more jittery in the replay, and Palace would undoubtedly have exploited his lack of confidence. In short, his axing may have won the cup for United. And it may also have saved Alex Ferguson's job.

Martin Edwards and his fellow directors have always insisted that they never even 'came close to sacking him. As a board, we never sat down to discuss Alex Ferguson's future.'[54] A few months afterwards Edwards claimed that, had the board wanted to fire the manager – as '60 to 70 per cent of fans would have wanted' – then the bad results in 1989 would have been a good 'excuse'. But the directors appreciated that Ferguson was a 'workaholic' and was making huge improvements at Old Trafford.[55]

Specifically, the Manchester United board have always denied any suggestion that they treated the third-round game at Nottingham Forest as his final test. 'The directors never ever, *never ever*, mentioned the possibility that there would be a change with Alex Ferguson, because we knew he was right,' says Bobby Charlton, who then sat on United's main board.[56] Charlton in particular had observed the radical improvements that Ferguson had made to the United scouting and coaching regimes, and the quality of youngsters who were now appearing in the reserve and junior sides. Charlton's opinion naturally carried great weight with the Old Trafford board, because of his football pedigree.

We should perhaps believe Edwards and his fellow directors' claims that they never discussed Ferguson's position, for no evidence has ever emerged that they did. Nonetheless, had United lost any of their FA Cup ties that season – from the Forest match through to the final against Palace – the board would have found it very hard to resist the clamour to replace their manager. Indeed, Edwards himself also said, specifically about Ferguson, 'I don't think chairmen sack managers. Supporters decide whether a manager goes. If people vote with their feet, and stay away, that's when a change might be made.'[57] As Ferguson remarked years later, 'only a fool would deny that, without the series of events triggered by that victory at Forest, the pressure to sack me might eventually have become irresistible'.[58] 'We knew if we didn't win the Cup that year he was going to be on his way back to Scotland,' says the player Clayton Blackmore. 'Everybody thought that.'[59]

It was almost certainly the most difficult season Alex Ferguson has ever endured as a manager, but his previous record saw him through. 'If I hadn't had success at Aberdeen I definitely couldn't do it at United. Unless you have a store, a surplus of experience, knowledge, talent and, just as important, guts, you wouldn't have a prayer,' he claimed.[60] 'To be at Manchester United, you have got to have bottle and real character ... I had to dig deep into my personal resources because when you get a lot of criticism doubts begin to creep into your own mind.'[61]

United's FA Cup run disguised the fact that their League results had barely improved in the second half of the 1989–90 season. They had gone eleven league games without a win between November and February – their worst run for eighteen years, though long-term injuries to Robson and Webb hadn't helped. Their final league position – thirteenth – was United's lowest placing since relegation in 1974, and higher than Manchester City only on goal difference. There had been little obvious return on the previous summer's £7 million investment in players. Home crowds had been dropping fast – the 40,274 against City was the lowest for a derby match since 1931. Fans were upset not just with the poor results but with the lacklustre style of United's football too. At Old Trafford a boring team is almost less acceptable than a losing one.

Many of the supporters who chanted Ferguson's name around Wembley on that balmy May evening had been calling for his head only a few months earlier. The result was as much a relief to his family as to the manager himself, and somehow his eighteen-year-old son Jason managed to scale the perimeter fence and race across the pitch towards his father. Two stewards ran in hot pursuit, before the United manager explained who it was. Alex Ferguson had not just won the famous FA Cup but had shown he could be a success in England. The extra cash released by the temporary presence of Michael Knighton had bought him valuable breathing space. Not even he could have foreseen what it would herald in the decade ahead.

Twenty-Five Years and Counting

*'It must not become an obsession. You could go through
the records and wonder where it all fell apart in a given
season, ask why they bought this or that player. What
good would that do? It's all history.'*

ALEX FERGUSON on the league title, 1991[1]

In the early 1980s, when Dave Sexton was manager, the failure of
Manchester United's new million-pound forward Garry Birtles to
score his first goal for the club prompted a topical joke. What did the
American hostages say when released after 444 days of captivity in
Iran? Answer: 'Has Garry Birtles scored for United yet?' By 1990,
Nelson Mandela's historic freedom after more than two decades'
imprisonment in South Africa suggested a modification. What did
Mandela ask as he was released from jail? 'Have United won the
League yet?'[2]

Manchester United might have just collected the FA Cup for the
fourth time in fourteen years, but the league title continued to elude
them. Fans began to feel the club was jinxed. Only three times since
last lifting the championship in 1967 – in 1968, 1980 and 1988 –
had United even finished as runners-up. Alex Ferguson once commented that it would be terrible to go twenty-five years without the
title returning to Old Trafford. He must later have regretted those
words.

The world wasn't convinced that Ferguson could translate his FA Cup triumph into immediate league success. Indeed, bookmakers offered odds of 5–2 on his losing his job by the end of the season. The reality was that Manchester United were still only a good cup-winning side, able to rise to the occasion in knockout ties, but unable to find the consistency to win the League. This was illustrated in the autumn of 1990, when the Reds beat the champions, Liverpool, 3–1 at home in the League Cup, and in the next round faced Arsenal at Highbury (who had just beaten United 1–0 in the League at Old Trafford). Wednesday 28 November 1990 has gone down in history as the day that Margaret Thatcher resigned after eleven years as Prime Minister, but United fans remember it for one of the most surprising results of their entire history. George Graham's team were at their peak, unbeaten since May, and enjoying a superlative league campaign that saw them lose just once, at Chelsea (the lowest number of league defeats in any twentieth-century season). To make matters worse, United were without Bryan Robson or Neil Webb.

Yet the Reds seemed to be on fire at Highbury, winning 6–2 with a hat-trick by Lee Sharpe, who established himself as a significant United player that night (having previously scored only three times in sixty-one games). Danny Wallace also put in a rare high-quality performance, and United were 3–0 up by half-time. It was Arsenal's worst home defeat since 1921, and more notable since they'd let in only seven goals in their seventeen previous games that season. United had beaten the two top sides in England, and then beat Leeds twice in a two-legged semi-final, which made history of its own by sparking a rare Ferguson apology to a referee. John Martin had allowed Lee Sharpe to be kicked 'from pillar to post' the manager claimed immediately after the game. Then, having seen the video-tape, Ferguson changed his mind. 'I have got to hold my hands up. I was wrong,' he said.[3] 'I have to admit the referee had a better game than I thought.'[4]

Having beaten three such formidable opponents in earlier rounds, United then crumbled 1–0 in the final to Second Division Sheffield Wednesday – now managed by Ron Atkinson, who savoured his revenge on the club that had sacked him. Ferguson admitted the team had 'under-estimated' Wednesday. 'My lot looked at their players and thought: How many of you could play for Manchester United? How many top players have you got? The answer was not as many as us, but they beat us anyway.'[5]

Consolation came in foreign parts. Two months after the previous season's FA Cup triumph over Crystal Palace, UEFA had lifted the ban on English clubs playing in Europe, which had been in force since 1985. United could now take part in the European Cup-Winners' Cup, and got an easy ride. After beating the Hungarian side Pécsi Munkás 3–0 on aggregate, the Reds were drawn against the Welsh Cup winners, Wrexham, then second from bottom of the Fourth Division. Absurdly, United had to stay in Wales the night before the away leg, to comply with UEFA regulations about visiting teams being in the country twenty-four hours beforehand. They won 5–0 on aggregate, and reached the quarter-finals without having conceded a goal.

Montpellier then provided sterner opposition, drawing 1–1 at Old Trafford, thanks to a Lee Martin own goal. It created a tricky situation for the second leg, as the French had the advantage of an away goal, but United won 2–0, and then easily disposed of the weakest of the semi-finalists, Legia Warsaw. The campaign so far had been marked by several curiosities. Seven of United's goals had come from defenders – with Steve Bruce top scorer with four. And four opposing players had been sent off. The prize was a final against Barcelona in Rotterdam.

On 15 May 1991, Manchester United fans outnumbered Catalan supporters several times over in the Feyenoord stadium. Many fans were soaked, as little of the ground was covered and it poured that night – just as it had when Ferguson had won the trophy in

Gothenburg. Barcelona were the only top-class opponents United faced in the competition that year, and they won the European Cup a year later, but in truth the Catalan side failed to play as well as they could. The game was far less important to Barça, since they'd already won their domestic league – the competition that really matters to Spanish clubs – the previous weekend. It was very important to Mark Hughes, however, after his failure to make much impression when he'd been on Barcelona's books. He was credited with both United goals, though the opening one, halfway through the second half, really should have been acknowledged as Steve Bruce's fifth in the competition: his header was already going over the line when Hughes gave it a last, unnecessary, touch. Barcelona got one back with a Ronald Koeman free kick, then had a goal disallowed for offside, before Clayton Blackmore cleared off the line from Michael Laudrup. United fans bit their nails almost to the cuticles in the final stages, but the cup belonged to Manchester. 'The last ten minutes seemed to last ten years,' said Ferguson. 'Sir Matt reckons he felt about 105.'[6]

Alex Ferguson had now matched the Barcelona manager, Johan Cruyff, in winning the Cup-Winners' Cup with two different clubs. United were the first English side to win a European competition since Everton had won the same trophy at the same venue six years before, and the first team from any country to win a European honour having won all their away games. As Sir Matt Busby jointly held the silver cup with the United manager, it naturally stirred memories of 1968. It was an unfair comparison. Considered objectively, the 1991 Cup-Winners' Cup was probably the easiest trophy of significance that United have ever won, and that year confirmed the suspicion that the Cup was the least challenging of the three main European contests. The eventual abolition of the competition in 1999 took a little more shine from United's achievement.

Shortly after the Rotterdam final, Alex Ferguson was approached by an intermediary who asked if he'd be interested in becoming manager of Real Madrid, but he chose to remain at United to achieve his restated goal of winning the championship. But United's league form in 1990–91 had been almost as disappointing as in the previous campaign, although sixth was an improvement on thirteenth. Any team would have found it difficult to match Arsenal that season, but United found themselves behind Crystal Palace, Manchester City and a resurgent Leeds United (complete with Gordon Strachan).

The second half of the season was notable for several debuts. Ferguson had been raving for months about a lad in the youth team, and in March 1991 Ryan Giggs – just seventeen – came on against Everton to replace Denis Irwin (a full-back bought from Oldham the summer before). Giggs then scored on his full debut against City in April.

But Ferguson was keen to protect his young star, who, like past United prodigies Sammy McIlroy and Norman Whiteside, was inevitably being dubbed the new George Best. Giggs had great balance and pace, and Ferguson compared him to 'one of those little cocker spaniels chasing a piece of floating, wind-blown waste paper around the park – They have their heads in the air, dancing in a dozen different directions, their eyes fixed on the paper and pursuing it all over the place.' Yet the United manager infuriated journalists by refusing all requests for interviews with the player – to the extent that Desmond Lynam regularly complained about the ban on *Match of the Day*. 'My prime concern was the clear risk of a repetition of the George Best scenario from the sixties or a Gazza syndrome,' said Ferguson. 'I bolted the Old Trafford door and made certain Ryan was safe inside.'[7] Giggs was even prevented from signing a boot deal that would have made him £250,000, and other youth players were told to expect similar restrictions. 'They will have enough time for that when they grow up,' said Ferguson.[8]

The Ukrainian and former Soviet winger Andrei Kanchelskis appeared for the first time in a 3–0 end-of-season defeat at Crystal Palace, while at Sheffield United in February Ferguson had brought on as substitute his own nineteen-year-old son, Darren, who then played in four other games that season in midfield.

Darren is the only one of the Ferguson boys to play football professionally, though all three were keen players in their teens. Manchester United has never prevented the sons and relations of managers and their assistants from playing for the club. Sir Matt Busby's son-in-law Don Gibson played for the 1952 championship side. Busby's successors Tommy Docherty and Wilf McGuinness both had sons in the United junior teams, as did assistant managers Pat Crerand, Tommy Cavanagh and Jimmy Murphy, whose son Nicky was twice named as first-team substitute but never played.

Darren's twin, Jason, played about twenty games for the United A and B teams, often alongside his brother, and once as substitute for him. Jason was a centre-forward, like their older brother, Mark, who had played for the British polytechnic side. Unlike Darren, however, neither Jason nor Mark took football seriously as a career option. In his childhood, Jason seems to have been more of a soccer 'anorak' than a boy who enjoyed playing. 'He'll tell you every football team and the name of every player,' his mother once remarked, 'but he's not interested in the actual game . . . He has to have all the football gear, but he'll just put it on to play on the swings.'[9] Later with United, says a colleague, Jason 'was like a battering-ram; he'd fly into challenges', while Mark, in contrast, was 'very gifted technically' and had 'a lovely touch'.

A football coach picking his son for a team presents obvious problems. The player Kevin Bond was always taunted as 'Daddy's boy' after following his manager father, John, from Norwich to Manchester City. There were fewer difficulties for Harry and Jamie Redknapp at Bournemouth, or for Brian and Nigel Clough at Nottingham Forest. At one point Clough had made strenuous efforts to sign the young Darren Ferguson, and Spurs also had him on trial. Alex was reluctant to take him. 'I don't think he really wanted to sign me,' Darren said later, 'as he knew it would be difficult.'[10] Brian

Kidd, Archie Knox and other members of the coaching staff insisted, however, that Darren was good enough for United and a great passer of the ball, though he lacked pace. Cathy Ferguson was delighted, as she wanted Darren to carry on living at home.

Mark Ferguson eventually went to Aberdeen Polytechnic, studied chartered surveying, and then did a business administration degree in Paris. Jason, whom Ferguson calls 'the mercurial member of the family', chose a career in television. Through his father's contacts he secured a highly sought-after job with the north-west ITV station, Granada, which was no small achievement for a teenager. He didn't stay there long, however, before he announced he was leaving to do charitable work in Eastern Europe.

Ferguson's biggest shock that season was the news in late April 1991 that his assistant, Archie Knox, intended to leave – the consequence of another round of managerial musical chairs. Knox wanted to become assistant to Walter Smith, who had just taken over at Rangers in succession to Graeme Souness (who in turn had gone to replace Kenny Dalglish, who had just resigned as manager of Liverpool). The timing of Knox's announcement was unfortunate, coming the day after defeat by Sheffield Wednesday in the League Cup final and two days before the second leg of the Legia Warsaw semi-final.

Why Archie Knox left Old Trafford has never been satisfactorily explained. The move was not to a more senior job, though Rangers were a more successful club at the time. Knox himself has always said he moved because Rangers offered a better deal, though Ferguson says he persuaded Martin Edwards to make a big improvement to Knox's terms in an effort to keep him. He also argued that United was on the brink of great things, and that success in England was far more prestigious than in Scotland. It was no use: Knox was determined to go.

'I never dreamt . . . that Archie would even think about leaving,' Ferguson said. He and Knox had spent almost nine years together –

four at Aberdeen and four and a half at United. Ferguson accused Rangers of 'hypocrisy' for taking a 'moral stance' and 'screaming blue murder' about Liverpool's poaching of Souness, when they 'were at it all the time themselves behind the backs of Manchester United'.[11] What had made it worse was that Rangers wanted to take Knox immediately, without allowing him to stay on for the European final.

'Fergie was angry when [Knox] left, and to be fair he was right to be,' says another member of the backroom staff. 'I remember the look of disappointment and sadness on his face around the time. He felt betrayed by Knox. His pal had left him for money.' They had been great mates as well as colleagues, and had often socialised together, but the relationship was never the same again, and it's said they didn't speak to each other for the next four years. Nonetheless, Ferguson was subsequently more praising of Knox than of some of his other former assistants. 'He had worked himself into the ground for us,' he wrote. 'He was always a beast for work.'[12] But the United boss made no attempt to bring Knox back once more when the job became vacant again.

In August 1991, after four months' reflection, and to many people's surprise, he chose Brian Kidd to replace Knox. 'At first I didn't want it,' Kidd later revealed. He would have preferred to carry on working with the youth players, but Ferguson was insistent. The two men were to forge a partnership which proved at least as successful as the Ferguson–Knox combination. 'Sometimes Alex and I argue like cat and dog,' Kidd observed.

> We're like an old married couple. But I think that it's healthy to have different views and opinions when you're discussing things . . . The Boss is a very honest and loyal man which means that everyone knows where they stand, and if he's got something to say to you he'll say it to your face, which I really appreciate in a person.[13]

Between the two finals in the spring of 1991, the directors of Manchester United had taken the controversial decision to join Spurs and Millwall in becoming a full public company, floating the club on the Stock Exchange as a means to raise new outside capital. Many fans opposed the idea, fearing that United would henceforth be driven by the interests of the City institutions who would inevitably control most of the shares. Ferguson was not enthusiastic about the flotation either: when friends asked whether they should buy shares he told them not to bother as they would probably fall in price (as they did at first), and he didn't purchase any himself. More important, Ferguson also refused to participate in the share-option scheme which the new United PLC directors created to offer senior management more incentive (not that Ferguson needed any, one assumes). Share options give someone the opportunity to buy shares in the company at a specified future date but at today's prices, so if the stock goes up in value the individual makes a gain. (The theory is that option-holders thus have an interest in performing better to boost the share price.) The unfortunately named finance director, Robin Launders, who was a member of the new PLC board, was offered 100,000 share options, while Ferguson and other senior United staff were allowed only 25,000. Ferguson thought this was most unfair, and boycotted the scheme.

However, the manager was mollified to some extent by a new four-year contract worth £200,000 a year. It was the first time Martin Edwards (who became chief executive of the PLC) had ever given any United manager a deal of more than three years in length. Ferguson's salary had fallen behind those of several other leading managers in recent times, including George Graham, Kenny Dalglish and Howard Kendall – but then these three could each boast at least one league title. The new contract only partly bridged the gap.

Ferguson started the 1991–92 season with a new goalkeeper. Peter Schmeichel was signed from the Danish club Brøndby for just £505,000, which makes him probably the best bargain Ferguson has ever purchased. He began with clean sheets in his first four games, though he received some criticism in his early days, particularly over his handling of crosses. A blond giant of 6 feet 4 inches, in one-on-one situations Schmeichel often got the better of opposing forwards by forming his body into a star shape, and more often than not he either deflected the ball or intimidated the striker into making an error. He soon became notorious for shouting at his defenders for the slightest mistakes – often his own.

United won eight of their opening ten games, and by Christmas it finally looked as if it could be their season to win the League. Ryan Giggs had broken into the team on the left wing, taking the place of Lee Sharpe, who was injured for much of the year, while Andrei Kanchelskis raided down the right. On Boxing Day, after an impressive 6–3 win at Oldham, United topped the table after five wins in a row. The biggest challenge came not from Liverpool or Arsenal, but from Leeds United, who had returned to the top division only eighteen months before. By a strange quirk, the draws that December for both the League Cup and the FA Cup were made on the same Saturday, and United got the worst possible pairing in both – Leeds United away. With an imminent league fixture at Elland Road too, it meant United were due to play at Elland Road three times in the course of eleven days in three different competitions (though it turned out to be eighteen days, as the FA Cup tie had to be postponed).

United emerged from the sequence pretty well, drawing the League game and winning both cup matches. However, the cup knockouts freed Leeds to concentrate on the League, in which United had begun to falter. The Reds' most surprising result was a 4–1 defeat at home to Queen's Park Rangers on New Year's Day, the result not of overnight partying, it seems, but of several players suffering from flu. Commentators often stress that championship contenders can't afford to lose more than six games, but unexpected draws can prove almost as damaging to a team's prospects under the modern system of one point for a drawn game and three for a win. Points were lost two by two in silly draws at Notts County and Coventry, and at home to Sheffield Wednesday, Chelsea, Wimbledon and Manchester City. Yet even in late February United were still favourites, quoted at 9–2 on to win the championship.

Leeds, however, were hanging on; after Lee Chapman was injured in the FA Cup game against United, their manager, Howard Wilkinson, went out and bought a French international forward who had a reputation both for touches of brilliance and also for being undisciplined and awkward. His name was Eric Cantona.

With five games left to play, United had seventy-four points and were still considered champions-in-waiting, while Leeds were two points behind with only four games remaining. But United's campaign collapsed around Easter weekend. On Thursday 16 April they beat Southampton at home before travelling to relegation candidates Luton on the Saturday. A 1–1 draw there suggested frailty, and two days later, on Easter Monday, they fell 2–1 to Nottingham Forest. 'It's all our own fault,' Ferguson acknowledged.[14] 'We have got ourselves into a ridiculous position.'[15]

But United could still win the title if they won their three remaining games: away to West Ham and Liverpool, and at home to Spurs. On past history, the east-London fixture was a harder prospect than that at Anfield, since West Ham had the Reds' worst away record of all the clubs they visited regularly. United had won just eight times at Upton Park in their history (and only once since 1967, when a 6–1 win had clinched United's last League title). Surely this year would be different, for West Ham were already certain to be relegated. But the fact that they were already doomed made the Londoners relax, while United were very nervous. West Ham won 1–0, thanks to a freak goal near the end, and Ferguson described it as 'obscene' and 'almost criminal' that West Ham should have raised their game when it was too late to prevent relegation.[16] Now the initiative lay with Leeds, who were confirmed as champions by winning 3–2 on the Sunday at Sheffield United. That same afternoon United had to visit Anfield. Ian Rush, who had never previously scored against the Reds in twenty-four attempts, finally broke his duck as the Merseyside club won 2–0. That it was Liverpool who administered the *coup de grâce* only intensified United's pain.

Alex Ferguson would exploit the agonies of that season's run-in to good effect, however. He told his men never to forget incidents such as when Liverpool fans asked for Lee Sharpe and Paul Ince's autographs and then tore them up in their faces. 'Remember this day and just how important you are at Manchester United,' he said. 'What has just happened should tell you all how much people envy you. They wouldn't have done that otherwise. It proves how big we are.' The following season he pinned up in the dressing room a photograph known as 'Dante's inferno', showing the distraught faces on the United bench at the moment Steve Bruce missed with a late header against Forest. It was 'to make sure it never happened again'.[17]

But Ferguson was also aggrieved about United's fixture congestion at the end of the season. They had been forced to squeeze in four games in seven days between 16 and 22 April (against Southampton, Luton, Forest and West Ham), because the FA wanted the season to end early to allow England to prepare for the forthcoming European Championship. Later, he suggested United should have taken a stand, refused to play one of the fixtures, and told the authorities, 'Take the points off us – we're not going to play such a spate of games.'[18]

To play four matches in just seven days was quite unusual, though four in eight was fairly common, and in the past it had been traditional to play three games over the four days of the Easter weekend. Even without United's workload, however, Leeds would probably have taken the title – after all, they won by four points, and also boasted the better goal difference. Nor were United distracted during the final run-in by other competitions, as they would often be in the future, and as many past championship contenders had been. They'd been eliminated by Atlético Madrid in the second round of the Cup-Winners' Cup the previous autumn, and by Southampton on penalties in the FA Cup in February.

The real issue was that United had suddenly stopped scoring goals in the new year: 42 of United's 63 league goals – exactly two-thirds – came in the first half of the season. 'We simply did not score enough goals as a team to even deserve winning the title,' Ferguson would admit.[19] It might have helped had the Old Trafford pitch dried up too: it was hardly conducive to United's style of play. Ferguson later conceded he might have overcome both problems had he redoubled his efforts to sign the Luton striker Mick Harford, as 'he may well have won the championship for the club'.[20] Harford, who was still deadly with his head despite being thirty-three, might have encouraged United players to keep the ball in the air and away from the wretched Manchester playing surface.

At least there was some consolation in winning the League Cup – the only time United have ever won the trophy. After seeing off Cambridge, Portsmouth, Oldham, Leeds and Middlesbrough in earlier rounds, they beat Nottingham Forest 1–0 in the final. Ferguson also collected the European Super Cup for the second time, after beating the European Cup-winners Red Star Belgrade 1–0 at Old Trafford, though even he concedes it was a 'fairly outrageous victory'.[21] United gained a huge advantage when UEFA decided to confine the contest to one match in Manchester, because of the political troubles in Yugoslavia. Red Star dominated the fixture, but squandered their chances before a shot from Neil Webb hit the post and Brian McClair tapped in the rebound.

Another highly significant consolation in the spring of 1992 was provided by the Manchester United under-18 team, which won the FA Youth Cup for the first time since George Best was a teenager. The Manchester United youth sides of the 1950s had been truly formidable, including players such as Duncan Edwards, Eddie Colman,

Billy Whelan, David Pegg and Bobby Charlton. But the young Manchester United team of 1992 may well lay claim to be the greatest FA Youth Cup winners of any club or any era, having swept aside Tottenham Hotspur 5–1 in the two-legged semi-final and then Crystal Palace 6–3 over two games in the final. The youngsters' playing style reflected that of the senior side, with an emphasis on fast, attacking wing-play; but that was hardly surprising when the side included four footballers – Ryan Giggs, David Beckham, Ben Thornley and Keith Gillespie – who would make their professional name as wingers (though Thornley and Gillespie were the two wingers in the youth team, with Beckham playing in central midfield and Giggs as an outright striker). Of the fourteen lads who appeared in the final, only three never played for the United first team. Seven would go on to represent their countries, including Gary Neville, David Beckham, Nicky Butt and Ryan Giggs (who had already played for Wales), and Robbie Savage and Keith Gillespie (who eventually joined other clubs). The United team which reached the semi-final of the Lancashire FA Youth Cup in 1992 included another future international, Paul Scholes.

At the age of 17 years and 321 days, Ryan Giggs had become the youngest international player in Welsh history when he was a substitute against Germany in October 1991 (a record subsequently taken by Ryan Green). Giggs, who was already a regular in the Manchester United first team, and was chosen as PFA Young Player of the Year that season, had returned to captain the Youth Cup side in the second leg of the final. Having already represented his country, Giggs acted as a mature father figure to his teammates, none of whom had yet graduated to the United senior squad. However, Alex Ferguson had been somewhat less impressed with his maturity three weeks earlier, during the hectic final ten days of the unsuccessful race for the championship.

Ferguson was shocked to learn that, on the evening of Easter Monday – the day United lost 2–1 at home to Forest – Giggs and Lee

Sharpe had gone clubbing in Blackpool, even though it was less than forty-eight hours before the team's decisive trip to West Ham. Ferguson didn't learn of the youngsters' escapade until he was at a dinner in Morecambe on the Thursday night, the day after losing in London. He raced back to Manchester as soon as he could politely get away, and – still dressed in bow tie and dinner jacket – drove round to Lee Sharpe's house to find the street packed with cars, music blasting from Sharpe's windows, and the house full of girls. He 'burst in with all guns blazing', he says, and found twenty people holding a party, including Sharpe, Giggs and three of his junior players. 'I went berserk. I ordered everybody out of the house and as each apprentice passed I gave him a cuff on the back of the head.'[22] The comic thing, according to Ryan Giggs's then girlfriend, Joanna Fairhurst, is that 'he didn't call them by name. He just yelled 'ELEVEN!', then 'FIVE!', and ordered them to join him in the living room.'[23] Eleven and five were Giggs and Sharpe's respective shirt numbers.

Lee Sharpe had bought the house only recently, after moving out of club digs, and had also used his new-found wealth to buy a jeep and the expensive drum kit which had been responsible for much of the racket that greeted his manager's arrival. The player later told how Ferguson applied his notorious 'hair-drier' treatment, yelling that Sharpe had to get rid of everything – even his new drums and pet dog – and go back to lodging with a United landlady. Says Sharpe, 'It was like "Get rid of the lot. You're back in digs again." So that was it – back in digs. House sold. Girlfriend back to Birmingham. That was the last I seen of her I think.'[24]

Ryan Giggs's former girlfriend Joanna Fairhurst recalls that Ferguson threatened to phone the player's mother, and didn't confine his fury to the Manchester United employees. 'I was astonished when he turned on me and my pal, called us silly schoolgirls then ordered us out!' she says. 'When I spoke to Ryan next day he said he'd been fined a month's wages . . . I really liked Ryan but Alex

341

ruled the roost and I didn't stand a chance . . . That crazy scene really put the boot into my romance with Ryan.'[25] Sharpe and Giggs had also invited Darren Ferguson to come with them to Blackpool, and he was always grateful to have rejected the offer. 'After he'd finished with Sharpey,' Darren later related, 'Dad phoned me up and asked where I was. He was checking to make sure I wasn't hiding in a wardrobe.'[26]

At times that season Ferguson found the pressure relentless. He faced the accusation, which has surfaced regularly throughout his career, that he changed the team too much – though another wave of injuries didn't help. Towards the end of the season he also had a row with Neil Webb, who was dropped for several games, including the League Cup final against his former club, Forest.

The problems had started when Ferguson pulled Webb out of the England party which was due to visit Czechoslovakia for a friendly in preparation for that summer's European Championship. Having missed so many England games in recent years through injury, Webb was keen to impress the national manager, Graham Taylor, and secure his place in the side. But word went round the United dressing room that Ferguson didn't want players to go off and play in what he regarded as a meaningless friendly. Somewhat to his surprise, Webb found himself being substituted towards the end of a home game against Wimbledon. Afterwards, according to Webb's then wife, Shelley, the United physiotherapist 'informed Neil he was going to ring Graham Taylor and tell him he had picked up an injury and couldn't join the England squad. Manchester United paid his wages, so, though it broke his heart, he had no choice.'[27]

When Graham Taylor rang Neil Webb's home to ask about the injury, the player's mother-in-law answered the phone. 'No,' she reportedly told him, 'Shelley's just rung. He's perfectly OK.' Taylor was furious with Ferguson; the row was picked up by the press, and the FA decided that henceforth all withdrawals from the England squad had to be supported by doctors' certificates. 'Alex Ferguson never forgave Neil,' says Shelley Webb, who thinks her ex-husband might have accepted the situation had the United manager explained to him what he was doing.[28]

'The upshot,' says Ferguson himself,

> was that Neil chose to inform the England manager that he
> was actually fit and that he was only withdrawn on my
> instructions. I felt he was totally out of order and I did not
> like the attempts made by Graham Taylor to inform the press
> about United's role in the withdrawal of players . . . I was still
> inclined to pick Neil but he had to be taught a lesson to ram
> home how important Manchester United is to me, to the
> supporters and everyone else committed to the club. He
> knew he was in the wrong and after a couple of weeks he
> apologised.[29]

Yet, significantly, Ferguson did not deny the Webbs' allegations.

Alex Ferguson's stance towards his players' international careers reflects the pressure he was under as he tried to ensure that United won the championship for the first time in twenty-five years. Certainly during his own spell as an international manager he had been suspicious when claims of injury kept players out of the Scotland squad. However, his attitude runs deeper than that. As a club boss, Ferguson has always been clear that the club comes first. Indeed, his ability to instil this belief in his players has been one of the important ingredients in his success. At the same time Ferguson knew that, if United lost the championship because Webb was unfit to play in the final matches of the season, the England manager would scarcely take the blame for it. As it was, the serious injury that Webb had picked up while playing for his country just after joining United in 1989 had been one of the reasons why the Reds had stuttered that season.

Ferguson felt Webb had never quite recovered his previous form or pace (which partly explained why he also dropped him in favour of Mike Phelan for the Cup-Winners' Cup final). Indeed, Manchester United had suffered more than their fair share of misfortunes from players' injuries with England. Bryan Robson had been a regular casualty with the national team, and the mishaps which ended the careers of both Steve Coppell and Gary Bailey occurred while they were away on international duty. Ferguson's first row with a national team manager had been as early as May 1988, when he'd withdrawn Brian McClair and Gordon Strachan from a Scotland friendly against Colombia, so that they could play for United in their own prestigious friendly against the Italian champions AC Milan. Ferguson said the game had been planned long before, and to sell TV rights United had agreed to field their strongest side. The Scotland manager, Andy Roxburgh, duly retaliated by leaving both men out of his team to play England at Wembley a few days later.

Amazingly, considering that he himself had once been an international manager, Ferguson actually used to prepare an advance list of the United players he wanted to claim were injured and should therefore be withdrawn from their national squads. According to one account, Ferguson would give his 'injured' list to the club physiotherapist, Jim McGregor, the week before international games were due to take place. This then gave McGregor time to pretend that those listed had been injured during whatever match United played just before the internationals. 'The really funny thing,' says this witness,

> is that the list would increase in size if we'd lost on the
> Saturday. If we had, he'd be in one of his moods and just add
> a couple of names. Quite often he'd say, "You were shit;
> you're not going to England." So, if you played shit, you
> knew he might make you miss an international game. So
> maybe it was another strange form of motivation.

Such petty disputes would rumble on with national managers over the next few years, and a suspiciously large number of United players seemed to develop injuries just before international games only to experience quick recoveries immediately afterwards. In time, Ferguson reached understandings with most of the national team bosses from the British Isles, whereby some United players were released for friendly games and others were held back. A good example was Ryan Giggs, whom Ferguson was especially reluctant to release for Wales. A colleague says:

> He seemed to be really wary of letting him go. He genuinely
> feared what playing for Wales would do for Giggsy. He didn't
> like the fact that they were so bad that he'd have to do all
> the running. Ferguson really used to hate how much
> responsibility they'd put on such a young man. You could see
> his point really.

Ferguson tacitly agreed with the Wales manager, Terry Yorath, and his successors that Giggs would be available only for competitive fixtures: in the subsequent decade the winger played only one friendly for Wales and fewer than half his country's international games. Yet Ferguson's restrictions made Giggs very unpopular with many Welsh fans.

Alex Ferguson's response to international call-ups is a good illustration of how power has shifted to clubs in recent times. In the past, players were often obliged to play international fixtures on days when their clubs were also playing. In May 1958, for example, Manchester United faced AC Milan in the European Cup semi-final, and were still recovering from the devastation of the Munich crash. Yet the FA insisted that Bobby Charlton should play in a couple of friendlies for England rather than in the important semi-final games for United, whose needs were demonstrably greater.

Ferguson's relationship with Neil Webb did not improve after the

England row, and the player found himself increasingly overlooked by the United boss. 'His tenure had already degenerated into farce' when the squad travelled to an away game at Southampton early the following season, says Shelley Webb. Ferguson spotted the Webbs enjoying a bottle of wine over lunch in the team hotel, so he fined the player two weeks' wages (subsequently reduced to one after intervention by the PFA) and sent him home to Manchester. 'The weeks of being ostracised turned to months,' says Shelley Webb. 'Ferguson didn't want to play him but he didn't seem to want to let him go either.' The final straw came when Shelley, who is a journalist, did an item on the BBC2 football programme she presented, *Standing Room Only*, in which she reviewed Ferguson's latest book, *Six Years at United*. The publication had already prompted Paul McGrath and Tony Collins to threaten legal action, but Shelley Webb chose not to mention the additional criticisms of her husband. Instead, with Neil Webb's full consent, she lambasted the numerous attacks in Ferguson's book on players who had refused to join United in the past, such as Paul Gascoigne, or those who had left the club, like McGrath. Not long after the broadcast Neil Webb was sold back to Forest for £800,000 – barely half what United had paid for him three years before. 'Mission accomplished,' wrote Mrs Webb.[30]

Like other players bought by Manchester United from Nottingham Forest (notably Garry Birtles and Peter Davenport), Neil Webb had never really succeeded at Old Trafford. Although he holds a unique club distinction of scoring on his debut in four different competitions (the three main domestic contests and the Cup-Winners' Cup), Webb managed only 11 goals in 109 games – far below his Forest record of a goal almost every three matches.

Some Manchester United fans questioned whether the club would ever recover from the dreadful finish to the 1991–92 season. It was the third time, following 1972 and 1986, that United had been odds-on favourites for the title, only to see their dreams dashed. Was there some flaw in the club's make-up, they wondered – perhaps something psychological which would prevent them ever winning the championship?

The spring of 1992 had been an agonising period for Alex Ferguson and, exceptionally, he booked a whole month's holiday to recuperate. 'It was like a death in the family,' he declared. 'But you have got to get over it.'[31]

The Can-Opener

'Of all the many qualities a good team must possess, the supreme essential for me is penetration. And Eric brought the can-opener.'

SIR ALEX FERGUSON[1]

Liverpool fans may not appreciate the fact, but the man who is now their club's manager, Gérard Houllier, partly inspired the transfer which was to transform Manchester United's recent history and turn Alex Ferguson from a good manager into a great one. Martin Edwards was sitting in his office at Old Trafford in November 1992, chatting to Ferguson about United's need for a new striker, and mulling over possible targets. Ferguson suggested it was a pity that they'd never got to hear about Eric Cantona before he joined Leeds United earlier in the year. Houllier, who was then manager of Paris Saint-Germain, had recently been singing Cantona's praises, Ferguson explained. Steve Bruce and Gary Pallister had also been impressed with the Frenchman when United beat Leeds earlier in the season. Within seconds of Ferguson's comment, the Leeds managing director, Bill Fotherby, came on the phone to Edwards. 'The timing was weird,' Ferguson wrote later, 'absolutely uncanny.'[2]

Fotherby wanted to know if United were willing to sell their Irish full-back, Denis Irwin. The move would have taken Irwin back to the club where he had begun his football career, but he had settled well at Old Trafford after his transfer from Oldham two summers before, and there was no question of United selling him. (He would go on to win more honours than almost any player in the club's history, and make more than 500 appearances.)

Edwards then began probing Fotherby about players *he* might want to sell, mentioning the Leeds forward Lee Chapman, who'd already scored against United for five different clubs (and would go on to make it six). Ferguson tried to attract Edwards's attention, mouthing that he should ask about the other Leeds striker, but his boss didn't seem to understand. Eventually the United manager seized a piece of paper and scribbled Eric Cantona's name.

Having finally grasped his manager's point, Edwards enquired whether Cantona might be unsettled, and mentioned rumours of a dressing-room bust-up. To his surprise, Fotherby admitted there were problems with the French player. 'Any chance of you selling him and we'd be interested,' Edwards added. 'Need to be pretty quick, mind you, because we have the money for a striker and want to do some business now. If Eric's not available we'll go elsewhere.'[3]

The French forward had made quite an impact at Elland Road, having scored 14 goals in 35 games, including a couple of hat-tricks. He'd also won championship medals in two different countries in successive seasons – at Marseilles in 1991 and at Leeds in 1992, although his role in the Yorkshire club's title campaign should not be exaggerated, since he played only six full games, plus nine more as substitute, and scored three times. He was, however, hugely popular with the Leeds fans, who initiated the famous chant 'Ooh, aah, Cantona'. But the striker had fallen out with the Leeds manager, Howard Wilkinson, who punished him for breaches of discipline and dropped him from the team. Fotherby agreed to consult Wilkinson.

Edwards couldn't believe his luck when Fotherby rang back shortly afterwards to say 'Yes'. Even better was the price. He rang

Ferguson on his car phone to break the news. 'We've got him,' Edwards exclaimed, and then began teasing his manager about the fee he'd agreed. Ferguson picks up the story:

> Trying to be realistic, I suggested £1.6 million. 'Wrong.' So
> then I rattled off three or four more attempts. They were all
> so far off the mark, it was like one of those TV quizzes.
> Higher, lower, not even close. Eventually the chairman
> declared the true figure: £1 million. I just couldn't believe it.
> 'That's an absolute steal,' I blurted out.[4]

Leeds United, it seems, merely wanted to recoup the money they had paid the French club Nîmes for Cantona earlier in the year.

With his cocky, strutting posture – head up, chest out – and collar turned up, Eric Cantona looked like no other player. And, as he strode on to the Old Trafford pitch for the first time, and looked around, he must have suspected that Manchester United was a club that was big enough for his talents. At a time when Ferguson could still do no right in many commentators' eyes, some dismissed the decision to buy Cantona as another mistake: they couldn't see how he'd fit in to the United team. Ferguson later admitted to having had doubts on the first day or two.

Cantona had never managed to stay anywhere very long: this was his eighth move in ten years. What's more, he had a long record of dissent. His career was marked by regular sendings-off, suspensions, rows with his managers, and fights with teammates – similar to Alex Ferguson's own playing career, though far worse. Cantona was larger than life in everything he did, good and bad. In a notorious television interview, he had once compared his French team manager, Henri Michel, to a *sac à merde*, or shitbag, and said that Michel was one of the most incompetent managers in the world. In another famous incident, shortly before he left France, Cantona threw the ball at a referee's legs, was sent off, and at the subsequent French FA disciplinary hearing addressed each member of tribunal, one by one to their faces, as 'Idiot'.[5] The committee seems to have been surprisingly lenient, and suspended him for just two months. After that he turned his back on France, had a week's trial with Sheffield Wednesday – who couldn't make up their minds – and ended up at Elland Road.

Ever since November 1992, fans of the two Uniteds – Leeds and Manchester – have wondered why the Yorkshire club let him go, and so quickly and so cheaply. There was all sorts of speculation and gossip about Cantona being a disruptive influence on team unity. Howard Wilkinson later spoke of the player's 'tantrums, disappearances, sulks and an intolerance of being dropped'; he feared that Cantona would suddenly leave, as he had at previous clubs, never to return, which would make it difficult for Leeds to recoup their investment.[6] Wilkinson admitted to a nagging vision in his mind – 'the sight of the Frenchman disappearing over the horizon astride his Harley-Davidson with paint brushes and easel strapped on his back. It is an illusion that might yet come to haunt Alex Ferguson at Old Trafford.'[7]

Cantona found it difficult to get on with other Leeds players; he wouldn't do as he was asked in training, or adapt his role on the pitch when the manager thought it necessary. He was not enough of a team player, Wilkinson felt, and was too easily tamed by skilful opponents. Rather than try to change him, it would be far better, the Leeds boss thought, simply to get back what they'd paid and invest the money in a more reliable forward. In short, Howard Wilkinson hadn't found a way to manage the Frenchman. In November 1992, after he was dropped by Wilkinson for the second time in a fortnight, Cantona demanded a transfer. Leeds had in fact been trying to sell him for several days, but with no takers, when Edwards popped Ferguson's opportunist question.

Alex Ferguson had been looking for a new striker since United stopped scoring goals at the start of 1992. During the summer he'd tried to buy Southampton's twenty-two-year-old forward Alan Shearer. Southampton were happy to accept £3.3 million, but when they spoke on the phone Ferguson found Shearer surly and argumentative, and the player was clearly tempted by a more lucrative offer from Kenny Dalglish, who was now the manager of Blackburn Rovers. United weren't willing to break their careful pay structure by matching the Lancashire club's terms. Blackburn had been spending lavishly since they were acquired by the wealthy steel tycoon Jack Walker, and Ferguson could counter only by stressing United's prestige and potential, suggesting that Dalglish himself would never have joined Blackburn Rovers as a player. 'I was disappointed in the conversations with him,' says Ferguson. 'He surprised me, the lad. Money seemed to be the main thing to him . . . there was really nothing else I could do at that point.'[8] The United manager had been upset to find that Dalglish had phoned Shearer regularly towards the end of the previous season, while Ferguson had promised the Southampton manager he'd leave any approach until the summer. This had made Shearer think United weren't that interested in him, and also illustrated the problems which can arise if managers obey the rules on not tapping players. 'I felt that maybe I lost the inside rail on the deal by talking solely with his manager,' Ferguson claimed in his diary. 'But that's the way we do things, the way I do things.'[9] Well sometimes, one should say. The cases of Paul Gascoigne and Jim Leighton would suggest otherwise, as would several more examples in the future.

Instead Ferguson spent £1 million buying Dion Dublin from Cambridge United, after seeing a videotape sent by the club's manager. Dublin had already agreed to go to Everton, in fact, but couldn't resist United, according to the Merseyside club's boss, Howard Kendall. 'Dion said to me, "How can I turn down Manchester United?"'[10] But, in only his sixth appearance for United, Dublin broke his leg, and was expected to be absent for six months, which left Ferguson as short of strikers as he'd been in the previous season.

He faxed a £3.5 million offer for David Hirst of Sheffield Wednesday, but the South Yorkshire club weren't interested, and their manager, Trevor Francis, publicly complained about the heavy-handed nature of the approach. Then Hirst, too, suffered a bad injury.

United's lack of firepower had become a serious embarrassment, with just 17 goals in 16 games by the time they bought Eric Cantona in late November. Nothing illustrated the problem better than their exit in the first round of the UEFA Cup, beaten by Moscow Torpedo on penalties after two goalless draws.

Alex Ferguson would describe Eric Cantona as the 'can-opener' who unlocked his side's potential, a catalyst who sparked an almost immediate reaction. He was broken in gently at first, playing a friendly in Portugal, then being brought on as substitute against Manchester City, and he didn't score his first goal for another two games, at Chelsea. But over Christmas everything suddenly clicked. It began on Boxing Day, when the team were 3–0 down at Sheffield Wednesday with half an hour to go, but came back to draw 3–3. United then notched up two of the best Old Trafford performances of the 1990s: a dazzling 5–0 defeat of Coventry (who'd just thrashed Liverpool 5–1), then a 4–1 win over Spurs a fortnight later.

It wasn't that Cantona scored lots of goals: instead, he added a new dimension. Operating just behind Mark Hughes, he acted like the conductor of an orchestra with his clever flicks, precisely weighted passes and ability to spot openings others hadn't noticed. He was remarkably quick on the ball, though economical with his movements. His only fault was a complete inability to tackle: 'He couldn't tackle a fish supper,' Ferguson would later remark, and he kept urging Cantona not to bother.[11] Suddenly, from a situation where nobody was scoring, now everyone was. As 1992 gave way to 1993, eleven different players were on target in the course of just four games. Cantona had elevated United's football to a different level.

What impressed Alex Ferguson, especially considering the stories of Cantona's dissent and ill-discipline, was the player's dedication. Whereas at Leeds United he might miss training sessions, or disobey the coaches if he disagreed with them, on the western side of the Pennines he became a model professional. Colleagues were amazed when, one day early on, he approached Ferguson after morning practice and asked if two youth players could help him with extra work. It became a habit, and others soon joined in. His enthusiasm and professionalism were infectious, especially among the talented younger players hovering on the edges of the first-team squad.

The challenge was to keep Cantona contented and so dissuade him from moving on again. Ferguson found the Frenchman less confident than he appeared, and realised he needed constant encouragement, reassurance and praise. Gordon Strachan had warned publicly that Cantona got depressed if his team weren't winning or playing well. Fortunately they now were. Ferguson took a philosophical approach to the idea of Cantona suddenly departing on his bike, and once remarked, 'I think if he is here today, tremendous, but if he is gone tomorrow we just say: "Good luck, Eric, thanks for playing for us; you have been absolutely brilliant."'[12]

What had made the difference? In part, Eric Cantona clearly felt he'd arrived somewhere equal to his talents and aspirations. A second factor was undoubtedly his skilful handling by the United boss. Cantona was excused from some of Ferguson's more minor rules – for instance, the club's strict dress code – and he was one of the few players with whom the manager never lost his temper. (Two others were Willie Miller and Bryan Robson.) 'I have never purposely, or separately, asked Eric to stick to our rules,' Ferguson admitted. 'Everyone on the playing staff accepts there must be a recognised and acceptable level of behaviour and Eric has never stepped out of line.' He also confessed that he'd changed his whole attitude with Cantona, and had had to perform 'a bit of a U-turn on my usual policy, and accept that we have a different type of player around the house'.[13]

And, apart from in his first game, Ferguson was careful never to demote Cantona to the substitute's bench – one of the player's prime grievances at Leeds. Indeed, Cantona was rarely pulled off for a sub-stitute either. Alex Ferguson was the first manager whom the French player totally respected, though he had been managed by a roster which included distinguished names such as Michel Platini, Guy Roux and Franz Beckenbauer.

Curiously, given Ferguson's complaints about fixture congestion at the end of the 1991–92 season, United had undertaken a punish-ing overseas tour the previous summer. It was organised by the Norwegian agent Rune Hauge, to whom they would later pay £21,000 for his efforts. The schedule began against Start Kristiansand in Norway, then involved an astonishing dash to Glasgow for a friendly against Celtic the following night, before the squad immediately flew back to Scandinavia for three more matches – against Lillestrøm and Rosenborg in Norway, and Elfsborg in Sweden. It entailed five games in eight days; and, whereas teams on close-season tours often involve numerous reserve players, United fielded strong sides on every occasion. Six players – Irwin, Pallister, Wallace, Giggs, Phelan and Darren Ferguson – appeared in all five matches, and, as might be expected, several members of the squad were left complaining of muscle injuries.

It could also come as no surprise that the start of the 1992–93 league season, before Cantona's purchase, was United's worst since Ferguson arrived. They lost 2–1 at Sheffield United, and then 3–0 at home to Everton. Indeed, Sheffield's opening strike – from Brian Deane after just five minutes – was the very first goal in the new Premier League. The top of English football had been reorganised after the twenty-two clubs in the old First Division of the Football League had broken away under the auspices of the Football Association. Their new FA Premier League was designed to negotiate its own deals with the television companies, and to grab an even bigger share of football monies for the big fish. In reality, aside from

the financial details, little had changed: the elite division still consisted of twenty-two clubs who played each other twice a year, of
which three would be relegated at the end of the season and replaced
with sides promoted from the remaining Football League below. In
his book *Six Years at United*, published in the autumn of 1992,
Ferguson described the new arrangement as 'a piece of nonsense'.
His remark seems somewhat ironic now, given that his teams would
go on to dominate the first decade of the new league in a way that no
club had ever done before in English football, winning seven of the
first nine championships. 'It would hardly behove the manager of a
leading club,' he said, 'to suggest that people both in and out of the
game have been conned, but I can well understand the ordinary fan
in the street wondering.' The new league, Ferguson added, had 'done
the reputation of the clubs no good whatsoever and . . . alienated a
great many supporters'.[14] In the event, Manchester United's support
and crowds under the new regime would scale new peaks.

Ferguson was also forthright in denouncing the Premier League's
£304 million television deal with BSkyB, even though, as he
acknowledged, his own twenty-year-old son Jason now worked as a
journalist with the pay-television company. The contract was 'a plain
and simple rip-off' in which 'the Sky people would fleece the fans'.
The deal, he wrote, 'sells supporters right down the river, and hits
hardest at the most vulnerable part of society, the old people', who
could not afford the new satellite dishes. 'I know Sky are putting a
lot of money into football, but it's the fans who are paying the price
and I don't like that,' he declared, describing as 'diabolical' the tele-
vised Monday-night fixtures at distant venues which meant that
travelling supporters had to take time off work to get there.[15]
Ferguson also warned he wouldn't necessarily give interviews and
filming opportunities to Sky whenever it wanted them.

Ferguson was clearly taking a risk in being so outspoken, since
Manchester United had played a leading role in the development of
the Premier League, and stood to gain handsomely. His immediate

boss, Martin Edwards, who was still the largest shareholder in the new Manchester United PLC, would soon be worth tens of millions of pounds, thanks partly to a more entrepreneurial attitude at Old Trafford, but largely to the success that Ferguson was starting to achieve on the pitch. In time, the growing disparity between what Edwards reaped from Ferguson's efforts and what the manager himself earned would rupture their previous friendship to the extent that Ferguson came close to leaving United on several occasions.

Alex Ferguson has always been more publicly sympathetic to ordinary supporters than have most football managers, and has gone out of his way to support their interests. He firmly allied himself with the radical movement then spreading within the game centred around fanzines and new independent supporters' associations which operated independently of their clubs – the ISAs. Ferguson also voiced fears in his 1992 book that United's less affluent and working-class supporters would be priced out of the game, and in particular he expressed anxiety about the rebuilding of the famous Stretford End at Old Trafford – the half-covered terrace where 10,000 of United's most vocal fans traditionally stood. 'I cannot help but feel they will have torn the heart out of the ground,' he wrote, at a time when the old Stretford End had just been pulled down and was being rebuilt as an all-seater cantilever stand in keeping with the other three sides of the stadium. The government had forced all leading British clubs to get rid of standing areas by 1993, in response to recommendations made by Lord Justice Taylor following the 1989 Hillsborough disaster, in which ninety-five fans had been crushed to death. 'Personally,' Ferguson said of the move to all-seated grounds, 'I can't say I like it.'[16]

On the pitch, United rose from tenth at the start of November 1992 to the top of the table after the Cantona-inspired defeat of Spurs in early January. Their main championship rivals were Aston Villa, managed by Ron Atkinson (who had a now well-behaved Paul McGrath commanding the defence), and Norwich City, who had led the table for much of the autumn thanks to fifteen goals by Mark Robins, the hero of the 1990 FA Cup run, who'd left United for £800,000 during the previous summer in frustration at not winning a regular first-team place. It would be tempting to suggest that United's season was plain sailing after Eric Cantona arrived, but there were still setbacks. The worst was a 1–0 defeat at Oldham, where (without Cantona) United spent a fruitless evening pumping long balls to Mark Hughes. That mediocre display was followed by three wasteful draws.

The crescendo began, however, on 5 April, with one of those Monday-night Sky TV matches which Ferguson had so decried, at their far-flung rivals Norwich City, who'd kept up the pressure by beating Villa in their previous game. United suddenly clicked back into devastating form, and the overwhelming memory is of the sheer speed of the Reds' attacks. With Kanchelskis and Sharpe raiding down the wings and Giggs through the middle, United took a 3–0 lead in just twenty-one minutes, though Norwich got one back in the second half. Ferguson had told his team to enjoy themselves, reminding them that if they won their last seven games they would be champions.

But everyone remembered only too well what had happened at the same stage of the previous season. And the next game, at home to Sheffield Wednesday on Easter Saturday, seemed to have echoes of the holiday home fixture against Forest the year before – especially when the visitors scored a penalty in the sixty-fifth minute. Bryan Robson was brought on as substitute, but Wednesday were still ahead with five minutes to go, and thousands of fans had already left the ground in despair. Suddenly, to huge relief, Steve Bruce equalised from a corner. Alex Ferguson would have been happy with that, since he'd just heard that Aston Villa had managed only a draw. Earlier, however, the match had stopped for several minutes when the referee was injured and had to go off, and the substitute official made due allowance in adding injury time. The Sheffield Wednesday manager, Trevor Francis, calculated there had been seven minutes and fourteen seconds of additional play when Bruce popped in a second header to make it 2–1. It provided one of the most powerful pictures of the season: Alex Ferguson and Brian Kidd dancing on the pitch after Bruce scored his second. They were confident the title was finally in their grasp, though wins against Coventry, Chelsea and Crystal Palace were required to make sure.

To the disappointment of many United fans, the League was finally clinched when the team weren't playing, as Villa unexpectedly lost 1–0 at home to Oldham, who were still fighting against relegation. Alex Ferguson was playing golf at Mottram Hall in Cheshire with his son Mark that afternoon, having decided he couldn't endure the agony of watching the Villa game live on Sky. As he reached the seventeenth hole, a complete stranger ran up. 'Mr Ferguson,' he cried, 'they murdered Villa. Oldham have won. It's all over. United are champions!'[17]

In later years Manchester United supporters would deride their City rivals for not having won a trophy for twenty-six years, draping a banner from the balcony at the Stretford End with movable numbers to ram the point home. ('026 YEARS' it simply read.) But twenty-six years is how long United fans had had to wait since their previous league triumph, during which time titles had gone to unfashionable sides such as Derby County (twice) and Nottingham Forest, and, more painfully, to Liverpool on no fewer than eleven occasions. Now, 1993 was a victory to savour. The players immediately rushed to Steve Bruce's house to celebrate, ignoring Ferguson's rules on drinking, even though they were due to play Blackburn the following evening. Simultaneously, and spontaneously, hundreds of delirious fans gathered outside the stadium at Old Trafford and in bars and pubs all over the city. When Lee Sharpe drove down to the stadium to observe the festivities, he was carried shoulder high all round the outside of the ground.

The following day turned into one long Manchester United

carnival. Tickets for the Blackburn game went on the black market for more than £100, while Old Trafford and the surrounding area became a heaving, noisy, celebrating sea of red, white and black. Blackburn lost 3–1, with Gary Pallister scoring in the final minute – the last regular outfield player to get his name on the score sheet that season, before Robson and Bruce, who had both captained the side, jointly collected the new Premier League trophy. Even Cathy Ferguson, who didn't normally attend even cup finals, was there for this historic occasion. Alex later described it as 'the day I truly became manager of Manchester United . . . there was a sudden, over-whelming realisation that now I was master of my own destiny'.[18]

In the end United won the title by a comfortable ten-point margin over Aston Villa. It had taken him six and a half years, but Alex Ferguson had at last done as he had promised, becoming the first manager to win the League in both England and Scotland. He claimed to have learned more in those six-plus years than in his previous forty-five.

Eric Cantona, meanwhile, had scored nine goals – but that was only part of his contribution. His inspiration and ability to create openings for others were widely credited with having made the difference. 'He's the brainiest player I've ever seen,' said Bobby Charlton.[19] Cantona now had the unique record of winning three league titles in three seasons with three different sides. He had quickly become the biggest hero at Old Trafford since Denis Law reigned as King of the Stretford End, with fans waving tricolours, singing to the tune of the Marseillaise, and gloating over the fact that their hated Yorkshire rivals had let him go so cheaply.

Many people predicted that, having won the League once, Manchester United would pick up several more titles in the years ahead, though it was never explained why this should happen. 'Let's not get carried away,' said the Arsenal manager, George Graham. 'The days are over when one club can dominate our game.'[20] In truth they were only just beginning. Yet Graham supported Alex

Ferguson's cause that summer when the United manager tried to negotiate a better pay deal in reward for his achievement. Ferguson had been shocked to discover that Graham earned twice his own salary, and it also irked him that he was getting only a third of Eric Cantona's pay. Martin Edwards did not believe what his manager said about Graham's terms. 'The chairman refused to budge an inch,' Ferguson says, 'and I had to accept what was an improved contract but one that left me at a pay level far below that of either Graham or Cantona.'[21] Ferguson's problem was that he was now so emotionally committed to Manchester United that none of the directors believed he would walk out. It was borne out by small gestures such as his regularly wearing a special red version of United's 1968 European Cup-final shirt (the strip on the night itself had been blue). 'I would only leave United on a point of principle,' he confessed that summer. 'Something would alter dramatically in the parameters of my duties to shift me . . . I just cannot see myself ever being in charge of another club, in Britain or abroad. The determination now is to finish my life at United and, I hope, that parting is still many years away.'[22]

Ferguson said that winning 'a trophy every year I'm in charge' would be 'the fundamental, all-important driving force in shaping the seasons to come'.[23] It was a goal he would achieve with some leeway. After United had collected four different trophies in four years, the European Cup was the last remaining prize, and the league title now enabled them to enter the competition for the first time since 1969. Ferguson strengthened his squad over the summer by buying the twenty-one-year-old Irish midfielder Roy Keane from Nottingham Forest for £3.75 million. Jack Charlton, the Ireland manager, likes to think he made the decisive recommendation. 'I said, "He's got an engine like you've never seen before, Alex. Get him bought. You'll be able sell him if you want in a couple of years to Europe. And you'll make a bloody big load of money on him." And Alex signed him the following day.' Charlton puts Keane's subsequent maturity as a player almost entirely down to Ferguson's influence, though the move was bad news for the manager's own midfielder son, Darren, who had played fifteen games in the championship campaign and collected a second medal for the family.[24]

It was the second time, after buying Neil Webb, that Ferguson had raided the Nottingham club for a replacement for Bryan Robson, and this time it was successful. Keane was a tough, combative midfielder who rarely gave the ball away and struck a useful number of goals. One drawback was his nationality, which would increase the problems United would have with a new rule that UEFA had just introduced, limiting the number of foreigners that clubs could use in European games. Clubs would be allowed to field only three foreign players, plus two more who might have foreign nationality but who could count as 'assimilated' if they had been groomed as youth players and played in their club's home country for more than five years. The headache for English clubs was that Welsh, Scottish and Irish players all counted as 'foreign'. The rule would have caused severe difficulties for many of the English winners of European trophies had it applied in the past (though United's 1968 European Cup team would have scraped through, and the 1991 Cup-Winners' Cup team was mostly English). But now United had Schmeichel, Irwin, Keane, Kanchelskis, Hughes, Cantona and Giggs all competing for the five foreigner places, along with Brian McClair and Darren Ferguson on the fringes of the team.

United successfully jumped their first European Cup hurdle, beating the Hungarian champions Kispest-Honvéd 5–3 on aggregate, and then faced what looked like another straightforward tie, against the Turkish club Galatasaray. It looked even easier when United took a two-goal lead at Old Trafford within the opening quarter of an hour. But the Turks fought back, equalising by half-time and scoring again afterwards to lead 3–2. United's record of being unbeaten in fifty-one home European games since 1956 looked in peril until Eric Cantona scored a late equaliser. With the advantage of three away goals, the Turks maintained the upper hand amid the fire-works and noise of the Ali Sami Yen stadium in Istanbul, where United players and fans were attacked by the home crowd and Turkish police alike. Mark Hughes was sacrificed to the 'foreigner' rule, and United failed to create a single clear-cut chance as they tumbled out of Europe with a goalless draw. In the six times they'd entered the European Cup, it was the first occasion that they'd failed to reach even the semi-finals. As the players were leaving the pitch, Eric Cantona received a red card for protesting about the referee, and then suffered double punishment with a blow to the head from a police baton.

Yet in England Manchester United swept everything before them – or almost everything. Before the season began, Ferguson had challenged his players as to whether they were hungry enough to do it all again. He told them he'd put in an envelope the names of six players he feared weren't up to it, and he would review those names at the end of the season if United failed to retain the league title. It proved to be a 'psychological ploy'. Was there really an envelope with names? 'Ach no,' he admitted later. 'The only name in it is my own.'[25]

Having beaten Arsenal on penalties in the 1993 Charity Shield, United reached the halfway stage in the League having won sixteen games out of twenty-one, drawn four, and lost only once. Bobby Charlton – former Busby Babe and member of the 1968 European Cup-winning team – said this was the 'best ever' Manchester United side he'd seen.[26] Its nearest challengers were Leeds United and Blackburn Rovers – the latter now blessed with Alan Shearer's fire-power, and having Kevin Moran playing occasionally in defence.

It was a sign of United's superiority that they held a thirteen-point lead over both sides at Christmas. And they were in magnificent form in the opening stages at Anfield one evening in early January, having swept into a 3–0 lead over Liverpool with barely twenty minutes on the clock. But then they fell apart. The

Merseyside team scored twice before half-time and bombarded United's goal throughout the second half until Neil Ruddock equalised. Such was the Liverpool pressure that United could easily have lost, which would have prevented Alex Ferguson's later proud boast that in twenty-eight years of management he had never been defeated after taking a two-goal lead (though in this case, of course, it was three goals). Memories of this feast of football were sullied, however, when later that year the *Sun* newspaper alleged that the Liverpool goalkeeper, Bruce Grobbelaar, had been bribed to concede goals in that particular match and several others – though it didn't look like that on the night. (The accusation has yet to be resolved in the courts: juries failed to reach verdicts in two successive criminal trials, and the Appeal Court then overturned Grobbelaar's £85,000 libel victory against the *Sun*.) The irony is that, immediately after the game, the goalkeeper being criticised was not Grobbelaar but United's Peter Schmeichel. Indeed, the Dane almost lost his job.

Schmeichel claims that by this time his authority was so established at Old Trafford, with his reputation for mental toughness, that he had become one of the players who filled 'a kind of scapegoat role' whenever Ferguson got angry about the team's shortcomings. (Another was Gary Pallister.) In the dressing room after the 3–3 draw the United manager launched a tirade against his goalkeeper, not for any of the goals he'd let in, Schmeichel claims, but for the poor quality of his goal kicks:

> He wasn't just livid, he was absolutely hysterical . . . He didn't
> just criticise some of my goal kicks, he more or less heaped
> derision on *all* the goal kicks I had taken in the entire
> game . . . neither of us truly meant what followed: a gigantic
> argument which with the speed of lightning reached such a
> personal level that I don't care to mention what was said . . .
> It turned into a fight between two willpowers, neither of

which was interested in or capable of backing down. I said
the most awful things. I questioned his capabilities as a
manager. I aired doubts about his personal qualities.
Ferguson didn't keep anything back either, and at one point
he threatened to throw a cup of tea in my face. In the end I
just turned my back on him and headed for the showers,
embarrassingly aware of the fact that it had grown deadly
silent in the changing room.[27]

One witness says that at half-time Ferguson even told Schmeichel
to get into the bath as he was going to be substituted. 'Then five
minutes later, when Fergie had calmed down to a sane level, he just
said, "Right, fucking get out and put your kit on." Suddenly he
hadn't been substituted.' What had really upset the United manager
was that his team should have collapsed so easily, on live television,
when everything had looked so straightforward – and against their
arch-rivals, Liverpool. Having once been a great admirer of
Liverpool, Ferguson now hated the club even more intensely than
most United fans did.

After the row, Schmeichel immediately rang his agent and asked
him to find a new club, and the keeper mentally prepared himself to
leave Old Trafford. He knew that what he had said had gone well
beyond what his boss could reasonably tolerate. His fears were confirmed when the two met in Ferguson's office two days later. 'I
suppose you realise that I have no choice but to give you the sack?'
Ferguson said, according to Schmeichel's account. The goalkeeper
apologised, but his boss replied that it made no difference: he would
still have to leave.[28]

Peter Schmeichel then went off and apologised to his teammates,
confessing that his behaviour had been 'childish . . . embarrassing
and unforgivable'. Unbeknown to Schmeichel, however, Ferguson
was listening to every word from behind a door, and he later told the
goalkeeper's agent how surprised he'd been that the player had been

able to eat his words and swallow his pride. 'Perhaps', Schmeichel suggests, 'that was the reason why my verbal sacking never materialised as a formal notice of dismissal.'[29] By apologising so freely, and admitting he'd been at fault, Schmeichel had restored Ferguson's authority and dignity.

It was years before the story reached the outside world, however, and Ferguson made no mention of it in his autobiography five years later. A rather more surprising omission from the book was the departure a few days afterwards of his son Darren, who joined First Division Wolves for the modest fee of £250,000. Despite his championship medal, Darren had found it increasingly difficult to get into the side now that Roy Keane was guaranteed a place in midfield, yet it was difficult to complain or get angry when the boss was also his father. Nobody has ever suggested that Alex Ferguson showed favouritism towards Darren at Old Trafford; indeed, Andrei Kanchelskis noticed that he 'probably criticised his son's mistakes more severely than anyone else's'.[30] 'I had to get away,' Darren explained years later, 'I was twenty-one, Ince was playing as well as he ever has and they'd just signed Keane. I felt that I wasn't getting as many games as I wanted.'[31] He'd been particularly upset the previous season after playing well and then being dropped for Bryan Robson.

Alex Ferguson himself negotiated Darren's contract with Wolves, who were now being managed by the former England boss Graham Taylor. The move was a mistake. Wolves have long seemed a good bet for an imminent return to the top flight, but season after season they have failed to live up to their potential. Years later Darren acknowledged he 'should have stayed' with his father at Old Trafford.[32]

The collapse at Anfield had no long-term repercussions, and United's season seemed to proceed as serenely as ever until March, when results dipped and they had four players sent off in the space of five matches. First Peter Schmeichel was dismissed against

Charlton Athletic in the FA Cup quarter-final for racing out of his penalty area and then both toppling an oncoming forward with a two-legged tackle and handling the ball. (Absurdly, Ferguson said the referee would be embarrassed when he saw the incident on television.) Eric Cantona then collected two red cards in two games: first after stamping on John Moncur at Swindon (which even Ferguson couldn't excuse), and then, harshly, for a second bookable offence at Highbury three nights later. The Frenchmen was now displaying his nasty streak a little too often, and had been lucky to escape being sent off for a vicious foul on the Norwich player Jeremy Goss in the FA Cup fourth round a few weeks earlier. It was witnessed by millions on live television, though not by the referee, it seems, and Cantona went unpunished. It spoilt an accomplished 2–0 victory by United, and prompted the BBC pundit Jimmy Hill to describe the incident as 'despicable and villainous'; Ferguson responded by calling Hill 'a prat'.[33] Earlier, in the third round, Mark Hughes had been dismissed for lashing out at the Sheffield United defender David Tuttle, and again Ferguson immediately came to Hughes's defence in his post-match comments.

After this spate of dismissals and unpleasant attacks, Alex Ferguson's side was rapidly losing public sympathy and faced increasing hostility from the media and opposing fans. Already, five different players had been sent off that season (Robson, Hughes, Kanchelskis, Schmeichel and Cantona), and commentators were turning against the aggressive, snarling attitude of players such as Ince, Hughes, Cantona and Keane, and the way they seemed to dispute clear-cut decisions by referees, and to accept nothing with either good grace or sportsmanship. People drew contrasts with the last great Manchester United side, the Busby team of the 1960s. It was difficult to conceive of Busby ever calling a TV commentator 'a prat', though Sir Matt, too, had his problems with unruly players. Hotheads such as Stiles, Crerand, Law and Best accumulated almost as many sendings-off as their 1990s successors, in an era when dismissals were much rarer.

Significantly, one of the most vocal critics of this new bad-tempered United was the respected journalist Hugh McIlvanney, who was such a close friend of Ferguson that he occasionally stayed at his home:

> Self-control deserts several of their most important players
> so readily and comprehensively that they can plummet in
> seconds from standards of football that would do credit to
> Maracanã or Bernabéu to antics, physical and verbal, which
> would disfigure a game between pub teams on Hackney
> Marshes.
>
> It was nothing short of extraordinary that he [Ferguson]
> went out of his way to make justifying noises some time ago
> after Mark Hughes was so lamentably unprofessional as to
> direct a petulant kick at a Sheffield United player's rear. More
> recently, his suggestion that the dismissal of his goalkeeper,
> Schmeichel, from the FA Cup tie with Charlton Athletic
> should have embarrassed the referee involved was unlikely to
> draw widespread sympathy.[34]

To some extent Ferguson was the victim of his own self-imposed ordinance never to criticise his players in public – something he'd learned from Scot Symon, his manager at Rangers. 'Once you do that, you have lost the bolt off the dressing-room door,' Ferguson said.[35] It meant he would not reveal when players had been punished internally, or respond to demands that he should crack down on them. In fact Ferguson later did reveal that around this time, rather bravely, he hauled all the main culprits into his office at once. 'No more,' he apparently insisted. 'That's it, finished, OK?'[36] On the other hand, the outside attacks also suited Ferguson's purposes, bolstering team spirit by creating a siege mentality, as so often in the past. 'It feels as though we are not only playing the world,' he remarked at one point that spring, 'but Mars as well.'[37]

Yet five years later, in his autobiography, Ferguson seemed to concur with many of the complaints made in 1994 – influenced perhaps by Hugh McIlvanney, who helped him compose the book. Ferguson now admitted that Mark Hughes had 'almost dislodged Tuttle's testicles' at Sheffield United, but it wasn't until later, he said, when he saw the videotape, that he realised that he himself had been 'defending the indefensible'. There were also times, Ferguson conceded, when 'Cantona was not at all the innocent party'. In particular the Frenchman's foul on Jeremy Goss was 'not only hor- rendous' but 'despicable'. (The latter, astonishingly, was one of the two offending words which had caused the manager to deride Jimmy Hill as 'a prat'.) 'It was an even more serious offence,' Ferguson said of Cantona, 'when he stamped on Swindon's skilful midfielder, John Moncur, and that was the first time I lost my temper with him. There was no way I could condone what he had done.'[38]

Despite the criticism, the beleaguered Manchester United party travelled to the League Cup final at Wembley on the last Saturday in March looking as if they might win a domestic treble of League, FA Cup and League Cup. It was an achievement which was common in Scotland, but unprecedented south of Hadrian's Wall. Only once before had any team even managed to win both domestic cups – Arsenal, in the previous season – let alone the league championship as well.

Their opponents in the League Cup final were Ron Atkinson's latest employers, Aston Villa. The inevitable happened: Villa won 3–1, and Andrei Kanchelskis was sent off for handling on the line (only the second player, after United's Kevin Moran, to be dismissed in a Wembley final). For the second time in four years Atkinson had beaten Alex Ferguson in the League Cup final (having also knocked United out in an earlier round the previous year). It would, however, be the last time that Ferguson took the competition seriously, and already in earlier League Cup ties that season he had started to field teams that were slightly below full strength. The Football League chose not to apply their rules and stop him.

Would the upset at Wembley, combined with a rash of suspensions and the sudden dip in form, deflate United so much as to ruin the rest of the campaign? Comparisons were made with the Leeds United of 1970, who had also looked capable of winning three major trophies but had ended the season with nothing. That was the grim thought a week later when Alan Shearer helped Blackburn to a 2–0 win over United and cut the Reds' lead – once a mighty fourteen points – back to just three.

United's season looked in even worse shape when they returned to Wembley for an FA Cup semi-final and deservedly fell a goal behind to Oldham Athletic. It was the team's worst performance all season – sluggish, unadventurous and outwitted. All seemed lost until, with less than two minutes to go, Mark Hughes volleyed an extraordinary equaliser. Oldham were outplayed in the replay at Maine Road three days later, when Andrei Kanchelskis tantalised the opposing left-back, and Bryan Robson scored his ninety-ninth and last goal for United (making him, at the age of thirty-seven, the club's oldest post-war goalscorer). Almost as important, Mark Hughes's goal at Wembley had given United valuable breathing space in the League, as a difficult game at on-form Leeds was postponed until they were back on song.

In the end Ferguson's men won the League at a canter, with the deciding result coming when Blackburn lost at Coventry. United finished with ninety-two points – a new record under the system of three points for a win, and eight ahead of runners-up Blackburn. The FA Cup final against Chelsea still looked a dangerous prospect, however, since the London club had beaten United at home and away in the League. On the day, they had the best of the first half, but the worst of the second.

The final scoreline flattered United. Their 4–0 victory came thanks to two spot kicks by Eric Cantona, who had quickly established himself as a lethal penalty-taker. Twice at Wembley the Chelsea goalkeeper, Dmitri Kharine, dived to the wrong side. Cantona claims he could always tell which way goalkeepers would dive: only twice in his twenty Manchester United penalties did he send the ball the same way as the keeper.[39]

Again there had been no room for sentiment by Ferguson in his Wembley team selection. Bryan Robson wasn't picked even as a substitute, though it was known to be his final season at Old Trafford. The United club captain, who was already lined up to become player/manager of Middlesbrough, thereby missed his chance of collecting the cup for a record fourth time, and of reaching 100 goals for United. Ferguson later admitted he'd been too heartless, and that Robson should have been on the bench (just like Stuart Kennedy, Aberdeen's unusable substitute, in the 1983 Cup-Winners' Cup final).

Preston North End in 1889 and Aston Villa in 1897 were both early winners of the celebrated double of league championship and FA Cup, but for much of the twentieth century many people questioned whether the demands of modern football were too great for the feat to be repeated. It wasn't until 1961 that Tottenham Hotspur proved them wrong, and then as the century approached its close the double was achieved with increasing regularity. Arsenal did it in 1971, Liverpool in 1986, and now Manchester United eight years later. And before the new millennium three more doubles would be collected, with Manchester United playing a leading part in the drama each time.

Overall, the team had won 41 games – a new United record – 22 of them away, and had also set new club records for successive games undefeated (34), consecutive away wins (7) and undefeated home games (36). Eric Cantona collected the PFA Player of the Year award, and Alex Ferguson – inevitably – was Manager of the Year for the second season running. 'He's right up there already with all the

Scottish greats,' said his playing hero Denis Law – 'Sir Matt, Shanks, Big Jock. To the Manchester United fans, he's the son of God.'[40]

Sadly, none of those Scottish peers had lived to witness Ferguson's achievement – not even Busby. Sir Matt himself had come very close to the double with his Busby Babes in 1957, only for his goalkeeper, Ray Wood, to suffer an injury in the cup final (in the days before substitutes), which led to Aston Villa's 2–1 victory. Busby had died four months before the 1994 final, at the age of eighty-four, though he lived long enough to see Manchester United regain their place at the top of English football. With six major trophies in five seasons – two Leagues, two FA Cups, the League Cup and the European Cup-Winners' Cup – Alex Ferguson was now close to matching Sir Matt's managerial record of eight senior honours (five Leagues, two FA Cups and the European Cup). People were starting to compare Ferguson with his illustrious predecessor.

Losing the Plot

'The next day Hughesy is sold to Chelsea. What are the club playing at? The first two months of the season it looks as though it will be a case of bring your own boots along.'

IMUSA newsletter, July 1995

To this day, many fans consider the team which clinched the 1994 double to be Manchester United's greatest-ever line-up – better even than the European Cup-winning side of 1968. The team which beat Chelsea at Wembley was Schmeichel, Parker, Irwin, Bruce, Pallister, Keane, Kanchelskis, Ince, Cantona, Hughes and Giggs (while Sharpe and McClair came on as substitutes). That starting eleven began just twelve games during the season, and won every one of them, with an aggregate score of 28–4. Sadly, Alex Ferguson was never able to pick the same combination again. In the eighteen months after the double, that great team was slowly broken up.

The main target for the 1994–95 season was the European Cup – the one competition in which Ferguson had so far failed to emulate Sir Matt Busby. United had succumbed in the season before to the Turks of Galatasaray, and Ferguson also had had an undistinguished record in the European Cup with Aberdeen, winning just three ties in three seasons. After losing to Liverpool in 1980, his team had been knocked out by Dynamo Berlin in 1985 and by Gothenburg the following year.

And Gothenburg were among United's three opponents in the first stage of the European Cup in 1994 – the first year in which the competition adopted a small-league format for the opening stage, with teams playing each other at home and away in groups of four. But the Swedes were probably the most welcome members of the group, since the quartet also included Galatasaray, again, and Barcelona, who now boasted the Bulgarian and Brazilian strikers Hristo Stoichkov and Romario among their galaxy of stars.

The three home fixtures posed few problems, and United did well in a 2–2 draw with Barcelona. But they came unstuck away from Manchester. Eric Cantona was suspended for a previous sending-off when they travelled to Barcelona in October 1994, but another first-team regular also had to be left out to accommodate UEFA's 'five-foreigners' rule. Peter Schmeichel was omitted in favour of Gary Walsh, and the Reds lost 4–0. Stoichkov scored twice, and Romario added another. Ferguson called it the 'most emphatic defeat' of his Old Trafford career.[1] It was the equivalent of Aberdeen's 1980 drubbing by Liverpool.

Paul Ince took the manager's fire in the dressing room when the team came in 2–0 down at half-time. Ferguson was furious with Ince's growing habit of going forward to operate as an attacking midfielder rather than sticking to his task of breaking up Barcelona's attacks. 'It was as close to a fist fight as you can get without it kicking off,' says reserve goalkeeper Kevin Pilkington. 'Barcelona played the most devastating football I've ever witnessed, but the gaffer came and let rip, as if the lads hadn't tried,' he says.

The boss ripped into Incey – went mad. 'You fuckin' bottler, Incey! You can't handle the stage, can you? You're getting pissed on 'cause you're a fuckin' bottler!' Incey went, 'I'm not a bottler. Don't you dare call me a bottler, gaffer. Don't you dare.' So then the gaffer leant down and, one more time, shouted right in his face, 'You are a fuckin' bottler!' That was deliberately provoking Incey, so Incey jumped up and squared up to him – eyeball-to-eyeball stuff. Kiddo [Brian Kidd] and Brucey jumped in and separated them, and just about stopped it. It was amazing that this was at half-time, not the end. We still had half the game left after that! The lads were stunned – we had just watched in amazement really.[2]

Alex Ferguson was beginning to wonder about Paul Ince. In the years immediately after the player's arrival from West Ham in 1989, he had been impressed by how the Londoner had matured:

He was a young man that you looked at and said, 'He's at war with the world.' He had a difficult upbringing. He came to us with his energy not channelled the right way. He was argumentative, competitive, belligerent . . . But bit by bit we got the message over that we were on his side and we wanted him to become the best player in England.[3]

He felt Ince's maturity had been helped by finding a wife. 'I like all my players to be married,' Ferguson once said, 'with a couple of toddlers around the house. You are guaranteed a consistent level of behaviour when a footballer has a stable family background.'[4]

Yet now the United manager was starting to feel that Ince lacked 'humility' and often 'got carried away'.[5] The midfielder began styling himself as 'the Guvnor', and bought a car number with the letters GUV. Ferguson also worried that Ince might be becoming a bad influence on the young Ryan Giggs, who'd become a close friend.

In the next European away game, in Gothenburg, Ince was sent off for dissent as United went down 3–1. The defeat meant that, even if they beat Galatasaray in their final home game, further progress in the competition depended on Gothenburg winning in Barcelona at the same time. United duly beat the Turks 4–0, but the Barcelona game was drawn. Once again United had been eliminated before Christmas.

For some time Ferguson had been seeking to strengthen his forward line, especially since Mark Hughes was now in his thirties. Because of UEFA's 'foreigners' rule, he really needed an English striker, and, with Alan Shearer sewn up by Blackburn, an obvious target was the Nottingham Forest forward Stan Collymore, who had not at that stage acquired his later reputation for being wayward. It seems that Ferguson promised his friend Joe Royle, who'd just become manager of Everton, that once he'd landed Collymore then he'd sell him Hughes. Everton knew their Scottish striker Duncan Ferguson was likely to be jailed for assault. 'Alex actually came to me offering Hughes,' says Royle, 'not the other way round.'

> He came and said, 'When we get Collymore, Hughes will not be happy playing second fiddle and sitting on the bench. Do you want him when I get Collymore?' From myself and Alex's point of view, the deal for Hughes had been done. We were a big club and he lived in Cheshire, so he wouldn't have to move house.[6]

'Alex was persistent when he wanted someone,' says the former Nottingham Forest manager Frank Clark. 'He used to ring once a week about Collymore. He really wanted him.'[7] Clark confirms that Collymore was keen to move to Manchester, but Clark was equally keen on keeping him, at least until the end of the season.

Joe Royle remained determined to buy Mark Hughes for Everton, and, when, around the start of 1995, he realised that United seemed to be getting nowhere with Collymore, he drew Ferguson's attention to another prolific striker. 'I tipped him off that Andy Cole was available. I'd heard from a contact that Newcastle had made a bid for Chris Armstrong at Palace. That showed they might let Cole go.'[8]

Andy Cole was the most successful goalscorer in England at that time, having hit the net forty-one times the season before – the highest total for seven years (and that was without taking penalties). Ferguson had asked the Newcastle manager, Kevin Keegan, earlier in the season whether he might be willing to sell Cole, but was told not.

As the Collymore situation dragged on, Ferguson considered other possibilities – among them Les Ferdinand of QPR and Teddy Sheringham of Spurs, though he concluded that the latter was 'too old for my liking' (he was then twenty-eight).[9] Then, in January, Keegan rang Ferguson to ask if he'd be willing to part with his young Irish winger Keith Gillespie, who'd played well in a couple of games against Newcastle that season. Ferguson's answer was also 'No', but he took the opportunity to enquire again about Andy Cole. This time Keegan's refusal seemed less firm.

Stan Collymore remained the principal target, but, on the day that Ferguson rang Frank Clark to make a substantial offer, the United manager was told that Clark had flu and couldn't talk. That did it. Ferguson decided Forest were fobbing him off again, just as they had several years before over Stuart Pearce. He was sceptical about the flu, though Clark insists he really was ill.

So Ferguson had a third go at Keegan. This time the Newcastle manager was definitely interested, provided he got Gillespie in return. It took three days to agree the deal, with Cole valued at £7 million and Gillespie £1 million, and United paying Newcastle the difference. It was a new British transfer record – almost twice what Ferguson had paid Nottingham Forest for Roy Keane eighteen months before. Kevin Keegan came under heavy criticism from Newcastle fans, who were tired of losing their best players to bigger clubs, and who regarded Cole as their greatest goalscorer since Malcolm MacDonald in the 1970s.

'History was altered in a weekend,' says Frank Clark. 'It could so easily have been Stan not Cole that was part of that United era. When Cole signed, Stan was gutted. He knew that that was it, his chance had gone.'[10] In retrospect, Alex Ferguson must be relieved that Clark's stubbornness and ill health prevented Collymore from going to Old Trafford. The Forest forward eventually joined Liverpool, before moving to Aston Villa and Leicester as his scoring rate declined amid increasing personal problems. On the other hand, Ferguson might have been the manager to sort out those problems.

Mark Hughes, meanwhile, was now expected to join Everton. When the Cole deal went through, Ferguson apparently sat the Welsh striker down and told him he could leave if he now wanted, but he'd prefer it if he didn't. According to Ferguson's diary, he told Hughes, 'We're not interested in selling you, but in the situation as it is, I don't want you feeling that we aren't recognising your contribution to the club. You can still be a great player for this club.'[11] That statement seems to be flatly contradicted by Joe Royle's version, in which Ferguson rang several times to offer to sell Hughes once United had got a replacement.

By coincidence, United were due to visit Newcastle a few days after signing Cole. Given the tense situation on Tyneside, it was thought prudent not to field the Reds' new recruit, and Hughes kept his place. The Welshman badly injured his knee while scoring United's goal, so any move to Everton was put on hold – which was just as well as events unfolded.

The young player who'd gone to Newcastle in exchange for Cole, Keith Gillespie, was a good prospect and highly regarded by the fans, but the move made sense from United's point of view. Coming from Northern Ireland, he was officially a 'foreigner' under UEFA's new rules, whereas Cole was English. Generously, Alex Ferguson offered to negotiate on Gillespie's behalf the details of his new contract with Newcastle, and the player says Ferguson overstated Gillespie's wages at Old Trafford so as to increase the amount that

Newcastle would offer. 'I think he was lying a bit when he said how much I earned at United,' says Gillespie. 'I can't really remember what the exact amount was, but he obviously exaggerated a little bit!'[12] He was still not twenty, and overnight his earnings increased from a meagre £250 a week in Manchester to about £2,000 on Tyneside. Much of this sudden wealth would be frittered away in feeding a habit which had increasingly gripped the player while he was on United's books.

'There is something about the football fraternity that likes a gamble,' Alex Ferguson once observed, 'but Rangers taught me a lesson and I won't have it at Old Trafford.' It was 'hardly conducive to team spirit', he felt.[13] The defender Colin Gibson tells a different story, claiming that in his time at United 'it wasn't unheard of for someone to lose £200 a time, when they were earning around £1,000 a week. Fergie used to bet on cards, and on the coach he used to bet a bit.'[14] Ferguson's laxness in this area sits uncomfortably with his insistence on strict discipline in other aspects of his players' behaviour.

Keith Gillespie's gambling habit seems to have been reinforced by the fact that Ferguson, along with several senior players and coaching staff, used to employ the teenager as a 'runner' to and from the local bookmaker's shop near The Cliff. 'Alex Ferguson used to give me money,' he says, 'and I used to run to the bookie's to put the bets on.' Gillespie remembers that it wasn't unusual for Ferguson to get him to place a £50 bet on a dog or a horse, and he then collected everyone else's bets – rather like a lunch list. 'Alex Ferguson used to put on more than anyone,' says Gillespie, who usually took the opportunity to place bets himself.[15]

The Irishman admits he was a natural choice for the job: he was already gambling, and his colleagues knew he'd be going to the bookie's anyway. But, while he was with Manchester United, he doesn't recall the manager ever warning him that he was betting too much.[16] His story is confirmed by his friend and playing colleague

Gary Twynham, who says he often accompanied him to the book-maker's shop. 'When there was a hot tip for the races or the dogs Keith would be the runner,' Twynham says.[17] A senior source at the club adds:

> Gillespie was Fergie's runner. Everybody knew that. Fergie used to send him down to the bookie's all the time. With the horses, we used to call Fergie, Robbo and Incey the 'Big Three', because they loved it. They were always at it. I don't know how much Fergie put on: it was a lot – hundreds definitely. Ferguson saw drinking as the enemy, not gambling. He liked a gamble himself, and understood that players got bored and had disposable cash.

At one point, after leaving Newcastle United, Gillespie was exposed in the press as having lost £47,000 in a single day. The player's mother was so concerned that, even though he was no longer Gillespie's boss, she rang the Manchester United manager to beg him to persuade her son to give up the habit. Ferguson duly read him the Riot Act.

Publicly, Alex Ferguson had a far more troublesome player to contend with, however. In January 1995, only days after the Cole–Gillespie deal, Eric Cantona caused a scandal when he attacked a Crystal Palace fan at an evening league match at Selhurst Park, after being sent off for kicking the defender Richard Shaw.

At first Ferguson didn't realise how serious the incident was. He was more concerned to reorganise his depleted team, and was annoyed with Cantona for being dismissed for the fifth time in fifteen months, for a silly, provoked foul. 'I only saw the aftermath, a punch being thrown,' he said later. 'Then I saw Eric lying over a hoarding and I thought maybe he'd been dragged into the crowd or something. I didn't fully understand how serious it was that night, even having spoken to the police.'[18]

When the United boss got home in the early hours, after flying back from London, Jason Ferguson told his father that Cantona had attacked the fan with a kung-fu kick. Alex Ferguson couldn't believe it, and declined his son's suggestion that he see for himself on the video. Instead he went to bed. But he couldn't sleep, so he got up around 5.30 a.m. and watched the tape. Only then did the United boss appreciate the seriousness of what had happened. It was a full-blooded assault by the Frenchman, who had jumped over a McDonald's hoarding to direct a kick right into the chest of a fan who'd run down a gangway to taunt him about the sending-off. They'd then thrown punches at each other. 'Jesus Christ,' said Ferguson. 'It was terrible. I couldn't believe it. How could Eric have done it?'[19]

The story became headline news on television and radio bulletins, and dominated every front page. It was by far the biggest crisis since Alex Ferguson's arrival at the club. Cases of players attacking each other are common enough on the football pitch, but it is quite rare for a footballer to assault a spectator. Both United and the FA were under pressure to discipline Cantona severely, and the police were also investigating. Paul Ince, too, was suspected of having attacked someone that night.

Cathy Ferguson told her husband to do the right thing and take a tough line with Cantona, even if it cost him a third championship. 'Make sure you don't give anybody room to say that you're the type of manager who is only interested in winning at all costs,' she told him. 'You'd better let everybody out there know you have values that rise above results, and that you have the same concerns with the standards of Manchester United as Sir Matt Busby had.'[20] Many people, including some United supporters, said the club should get rid of the player. 'My initial feeling was for letting Eric go,' Ferguson said in his diary. 'I felt that this time the good name of Manchester United demanded strong action. The club is bigger than any individual. I related that to the board and they agreed.'[21] Ferguson also

381

feared that, in any case, the media spotlight and the ensuing provocation by other supporters would make it difficult for Cantona to carry on in the English game. However, the club solicitor, Maurice Watkins, came to the Frenchman's aid. He warned that tough action by United, or an apology by the player, might prejudice any criminal case, and could also be tricky under the terms of Cantona's contract. In the player's defence, it should be noted that he had been the victim of several unpunished fouls during the game, and he was also annoyed with himself for retaliating and being sent off.

Another voice urging Ferguson to show understanding towards the player was Sir Richard Greenbury, the chairman of Marks & Spencer, a United fan who had become a personal friend of Ferguson's. He rang the United manager on his mobile and pointed out the parallels with the tennis star John McEnroe, who was well behaved off the court, but couldn't control his temper on it. 'I said he had to be punished,' says Greenbury, 'but to bear in mind the background to it all. With that territory goes a will to win which from time to time will boil over, and then you have to pay the price for it.'[22]

On the night following the assault, Ferguson and other key figures at United met in a hotel in Alderley Edge, in Cheshire, and decided to suspend Cantona from playing until the end of the season; they also fined him two weeks' wages – £10,800. This was done after consultation with the Football Association, which was seeking a worldwide ban from FIFA, the world football authority, while the French FA stripped him of his country's captaincy. A month later the FA then imposed its own £10,000 fine on Cantona, and added a further punishment by banning him from playing until the following October, which meant he would miss six months of football instead of the four months envisaged by United. This action infuriated United: the club believed it had an understanding with FA officials that its suspension of the player for the rest of the season would be sufficient.

Two months later, on the morning of 23 March, Ferguson went to Buckingham Palace to collect a CBE (to add to his 1984 OBE), but his day was spoilt by the news from Croydon magistrates' court, where Eric Cantona, despite pleading guilty, had been given a two-week jail sentence for common assault. It was a stiff punishment for a first-time offence, but the bench took a tough line because of Cantona's fame and the fact that he was a role model to many young people. 'Ooh, aah, Prisona,' said the *Sun*'s headline the next day.[23] But, thanks to quick action by his lawyers, the star didn't go to jail. On appeal his punishment was reduced to 120 hours' community service, which involved him coaching Salford schoolchildren at The Cliff.

Many had feared that, without the 'can-opener', Manchester United's season would be ruined. Far from it. Andy Cole did well at first, and broke numerous records in only his seventh game for the club, when he scored five times in a 9–0 win over Ipswich. It was the most goals ever scored by United in a league game, and the club's best-ever win at Old Trafford. It also matched the best previous result of Ferguson's managerial career, when Aberdeen had beaten Raith Rovers by the same score in the Scottish League Cup. Later Ferguson said he had been praying that United wouldn't reach ten, as he felt sorry for the Ipswich manager, George Burley.

Blackburn Rovers had led the table since late November, but United gradually eroded their lead and were grateful that Mark Hughes had been unable to join Everton because of his injury, for once he was recovered he was needed to replace Cantona. Towards the end of the season, with Blackburn still in front, Ferguson resorted to psychological tricks to upset his rivals, having noticed signs of strain on the face of their manager, Kenny Dalglish, in post-match interviews. 'Blackburn can only throw the League away now,' he declared. 'We must hope they do a Devon Loch,' he added, referring to the Queen Mother's horse which had inexplicably pulled up within yards of winning the 1956 Grand National.[24] It was a clever way of upsetting Dalglish, who had resigned as Liverpool manager in the middle of the season four years earlier because he couldn't cope with the pressure. Ferguson had also been playing for Rangers in 1968 when Jock Stein had declared that the league title was theirs to throw away, which they then did. The United manager also attacked Blackburn's dull style of football, while again appearing to concede that the league title was theirs. 'I could not be wholly satisfied with winning the Premiership if my team had played like Blackburn Rovers this season. We always try for more than just the win. Anything else isn't our way.'[25] Ferguson later confessed that he had enjoyed playing on Blackburn's likely nervousness as front-runners. 'I was just stoking it up. I just found it hilarious,' he said – though that didn't seem to be his mood at the time.[26] 'I don't think it affected Blackburn,' says Dalglish of the Devon Loch comment. 'It wasn't going to bother me, something like that.'[27]

The championship saw the most nail-biting finish since the dramatic showdown between Liverpool and Arsenal in 1989. By the final Sunday, Blackburn were two points ahead, but United had the superior goal difference. Blackburn faced a tough fixture at Anfield, though cynics suggested that Liverpool might want their former favourite Dalglish to see off their traditional Mancunian enemies. United, meanwhile, had an equally tricky encounter at West Ham, where results rarely went the Reds' way. The club had won the title at Upton Park in 1967, but had effectively lost it there in 1992. If Blackburn won, the League was theirs, whatever the result at West Ham. If they drew or lost at Anfield, Manchester United would be champions if they defeated the London club.

Alex Ferguson started the match with Mark Hughes on the subs' bench, playing with five in midfield and just one striker. West Ham took an early lead, before Ferguson brought Hughes on at half-time. McClair got an equaliser early in the second half, and United spent the next forty minutes bombarding the West Ham goal. But Ludek Miklosko stopped everything flung in his direction. Andy Cole simply couldn't score. Later, Mark Hughes's agent, Dennis Roach, observed Ferguson's tendency to drop the striker for important matches – such as the home games against Palace in 1989 and Forest in 1992, and away to Galatasaray in 1993 – only to find that it didn't pay off.

To add to the frustration, at Anfield Liverpool had overturned Blackburn's early goal to win 2–1. United's draw meant that they finished a point behind the new champions. 'Well, that's Manchester United,' Ferguson remarked afterwards.[28]

United had failed to emulate Huddersfield, Arsenal and Liverpool in winning three titles in a row. Yet, under the old system of two points for a win, the outcome would have been reversed. Blackburn and United would have finished with equal points, and the Reds would have triumphed on goal difference (and also, for real traditionalists, on goal average).

While jockeying with Blackburn in the League, United had also reached the FA Cup final again, despite the absence from the cup competition of Andy Cole (who was 'cup-tied', having already played in that season's competition for Newcastle). United's biggest scare was when they managed their usual semi-final trick of going a goal behind to Crystal Palace – twice – before winning 2–0 in a poorly attended replay in which Roy Keane was sent off for stamping on Gareth Southgate. Their Wembley opponents were Everton, who had finished only fifteenth in the League.

Some thought the FA Cup final might provide consolation for the Reds' narrow loss in the League, but the West Ham result only made things harder at Wembley. 'They were so under pressure and really needed to win the FA Cup to save their season,' says the former Everton manager Joe Royle. 'It was a great time to play United. We were the underdogs, so there was no pressure.'[29] United were sluggish on the day, and Everton duly won 1–0.

Years later, in his autobiography, Ferguson showed the 'bad loser' side of his nature by saying it was 'just not acceptable' to lose to 'a team as ordinary as Everton'.[30] Joe Royle was so angry that he complained to Ferguson: 'The thing about Alex is that he can't see past Manchester United and he is obsessed with them winning. Being unfair after a defeat sometimes, that's his way of coping with losing. Alex is not a good loser. That's not his strong point.'[31]

It was nonetheless an impressive achievement by United even to come close to a second double, especially when Eric Cantona had been absent for the last third of the season. No previous English double-winners had ever looked likely to repeat their triumph the season afterwards. Aston Villa, Spurs and Arsenal had all dropped down the League the following year, while Preston and Liverpool had suffered early defeats in the FA Cup. United had come within three goals – one in the League and two at Wembley – of winning both again. At the back, United had been superb all season, with Schmeichel, Pallister and Bruce forming a defensive triangle that was as effective as the Leighton–Miller–McLeish combination at Aberdeen. At home they conceded only four league goals (two of them against Nottingham Forest), and the eighteen clean sheets at Old Trafford were almost certainly an all-time league record. Schmeichel played one stretch of almost twenty-six hours at Old Trafford without conceding a league goal. The problem was in the 'goals for' column: having broken the transfer record to sign a prolific striker, United had not scored enough (though Cole got twelve in all). Eric Cantona would surely have prevented at least one of the goalless home draws late in the season against Spurs, Leeds and Chelsea.

A mood of depression hung over Old Trafford that summer. First there were questions over Eric Cantona's future at the club, with predators such as Inter Milan reportedly ready to offer him £25,000 a week (five times his existing pay). Cantona had signed a new three-year contract worth £750,000 a year with United before the season ended, with the proviso that he was available to play. But there were still doubts as to whether he'd be seen in a red shirt again. If he was, would he be able to tame his temper without losing his brilliance?

Eric Cantona was not the only summer headache. Another was Mark Hughes's surprise decision to move to Chelsea. The Welshman knew he'd always be third choice behind Cantona and Cole, and Ferguson had been ready to sell him to Everton a few months earlier. What the boss hadn't realised was that Hughes had never signed the new contract he'd been offered four months earlier. There had been a query over his pension rights which had not been resolved. Fans were disappointed with the news, but not despairing. 'Sparky' was a popular player, but they appreciated that, at thirty-one, his best days were past him.

Supporters were rather more aggrieved by the departure of Paul Ince to Inter Milan for £6 million. Ince's performance in the FA Cup final had hardened Ferguson's view that the player should go; in particular, he was furious that Ince's surge forward with the ball had opened up the space which allowed Everton to score after Dave Watson won the ball from the United midfielder. From Barcelona to Wembley, Ince had upset the United manager by going forward too much. Ferguson later revealed that he felt Ince had played only 'four really good games' that season, 'and it reached the stage where I wasn't sure he was earning his place'.[32]

Ferguson had heard from a Dutch agent that someone claiming to represent Ince had been trying to sell the player to an Italian club. Ince himself had also been chatting about going to Italy. According to the singer Mick Hucknall, a close friend of both Ferguson and Ince, who had a home in Milan, 'He was telling me for a long time he wanted to go abroad. There's no doubt in my mind that he wanted to go – he was forever telling me, "I'm coming, Micky, I'm coming."'[33] Hucknall says he didn't mention this to Ferguson until after the official deal was done, but it's unlikely that other reports didn't get back to the United manager. Whether Ince was set on playing in Italy isn't clear. It may have been boastful talk, or even a negotiating ploy to improve his terms at Old Trafford. If so, it backfired badly.

We now know from Ferguson's autobiography that he told a shocked Manchester United board on Tuesday 16 May, four days *before* the cup final, that he wanted to sell Paul Ince. This is completely at odds with what Ferguson told the outside world, and the player himself, in the subsequent weeks. When it became known that Inter Milan had bid for him, he insisted that Ince was staying. 'Paul Ince is not for sale. I'm adamant about that,' he said on 5 June. 'There has been interest from Inter. They came in at the weekend but we just weren't interested. They were turned down flat. We want all our players to stay at Old Trafford.'[34] Two weeks later Ferguson claimed to have just spoken to Ince 'and again told him he was wanted by Manchester United'.[35]

One side effect of Ince's transfer saga was to give a higher profile to the Independent Manchester United Supporters' Association (IMUSA), which had been formed earlier in 1995. The group found itself in a difficult position at a time when it was still finding its feet and establishing the best way to work with the club. It had been set up to campaign publicly against what it perceived as a growing commercial exploitation of the fans by United, and the lack of consultation with them. It had decided early on not to comment on team matters.

But the events of the summer of 1995 made it hard to stick to this resolution. Many members were urging it to intervene to try to prevent the breakup of the double-winning team, and some leading members of IMUSA knew that what was being said in public did not square with what they were learning from inside sources.

IMUSA's press officer, Richard Kurt, was getting regular updates from a close friend who was going out with Martin Edwards's daughter at the time. Kurt's comments on behalf of IMUSA were coloured by the knowledge that Edwards had told his family that Ferguson was determined to sell Ince. The United chief executive found Ferguson increasingly irrational, and thought he was losing the plot.

Edwards was also infuriated that the manager did not keep him informed about what was going on. Kurt recollects:

> I knew from a very early stage that Alex Ferguson was not
> telling the truth about Ince, and that's what made me cross. If
> he had said right from the start, 'Look, I just don't want him.
> I want to sell him. Right, endgame', it would clearly have
> been so much better. Because so many people didn't think he
> was telling the truth, and because so many people were just
> upset by the fact that these players were being sold, it just
> rumbled on and on.[36]

At one point an IMUSA delegation went to Paul Ince's house and spent ninety minutes with the player and his wife trying to persuade them to stay in Manchester. According to that summer's IMUSA newsletter, 'He [Ince] asked of us that we tell all Reds that he himself did not make any noises about wanting to leave and would still be with us if the Inter bid had not been accepted.'[37] Paul Ince, it seems, was also being less than frank. Ferguson noticed that the player was remarkably familiar with the Inter president when the latter came to Manchester to clinch the deal in June 1995.

'To us a monumental thing was happening,' says Richard Kurt, 'the breakup of our best ever team. All we ever wanted was to talk to Ferguson, but it never got to that stage, and it was conducted through the press.'[38] Kurt himself then went too far, angering Ferguson by telling a Sunday newspaper that it might be time for the United manager go. 'This is a personal view but I believe United have seen the best of Alex Ferguson,' he was quoted as saying. 'Maybe he is coming to the end of his shelf life.'[39]

Kurt claims that his views were misrepresented, and that he was speaking personally, not for IMUSA, but his comments were inevitably seized on by other papers. In truth, many fans – though not a majority – were beginning to concur that Ferguson might be losing his touch.

Kurt resigned as IMUSA press officer to save the group embarrassment. Two of the organisation's other officials thought they had patched things up with Ferguson when they chatted to him at a United funeral. To their astonishment, a few days later the manager lambasted the supporters' group in the pages of the *News of the World*, and mocked its campaign for lower ticket prices. They were making United look like a 'laughing stock' Ferguson said, and were only speaking out 'for their own egos and to get themselves projected . . . They are the people always going on about ticket prices. I think sometimes they want to get in for nothing.'[40] 'I used to be a Fergie-lover,' says Richard Kurt:

> But frankly the episode was the final souring, from my point
> of view. I've never felt the same about Ferguson since. It was
> unnecessary for him to go over the top as it were, with a two-
> footed tackle on the Sunday and to slag off IMUSA, having
> apparently made peace with everybody. When people say that
> they have problems with Ferguson as a personality, or as a
> man, I usually cock a sympathetic ear, because I can
> understand where they are possibly coming from.[41]

Later, Alex Ferguson would talk of the departures in the summer of 1995 as if they were part of a carefully considered strategy. 'I needed to change the direction of the club,' he said, 'to get the next six or seven years of real success again.'[42] In reality, Manchester United had lurched through a series of summer crises brought about by a lack of openness on his part and by others.

It's also clear that the Paul Ince affair caused huge tensions both between Ferguson and his chief executive and with the manager's assistant, Brian Kidd. Martin Edwards was under considerable pressure from United fans, who believed Ince was being sold only for financial reasons, and Ferguson did nothing to dispel that idea. Edwards was furious: he thought his manager was deliberately stirring up fans' anger against him (he was an easy target), when it was really Ferguson who wanted to sell Ince while Edwards didn't. The United chief executive urged Ferguson to change his mind, pointing out that Kidd, too, thought that Ince should stay at Old Trafford. 'That was a surprise,' Ferguson wrote later. 'Brian had never voiced such an opinion to me.'[43] The Ince affair was an important stage in the emergence of a rift between chief executive and manager, and planted suspicions in Ferguson's mind that Edwards and Kidd were ganging up against him.

The departure of Andrei Kanchelskis was equally acrimonious, but the disputes in that were more long-standing, and the whole affair was overlaid with frightening aspects of post-Soviet gangsterism, corruption and threats of violence. It was 'real Godfather stuff . . . amazing stuff', Ferguson said later. 'There were a few threats all right.'[44] One disturbing fact was that the entire board of Kanchelskis's former club, Shakhtyor Donetsk had been murdered – apparently by the Russian mafia.

Andrei Kanchelskis had had a difficult relationship with Ferguson since joining United in the spring of 1991, and the manager in turn was often unhappy with the winger's performances. The Ukrainian rarely enjoyed long runs in the team. In December 1992 Ferguson was so weary of him that he told Kanchelskis he was being demoted to training with the reserves. When Kanchelskis laughed and refused to obey the order, Ferguson erupted and warned that if he did not keep fit he would 'go to rot on the subs' bench and would not be ready if ever needed'. Kanchelskis says he relented immediately:

> You do not tell the manager what you think he should be
> doing; you do what you are told . . . The remark about me
> going to rot had cut me to the quick. If the Boss had wanted
> to shake me up, he had done just that. It inspired me to train
> and work overtime to keep at the peak of fitness.[45]

Nonetheless, he asked to leave, first in April 1993, and again a year later, when supporters chanted for him to stay.

The 1994–95 season had been the winger's best. Kanchelskis finished as United's top scorer, and fans will always remember him fondly for three excellent goals in a celebrated 5–0 win over Manchester City – United's first league hat-trick for more than five years. Yet Ferguson later alleged that even during the early part of that season other clubs were being contacted by somebody with offers to sell the player. 'I've seen the faxes myself,' he claimed.[46] The following spring the Ukrainian attacked Ferguson in a tabloid newspaper for not giving him enough games. By now, unknown to Ferguson, the player had a huge incentive to leave, since his new contract, signed in 1994, contained a clause which entitled him to a third of the transfer fee if he did move on, with a big payment to his former club, Shakhtyor Donetsk.

By the time Kanchelskis was eventually transferred to Everton for £5.5 million in the summer of 1995, both the player and his agent, Grigory Essaylenko, had blamed Alex Ferguson for his departure, claiming that if anybody else were in charge then Kanchelskis would have stayed. 'He cannot work with the manager,' said Essaylenko. 'It is a personal thing – man-to-man. He is not happy.'[47] Kanchelskis echoed his agent: 'My heart is with Manchester United but I can't stay for one reason and that is the manager. Our personal problems are just too big.'[48] However, these statements don't really square with the tone of Kanchelskis's book, which had come out a few weeks earlier, in which the player was positive about Ferguson and particularly grateful for the manager's sympathy over a miscarriage his wife had suffered. The suspicion is that the differences between Ferguson and Kanchelskis were subsequently exaggerated to justify the winger's request to go.

In his memoirs four years later Ferguson detailed some of the threats and strange events involving Kanchelskis. In particular he alleged that late one night in 1994, in a hotel car park near

Manchester Airport, Grigory Essaylenko had presented him with a 'handsomely wrapped box'. When Ferguson got home, he and Cathy were shocked. 'What the box contained was money, bundles of the stuff,' he wrote. 'We counted it and in all there was £40,000.' Fearing someone might have filmed the agent giving him the present, Ferguson took it into Old Trafford the next day, and the club solicitor, Maurice Watkins, advised that the cash should be lodged in the United safe. Ferguson was puzzled as to why Essaylenko should want to pay him, as he hadn't been involved in negotiating Kanchelskis's new contract (hence his ignorance about the clauses under which both Shakhtyor and Kanchelskis were paid if the player was transferred). Ferguson presumed the cash was to encourage 'co-operation in the future'.[49]

Essaylenko himself denies ever making such a payment. 'It's all nonsense,' he said in 1999. 'There were no parcels of any kind because that would not be ethical.'[50] Ferguson says he finally returned the £40,000 when the agent next visited Old Trafford, in the following spring, though he claims Essaylenko tried to persuade him to keep the gift. Later at the same meeting Essaylenko demanded that Kanchelskis be granted a transfer, and, according to Ferguson's account, warned Martin Edwards, 'If you don't transfer him now, you will not be around much longer.'[51] It came across as a threat, and Maurice Watkins advised his colleagues that selling the winger was the only sensible option.

The most intriguing aspect of Alex Ferguson's story is that he and the United directors didn't return the £40,000 at once. More curious still, the club does not appear to have called the police. Nor did it report the matter either to the Football Association or to the FA Premier League inquiry which, coincidentally, was in the process of examining allegations of bribery within the game, or what are known as 'bungs'. The investigation had been set up in 1993, under a QC, Robert Reid, originally to look into 'bungs' paid by Tottenham Hotspur for various transfers. Its scope was quickly expanded to cover numerous other moves, including Andrei Kanchelskis's transfer to United in 1991, which makes the club's failure to report the £40,000 gift from the same player's agent all the more surprising.

The Reid inquiry had been given impetus in 1994 by the revelation that the Arsenal manager, George Graham, had received £425,000 in cash from the Norwegian agent Rune Hauge over the purchase of two Scandinavians, Pal Lydersen and John Jensen, in 1991 and 1992. Graham was caught when a Danish television reporter noticed a discrepancy between what the Copenhagen club Brøndby claimed to have received for Jensen and what the London side said it had paid. As a result, Arsenal sacked Graham in 1995, even though he had been their most successful manager since the war, and had returned the money to Highbury with interest. Ferguson said he had 'a lot of sympathy' for the disgraced manager, since Graham would effectively be out of football for eighteen months because of a one-year ban subsequently imposed by the FA (along with a £50,000 fine). 'In prison terms that's probably the equivalent of a three-year sentence,' he said. 'Did the FA get it a bit out of perspective? Yes, I think so.'[52] Graham, of course, had been supportive of Ferguson's tussles with the Old Trafford board over pay.

Suspicions were aroused because Alex Ferguson had himself used Rune Hauge in 1991 to acquire both Andrei Kanchelskis and Peter Schmeichel, the latter from the same club, Brøndby, involved in the John Jensen deal. But Ferguson firmly refuted any implication that he too had taken 'bungs', and later said of the Schmeichel transfer:

Mr Edwards and another of our directors went across to Denmark. I understand that they did not even allow Hauge into the room while the deal was concluded though they did do the salary negotiations through him . . . It has always been a particular rule of mine to ensure that I do nothing underhand when it comes to any dealing with players so I know that I am as clean as a whistle in this.[53]

Perhaps understandably, in his memoirs Ferguson downplays his connections with Rune Hauge. 'I am not on terms of close friendship with Rune, but I have never had any hesitation in dealing with him since he is a brilliant judge of a player and a real professional when it comes to finding the best talent.'[54] Ferguson says he first met the agent in 1984 when Aberdeen visited Germany for a summer tournament, and it is clear that by the early 1990s the two men were meeting a lot. Hauge was frequently seen at The Cliff, and he was closely involved in organising several of the club's regular summer tours to Scandinavia. 'I remember in Oslo one year,' recalls Russell Beardsmore, 'Hauge gave us a guided tour around the city and showed us museums. He met us in the airport, then stayed with us in the hotel for days. I remember picking up the papers when the George Graham thing came out and thinking, "Jesus, that was him!"'[55]

In 1991, Ferguson says, he asked Hauge for advice on acquiring a right-winger. The agent recommended Kanchelskis, and sent him a tape of the player in action. Ferguson also says that, on the only occasion Hauge ever mentioned money to him, he was immediately referred to Martin Edwards. Subsequently the Norwegian would also act for two other players who joined United: Henning Berg and Ole Gunnar Solskjaer. The 1991 Kanchelskis deal, however, was the only transfer involving Ferguson which was specifically investigated by the FA Premier League inquiry.

Reid's panel, which also contained the former United player Steve Coppell and the Premier League chief executive Rick Parry, did not interview Alex Ferguson. But they did examine the four payments which made up the £1.2 million paid by United for Kanchelskis, as well as several much smaller sums which the club had paid Hauge over the years for items such as summer tours. The inquiry's three-page report on Kanchelskis concluded in 1997:

There is no evidence to suggest that there was any
irregularity in any of these payments or that any part of any
payment found its way back to anyone at Manchester
United . . . there is no evidence to suggest that any irregular
payments were made by Mr Hauge to anyone at Manchester
United.[56]

What's more, the inquiry noted that the transfers in which the panel were sure the Norwegian gave people 'bungs' always involved a different Hauge company from the firm employed in the Kanchelskis deal. Reid did decide, however, that the Norwegian agent's very involvement in the 1991 Kanchelskis deal breached the rules of both the FA and FIFA, which at that time prohibited payments to agents in player transfers.[57] By the early 1990s, irregular payments to agents had become so widespread in football, and so unpoliced by the authorities, that the FA deserved to face one of its own charges of bringing the game into disrepute, for having a rule it never enforced.

Looking back seven years later, it's hard to appreciate how concerned many Manchester United supporters were in the middle of 1995 as Alex Ferguson sold stars of the calibre of Hughes, Ince and Kanchelskis. He appeared to be placing a huge weight on the emerging youth-team players, with no experienced blood to replace the departures. It proved to be the only summer in Ferguson's sixteen years at Old Trafford that he signed no significant new players.

At one point the *Manchester Evening News* even conducted a phone-in poll on whether Alex Ferguson should go. The verdict was against him: 53 per cent of callers thought the United manager should resign, and 47 per cent that he should stay. It was a completely unrepresentative exercise, as there was nothing to stop fans of hostile clubs such as Manchester City adding their voice to get rid of Ferguson, or to prevent people from voting several times. Yet leading United supporters acknowledge that there was a strong body of opinion against Ferguson at that time. Had a truly scientific survey been conducted, his critics could easily have reached the 40 per cent mark.

The instability following the transfers of Hughes, Ince and Kanchelskis was bad enough. To make things worse, there were suddenly fresh doubts about Eric Cantona, despite the new contract he had signed. The player wasn't allowed to play again until 1 October, when United were scheduled to play a home fixture against Liverpool of all teams. To help him get back to match fitness, the club had arranged a series of private summer practice games against local league sides at The Cliff. When details of the first of these – against Rochdale in July 1995 – reached the press, the FA announced that the games breached Cantona's ban. The following Monday, Ferguson flew into Manchester Airport from a funeral in Glasgow to receive an urgent message to ring Martin Edwards. The United chief executive told his manager that 'Eric wants away'.[58] Cantona had been so annoyed by the attitude of the English football authorities that he had immediately gone to Paris, while his agent renewed contact with Inter Milan. It was feared the player would never return.

Alex Ferguson admits he was inclined to let Cantona go, but his attitude was tempered by his wife, Cathy, who said it was not like him to give in so easily. The United manager flew to Paris and checked into a room at the expensive Hôtel Georges V. The press were close behind, because Ferguson had foolishly told reporters at a dinner the night before that he was off to see the Frenchman. The hounds were thrown off only when Ferguson escaped through the hotel kitchen and was handed a motorcycle helmet by Cantona's agent, Jean-Jacques Bertrand, before they sped off on Bertrand's bike to the player's favourite restaurant. The owner had closed the premises to other customers to allow Ferguson, Cantona and the agent to talk privately over dinner. It was all a matter of reassurance, it seems. 'I believe he wanted me to put an arm round him and convince him that everything would be all right,' says Ferguson, adding that they spent much of the meal chatting about old football matches. 'Those hours spent in Eric's company in that largely deserted restaurant added up to one of the more worthwhile acts I have performed in this stupid job of mine.'[59] Cantona agreed to come back, and the FA relented, agreeing that he could play in friendlies so long as they weren't 'official' and didn't last a full ninety minutes.

The 1994–95 season and the troubled months which followed had been almost as difficult for Alex Ferguson as 1989–90, the year he won his first trophy. That summer he rejected an approach by Inter Milan, though he failed to secure a better-paid contract with United covering the six years until he reached the age of sixty. He went to negotiate with the PLC chairman, Sir Roland Smith, at his home on the Isle of Man, and this time he was armed with a copy of George Graham's old contract to make his case for being equally well rewarded (though Graham had since been sacked). Smith rejected the demand, observing on the question of length that the recently published Confederation of British Industry report on directors' pay disapproved of contracts of more than three years, and this extended to top executives as well. Indeed, these new recommendations on pay had been drafted by Ferguson's friend Sir Richard Greenbury. Smith put Ferguson further on the defensive by questioning whether he might have taken his 'eye off the ball' in the previous season: people at United felt he hadn't been as 'focused' as in the past, he said.[60] Ferguson expressed his surprise that Martin Edwards had never raised any such complaint with him.

Yet weeks later Ferguson himself would admit to having spread himself too thinly over the past twelve months, rather than concentrating on the absolute priorities. 'Everyone was wanting a bit of me. The whole thing was becoming a monster. I have to get back to focusing on the ball again.'[61]

Manchester United supporters faced the coming season anxiously. Three big stars had left – unnecessarily it still seemed. Another would be absent until October, and the fear was that he might not play with the same verve if he had to keep his temper in check. In their absence, all Ferguson seemed to be able to offer to the club and supporters were the young players, still largely untested, who were beginning to emerge from Manchester United's youth programme.

Nothing With Kids

'The trick is always buy when you are strong, so he needs to buy players. You can't win anything with kids . . . He's got to buy two players, as simple as that.'

ALAN HANSEN, August 1995[1]

Keith Gillespie was puzzled. Somebody kept ringing his mobile from an 0161 number, which indicated that they were calling from the Manchester area. However, he was reluctant to answer without knowing who it was. All became clear when, while he was at home one evening that summer, Alex Ferguson's voice suddenly blasted out over his telephone answering machine. Gillespie quickly picked up the handset. Ferguson wanted to know if Gillespie was interested in coming back to United. The player was surprised, and keen to accept. 'Once I was out of Man. United, it had never ever crossed my mind that it would be possible to go back. He didn't really have to persuade me.'[2]

With the departure of Andrei Kanchelskis, Ferguson had suddenly had a vacancy on the right. On reflection he strongly regretted his decision to let Gillespie go to Newcastle six months earlier – especially now that UEFA's troublesome rule which restricted the number of foreign players had been removed by a legal challenge. He had considered Darren Anderton, but the player had just signed a

400

new contract with Spurs, so Brian Kidd suggested that Ferguson should try and get the young Irishman back. Once again, of course, if Ferguson hadn't spoken to Keegan first, he was breaking the FA's rules on tapping players. 'He said, "Keep it hush-hush,"' Gillespie recollects, though his proposed return to Manchester eventually came to nothing.[3] The player learned via Gary Neville, some weeks later, that Kevin Keegan had vetoed the idea – which wasn't surprising, since Gillespie had been playing well, in a successful and promising Newcastle team. An obvious drawback would have been that Newcastle fans would have felt that Ferguson had got the better of Keegan over both players involved in the exchange of January 1995, Cole and Gillespie.

Had Keith Gillespie returned to Old Trafford, or Anderton been bought, or Kanchelskis not left, it would have delayed further the emergence of the most famous of all the home-grown stars nurtured under Alex Ferguson at Manchester United. For each of these players would have filled the right-wing position which David Beckham was soon to make his own. And David Beckham was the most exciting of the crop of youngsters given the chance to follow Ryan Giggs into the first team, following the departures of Hughes, Kanchelskis and Ince that summer.

It was not an auspicious start in August 1995. United's starting line-up at Aston Villa on the opening day of the season contained four youngsters – midfielder Nicky Butt, forward Paul Scholes, and the brother defenders, Gary and Philip Neville – while Beckham and another defender, John O'Kane, came on as substitutes. United were 3–0 down at half-time, and, though Beckham pulled a goal back in the second half, the performance prompted Alan Hansen's famous remark on *Match of the Day* that night: 'You can't win anything with kids.'[4]

Alex Ferguson had been trying to blood his young players for several years. Two years before, he'd said, 'I have seven or eight kids waiting patiently for the opportunity, young footballers on the threshold of the big time . . . I don't think it is possible to manoeuvre eleven through the ranks together, but in slow stages, I believe it is the dream that can be realised.'[5] He gave many of them first-team experience in the early rounds of the League Cup, a competition to which he attached increasingly less importance. The first time he did this, in September 1994, it caused an outcry in the Potteries, where United had been drawn to play Port Vale and the Staffordshire club expected a full house eager to see Eric Cantona, Ryan Giggs and other stars from the double season. Instead they watched one of the youngest teams ever fielded by Manchester United. A local MP accused United of letting Port Vale sell tickets under false pretences, and critics called on the Football League to enforce its rules obliging teams to field their strongest teams in its cup competition.

The last laugh was on United, who won 2–1 at Port Vale with two goals from Paul Scholes. The team for the second leg two weeks later was even younger, with six players aged under twenty, yet they did even better, winning 2–0. In the next round an equally youthful eleven held out for eighty minutes against high-flying Newcastle at St James's Park before conceding two goals in the dying minutes. Years later spectators at all three games could reflect that they were among the first to see Alex Ferguson's youngsters playing for the first team.

Publicly, Ferguson denied fielding 'an under-strength team': United were giving the cup 'our best shot', he insisted, and not treating it 'in a cavalier manner'.[6] Yet it's clear from his diary that he was happy to take some risks with team selections for these cup-ties because he was always in two minds about whether he wanted to win them. His head said the League Cup wasn't worth bothering with; but his heart hated losing, no matter what the contest. The compromise was to tell the lads to enjoy themselves and not to worry too much about the result. 'If they are not given a chance now it will be too late,' said Ferguson at the time of the Port Vale game – 'they will go to other clubs who will get the benefit of the training they've had at United.'[7]

Of the fourteen players who'd won the 1992 Youth Cup, only Ryan Giggs was already a first-team regular. In January 1993 Ferguson had given eight other members of the side professional contracts, which was a large number for just one generation of players: normally the attrition rate is far higher as players emerge from the youth ranks into the world of league football. The next to make his debut had been the midfielder Nicky Butt, followed by the defender Gary Neville. David Beckham was one of the last to mature – a 'late developer' said Ferguson.[8] Four of these youngsters – the Nevilles, Scholes and Butt – had all come from one local junior club, Boundary Park Juniors in Oldham (which, despite the name, has nothing to do with Oldham Athletic's ground, Boundary Park). While that quartet and Ryan Giggs were all from the Manchester area, Beckham was a Londoner. Nobody could question his Manchester United credentials, however, for Beckham's parents, Ted and Sandra, had been following United for years, travelling with other Cockney reds by train and coach. In 1986 the twelve-year-old David had even been United's mascot for a visit to West Ham.

Despite the opening-day defeat in 1995, the youngsters retained their places. United won their next five games, and spent the rest of the season proving Alan Hansen wrong. There were setbacks, however. United's League Cup performance was less distinguished than in the previous season, as they lost 3–0 at Old Trafford to Third Division side York City (and the young defender Pat McGibbon was sent off in his sole game for the club). The following week saw an equally embarrassing exit in the first round of the UEFA Cup. The Russian side Rotor Volgograd went through on away goals, and United preserved their unbeaten European home record only when Peter Schmeichel left his penalty area in the last minute of full time and scored from a corner.

Eric Cantona's return against Liverpool on 1 October provided quick consolation and some cause for celebration, as he made the opening goal for Nicky Butt after a minute, and then scored a penalty in a 2–2 draw. Cantona went on to have an outstanding season, scoring nineteen goals while controlling his temper and ending up as the football writers' Footballer of the Year.

But the 1995–96 championship will always be remembered for the fate of Newcastle United and their manager, Kevin Keegan. By mid-January the Tyneside club had amassed a seemingly unassailable twelve-point lead at the top of the table. Then, as Aberdeen had done to Celtic in 1980 under Ferguson, United slowly reeled them in. And, as with Aberdeen, the psychological turning point came when United visited their rivals and beat them, in early March. Newcastle, who'd won all the thirteen games they'd played at St James's Park so far, dominated the first half, but were prevented from scoring by a string of magnificent saves from Peter Schmeichel. Then Eric Cantona scored shortly after half-time and Keegan's team could find no response.

The final games of the season were notable for two colourful events (literally in one case). The first was at United's game at Southampton, where they were losing 3–0 at half-time. Ferguson decided the problem was the club's second-choice grey shirts, which he thought made it difficult for his players to spot each other. They were replaced by the club's third-choice blue-and-white strips for the second half, though United still lost 3–1; afterwards the shirts were dropped for good. United's then marketing director, Edward Freedman, estimates that it cost the club at least £200,000 in lost sales, but nobody at Old Trafford could stop Ferguson, and United had taken just one point in five games dressed in grey. 'There was no way we could do anything about it. The chairman wasn't going to insist. Football came above everything.'[9]

The second event occurred after Leeds United came to Old Trafford and narrowly lost 1–0. They played far better than they had managed for most of the season, even though their goalkeeper was sent off early in the game and had to be replaced by a defender.

'You wonder if it is just because they are playing Manchester United,' said Ferguson, who clearly wanted to ensure the Yorkshire club played equally well when they met Newcastle twelve days later. 'I think we can accept any club coming here and trying their hardest as long as they do it every week. No wonder managers get the sack.'[10] He added, 'On that performance they should be a top six team. They're not. They're struggling so they've been cheating on their manager.'[11] Ferguson may also have maintained he was coming to the aid of his friend, the Leeds manager Howard Wilkinson, yet his intervention infuriated and embarrassed Wilkinson, both by suggesting he had lost his players' support and also by linking him with dismissal.

When Newcastle then beat Leeds 1–0 – thanks to a goal from Keith Gillespie – Keegan couldn't suppress his anger. His ferocious and untypical post-match outburst against Ferguson on Sky TV illustrated the intense pressure Keegan must have been feeling as the championship slipped away from his team.

> This has really got to me . . . We're still fighting for the title, and he's got to go to Middlesbrough and get something. I'll love it if we beat them . . . A lot of things have been said over the last few days, some of it almost slanderous . . . It's not part of the psychological battle, when you do that with footballers – like he said about Leeds. I've kept quiet, but he went down in my estimation when he said that. The battle is still on and Manchester United have not won it yet, not by any means.[12]

But United had beaten Nottingham Forest 5–0 the day before, and went on to clinch the championship with a 3–0 victory at Middlesbrough – thus finishing four points ahead of Keegan's men. More remarkably, they also reached the FA Cup final for the third year running, and faced Liverpool. In one of the most boring finals

Wembley has witnessed, United clinched it after a Beckham corner was pushed away by the Liverpool keeper David James but then volleyed through the packed defence by Eric Cantona, with only five minutes remaining. It was United's second double in three seasons, and they'd become the only club to manage the feat twice. And, apart from Eric, it had been done largely with kids.

The Wembley final might easily have been made much more dramatic had Ferguson carried out a threat he issued on the eve of the match. The United boss was so exasperated by the lack of progress in his attempts to get a better contract that he threatened not to perform the manager's traditional proud duty of taking his men out on to the Wembley turf side by side with the opposition boss. 'There was a terrible bust-up,' says a senior United source. 'Ferguson said he wouldn't come out with the team unless they agreed his new salary.'

In February, as United overhauled Newcastle in the title race, Ferguson had expressed his impatience at not being offered a new deal. 'I want to stay here,' he said, 'I've been waiting to see what the chairman is going to do, and I'm still waiting.'[13] By the time of the cup final, three months later, he was convinced the United board were dragging their heels. The night before the game Ferguson had a 'furious row' on the phone with the director Maurice Watkins, who was usually an ally in club politics and who had tried to reassure him that a deal would be agreed.

> I was absolutely disgusted. It was annoying that they had insisted on leaving the business until the end of the season in the first place and now their words, 'We'll look after you,' seemed utterly hollow . . . it got to the point where I was not prepared to be ridiculed and felt that on a matter of principle I might have to resign.[14]

Ferguson had let it be known that the Irish FA had recently offered him £300,000 a year to take over the Republic of Ireland side after the retirement of Jack Charlton. An even more improbable alternative had arisen when Terry Venables had announced that he would step down as England manager after the European Championship in the summer of 1996 (supposedly to have time to prepare for a libel case relating to his business affairs). Ferguson was contacted by the former England player and Leeds manager Jimmy Armfield, who was acting for the FA as a headhunter. Armfield simply sought Ferguson's advice about possible contenders, but, according to the former FA chief executive Graham Kelly, 'it soon became clear that [Ferguson] was interested in succeeding Terry Venables as England coach'.[15]

Kelly says the obstacle was that the Manchester United board wouldn't give the FA permission to talk to Ferguson, even though the Old Trafford directors had not offered him the new contract he wanted. And the Football Association wasn't in the business of tapping people. Kelly claims that when he met Ferguson at a dinner a few weeks later 'he made it clear to me how disappointed he was at not having had a chance to discuss the England post'. According to Kelly, Ferguson's brother, Martin, 'was keen for him to have a go at it'.[16] Given the United manager's fervent patriotism, it seems unlikely that he took the idea seriously, and certainly he has never suggested this subsequently. He may have been using the England job as a bargaining counter with the United board.

At the same time, it appears that Martin Edwards was contemplating replacement managers as a precaution if Ferguson did walk out. His prime target was the man who would have been his alternative choice back in 1986: Terry Venables. It would have been a strange choice, given that Venables had resigned as England manager to deal with his legal problems, for running a club is a far more pressing occupation than looking after a national team. When Edwards mentioned the name to his marketing director Edward Freedman, who had worked with Venables at Spurs, Freedman said, 'You must be mad.'[17]

Ferguson's problem, as ever, was that the directors knew how emotionally committed he now was to United. In his own words, he was 'embroidered into the fabric of the club'.[18] Having invested so much effort in United's future, he was unlikely to walk away. A week after the cup final Ferguson's accountant, Alan Baines, spent six hours negotiating with the Old Trafford board. The outcome was a new four-year deal worth up to a £650,000 a year, and potentially a lot more with bonuses. 'I was not given what I believed I was worth but, nonetheless, I had made huge strides in relation to my existing agreement,' Ferguson says.[19] He then proceeded to weaken his bargaining position in future contract talks by saying 'it was never in my mind to walk out . . . you don't quit this job or this club. You have to see it through.'[20]

During the 1995–96 season Alex Ferguson had seen off the critics from the summer before, and had shown how right he was to hold his nerve in the face of huge public pressure and not make panic buys. Eric Cantona had been able to control his temperament without its affecting his game, and the youngsters had excelled themselves in a way that not even Ferguson could have expected. But he had also had more than a fair share of luck. Nobody would have expected serious championship contenders to collapse as dramatically as Newcastle did in the second half of the season, when, during one stretch of eight games, they picked up only seven points. It had looked like a masterstroke in February when Kevin Keegan strengthened his squad by buying the exciting Colombian forward Faustino Asprilla, but the player's arrival seemed instead to upset the rhythm of the Tyneside team. Keegan never really recovered from the failure, and resigned as Newcastle manager the following January.

Manchester United's squad, in contrast, had been rejuvenated by the infusion of Ferguson's young players. After the 1992 Youth Cup victory, United's teenagers had reached the final again the following year, but lost to Leeds, and had then won the trophy once more in 1995. Now many of the class of 1992 and 1993 were not just playing first-team football for United, but also being selected for England. Gary Neville had made his national debut in 1995, and was now joined by his younger sibling Philip – the first brothers to play together for England since Bobby and Jackie Charlton. David Beckham won his first international cap in the autumn of 1996, and Nicky Butt and Paul Scholes followed within a year.

Yet amid the accolades for the Manchester United youth programme came strong claims from other clubs that Alex Ferguson's development staff had used unfair methods to sign junior players. In particular they were accused of poaching two teenagers – David Brown from Oldham Athletic and Matthew Wicks from Arsenal. The FA's rules state that no club should approach a boy who is registered as an associate schoolboy with another team. Arsenal and Oldham were aggrieved that they'd spent several years honing the youngsters' skills, only for United to march in and sign them up.

In the case of Matthew Wicks, the sixteen-year-old son of the former Chelsea player Steve Wicks, Arsenal sought £1.5 million in compensation after the youngster had spent six years at Highbury. In January 1996 the FA found United guilty of making an illegal approach, but the Reds escaped punishment because Wicks had become homesick in Manchester and returned to Arsenal anyway.

Only two weeks later the FA fined United £20,000 for making an illegal approach to David Brown, the schoolboy formerly with Oldham Athletic.[21] In a separate judgement by the Football League, United were also ordered to pay the Lancashire club an immediate £75,000 in compensation, and were told the figure could rise to as much as £500,000 if Brown made a substantial number of appearances for his new club, or played for England. The Oldham chief scout, Jim Cassell, described United's taking of his player as 'disruptive, demoralising and very, very disheartening' to the club's youth programme, and in protest Oldham stopped playing United at junior level.[22]

Manchester United insisted, however, that they'd acted within the regulations on signing young players, but that the rules were difficult to interpret. David Brown had yet to sign a new agreement with Oldham, so United took the chance to swoop. 'We have done nothing outside the rules,' Ferguson claimed.

> With young players it's a case of some you win and some you lose. Nick Barmby slipped through our fingers when he went to Tottenham . . . One of these boys approached us, another had not been contacted by his club for a year and the third felt that we offered better prospects after his club changed managers and were relegated.[23]

Sadly, none of the players in dispute fulfilled their promise. None ever played Premier League football, though both Wicks and Brown played for lower-league sides. Assessing the rights and wrongs of the poaching allegations against Manchester United is not easy. It's perfectly understandable that many young boys should jump at the chance of going to Old Trafford once they hear that United are interested in them. Nor should teenagers be prevented from switching clubs if they wish. On the other hand, it is important that clubs should be rewarded for the efforts they put into developing young players. It is also true that larger, more glamorous, clubs don't always provide the best opportunity for youngsters to prosper.

Alex Ferguson has always been adamant that, unlike in the Busby era, United have never made illegal payments to parents. This may have meant that some prospects have slipped through the net. The England striker Michael Owen, for example, was coached at Old Trafford when he was eleven and twelve. 'We wanted to sign him,' Ferguson once said, 'but we weren't prepared to meet his father's requirements, so he signed for Liverpool.'[24]

Four years later, in 2000, Manchester United were again in trouble, when the Football League ordered them to pay Wolves £200,000 in compensation for taking the former England schoolboy Daniel Nardiello, with further payments becoming due if he made the grade. (He eventually made his senior United debut in the League Cup in 2001.) The Wolverhampton Wanderers chief executive, Jez Moxey, claimed the compensation award sent a 'message to predatory clubs that they cannot get away with cherry-picking the outstanding talent being developed by Wolves.'[25] If so, it had little effect, for a year later United were ordered to pay Wolves another £200,000 for taking a second England schoolboy, Kris Taylor. Although it is often said that poaching is common throughout youth football, the authorities and many clubs believe that United have been bigger offenders than most, and too aggressive in their quest to find the talent of tomorrow. Even one of Ferguson's closest managerial friends believes that United have been unfair in the methods they have used in his time to sign young players: 'They didn't stop at much to get them,' he says. 'They got good players by any means necessary. I'm sure Alex would have a smile on his face about it if you asked him now, but I know clubs have been very upset with United while he's been there.'

Both Nardiello and Taylor had been coached by Wolves since the age of about nine. The director of the Molineux youth academy, Chris Evans, says

> you have clubs who are affluent enough and have a
> philosophy whereby they believe that they have to recruit the
> best talent in the game. The chequebook is the be-all and
> end-all of everything. Halifax cannot come in and take Taylor
> or Nardiello from us. Manchester United can, and do. They
> have vast budgets and vast status. They can come and take
> our best players, and there is absolutely nothing we can do
> about it. I would like to see them take the same chances as
> every other club by spotting and developing their own talent

and not wait to see what everyone else does and then take theirs.[26]

Nowadays Evans still has to fight against scouts from Manchester United and other top clubs turning up at Wolves games unannounced, contrary to what the FA says is good practice.

'How can you control such wealthy clubs?' asks a Football League official. 'Manchester United have a track record in failing to recognise they have a commitment to pay adequate compensation for obtaining the best players from other clubs.' It is difficult for Alex Ferguson to disclaim responsibility when he is in overall charge of the Manchester United youth scheme. He has always prided himself on taking a close interest in his young players, even if he is now much less actively involved in their development than during his early years at Old Trafford. 'He cannot abdicate responsibility for what is going on at youth level,' says the Football League official.

One curious aspect of Manchester United's youth programme under Ferguson has been its failure to produce good strikers. Paul Scholes is the only exception, and he eventually became a midfield player instead. All Manchester United's main goalscorers in recent times have been bought by the club, and in the summer of 1996 Alex Ferguson made a second attempt to buy Alan Shearer, who was then at the peak of his powers for both Blackburn Rovers and England.

For several weeks the other leading clubs trembled as United appeared to be favourites to sign the player (though Newcastle were also in the running). Having just won the double again, it looked as if Manchester United would become almost unbeatable with a forward who scored around thirty goals a season. In early July Shearer's agent told Ferguson that the player was 'ready to leave Blackburn and would like to play for United', and the Reds' boss got the same message from Old Trafford players who spoke to Shearer during that summer's European Championship.[27]

But Ferguson was always sceptical that Shearer would sign for him, because of the way the striker had rejected United four years before. Moreover, neither Blackburn's owner, Jack Walker, nor his chairman, Robert Coar, could stomach the idea of their star player going to United, whom they saw as local rivals. Shearer himself was worried about how United fans might treat him, particularly if things went badly. On the other hand, he also thought that Newcastle, where he had been brought up, might prove to be something of a goldfish bowl. And he didn't want to go abroad – the other option. The club he really wanted to join was Liverpool, which he thought was becoming a serious contender again, and his former manager at Blackburn, Kenny Dalglish, had regaled him with stories about the glory days at Anfield. But Liverpool couldn't afford him.

When Ferguson met the player and his agent, Tony Stephens, he became 'convinced that Shearer is interested in joining us'. Could he take penalties at United? the striker had asked Ferguson. And could he wear the number-9 shirt? The United manager pointed out that Eric Cantona never missed penalties, so he would retain the job for the time being, but there shouldn't be a problem with the shirt (which then belonged to Brian McClair). A week later, after much waiting for his mobile phone to ring, Ferguson heard from Tony Stephens that Shearer had instead chosen to join Newcastle United, for a new British record fee of £15 million. 'I had this terrible gut feeling all along it wouldn't happen, simply because Jack Walker hates United,' Ferguson said afterwards.[28] He felt 'sick and then angry' at first, but it wasn't as big a blow as the transfer failures of the late 1980s.[29]

Having not spent his transfer budget on Shearer, Alex Ferguson instead acquired five foreigners over the summer – in contrast to the year before, when he had bought nobody. The biggest names were the Czech winger Karel Poborsky and Johan Cruyff's son, Jordi, a versatile midfielder and forward from Barcelona. Both had excelled in the European Championship, which had been held in England that June, though they later proved to be the most disappointing of the bunch. The Norwegian Ronny Johnsen gave Ferguson more options in central defence now that Steve Bruce had joined Birmingham City, and could also play in midfield, while the Dutchman Raimond van der Gouw was a back-up goalkeeper. As for the young Norwegian striker with the strange name, Ole Gunnar Solskjaer, nobody knew much about him.

If Alan Shearer was a serious loss, it didn't show when United thrashed his new club, Newcastle United, 4–0 in the Charity Shield, nor when United won 3–0 at Wimbledon in the opening league fixture of the 1996–97 season and David Beckham scored one of the most remarkable goals of all time. Noticing that the Wimbledon goalkeeper, Neil Sullivan, had wandered off his line, Beckham lobbed the ball from behind the halfway line, more than fifty yards from the goal, and beyond the keeper's despairing lunge.

But Newcastle showed they were still formidable opponents. Indeed, in the autumn of 1996, at the very time when Ferguson was about to celebrate ten years at Old Trafford, the Tyneside club inflicted the first of a string of horrendous defeats, beating United 5–0 at St James's Park. To lose 6–3 at Southampton six days later was an even greater humiliation for the Reds (even if it was with ten men, after Roy Keane was sent off). The following week United's glorious record of never having lost at home in Europe ended with a 1–0 defeat by the Turkish side Fenerbahçe, which United had earlier beaten 2–0 in Istanbul. To cap it all, Chelsea then visited Manchester and ended an unbeaten home league run which stretched back thirty-five matches – two short of the club record. 'Fourteen dismal days in ten fantastic years,' said Ferguson. 'So much for my sense of timing.'[30]

But there were plenty of bright spots too. Perhaps the brightest was twenty-two-year-old Ole Gunnar Solskjaer. Ferguson had intended to bring him on slowly, perhaps initially in the League Cup, but was so impressed with Solskjaer in practice games that he blooded him in only the third match of the season, at home to

Blackburn. 'From the first training session he made everyone sit up and take notice,' Ferguson wrote in his diary. 'The improvement he makes each week is startling.'[31] Solskjaer scored just nine minutes after coming on as substitute against Blackburn, and went on to finish his first season as United's leading scorer, with nineteen successful strikes – well ahead of Eric Cantona and Andy Cole.

In the European Cup, the Reds progressed further than ever before under Ferguson, with a particularly impressive 4–0 demolition in the quarter-finals of Porto, the Portuguese champions, who had been unbeaten until then. The German side Borussia Dortmund looked a relatively easy proposition in the semi-final, only for United, without Peter Schmeichel, to lose 1–0 in Germany. They lost again by the same score at Old Trafford, and Borussia went on to beat Juventus 3–1 in the final in Munich.

Manchester United won the League for the fourth time in five years; for Eric Cantona, with his previous successes at Marseilles and Leeds, it was his sixth championship medal in seven seasons. In truth, the Frenchman hadn't been at his best, though he still played a significant creative role for the team. In the final weeks Ferguson noticed that Cantona seemed to be preoccupied, and suspected he was upset at failing to achieve his 'personal Holy Grail' of winning the European Cup. 'I think he has reached a crossroads in his career,' Ferguson told his diary the day after the second defeat by Borussia. 'It looks as if the chances he missed – not to mention his relatively quiet performance – have prompted him to question his future.'[32] Two weeks later Cantona confirmed Ferguson's fears: he had decided to give up football and hoped to pursue a career as an actor. Ferguson had considerable sympathy with two of the reasons Cantona gave for leaving – that he didn't like being a pawn of the United merchandising operation, and that he also felt that the board had been unadventurous in acquiring star players. United waited for nine days before announcing the news to the outside world.

Manchester United had done well to get four years of football out of Cantona. Alex Ferguson had succeeded where several previous managers had failed, by accepting that Cantona was a rare talent and had to be handled as such. At first the other United players resented it when Ferguson gave the Frenchman this leeway. He was allowed to turn up late for training or for the team coach; he ignored the club dress code, and was often unshaven. Yet Alex Ferguson rarely reprimanded him. Paul Ince pointed at Cantona on one occasion, complaining to his manager, 'You never shout at him.' Similarly, Lee Sharpe tells of once being told off by Ferguson for arriving at a civic reception at Manchester town hall dressed in a trendy suit, only for Cantona to turn up wearing trainers.

'What was genius,' says one United insider, 'is that Fergie knew if he carried on treating Eric like royalty he would start performing like the king, and then automatically all the players would accept that their king should be treated a little differently.' Once the rest of the squad came to appreciate that Cantona was the special ingredient which raised everyone's game, the grumbling from colleagues stopped.

'Now I'll tell you the really clever bit,' says the inside observer.

Once Eric realised that Fergie respected him and loved him, he started coming round to Fergie's way without being told! He did it out of respect. He started turning up on time, shaving, never late for the bus, even used to come in early. It was amazing – a complete turnaround. By the end, everyone was happy. Now that is phenomenal man-management. You need to know which players you can get away with treating differently, without totally losing the support of the others. He knew he could risk it with Cantona, and the players would eventually accept it.

Traditionally, the employment of highly talented egos has been confined largely to the fields of show business and sport. Perhaps the main thing to be learned from Ferguson's handling of Cantona is how specific the approach has to be for each employee, and how hard it is to balance what is necessary to get the best from the individual with its effect on the other members of the team. Other gifted but difficult players – Paul Gascoigne, for instance – would have needed an entirely different approach.

The fact that Cantona was French and was so unusual and eccentric for a footballer – a man who loved painting, and read Baudelaire and Jean-Paul Sartre – helped give him an aura of genius. It also helped that Cantona's period at United coincided with an influx of very young players who regarded the Frenchman as a talismanic father figure. The Manchester United team inherited by Ferguson in 1986 would have been somewhat less forgiving of such inconsistent standards by their manager. The other vital ingredient, of course, was United's almost non-stop success: without that, Cantona might have left much sooner.

The worrying question was whether Manchester United could now succeed without the catalyst who'd turned inconsistent cup-winners into a regularly winning team. The player's importance had been underlined in 1994–95, when Cantona had (through his own fault) been absent for the closing stages, and the team had won nothing.

That importance seemed to be borne out in the following season, 1997–98, after Ferguson paid Spurs £3.5 million for Teddy Sheringham (even though he was now thirty-one) and the player failed to fill the gap left by Cantona's retirement. It did not help, however, that Roy Keane was injured for most of the season after a foolish tackle on Alf-Inge Haaland at Elland Road, or that Ryan Giggs was also absent for a long stretch with a torn hamstring. Despite this, United still led the title race for much of the season: one autumn spell saw them score twenty goals in just four league games. A United-supporting Manchester bookmaker, Fred Done, was so certain his favourites would be crowned champions that he

417

paid up on bets in advance. Indeed, United amassed enough points to finish comfortably on top in most seasons, which would have made it three titles in a row.

But Arsenal, under their new French manager, Arsène Wenger, suddenly usurped Manchester United's position as the masters of English football. That spring they won the double for the second time in their history (the third time the feat had been achieved in five years, compared with just three doubles in the previous one hundred years – a sign of the increasing concentration of power in the English game). The turning point was when Arsenal visited Old Trafford in March 1998 and left with a 1–0 win after a fine goal by Marc Overmars, a player United had once fancied. The Gunners put together a run of ten straight victories, playing some of the best football produced by any English club in modern times. In the end United lost the title by only one point, but, given the clear superiority of Arsenal's football, a significant gulf seemed to have opened between the two sides.

Nor was there better news in the European Cup, where United went out to Monaco on away goals in the quarter-final. The French League club were regarded as the weakest of the other quarter-finalists, but Ferguson overreacted in concluding that United had been too adventurous against Borussia the year before. This time his team were rather too cautious and came home from Monte Carlo with only a goalless draw. The Monaco ground can be difficult for visiting sides, because the pitch is very hard on account of being constructed above an underground car park. So Ferguson ordered the Old Trafford groundsmen to water the pitch heavily for the second leg, reckoning that the French team would not be comfortable on a soft surface. 'I don't care how much water you put on the fucking thing,' he shouted at the United groundstaff. 'Get it flooded.' 'That's not cheating,' remarked the head groundsman, Keith Kent. 'That's playing to your advantage.'[33]

But, when David Trezeguet scored an early goal in Manchester, this left United needing to score two to win the tie, because of the away-goals rule. The match ended in a disappointing 1–1 draw. Afterwards Ferguson took his frustration out on Nicky Butt for giving the ball away. According to the reserve goalkeeper, Kevin Pilkington, 'The gaffer came in and shouted, "I'm out the fuckin' European Cup now, Butty, and it's your fuckin' fault! What were you fuckin' doing?" But Nicky was a young lad. He was hurt. We all felt for him.'[34]

One can understand how Ferguson felt too. For the fourth time in four attempts his Manchester United side had failed to make an impact in the one competition where their greatness had traditionally been measured.

The summer of 1998 was as gloomy as that of three years before. At least in 1995 nobody believed that Blackburn Rovers could sustain their success. Now many feared that Arsenal might have taken Manchester United's mantle for good.

23

'Football, eh? Bloody Hell!'

'Deep down, I know it would be impossible to win the League, the Champions' Cup and the FA Cup.'

ALEX FERGUSON, 1997[1]

It was a sign of the extent to which Manchester United had become a commercial organisation, owned by large financial institutions, that during the summer of 1998 some of the most important meetings in the club's history took place in the City of London. The British headquarters of HSBC – once the Hongkong and Shanghai Banking Corporation – occupy the old Vintners' Hall, an imposing grey building on the north bank of the Thames next to Southwark Bridge. HSBC both acted as United's financial advisers and gave the PLC chairman, Sir Roland Smith, a London base. And it was at the HSBC building in July 1998, faced with criticism from Smith and United's chief executive, Martin Edwards, that Alex Ferguson suddenly asked the extraordinary question 'Do you want to call it a day?'[2]

'No, no,' both directors insisted, realising they had gone too far. But they'd hit home. Just as in the summer of 1995, Edwards was worried that Ferguson might have taken his eye off the ball: now the concern was that he was spending too much time on his new hobby of owning racehorses. Ferguson replied that he needed an outside activity to provide some kind of release from his seven-day-a-week job, reminding Edwards that he had long suggested that his manager should find some way to relax.

Edwards and Smith were also anxious about Ferguson's plans to buy the Aston Villa striker Dwight Yorke, and asked whether he was worth the likely fee of around £12 million. Ferguson pointed to his successful record in transfer dealings over the previous decade, claiming that he had all but balanced the books, and also achieved great value for money. He had a point. By 1998 the earlier disappointments such as Neil Webb, Danny Wallace, Jim Leighton and Ralph Milne were easily outweighed by undoubted bargains such as Brian McClair, Steve Bruce, Lee Sharpe, Mark Hughes, Gary Pallister, Paul Ince, Denis Irwin, Peter Schmeichel, Eric Cantona and Roy Keane. 'If you don't recognise that I am the best person to judge which players should be bought by the club,' he warned, 'I may as well leave now.'[3]

The two directors' anxiety reflected the despondency which had surrounded Old Trafford since the end of the previous season. Not only were Arsenal the new top dogs in English football, but the defeat by Monaco illustrated a pattern. Under Ferguson, United had not been knocked out of Europe by the leading sides such as Juventus, the Milans, Barcelona, Real Madrid or Bayern Munich. Instead they had failed repeatedly against much lesser names – Atlético Madrid, Moscow Torpedo, Galatasaray, Gothenburg, Volgograd and Borussia Dortmund.

It also seemed as if the financial constraints imposed by being a public company would prevent United from acquiring the world-class players that many observers felt the club needed, both to compete with Arsenal domestically and also to succeed at the European level. The financial stringency required by the City made it much harder to gamble on expensive transfer deals.

Alex Ferguson had nonetheless spent almost £28 million in the summer of 1998 trying to match the London club. The money went on just three players – the PSV Eindhoven defender Jaap Stam, who cost £10.6 million; the Swedish winger Jesper Blomqvist, who had caused United much trouble playing against them for Gothenburg back in 1994, and cost £4.4 million from Parma of Italy; and Dwight Yorke, who eventually moved from Aston Villa for £12.6 million.

But what concerned many United fans were the players who had failed to come to Manchester. That summer the Dutch striker Patrick Kluivert was reported to be on the point of moving to Old Trafford, but then it emerged that he refused even to talk to United. He said Arsenal were the only English team he would consider, and then joined Barcelona instead. The Argentine forward Gabriel Batistuta had long been a Ferguson target, but United simply couldn't afford him. Batistuta, Martin Edwards explained, 'would have cost £12 million or £13 million, which in itself may have been acceptable but his personal terms were five times greater than our biggest wage-earner. It would not have been responsible for us to have bought Batistuta because the next time . . . our players' contracts came up for negotiation the benchmark would have been Batistuta's wages.'[4]

The player most coveted by Manchester United fans was the young Brazilian forward Ronaldo, who was then considered to be the best player in the world. Ferguson had been offered Ronaldo by his agent in 1996, but United couldn't afford either the £20 million fee or his £50,000 a week wages. 'Can you really justify that kind of outlay when you are a public company?' Ferguson asked. 'Perhaps I could steal the crown jewels – but how would the rest of our players feel? . . . And what guarantee would we have that the same agent wouldn't be hawking him around again in six months' time?'[5]

Ferguson felt that, over the years, the constraints of being a PLC had prevented United from translating their domestic success into glory on the European and world stages. Eric Cantona had cited the club's lack of ambition in buying players as one of the reasons he wanted to retire. 'My hands were tied,' Ferguson claims, 'because Manchester United's policy on salaries gave me no chance of providing the financial packages required to secure those great players' contracts. I think the restrictions applied to wages prevented us from being the power in European football that we could have been in the Nineties.'[6]

Manchester United's wage structure at this time paid many of the club's top players about the same amount: around £23,000 a week. Such parity was good for encouraging team solidarity, especially among those who'd grown up together, but the wage ceiling was also a deterrent to potential world-class recruits. Just as Ferguson felt that a talented star such as Eric Cantona could be allowed to operate under different rules of behaviour, he also thought it was right to reward more highly the two or three individuals who might enable United to compete in Europe. 'The world of the PLC can be very frustrating for me,' he wrote later. 'I understand that the interests of shareholders have to be carefully considered, especially those of the institutions that have invested heavily in the club. But what about the 55,000 supporters who turn out at every home match?'[7]

Ferguson occasionally warned his directors that they were being too cautious. 'The club has got to get to grips with what actually makes a winning club in Europe', he said publicly in April 1998:

> It is not even anywhere near that. It is not a Barcelona, it is not an AC Milan, it is not a Juventus, it's not a Real Madrid . . . What may happen after I leave is that it will dawn on them that, when a new manager comes in, he may ask for £60 million to build a team to win in Europe.
>
> But they may not get the best manager to replace me. And then the dawning part comes in and they will say: 'I wish we had done that five years back down the road.' There are big strides this club has got to take, but when they will do it, I do not know.[8]

Yet one United director says Batistuta was the only case where the board blocked a transfer. In 1998, when Ferguson tried to buy the Chilean striker Marcelo Salas, who'd troubled England with two goals at Wembley in February that year, Martin Edwards made it clear that the board were willing to pay the £9 million demanded by Salas's club, River Plate of Argentina, and could also meet his salary demands. But he was never signed. 'Salas was not my decision and not the board's decision,' said Edwards. 'Salas was Alex Ferguson's decision. We said to Alex, "Look, is Salas going to play or Cole?" and Alex withdrew on Salas.'[9] Edwards resented the way Ferguson was trying to blame him for the failure to sign Salas, just as back in 1995 Ferguson had implied that Edwards was responsible for Paul Ince's departure.

Many supporters – perhaps even a majority – believed that salvation from the financial straitjacket had arrived in September 1998, when news broke that Rupert Murdoch's satellite-television company BSkyB was making a £624 million takeover bid for Manchester United. Martin Edwards was to join the Sky board, and would receive £87 million for his shareholding. Both the PLC board and BSkyB suggested that becoming part of a multi-billion-pound global media empire would give United the financial clout to pay the transfer fees and wages needed for players of Ronaldo's and Batistuta's calibre, though Murdoch's men were careful never actually to make such a promise. Indeed, nobody familiar with the way in which Sky and Murdoch's News Corporation companies were run would have expected them to.

Final details of Sky's offer were thrashed out in late-night meetings at HSBC on the Thames. Alex Ferguson was excluded from the secret discussions which preceded Sky's announcement, because by now Martin Edwards distrusted him. It may have been a fatal error.

Relations between Ferguson and Edwards had deteriorated badly over the previous two or three years. As late as November 1996, when Ferguson chatted at length to this author at a party, the United manager still had great respect for his chief executive, and expressed his gratitude for the way Edwards had stood by him during the difficult years of the late 1980s. But that relationship had gradually broken down during successive rows such as the Paul Ince episode, repeated tensions over money for new players, and, above all, disagreements about Ferguson's own remuneration. 'Always the disharmony has developed over money,' Ferguson later explained. 'I feel I should have received a better salary over my period at United than was forthcoming from Martin, who is extremely guarded with money.'[10] He thought Edwards was being particularly miserly when the chief executive himself had made millions out of the club through a variety of means – the share-option scheme, regular dividends, and his pay and bonuses, but above all the ever increasing value of his shares during United's successes under Ferguson. 'Ferguson was always pissed off that Martin had made £100 million and he didn't make anything,' says a club insider.

Whereas Ferguson and Edwards had operated in close partnership during the manager's early years at United, chasing round Britain together in pursuit of new players, they had became increasingly estranged. With so many more people now involved in the management of the rapidly expanding enterprise, they no longer needed to work so closely anyway. Nor did it help that the big decisions were now taken at PLC board meetings, to which Ferguson was not normally invited: he was limited to meetings of the directors of the football club, a subsidiary of the PLC. By the late 1990s the tensions were so great that the manager and the chief executive spoke to each other only when they had to.

Although born only three years apart, Ferguson and Edwards were products of vastly different backgrounds – the one from a crowded tenement block in the shadow of the Govan shipyards; the other brought up in an affluent part of Cheshire, and educated at a private school in Oxfordshire. While one boy watched Rangers by scrambling over the wall at Ibrox, the other sat with his parents in the Old Trafford directors' box. One United insider says he always felt Martin Edwards regarded Ferguson as 'trade', or just another employee like the ticketing manager, rather than as an exceptional talent who should be treated like one of the club's star players. They also had very different political loyalties. While Edwards was a committed Conservative and contributed money to the party, Ferguson was becoming increasingly public in his support for the Labour Party.

According to Mihir Bose's book *Manchester Unlimited*, Sky executives were surprised in the summer of 1998 at the degree of hostility between the two men. 'He has got very close to New Labour and to Number 10,' Edwards reportedly told the Murdoch team about Ferguson (without appreciating that they too were close to New Labour). 'He is very friendly with Alastair Campbell. He is a socialist, you know. Very strange. And all this friendship with New Labour and Campbell I do not understand.' The United chief executive warned that Ferguson could not be trusted if they told him confidentially about the deal in advance. 'Christ, no! You don't want to see him. He's a troublemaker. If you tell him, he'll leak everything. He's totally hostile and I've just written him a letter warning him.' When Sky suggested it might help win Ferguson's backing if they ensured that he would benefit from the takeover financially, Bose says Edwards responded, 'Don't give him money for Christ's sake. The man's useless.'[11]

Edwards subsequently denied saying the words attributed to him, but nobody disputes the rift they reflected. Ferguson seemed to come to his boss's aid by describing the remarks as 'such blatant nonsense' that he could never believe that Edwards was 'capable of uttering them'. But then, with a clever sideswipe, he added that one couldn't say that his own record at United showed him to be useless with money, 'considering that Martin's fortune has swollen by upwards of £120 million over the past ten years as a result of his shareholdings in the club'.[12]

So news of the Sky bid came as as much of a surprise to Alex Ferguson as it did to Manchester United supporters. Although at first many fans welcomed the bid, there followed a seven-month battle in which active supporters' groups such as the independent supporters' association, IMUSA, and a specially founded sister organisation, Shareholders United Against Murdoch (of which this author was a leading organiser), campaigned to stop the takeover. Within a few days the Office of Fair Trading announced that it would investigate the bid. By the end of October, Sky was close to gaining enough 'Yes' votes from United shareholders. Then, after two months of intense lobbying and media activity by fans' groups, and opposition from MPs and from the Football Association (which said the bid was 'not welcomed'), the Trade Secretary, Peter Mandelson, referred the proposed takeover to the Monopolies Commission. The following April the Commission found that if Sky did acquire United it would damage competition between broadcasters and also harm the quality of British football. So Mandelson's successor, Stephen Byers, blocked the takeover.

The BSkyB bid had put Ferguson in a difficult spot. His political instincts, as a Labour supporter and a former trade-union activist, might have made him hostile to the idea of Rupert Murdoch becoming his ultimate employer (though, equally, many of his Blairite friends had become quite cosy with the media tycoon). Ferguson had never been a huge fan of Sky from the time it secured the Premier League TV contract in 1992, even though his son Jason had worked for it almost ever since, specifically on football. More than once Ferguson had boycotted the station because of how it had treated United. However, he frequently earned money from ghost-written articles and interviews for Murdoch's newspapers. Everyone agrees that, if Alex Ferguson had taken a stance on it from the outset, it would have had a huge influence on the bid's prospects one way or the other. In particular, if Ferguson had backed the takeover then much of the opposition of supporters would have crumbled immediately.

Sky had promised to keep Ferguson as manager if its bid succeeded; indeed, anything else would have provoked an even greater outcry from the fans. However, his exclusion from the talks with Sky almost certainly made him feel slighted. The world saw him as 'Mr Manchester United', and yet he'd been kept in the dark about one of the most important developments in the club's history. It must have prompted in him the same feelings of humiliation which had driven him so much in his early career. Although Ferguson said little about the bid in public, nothing he did say could be construed as support for it.

'The Sky thing is irrelevant,' he remarked. 'My priority is to remain the manager of Manchester United, no matter who's in control.'[13] As for Rupert Murdoch, 'I don't know him. You have got to know people before you can have views on them.'[14] Oddly enough, the two men are similar characters: very charming in person, but also driven, energetic empire-builders. They love exercising power, and are gamblers by nature – both in their work and on the horses. 'Alex Ferguson is like Rupert Murdoch,' says someone who has worked with both men. 'He has the ability to inspire people, to make them think that they are the only person that matters for him, but is then ruthless when it comes to moving people on.' For every Willie Garner, Jim Leighton or Paul Ince, there are Murdoch editors and News Corporation managers who still don't understand why they were unexpectedly discarded.

Even today it is difficult to say what Alex Ferguson really thought about the Sky bid. He was possibly never that sure himself. He gave mixed signals, partly depending on his audience. In Ferguson's memoirs a year later he expressed some concerns. 'My own feeling is that the club is too important as a sporting institution, too much of a rarity, to be put up for sale.'[15] And during their battle to stop the takeover IMUSA leaders were convinced that, privately at least, Ferguson was fully on their side.

After the public differences during the summer of 1995 between Ferguson and the fledgling independent supporters' association, relations were repaired remarkably quickly, and the following year the United boss addressed an IMUSA members' meeting. When Ferguson had to postpone his talk at the last moment, he offered to come twenty-four hours later instead and to pay for overnight accommodation for any members who'd travelled long distances to hear him (though the idea wasn't practical and the arrangement was put off to a later date). Ferguson had also met IMUSA delegations, spoken occasionally to IMUSA officers on the phone, and promoted the association's idea of a flag-waving day to improve the crowd atmosphere at Old Trafford. Now, during IMUSA's fight against Murdoch, Ferguson spoke regularly on the phone to the organisation's chair, Andy Walsh.

They talked at least once a week during the early stages of the campaign, sometimes for as much as half an hour at a time. The United manager encouraged Walsh to keep up his efforts, and raised his spirits during moments when Walsh felt demoralised and didn't think the campaign could succeed. So Walsh was astonished months later, after the takeover had been blocked, to read an interview with a *Guardian* reporter, Simon Hattenstone, in which Ferguson said he'd been 'indifferent' to the bid, 'because I always felt if it did happen, as long as I had a football team I was happy. And that is really the nub of my life – so long as I'm controlling the team.'[16] That wasn't the Alex Ferguson that Walsh had regularly heard on the telephone, boosting his morale and urging him to keep fighting.

Walsh later concluded that the United manager, like any skilful operator, had primarily wanted to chat so as to glean the latest gossip about what was going on, and to work out whether the Murdoch bid was likely to succeed. Ferguson was too much of a political animal (with a small 'p') ever simply to ignore the huge public dispute that was raging over the ownership of his club.

Yet his public talk of the takeover as being 'irrelevant', and of being 'indifferent' to it, hides the fact that behind the scenes Ferguson was encouraging alternatives to Sky. He may not have shared many of the direct concerns of the anti-Sky campaigners – there was, for instance, no re-emergence of Ferguson the trade unionist, no worry about Murdoch as the anti-union newspaper publisher of Wapping. Nor was it a case of Ferguson the socialist being horrified by the tycoon's Thatcherism. It was more a view that if Manchester United were to have a new proprietor then he'd like some say in that ownership.

At an early stage in the Sky story Ferguson recruited an upmarket solicitor, Kevin Jaquiss, who was then with the Manchester partnership Slater Heelis and had been recommended to the manager by a firm in the City of London. This was a significant move, because Ferguson already had a lawyer – his long-standing Aberdeen solicitor and family friend Les Delgarno. If he needed advice about where the bid left him as a Manchester United employee, Delgarno could certainly have given it. But in the autumn of 1998 Ferguson was told he needed more expert advice, and Kevin Jaquiss specialises in corporate work. And, in the seven months of public debate about the bid, Jaquiss partly acted as a go-between with IMUSA.

What can now be revealed is that Alex Ferguson was secretly trying to buy Manchester United himself. The work on this was done in a private capacity by Ferguson's son Mark, who was then a fund manager with the Schroders securities house in the City of London. As soon as the Sky bid was announced, Mark began sounding out sympathisers at Old Trafford, along with wealthy friends of his father and other potential investors who might join a consortium. Today, Mark Ferguson denies any such activity, but it has been confirmed by one of his father's closest friends and a leading businessman whom Mark visited, and many others also heard rumours about his search. He made little progress, however, largely because Martin Edwards and his allies on the United board were so keen on Sky that they weren't willing to take rival bids seriously. Ferguson's attempt never got to the point of a formal approach to United's financial advisers, HSBC. 'I'm not sure how seriously it was treated,' says Keith Harris, who led the HSBC team working for United on the Sky bid. 'It was picked up that he [Mark] was trying to put together a financial consortium to make a bid, but there were an awful lot of rumours at that time.'[17]

The remarkable thing, given the intense media interest in the Sky bid, is that Mark Ferguson's activities were never exposed back in 1998. The Fergusons were taking a big risk, since it would have been highly embarrassing to Alex had word of Mark's efforts ever got out. Potentially it could have cost him his job, since he was undermining the main plank of the PLC board's policy. It was also a sign of how Alex Ferguson saw (and still sees) his long-term role at Old Trafford as being more than that of a successful football manager. 'Alex was always interested in trying to buy the club,' says one United director. Such ambitions would have to wait while he concentrated on football.

As the 1998–99 season progressed, Manchester United's performances on the pitch began seriously to undermine the argument that they needed Murdoch's millions to be successful. In 1997, for the first time since the 1950s, the European Cup had been expanded beyond simply the champions of each national league, and now included one or two runners-up from the bigger football powers (which made the competition's new name, the Champions League, even more inappropriate, since it was neither a proper league nor confined to champions any more). This meant that, although United had only come second to Arsenal in the previous season, they could play in the European Cup again. Ever a football traditionalist, Ferguson said he thought briefly about not entering the cup 'on principle because I had always felt that the competition should be

431

what it said – champions!' Such thoughts were indeed brief: they 'lasted a millisecond', he added.[18]

After beating the Polish side ŁKS Łódź in a pre-season qualifying round, United were pitted against two tough opponents in the group stage – former champions Bayern Munich and Barcelona – along with the Danish team Brøndby. The Danes were easily dispatched, 6–2 away and 5–0 at home, and United drew all four games against the German and Spanish sides, though they could have won in both Munich and Barcelona. The thrilling 3–3 draw in the Nou Camp was a vast improvement on United's 4–0 humiliation there four years earlier, and saw the new forward partnership between Andy Cole and Dwight Yorke at its dazzling best. Like all the best striking combinations, the two seemed to operate telepathically, and Cole had benefited from his growing friendship with his more laid-back partner, after years in which he had looked uncomfortable first with Eric Cantona and then with Teddy Sheringham (with whom he wasn't on speaking terms). 'He's a clever boy, Andy, bright,' said Ferguson. 'He looked at how Yorke was, how relaxed, and he thought, this is possible.'[19]

The success of the Yorke–Cole pairing meant there was little room for either Sheringham or Ole Gunnar Solskjaer, and the board were also keen to recoup some of their £28 million summer outlay. Over the summer of 1998 a £5 million deal had been arranged for Solskjaer to join Tottenham Hotspur. On his own admission, Ferguson was prepared to let him go, but the player changed his mind at the last moment and decided he'd prefer to stay at Old Trafford even if it meant sitting on the substitutes' bench. How different history might have been had Solskjaer gone to London instead!

More worrying for Alex Ferguson was the actual departure, in December 1998, of another popular United hero. During the summer, Brian Kidd had rejected an approach to become manager of Everton, for whom he'd once played; but when Blackburn Rovers sacked their latest boss, Roy Hodgson, that autumn Kidd could not resist the offer to replace him. Ferguson says his assistant 'never did explain to me' why he left, though Kidd himself insists it wasn't for more money.[20] Indeed, Ferguson had worked hard during the summer to keep Kidd at United. At the HSBC crisis meeting he had urged Sir Roland Smith and Martin Edwards to improve his assistant's contract to dissuade him from accepting the Everton offer. When the United directors did as he asked, it made Ferguson wonder why he himself never found it quite as easy to get a pay rise.

Ferguson suspected that the Everton approach had stirred Kidd's ambition sufficiently that he then said 'Yes' when Blackburn made their offer. It does seem that Kidd wanted the challenge of managership more than money. He was almost fifty, and had spent most of his career on the backroom staff after short, disappointing spells in charge of Preston and Barrow in his early thirties. 'Me and the gaffer have worked really closely and I've nothing but admiration for him,' Kidd said as he left. 'If I've not learnt from him then there must be something wrong with me.'[21]

As with Archie Knox's departure, Ferguson took it badly, although he mostly disguised it at the time. Indeed, his comments seemed quite generous. 'You can never underestimate people's ambitions,' he said of Kidd, 'and you have to encourage that.'[22]

Ferguson and Kidd had worked as a highly effective partnership for more than seven years. Over that time United had been more successful than in any other period in their history, having collected seven trophies – four championships, two FA Cups and one League Cup. Indeed, there were some who argued that it was only once Brian Kidd had replaced Archie Knox in 1991 that Ferguson really began to excel (and one senior United official even suggested privately in 1998 that the wrong man was leaving). Kidd was adventurous and eager to learn new methods. He would frequently travel to study training techniques at top foreign clubs, and then try out the best of what he'd learned back at The Cliff and Old Trafford.

Gradually Ferguson had given his assistant more and more responsibility for working with the players, and Kidd had developed a
particularly good rapport with those whom he had initially coached
in the Manchester United youth teams in his earlier roles at Old
Trafford.

The players Ferguson had bought were also huge admirers of
Brian Kidd. 'Nobody has ever helped, cajoled and nursed me through
the traumas on the training field more than Brian,' says Andy Cole:

> He was always the ear I could bend, particularly when I felt
> down in the dumps . . . He was comforter, adviser, confidant,
> protector and coach all rolled into one . . . The working
> relationship between Kiddo and the manager was akin to the
> good-cop, bad-cop routine. When the gaffer was losing it,
> Brian would sit down and talk to the players and analyse
> maybe what had gone wrong during the game. If the manager
> was flying off the handle and very angry, the message could
> be a little blurred. Kiddo, subsequently, would take a quiet
> moment to detail exactly what the manager wanted from
> us . . . Kiddo always praised, never carped and when he
> exposed the faults it was always in a positive, objective way.
> He raised my depleted morale no end and Brian was
> exceptionally helpful with all the United players, not just
> me . . . All of us, I don't mind admitting, were heartbroken
> when he left the club. Not one of us expected it to happen. It
> was like a thunderbolt striking the whole dressing room.[23]

The United physiotherapist Dave Fevre, who eventually followed
Kidd to Blackburn, says it felt like a 'bereavement' when Ferguson's
assistant left. 'The place was like a morgue. There were tears from a
few. The players were gutted.'[24]

Once again, Ferguson didn't rush to find a new assistant. For the
first time in years he had to get involved in training, while he asked

the chief scout, Les Kershaw, and the former youth coach Eric Harrison to put out feelers to find the best up-and-coming managerial talent in football. After two months they recommended Steve McClaren, who was deputy to Jim Smith at Derby County. (Their reserve was David Moyes, then manager of Preston, and a Drumchapel graduate.) McClaren was known for being a greater student even than Brian Kidd of foreign methods, a coach who was keen to learn both from other football clubs and from other sports such as American basketball.

McClaren's appointment was 'a masterstroke' says Dave Fevre, who had thought Ferguson would have difficulty finding someone to fill Kidd's shoes so quickly and neatly. 'Steve came in, and within a few weeks had got into that situation where he followed on from what Kiddo had done.'[25]

Rarely can any coach have joined a football club at a more opportune moment. By February 1999 Manchester United were flying – in serious contention in the League, the FA Cup and the European Cup. No United season can have witnessed so many outstanding games as 1998–99. Early in the new year the Reds had won 6–2 at Leicester City, thanks to a hat-trick from Dwight Yorke, and three weeks later they returned to the East Midlands to play bottom-placed Nottingham Forest. The 8–1 scoreline was the biggest away win in their 121-year history, but still more remarkable was the performance of the substitute Ole Gunnar Solskjaer. He came on with just eighteen minutes to go, with the score at 4–1, and established what is thought to be the only occasion in top-class English football of a substitute scoring four goals. Every time the Norwegian touched the ball it seemed to fly into the Forest net. His four successful strikes spanned just 13 minutes and 48 seconds.

But two of United's greatest games that season, including another Solskjaer substitution act, were reserved for the FA Cup. Manchester United did not have an easy cup run in 1999. Over the course of six ties they met all the five other teams who had contested the three previous finals – Middlesbrough, Liverpool, Chelsea, Arsenal and Newcastle United. Alex Ferguson reckons the fourth-round home tie against Liverpool in late January provided the springboard for United's ultimate success that season. The team conceded a third-minute header to Michael Owen, and the score remained 1–0 until two minutes from time. Then Dwight Yorke equalised from a Beckham free kick, leaving United fans feeling relieved to have escaped with a replay at Anfield. But the game wasn't over. Two minutes later a left-foot shot from Solskjaer left Liverpool suddenly trailing and with no time to respond. It was a pattern to be repeated.

The semi-final replay against Arsenal at Villa Park was even more remarkable. David Beckham opened the scoring after seventeen minutes, before Dennis Bergkamp equalised halfway through the second half with a shot which deflected off Jaap Stam. Things looked bleak when Roy Keane was sent off five minutes later for committing a second bookable offence; it was his second dismissal in a Villa Park semi-final replay, and the third time he'd been sent off by the referee David Elleray (a fourth instance followed two years later). It was also the first semi-final in eight attempts where United hadn't gone a goal behind, though they certainly looked under the cosh in injury time, when Arsenal were awarded a penalty for Phil Neville's trip on Ray Parlour. But Peter Schmeichel dived the right way to pull off a brilliant save from Bergkamp and took the tie to extra time.

Those first ninety minutes at Villa Park had contained many of the ingredients of the finest football dramas – England's two best sides; two good goals; a sending off; and a late penalty save. But the match will go down in history for Ryan Giggs's winning strike in the second period of extra time. Intercepting a careless pass from Patrick Vieira in the United half, he ran more than sixty yards and outwitted at least five Arsenal men to shoot above a flailing David Seaman in the opposition goal. Given the circumstances – the FA Cup semi-final replay; his team down to ten men; the second period of extra time; and against United's most dangerous rivals – it has strong claims to be one of the greatest goals of all time.

United had won their tenth FA Cup semi-final in a row. Yet there were still several dramas to come. The Reds had already reached the European Cup semi-finals with a decisive 3–1 aggregate win over Inter Milan, but then faced even more formidable Italian opponents in Juventus. The Turin club, with its glittering midfield of Deschamps, Davids and Zidane, dominated the first forty-five minutes at the first leg in Manchester, but had only a 1–0 lead to show for their superiority. United came back after half-time, and Giggs equalised in the last minute to finish 1–1. The problem was that Juventus had now scored, and history didn't augur well for the foreign leg. United had never won a serious match in Italy; indeed, the Inter Milan game in the previous round was the first time they'd even drawn there. In fact United hadn't beaten any leading European club in an away tie since a remarkable 5–1 win over Benfica in Lisbon in 1966.

Alex Ferguson assured reporters that United would definitely score at least once in Turin, and had thought carefully about the complex implications of the away-goals rule. 'I took this positive attitude with the players, too,' says Ferguson. 'I said in my pre-match talk that if Juventus scored it mattered not, because after drawing 1–1 in the first leg, just one away goal would put the game back in our court.'[26]

Ferguson's optimism seemed misplaced when Juventus went 2–0 up in eleven minutes, and the situation started to look depressingly familiar. Yet the Italians' two goals weren't completely disastrous: if they could level the score, United would now go through on away goals. What followed was one of the most fluent performances in Manchester United history. By half-time United were firmly in the driving seat after goals from Roy Keane and Andy Cole had indeed made it 2–2. Cole's winner, six minutes from time, was a bonus as United achieved their first-ever win in Italy. Alex Ferguson had reached the European Cup final at his eighth attempt. He described it as 'the greatest performance ever produced by a team under my management'.[27] However, the performance did not come without cost: both Roy Keane and Paul Scholes had been booked in Turin and would be suspended for the final.

English teams have an excellent record in the finals of the European competitions, perhaps because they take the domestic knockout cups more seriously than do their foreign rivals, and are therefore used to excelling in the one-off game of a ninety-minute European final (in contrast to earlier rounds, which take place over two legs). By 1999, English teams had won twenty-six times in European finals – twice as often as they'd lost.

But before United faced Bayern Munich in Barcelona there were several items of domestic business to attend to as the Reds' season moved towards an unforgettable eleven days in May. The championship race had produced the tightest finish since 1995. With four games to go, United were winning 2–1 at Liverpool, only for Paul Ince to equalise in front of the Kop in the ninetieth minute. It was a very public revenge on Ferguson for their acrimonious parting in 1995, and also for the United manager's description of Ince, in a recent television documentary, as a 'big-time Charlie'.[28]

When United drew their penultimate match 0–0 at Blackburn it was enough to relegate Brian Kidd's side. The result meant that United had to beat Tottenham at home the following Sunday to be sure of outpacing Arsenal. Spurs caused a fright by taking the lead midway through the first half, but Beckham scored just before half-time, and then Ferguson brought on Cole to replace Teddy Sheringham. It worked. Cole's strike within three minutes of coming on – floating the ball over Ian Walker – proved enough to secure the first pillar of a treble which Alex Ferguson had once suggested was beyond any team's capabilities.

Ferguson was now confident that his side's buoyancy after winning the League would carry United through to the other two trophies, just as losing the League at West Ham in 1995 probably deflated United for the subsequent cup final against Everton. 'I felt that if we could make it as champions then everything else would fall into place.'[29]

The second stage of the treble came against Newcastle United at Wembley a week later. Never before can any manager have knowingly fielded less than his best team in an FA Cup final. But that's the gamble Ferguson took in 1999, having already picked less than full-strength sides in cup-ties in earlier rounds. Denis Irwin was suspended for Wembley, but Ferguson also risked leaving Nicky Butt, Jaap Stam and Dwight Yorke out of his starting eleven, to keep the players fresh for the European final. In Dwight Yorke's case Ferguson knocked on the door of his hotel room at 10 a.m. that morning to deliver the news. The striker was upset, even after his manager assured him he was being kept back as one of the ace cards for Barcelona.

Ferguson was risking defeat at Wembley to ensure United won in Spain. 'Europe had become a personal crusade,' Ferguson later explained. 'I knew I would never be judged a great manager until I won the European Cup, and so I had to make sure we were ready and fresh for the big one in the Nou Camp.'[30]

In the event, Ferguson could probably have won the cup final that year by fielding the Manchester United youth team. Newcastle were a shadow of the side previously managed by Kevin Keegan, and were dispatched with relative ease thanks to an early goal from Teddy Sheringham, three minutes after he came on to replace the injured Roy Keane. Scholes made it 2–0 in the second half. It was all a bit of a stroll: Newcastle's performance was feeble, and nobody doubted that United could have scored more if necessary.

Amid the anticipation of the European Cup final in Barcelona four days later, it was easy to forget that United had just completed their third double in six seasons. Seen from another angle, of the seven English doubles won during the twentieth century, three belonged to Manchester United. No other manager had won two English doubles, let alone three.

Manchester United flew out to Spain on Concorde with a large back-up team which included a nutritionist and the club chef. They stayed in a luxury hotel on a rocky outcrop overlooking the holiday resort of Sitges, just down the coast from Barcelona. But Ferguson was not pleased to find the building crawling with United fans. He lost his temper and shouted at them to give the players some peace. They'd be the first to complain, he cried, if the team lost. 'I regretted I had done it,' he said later. 'I place great importance on supporters, and I was out of order. I later apologised to them.'[31]

Just as when Aberdeen went to Gothenburg for the 1983 Cup-Winners' Cup final, Ferguson was keen, despite his outburst, to make the atmosphere as relaxed as possible. 'The mood was almost like the preparation for a third round Milk Cup tie at some Division Three club,' says Andy Cole. 'We didn't do anything special; a rest in the afternoon, then listening to the gaffer's pre-match talk-in which seems to get longer and longer as the seasons go by.'[32] 'He didn't make a big spectacle about it being this particular game or that particular game,' says Dave Fevre. 'It was just a standard procedure in how he went about it.'[33]

Without Roy Keane and Paul Scholes, Alex Ferguson took another gamble and switched his team round. David Beckham played in the centre of midfield – his preferred place – alongside Nicky Butt. Giggs took Beckham's normal place on the right, and Blomqvist replaced Giggs on the left, in a side which included eight different nationalities. Ferguson tried to encourage his men by telling them that Bayern were not as good as Arsenal, over whom they'd already got the upper hand that season.

As against Liverpool in the FA Cup, they started poorly. After only six minutes the defender Ronny Johnsen gave away a free kick on the edge of the United penalty area when he challenged Carsten Jancker. Mario Basler then worked his shot round both the United wall and an unsighted Peter Schmeichel. Late in the second half the Germans might easily have made it 2–0 or more when they hit the woodwork twice. 'The spark appeared to be missing,' says the defender Jaap Stam. 'We weren't playing well as a team and the chances we normally carve out, seemingly without breaking sweat, simply weren't coming along.'[34] Most observers say Bayern Munich were the superior side for most of the game, though Ferguson disagrees. 'We were much the more convincing team for the bulk of the hour and a half,' he claimed, 'and we were infinitely the more ambitious.'[35]

'Most managers earn their money just in the half-time team talk alone,' Ferguson once remarked, and he certainly did so that night.[36] Rather than berate his team for their mistakes, Ferguson claimed they'd had lots of chances to score in the first half. It wasn't true, but it gave the players hope. Further inspiration had come from an encounter the night before with his former Aberdeen striker Steve Archibald, whom he'd met while the squad were training at the Nou Camp. Archibald, who'd gone to play for Barcelona after his spell with Spurs, said he would never forget the agony, after losing the European Cup final in 1986, of being within a few feet of the trophy at the end of the game, and yet not being allowed to handle it. Archibald recalls Ferguson saying, 'I cannae tell 'em that – it's far too much pressure!'[37] But, when you're losing 1–0 in the European Cup final, risks are required.

'Lads, when you go out there, if you lose you'll have to go up and get your medals,' the manager reportedly said.

> You will be six feet away from the European Cup, but you won't be able to touch it, of course. And I want you to think about the fact that you'll have been so close to it and for many of you that will be the closest you will ever get. And you will hate that thought for the rest of your lives. So just make sure you don't lose. Don't you dare come back in here without giving your all.[38]

441

It was 'one of those inspirational speeches that turn fearful men into world-breakers', says Jaap Stam, 'and the gaffer delivered in some style.'[39] Says Ryan Giggs, 'Just when we really needed it, the thought of having to walk right past the European Cup and not touch it spurred us on.'[40] 'You have got to find a way to affect people's lives through motivation,' Ferguson later explained to the press. 'But you have to have players who can be motivated. Some people can just melt.'[41]

If anything, however, the game turned on Ferguson's substitutions. The Cole–Yorke combination, which had produced fifty-three goals that season, was subdued, and midway through the second half Teddy Sheringham came on for Jesper Blomqvist. With nine minutes left, Ferguson pulled off Andy Cole and sent on Ole Gunnar Solskjaer. But when ninety minutes came up on the clock Bayern were still winning 1–0 as the fourth official indicated that there were three minutes of injury time. It was the cue for the most dramatic finish ever seen in forty-four years of European Cup finals, or that the Continent may ever see.

United won a corner on the left. As David Beckham went to take the kick, Peter Schmeichel galloped up to cause confusion in the German penalty area and he claims to have brushed the ball as Beckham's corner flew over. Half pushed away by a German defender, it came to Giggs, who mishit his shot. But it was tucked inside the post by a grateful Teddy Sheringham.

United fans couldn't believe it. The Reds were back in the game, and looked favourites to win in extra time against a Bayern side that appeared utterly demoralised by the late equaliser. But extra time was not required. Within a minute of the restart United won another corner on the same side. It was headed on by Sheringham to Solskjaer, who volleyed it into the roof of the net. This author swears he detected a moment of silence as people took in what they had just witnessed, as if time froze for an instant. Then came pandemonium.

Just 103 seconds had elapsed between the two goals, including the celebrations after the equaliser. Fifteen seconds after the second restart the referee's whistle proclaimed United as European champions for the first time since 1968. Appropriately, the day would have been Sir Matt Busby's ninetieth birthday.

Peter Schmeichel, the captain in Roy Keane's absence, collected the trophy after his last game for United. The players spent almost an hour on the pitch. After winning their third trophy in less than a fortnight, they entertained the 50,000 United fans with a series of dances and songs. The suspended Roy Keane and Paul Scholes were persuaded to join the festivities, even though they were dressed in suits. The celebrations were orchestrated by David May, who'd manoeuvred himself into the most prominent place in every group picture. The defender had won a European Cup medal as one of the seven substitutes, even though he hadn't played a single game in the competition all season. Nobody seemed to mind. May now persuaded the fans to go silent for each of his colleagues as one by one they improvised different acts holding the trophy.

Manchester United had won the treble of the European Cup and their two main domestic honours. Only three sides in Europe had ever achieved the feat before – Celtic in 1967, Ajax in 1972, and PSV Eindhoven in 1988, and nobody would pretend the Scottish or Dutch leagues were as competitive as the English.

Some said Alex Ferguson had been lucky, and fortune plays a role in most sporting triumphs. They cited the late comebacks against Liverpool and Arsenal, Schmeichel's penalty save from Bergkamp, and the fact that United had suffered few injuries. One might also have added Solskjaer's decision not to join Spurs. On the other hand, the cup draws did United no favours. Quite apart from a succession of tough ties in the FA Cup, it had taken United a record thirteen games, all of them unbeaten, to win in Europe. After emerging from the so-called 'group of death', it was a worthy achievement to dispose of Inter Milan, Juventus and finally Bayern Munich. And key players had been absent from both finals through suspension.

'Football, eh? Bloody hell!' remarked a beaming Ferguson, still reeling from the game's dramatic climax, as he was interviewed live on television in the Nou Camp. 'It's been the greatest night of my life.'[42]

Taking on the World

'What I tend to do is give myself other challenges. One was to learn to play the piano . . . it's good to have a challenge all the time to stretch yourself. I keep saying I'm going to go back to learning languages. I'm going to educate myself again.'

ALEX FERGUSON[1]

As fans gathered for the 1999 FA Cup quarter-final replay at Chelsea, few of them noticed the tall figure standing with his young son, Rory, beneath the seats which had been allocated to the several thousand Manchester United supporters. 'I didn't really want to come tonight,' he said while chatting to this author, 'but Alex specially biked two tickets round to Number 10, so I felt I had to be here.'[2] Alastair Campbell might have been one of the most influential men in Britain, sometimes even described as the real Deputy Prime Minister, but he couldn't disappoint Alex Ferguson.

Campbell was more enthusiastic about the invitation ten weeks later to travel with Ferguson's official party to the European Cup final in Barcelona. Blair's press secretary enjoyed one of the best seats in the Nou Camp, and basked in his friend's greatest moment. And within days of Manchester United winning the European Cup a call came from Number 10 to the manager at his holiday villa in the south of France. It wasn't from Campbell, but from the office of the Downing Street honours secretary. Would Ferguson like to accept a knighthood?

Curiously, Ferguson had doubts about receiving this latest honour, despite having accepted the CBE and the OBE in the past. His wife wasn't keen on the idea of becoming Lady Cathy, and was worried about the extra commitments the title might involve. 'I put it to the family,' Ferguson later revealed, 'and Cathy was a bit "Oh, I don't know, what would your father think?" and my son said, "Mum, it's nothing to do with my Dad's parents; they're gone; they'd be proud of him. You can't refuse this, it's recognition of what he's done." We had a discussion and decided it was right.'[3]

Alex Ferguson was squeezed into the Queen's birthday honours list at the last minute in June 1999. He thereby joined Matt Busby and Bobby Charlton among Manchester United's footballing knights. (Sir Walter Winterbottom, who played for United in the 1930s, was also knighted for his work as England manager.) Ferguson found the title uncomfortable for a while, and refused to sign himself 'Sir Alex' when asked to by a woman autograph-hunter shortly afterwards.

The combination of treble and knighthood was excellent news for Alex Ferguson's publishers, who, with fortuitous timing, planned to bring out the manager's autobiography in the summer of 1999. The publishing world had gasped when Hodder Headline agreed to pay a £1.1 million advance for the book; no one could see how they'd possibly earn it back, even if sales were combined with extensive newspaper serialisation. Ferguson's former publisher, Bill Campbell of the Scottish house Mainstream, had pulled out of the bidding at £650,000. 'I never felt so relieved to lose a book,' he says, having feared that even an advance of that size could have entailed huge losses.[4]

To help write the book, Ferguson had recruited his long-standing journalist chum Hugh McIlvanney. But unlike most football memoirs, and indeed the manager's previous books, which were largely dictated, either to a reporter or on to tape, much of the 458-page

Managing My Life was physically written by Sir Alex himself. The eighteen-month project must have taken extraordinary discipline. Whenever he found spare moments, Ferguson sat down and wrote on a pad in longhand; good opportunities came on European away trips, where there is often time to kill while hanging round in the team hotel before the game. Ferguson's text was then typed up, before McIlvanney polished his words. The project also involved several researchers and fact-checkers, both in Glasgow and in Manchester, and Ferguson and McIlvanney gathered together groups of old Scottish friends to prompt memories of distant parts of his life.

Managing My Life was a spectacular success. Ferguson undertook an extensive signing tour, on which publishers and bookshop managers who'd only seen him on television were surprised both by his great charm and by his willingness to do whatever they asked. At some shops in Manchester and London the demand was so great that customers had to be turned away without a signed copy, though he agreed to return at a later date. Rupert Murdoch's News International group bought the serialisation rights for £650,000, and ran extracts of the book simultaneously at both ends of the market, in *The Times* and the *Sun*. It was later chosen as the 1999 Book of the Year by the publishing trade, and by the start of 2002 it had sold more than 216,000 copies in hardback and over 100,000 in paperback. These phenomenal figures easily repaid the huge advance.

Ferguson's 1999 autobiography was even more candid than his five previous volumes. His pages were crammed with anecdotes and benefited from his striking memory for detail (though, despite the fact-checking, there were plenty of errors too). It was also unusually vituperative for a football book, especially about a number of former associates. The whole tone sat uneasily with his very last sentence: 'Loyalty has been the anchor of my life and it is something that I learned in Govan.'[5]

Several past colleagues might have questioned that sense of loyalty – among them Gordon Strachan, Tony Collins, Alan Hansen,

Jim Leighton and Paul Ince – as might his boss at United, Martin Edwards. Indeed, some of the criticisms in *Managing My Life* were just as strong as the comments by Graeme Hogg and Paul McGrath for which, a decade earlier, Ferguson and United had successfully pressed the FA to bring disrepute charges. But his most surprising attack was on Brian Kidd, his assistant who had left Old Trafford to become manager of Blackburn nine months before, after working with Ferguson for more than a decade.

Ferguson admitted in the book that he was annoyed with himself for having let Kidd exert too much control over the Manchester United squad's training sessions in the mid-1990s, having himself become preoccupied each morning with all the other demands on a football manager's time – calls, meetings, press queries, invitations, letters and endless paperwork. But then Sir Alex proceeded to attack Kidd's reputation. 'I saw Brian Kidd as a complex person, often quite insecure, particularly about his health,' he wrote. 'He also worried about how good he was at coaching, and concerns over whether I still wanted him as my assistant and what would happen to him if I retired were common themes on his regular doubting days.' Ferguson questioned whether Kidd could ever restore Blackburn to the championship glory of 1995, let alone succeed if he returned to become manager at Old Trafford. 'Deep down,' Ferguson said, 'I would have had serious reservations about Brian ever taking charge of United. I suspect that the constant demand for hard, often unpopular, decisions would have put an intolerable strain on his temperament.'[6] This echoes a comment that Ferguson had made to one newspaper at the time of Kidd's departure. His assistant, he said, used to put his arm round players and tell them they were wonderful. 'And they all believed him. Me? I was the one who told them they were dropped.'[7]

Ferguson's comments about Kidd in his autobiography weren't all negative, of course, but even some of the positive points he made were backhanded. He suggested again, for example, that Kidd had the ability to make himself all things to all players. 'His forte was training players and with us he revealed a gift for getting close to them. Each individual in the squad came to feel that Kiddo wanted him in the team.'[8]

These 1999 remarks about Brian Kidd were in complete contrast to many of the things that Ferguson had said about his assistant in the past. On the team coach after winning the double at the 1994 cup final, for instance, a jubilant Ferguson said Kidd had done 'fantastically well', and added that 'the other great thing is he is loyal to me', before plonking a kiss on his assistant's cheek.[9] On several occasions Ferguson himself had suggested that Kidd should take over when he eventually retired from Manchester United. 'If my opinion counts for anything, I recommend Brian as my successor,' he remarked in 1995. 'As far as I'm concerned, he's got it if he wants it. He has done a terrific job for this club and I want him to have a big say in its future.'[10] Another time he said, 'Brian Kidd is instrumental to the future of the club and . . . if he wants to be the manager he has every right to expect it.'[11]

Ferguson seemed to have misjudged the sentiments of many United fans, among whom Brian Kidd had always been popular. Had the book not been published in the aftermath of the 1999 treble, when to most supporters he could do no wrong, the United manager might have suffered more of a backlash. He quickly attempted to explain what lay behind his comments: 'I was trying to show how vulnerable I felt last summer and I tried to relay the facts as they happened,' he said. 'It was a period when I felt vulnerable and isolated. People who have been managers will understand that. It's not the easiest position to be in.'[12] It is a sign of the surprising unease Ferguson has about working on his own that he should also have used the same word – 'vulnerable' – at the time of Archie Knox's sudden departure in 1991.

Many people in football were shocked at how far Ferguson had gone in disparaging his former deputy. Fellow manager David

O'Leary, who now employs Kidd at Leeds United, says, 'The vitriolic tone of Alex's comments stunned many people at Old Trafford as well as managers and coaches elsewhere.'[13] Howard Kendall, normally an admirer of Ferguson, asks, 'Why did he do it? He didn't need to do it, didn't need to say it, and I think this was the general opinion within the game. That was disappointing. But that doesn't alter my thoughts of him.'[14] Some suggested that Ferguson had been trying to spice up his book to make it more attractive for newspaper serialisation.

Brian Kidd got advance notice of Ferguson's remarks from a journalist friend. Despite the obvious temptation to respond, and lucrative offers from newspapers, he has never done so point by point, though he gave a quick if pained reaction at the time. 'Walt Disney is trying to buy the film rights to this book as a sequel to *Fantasia*,' he suggested:

> If you work for a person for more than ten years, you get
> to know a lot about them. I've chosen to respect that
> relationship. Clearly Alex Ferguson has not. But I'm not
> going down the road of who said this and who did that – it's
> laughable. I've more important things to do. I have a job to
> finish here and I can't be bothered. I mean, what do you tell
> your kids? I'm struggling for words about this.[15]

Kidd's friends confirm that he was deeply wounded by Ferguson's remarks. 'Kiddo was absolutely devastated,' says the physiotherapist Dave Fevre, who had followed him from Old Trafford to Ewood Park. 'He felt that it had tarnished his time at the club, soured things, and all due to one man who had to get nasty.' In particular, Brian Kidd believes that Ferguson's comments, much publicised in the summer of 1999, undermined his standing with Blackburn's owner, Jack Walker, and contributed to his sacking only three months later, after less than a year as manager at the Lancashire club. 'Kiddo thinks that it sowed the seed of doubt in Jack's mind,' says Dave

Fevre. 'I mean, if you're Jack Walker, the club's going through a rough patch and you read that Alex Ferguson doesn't think Brian Kidd is right for management, you're going to wonder, aren't you?'[16]

Ferguson's hostility towards Kidd seems to have gone beyond the animosity he'd shown towards other departed assistants. He felt that they had betrayed him only by leaving, but concluded that Kidd had been disloyal to him while he was still at Old Trafford, moaning about his decisions to Martin Edwards and other senior staff at the club. He clearly felt that Kidd had forged something of an alliance with Edwards, at a time when he himself had come to regard his chief executive with contempt. This had first shown itself when Edwards and Kidd tried to persuade Ferguson not to sell Paul Ince in 1995. They also shared doubts about buying Dwight Yorke three years later: Kidd, according to Ferguson, had even suggested to Martin Edwards that United should go for the West Ham (and later Celtic) striker John Hartson instead. And Ferguson says that Kidd had grumbled to colleagues at Old Trafford about the failures of the 1997–98 season, when Arsenal won the double.

It might be tempting to dismiss Ferguson's comments about Kidd as paranoia, and typical of a great sense of betrayal he often feels about assistants who suddenly leave his side. But sources at Old Trafford confirm that during his final years at the club, Kidd often grumbled that he 'had to do all the work', and that behind Ferguson's back he was not always totally supportive of his boss.

The two men also had heated disagreements over politics. Brian Kidd makes no secret of being a Conservative, and was never frightened to argue with his socialist boss in front of their colleagues. 'They used to have some right rows,' says one former United insider. 'They often got very heated, because both thought their views were the right ones. But Kiddo would stand his ground. He has a very sharp temper too – it's not just Alex. Kiddo's a really calm guy most of the time, but when he loses his rag everyone knows about it. He can erupt and really give it.'

However, the physiotherapist Dave Fevre, who says he's still a friend of Sir Alex, suspects that, deep down, Ferguson was jealous of his former assistant's crucial role in grooming the great Manchester United youth team of 1992:

> Alex knows that it was Kiddo who really has played the massive part in the lads' development, and that bothers him. It was Brian that made Giggsy and Scholesy and the like into superstars, not Alex. And people at the club know that. I think Alex thought Brian was getting too much credit from the players, so he thought he'd blacken his role at the club and put a stop to it all. Remember, Kiddo was a United legend as a player too, whereas Alex wasn't even a top player; that could have added to things. The other thing is how popular Kiddo was, and is, with the players – he's far more liked than Alex. I think that is a cause of jealousy too.[17]

Yet, bizarrely, early in 2000, just six months after *Managing My Life* was published, Ferguson briefly considered bringing Brian Kidd back to Old Trafford to work on the youth programme. Kidd was even approached, but Ferguson had second thoughts, and concluded it wasn't a 'feasible proposition'.[18] Instead, Kidd became head coach at Leeds United. His manager, David O'Leary, says there was an 'embarrassing moment' when Ferguson visited the Leeds coaches' room for a drink after United played at Elland Road in 2001. 'You could have cut the atmosphere with a knife,' O'Leary says. The former partners didn't exchange a word, it seems. 'Brian quickly changed while Alex just kept talking, and never blinked an eye as Brian walked by. I just thought it was a sad way for two men to behave after all they had shared at Old Trafford.'[19] 'It is a very sad tale,' agrees Dave Fevre. 'They achieved so much together, and now there's no relationship between them at all.'[20]

The biggest revelation in Alex Ferguson's autobiography, made for

20. The Ferguson clan as Alex collects his OBE in 1984. He was awarded the CBE in 1995 and a knighthood in 1999. Some predict the United manager will eventually secure the first football peerage.

35. Keeping his eye on Tony Blair, 1996. Ferguson has supported New Labour publicly and financially, and is very close to Blair's press secretary Alastair Campbell.

36. The other side of 'The Boss', with his full zest for life, seen with the chef Kenneth Hom. Ferguson loves cooking; he trained as a chef and once hoped to open his own restaurant.

the first time, was the extraordinary story of the £40,000 handed over by Andrei Kanchelskis's agent in 1994. The tale was immediately picked up by the press, and naturally prompted the question of why Ferguson and Manchester United hadn't reported the attempted gift to the football authorities at the time it was made, especially when an inquiry was specifically looking into 'bungs' and Kanchelskis in particular. The inquiry's former chairman, Robert Reid, expressed surprise at what Ferguson had written, saying he would have 'liked to have known' about the £40,000.[21]

It was too late to ask Reid to re-examine the matter, since his inquiry had concluded its investigation in 1997, after four years' work, and he himself was now a judge. Instead, the FA asked its compliance officer, Graham Bean, to investigate the story. Bean questioned Ferguson, the United solicitor, Maurice Watkins, and other club officials, and quickly concluded that the manager himself had behaved properly in reporting the 'gift' to his employers. Manchester United's behaviour, however, was another matter, and Bean never got an adequate explanation of why the club had never reported the incident to the authorities. But the episode was quietly forgotten. 'Everyone was scared of United,' says a source at the FA Premier League. 'The feeling was, and still is, that Fergie and United should have had the book thrown at them. It was a complete breaking of the rules not to report the thing in the first place.' The reason why the matter was never pursued was simple: during the latter part of 1999 the FA needed co-operation from United and Alex Ferguson over a more important matter.

The world football body, FIFA, was planning a club equivalent of the World Cup. The new World Club Championship, due to be played in Brazil in January 2000, was to involve the top teams from each continent. Manchester United were invited as holders of the European Cup, but the competition would mean being away from domestic commitments for almost two weeks. Nonetheless, the Football Association was keen for United to play in the tournament, and feared that a refusal would reflect badly on English football and undermine the FA's bid to stage the World Cup in England in 2006. Worse, if United didn't go, their place in Brazil would almost certainly be offered to their defeated opponents in the 1999 European Cup final, Bayern Munich, which would boost Germany's rival World Cup bid. In the circumstances, the English authorities were hardly likely to reprimand United over the Kanchelskis gift. 'United got off because the FA didn't want it pushed due to the whole Brazil thing,' says one senior source at the Football Association. 'The FA put pressure on United to go to Brazil, so they could hardly turn round and say, "By the way, we're going to do you on that Russian agent business."'

The World Club Championship in Brazil would embroil Ferguson in his biggest controversy since Eric Cantona's assault on a Crystal Palace fan in 1995. The FA and United concluded that, to take two weeks out of the domestic season to go to Brazil, the club would have to withdraw from that season's FA Cup, since the fourth round was due to be played while they were away. It would be the first time in the competition's 127-year history that the holders hadn't defended the trophy. The concern was fixture congestion. The European Cup had been expanded that year to include an additional group stage of six matches, and, as the European champions, United already also faced extra games in the coming season in both the European Super Cup and the Inter-Continental Cup (which, confusingly, had also been called the World Club Championship in the past).

Manchester United were placed in a difficult position. There was talk of the club being given a bye to a later round of the FA Cup, or being allowed to field a youth team, but neither was satisfactory. Yet United accepted the Football Association's suggestion of withdrawing from the FA Cup a little too quickly. With a bit of imagination, the fixture list could have been juggled to accommodate their trip to South America. And, historically, the FA Cup was used to coping with fixture congestion. In the severe winter of 1963, for instance, United didn't play their first cup-tie until March, yet still triumphed at Wembley in May.

The United manager was torn. Ferguson the football romantic naturally felt it was a huge pity not to defend the world's most famous knockout trophy. On the other hand, Ferguson the ambitious pioneer liked the idea that Manchester United might be recognised as world champions; and, just as in the 1950s Matt Busby had led the way with English participation in the European Cup, Sir Alex also fancied the idea of helping to develop an exciting new competition. As a result, Manchester United and Alex Ferguson will for ever be accused of helping to undermine the prestige of the FA Cup by not participating in 1999–2000. In fact, however, the competition was already losing its gloss, because of the way the FA had tinkered with so many of its traditional features in the 1990s. Ferguson insists that the 'notion that I would willingly belittle the competition is crazy' and that it hurts him to see the Cup in decline.[22] Any criticism of Ferguson over his treatment of the FA Cup should be not about the events of 1999–2000 but about the way in which, contrary to his claim, he has regarded it as the third-choice contest, way behind the League and the European Cup. For several seasons he has routinely fielded weakened teams in the competition. While he has never done this on the scale of his youthful line-ups in the League Cup, nonetheless since 1997 Ferguson has rarely picked United's strongest possible side in the FA Cup – even in 1999, when he was pitted against teams of the calibre of Chelsea and Arsenal. When players sense that their manager is not taking a tournament as seriously as other competitions, it inevitably undermines their determination to win. In 1997 and 1998, and again in 2001 and 2002, United were knocked out by mediocre Premier League sides which Ferguson's men easily defeated in the corresponding league fixture that year (successively Wimbledon, Barnsley, West Ham and Middlesbrough).

Alex Ferguson and other members of senior management at Old Trafford felt aggrieved at how United were left to take the flak, even though they'd withdrawn from the Cup only after both the FA and government ministers had insisted on the importance of the Brazil tournament. The *Mirror* in particular mounted a huge campaign against the decision. At one point Ferguson was so angry with ministers criticising United for pulling out of the Cup – in complete contrast to their private pressure to play in Brazil – that he rang Downing Street early one morning and managed to speak directly to Tony Blair. Kate Hoey, who'd just become sports minister in succession to Tony Banks, later said that Alastair Campbell had warned her on her very first day, 'Don't say anything to the press about Manchester United pulling out of the FA Cup to play in Brazil . . . Alex is angry about the *Mirror* campaign and we don't want to rock the boat.'[23]

It's doubtful whether more than a handful of Cabinet ministers could have rung Number 10 early in the day and got through to the Prime Minister – Gordon Brown, Jack Straw, David Blunkett, Robin Cook and Lord Irvine perhaps, but lesser members of the Cabinet might have had trouble. Yet Alex Ferguson's swift knighthood in the aftermath of Barcelona had been the culmination of an increasingly cosy relationship between the United boss and New Labour. He'd contributed supporting messages to Labour campaign documents before the 1997 election, and had donated at least £5,000 to party funds. Ferguson was filmed kicking a ball about with Tony Blair, and the Labour leader visited the Manchester United dressing room after the team won 1–0 at St James's Park in December 1997. In the run-up to Labour's election victory, Ferguson was also consulted by Alastair Campbell about how the party's front-benchers and key organisers should keep themselves physically and mentally fit during the punishing twenty-hour days of the election campaign. Staff at the Labour headquarters in Millbank have Alex Ferguson to thank for the ban on alcohol during the six-week battle. Ferguson also advised Labour organisers not to think that they should work all the time, but to 'Switch off. Take a break. Nip home to see the family' – though it's not advice that Blair's team seemed to heed that much, nor Ferguson himself.[24]

Alex Ferguson's closest Labour ties were always with Campbell, to whom he had originally been introduced by his late friend Jim Rodger, a former colleague of Campbell's on the *Daily Mirror*. During the 1997 election, when United were battling to win the League and the European Cup, Ferguson would frequently pick up his mobile phone, ring Campbell on the campaign trail, and offer further titbits of advice. 'Never forget, that you are inside a bubble and you have to lift yourself out of it,' he told him, advising the Labour team to put themselves in the minds of ordinary voters. 'Remember that the journalists and politicians inside the bubble are not thinking in the same way as the people outside it.' Another suggestion was to cut down on unnecessary thought: 'Don't allow anything inside your head that you don't need to be there.'[25]

Alastair Campbell is a dedicated supporter of Burnley, and still manages to go to many of the club's games despite his schedule in Downing Street. He has tried to bring up his two sons to support the team as well, only to have the older boy, Rory, defect to Manchester United, in spite of acting as the Burnley mascot when he was five. Rory Campbell's conversion came when Ferguson gave the family a personal tour of Old Trafford. Alastair Campbell may be a master of public persuasion, but he admits that the United manager 'indoctrinated' his boy 'rather more powerfully than I have'.[26]

Campbell and his son Rory can often be seen tucked amid the away fans when Manchester United play in London. The tickets come courtesy of Alex Ferguson, and Campbell is usually keener to use them than he was that night at Stamford Bridge. Before kick-off and at half-time, Campbell will have his ear glued to his mobile phone, keeping up with political developments.

It's often been observed that Alastair Campbell likes to befriend older men, who become influential father figures. In his early career as a journalist it was the newspaper owner Robert Maxwell who filled that role; later it was the then Labour leader Neil Kinnock, before Alex Ferguson, who is fifteen years Campbell's senior, became the latest paternal influence in his life.

At times – especially around the 1996–97 period, but often since then – Ferguson and Campbell have been known to speak to each other on the phone several times a week. 'Alastair is always a very good source about what is happening at United,' says one senior Labour figure. 'He's now a United fan as well, though he doesn't admit it. He likes to know everything that is going on.'

Politically, Alex Ferguson's commitment to the Labour Party has to do more with his family background and the traditions in which he was brought up than with a fervent ideology. 'I was born a Labour man and I'll always be a Labour man,' he once said, and has told friends he could never insult his father by voting Conservative.[27]

Despite his faux pas with Jock Stein when he failed to notice striking miners collecting money outside a football ground, he was a strong supporter of the National Union of Mineworkers during the great 1984–85 coal strike. One night during the 1984 European Championship, he and fellow managers David Pleat and Jim Smith had a heated argument in Marseilles about the merits of the dispute. 'They were right, you know, but they were badly led,' Ferguson said of the striking miners seven years later. 'You look at their forecast of what the Coal Board planned to do to the industry and see what happened after the strike; it was worse than they expected. They were more than justified in trying to protect their communities.'[28] In 1991 he gave his support to miners who were trying to keep open Parkside colliery in Lancashire. Yet, despite his own past union activity, Ferguson clearly feels the trade unions became too strong at one point. 'I was always very big for the unions,' he told Labour Party members in 1996. 'I completely understand the reasons why they became so powerful, but they reached that height and they were bound to fall.'[29]

Like Alastair Campbell's, Ferguson's socialism is pragmatic: like a committed football fan, his prime concern is to see his team win, worrying about the niceties of their performance only later. But pragmatism goes only so far. Unlike Tony Blair, but in common with many Scots, he displays a passionate dislike of Margaret Thatcher. 'Don't associate me with that woman,' he snarled when a journalist pointed out that they shared an ability to survive on only five hours' sleep.[30]

On the other hand, Ferguson has no qualms about giving significant financial support to Manchester Grammar School (MGS), even though it is a private school. The United director Maurice Watkins, who chairs the MGS bursary appeal, persuaded Ferguson to play an active role in drumming up funds even though Sir Alex has no personal links with the school and his own sons were educated within the state system. Appeal money is used to enable parents from poorer families to afford the school's annual fees of almost £5,700, and Ferguson has clearly been impressed by the quality of education at MGS. He has gone to the trouble of entertaining potential appeal donors on match days at Old Trafford, and his name is listed in the panelled MGS entrance hall as a substantial donor himself, alongside distinguished old boys such as the former England cricket captain Mike Atherton and the National Theatre director Nicholas Hytner. The school won't say how much money Ferguson has given, but the qualifying donation for the roll of honour is at least £25,000. 'There's nothing in this activity for Alex Ferguson at all,' says the school's high master, Martin Stephen. 'He has never baulked at a request to help. He's able to tell people, "I've given it some of my own money." His involvement in this is completely selfless. He's one of several left-wing figures whom we've been able to persuade. I owe him a lot.'[31] Although the Labour Party is no longer as hostile to private education as it once was, most socialists believe such schools harm the state system by creaming off the best pupils and teachers, and many would be delighted see places such as MGS closed down.

Despite his regular contact with Alastair Campbell, one of Britain's most skilled spin doctors, Ferguson and United failed to prevent the club's trip to Brazil in January 2000 turning into a public-relations shambles. By the time they flew off to Rio, so many journalists were hostile to the club's involvement that the team was certain to get a bad press. United came under fire for not doing more with the locals in Rio; Martin Edwards was exposed for picking up a prostitute in a seedy disco; and Ferguson was criticised for not holding enough press conferences, though he claimed there was no one to organise them.

It was worse on the pitch. First United had to cope with the temperature. After playing in freezing conditions at Sunderland nine days before, they faced almost 100 degrees in the famous Maracanã stadium, where United lost the toss for the first two games and their opponents began defending at the shady end of the ground. The Reds suffered from serious lapses by the players. David Beckham was sent off for a foul in the first game, against Necaxa of Mexico; Dwight Yorke missed a penalty, and the match ended in a disappointing 1–1 draw. With Beckham suspended, they then lost 3–1 to the Brazilian side Vasco da Gama, who were playing on their home ground. Two uncharacteristic errors in central defence by Gary Neville allowed Romario to score twice in the space of three minutes. Out of eight teams, United didn't even qualify for the third- and fourth-place play-off.

David Beckham's dismissal earned huge headlines back in England. It was cited as another example of the player's petulance and uncontrollable temper, though in fact it was only the second time he had ever been sent off. It was unfortunate for the player that the other occasion was on an even bigger stage: for England against Argentina in the 1998 World Cup in France. Then Alex Ferguson had reassured Beckham of United's support, when much of England seemed willing to lynch the player for supposedly wrecking the national side's chances.

Privately, however, Ferguson was growing increasingly concerned about the influence of Beckham's wife, the Spice Girl Victoria Adams. After their wedding in the summer of 1999 the couple spent much of their time at their Hertfordshire mansion, and it was widely reported that 'Posh' would prefer her husband to play for a London side. Ferguson had long been worried about the travelling Beckham was doing between Hertfordshire and Manchester. The player would often get up at 6 a.m. to be driven 160 miles to The Cliff for training.

Not long after Brazil, in February 2000, Ferguson finally lost his patience with Beckham when the player missed training on the grounds that his son, Brooklyn, was ill with gastroenteritis. The manager would have been more sympathetic had Victoria Beckham not attended a London Fashion Week event that night. United's next match was potentially the biggest fixture of the season – away to Leeds United, their nearest challengers in the championship race. Nonetheless, Ferguson fined Beckham two weeks' wages – £50,000 – and dropped him against Leeds. According to Beckham's wife, an enraged Ferguson questioned the player's commitment, warned him that nobody was bigger than the club, and even said he wanted the England star to leave United.[32]

A few months later Ferguson broke his own rule about not criticising his players in public with the publication of the updated paperback edition of *Managing My Life*. Beckham hadn't been 'fair to his team-mates' said Ferguson about the Brooklyn incident:

> I had to imagine how they would feel if David could adjust
> the schedule to suit himself. There was no way I could
> consider Beckham in the team to meet Leeds. That much was
> crystal clear in my mind before David worsened the problems
> between us when we met up on the Saturday by making me
> lose my temper badly, something I hadn't done for years . . . It

doesn't matter to me how high a player's profile is. If he is in the wrong, he is disciplined. And David was definitely in the wrong.[33]

Beckham had already clashed with Ferguson the previous summer after his wedding to Victoria, when the player got his agent, Tony Stephens, to ask Martin Edwards for two extra days off pre-season training to extend his honeymoon to ten days. Ferguson, who had enjoyed no honeymoon at all when he married Cathy in the middle of the season in 1966, was unsympathetic. Nor can it have helped that the player had gone behind his back and involved two men he disliked – Stephens (who was Alan Shearer's agent) and Edwards. He insisted Beckham had to come in on the first day of pre-season training and couldn't even have the four days off that he'd given the other England players to make up for their time that summer with the national squad. Victoria Beckham says that, when David complained that they couldn't go on honeymoon anywhere in less than a week, Ferguson replied, 'That's your problem, David. I don't give a shit.' She describes the manager's decision as 'vindictive' and 'unforgivable'. She also claimed that the United manager 'has never said more than "Hello" to me in the four years I have known David'.[34]

Beckham was pictured watching the Leeds match from the stand as United won 1–0 thanks to a goal from Andy Cole. But his suspension lasted only one game, and the result effectively confirmed yet another league title, as the Yorkshire club fell further behind. Rival clubs had failed to pick up many points during United's absence in South America, and the trip seemed to rejuvenate the players. By April the question was merely how many pages United could rewrite in the record books, as the club ended the campaign with eleven wins in a row. The ninety-one-point total was the highest ever under the three-points-for-a-win system. If one measured United's haul by the old system of two points for a win, then they'd claimed the highest percentage of points since Preston in the very first league season, 1888–89. The eighteen-point winning margin over Arsenal was also the greatest of all time (even when converted to the old points system). No wonder United fans sang about winning the league in 'second gear'.

It was a different story in the European Cup. United got through the two group stages easily enough, but faced Real Madrid in the quarter-final. A goalless draw in Spain, where the Reds had never beaten a home side, was followed by disaster in Manchester. An uncharacteristic own goal by Roy Keane was followed by two second-half strikes by the Spaniards. Never before had a foreign side been 3–0 ahead at Old Trafford, and although United pulled two back it wasn't enough. Real Madrid went on to claim the trophy for the second time in three seasons.

Nor was there any consolation in the European Super Cup, the annual challenge match between the holders of the two main UEFA trophies, which Alex Ferguson had won with both Aberdeen in 1983 and United in 1991. The game against the Rome club Lazio was played on neutral territory in Monaco at the end of August 1999, but it occurred in the middle of a heavy league timetable, and Ferguson chose not to take it seriously. Once United went a goal down, instead of reinforcing the team he made several substitutions which seemed designed mostly to give players first-team experience rather than to pull the Reds back into the game.

The Inter-Continental Cup match played in Japan against the Argentine club Palmeiras was a very different proposition. No British team had ever won the contest in six attempts stretching back to 1967, when Celtic had been beaten by Racing Club of Argentina. Indeed, Willie Morgan's goal for United against Estudiantes the following year had been the only occasion when an English team had managed even to score in the competition. Ferguson says he treated the game as 'one of the most important tests' he had faced as manager.[35] Palmeiras also took the challenge so seriously that they arrived in Tokyo ten days early to acclimatise. Yet United pulled off the first British victory in the contest, thanks to a first-half goal by Roy Keane. Ferguson regarded it as one of the most satisfying results of his career, in a far more distinguished world contest than the FIFA tournament in Brazil.

Ferguson also acknowledged a superb contribution to the Tokyo game from the Australian goalkeeper Mark Bosnich, who had rejoined United that summer in place of Peter Schmeichel. Yet Bosnich's return was fraught with difficulties. Ferguson had tapped the player while he was still with Aston Villa, but began to have doubts when Bosnich arrived overweight in July, his 'fitness was not what it should be', and was involved in an incident in a nightclub around the same time.[36] There may also have been residual unease about what had happened when the Australian was forced to leave Old Trafford in 1991 because he couldn't get a work permit. Aston Villa lured him back to England in 1992 when their manager, Ron Atkinson, came up with the bright idea that he marry a British girl. When United complained that this was poaching, the FA fined Villa £35,000. It must have been satisfying for Ferguson to get the player back from Villa, and the 1995 Bosman European court ruling meant that no fee was required, because his contract had expired. The real cost, however, was the 'keeper's high wages, and there was also a lingering question about Bosnich's commitment to United, since he had seemed quite happy to go to Villa in 1992, instead of returning to Old Trafford.

Early in the 1999–2000 season Ferguson bought another keeper, Massimo Taibi, from the Italian club Venezia, but Ferguson found him even more unsatisfactory. After a good first appearance at Anfield, Taibi suffered the indignity of letting a gentle shot run between his legs against Southampton. In the next match, at Chelsea, he came out for a cross in the opening minute, but failed to make contact with the ball at all and allowed Gus Poyet to score as Chelsea began a 5–0 rout. Taibi's career at Old Trafford lasted just four matches, in which he let in eleven goals, earning the cruel description 'the blind Venetian'.

Manchester United seemed in 1999–2000 to have returned to a problem familiar from the 1990s: they could win their domestic league with relative ease, but it was hard to make the same impact in Europe. Some people wondered whether United's failures on the Continent were because the competition at home seemed so feeble. It was noted that the one recent season in which they'd been driven to the wire to win the title, by Arsenal in 1999, was also the year they won the European Cup.

As United collected the league title with four games to spare, Ferguson sought reinforcements for Europe by agreeing to buy a prolific twenty-four-year-old Dutch striker, Ruud van Nistelrooy. He had originally been recommended by Darren Ferguson, while the manager's son was on a loan spell in Holland in 1999. 'Dad, you've got to sign this fellow,' Darren reportedly said. 'He's fantastic.'[37] United had quickly watched him, but PSV Eindhoven got there first, paying just £4.2 million.

Now United and PSV had agreed a £19 million transfer fee, but Ferguson was furious when the Dutch club announced the deal before United had ironed out the details. Worse was to come: the deal was delayed, and the press conference at Old Trafford cancelled, when van Nistelrooy was found to have medical problems, and photographers were left snapping pictures of his empty chair. Then a few days later the striker collapsed in training back in Holland, suffering serious problems with his cruciate ligament. These meant he would be out of football for about a year.

What followed showed both the persistent and caring side of Alex Ferguson and the way in which the United manager was happy to bend the rules when it suited him. Ferguson rang the player from Spain, where he was taking a short break, to offer his sympathy; then, about ten days after van Nistelrooy had been injured, the United manager flew to Holland and turned up unexpectedly at the striker's flat. Ferguson had come to give him reassurance, and cited several examples of players who had come back from similar injuries in the past, including Roy Keane and the Bayern defender Lothar Matthäus. Later that summer Ferguson even offered to let van Nistelrooy come and train at United when he was fit enough to do so. In similar circumstances many managers would have given up on the player, left it to PSV to sort out his injury, and waited to see if he got better. Remaining in touch proved to be a typical Ferguson master stroke.

Yet the United boss had gone to see van Nistelrooy behind the back of the player's club, PSV. In effect, this again amounted to Ferguson tapping, and PSV were understandably angry. 'Ferguson should be ashamed of himself,' said the Dutch club's president, Harry van Raaij:

> He has overstepped all the bounds of good manners. He must really think he is the king of football. I am as angry as hell and I'm looking thoroughly into this matter . . . Ruud is under contract to us. We have paid for the operation, we are continuing to pay his salary and we are also funding his personal rehabilitation, which is taking place under the supervision of PSV's own medical staff . . . We have spent a lot of money on his recovery and now someone is disturbing the process.[38]

A year later, in the spring of 2001, when the transfer finally went through, van Raaij went back on the warpath, describing as 'scandalous' Ferguson's invitation to train at United. 'Fergie played it well but not fairly.'[39] But van Nistelrooy himself was exceedingly grateful for Ferguson's encouragement and interest at a time when his dreams of playing for United seemed to have been dashed and he feared he might never play again. 'For him to then turn up on my doorstep after the injury was just amazing. Imagine it, to have such a big club at your door. He showed me such warmth, and he stayed in touch with me throughout my rehabilitation.'[40]

Ruud van Nistelrooy's words are reminiscent of things that former Aberdeen and United youth players have said about the exceptional personal attention which Ferguson used to pay them in their early careers. Yet Ferguson's interest and compassion were selective. He took far less notice if a player was no longer of use to United. By the end of the 1999–2000 season both Massimo Taibi and Mark Bosnich were languishing at Old Trafford with little sympathy from a manager who seemed to have a thing about dealing with goalkeepers. Despite his outstanding game against Palmeiras, and several other good performances, Bosnich's career at Old Trafford never recovered after he lost his place through injury in April 2000. He was clearly a great shot-stopper, but his distribution was poor, especially in comparison with Peter Schmeichel's. At one point a United striker was deputed to teach Bosnich how to kick, but it made no difference.

By the summer of 2000 the Australian's career at Old Trafford looked to be over when Ferguson signed Fabien Barthez, the goalkeeper who'd starred in France's 1998 World Cup team. Suddenly, rather like Jim Leighton ten years earlier, Bosnich found himself at the start of the 2000–01 season not just displaced by Barthez (which on merit was understandable) but also behind Raimond van der Gouw and even the inexperienced teenager Paul Rachubka in the United pecking order. As the first-team squad flew to a prestigious pre-season tournament involving Real Madrid and Bayern Munich in Germany, Bosnich was filmed by TV cameras playing a friendly with the reserves at non-league Chelmsford Town.

Ferguson tried to set up a deal for Bosnich to go on loan to Celtic, but the player declined it, insisting, rather like Leighton ten years before, that he would fight for his place at United. Indeed, he probably consulted Leighton on how to handle Ferguson, as the two keepers had become friends from their days together in Bosnich's first spell at Old Trafford. The Australian's refusal to move left

United paying extremely high wages to an occasional reserve player, yet Bosnich's obstinacy seems to have made Ferguson even less inclined to play him, and he never appeared in the first team again. Eventually, in January 2001, Bosnich joined Chelsea, though he would find first-team opportunities there almost as limited.

Nor would some Manchester United youth players recognise the care that Alex Ferguson displayed towards Ruud van Nistelrooy. By the late 1990s the United youth set-up had become rather less of a family institution than in the days when Brian Kidd was running the show and Ferguson was directly involved. Paul Wheatcroft, who is now in the first-team squad at Bolton Wanderers, used to be a youth player at United. He recalls that in February 2000 United set up a trial game at The Cliff against Halifax for all the youth players they didn't want, and invited scouts from other clubs. However, they failed to tell the players the purpose of the game. The youngsters realised what was happening, and worked out that their United careers were over, only when they spotted dozens of scouts surrounding the pitch. 'It was like a cattle-market,' says Wheatcroft. 'I thought it was disgraceful . . . I am a talented footballer – I don't need to be treated like that. We just felt like pieces of meat, really. Some of the lads were really upset about it and they couldn't perform in the game because they just couldn't take it in . . . It's an unbelievable way of going about things.'[41]

Gone were the days when Alex Ferguson took a close interest in each individual youth player, though he still knew their names and met each lad and his parents as he joined the club. By the time of the millennium Alex Ferguson's lifestyle was significantly different from that of the younger man who'd arrived from Aberdeen in 1986. His commitment to football was still enormous, but it was no longer obsessive. Over the years, Ferguson's growing status, reputation and security had enabled him to become a more rounded person, enjoying his wealth, making new friends, satisfying his intellectual enthusiasm and curiosity by taking up new interests and hobbies.

'He's learned to enjoy the rich tapestry of life,' says the singer Mick Hucknall of Simply Red. 'His intention is to live life to the full.'[42]

Yet nobody can criticise Alex Ferguson's devotion to his work at Manchester United. Having risen at 6 a.m., he still arrives at the United training ground around 7.15, spends half an hour in the gym, then perhaps reads the papers in the canteen over a typical breakfast of tea, cereal and toast. The early morning is also the time for meetings. Journalists who want to interview Ferguson, or other outsiders who need to meet the boss face to face, will often be told to report to the training ground at 8.00 a.m. He still needs only four or five hours' sleep, and often survives on less if United have returned from an evening match at the other end of the country, or flown back overnight from abroad. He'll then make do with an hour or two in bed before clocking in at his usual time.

Several players have remarked on how much Ferguson seems to have mellowed. He still loses his temper occasionally, but the tantrums are much less frequent – the result of being older and more experienced, and of the increased personal security which flows from success. The nervous cough of his early managerial career has disappeared, though an operation to cure it in the early 1990s seemed to make the problem worse. It may have been helped when he later adopted the habit of chewing gum during games, and became well known for getting through several packets as he stood on the touchline.

With his knighthood, Sir Alex Ferguson has now established himself as the senior statesman in British football. When clubs are picking new managers, he is often asked for advice on candidates. The English FA consulted Ferguson when it again needed a new coach in the autumn of 2000, and the Scottish FA likewise asked his advice about the successor to Craig Brown; he was consulted too about the appointment of his former Aberdeen defender Alex McLeish as the new Rangers boss at the end of 2001. Ferguson has also been an active member of the League Managers' Association; he rarely misses one of its committee meetings, often promotes the LMA's work publicly, and argues vehemently against the worsening trend among clubs of ditching their coaches at the slightest drop in form.

Sir Alex has also given backing to the government's efforts to encourage football supporters to get more involved in the running of clubs. He willingly lent his name to Supporters Direct, the body established by the then Culture Secretary, Chris Smith, in 2000 to help fans acquire a direct say. Ferguson has held several long meetings with the leading lights of Supporters Direct, and he gave public backing to their aim of getting football clubs more closely involved with their communities. And Ferguson's Manchester solicitor, Kevin Jaquiss, has given Supporters Direct considerable legal advice, helping to devise the model trust structure which the organisation recommends fans should adopt to obtain and pool shares in their teams. Sir Alex welcomed 'the creation of supporter–shareholder groups who are demanding a say in their clubs. Quite right,' he said. 'Why should the future of their club lie solely in the hands of financial institutions in the City of London?'[43] And publicly he encouraged Manchester United supporters to 'get involved' in the Old Trafford group, Shareholders United (of which this author was a vice-chairman from 1999 to 2001).[44]

But the biggest change in his lifestyle was the way in which Ferguson began to explore new worlds beyond football. In 1995 he took up playing the piano after meeting a Canadian cousin who had learned to play late in life, and Cathy gave him a piano for Christmas. He read more – biographies in particular. He was fascinated by the assassination of President Kennedy, and also loved reading about the late American oil tycoon Armand Hammer. 'You can't talk about drive, ambition and achievement without talking about this guy,' said Ferguson. 'He built himself up from nothing. He had drive, perseverance and foresight, all good qualities in my business.'[45] Ferguson might also have added that Hammer was ruthless.

He began collecting clarets, increasingly enjoyed going to the best restaurants in London and Manchester with friends, and also spent more time preparing meals in the kitchen at home. His love of food and drink led to an involvement in an Internet venture, toptable.co.uk. The chef Gary Rhodes, a United fan, was also involved in this restaurant booking service, which had originally been suggested by one of Ferguson's sons. Unlike many Internet businesses, toptable.co.uk continues to develop.

Ferguson also went out of his way to re-establish relationships with friends from his boyhood, some of whom he had not spoken to for twenty or thirty years. And he has enjoyed making completely new friends, particularly with people who have been successful outside football, such as Alastair Campbell, Mick Hucknall, the racing trainer Charlie Brooks and former Marks & Spencer chairman Sir Richard Greenbury. 'Alex has a wonderful sense of humour and he's a man who is interesting to talk to about a whole range of things,' says Greenbury. 'We talk about everything, from politics to history, you name it. Now that's a side of him that people don't see.'[46] Away from football, people encounter a very different Alex Ferguson from the public persona. Complete strangers are often astonished by how charming he can be, and he will often treat someone he has just met for the first time as if they have been lifelong friends. When he's relaxed and able to forget the pressures of his job, Alex Ferguson seems an incredibly happy person.

It does not seem to matter that some of his friends, including Campbell, Hucknall and Brooks, are far younger than Ferguson. He is fascinated by the parallels between their various professions – the similarities between football management and politics, or running a soccer team and a successful band, or between assessing footballers and judging good horses.

Ferguson and Alastair Campbell have much in common. Neither is afraid to provoke public rows to get what they want. They have clearly spent much time comparing tactics when it comes to

handling the media, and both are well known for bullying journalists and for being cavalier with the truth when it suits their purposes.
Campbell agrees that the two jobs have similarities:

> Reporters are always asking him about David Beckham and
> the latest saga involving Beckham's wife, Victoria, and the
> Spice Girls . . . So you have this feeling the media are having
> a kick at us the whole time and our job is to see them off . . .
> One of the things that Alex Ferguson and I talk about – and
> we do talk quite regularly – is the whole business about
> dealing with different pressures . . . how to deal with
> [journalists] when they're trying to get you on to their
> agenda and you're trying to get them on to yours . . . And it's
> difficult, because you've got all sorts of people and papers
> and TV and radio wanting a bit of you, wanting you to be
> focusing on what their interest is, and your job is to keep
> absolutely focused on the main event, the way forward and
> the next game.[47]

Hucknall also sees similarities with his business: 'Musicians, like
football players, have got healthy egos; they demand extra-special
attention. As you're working in a team environment, you've got to
play people off and see how they relate to the whole team.'[48]

Charlie Brooks, the former trainer who is now a journalist, is a
friend Ferguson acquired through a new involvement in racing. He
had always loved a bet, of course, but his enthusiasm was renewed
when he and Cathy were taken to the Cheltenham festival in 1997
as guests of Mike Dillon, the head of public relations at the bookmakers Ladbrokes. All of sudden this opened up a whole new
sporting hobby, and with Dillon's help he started acquiring shares in
several racehorses and teaming up with many of the leading players
in the industry. Ferguson found it particularly attractive as an interest as it was something he could pursue with his wife.

The knighted Alex Ferguson had also become even more of a magnet for voluntary organisations and public campaigns which each wanted a little of his time and patronage. For several years he had aided charities such as HAWC (Help Adolescents with Cancer) and Destination Florida (which enables children who have life-threatening diseases, or who are disabled, to take holidays in America). In his native Govan he assisted the football club for which he'd played as a teenager in renovating its premises. Harmony Row committee members were delighted one Sunday morning when Ferguson attended their meeting to offer general fund-raising advice, and were amazed when he immersed himself in the detail of what specific repairs needed doing.

During the spring of 2001 Ferguson also teamed up with the Chancellor of the Exchequer, Gordon Brown, on a trip to Salford to promote a local drugs campaign called Positive Futures. At a subsequent anti-drugs event in Govan, Sir Alex revealed that Brown had asked if he'd think about leading the government's 'war on drugs'. Ferguson said he was too busy, but added that it was the type of challenge he 'would relish' when he retired.[49]

Jason and the Larger Noughts

'Jason is more like my dad, with a short temper.'

DARREN FERGUSON[1]

In the autumn of 2000 the Manchester United accounts department received an invoice for £25,000. It was delivered on behalf of a Manchester-based football agency called L'Attitude, for their work in selling Alex Ferguson's gaffe-prone goalkeeper Massimo Taibi back to Italy. After conceding eleven goals in four games in the autumn of 2000, Taibi had become a great personal embarrassment to Ferguson, and was probably his poorest purchase in twenty-six years of management. L'Attitude were employed once the United manager decided the keeper had no future with the club, and after the player had spent several months back in Italy on loan. In August 2000 the agency arranged for Taibi to join the Italian club Reggiana for £2.5 million – a fee United considered satisfactory given his disastrous and brief career in England, though it was £2 million less than United had paid for the goalkeeper almost exactly a year before.

Such transfers take place almost every day of the year in football, and increasingly in the modern game agents take commission for setting them up – and usually a much more generous cut than the

1 per cent that L'Attitude received in Taibi's case. But officials at Old Trafford seem to have been nervous about paying the agency for this transfer. Nobody disputed that L'Attitude had done the work; it was simply that one of L'Attitude's directors was Jason Ferguson, the manager's son.

It was a curious development. For many years Alex Ferguson regarded football agents as the great pests of his working life – parasites who siphoned money out of the game and were all too ready to feed off his players. His stance was understandable. With large sums of money to be earned from a cut of transfer fees, agents were often disruptive influences who encouraged transfers in pursuit of more money for both players and themselves. (Ferguson regarded Mark Hughes's reluctant move to Barcelona in 1986 as a good example.) 'There is a rat race and the rats are winning,' Ferguson said in 1989. 'I don't understand why the top players want agents. In transfer discussions you are not going to offer a top player a pittance. So why does he have to be involved with extra people?'[2]

In fact for Ferguson the problems were about power as much as money. The manager knew that agents interfered in the tight control he generally exercised over his players. If a United player had no agent, Ferguson could expect to be the overwhelming influence and authority in his life; with an agent, young players had an alternative source of advice.

'There is so much intrigue when dealing with agents,' he wrote in 1994, 'that's why you try to avoid having any contact with them.'[3] When the Bosman ruling the following year allowed footballers to move at the end of their contracts without any transfer fee, the clubs saw further difficulties whereas the agents saw more business. Ferguson was asked at the time to name the biggest problem in football:

I would have to say agents. I don't think they've done the sport any good at all; I think the PFA and the clubs can look after the players perfectly well. I'm not saying that all agents are bad, but I can't see what good most of them do. It is better for players to get the PFA to represent them. That way, they are keeping the money spent on them within the game . . . Since Jean-Marc Bosman's successful court case I have been receiving letters every day from people who want to 'take care' of our players. They've all seen the gravy train arriving and they all want to jump on.[4]

In the early 1990s nobody could have predicted that one day Alex Ferguson would eventually help his own son Jason jump on to that gravy train. 'In the past,' says Mike Williams, an agent who has worked for Jaap Stam, 'if I approached a young United player there would have been a problem with Ferguson. He was very protective of his young players, and of agents he used to say, "Don't trust them."'[5]

Yet around 1995 Ferguson did allow one agent, an attractive former model called Wendy Bracken, to represent his young players in commercial deals. Among the boot contracts Bracken negotiated for 20 per cent commission were Nicky Butt's deal with Diadora and David Beckham's with Cica. 'She suddenly burst on to the scene,' says one Diadora employee, 'and introduced herself as the person Alex Ferguson wants to represent the players.' Then suddenly, after about six months, Bracken disappeared.

Despite Ferguson's general distaste for agents, Ted Beckham was anxious for his son David to acquire an agent, and indeed the flamboyant Eric Hall says he once took a call from Beckham senior, but then, to his eternal regret, lost his number. Instead, in a meeting at Manchester airport one evening in August 1996, David Beckham signed a contract to be represented by Alan Shearer's agent, Tony Stephens.

Later that evening Stephens drove round to Ferguson's home, which is nearby, walked up to his front door and told the United manager about the agreement face to face. Stephens insists the encounter was 'amicable' but it is hard to believe that Ferguson would have welcomed an unexpected and highly unorthodox home visit from a member of his least favourite profession, especially since he had already made it clear that he felt Beckham did not need an agent. Several others who know both men say the meeting was very acrimonious. Says one source: 'Fergie went mental, he was raging . . . He started effing and blinding and chased him down the drive. Fergie was giving it, "How dare you come to my fucking house. Get the fuck out of here!"'

Stephens admits that Ferguson subsequently told Beckham to leave Stephens, and, according to the alternative account, the manager told Beckham this the very next morning, but the player refused. 'Well, if you don't leave him you can use your fucking agent to transfer you to another club!' Ferguson reportedly shouted. 'OK, going then,' Beckham replied, showing early signs of his stubborn streak.

David Beckham called Ferguson's bluff, it seems, and it worked. It is also said that a week later Ferguson offered Stephens a compromise, whereby the agent would handle Beckham's commercial deals but not his playing contract, but the agent rejected this. Relations between Ferguson and Stephens have never recovered.

Tony Stephens is one of several agents Ferguson personally dislikes. Another is Mel Stein, the lawyer who acted for Paul Gascoigne when the player chose Spurs instead of United in 1988. The fullback John O'Kane, one of the more obscure members of the 1992 Youth Cup team, also defied his manager by signing up with Stein. 'From the moment he picked Mel,' says a friend, 'Fergie's attitude towards him got nastier.'

O'Kane's career at Old Trafford made little progress, and in January 1998 he agreed a £250,000 transfer to join Everton, who were then managed by Howard Kendall. Mel Stein was close to securing wages of £4,000 a week for O'Kane, but suddenly the atmosphere changed. 'Out of the blue,' the friend recalls,

Kendall just went, 'Four grand? No way are we paying that –
Alex Ferguson has just phoned and he says you only got
£1,800 at United. So we ain't going much higher.' John was
livid. It didn't matter to United what he got, and Everton
were very keen and would have paid £4,000 till Fergie called.
Fergie had halved John's wage packet. It was his way of
getting the last word.

Howard Kendall confirms that 'Alex gave me the low-down on the
lad, and then it was my decision what we would offer. Managers do
help each other at times and make calls to give each other tips.'[6]

Over the years, Ferguson grudgingly accepted that some agents
had their uses, though he wasn't always a good judge of which ones.
Quite apart from his admiration for the notorious Norwegian agent
Rune Hauge, he was also impressed by Ambrose Mendy, who negotiated Paul Ince's transfer in 1989, but who later received two jail
sentences for fraud. Despite his dislike of the profession, in 1995
Ferguson asked the Manchester-based agent Paul Stretford to help
his son Darren. The player was having a difficult time at Wolves,
where he was playing in the reserves and had got into trouble after
a drinking spree; he needed a change of club to revive his career.
(Darren later employed the Dutch agent Tom van Dalen to arrange
an eight-month loan from Wolves to Sparta Rotterdam in 1999.)

Perhaps the turning point in Alex Ferguson's stance came in 1997
with the establishment of a new Manchester agency called L'Attitude
Sports Consultancy Ltd. It was founded by two of Ferguson's friends,
Andy Dodd, whom he knew through the singer Mick Hucknall, and
Kieran Toal, a former United youth player, who had subsequently
trained to be a barrister. Ferguson quickly became aware of the company's existence, and some suspect he was keen to help a friendly
agency curb the role of existing operators, whom he thought were
increasingly malign influences.

Dodd and Toal seemed a good combination. Dodd was Mick

Hucknall's manager and had also been successful in property; he brought both financial experience and sufficient capital to develop the new business. He spotted that huge money could be made from football, and 5 or 10 per cent commission on a £10 million transfer could keep the business going for several years. Toal provided a lawyer's respectability and, more important, he had enviable contacts at Manchester United. He knew Alex Ferguson, and was also close to both his twin sons, Darren and Jason, with whom he had played in the United junior sides and had also been on holiday. (On one terrifying trip Toal and Darren were robbed by armed muggers in New Orleans.)

As a child, Jason Ferguson had always been considered the most troublesome of the Ferguson boys. Officials at Aberdeen remember that he would run around the directors' box during matches and pester the catering staff, to the irritation of the club chairman, Dick Donald. Much of Jason's subsequent career has been aided by his father and his father's connections. Despite a few games with the United A and B teams, and a handful later on for Peterhead in the Highland League in Scotland, professional football was never a realistic option for him. Instead he chose one of Alex Ferguson's other least favourite professions – journalism – securing entry to a media-studies course at Lancashire Polytechnic in Preston (now the University of Central Lancashire). At the last moment he turned his place down, having landed a trainee researcher's job in the sports department at Granada Television. Paul Doherty, the ITV station's then head of sport, and a friend of Alex Ferguson, advised the family that Jason would learn more working at Granada than on any academic course. But Doherty says he also warned the Fergusons that, if Jason wasn't up to the job, then he wouldn't be kept on just because of his family connections.

They need not have worried; Jason did well at Granada, and showed many of his father's best qualities – as well as the occasional negative one. He worked on local sports programmes – mostly football – and 'was an asset by his own abilities' says Doherty. 'He recalled incidents, goals, pictures from previous years with a photographic memory. I liked him and his enthusiasm quite a lot. His fiery nature came from family genes, I'm sure. He wasn't calm when I felt he deserved a bollocking.'[7]

Jason's employment at Granada coincided with the great upheavals in Eastern Europe following the collapse of the Berlin Wall. One day Paul Doherty says he came into the main sports office and noticed two great boxes of clothes. When he angrily asked whose they were, he was told they belonged to Jason.

> 'Get them out,' I ordered. 'This is a TV sports production area not an effing market trader's HQ.' Then I found out the truth: they were clothes Jason had been quietly collecting in his own time to send to the dispossessed in Romania. It was my first clue that his social conscience was driving his life in another direction. Pig that I could be, I still made him remove them![8]

Jason was so single-minded about the plight of Romanian orphans that he abandoned his £12,000-a-year job at Granada and set off for Bucharest to help them directly, earning wages of just £150 a week. Cathy and Alex Ferguson had understandable doubts about Jason's move, but were also proud of what he was doing.

On his return Jason took a teacher-training course in Aberdeen, and then Alex Ferguson had a word with Andy Melvin, whom he'd once known as a football reporter on the *Aberdeen Evening Express*, but who was now in charge of live football coverage at BSkyB, the young satellite company which, at great cost, had just acquired the new Premier League's franchise for live football. Melvin agreed to take Jason as a junior producer, but the new recruit rose quickly. He ran Andy Gray's *Bootroom* programme, then trained as a director, and eventually became Sky's senior football director – an astonishingly precocious appointment for someone who was only in his mid-twenties. Yet nobody disputed that he merited the job. Jason was well regarded by his colleagues, and dispassionate when covering United matches. On one famous occasion, spotting his father grimacing at a tense moment, Jason is said to have yelled, 'Get the camera on Fergie, he's looking angry.'[9]

Jason's privileged access to his father sometimes gave Sky an edge. In 1995, for instance, he had knowledge of Andy Cole's transfer from Newcastle four days before it was announced. He couldn't tell his bosses at Sky, but ensured that the broadcaster had the first TV interview with his father when the story broke of what was then the biggest-ever transfer in British football. Alex saw it as reward to his son for keeping the information to himself.

What's clear is that in 1999 Alex Ferguson also played a decisive role in redirecting his son's career, even though Jason was now twenty-seven and quite capable of looking after himself. Again the shop steward, Ferguson agreed with his son that Sky wasn't paying Jason enough and that he should leave the company. Then he helped find him a new job in another business he'd always decried – as a football agent.

One of the first people to hear of Jason's unexpected career move was Paul Stretford, who is based in Wilmslow in Cheshire, not far from the Ferguson family home. Stretford's agency, Proactive Sports, is one of the biggest in the world – a public company which is even quoted on London's Alternative Investment Market. 'Alex had mentioned that Jason was looking to get into this business,' says Stretford, who invited him to come and talk about the possibility of working for Proactive. 'Maybe he thought he could have a higher standard of living as an agent; maybe his father wanted that for his son. But it was a surprise that he was looking to be an agent.' Eventually Jason joined Kieran Toal at L'Attitude instead. 'I think Alex asked L'Attitude to take Jason on,' says Stretford. 'I think he approached them about it, because obviously he knew Dodd and Kieran Toal too.'[10] Initially, in

March 1998, while still working at Sky, Jason had taken a 10 per cent shareholding in L'Attitude, though the shares were in the name of his wife, Tania. In 1999 he joined the company full-time.

Sources close to L'Attitude say that Andy Dodd and Kieran Toal had little choice but to hire Jason, despite knowing he could be difficult and moody to work with. Though their contacts at Manchester United were good, they couldn't afford to jeopardise them by annoying the boss. 'It had been made very difficult for Andy and Kieran to say "No" to the idea of Jason joining L'Attitude,' says a close colleague:

> They didn't really have any choice at all. Dodd and Toal had been operating pretty successfully with United so far anyway, before Jason. They were doing all right. The club was happy with what they were doing. It was put to them by Alex that these relations with United would not continue to be so profitable and cosy if Jason wasn't on board. Alex wanted him in – so that was that. What could they do? So much of their business at that point was going to rely on their relationship with Alex and United.

The harder question, however, is why Alex Ferguson got so involved in helping his son with a new career move, especially when he risked accusations of nepotism and misuse of his position. The answer is probably that, first, he was keen for all three of his sons to become rich and successful in their own right. Indeed, Ferguson's attitude to his family in some ways reflects the Glaswegian culture in which he was brought up, in which the success of your sons is a reflection of your own success. A close observer of the family says:

> He's motivated by a desire to see his son do well and have a decent career with good earning power, like many fathers. There's certainly an element of arrogance: he's the big man, so

it won't do for his son not to be someone big too. It's an ego thing: he wants his son to be seen to be doing well. It's the same with all his sons – he's desperate for them to do well, and will help in any way.

While Darren was languishing at Wolves, Mark Ferguson was already doing well, having landed well-paid jobs in the City, first with Schroders, and then with the American bank Goldman Sachs. Named as the City's Fund Manager of the Year in 1999, he was already well on the way to becoming a millionaire through the combination of a high salary, large bonuses and the share options allocated by Goldman Sachs to leading employees.

Equally powerful, perhaps, was Alex Ferguson's sense of guilt at having neglected the boys when they were growing up. Every football manager talks of it being a seven-days-a-week job, but Ferguson took his commitment to his work to excess. One has only to read the two diaries he published in 1995 and 1997 to see how, even when Ferguson wasn't actually watching games, he was occupied most evenings with dinners, speeches and other football, media and charity engagements. Ever since going full-time at St Mirren he had devoted almost every waking hour to work, and he had had little time for his children beyond taking them to school each morning. 'I did not see them grow up, but I saw an entire generation of young players grow up,' he admitted in 2001 while discussing the retirement he planned for June 2002 and which he'd announced two years before.[11] 'That is why they see me more as a friend than a father. That is, perhaps, one of the reasons why I am leaving. I hope I can make up for lost time.'[12]

Alex Ferguson's efforts to help his son Jason were followed at the start of 1999 by the appointment of the manager's brother, Martin, to become Manchester United's chief foreign scout. The brotherly concern was understandable after Martin had suffered the loss of his wife, Sandra, from cancer at the end of 1998. And he had a respectable record as a player in both Scotland and England, and also as a manager. While he had achieved nowhere near the successes of his brother, he did win the League of Ireland as player/manager of Waterford in 1970 at the age of only twenty-seven. As United's overseas scout, Martin had two roles – to cast an eye over prospective transfer targets and to compile extensive background reports on upcoming European opponents. It was a plum job, involving extensive travel around Europe, and sometimes beyond, from his home near Glasgow. His weekly itineraries would often involve numerous flights from venue to venue on the Continent.

On the question of Jason, Alex Ferguson might also have reckoned that having his son work as an agent could help extend his own expanding influence within football. L'Attitude had started with several deals involving players at lower-division clubs, though none were big names. The partners put in hundreds of hours trying to sell lesser-known Manchester United players – potential transfers which Alex Ferguson had put their way. Among them were Jonathan Greening, a striker who'd joined United from York City in March 1998 and made a few dozen senior appearances, and two midfield players: Mark Wilson, who'd played in the first team, and Richard Wellens, a regular member of the reserves. Impatient to get results, Jason persuaded his colleagues to send faxes to several league clubs where they had no personal contacts, giving details of these and other United players whom they claimed were available for transfer. No club was interested. Wellens eventually joined Blackpool in 2000, while Greening and Wilson continued to attract Jason's interest until they left United in 2001.

The only money that L'Attitude did make from United was the £25,000 for the Massimo Taibi transfer, and even then they were upset not to get more than 1 per cent commission. 'They were gutted and were expecting more,' says a United insider. 'Jason was very annoyed and had words with his dad, but Alex would only push it so far. The club clearly weren't jumping for joy about the whole thing with Jason, even back then. Alex was clever enough not to push it at such an early stage for Jason.'

The Taibi money was a small reward for the time and effort that Jason and his colleagues had expended. Jason in particular was frustrated by the lack of results. Yet few directors at Old Trafford, if any, knew what L'Attitude had been doing, ostensibly on United's behalf, and nobody thought to tell the board. According to one informed source:

> Jason knew he was protected by the fact that his father was Alex Ferguson, and that the club was wary of complaining too hard to Alex. At the end of the day they were getting things done assisted by Alex's influence and not their own ability. L'Attitude assumed they'd be heavily reliant on work coming through Alex, and Jason wasn't content to sit and watch the business grow in a healthy and steady manner. He just wanted to push things more and more.

Alex Ferguson perhaps rationalised giving the work to his son by thinking that, if an agent had to profit from United transfers, it might as well be Jason. 'He was helping his son to do well,' says one observer. 'That is the natural and totally obvious thing to do. It's a story about nepotism, and money being channelled in certain directions in order to help someone he loved.' Ferguson may also have seen it as some indirect redress for, in his eyes, having been seriously underpaid by United over the years, at a time when Martin Edwards had made almost £100 million from the club. Yet even in 1999 Ferguson was still criticising other agents. 'The money they make goes out of the game and remains out of the game,' he wrote in a column in the *News of the World*. 'Their place in football needs to be closely looked at and defined. They should be controlled a lot better.'[13]

Yet Alex Ferguson did not just help his son in acting as a possible middleman in United transfers: he also nudged players towards appointing Jason as their personal agent. Perhaps the most worrying example occurred in 2000, when United released an unusually high number of junior professionals. Jason Ferguson expressed interest in representing the two players who had the best chance of succeeding at other clubs: Paul Wheatcroft, a striker, and Josh Howard, who plays in central midfield.

Howard, who had been captain of the United Under-19 team, remembers Alex Ferguson suddenly enquiring whether he had an agent:

> He said to me, 'We could keep you, but we don't think you're gonna play first-team football here. A lot of teams have come in for you, and you'll make a living out the game.' . . . He asked me who I had representing me, and said I would need some help . . . Then, out of the blue, I got a phone call off that Jason Ferguson, and he was asking me to sign with him. I thought it was a bit strange how he got my number. Jason wanted me to come and meet him, so I went and met him in his offices in Manchester. It was a company called L'Attitude, and he was with some other fellow called Kieran Toal. Jason said, 'Look, we'll get you some clubs interested. You can sign with us if you want to.' He said he had a lot of contacts at other clubs.[14]

But Josh Howard got cold feet. L'Attitude wanted between 5 and 10 per cent commission, whereas Mel Stein, who had also expressed interest in representing the midfielder, said he would charge only 3 per cent. It didn't take long for Alex Ferguson to discover that Howard not only had rejected his son but, much worse, had also signed with his least favourite agent. He was also upset that Howard's friend and colleague Dominic Studley, a left-back, had also committed himself to Stein.

Both players were soon summoned to Ferguson's office. 'He called us in,' explains Howard, 'and said, "What the fuck are you doing signing with him?" Then he just said, "You can fuck off out of here. I hope he gets you a club, because I won't. You'll never get any fucking help from this club."'[15]

In the view of Josh's mother, Beverley Howard, 'I knew that Ferguson had threatened that they wouldn't get anywhere in football. It was because Josh didn't sign with the person Ferguson wanted him to sign with – Josh hadn't gone with his son. I'm really cross with him. It was disgraceful . . . He intimidated him. He intimidated all of them.'[16] His friend Paul Wheatcroft recalls that Dominic Studley was in tears as the two young players left Ferguson's office.[17] 'I was upset,' says Studley, 'thinking, "I'm not gonna get a club."'[18]

That night the two players told Mel Stein what had happened. The lawyer immediately wrote to Ferguson, detailing the players' account and threatening legal action. Studley remembers that Ferguson summoned them back to his office.

But he was a bit slimy this time. He had Mike Phelan, the reserve-team coach, in the office with him as well, and me and Josh felt a bit intimidated by this, because we were only young – only nineteen. He read out the complaint that Mel Stein had written to him, and said to us, 'Why have you told Mel Stein I've told you to fuck off and all this? I didn't say this.' Me and Josh just agreed with him, because we felt intimidated. We said to him, 'We didn't say those things to him. Mel must be making it up.' Then he just nodded at Mike Phelan and said, 'You're my witness.' It just takes the piss. The way he *did* say it, and then got us in the office again and had the cheek to say that he actually didn't say it. He probably thought to himself, 'Oh no, I might have got myself in trouble, I'd best make them change their minds.' He was just really nasty, to be honest. People who go and watch the matches, they don't know what goes on inside the club at all.[19]

'We were only nineteen,' says Josh Howard. 'It was a bit like he was a school headmaster.'[20] Howard now plays for Hyde United in the Unibond League. Dominic Studley never found another club, and eventually left the game.

L'Attitude's biggest contract didn't involve United players at all, but was to organise the United manager's testimonial year in 1999–2000, following the glorious treble triumph. Andy Dodd chaired the official testimonial committee, and L'Attitude staff were under pressure from Alex Ferguson to deliver a programme which would both reflect his achievements at Old Trafford and raise a substantial sum of money. Jason relished the challenge, stomping round the agency's offices in the centre of Manchester barking out commands which everyone knew came from his father. One of the highlights of the programme was to be a star-spangled dinner at the city's biggest indoor hall, the G-Mex centre, with 2,200 diners and scores of friends and faces from Ferguson's past. Much effort was put into deciding who would be invited, how the venue would be laid out, and how it could be lavishly decorated so as to reflect the grandeur of the occasion.

While every expense detracted from the likely profits, diners also had to be reassured that they were getting good value for their tickets, since a table for ten cost £1,500. Something special was required.

Jason then issued the order which became legendary among the L'Attitude staff: 'Get me the fucking flaming columns!' Get them they did. The plan was to hire pillars of fire which would be placed around the hall. They would be expensive, but would also look impressive – giving the United manager more the aura of a Roman emperor than of a football gaffer. 'They were twelve foot high,' says one testimonial organiser, Steve Lock – 'huge things – and there were eight or more of them. They were everywhere. It was amazing – very epic. A big, tall, green, Roman-style column with a huge blanket with a light inside, and air blowing to move it all around. It did look like flames.'[21] 'They were massive,' says another colleague – 'ridiculously big. But things had to be dramatic to justify the ticket prices.' It was just the kind of grandiose touch that Alex Ferguson wanted to celebrate his reign. 'Alex's ego is as big as anybody's,' says one organiser, 'and he wanted something really grand, really over the top in many people's eyes, to match his sense of achievement in life. He wanted it to be a big, huge event, and Jason was really his mouthpiece in organising it. Alex wanted the flaming columns as much as Jason did.'

The dinner went well. Ferguson was introduced to the sound of Scottish pipers; the TV presenter Eamonn Holmes acted as master of ceremonies; Mick Hucknall sang; and Tony Blair delivered a video-taped tribute (though it provoked jeers). Shirts signed by David Beckham and Roy Keane went for £15,000 and £17,000 respectively. In the raffle, Blair's press secretary, Alastair Campbell, won two tickets to Canada to see the singer Bon Jovi.

The most dazzling jewel in Ferguson's testimonial crown was a match at Old Trafford between Manchester United and a Rest of the World XI. Testimonial matches are a relic from the days when footballers' earnings were restricted by the maximum-wage rule. The idea was to encourage loyalty to one club by raising a lump-sum payment at the end of a player's career, effectively from the club's supporters, to help fund whatever he did in life afterwards. Officially such benefit games are always organised by friends of the employee, and without the involvement of the club beyond providing the use of the stadium: the Inland Revenue then regards the match as a gift and therefore not subject to tax. Manchester United have granted more testimonial games than most clubs in recent times – almost one a year for players who have been on the books for more than a decade. If Ferguson's testimonial match in 1999 was agreed by United as part of his latest contract, it is questionable whether its proceeds should have been exempt from tax.

As expected, the match at Old Trafford in October 1999 was easily the most lucrative event of Ferguson's testimonial year, attracting a capacity crowd of almost 55,000 (bettered historically only by the 60,000 for Bobby Charlton's testimonial in 1973, when the stadium was larger). United lost 4–2 to the Rest of the World, whose players included Gianluca Vialli, Paul Gascoigne, Eric Cantona and Peter Schmeichel. At one point the guest team was withdrawn and replaced by a United old boys' eleven which included Bryan Robson, Mark Hughes, Lee Sharpe, Steve Bruce, Gary Pallister, Paul Parker and the manager's son Darren, all of which left the fans wondering which team to support.

Nonetheless, many of United's regular fans stayed away that night. This reflected no disrespect for their manager, but disillusionment with testimonial matches in an era when players and managers are richly rewarded compared with the average football supporter. 'Testimonials are about money,' declared Andy Mitten, the editor of the fanzine *United We Stand*, who dared to express the view that Ferguson didn't need the money:

> This season is already expensive enough for United fans
> without another full-priced game to attend. Can't the club
> put on a genuine celebration where the loyal fans are spared
> the £20 ticket charge? . . . It also seems hypocritical of Fergie
> to complain about too many games on the one hand and yet
> he is prepared to field a full first team for his testimonial.[22]

Ferguson was not pleased with Mitten when they next met.

Other events in Ferguson's testimonial season included two golf days, a race day at Haydock Park, which was attended by 15,000 people, and a Simply Red concert at the same venue. After United's 2–1 win at Highbury in August 1999, Ferguson was flown to the concert by plane and helicopter thanks to the Manchester millionaire and United fan Ron Wood, who also sat on the testimonial

committee. Ferguson then paraded on stage with several of his players and the three treble trophies. This last event was really designed
just as a celebration of the United manager, as none of the profits
went to his testimonial fund. But other monies were raised from selling 750 limited-edition prints of Ferguson at £395 each, as well as
from sponsorship, programmes and the TV rights from the game at
Old Trafford, which was shown on BSkyB. Companies were encouraged to make block bookings for a series of testimonial events,
graded at different prices: silver £12,000, gold £20,000, and the plat-
inum level at £100,000 – the last of which entitled firms to 200
tickets for both the match and the concert, advertisement hoardings
at Old Trafford, a champagne lunch, and the chance to meet golf
stars such as Tiger Woods, as well as Sir Alex himself.

In all, Ferguson's testimonial fund raised about £1.3 to £1.4 million. The organisers had promised that a 'substantial donation' from
the proceeds would be made to two charities: the Manchester-based
organisation From Street to Stadium, which helps poor children get
involved in sport, and Ferguson's mother's cancer charity, the
Elizabeth Hardie Ferguson Charitable Trust. In the end, From Street
to Stadium received £100,000 and the cancer trust £10,000, which
means that about 8 per cent of the testimonial profit went to these
charities.

The testimonial effort had raised a huge sum of money for a man
who was already one of the richest people in football, but Ferguson
had been expecting to receive at least the £2 million mentioned in
press speculation. 'Alex was disappointed with the amount of money
we made,' says one of his testimonial team. 'But there's realistic
expectations and there's Alex Ferguson expectations. There was a bit
of an ego thing going on. He had a certain picture of what he should
make.'

Jason had conveyed his father's worries to his fellow organisers as
the programme of events progressed. Dodd, Toal and other L'Attitude
staff found it increasingly hard to maintain a reasonable working

relationship with Jason. A good example occurred when he clashed with a former journalist, Andy Spinoza, who ran an associated public-relations company, aptly named Spin Media. On the Monday after the G-Mex dinner, several witnesses saw Jason attack Spinoza about the press coverage of the event. The dinner had been considered a huge success by everyone who attended, but Jason was angry when the papers said that David Beckham and his wife hadn't turned up on time, and was especially upset about a picture whose caption in Spinoza's former paper, the *Manchester Evening News*, described the Beckhams as 'the last guests to arrive'.[23] 'It was terrible,' says one observer. 'Really, really unpleasant screaming and swearing at Spin. I think that was the nail in the coffin, the final straw.'

Jason reported his father's eventual disappointment with the testimonial profit, even though his partners felt he shared the responsibility for it. Finding it increasingly difficult to cope with his 'hurricane personality', Dodd and Toal finally parted company with Jason at the end of 2000. But, without the Ferguson patronage, transfer business became very difficult – particularly if it involved United. L'Attitude also lost financially on the testimonial, because, says one observer, 'money they'd been told they'd get didn't come'. It was hard to chase debts, as they felt the United manager himself 'wasn't gonna be too helpful' now that the family link had been severed. L'Attitude folded early in 2001, with Andy Dodd bearing the brunt financially.

Meanwhile Jason had been planning another tribute to his father – a three-part television series which would be broadcast in 2002 towards the end of the manager's intended final season at Old Trafford. It would include a fly-on-the-wall documentary covering the last twelve months. He teamed up with Steve Lock, the producer whose firm, Big Eye, had supplied TV screens for the G-Mex dinner. Lock says they spent nine months planning the show:

I was on the verge of a great deal for his dad – really good financially, but also a decent amount of editorial control, you know: at least a good say in how it was done. The BBC were the keenest, and it was in the bag really. Then Jason decided he was going to set up his own TV production company and just suddenly said, 'I'm doing the retirement programme for my company.' I was livid. I couldn't believe it. I was very disappointed in Alex Ferguson. I used to respect him, but not now.

I wrote to him to complain about the whole thing, and his lawyer wrote back saying in legal jargon that I didn't have any rights regarding the idea. He knows his son was in the wrong and that Jase shafted us. I think he knows what a prat Jason sometimes is. But, you know, blood's thicker than water. I regard Jason as the Prince Edward of the Ferguson clan. He's often an idiot, but everyone just accepts it because of who his dad is. I question whether he would have got anywhere without his dad.[24]

The BBC rejected Jason's documentary as they felt the £100,000 fee he wanted was ridiculously high, even though he was offering an unusual level of access to Sir Alex and the team. Jason was eventually forced to abandon the idea when the club refused to accept it.

Colleagues may have found Jason Ferguson difficult to work with, but nonetheless he had earned a reputation as a good negotiator. The former Wrexham manager Bryan Flynn says Jason talked the Welsh club into giving his brother Darren an excellent deal in 1999.[25] If Darren did well out of it, his new club also benefited. By the summer of 2000 strong links had been forged between United, Wrexham and the Ferguson family. Over the next twelve months United sides visited the Second Division club's Racecourse Ground for three separate friendly fixtures – a startling commitment given United's league and European Cup programme and the heavy demand for Ferguson's teams to play additional non-competitive matches. The last game was a joint testimonial for Flynn himself and his deputy, Kevin Reeves, in August 2001, only a few weeks before they were sacked by the club. And Jason Ferguson again sat on the testimonial committee.

Darren Ferguson, in contrast to his twin brother, appears not to have benefited much from his father's connections. If anything, the opposite is true. 'I think a lot of managers are scared about the baggage that comes with me,' he once observed. 'They think he's going to interfere but he doesn't. He's just a normal father.'[26] The former Aberdeen player Mark McGhee, who took over at Wolves in 1995 while Darren was on the club's books, might disagree. He had gone to Wolves reluctantly, at the insistence of Alex Ferguson, and was accused of disloyalty over the manner in which he left his job at Leicester to do so; but he did little to resurrect Darren's career. This failure caused the end of a friendship between the two men that dated back to their triumphs together at Pittodrie in the early 1980s.

After leaving L'Attitude, Jason effectively became Alex Ferguson's own agent. His most important task was to negotiate with Manchester United over his father's post-retirement package. But he also began setting up a range of other deals which would ensure that Alex Ferguson, already a multimillionaire, would become even richer. Paul Stretford, for example, recalls negotiating a substantial contract with Jason for Sir Alex to promote the PlayStation computer game 'Premier Manager'. Stretford and the game's owners, ANCO, had concluded that Alex Ferguson was the only man for the job:

> Jason was actually very impressive as a negotiator. I'd heard all the stories about how difficult he can be, and the suggestions of arrogance, but I think the problem with the temper comes when you fall out with him – he's got a very similar temper to his dad, there's no doubt about that. He's very much his father's son.
>
> He was tough – very tough. He drove a hard bargain, but

remained calm and polite. He was very good at being aware of what the name 'Alex Ferguson' means, the prestige it carries, and the value that comes with that. He knew his father's worth. Jason negotiated a sizeable fee for Alex, and rightly so.[27]

In the spring of 2001 Jason also became a director of a new football agency, Elite Sports Group, which had just been set up by Francis Martin, a Spanish-born football agent who had been operating in the north-west for a couple of years and was officially registered with the world football body, FIFA. Martin's clients included Jordi Cruyff, the Dutch player who was with Manchester United at that time, who was a close friend. The other director of Elite is David Gardner, who, like Jason and Kieran Toal, had come through the United youth teams in the late 1980s and early 1990s and was good friends with both David Beckham and Ryan Giggs. Gardner chaired Giggs's testimonial committee in 2001, while Beckham names Gardner as one of his two 'best friends' (along with Gary Neville).[28] Gardner had been best man at Philip Neville's wedding, and his sister Emma had once been Ryan Giggs's girlfriend.

The name 'Elite' summed it up: instead of messing around with trifling deals for United reserve players or out-of-favour Italian goalkeepers, they planned to work on multi-million-pound transfers which might yield big money very quickly. Francis Martin's model was the highly successful SFX agency run by Tony Stephens and Jon Holmes, whose clients include Alan Shearer, Michael Owen, David Beckham and Dwight Yorke. 'They've done a good job,' Martin says of SFX. 'You never hear them in the press, or talking to anybody. They just get on and do their job professionally and quietly. That's what we're trying to achieve – to do a professional job, keep it quiet, and make our clients happy.'[29] Ironically, in January 2002 Alex Ferguson would attack SFX for disrupting the proposed sale of Dwight Yorke to Middlesbrough.

Few football deals came bigger – or were kept less quiet – than the controversial transfer of Jaap Stam in August 2001. (The background is covered in Chapter 27.) It was certainly good business. To receive more than £15 million for a twenty-nine-year-old who had had regular injuries was doing well, especially when he'd cost United only £10.6 million in 1998 and Alex Ferguson felt he was no longer the player he once was.

As the football world debated why Ferguson had got rid of Stam, an intriguing sub-plot emerged at the press conference where the Rome club Lazio unveiled their clearly shell-shocked new defender. Lazio officials chose to thank Mike Morris, an English agent based in Monaco. Morris has a good relationship with the Elite director David Gardner, who at one time used to act as Morris's driver whenever he was in Britain, and many people in football say that Morris is effectively the fourth partner in Elite. The Manchester United communications director, Paddy Harverson, soon confirmed that Jason's firm Elite had played a leading role in the Stam sale. Jason's partner Francis Martin says Elite did not bill United for their work over Stam, but sent their invoice to Lazio.

Yet strangely, the Manchester United chief executive Peter Kenyon, who handled the Jaap Stam deal, claims not to be aware of any involvement by Elite in the transfer. Kenyon says he only dealt with two agents in selling Stam – Mike Morris and Bruno Pasquale, an unregistered Italian agent who once played in Scotland for Hearts. Kenyon says he was approached by Morris, acting on Lazio's behalf, and enquiring whether Stam might be available for transfer.[30]

Bruno Pasquale himself claims to have initiated the idea of transfer when he noticed Stam had been dropped:

I saw Stam wasn't playing and knew of his problems with
Ferguson. Things did not seem to be resolving themselves so
I said to myself, 'Why don't we give it a try?' It was Thursday
morning. I called my friend Mike Morris. I asked him to give
United a ring to see if they were willing to deal for Stam.

Mike called me back and said they were interested and
wanted £17 million.[31]

Pasquale says he approached Roma and AC Milan, but got most
interest from Lazio. Kenyon and Pasquale's accounts of what happened tally with each other, suggesting it was a clever hunch by
Pasquale, channelled through Mike Morris. But the United chief
executive can offer no explanation as to what role Elite played in the
transfer, or why Elite should have invoiced Lazio, rather than Mike
Morris himself simply sending them a bill.

A plausible alternative to the official Kenyon explanation is that
Elite actually contributed to the Stam deal a crucial piece of information to which no other agent had access: the fact that Alex
Ferguson wanted to sell the Dutchman. It was this, perhaps, which
sparked Morris's inquiry to Peter Kenyon rather than shrewd guess-
work by Bruno Pasquale. In a world where knowledge is currency,
this information was potentially worth hundreds of thousands – if
not millions – of pounds in commission. This alternative theory is
supported by the fact that when Francis Martin was asked to explain
Elite's role in the Stam deal, he didn't mention the Pasquale hunch
and Morris enquiry to Kenyon, but said instead: 'Clubs will come to
you and ask you to move the players on for them.'[32] Considered in
general terms, 'buying' clubs may be willing to pay handsomely for
the information that another club wants to get rid of a player, so long
as that information is exclusive to them.

So when Jason Ferguson's agency sent their bill to Lazio, the
Rome club were perhaps charged for a valuable tip-off Elite may
have obtained that Stam was available, and which was conveyed to
the Italians via Mike Morris. 'Mike's got a lot of contacts,' says
Francis Martin. 'He's been in the game a long time, and I think he
can just put players to different clubs. He's a well-known person.'[33]
Paul Stretford, a highly experienced operator who knows Mike
Morris and is sympathetic to both Fergusons, thinks 'Jason was the

absolute key to the Stam deal'. He speculates as to the role played by Sir Alex's son:

> Elite were more able to be in there from the very start because he [Jason] would have heard off his dad that the player was available and that's the real bottom line; he will have realised that his company would make a fair whack. That means Elite could operate as the only people who knew that Stam would be going in a big-money move, and find a suitable buyer. I assume that's where Morris got involved. Jason didn't have the contacts to pull the deal off in Italy, but Morris has a way into Lazio, so they got him involved.

If this seems complicated, these three – Elite, Morris and Pasquale – weren't the only entities at work. Jaap Stam's personal Dutch agent, Tom van Dalen, who had once fixed Darren Ferguson's loan spell at Sparta Rotterdam, was also paid to negotiate the player's new pay and conditions with Lazio.

Despite the involvement of so many parties, the deal was also intriguing for its unusual haste. The official explanation for this was that Stam needed to join his new club before the UEFA deadline of Friday 31 August if he was to qualify to play for it in the first group stage of the European Cup. This argument does not impress Stam's UK agent, Mike Williams, who wasn't directly involved in the deal but was that week negotiating another rushed transfer, of the Polish goalkeeper Jerzy Dudek to Liverpool. Whereas Stam's move was completed on the Monday, four days before the deadline, Dudek's went through with only ten minutes to spare. In the world of football transfers, the four days' grace offered ample time to seek rival bidders for Stam. Williams's version is that

> the deal was cut and dried and put in a box with some ribbon round it by Alex Ferguson and his son, and before you knew

it the transfer had happened. There was no question: the way it was done was to make sure that other alternative options had no chance to make an offer. Jaap went along with the line that they wanted him to, and I think he should have taken a bit more time over it. I think events just overtook him.[34]

Stam himself seems to have been so stunned by his abrupt sacking by Manchester United that he didn't really care where he went, so long as he could continue playing at the highest level, and provided the deal was settled before he joined the Holland squad for their World Cup qualifier against Ireland. Indeed, had he stopped to reflect, Italy would probably have been low on his list of preferred destinations. In his autobiography, Stam explains that when he left Holland to join United in 1998 he didn't bother to consider Italian sides, as he had 'no intention' of playing in the Italian league:

> The style of the football over there just doesn't interest me. I love following games with goals galore, whereas in Italy it's all about clean sheets punctuated by the odd goal . . . I'd heard that in Italy a lot of clubs locked their players away in hotels for several days before games. That didn't appeal much and neither did the feedback I got about the lack of everyday privacy from some of the Dutch players plying their trade in Italy.[35]

In an updated edition of his book, Jaap Stam later revealed that Inter Milan and Real Madrid had also expressed interest at the last moment in 2001, but 'I had made my decision by then'.[36] The momentum driving him towards Lazio was unstoppable, amid the urgency created by the UEFA deadline. 'Lazio announced the thing in Italy at five o'clock,' says Mike Williams. 'He'd only just arrived in Italy at that point, and they were saying he had signed. Well, he hadn't even sat down and discussed it at that point.'[37] The crucial factor, Williams reckons, is that neither Elite nor Mike Morris had the contacts necessary to earn a commission from any transfer to Real or Inter, so they had no interest in these clubs bidding for the player, no matter how much they offered United.

Yet competition between two or three clubs, rather than a private deal with just one, should have been in the interests of the 'selling' party, Manchester United, since this ought to have bid up the price. The then chairman of Manchester United PLC, Sir Roland Smith, was puzzled as to why the transfer needed to involve four different agents, and was especially concerned that one of them was his manager's son. In the autumn of 2001 Smith delivered Alex Ferguson a stern warning that, in a public company such as United, everything should be above suspicion and nobody should expose themselves to potential conflicts of interest.

The most basic question is why the deal had to involve any middlemen at all. One United source says that Lazio had already expressed an interest in buying Stam during the summer, when Ferguson bought the Argentine midfielder Juan Sebastián Verón from the Italian club. On the face of it, therefore, there seems no reason why in late August someone at Old Trafford could not have rung Lazio to tell them that Stam was now up for sale. No agent need ever have got involved in the transfer, let alone three or four of them.

News of Jason's role was obviously a severe embarrassment to United at a time when many people questioned whether it had been wise for Alex Ferguson to sell Stam at all. United's communications director, Paddy Harverson, stressed that the agency did not have exclusive rights to conduct United transfers. 'We use different agents for different deals, and we always use FIFA-registered agents.'[38]

Estimates of how much Elite made from the Stam deal go as high as £1.5 million. Although the true figure is probably lower than that, it does appear that the three main middlemen – Elite, Morris and Pasquale – shared more than £1 million between them.

According to Bruno Pasquale, Lazio paid £16.5 million for the player – halfway between their opening bid of £16 million and United's demand for £17 million.[39] Yet United's annual report gives the proceeds as £15.3 million, so it would not be unreasonable to suppose that the £1.2 million difference represents what the various agents collected.[40] This is in the middle of the typical range of commission payments, which are usually between 5 and 10 per cent of the total fee. One prominent agent, who has discussed it with others in the business, reckons that in the Stam deal alone Elite had made more money out of United transfers than any other agent or agency in the past.

If Elite did indeed obtain and pass on the tip-off which started the process, then they are likely to have claimed the largest share of the commission. Yet Elite can claim that there was no conflict of interest, since officially they acted for Lazio and invoiced the Italian club. The reality, of course, was rather more complicated. Any extra fees that Lazio had to pay to intermediaries would probably have reduced the amount that they were willing to pay the selling club. United would have lost out from that, and it's hard to see how Jason's agency's involvement was in the financial interests of either the club or its shareholders. United sources dismiss such concerns and insist that Sir Alex has done nothing wrong. No rules or laws were broken, they say, while adding that agents are now an inevitable feature of the modern game.

Elite were also involved in another United transfer in 2001: the purchase of the goalkeeper Roy Carroll from Wigan Athletic for £2.5 million. Their other significant activity was organising Ryan Giggs's testimonial, a match between United and Celtic at Old Trafford in August 2001; the Elite director David Gardner chaired Giggs's testimonial committee. Elite, and Jason Ferguson in particular, also tried to fix up a newspaper column for Juan Sebastián Verón, without success. Similarly, Jason also tried to negotiate a Sunday-newspaper column for his father at £20,000 an issue. The *Sunday Times* sports editor, Alex Butler, was heard to say that if they'd accepted Ferguson's proposed terms it would have bankrupted his paper's sports department.

Verón was also one of the players involved in a far less lucrative venture when Elite began selling football shirts signed by him and other United stars, including Ryan Giggs, Paul Scholes and Ruud van Nistelrooy. (Leeds and Sunderland players were involved too.) Advertisements appeared in the journal *World Soccer* and also in Manchester United's own glossy magazine, advertising the shirts at £346 each, mounted in a glass frame with two photos and a certificate of authenticity, though the players had never actually worn them.

Elite ran into trouble with this scheme almost immediately when David Beckham's agency, SFX, insisted that Jason's firm was not allowed to sell shirts with Beckham's signature. 'These rights are owned by David and SFX in partnership and are part of the current negotiations. No deal has been done by Elite Sports Group who have no rights in the matter.'[41] SFX clearly feared that this was only a start, and that Elite were trying to poach all their Beckham business.

Manchester United officials were also unhappy with Jason Ferguson's shirt enterprise, and one official describes it as 'grubby'. Legally, however, it was hard to prevent, since the magazine ads showed only the backs of the shirts with the autograph on the white fabric of the player number. Since they didn't show the club crest, they probably didn't infringe Manchester United's trademarks. 'The club has not licensed this operation and does not receive any financial gain from the deal,' said a United spokesman. He added, pointedly, 'Manchester United provides many autographed shirts for charity auctions only and will continue to do so. The players, however, are free to do as they want.'[42] By selling such items Elite were devaluing the autographed shirts which Manchester United traditionally donate to charitable causes for nothing, and which the organisations typically auction to raise funds.

Yet by the end of 2001 Alex Ferguson's success in winning a generous post-retirement contract had altered the balance of power within the club. For once the board now found themselves in the weaker position. This meant that Ferguson and his son could do almost as they pleased. United officials acknowledged privately that they were powerless.

Elite's autographed shirts may be beyond the means of the average fan, but it's nonetheless surprising that well-paid stars should bother to get involved for the sums concerned. While the players themselves could expect to receive £100–150 on each sale, such payments are negligible when compared with the rest of their income. 'Why are they bothering?' Mike Williams asks of Elite. 'There's not much money in it. It was pretty cheap doing that, really. It was desperate.'[43] However, the shirt scheme appears to offer a way for the agency to gain access to leading players whom they don't already represent, in the hope perhaps of picking up their custom. And which United player would want to upset the manager's son?

Perhaps the most worrying aspect of Elite's close relationship with Manchester United is the way Alex Ferguson actively encouraged young United players to use Jason as an agent, albeit unsuccessfully. The Northern Ireland striker David Healy, who moved from United to Preston for £1.3 million in December 2000, says he was one of those urged by his former manager to hire Jason. 'When I was moving, he just asked, "Have you got an agent?" And I said, "Yeah." And he said, "Because if you don't, my son Jason, he'll sort you out with your stuff." He just said, "You know, if you're stuck for anybody."'[44]

Several less well known, yet promising, United players were also urged to use the manager's son. In some instances Ferguson got very annoyed when they chose other agents instead. 'He bullies young players into joining Jason,' says a rival agent. 'It is quite appalling, really. He will take a young player and try and use his power to push them to Jason. He is quite blatantly abusing his power.'

The most stark attempt to get players to sign with Jason occurred in the summer of 2001. It was almost a carbon copy of the Josh Howard and Dominic Studley story, only this time it involved two players who might prove highly lucrative to any agent. Jonathan Greening and Mark Wilson had been among the young United reserves Jason had tried to sell in 2000, while he was at L'Attitude. They had each played several dozen games in the United first team, and also for the England Under-21 side, and it was obvious they would go for several million pounds when transferred, and command large salaries. Greening, a two-footed winger, was particularly sought after.

Before long the story was circulating widely in football and media circles around Manchester that there had been some kind of bust-up between the players and Alex Ferguson over them refusing to use Jason as an agent. 'I heard that he was having a try with Jonathan Greening and Mark Wilson,' says John Curtis, the full-back who had left United for Blackburn in 2000. 'But both of them said "No" and stuck with their existing agent, Mel Stein. They just refused to do what Fergie said.' Curtis, who remains good friends with both players, felt it was 'understandable' that Ferguson should want to help Jason out in this way.[45]

Greening and Wilson themselves were less understanding. The pair felt intimidated by Ferguson's bullying manner as he urged them to dump Stein, using seriously derogatory comments when referring to the agent. 'Fergie had them in regularly to yell at them,' say a former United player:

> He just used to berate them and shout,'Why are you with that
> fucking Mel Stein? You can use Jason. He'll do well for you.
> You're fucking leaving Stein, right now.' He couldn't
> understand why they wouldn't go with Jason. He didn't get it.
> Players don't drop their agents at the drop of a hat, unless
> they've had a problem. At first, Jonathan and Mark were so

upset they did consider ditching Stein, but after a while they thought, 'No, why shouldn't we choose our own advisers? We don't want the gaffer's son.' You've got to admire that.

By 2001, with limited first-team prospects, both players were keen to leave Old Trafford. Transfers were mooted with several clubs, selling them together as a package, rather unusually, but proposed deals with Preston and West Ham fell through. That summer Ferguson said he would refuse to sell them unless they dropped Stein. 'He knew how much they wanted a move,' says the ex-United colleague, 'and was using all his power to get them to follow Alex Ferguson's agenda, not their own. He shouted at them, "You can fucking well rot in the reserves!"'

'Greening was livid, but Mark probably even more so,' the friend says. 'Mark was willing to take it all the way to court.' It wasn't until Mel Stein threatened Ferguson with legal action that both players were granted a transfer, and in August 2001 they signed for Middlesbrough in a deal worth £3.5 million. But Ferguson and United had also realised how damaging it might be if more details of the long-running row came out in public or the players sold their stories to the press. The dispute had provided the most graphic illustration yet of how Sir Alex tries to push business towards Jason, and bullies young, vulnerable employees to leave their existing advisers. Only in this case the players concerned weren't obscure teenagers but relatively well-known footballers.

Under the legal settlement Stein and the two players were obliged to accept a confidentiality clause which seems to have been designed to hide one of the less attractive sides of Alex Ferguson's much-praised style of man-management. Manchester United fans might not have been impressed to discover that as compensation for their manager's defamatory remarks about Stein, money was paid to a charity nominated by the lawyer. Stein himself, who is normally happy to give interviews, refuses to discuss the episode beyond saying he is bound by the confidentiality agreement, although the story had already been circulating freely in the Manchester football community.

Ferguson also encouraged the defender Wes Brown to leave his existing agent, Jonathan Barnett of Stellar Promotions, whom the United manager seems to dislike almost as much as he hates Mel Stein. 'He just put pressure on the kid,' says Barnett – 'general pressure on a young boy. He made life hell for him, made comments, more innuendo than anything. And he wrote a letter to somebody who works for me, one of my fellow directors, banning him from the training ground because we acted for Wes Brown, when in fact he'd never actually been to the bloody training ground!'[46] Jonathan Barnett isn't sure, however, whether Ferguson actually recommended that Brown go to Jason instead. But another agent who pitched to represent Brown around that time recalls the player saying he was under pressure from Sir Alex to join his son. 'He said, "No, no, no, I've got to leave Jonathan Barnett. The gaffer's kicking up a fuss. I've got to leave him. He wants me to go with Jason Ferguson."' Although Brown did leave Jonathan Barnett, he teamed up instead with the lawyer Michael Kennedy, who'd been recommended by the United captain Roy Keane, whom Kennedy also represents.

Not all Jason's work involved United. In February 2002 the Bolton chairman Phil Gartside personally thanked him for bringing the experienced French player Youri Djorkaeff to his club. Earlier, Jason was involved in attempts to take a couple of players from Spain to Middlesbrough, including the England and Real Madrid winger Steve McManaman, but the former Liverpool star preferred to stay put.

According to his friend Hugh McIlvanney, writing in February 2002, Alex Ferguson felt that attempts to generate controversy over Elite were 'malicious', and he was 'content in the certainty that, far from risking a conflict of interest, the transactions were straightforward and honourable and blatantly to United's benefit'. Ferguson

also stressed that Elite had been involved in only two United transfers – presumably those of Stam and Carroll.[47]

The agent Paul Stretford points out that Jason Ferguson is only
one case where the son of a famous football figure is involved in
agency work – among the others are the sons of the Arsenal vice-
chairman, David Dein, and the Bolton manager Sam Allardyce. 'Alex
and Jason Ferguson come in for unfair stick,' says Stretford. 'That
might be because some other agents are jealous. A major part of any
business is having good contacts. Besides, what father wouldn't want
to help their son in life? It's only football where people seem to
want to look at these things and get the wrong idea. Many businesses
are run by keeping things in the family . . . nepotism is not a
crime.'[48] What Stretford seems to overlook, however, is that
Manchester United is no longer a family business, but a public company, and therefore subject to much more stringent rules of conduct.

Through Sir Alex, Elite have already approached the former Derby
County manager Jim Smith to ask if he would join them (Smith
chose to become assistant manager at Coventry instead), and the
word in football is that Ferguson himself will be invited to become
a director of the agency when he eventually retires from Old Trafford
around 2005. This would give Elite enormous credibility, in much
the same way that Kenny Dalglish enhances the status of its com-
petitor, Proactive, by being on its board. If Ferguson does join his
son, he will do so in an environment in which the FA Premier
League has started to scrutinise the practices and standards of the
agency business far more closely. But that's just what the United
manager has often said should happen. 'The role of agents has to be
reconsidered,' he said in February 2002. 'Agents stand to make so
much money they sometimes stand in the way of deals.'[49]

Sir Alex Ferguson will then have come a long way from the days
when he compared football agents to rats. But, as ever with an eye on
the way the game is changing, he did say that 'the rats are winning'.

'You Know the Rules Here'

'When Paddy [Crerand] introduced me to Sir Matt
when I was still a player I was trembling. I was in awe.
Those managers had control of their clubs and they had
control of the Press.'

ALEX FERGUSON[1]

'Ⅰf you're doing a book on Alex Ferguson then we wouldn't co-operate, as we don't want to upset them,' said David Thomas, the head of syndication at the *Manchester Evening News*. I found it hard to believe what I was hearing, and began to wonder if perhaps I had been transplanted to Cold War Eastern Europe, or Robert Mugabe's Zimbabwe. Thomas explained that I would need the approval either of Sir Alex himself or of Manchester United before my researcher could go through the paper's cuttings' files, even though all the material had already been published. Normally the *Evening News* is happy for researchers to come and peruse its archives, and I was willing to pay its £75 a day charges. 'If someone can fax us a letter from United saying it's with their knowledge and approval then it's OK,' Thomas continued, stressing that nothing could be done without this. 'It's just not worth it. If you did two days in our library and that was to get back to United, that can backfire.' When I expressed my astonishment that an independent newspaper should be so beholden, Thomas commented, 'You obviously don't know him as well as we do.'[2]

Appeals to David Thomas's superiors got nowhere: I am still waiting for Paul Horrocks, the editor of the *Evening News*, to reply to my two e-mails. British newspapers normally pride themselves on their independence from the organisations whose affairs they report on, analyse and sometimes criticise. They usually argue that such independence is essential to their credibility with readers, and to earning and keeping the trust of their news sources. So it is eye-opening that one of Britain's most respected provincial newspapers, part of the supposedly liberal Guardian Group, should be so deferential to a powerful local institution such as Manchester United. It was as if the *Guardian* itself had refused access to its cuttings on Tony Blair without first getting approval from Downing Street. But it is a sign of the hold that Sir Alex Ferguson has established over much of the British media, and of the fear he can engender among sports journalists and their editors.

This wasn't the only instance during the preparation of this book when I found media colleagues afraid of upsetting the Manchester United boss. When I approached the Sky Sports executive Andy Melvin to talk about his time as a football reporter in Aberdeen, he said, 'knowing that Alex doesn't want this work published I have to decline the offer to take part'.[3] The Popperfoto picture agency was initially happy to discuss supplying photos for the front cover, only for its boss, Monte Fresco, to write to the publishers to say, 'we understand that this book is an unauthorised biography and . . . we feel that it would be inappropriate for us to have any involvement'. Fresco sent a copy of his letter to Sir Alex's son Jason.[4]

By the new millennium Sir Alex Ferguson was so powerful that many newspapers and broadcasting companies were frightened of offending him. This meant that reporters were unwilling to call the Manchester United manager to account – a basic journalistic task – for fear of losing what they perceived to be essential access to him and his players. Ferguson can turn on and off the tap of interviews, comment and access without any penalty from his frustrated employers at Old Trafford, or from the football authorities.

From the day in 1958 when the teenage Alex Ferguson wrote to the Scottish journalist Malcolm Munroe to apologise for his careless performance for Glasgow Schoolboys, he has always understood the importance of handling the press. Indeed, his media skills were noticed by the 1978 industrial tribunal into his sacking as manager of St Mirren, which commented on how he had briefed journalists in the middle of an important board meeting. At Aberdeen he was famous for recording how often Glasgow reporters covered his matches.

In recent times Ferguson has become increasingly hostile to the media. To some extent one can understand his attitude. Manchester United have long been a big story for the sports pages, but since the club became more successful in the 1990s, and as TV money has made football both glamorous and fashionable, media interest has grown relentlessly. Most of the north-west football writers are based in Manchester, and, although they are nominally meant to cover other clubs as well, many of them have become Manchester United correspondents in all but name. They are under enormous pressure from their sports editors – and increasingly from their news desks as well – to produce stories, and preferably exclusives, every day of the week. With fierce competition between papers, in particular the mid-market and down-market titles, the penalties for failure are tough. Some reporters are tempted to cut corners, to exaggerate trivial incidents, and sometimes to make things up altogether. An Old Trafford manager could easily spend his whole life dealing with the media. As Ferguson once wrote, 'We need to cut back on publicity, because at times it threatens to drown us and stop us doing our proper jobs.'[5] There is, however, a difference between limiting access to get one's job done and using it as a form of media control.

Ferguson occasionally claims to pay no attention to what is in the papers. 'I have a mechanism that says, "Forget it", and I don't read the tabloids,' he once wrote, before adding with a hint of menace, 'My legal department does that.'[6] Yet the former United player Russell Beardsmore might testify otherwise. In 1994, a year after leaving Old Trafford, Beardsmore did an interview with the *Sunday People* in which he was quoted as warning young players that it was 'the hardest thing in football to make it at United . . . Forget any big ideas – that way you won't be gutted like I was.'[7] When he bumped into Ferguson three years later, the United manager expressed his fury in typical fashion at comments that could have deterred future recruits. 'He slaughtered me – really slaughtered me,' says Beardsmore.[8] Ferguson backed down when the player explained he'd obtained an apology from the paper for being misquoted, and the United manager later arranged for Ryan Giggs and Nicky Butt to play in Beardsmore's testimonial.

'Fergie is a master manipulator of the media,' says David Anderson, who reports on United for the Press Association.[9] 'He knows exactly what a journalist wants,' says Bob Cass of the *Mail on Sunday*.[10] Ferguson once said he would 'hate' to be a football journalist, especially 'a reporter on the tabloids' – which was odd for someone who had helped his own son to go into sports journalism.[11] Given his skill at playing the media game, and the fun he derives from it, Ferguson would have done the job brilliantly, however. His fantastic knowledge of football, his determination to beat everyone else to the best stories, his ability to apply charm or aggression depending on the circumstances, and his recklessness with the facts would all have been great assets as a tabloid sportswriter.

Ferguson's pre-match press conferences are carefully thought through in advance to have the maximum effect on United's opponents. The BBC pundit and former Liverpool captain Alan Hansen has observed how Ferguson will often say how such-and-such a player in the opposing team is particularly good, thereby adding to the pressure on the individual. Or he may even praise the referee in advance, hoping, it seems, that the official will feel flattered and not want to upset Ferguson's high opinion of him.

After games, Ferguson has perfected the art of offering journalists a juicy distraction if United have lost, or have been involved in an embarrassing incident. One example occurred in August 1994, when Eric Cantona was sent off in a pre-season game against Rangers at Ibrox: Ferguson attacked the home fans (of which he'd once been one himself) for being too hostile to United. It had the required effect: the papers had their story, and there was little space left to mention Cantona's dismissal. 'Like a conjurer,' the *Times* reporter Kevin McCarra says of the incident, 'Ferguson had misdirected an audience who enjoyed the deception.'[12] Ferguson himself later admitted in his diary, 'I wanted to give them something to talk about other than Eric.'[13] His other frequent ploy is to criticise a doubtful decision by the referee.

Similarly, when United lost 2–1 to Nottingham Forest at Old Trafford four months later it was the Reds' first and only home league defeat of the season. Afterwards Ferguson accused the Forest full-back Stuart Pearce, whom he'd once tried to buy, of having made racist remarks to Paul Ince during the game. The Forest manager, Frank Clark, believes it was a deliberate ploy to distract attention from United's rare defeat. 'These type of allegations are made all the time in football in regard to things that happen on the pitch,' says Clark. 'I suspect he did it purely to take the pressure and the focus off defeat. He knew the press would stir it up so that then there's nothing in the press about the Man. U. loss and losing their home record.'[14]

Equally, Ferguson seems to have no qualms about using journalists to feed disinformation to United's opponents about possible team line-ups, injuries and tactics. Football writers have lost count of the number of times he has told them that such-and-such a player is injured, only for whoever it is to recover overnight in time to play the following day. Indeed, journalists regard the details about Manchester United's likely eleven which are released for the

Saturday-morning papers as all but worthless. 'It's just frustrating to be asked by your desk to produce these teams for the paper,' says a reporter who is close to Ferguson. 'You know it's going to be a guess. You can disregard anything Alex tells you about team selections, injuries, who's playing and so on. Frankly, he blatantly lies to you. He's rationalised it in advance, of course, by deciding it suits his purposes to confuse the media.'

'Journalists who don't play the game Ferguson's way,' the BBC Radio 5 Live reporter Pat Murphy once observed, 'are consigned to the gulag of indifference, frozen out. Ferguson would prefer questions from the media to be about as demanding as an interview in *Hello!* magazine.'[15] The manager can be as intimidating and foul-mouthed with reporters and photographers who upset him as he is with team members, even though they are not his employees. On one occasion at The Cliff he even tried to make a *News of the World* photographer, Billy Griffiths, open his camera and hand over his film, peppering his blast with plenty of swear words beginning with F, C and B. 'He didn't seem to mind that there were small children around to hear the foul things he was saying,' Griffiths said afterwards. 'When he asked me for the film, I said: "No way, it is mine."'[16]

Many reporters have similar tales. David Anderson was one victim after stating incorrectly that Peter Schmeichel was out of the team for family reasons. 'He launched into a tirade: "Fucking check your facts." I was absolutely stunned. It's the way he switches on Mr Anger and all the expletives, the finger-jabbing, right in your face, eyes blazing, lots of "fucking". I was reeling from this. To be fair, I had made a mistake.'[17] But Anderson was even more astonished a few moments later when Ferguson suddenly turned off the anger and gave one of his best one-on-one interviews.

Ken Lawrence, a Manchester-based freelance journalist who has worked for several tabloids in his time, suffered a similar blast in 1991 when he complained to Martin Edwards on behalf of the rest of the north-west reporters about Ferguson delaying his post-match comments after a game in Athens. When Lawrence got on the plane home, Ferguson began shouting at him and told the reporter never to report him to Edwards again. Lawrence says he told Ferguson that if he had to he would. 'Then he lunged into me, jabbing at my chest with his finger. Brain Kidd had to pull him away, and he was led away ranting down the plane.' Lawrence had to persuade his colleagues not to write about the incident, and adds that Ferguson did apologise to him later that week. 'That was the first time press people in Manchester saw the other side of him. Until the FA Cup win in 1990 he was under great pressure, so he was far more get-at-able and user-friendly. Then he embarked on a campaign of control over the press.'[18]

Reporters who continue to offend find themselves banned from his briefings. Ferguson may even put pressure on their news desks to have them removed from the United beat. The offence need not involve making factual errors, but simply asking the manager questions he doesn't like, says David Anderson:

> It's almost a climate of fear. Normally at Fergie's press
> conferences you don't ask critical questions. He has us all
> frightened and in the condition where no one dares ask
> daring questions, otherwise he has them thrown out and
> banned. Or you tie yourself in knots making a fool of
> yourself trying to ask a question that's acceptable. It's very
> much a classroom atmosphere. He'll pick on people who
> make mistakes in their questions – 'What an idiot, he doesn't
> know his two times table.'[19]

The situation at Manchester United would be familiar to journalists who reported Aberdeen's affairs in Ferguson's time between 1978 and 1986. 'Many sports writers would do anything rather than upset the guy,' remembers Frank Gilfeather, who then worked for the local ITV station, Grampian, and also for Radio Clyde. 'And if he bollocked them they would crawl back five minutes later just to get the quotes.'[20] Frank Gilfeather admired Ferguson's stamina, non-stop work, and ability to think ahead, but hated how most journalists were cowed into submission. What he disliked above all was that Ferguson was so unpredictable.

On one of the Friday-night programmes he presented for Grampian, Gilfeather suggested in a background report on Aberdeen that Joe Harper might not have a future at Pittodrie. His report included several 'vox pops' with Dons' fans who said Harper was their 'king' and asked what Ferguson was playing at. The manager's response came after the game the following day, when Gilfeather turned up for the traditional post-match comments in Ferguson's office:

> I'm walking up and hear this torrid abuse, and I turn and see
> him shouting and bawling at me, 'You put that out last night,
> about Harper and all.' There were policemen there and club
> officials going about. They were quite shocked. I later
> explained in print that he sees any mild criticism as criticism
> of his 'baby'. It was as if the club was his family, a thing he'd
> built, and anything you said against it you were seen to be a
> traitor, if you like.[21]

Of course Frank Gilfeather had been correct: Joe Harper didn't last much longer under Alex Ferguson at Pittodrie.

There were also rows about Gilfeather not obtaining Ferguson's permission when he interviewed Aberdeen players: it was the players' responsibility to get such approval, the reporter insisted, not his job. But the biggest dispute occurred when the Aberdeen manager came into Grampian one Friday evening and told the TV presenter that Jim Leighton wouldn't be playing the next day because he was injured. The following lunchtime, before the game, Gilfeather heard from a senior source at the club that the goalkeeper had actually been dropped. So Gilfeather announced this detail on Radio Clyde, pointing out the inconsistency with what Ferguson had told him only the night before. The following Monday, Ferguson accused Gilfeather of calling him a liar, and said he would be banned from the post-match gatherings in future. A few weeks later Ferguson rang Gilfeather's boss at Radio Clyde and demanded that the station assign another reporter to Aberdeen's games.

In time, Joe Harper himself became one of Ferguson's media victims, when the manager started boycotting the local Northsound radio station because Harper presented programmes for it. Harper claims that 'He said to them, "If you're going to keep Harper on that show, you're not going to get any access to me or the players." So they put me off the show, because they didn't have enough clout at the time. So basically he put me out of a job. It was only a part-time thing, but it was a job.'[22]

Such experiences in Ferguson's Aberdeen days have echoes at Manchester United. In some cases the manager has refused to do post-match press conferences until an offending reporter has left, and many football writers who specialise in covering United have been barred from the briefings Ferguson has traditionally given at the club training ground on Friday lunchtimes before a weekend game. This might be understandable in the case of some tabloid papers, whose journalistic standards are often poor when it comes to covering football, and which often run stories which are largely fabricated. Yet the Press Association – the British agency which serves most other media outlets – is hardly known for sensationalism. Indeed, the PA is notoriously cautious in its coverage. Yet, despite this, the PA reporter David Anderson has long been excluded from Ferguson's Friday sessions. At the time when Anderson was admitted to such briefings it was considered traditional for the PA man to set the ball rolling with questions on the obvious topics of the day. After a few minutes he would shut up or leave to give the newspaper journalists their chance. But Ferguson would unsettle him,

Anderson says, by giving very short answers to his opening queries – 'Yes', 'No' or 'No comment'. This gave the reporter no time to think of follow-ups. On one occasion Ferguson spotted the questions Anderson had listed beforehand in his notebook, and told him to strike off the first two 'for a start'.[23]

Anderson says his problems started towards the end of the 1998–99 treble season. Martin Edwards had publicly said that Ferguson could keep his job for life, so Anderson tried to ask the United manager about his next contract. 'He said, "I don't want to talk about that. I've had enough of you. Get out. You ask too many questions."' Anderson says he wasn't able to attend the next briefing anyway, but when he turned up on the subsequent occasion Ferguson again told him to get out. 'I've been banned ever since,' he says.[24]

In the case of the *Daily Mail*, it's not an individual journalist who is barred but the whole newspaper. In the mid-1990s the paper ran several stories linking the United manager with the notorious Norwegian agent Rune Hauge. Ferguson was furious that the *Mail* seemed to be declaring him guilty by association (though, given the Norwegian's reputation, it was perhaps unwise for Ferguson to maintain his friendship and dealings with him). Nor did it help the *Mail* that its then sports editor, Brian Cooney, had in 1987 tipped off the newsdesk where he previously worked, the *Daily Star*, about Ferguson's affair with the Aberdeen waitress Deirdrie McHardy. The *Mail* ban seems to be the strongest of all: when Ferguson briefs the press informally in a small huddle – for example in an airport baggage area on a European trip – he will always ensure that no *Mail* journalist is present before speaking. The boycott continues even though Cooney left the paper in 2000 and his successor, Colin Gibson, travelled to Manchester early the following year to meet the new United chief executive, Peter Kenyon, and the club's communications director, Paddy Harverson, to try to restore relations. Ferguson, however, refused to see Gibson, and things remained unresolved – with the result that in 2001, unusually among the media, the *Mail* had no compunction about asking pertinent questions about Jason Ferguson's activities. This only prompted Ferguson to accuse it of 'running a campaign against myself, my son, and the club . . . It's a disgrace, it's a vendetta.'[25]

At the formal press conferences which take place after games, or which are required by UEFA on the day before European fixtures, Ferguson will enter the room scanning it for potential dissidents, hoping, it seems, to scare off trouble. 'Stupid question!' he will often say to reporters who ask something awkward. In 1993, after he'd had a row on the touchline with the QPR manager Gerry Francis, he stormed out of a press conference when journalists tried to press him about the incident, which had followed a ferocious tackle on the United defender Paul Parker. 'You guys go too far, you are a pain in the arse,' he shouted. 'You don't stop, do you? I am going to end this right here.'[26] Sometimes, as press conferences come to a close, Ferguson is known to bark, 'Away and write your shite!'[27]

The man who once refused to take part in a Falkirk team photo because he didn't like one of the photographers present has turned the media boycott into an art form. In 1992, for instance, he was angry about remarks made by Tommy Docherty on the Piccadilly radio station in Manchester, where the former United and Scotland manager worked as a summariser on United games. Docherty had suggested that the defender Gary Pallister had been an expensive mistake, particularly when he missed a number of games through injury. Ferguson both boycotted Piccadilly and tried to get Docherty banned from making further radio broadcasts from Old Trafford. Docherty says the United board overruled Ferguson, 'and said everyone's entitled to their opinion'.[28] On at least two occasions Ferguson has boycotted Sky Television, even though his own son Jason worked there as a producer at the time. His first such protest came in 1993, when Sky showed pictures of Ferguson's touchline row with Gerry Francis: Ferguson banned United players from talking to the station. The following year he was annoyed with Sky's treatment of Eric Cantona, especially when the station edited a series of the player's illegal tackles and set the sequence to music.

But Ferguson's least favourite broadcast outlet must be the BBC's Radio 5 Live. The station upset the United manager one Monday morning in 1996, after United had lost 6–3 at Southampton, when a presenter said the six goals that United let in had made her weekend – a sentiment with which her fellow presenter apparently concurred.

Later Ferguson began a complete boycott of Radio 5 Live after the commentator Alan Green described Roy Keane as a 'lout' while explaining why he wouldn't vote for Keane as Footballer of the Year – though Green added that he didn't actually have a vote in the contest. Green quickly withdrew the comment, but BBC bosses were convinced that it was these incidents and Ferguson's hostility that lay behind Manchester United's decision in 1998 to award its radio contract for European games to Talk Radio, even though the BBC believed it had matched its rivals' price.

Ferguson's biggest row with the BBC occurred in the autumn of 2000, after the corporation's monthly magazine *Match of the Day* published a profile of Ferguson. 'During his reign,' said the opening strap line, 'he's been branded a bully, cheat and back-stabber, and there is plenty of evidence to show that the flip side to his character has been crucial in Ferguson's success story.'[29] Ferguson was understandably offended by the words 'bully, cheat and back-stabber' and sued the BBC for libel, with the help of the United solicitor, Maurice Watkins, who described the article as a 'character assassination'. Ferguson boycotted the whole of the BBC, and applied particular pressure to its Saturday night *Match of the Day* highlights programme by refusing it any interviews with United players. The BBC pointed out that the programme had no connection with the magazine of the same name, and that the corporation's publications are remote from its broadcast programmes, but this made no difference.

Ferguson's boycott lasted several weeks, and the *Match of the Day* presenter Gary Lineker announced several times on air that the United manager wouldn't do interviews because of the dispute. The irony was that the author of the article, Tim Glynne-Jones, who also edited *Match of the Day* magazine, is a keen Manchester United supporter, and in the 1980s had started one of the earliest Old Trafford fanzines, the *Shankhill Skinhead*, named after Norman Whiteside. 'I would have thought,' Glynne-Jones says, 'that a man who has achieved what he has achieved would be able to shrug off that sort of criticism. What I was really saying was that he was cunning. I'm surprised that reading that would shock him. I would have thought he would just chuckle and say, "Yeah, I'm good at that."'[30]

Glynne-Jones and the BBC lawyer assigned to the case were keen to fight it. They gathered evidence to support the 'bully, cheat and back-stabber' claim, though that hadn't in fact been the overall thrust of the article, but in the end Ferguson won because the boycott was hurting the *Match of the Day* programme too much. In a meeting with Maurice Watkins at the Royal Lancaster Hotel, the BBC agreed to pay £10,000 to the cancer trust named after Ferguson's mother and to publish an apology in the magazine. 'At the end of the day,' says a senior BBC executive, 'he's an important person and they're an important side. I guess we decided that he was making it rather difficult for some of my colleagues in BBC Television.'

'Ferguson intimidates as many broadcasting executives as he does journalists,' says Alan Green.[31] In October 1995, when Roy Keane was sent off in a 2–0 win over Middlesbrough – his third dismissal in fourteen games – the then BBC head of sport, Brian Barwick, urged the commentator John Motson to question Ferguson about the incident in his post-match interview for that night's *Match of the Day* programme. Motson is no Jeremy Paxman, and his question was couched in the mildest terms – indeed, he almost suggested the answer as he asked if United would deal with Keane inside the club. 'Well, John, you've no right to ask that question,' Ferguson calmly replied. 'You're out of order. You know full well my ruling on that. Right, that's the interview finished.' It was only once Ferguson had walked out of the shot that he erupted, though he was still in microphone range and being recorded. He warned the popular commentator not to let their exchange be broadcast: 'I don't want to fucking watch it! Cancel it! Fucking make sure that does not go out!' Motson meanwhile pleaded that he'd been 'asked to ask' the question. 'You fucking know the rules here!' Ferguson shouted back, revealing his view that he has a unwritten understanding with football journalists that they don't ask about awkward subjects.[32] The ridiculous thing was that Motson's question had actually been very soft. It would have been easy for Ferguson to smile and to brush it off with something like 'As you say, John, it's an internal matter, and we'll keep it that way.'

A debate ensued in the *Match of the Day* office as to whether to show the outburst on the programme that night. The presenter Desmond Lynam was in favour, suggesting they could bleep out the swear words and that it would show viewers another side of Ferguson. His editors, however, preferred not to upset the United manager further. Yet had a government minister reacted the same way to a question on *Newsnight* the exchange would certainly have appeared on the programme and received wide coverage elsewhere.

Just as many Conservative and Labour politicians believe that the BBC is biased against their parties, so Alex Ferguson appears convinced that the corporation is not just biased against Manchester United but is strongly pro-Liverpool – an opinion which is shared by many United supporters. (Most other football fans, of course, think the whole media industry is biased *towards* United.) The regular presence of two former Liverpool defenders, Alan Hansen and Mark Lawrenson, as pundits on *Match of the Day* is seen as evidence of this, along with the fact that the former BBC head of sport, Brian Barwick, was openly a Liverpool fan (though the programme's editor, Niall Sloane, is a United supporter, as is the reporter Tony

Gubba). Ferguson couldn't understand why United were never chosen as Team of the Year in the BBC Sports Personality of the Year awards, especially after winning the double in 1994 and 1996. It was only after Barwick left to go to ITV that United finally won the accolade in 1999. Privately, senior BBC sources believe that Barwick's partisanship may indeed have prevented Ferguson's team from winning the award before then.

Ferguson's approach to the media has undoubtedly changed during his time at Manchester United. During the early years, when he was still trying to establish his reputation in England and bring success to Old Trafford, he understood the power which journalists have to destroy a struggling football manager. As a result he remained on sociable terms with most reporters. In the early 1990s, however, as he won English honours, maintaining good relations was no longer so important. 'I just don't need the press any longer,' he was heard to remark. 'Confidence came with his success,' says Alan Green, 'and his tone seemed to become more aggressive and arrogant.'[33] The outspoken BBC Radio 5 Live commentator says he now dislikes Ferguson 'intensely', even though they were friendly in the 1980s, and he regards it as 'a badge of honour' that he is one of the few journalists to stand up to him.[34]

Whereas reporters had once been encouraged to stay in the same hotel as the players when United had an away fixture, now the team and the press stay at different locations. The easy access that journalists once had to the training ground has gradually been reduced, especially since 2000, when United moved from The Cliff to new training facilities at Carrington. The site soon became known as 'Fortress Carrington', because fans and the media find it so difficult to locate and get into. 'It keeps those fuckers from the media out,' Ferguson once boasted to a football colleague.[35] At the same time, young Manchester United players are given training in handling interviews, so that when they do talk to journalists they get the message across in the best way.

This tension between hostility and a careful use of the media has run throughout Ferguson's career. From his days as a player he has gone out of his way to establish good relations with a small band of friendly journalists such as the late Jim Rodger of the *Daily Mirror*, though such relationships have always been on his terms. Ferguson's favourites have tended to be older reporters, often Scots, whom he has known for many years and feels he can trust. They include Hugh McIlvanney of the *Sunday Times*, who helped write his autobiography; Bill Thornton of the *Daily Star*; Gerry McNee, who covers Scottish football for the *News of the World*; another Scottish reporter, Glenn Gibbons, who writes for the *Observer* and the *Scotsman*; and Peter Fitton and Bob Cass, who are both with the *Mail on Sunday*. Cass, who is based in the north-east, first got to know the manager when he went up to Scotland to cover one of Aberdeen's European games for the *Sun* in the early 1980s and Ferguson went to the trouble of driving out to meet him at the airport, 'even though he didn't know me from Adam'.[36] Despite his aggressive treatment of much of the press, such acts of generosity are not unusual. The football writer Steve Curry says that, when he lost his job on the *Express*, Ferguson was 'one of the first on the phone' to offer sympathy (as he often is, too, when fellow managers get the sack).[37]

Another journalist who has always got on well with Ferguson, and has collaborated on four of his books, is the former *Manchester Evening News* football correspondent David Meek. Meek covered United for almost forty years, from the Munich air crash in 1958 until his retirement from the paper in 1995, and always enjoyed special treatment. Since his departure as the *Evening News* United correspondent the relationship between the newspaper and the club has deteriorated, which may explain the reluctance of the paper's management to allow this author to look at its cuttings files. 'I don't feel our local paper does us any favours these days,' Ferguson wrote in his diary in 1997, 'so I'm reluctant to do them any in return.'[38] He was particularly upset by the phone poll the *Evening News* conducted in the summer of 1995, which suggested he should quit as United manager. He felt it was a kick in the teeth after the help he'd given Meek over the years, and Meek's successor, Stuart Mathieson, has never enjoyed the same kind of access.

Alex Ferguson has long understood that football is unlike many other specialist areas of journalism, where reporters will find alternatives if one source is denied to them. In effect, each club is a local monopoly. If the manager of Aberdeen won't speak to a local sports reporter, or Manchester United boycotts the *Daily Globe*'s correspondent covering north-west football, it can seriously affect the journalist's output and damage their standing with their editors. Many reporters prefer to avoid asking difficult questions or reporting embarrassing facts, simply to preserve some kind of relationship which gets them access to stories and quotes from the manager. It has even got to the absurd stage occasionally where if one reporter has an exclusive story that will annoy Ferguson he will deliberately share it with rivals from other papers to avoid suffering a personal backlash from the United manager.

Since Manchester United are the biggest story in football, Ferguson has huge power in controlling the media agenda, and it is a power which he has become adept at exploiting. His public comments are usually highly newsworthy, and because of his status, influence and connections within football he is often able to supply friendly reporters with strong stories which have nothing to do with his club. But even those with special access will find themselves used by Ferguson when it suits him. In 1997 the editors of the *Mail on Sunday* were tipped off that Eric Cantona was about to retire, and they naturally asked Bob Cass to check the story with Ferguson. The United manager denied it to Cass more than once, only for Cantona to announce he was quitting at a press conference two days later. Cass nearly lost his job for killing one of the biggest football stories of the year, though Ferguson did apologise to him afterwards. He explained that he'd promised Cantona not to release the news, and promised to make it up to Cass later. Ferguson had also denied the story to Peter Fitton, then on the *Sun*, who had also been tipped off about Cantona. The United manager's friend Gerry McNee of the *News of the World* was similarly misled in the summer of 2001 when the paper was given what seemed a highly improbable tip that Ferguson wanted to sell the defender Jaap Stam. Ferguson's denial killed the story, yet Stam was duly sold to Lazio only a few weeks later.

While obstructing large sections of the media, Alex Ferguson rarely fails to get his opinions across on most issues. He uses United's own outlets prolifically, with long columns in the club programme and articles in every edition of the monthly magazine and the annual handbook. Ferguson was delighted in the late 1990s when United set up first its own local radio station and then a television channel, MUTV, for which he does regular interviews, confident he can count on a comfortable ride. Although he often complains about the incessant pressures for interviews and comment, he has still found time to 'write' his own well-paid columns in the national press, though in practice they are usually ghost-written for him on the basis of interviews. During the 1998 World Cup, for instance, when he also acted as an ITV pundit, he did a weekly analysis from France for the *Sunday Times*. In one famous article he strongly criticised Glenn Hoddle, the England manager, for putting David Beckham on the platform at a press conference just after he had unexpectedly dropped him. 'It is something I would never have allowed,' Ferguson wrote. '[Beckham] must have been devastated emotionally, and asking him to bare his soul in public was not likely to help anybody but the headline-writers.'[39] Hoddle retaliated by saying that Ferguson had been unprofessional in criticising a fellow manager, and accused him of disrupting England's preparations for their next game.

During the 2000–01 season Ferguson was paid £100,000 to contribute about eight articles over the course of the year to the *News of the World*, though part of the outlay was met by the column's sponsor, the brewers Carling. This is about the going rate for articles by celebrities, and generally Ferguson gives value for money, expressing his views in pungent style, with plenty of controversy.

Nobody is more keenly aware of his value as a media contributor than Ferguson. In his Aberdeen days, it upset Frank Gilfeather that the manager always demanded payment before agreeing to speak on camera to the local ITV station. 'The first thing he always asked was "How much?"' Gilfeather recalls:

> And at that time it was something like twenty-five quid or whatever. I'd say, 'Look, it's only a couple of minutes, Alex.' 'Yeah, well how much will I get? I get £35 from STV when I do a thing for their news or for *Scotsport*, so how much for you guys?' Afterwards he would pull me into a room and say, 'Remember how much I am getting.' I thought, 'This guy is money crazy.' He was very into money.[40]

On one occasion Ferguson justified his claim for payment by reminding Gilfeather that Grampian had recently announced good profits. The TV presenter says he raised Ferguson's constant financial demands with Chris Anderson, the Aberdeen club's vice-chairman. While Anderson agreed that Ferguson ought to do such interviews for free, as part of his managerial duties, the Aberdeen directors felt powerless to stop him demanding money.

Alex Ferguson's poor relations with large parts of the media have also been a matter of concern to the senior management and directors at Old Trafford, especially since 2000, when the club appointed a director of communications, Paddy Harverson, a former *Financial Times* reporter, whose job it is to improve United's public relations and image. But few Manchester United supporters care that the manager has such bad relations with newspapers and broadcasters; many believe that the press is biased against their club anyway. Ferguson can rightly claim that his boycotts and bans against particular reporters and media outlets have no effect on the team's results or on his relentless accumulation of trophies. Indeed, the fact that particular journalists, major broadcasting companies or national newspapers are banned from time to time, or that he sometimes refuses to speak to the press as a whole, adds to the siege mentality which he has always inculcated in his players. His attitude might appal public-relations experts, but Ferguson has thrived on the so-called 'ABU syndrome' – the idea that the rest of the world backs Anyone But United. Above all, he has become a master of manipulating the emotions and passions which football generates.

In appointing Harverson, United were one of the last major clubs to employ a full-time PR man – mainly because Ferguson had always opposed the idea. He believed that PR people consider it their duty to get more publicity, whereas he feels that United need less. In 1997 Ferguson said that the media had become a 'monster', and that many of the younger journalists had become too egotistical and all-demanding. 'They want exclusive stories and confidential background; they want their cards marked; they want gossip. And believe me if they don't get it, you're in trouble.'[41]

Relations between Alex Ferguson and the press reached a new low in November 2001, when Manchester United hit their worst run of form since 1996. The manager suddenly announced that he wouldn't give any more media interviews; there would be no more press conferences or Friday briefings, and henceforth the only comments he would make would be to Manchester United's own radio station and TV channel. Broadcasters were allowed to use clips from these interviews, so in effect they had to recycle public-relations handout material. This practice is normally discouraged or even forbidden in broadcast journalism, because it gives reporters no chance to put the subject on the spot. But as United returned to form in December 2001 Ferguson's ban was slowly relaxed: he soon agreed to television and radio interviews again, and he was in any case obliged under UEFA rules to do press conferences before European games.

Yet his boycott was in breach of Manchester United's contract with the FA Premier League, which states that managers must make 'their best endeavours' to speak to the press before and after games. 'The press ban gave us a major headache,' says one Premier League official. 'Journalists were ringing up going, "What's going on? He can't do this. Look at the Premier League contract." And they're right. He's a law unto his own – that's what everyone says. It's another example [of how] he gets an easy ride from the footballing authorities because he's so big and powerful.' Like the Football Association previously, the Premier League failed to enforce its rules.

Ferguson's behaviour was also personally embarrassing to Paddy Harverson, as he'd been employed specifically to stop such disputes. In December 2001 he brokered a compromise whereby Ferguson would brief one daily reporter – Bill Thornton of the *Daily Star* – and one Sunday journalist – Bob Cass of the *Mail on Sunday* – and it was understood that they would then pass on the quotes to their respective colleagues. The Sunday briefings quickly broke down, however, at the end of December 2001, when Ferguson seemed to hint in his briefing with Cass that he might think of reversing his decision to retire in May 2002. 'At the moment my mind is made up about retiring at the end of the season,' he said. 'Is there any possibility of me changing my mind? I don't think so but you never know what might happen. The club are looking for my successor but when the thing comes, nearer the time, who knows what will happen? But at the moment my mind is fixed on retiring.'[42]

Cass himself made little of the manager's comment in the *Mail on Sunday*, but it was seized on by most of his Sunday rivals, which resulted in a series of back-page 'exclusives'. The headline 'FERGIE: I'LL STAY' in the *News of the World*, was typical.[43] Ferguson and Cass were so annoyed that his words had been interpreted in this way that two days later the United manager gave a follow-up interview, to Glenn Gibbons in the *Scotsman*, in which he insisted he was sticking by his decision to retire. 'I'm going, all right,' Ferguson announced, 'that's been settled for some time now.'[44] The resulting article was an obvious attempt to rewrite the Sunday headlines.

Alex Ferguson and Bob Cass both claimed to be so upset about how the manager's remarks had been hyped up that they abandoned the pooled Sunday briefing after that. And Manchester United officials even cited the incident as an example of how journalists would seize on the slightest ambiguity to make an inaccurate splash on the back pages.

Six weeks later, however, the 'hype' would prove to be no exaggeration at all.

Extra Time

'We were just assuming that he was leaving at the end of the season. I've said before – the wives make decisions, the big ones.'

David Beckham[1]

The call came through while I was in St Helen's on Merseyside, compiling a film for BBC *Newsnight* during the May 2001 general-election campaign. It was from Alex Ferguson's Manchester solicitor, Kevin Jaquiss, whom I had known since we were at school together in the 1970s. Sir Alex, he explained, had reached a dead end in his negotiations with the club over the role he was to fulfil at Old Trafford after his retirement as manager in 2002. For months Manchester United had been talking publicly about a consultancy or 'roving ambassador' role, but so far, said Jaquiss, the details had been 'derisory'. It now looked as if he would simply leave United when his contract expired in June 2002, never to return. Jason Ferguson, the solicitor explained, was keen to get this fact into the public domain, but in such a way that the story did not have any Ferguson 'fingerprints' on it. Could I help? When I suggested this might just be a negotiating ploy, Jaquiss assured me it was not: Ferguson had indeed reached the end of the road.

Even from St Helen's, it was straightforward to find a home for such a story: the *Daily Mail* was enthusiastic. Given Ferguson's strained relations with the paper (I didn't then appreciate just how strained they were), placing it there would disguise the story's origins in the Ferguson camp. The *Mail* ran it on its back page the following day under the headline 'Fergie's future in doubt', though it downplayed the extent of the impasse, perhaps because it had been stung by Ferguson in the past.[2] The rest of the media ignored the story at first, partly because United said they were still confident of a deal. But three days later Ferguson confirmed the news himself when questioned by the club's TV channel, MUTV, and in subsequent interviews he said he was 'very disappointed' that United had not offered him a proper post-retirement role. 'All the talks on the subject are now dead. It is over. When my contract is finished I will leave United for good . . . I have decided I will not take any 'roving ambassador' role and will sever all connections . . . That's all there is to it. I am definitely going.'[3]

Suddenly the story erupted. It was now all over the back pages, and on radio and television bulletins, with widespread speculation that the United manager might even quit during the summer, a year early. As United lost 3–1 at Tottenham that Saturday, in the final game of the season, fans chanted, 'Every single one of us loves Alex Ferguson' to the tune of 'Down by the Riverside'. The anthem went on for thirty-one minutes.

The fans had good reason to sing. Although the Spurs game was the third defeat in a row, United had already won the League with ease. It was Alex Ferguson's seventh title in nine years, and he had also become the first boss in English club history to win three successive championships. (The previous hat-tricks, by Huddersfield in the 1920s, Arsenal in the '30s, and Liverpool in the '80s, involved two managers at each club.) Indeed, had United not relaxed in the final weeks, they could have won by an even larger margin than the record-breaking eighteen points of the year before. Even so, they finished ten points ahead of second-placed Arsenal, whom they had beaten 6–1 at Old Trafford in February. The most notable feature of the season had been the contribution of Teddy Sheringham. The thirty-five-year-old striker won both the national player of the year awards, and also regained his place in the England side, after scoring twenty-one goals – almost as many as he'd managed in total in his three previous seasons at Old Trafford.

But there was again disappointment in Europe. United would probably have been eliminated in the first group stage of the European Cup had the Dynamo Kiev forward George Demetradze not missed a sitter five minutes from the end at Old Trafford. The second group stage was easier, but in the quarter-final Bayern Munich took revenge for the events of May 1999, winning both in Manchester and in Munich. Like United's conquerors in 1997 and 2000, Bayern went on to win the European Cup. The Bayern coach, Ottmar Hitzfeld, a good friend of Ferguson, was the only manager to beat United at home and away in a two-legged European tie, and he'd now done it twice, having previously achieved the feat with Borussia Dortmund in 1997. No wonder Hitzfeld was among those mentioned as Ferguson's possible successor. Others included Martin O'Neill, the former Leicester manager who'd revitalised Celtic, winning the Scottish treble in his first season; David O'Leary, who'd just taken a young Leeds United team to the semi-final of the European Cup; the Roma boss, Fabio Capello; and Sven-Göran Eriksson, who had revived England's chances of qualifying for the 2002 World Cup.

In May 2001 it looked as if the Manchester United board might have to choose a new manager rather sooner than they'd intended. Once again the directors were plunged into a summer crisis over Ferguson's future. Friends of Sir Alex say he honestly believed that the Spurs fixture might prove to have been his last game with the club. 'Privately he said, "I think I'm out of here,"' recalls his Aberdeen friend George Ramsay. 'He was really down in the dumps, angry and sad.'[4] His three sons had been so anxious that this might indeed be his last game for United that they had hastily made sure they were all present, while Jason told people his father would not be at United in the coming season.

The question of what to do with Alex Ferguson once he retired had exercised minds at Old Trafford for years. Martin Edwards was known to be worried by what he called the 'Busby syndrome'. Sir Matt Busby had become a United director after initially retiring in 1969, and had visited the ground almost every day. Edwards, who had been on the United board since 1970, had observed how three previous managers – Wilf McGuinness (1969–70), Frank O'Farrell (1971–72) and Tommy Docherty (1972–77) – had been affected by Busby's long shadow. Sir Matt was a powerful voice in club affairs, and also a magnet for disaffected players. Alex Ferguson was just as forceful a personality as Busby, and Edwards feared that if he stayed at the club after relinquishing the managership he would not be able to resist getting involved in football matters whenever things got rocky. After all, none of the home-grown players had ever known any club boss but Ferguson. But Edwards was no longer such a significant figure in United affairs, having stepped down as chief executive in the summer of 2000 to make way for Peter Kenyon, a former manager with the Umbro sportswear company. Edwards's attempts to succeed the retiring Sir Roland Smith as PLC chairman had been thwarted, but he remained a member of both boards and chairman of the subsidiary football company, and his fears that Ferguson would constrain whoever succeeded him as manager were undoubtedly shared by other influential voices at Old Trafford.

Martin Edwards hadn't always opposed the idea of Alex Ferguson serving the club in some other role after retiring from management. In 1993 he said it would be a 'great shame if Alex wasn't to be around in some capacity' after he stopped running the team, 'whether as a director or general manager on the football side.'[5] And the following year he said that, 'It might be appropriate that Alex takes his place on the board.'[6] Edwards's subsequent fears about Ferguson and the

Busby syndrome were part of the cooling in relations between the two men in the second half of the 1990s.

Ferguson was naturally hurt by the idea that the directors might insist that he leave the club completely, with no acknowledgement of his enormous contribution to the transformation of Manchester United over the decade. With his keen grasp of football history, he was very aware of how shabbily clubs had treated his great managerial heroes in the past – most notably Scot Symon, who'd been sacked by Rangers; Jock Stein, who'd been moved to run Celtic's pools operation; and Bill Shankly, who was given no other role at Anfield after retiring as Liverpool manager in 1974. Ferguson was not shy in responding publicly to Edwards's concerns that the Busby problem might be repeated:

> It's a different bloody era. Sir Matt didn't have the media war you have today, he didn't have the size of the club you have today. It's a different set of circumstances completely. You would think that the club would want someone of experience to stay on. I wouldn't have wanted any involvement with the first team whatsoever and I said that to Martin Edwards. I'm not sure they could grasp the situation. This thing with Sir Matt seems to be in Martin Edwards's head quite firmly, although I don't think it is a fair comparison.[7]

But part of the problem was of Ferguson's own making, for he had never been clear about the role he might fill after stepping down. He never said so, but he would have loved a place on one or both of the United boards, and he had of course served briefly as a director of Aberdeen. The title of club president, which Busby had eventually been accorded, would have chimed with Ferguson's sense of his place in the club's history. And he had also shown, with his behind-the-scenes manoeuvrings at the time of the Sky bid, that he was interested in playing some part in the ownership of the club –

though this was hardly something to broach with the United directors. (Nor, despite his personal wealth of perhaps £5–10 million, was he rich enough; United's stock-market value of around £350 million, as at the start of 2002, meant that any ownership role would have required other significant investors.)

There was talk that he might act as a club ambassador, rather as Sir Bobby Charlton has long done, promoting the development of United's marketing operations overseas. Another suggestion was that he might revamp the famous Old Trafford youth programme, which now involves ties with several foreign feeder clubs, but has been suffering from new FA rules which limit recruitment to teenagers who live within ninety minutes' drive of the club. And it was clear that, whatever the job, Alex Ferguson expected to be well-remunerated – partly to reflect his past work for United, which he continued to feel had been under-rewarded, as much as for any future contribution he might make.

United officials weren't impressed, however, by Jason's arrogant manner in negotiations, and by what they thought were unrealistic demands. On the other hand, Ferguson himself was particularly upset to hear that during the final meeting in May one director had said, 'He may be a good manager but he doesn't exactly sell the strips, does he?'[8] Sir Alex also suspected that Martin Edwards was plotting with Brian Kidd to bring Kidd's boss at Leeds, David O'Leary, to Old Trafford as his successor, with Kidd returning at his side. Indeed, Ferguson was so worried about this possibility that he told his journalist friend Gerry McNee about his concerns, and the story was promptly published in the *News of the World*.

Whatever their differences, the fact is that between May and July 2001 Sir Alex completely outmanoeuvred the club. After the careful leak through Kevin Jaquiss of the fact that he was angry, and his subsequent confirmation of the rift in an MUTV interview, supporters immediately rallied to his side. The chants at White Hart Lane showed the depth of their feeling, and the two main fans'

535

organisations, IMUSA and Shareholders United, denounced the United board for not giving Ferguson the kind of job he wanted and which they felt he deserved. The level of outrage may have surprised the directors, and they soon realised that without decisive action the manager might resign suddenly, or, just as damaging, the arguments could drag on publicly for months, with an inevitable effect on the morale of the players and the share price of the PLC. The fans who belonged to Shareholders United had previously never won much support from the City institutions who own around 70 per cent of the stock. But there was now a possibility that some institutions might join the pro-Ferguson campaign, especially as Shareholders United planned to table a resolution in his support at the PLC's autumn AGM. It could become as big a battle as the Sky controversy of 1998–99, with the media hungry for United stories and happy to give prominent coverage to those voicing their support for Ferguson.

In the face of all of this, the PLC chairman, Sir Roland Smith, and the new chief executive, Peter Kenyon, acted quickly. The task was to convince the three non-executive members of the company board of the need to reward Ferguson more handsomely – and also the finance director, David Gill, who, given his job, took a robust view of the matter. United's marketing director, Peter Draper, and communications director, Paddy Harverson, drafted internal papers setting out the financial reasons why Ferguson should have a well-rewarded post-retirement contract. These revolved around the idea that his continued presence would make a huge contribution to the Manchester United 'brand'.

Old Trafford sources say it also helped resolve the impasse that Jason Ferguson was now replaced as negotiator by his father's accountant, Alan Baines. Jason was 'out of his depth' according to one United witness. 'It's one thing to negotiate a fee for an after-dinner speech, but this was a big business matter.' Baines later explained that Ferguson 'had been insulted' by United's earlier post-retirement offer of £100,000 a year. 'I told the club they had a dilemma. The most successful manager they had in history was unhappy. He felt he had been let down on a loyalty basis and was in huge demand. He would have gone to Barcelona or Monaco. We had to get the temperature down.'[9] It is doubtful, in fact, whether Cathy Ferguson would ever have accepted the idea of Alex moving overseas, but there would certainly have been no shortage of offers. It's believed that the sportswear company Nike, for instance, had already proposed to Ferguson a deal worth £4 million over four years to act as its worldwide ambassador – an offer that Ferguson hadn't hidden from the United directors. Ferguson might also have expanded his work for UEFA, where he had already served for some years on a working party looking into the future of football. 'I am such a bloody talented guy,' he boasted. 'I might go into painting or something like that.'[10]

The outcome was that Ferguson got a five-year post-retirement contract worth more than £1 million a year. In addition, his pay for his forthcoming final season as manager was increased to over £3 million, or £60,000 a week, which meant that for the first time in his years at Old Trafford Ferguson would be better rewarded than any of his players, of whom the best-paid was Roy Keane on around £52,000 a week. 'I am a great believer that a manager cannot command respect from the dressing room unless he earns more than the players,' said Alan Baines.[11] This had been a constant refrain from Ferguson ever since St Mirren, though Baines's claim that underpayment reduced his client's authority is hardly supported by the facts. In the event, Sir Alex would hold his number-one spot in the Old Trafford pay league only briefly.

Ferguson had won hands down. His victory marked the end of Martin Edwards as a major force in Manchester United politics. Edwards's successor, Peter Kenyon, was much more willing to recognise that the United boss should be treated as a rare talent, akin to a superstar player. Indeed, Kenyon – who is far more sympathetic towards the club's fans, and known as 'Cuddly Pete' – had expressed his hope of persuading Ferguson to stay on almost as soon as he started his new job in the summer of 2000.

But Sir Roland Smith and Peter Kenyon soon found that they were under pressure not just from supporters' groups. Shortly after the Ferguson settlement, two Irish multimillionaires, J. P. McManus and John Magnier, had bought a 6.8 per cent shareholding in United. They later increased their stake to 8.6 per cent. The purchase, through a company called Cubic Expression, made them United's second biggest shareholders, behind BSkyB, and they were reported to have their eye on Sky's 9.9 per cent shareholding, though the TV company insisted it wouldn't sell. Both men take a keen interest in horse racing, being known as the 'Coolmore Mafia' after the stud farm which Magnier owns in County Tipperary, and from which he partly made his millions. McManus, who owns the great racehorse Istabraq, is a former bankrupt who made his money in currency trading.

The key fact was that they were also close friends of Alex Ferguson, to whom they had first been introduced, albeit briefly, by the Ladbrokes public-relations man Mike Dillon, when he took Ferguson and his wife to the Cheltenham Gold Cup on their wedding anniversary in 1997. 'When you meet someone who is successful,' Ferguson said of Magnier, 'you want to know more about them and what makes them successful. There's an ordinariness about John that makes you think there must be more than this. But he's so humble, with his feet on the ground, and you realise that's it.'[12] Ferguson was also a frequent visitor to the L'Ambassadeurs gaming club in London, a favourite haunt of the two Irishmen.

Alex Ferguson's interest in horse racing had developed rapidly since his 1997 trip to Cheltenham. The horses he owned, or mostly part-owned, had soon met with success. They were stabled with some of the best trainers in the business. Ed Dunlop in Newmarket had trained Ferguson's first horse, Queensland Star – bought for

17,000 guineas and named after one of the ships built by Ferguson's father. Jack Berry in Lancashire looked after both Harmony Row and another horse, Candleriggs, which cost 35,000 guineas and is named after a Glasgow street. Charlie Brooks, who was based near Newbury before retiring as a trainer in 2000, trained Yankie Lord, which he and Ferguson had hoped to run in the Grand National before it had fitness problems.

Several of Ferguson's horses were co-owned with either J. P. McManus or John Magnier, with Magnier's wife, Sue (daughter of the legendary Irish trainer Vincent O'Brien), or with Michael Tabor, who is also close to the Coolmore Mafia. When his horse Rock of Gibraltar won the Grand Criterium at Longchamp in October 2001 on Prix de l'Arc de Triomphe day – the biggest win of his racing career – Ferguson celebrated with the horse's co-owner, Sue Magnier, and her husband.

Many of his horses were trained by Aidan O'Brien (no relation) at the Ballydoyle stable in Ireland, which is owned by Magnier and closely connected to his Coolmore stud farm a few miles away. 'I can see the likeness between Aidan and myself as a young manager,' Ferguson said. 'His obsession with Ballydoyle. He never takes a holiday you know.'[13] Ferguson would frequently get up early in the morning, take a private plane to Newmarket or Ireland, and watch his horses out on the gallops, before having a big breakfast with his trainers and stable-lads.

John Magnier has been described by the *Racing Post* as the 'most powerful individual in racing'.[14] His bloodstock and training operation, which extends to 6,000 acres around Coolmore, and has large branches in Australia and Kentucky, has achieved an even greater dominance in the sport than Alex Ferguson has in English football. Magnier may be media-shy, but he and Sir Alex have much in common – not least the same highly focused aggression, desire for total control, and willingness to gamble for high stakes. 'Yes, he is ruthless and something of a control-freak,' says one observer, 'but if you support Magnier, then he will always support you.'[15] He could have been describing Sir Alex.

Although Cubic Expression's spokesman insisted that the United shares had been acquired only for investment purposes, members of the PLC board were understandably nervous, given the new shareholders' friendship with their manager. Their fear was that acquisition of a stake in the club was the prelude to a full-scale takeover bid which would give Ferguson an even more powerful role, and possibly endanger the positions of most directors and senior staff.

What particularly worried the Old Trafford management was that Magnier and McManus were also close to the Irish multimillionaire financier Dermot Desmond, who had recently acquired the biggest shareholding in Celtic. Indeed, they are known collectively in Ireland as the Three Musketeers. Cubic spokesmen tried to portray them as United fans, but it would probably be more accurate to describe the three as Ferguson supporters. Magnier has never even been to Old Trafford, while McManus comes from a family of Arsenal fans. McManus would later claim to have 'no interest in making a bid for the club. I'm just a passive shareholder. I've enough aggravation in my life without thinking of a take-over.'[16]

As well as securing his personal position in the summer of 2001, Ferguson also benefited from a loosening of the Old Trafford purse strings. Just as Kenyon was much more sympathetic towards the idea of rewarding Ferguson properly, he also took a more relaxed attitude towards both investing large sums of money in big-name players and paying them world-class salaries. Indeed, United's traditional pay cap had already been exceeded by Roy Keane's new contract at the end of 1999. The club had broken the British transfer record once in 2001, when Ruud van Nistelrooy finally signed for £19 million in April, almost exactly a year after his initial deal broke down. (His arrival led to Teddy Sheringham's return to Spurs on a free transfer.) In July, United broke the British transfer record again by signing the Argentine midfield player Juan Sebastian Verón from the Italian club Lazio for £28.1 million. Verón's wages were £80,000 a week, though his admiring boss didn't seem too bothered about losing his brief turn at the top of the United earnings table.

Ferguson also made strenuous efforts to sign the French defender Lilian Thuram from Parma, and told the United board that if the deal materialised then he intended to sell the Dutch defender Jaap Stam, whom he felt was a poorer player since recovering from his latest injury. Stam's potential availability was communicated to Lazio during the transfer negotiations for Verón, though none of this was known publicly at the time, or indeed mentioned to Stam himself. In the end Thuram joined Juventus, on terms which not even Peter Kenyon would have been willing to sanction. An attempt to sign Thuram's French colleague Bixente Lizarazu also failed.

Jaap Stam's prospects at Old Trafford were not improved, however, by a poor start to the 2001–02 season. He was outmanoeuvred by Michael Owen as Liverpool won the Charity Shield in Cardiff in August, and then again played badly as promoted Fulham scored twice in the opening game at Old Trafford, though United won 3–2. When United travelled to Blackburn the following Wednesday Stam was suddenly dropped, and not even named as a substitute. The world immediately assumed it was punishment by Ferguson for comments which the defender had made in his autobiography, *Head to Head*, which had been serialised in the *Mirror* the previous week, starting with the front-page headline 'SIR ALEX ACCUSED'.[17]

The *Mirror*'s coverage was undoubtedly hyped up, but several passages in Stam's book reflected badly on Ferguson. The defender revealed that the manager had tapped him while he was still a player with PSV Eindhoven, which was against the rules of both the Football Association and UEFA, albeit a common practice among managers. Stam explained that in 1998 his agent, Tom van Dalen, had arranged a meeting with the United boss near Amsterdam airport, while Ferguson and his wife were returning from a short break in France. The encounter took place in a flat, as both sides feared being noticed if they met in a hotel. 'While the meeting may have been technically against the rules, it happens all the time and has become an accepted part of the game,' Stam wrote, adding that Ferguson then suggested the Dutchman might help United take that 'extra step' towards winning the European Cup. 'Ferguson's passion was overwhelming and he was even clever enough not to try the hard sell on me,' he said.[18] The meeting was followed by several reassuring phone calls from Ferguson when there were difficulties in closing the deal.

Stam's revelation of an illegal approach was published only a day after the *News of the World* had accused Ferguson of trying to tap the Arsenal star Patrick Vieira that summer. Then the former Nottingham Forest manager Brian Clough got in on the act by saying that in the early 1990s Ferguson had tapped Roy Keane 'to the eyeballs'.[19]

Jaap Stam also embarrassed his boss by his book's recounting details of a violent half-time outburst at Sheffield Wednesday early in the 1998–99 treble season: this suggested that Ferguson might not have mellowed as much as was generally believed. United had been drawing 1–1 after a particularly inept performance in the first forty-five minutes. 'What the fuck are you lot playing at?' Stam quoted Ferguson as saying as the team returned to the dressing room: 'That is the biggest load of shite I've ever seen. Not one of you can look me in the eye, because not one of you deserves to have a say. I can't believe you've come here and decided to toss it off like that crap you're playing out there.'[20] Then, with his face growing red, Ferguson exploded and kicked out at a medical treatment table which stood between him and Stam, who recalled:

Drink bottles, rubs and tapes smacked me in the chest as I pulled my feet back and stuck my hands over my bollocks to try to save myself from damage. There were gasps around the dressing room as the metal-legged construction crashed to the ground just inches from my retracted toes . . . As he singled out players one by one for a personal verbal bashing, Ferguson picked up the plastic water bottles now scattered across the floor and hurled them into the shower.[21]

Stam also revealed that Ferguson had encouraged his players to dive for penalties. 'It has got to the stage where Ferguson has even told us: "Don't try and stay on your feet if you are in the box and get a slight kick. He wants us to copy other sides we face in European competitions and go down to win a penalty.'[22]

The problem wasn't just that Jaap Stam had said these things about his boss, but also the way in which they were skilfully exploited by the *Mirror* extracts, which ran over four days and were taken out of a context which overall was very positive about Ferguson. Other papers, including the *News of the World*, had read the book and rejected it, which meant that the *Mirror* secured the serialisation rights for just £15,000. The deal was remarkably good value considering how much the paper got from it.

It was widely assumed that a naive Stam had been duped into saying what appeared in the book – which, like most football memoirs, was ghost-written. Stam and his advisers were upset that the publishers had had little say in how it was serialised, and were astonished to see much of it appear on the news pages rather than in the sports section. But Stam's English agent, Mike Williams, says the player specifically requested that the tapping story be included. 'I said, "Are you sure you want it to be in there?" And Jaap just said, "Fine, I want it to be there." Because it was a true account of the situation. He is that sort of guy. He's quite an honest sort of guy.'[23]

Only three days after the Blackburn game and a week after the serialisation, it was announced that Stam was being transferred to Lazio for £15.3 million. It was generally assumed that the book was the reason, and that once again Sir Alex was cracking down on dissent. Ferguson insisted it was 'absolutely a footballing decision'.[24] The official United line was that the Dutchman had failed to command the United defence in the way that Steve Bruce and Gary Pallister had once done. Younger players such as Wes Brown and the Neville brothers needed a leader to hold the line, Ferguson argued, but Stam had not fulfilled this role. Statistics compiled by *The Times* seemed to support Ferguson's view that Stam hadn't been the same player since returning from injury. He had made barely half as many successful tackles per game in the 2000–01 season as in his first year at United, and only a third as many clearances.[25]

Jaap Stam was stunned by the transfer, especially after signing a new five-year contract at the start of 1999. 'I am surprised and am still trying to take it all in,' he said. 'I do not understand why this happened.'[26] He'd already apologised to Ferguson about his book, and thought his future at Old Trafford was settled. The defender didn't even have time to say goodbye to most of his playing colleagues. Afterwards, however, according to Mike Williams, Ferguson did take the trouble to write to Stam at his new home address in Rome to assure him that it was only for financial reasons that he had been sold. 'All that I can say is that Jaap read it,' says Williams. 'I can't say that he appreciated it.'[27]

Four days after Stam had gone, Ferguson acquired a replacement defender whom he felt was equal to the leadership role: the former French captain Laurent Blanc, who came on a free transfer from Inter Milan, and whom the United manager had twice tried to sign before. Blanc, however, was nearly thirty-six, and privately many people shared Alan Hansen's public observation that it made no sense to replace a defender who had lost half a yard of pace with one who was 'four yards slower'.[28] The episode evoked memories of the Whiteside–McGrath affair of 1988, and the Ince–Hughes–Kanchelskis transfers of 1995, as once again many United followers questioned Ferguson's judgement.

As the autumn fixtures unfolded, the substitution of Stam by

Blanc seemed to have been a disaster. The Frenchman was slow to adjust to the pace and style of English football; the United defence seemed shakier than ever, and there was little sign that Blanc had instilled fresh authority. On the contrary, by early December United had the second-worst defensive record in the Premier League, having conceded goals more quickly than at any time in the previous decade – twenty-six in just fourteen league games, only five fewer than in the whole of the 2000–01 season.

When United lost 1–0 at home to West Ham on 8 December it was their sixth defeat of the season – as many as in the whole of the previous campaign. Conventional wisdom has it that no championship team can afford to lose more than six times – a maxim to which Ferguson himself subscribes. In fact the exciting 4–3 defeat at Newcastle in September might easily have gone the other way, but the 3–1 losses at Arsenal and Liverpool were fully deserved. What upset Ferguson most about the Anfield defeat was that United seemed to have less hunger to win than Liverpool. At Highbury, United had been 1–0 ahead at half-time, if against the run of play, and they were drawing 1–1 until ten minutes from the end, before two elementary errors by the normally dependable Fabien Barthez. Afterwards, the French goalkeeper was so distraught to have messed things up in front of millions of viewers on television that he was in tears. To avoid press photographers, he was smuggled away from the ground in a car by David Beckham's agent, Tony Stephens.

The purchase of Juan Sebastián Verón seemed to have unsettled the side, as Ferguson began experimenting with formations and line-ups to accommodate the midfielder alongside Roy Keane and Paul Scholes. His solution was to revert yet again to a 4–5–1 formation, with Ruud van Nistelrooy as the lone striker. It was no more successful than it had been before, and by December the tactics had been abandoned for domestic fixtures. Verón had played well in the opening weeks of the season, but his game deteriorated as fans speculated that he might be keeping his best for the coming World Cup.

The player himself dropped various hints that he wouldn't mind returning to Italy. David Beckham, too, suffered a serious drop in form, until Ferguson 'rested' him for several games in December.

There were, however, some consolations during the first half of the season. The first was Ruud van Nistelrooy, who scored on his debut in the Charity Shield, again in his first league game, and regularly thereafter, impressing everyone with the power of a Mark Hughes and the pouncing ability of a Denis Law. The Dutchman's efforts meant that, even while United were leaking goals badly at the back, they were scoring regularly: the question in every game was whether they could score more goals than they conceded. The team's problems were captured best by the game away to Tottenham at the end of September. United were 3–0 down at the interval, only to make an extraordinary comeback in the second half to win 5–3. It wasn't quite as dramatic as Barcelona, but statistically it was the greatest comeback in Manchester United history.

The other encouraging sign was United's progress in Europe, where they marched through the two group stages of the European Cup with relative ease, and but for late goals by their opponents would have clocked up impressive victories away to the Spanish side Deportivo La Coruña and Bayern Munich. The 2002 European Cup final was due to be played at Hampden Park, the home of Queen's Park, Ferguson's first club as a player. But, given United's erratic domestic form, and the shakiness of the defence, it seemed unlikely that the location would provide the fairy-tale ending to Alex Ferguson's career which many had once discussed.

By late autumn, as he began his boycott of the press, commentators suggested that Ferguson was losing his grip. 'The day that Ferguson's empire began to crumble' the sports section of *The Times* headlined the Liverpool defeat, asking whether it was 'a season too far, a fight too many for the ageing heavyweight'.[29] The December defeat by West Ham left United ninth in the table, eleven points behind Liverpool, who also had a game in hand. The odds of United retaining the league title dropped to 10–1. Ferguson was accustomed to autumn blips, but this was his team's most prolonged dip in form since the dark days of 1989.

Various explanations were offered. It was said Ferguson was missing his former assistant Steve McClaren, who had left Old Trafford during the summer to become manager of Middlesbrough. There was something in this. Whereas Ferguson had reacted badly to the departures of Archie Knox and Brian Kidd, he was much more sympathetic to McClaren's leaving. It was appropriate to let him go, Ferguson felt, since his assistant would probably lose his job when he himself stepped down, as the United board were unlikely to promote McClaren as his replacement and a new manager would almost certainly bring his own coaching team with him. Similar thinking explained Ferguson's decision not to appoint a proper replacement for McClaren, as a new assistant would probably be in place for only twelve months.

Instead, Ferguson decided to take a much more active role in training sessions, promoting reserve coaches Jim Ryan and Mike Phelan to work with him. But Ryan, a former United player, was not as popular with the players as Steve McClaren or Brian Kidd. 'In the past, believe it or not,' says one close observer, 'the United lads actually liked going in to work every day. Now they had to put up with a bloke they thought was a prat telling them what to do all day.' A colleague who worked with Ryan when he was a coach at Luton Town says he was 'way out of his depth. He couldn't sort out United's defence if he was to try all year. At Luton he was just too lax. Ninety-nine times out of a hundred he'd just play some five-a-sides and leave it at that. I'm not surprised the United boys aren't responding to him.' Bryan Robson, whom McClaren had replaced at Middlesbrough, was also brought in to run occasional practice sessions, though taking training had never been his forte.

However, the most powerful explanation for United's autumn crisis seems to be that the players knew Sir Alex was leaving, and as a result he no longer had quite the same authority. Roy Keane later said that Ferguson's imminent retirement had been 'a factor' behind the slump.[30] Ferguson admitted in retrospect that it might have been a mistake to say in advance that he intended to go, and that it might have upset the team's unity. 'It changed the working atmosphere,' he said, 'and it may have derailed the players a bit.'[31] People were certainly surprised when in early November the normally well-behaved Paul Scholes refused to travel to Highbury for a League Cup game in which Ferguson planned to field a greatly weakened team. And the French defender Mikaël Silvestre was heard grumbling publicly about losing his place in the side, commenting pointedly that he would still be at Old Trafford after Ferguson had left.

But in mid-December United's form suddenly turned. A 5–0 home win over relegation contenders Derby County was followed by a 1–0 win at Middlesbrough and a 6–1 thrashing of Southampton. Over the next three months United won eleven league games out of twelve, the only exception being a 1–0 loss at Old Trafford to Liverpool – the fourth home league defeat of the season. Ruud van Nistelrooy was now scoring at the rate of more than a goal a game. He equalled the record of the Busby Babe Billy Whelan by scoring in eight consecutive league games, and in all competitions he found the target nine games in a row, breaking the club record. Despite the lows of early December, it took only six weeks for United to reach the top of the table as their rivals Liverpool and Leeds United now hit bad patches.

The most exciting game of this run was the FA Cup third-round tie at Aston Villa, where United went 2–0 behind early in the second half, after yet more poor defending. Ruud van Nistelrooy had been rested on the substitutes' bench, reflecting Ferguson's policy of fielding slightly weakened teams in FA Cup matches. His arrival on the pitch in the fifty-ninth minute prompted United to turn the game round with three goals in five minutes, two of them from the Dutch striker. A joyful Ferguson couldn't contain his excitement as he danced along the touchline. That game more than any helped re-inforce his doubts about whether he was doing the right thing in giving up, even though United were then knocked out 2–0 at Middlesbrough in the next round.

It seemed strange, too, that a manager who was due to retire in six months' time was still devoting so much effort to acquiring new players. In late January he paid £6.9 million to River Plate of Argentina for the young Uruguayan striker Diego Forlán, who'd been spotted by Ferguson's brother, Martin, on a scouting trip to South America in search of a defender. Forlán had been snatched from Steve McClaren's grasp, as the player had originally flown into Gatwick to sign for Middlesbrough, but having missed his connect-ing flight to Newcastle he was persuaded to fly to Manchester instead. As with every new player he signs, Sir Alex Ferguson was there in person to meet his new recruit as he arrived at Manchester airport.

Such personal touches have always been an important feature in Ferguson's style of management – small gestures which require little effort but which have a powerful effect on the recipient. West Ham's Italian striker Paolo di Canio was similarly impressed when Sir Alex rang him out of the blue on 31 December, ostensibly to wish him a happy New Year. (Ferguson is like a teenager on the phone, con-stantly ringing friends from his mobile and sending text messages.) The real purpose, of course, was to show how committed he was to bringing di Canio to Old Trafford: in effect, it looked like a mild form of tapping.

For years the Manchester United manager had admired di Canio's extraordinary skills, and at the start of 2001 the West Ham player had knocked United out of the FA Cup with a nerveless one-on-one confrontation with Fabien Barthez. Di Canio was now thirty-three, but as Ferguson approached the second half of the 2001–02 season he saw him as the final ingredient to ensure that the team ended up with some trophy – in much the same way that Eric Cantona had made the decisive difference almost a decade before. Like Cantona, di Canio was a mercurial character who combined brilliance with a long record of disciplinary problems. The most notable had been the occasion in 1998 when he pushed the referee Paul Alcock to the ground while playing for Sheffield Wednesday. As with Cantona, Alex Ferguson was confident he could tame the Italian's wilder instincts while also fostering his talent.

But the plan went wrong when Dwight Yorke refused to leave United to join Middlesbrough. Andy Cole had already joined Blackburn for £8 million, but with the arrival of Forlan another high-earner would have to be removed from Old Trafford's books if the club was to accommodate di Canio's pay demands. Middlesbrough were happy to pay the £6.2 million fee that United demanded, but Yorke wanted to increase his £24,000 a week wages to a whopping £58,000 – to compensate, apparently, for the much reduced media earnings which he believed would be entailed by playing on Teesside. Sir Alex believed Yorke was being poorly advised by his agent, Tony Stephens. 'Dwight's transfer has hit a snag because he is reluctant to move,' said a seething Ferguson, 'well, his agent's reluctance more like. We would like to bring in Paolo di Canio as everybody knows. But we will have to soldier on with the troops we have.'[32] Dwight Yorke would find it hard to play for United ever again. Ferguson seemed to have given up on the player once he'd signed Ruud van Nistelrooy, deciding he'd never talk Yorke out of his much-publicised lifestyle of women and drink.

The last week of 2001 was a pivotal time for Sir Alex Ferguson. The New Year's Eve on which he rang Paolo di Canio was also his sixtieth birthday: he had reached the age at which he had long said he would retire from team management. The experience of being alongside the sixty-two-year-old Jock Stein when he died of a heart attack during Scotland's World Cup qualifying match in Cardiff in

1985 had persuaded Ferguson not to continue in the game beyond sixty. He also felt he wanted the opportunity to enjoy his new interests in life, and to spend more time with his growing band of grandchildren than he had managed with his own sons. New Year's Eve 2001 was also the day when Ferguson misleadingly told Glenn Gibbons of the *Scotsman* that he still intended to retire at the end of the season (contrary to the interpretation that many Sunday papers had placed on his interview with Bob Cass a few days before).

For the world now knows that, while Alex Ferguson spent the Christmas holiday with his family, he took the big decision to do the very opposite of what he told Gibbons. Sir Alex claims it was his wife, Cathy, who suggested it first. She had realised that a restless husband at home all day with no football team to look after would be difficult to live with. 'Cathy said she'd had a chat with the boys. "We just don't think you should be retiring – you're too young," she said. That was basically how it started.'[33] After the sacrifices he'd expected of his family in the past, Ferguson claims it wasn't a suggestion he'd have raised himself. But 'I do have to confess that maybe it was an idea I was hoping deep down she would come up with.'[34] He still felt fit, and medical examinations gave him a clean bill of health.

Manchester United had become a drug to Alex Ferguson. As he watched the exciting, rejuvenated team of December and January, he couldn't bear the thought of letting somebody else take over his boys, whom he'd seen grow up into mature adults as if they were his own family. He never said so publicly, but it must have dismayed him to think that a successor might have achieved equal success with what for some years would remain largely the side he had built. UEFA had announced that the European Cup final was to be staged at Old Trafford in 2003. If United got to the final, Ferguson might have gone through the combined ecstasy and agony of seeing his players win the coveted trophy for another manager in the very stadium he believed had been rebuilt by his successes. He feared he might be making 'the biggest mistake of my life', and that it might be difficult to rectify later. 'What if I wanted back in after a year out? That would be the worst thing that could happen. You couldn't just walk back into a job like this.'[35]

So Sir Alex decided to stay. The extension would give him the chance to prove beyond doubt that he was the greatest British football manager of all time. As things stood, Jock Stein had won more major British trophies overall – twenty-six to Ferguson's twenty-three. While Ferguson had already overtaken the former Liverpool manager Bob Paisley in English honours, with fourteen trophies to thirteen, Paisley had won three European Cups to Ferguson's one. Even to win the European Cup once more would help dispel the lingering doubts that 1999 was a one-off. Ferguson always stressed that historically the great European sides – Real Madrid, Ajax, Bayern Munich, AC Milan and Liverpool – had all won the European Cup more than once.

And Bobby Robson, the manager of Newcastle, who was almost nine years older than Ferguson, showed that it was possible to continue to withstand the pressure of Premier League football so long as one still had the passion for it. Robson had transformed the team he inherited from Ruud Gullit, and had taken them that season to the top of the table – yet managing the Tyneside club involved similar pressures to being in charge at Old Trafford.

Sir Alex Ferguson also found the environment at Old Trafford more straightforward since Peter Kenyon had taken over from Martin Edwards as chief executive. Indeed, had Kenyon been in charge in 1999 Ferguson might never have announced his retirement:

I felt the circumstances at the club had changed . . . There are people at the club now on the same wavelength as me. They want what I want . . . Spending £28 million on Verón may have been the best thing the club has ever done in that it told other people and the supporters that we're prepared to try to become the best club in the world.[36]

Ferguson first broached the idea of staying on with his long-standing board ally Maurice Watkins, then approached the other directors after United beat Sunderland 4–1 on Saturday 2 February. Peter Kenyon was delighted and immediately dropped his search for a new manager – though he insisted that Ferguson should stay for another three years rather than the two years that the manager initially demanded. The news was announced the following Tuesday, and Ferguson gathered his squad together that morning at the training ground at Carrington and told them personally. 'When I had finished speaking there was a moment of silence,' he said afterwards, 'and then they started clapping. I was quite touched and got out of there pretty quickly.'[37] Curiously, Gary Neville gave a rather different account the next day, saying, 'there was no applause or anything'.[38]

It was a further three weeks, however, before the terms of Ferguson's new three-year contract were settled. The club agreed to increase his pay yet again, from £60,000 to £70,000 a week – though this was still less than Verón was getting.

Sir Alex's decision to sign a new contract seemed to release a logjam. A few days later Roy Keane agreed a new deal which was said to be worth £100,000 a week. And it looked likely that David Beckham, too, would sign a new contract after months in which he'd insisted on knowing the identity of his new boss before he committed himself, as well as arguing over the rights to his image.

Ferguson and the club also agreed that for his final three years he would be able to concentrate on those parts of the job which he did best, leaving others to take on much of the administrative burden. As for what would happen after 2005, Ferguson claimed he had 'no intention of staying at the club in any capacity whatsoever'.[39]

We'll believe that when and if it happens.

Epilogue

'It was *very* close,' admits the senior United official, laughing loudly and nervously. He is clearly haunted by the thought of how near the club came to losing Sir Alex for good, simply by agreeing a deal with the man they'd chosen as his successor. Had the Manchester United manager left it another day or two to make his dramatic U-turn, pondering a bit longer just to make sure, then it would have been too late. Once United had unveiled a definite replacement there could have been no going back. What nobody knew at the time was that the board was within hours of sealing an agreement for a new boss to take over at the start of the 2002–03 season. And the man whose services they were about to clinch was the England manager Sven-Göran Eriksson, who was all set to move to Old Trafford after the 2002 World Cup in Japan and South Korea.

The general impression during the early weeks of 2002 was that Manchester United weren't having much luck finding anyone of sufficient calibre to succeed Ferguson. Several prominent names had very publicly announced they weren't interested in the job or able to take it. In reality, the chief executive Peter Kenyon had made huge progress in his head-hunting, to the extent that the previous autumn he'd told IMUSA members they would be 'very pleased' with the man the board eventually selected.

Sven-Göran Eriksson undoubtedly fulfilled the criteria Kenyon had publicly laid down for the job – of being experienced and with an outstanding record of proven success. In less than twelve months, since succeeding Kevin Keegan as England coach, the academic-looking Swede had almost become the messiah of English football, especially after the extraordinary 5–1 win in Germany in September 2001, as the revived national side marched towards qualification for the World Cup. Eriksson also had a formidable record in club football, having won trophies with all the five teams he'd managed, including the UEFA and European Cup-Winners' Cups, and league titles in three different countries – with Gothenburg in Sweden, Benfica in Portugal, and Lazio in Italy. 'United offered the job to Sven,' says a senior source at the Football Association, his employers as England boss,

> and he was very keen to do it, and all set to go. It's amazing in some ways, but I don't think Sven enjoys being England manager that much. He has made plenty of noises about wanting to get back into the day-to-day drug that is club football and he looked at Old Trafford and the players they have and thought, 'Hey, that's the club I want. I can win European Cups there.' I think that Sven thought a good World Cup performance would empower him to be able to say: 'Look, I've done well for you, please let me get back to what I really love – club football.'

Quite apart from Eriksson's impressive record, Manchester United had another major reason to appoint the FA's national team coach.

The England captain David Beckham had publicly expressed his reluctance to sign a new contract at Old Trafford until he knew the identity of Ferguson's successor. Given the excellent relationship between Eriksson and Beckham, the Swede's appointment would have been the ideal way to clinch the player's next deal. 'United officials said the biggest pull with regard to Sven was Beckham,' the FA source explains:

> They stressed they had to go for Sven because they are a PLC, and by far and away the club's biggest asset on the pitch is David Beckham. So it was absolutely crucial that he stayed. Financially, and football-wise, him leaving would have been a disaster. They had seen Sven's special rapport with Beckham, which is undoubtedly very strong, and realised that he was a great way of getting him to stay. That was a big worry – that Alex going, and a change of manager, was a reason for Beckham to go.

But Sven-Göran Eriksson hadn't been United's only target, and sources close to the club say Peter Kenyon had an excellent alternative in reserve if the Eriksson arrangement had hit a last-minute hitch. United had asked the former Leeds United and Sheffield Wednesday manager Howard Wilkinson to sound out his friend Fabio Capello, the manager of Roma, to see whether he was interested in the job. Capello, too, had a very distinguished CV, having won league titles with AC Milan, Real Madrid and Roma, and the European Cup with Milan in 1994. Capello sent word back that he would love to succeed Ferguson. Because of Eriksson's interest, however, United only ever made him a 'half-offer'.

Sir Alex knew little about Peter Kenyon's efforts to find his successor, having deliberately distanced himself. His feeling was that Eriksson was the candidate being courted, but astonishingly Ferguson did not appreciate just how close United were to landing their man. About a week before announcing his U-turn, Sir Alex had even mentioned to a leading United fan that he would almost certainly change his mind about retiring. The friend was delighted to hear this, but also concerned when Ferguson admitted he hadn't yet told the club directors of his thinking. Hadn't he better do so, the United supporter suggested, before they chose someone else and it was too late?

Alex Ferguson ignored that advice for several days, and so came perilously close to ending his time at Old Trafford. It would have happened through uncharacteristic indecision and lack of communication: a ludicrous mix-up which would have trumped any of that season's notorious blunders by the clumsy Manchester United defence. One can imagine the personal torture Ferguson would have suffered seeing Sven-Göran Eriksson publicly anointed as his replacement, when he himself had already decided to stay on, but just hadn't got round to telling the people who mattered. Sir Alex could hardly have interrupted the press conference and announced: 'Sorry, Sven; sorry, Peter; I'd actually like to stay.'

It would have been a farcical, and terribly sad, way to end the most distinguished managerial career in British club football.

That sustained record, over almost thirty years, has been due to Ferguson's array of personal qualities and talents. The bulk of those attributes would almost certainly have brought impressive results in several of the other walks of life in which he has dabbled, as leading trade unionist, for instance, or as a businessman, a journalist or even a politician.

First, Alex Ferguson is blessed with a good brain, which gives him incisive analysis, insatiable intellectual curiosity, and an outstanding memory for faces, incidents and the smallest snippets of information. Physically he has a strong constitution and stamina, is rarely ill, and can keep going on little sleep. Then come his highly focused dedication, resilience, passion, energy, work-rate, hunger, and a drive bordering on the obsessive – mental qualities which seem to stem in part from his upbringing, his relationship with his father, and his disappointing lack of tangible success as a player.

Add to that mix Ferguson's skill as a judge of character, and his ability to motivate through a combination of fear, infectious enthusiasm and inspiration. Throw in the attention to detail, his constant long-term planning, and above all courage both in acting decisively and taking big gambles when needed, and you have the qualities of a successful leader.

Among the skills specific to football, Ferguson's ability to assess players, and to build a balanced team, is unsurpassed. Yet although he's remembered for particular flashes of genius when it comes to clever substitutions in big matches, Sir Alex will not be especially remembered as one of the game's finest tacticians.

Ferguson's friends and supporters cite other positive qualities which are easy to overlook in an assessment which concentrates on his professional career. They talk of the compassionate Alex Ferguson, a man who often displays unusual consideration, warmth and good humour. Take the case of Gary Twynham, the young player who accompanied Keith Gillespie on his trips as Ferguson's bookie's runner. Twynham was jailed not long after leaving Manchester United, convicted of a serious assault in a pub brawl. Ferguson sent a character reference for Twynham in court, and later wrote to the player in prison wishing him well, and stressing he could still get back into football. It undoubtedly boosted Twynham's spirits. 'This is the guy who is manager of the biggest club in the whole world,' he says, 'and he's got time to write me a letter and wish me all the best.'[1]

United supporters will tell of numerous occasions when Sir Alex has turned up late at night to some charity event in an obscure pub, for instance, when they half expected something more pressing would cause him to cry off. There's also the tale – perhaps apocryphal, but nonetheless in character – of a supporter who wrote to Ferguson explaining he wouldn't be renewing his United season ticket as he'd just lost his job and couldn't afford it any more. It's said that Ferguson paid for the ticket instead.

When he's not under pressure on the touchline, at a press conference or in front of the TV camera, Sir Alex Ferguson can be delightful company. 'He's always got a smile, a laugh or a song for everyone,' says the former United winger Jesper Blomqvist. 'He sings all the time.'[2] His habit of bursting into song, be it while ambling along a corridor, or alone in his hotel room, reveals a naturally contented person beneath the belligerent façade. Colleagues also know Ferguson the teaser and practical joker. An example occurred when one of the laundrywomen at Carrington inadvertently broke the local environmental regulations by using bleach in her washing machine. Ferguson rang the laundry a few days later pretending to be a council official, and asking why most of the ducks in the nearby lagoon had mysteriously vanished.

At times it is hard to square these engaging characteristics with the same individual whose darker sides have often surfaced in this book – with the Ferguson who bullies and intimidates; with the man of violent temper who acts ruthlessly against anybody who gets in his way; with the arrogance, hypocrisy and lack of honesty; and with the manager obsessed with money and aggrandisement. Most successful leaders, of course, display some of those traits. Ruthlessness is an essential ingredient of achievement in many fields, as the needs and hopes of individuals are sacrificed to the greater collective good. Few public achievers have pursued their careers without telling the occasional lie. Yet it's hard to justify the degree of ruthlessness Ferguson sometimes displays; to see how United benefits, for example, from maintaining grudges many years after the original grievance which sparked his anger.

Statistically he already outflanks every boss in English football history, and while Bill Struth of Rangers and Jock Stein of Celtic won a few more trophies, both were confined to Scotland and neither man proved himself in the far tougher milieu of the English game.

Perhaps only Brian Clough and Sir Matt Busby remain convincing contenders as Ferguson's equals if not superiors. Like Sir Alex, Clough achieved great success with two different sides, only in his case neither Derby County nor Nottingham Forest was a big club. Almost a quarter of a century after Forest first won the European Cup in 1979, it is increasingly difficult to understand how such a relatively small outfit twice became European champions. The answer, of course, was Clough's great knack of getting the best out of his men and moulding lesser players into a remarkably effective unit. Alex Ferguson is equally good at building, inspiring and cajoling a team, but when Manchester United finally matched Clough's Forest in 1999 by winning the European Cup for a second time, they were only achieving what was long overdue for one of the richest and best-supported clubs in Europe.

One cannot avoid comparing the two greatest United managers, both of whom were knighted for their achievements. Matt Busby took over in 1945, and from a bomb-wrecked stadium, and a traditional position as the mere number-two club in Manchester, he made United great. Sir Matt's record is statistically far inferior to that of Ferguson; his teams endured long spells of mediocrity in the early 1950s and early '60s; and the side Sir Matt bequeathed on his retirement in 1969 was so poor as to suffer relegation five years later. Yet who knows what greater heights Busby's men might have scaled in England and Europe, but for the tragedy of Munich?

Sir Matt Busby will never be remembered for relentlessly gobbling up silverware: he only won eight trophies in twenty-four years, and never more than one per season. Busby's legacy is much wider, not only in founding the modern Manchester United, but also as a pioneer of the post-war game. His name is primarily associated with developing his own young football talent – the Busby Babes – and then also for leading English clubs into Europe against the resistance of the old-fashioned football authorities. Sir Alex Ferguson has pursued commitments to both youth and Europe with just as much vigour and enthusiasm as Busby, but as a follower rather than a standard-bearer.

Great men are judged, in part at least, by the lasting differences they make to the world. Ferguson has always been very open to new ideas at the micro level, from adopting foreign training methods and nutritional systems, to employing a university orthoptician to advise on how to improve players' peripheral vision, and developing the art of using a large playing squad. But as things stand, Sir Alex will largely be remembered for the dimensions of his trophy cabinet, and for helping to transform Manchester United into a financial juggernaut, rather than for being a football visionary or revolutionary. That's not to question Ferguson's clear and romantic passion for the game, which still excites him as much as it did in the back courts, school yards and public parks of post-war Govan.

Ferguson also falls below Busby for the petulant and snarling image which his Manchester United team has often displayed to the world, though this is less of a problem today than it was in the mid-1990s. In deliberately building his famous siege mentality as an effective means of motivating players, and inculcating the philosophy of win at all costs, Ferguson has created a United which often lacks the humility of which he frequently talks, and the ability to accept defeat with good grace.

A world of bad losers would be a depressing place. Nothing better illustrated this less attractive feature than the notorious pictures in January 2000 of Roy Keane, Jaap Stam and several other players chasing the referee Andy D'Urso after he'd awarded Middlesbrough a penalty. With veins almost bursting from their temples they screamed and swore directly into the face of the beleaguered official. Ferguson later condemned this nasty outburst, both privately and, for once, publicly, but it stemmed directly from his own aggressive style of management, and echoed similar rows with referees from his own career, both as a player and manager.

For a team which supplies a large proportion of the England

national side, is commendably home-grown, and plays hugely enter-taining football, Manchester United ought to be much more popular with the wider public. The enmity they generate among those who are not United fans is the inevitable downside of a Ferguson policy which positively thrives on confrontation and people hating his team.

To some extent, the problem is more one of perception than of reality. Manchester United regularly do well in the annual fair-play table, and if Keane, Butt or Beckham are sent off it generates bigger headlines than with most other clubs, no matter what the offence. In part, United's public unpopularity also stems from excessive com-mercialism and the belief that they have purchased success. Most of Ferguson's senior management colleagues at Old Trafford would love to reduce United's unpopular standing, if only for commercial reasons, and to restore the kind of affection enjoyed by the Busby teams of the 1940s, '50s and '60s. It's a flaw which a man keen on his place in history should address in his three extra years, though one suspects Ferguson will feel there are more pressing priorities.

Sir Alex has already earned his place in the pantheon of great British football managers. He has time left to become the greatest of them all.

APPENDIX I

Playing Career Statistics

	League	Scottish Cup	Scottish Lge Cup	Europe	Other	Total
Queen's Park						
1958–59						
Games	8	0	0	–	1[1]	9
Goals	4	0	0	–	0	4
1959–60						
Games	23	0	0	–	1[1]	24
Goals	11	0	0	–	0	11
Totals	31	0	0	–	2	33
	15	0	0	–	0	15
St Johnstone						
1960–61						
Games	3	0	1	–	1[2]	5
Goals	0	0	1	–	1	2
1961–62						
Games	13	1	0	–	1[2]	15
Goals	5	0	0	–	0	5
1962–63						
Games	12	1	2	–	0	15
Goals	8	1	0	–	0	9
1963–64						
Games	9	1	0	–	2[3]	12
Goals	6	0	0	–	1	7
Totals	37	3	3	–	4	47
	19	1	1	–	2	23

1. Glasgow Merchants Cup
2. Dewar Shield
3. Summer Cup

563

	League	Scottish Cup	Scottish Lge Cup	Europe	Other	Total
Dunfermline Athletic						
1964–65						
Games	26	6	4	4	5[4]	45
Goals	15	3	3	0	1	22
1965–66						
Games	32	4	6	6	–	48
Goals	30	0	4	4	–	38
1966–67						
Games	30	5	5	3	–	43
Goals	20	5	2	2	–	29
Totals	88	15	15	13	5	136
	65	8	9	6	1	89
Rangers						
1967–68						
Games	29	5	6	6	–	46
Goals	19	0	2	3	–	24
1968–69						
Games	12	1	4	3	2[5]	22
Goals	6	0	2	3	1	12
Totals	41	6	10	9	2	68
	25	0	4	6	1	36
Falkirk						
1969–70						
Games	21	3	0	–	–	24
Goals	14	3	0	–	–	17
1970–71						
Games	28	1	8	–	–	37
Goals	14	0	3	–	–	17
1971–72						
Games	28	2	9	–	2[6]	41
Goals	9	1	4	–	0	14

4. Summer Cup
5. Glasgow Cup
6. Texaco Cup

	League	Scottish Cup	Scottish Lge Cup	Europe	Other	Total
Falkirk (cont.)						
1972–73						
Games	19	2	1	–	–	22
Goals	0	1	0	–	–	1
Totals	96	8	18	–	2	124
	37	5	7	–	0	49
Ayr United						
1973–74						
Games	18	4	0	–	2[7]	24
Goals	9	1	0	–	0	10
CAREER TOTALS						
Games	311	36	46	22	17	432
Goals	170	15	21	12	4	222

---

7. Texaco Cup

APPENDIX II

Managerial Career Statistics

From 1987 onwards three points were given for a League win compared with two points in the past. The figures in brackets in the points column are my recalculations of how many points Ferguson's teams would have gained under the old system. Throughout the table the percentages are then calculated according to two points for a win.

Key: D1 – Division 1 etc.; F – Final; Gp – group stage; Lge – League; (p) – won on penalties; QF – Quarter-final; R1 etc. – Round 1 etc.; SF – Semi-final; W – winners; WC – Winners' Cup.

EAST STIRLINGSHIRE (1974)

Season	Outcome	Played	Won	Drawn	Lost	Goals For	Goals Against	Points	%age
1974–75									
Scot Lge D2		12	7	2	3	24	19	16	66.7%
Scot Lge Cup	R1	5	3	1	1	12	8		
Total		17	10	3	4	36	27		

ST MIRREN (1974–78)

Season	Outcome	Played	Won	Drawn	Lost	Goals For	Goals Against	Points	%age
1974–75									
Scot Lge D2	6th	27	13	6	8	47	31	34	63.0%
Scot Cup	R2	1	0	0	1	1	2		
1975–76									
Scot Lge D1	6th	26	9	8	9	37	37	26	50.0%
Scot Cup	R3	1	0	0	1	0	3		
Scot Lge Cup	R1	6	1	2	3	5	8		
1976–77									
Scot Lge D1	1st	39	25	12	2	91	38	62	79.5%
Scot Cup	R4	2	1	0	1	5	3		
Scot Lge Cup	R1	6	1	2	3	7	12		
1977–78									
Scot Prem Lge	8th	36	11	8	17	52	63	30	41.7%
Scot Cup	R3	1	0	0	1	1	2		
Scot Lge Cup	QF	6	2	1	3	6	8		
TOTAL		151	63	39	49	252	207	152	59.4%

ABERDEEN (1978–86)

Season	Outcome	Played	Won	Drawn	Lost	Goals For	Goals Against	Points	%age
1978–79									
Scot Prem Lge	4th	36	13	14	9	59	36	40	55.6%
Scot Cup	SF	5	3	1	1	12	6		
Scot Lge Cup	F	8	6	1	1	25	7		
Euro CW Cup	R2	4	2	0	2	7	6		
1979–80									
Scot Prem Lge	1st	36	19	10	7	68	36	48	66.7%
Scot Cup	SF	5	3	1	1	16	3		
Scot Lge Cup	F	11	7	2	2	23	11		
UEFA Cup	R1	2	0	1	1	1	2		
1980–81									
Scot Prem Lge	2nd	36	19	11	6	61	26	49	68.1%
Scot Cup	R4	2	1	0	1	2	2		
Scot Lge Cup	QF	6	3	1	2	15	4		
European Cup	R2	4	1	1	2	1	5		
1981–82									
Scot Prem Lge	2nd	36	23	7	6	71	29	53	73.6%

Season	Outcome	Played	Won	Drawn	Lost	Goals For	Goals Against	Points	%age
Scot Cup	W	6	5	1	0	14	6		
Scot Lge Cup	SF	10	7	1	2	21	4		
UEFA Cup	R3	6	3	2	1	13	9		
1982–83									
Scot Prem Lge	3rd	36	25	5	6	76	24	55	76.4%
Scot Cup	W	5	5	0	0	9	2		
Scot Lge Cup	QF	8	4	2	2	19	11		
Euro CW Cup	W	11	8	2	1	25	6		
1983–84									
Scot Prem Lge	1st	36	25	7	4	78	21	57	79.2%
Scot Cup	W	7	5	2	0	11	3		
Scot Lge Cup	SF	10	7	2	1	23	3		
Euro CW Cup	SF	8	3	2	3	10	7		
Euro Super Cp	W	2	1	1	0	2	0		
1984–85									
Scot Prem Lge	1st	36	27	5	4	89	26	59	81.9%
Scot Cup	SF	6	3	2	1	10	4		
Scot Lge Cup	R2	1	0	0	1	1	3		
European Cup	R1	2	1	0	1	3	3		

Season	Outcome	Played	Won	Drawn	Lost	Goals For	Goals Against	Points	%age
1985–86									
Scot Prem Lge	4th	36	16	12	8	62	31	44	61.1%
Scot Cup	W	6	5	1	0	15	4		
Scot Lge Cup	W	6	6	0	0	13	0		
European Cup	R3	6	3	3	0	10	4		
1986–87									
Scot Prem Lge		15	7	5	3	25	14	19	63.3%
Scot Lge Cup	QF	3	2	1	0	8	2		
Euro CW Cup	R1	2	1	0	1	2	4		
TOTAL		455	269	106	80	900	364	424	70.0%

MANCHESTER UNITED (1986–2002)

Season	Outcome	Played	Won	Drawn	Lost	Goals For	Goals Against	Points	%age
1986–87									
League	11th	29	11	10	8	36	29	32	55.2%
FA Cup	R4	2	1	0	1	1	1		

Season	Outcome	Played	Won	Drawn	Lost	Goals For	Goals Against	Points	%age
1987–88									
League	2nd	40	23	12	5	71	38	81 (58)	72.5%
FA Cup	R5	3	2	0	1	5	3		
League Cup	R5	5	4	0	1	10	4		
1988–89									
League	11th	38	13	12	13	45	35	51 (38)	50.0%
FA Cup	R6	7	3	3	1	11	4		
League Cup	R3	3	2	0	1	7	2		
1989–90									
League	13th	38	13	9	16	46	47	48 (35)	46.1%
FA Cup	W	8	6	2	0	15	9		
League Cup	R3	3	1	1	1	3	5		
1990–91									
League	6th	38	16	12	10	58	45	59 (43)*	56.6%
FA Cup	R5	3	2	0	1	4	3		
League Cup	F	9	7	1	1	21	10		
Euro CW Cup	W	9	7	2	0	17	4		
Charity Shield	W	1	0	1	0	1	1		

* one point deducted for fighting v. Arsenal.

Season	Outcome	Played	Won	Drawn	Lost	Goals For	Goals Against	Points	%age
1991–92									
League	2nd	42	21	15	6	63	33	78 (57)	67.9%
FA Cup	R4	3	1	2	0	3	2		
League Cup	W	8	6	2	0	15	4		
Euro CW Cup	R2	4	1	2	1	3	4		
Euro Super Cp	W	1	1	0	0	1	0		
1992–93									
Prem League	1st	42	24	12	6	67	31	84 (60)	71.4%
FA Cup	R5	3	2	0	1	4	2		
League Cup	R3	3	1	1	1	2	2		
UEFA Cup	R1	2	0	2	0	0	0		
1993–94									
Prem League	1st	42	27	11	4	80	38	92 (65)	77.4%
FA Cup	W	7	6	1	0	18	3		
League Cup	F	9	6	1	2	19	9		
European Cup	R2	4	2	2	0	8	6		
Charity Shield	W (p)	1	0	1	0	1	1		

Season	Outcome	Played	Won	Drawn	Lost	Goals For	Goals Against	Points	%age
1994–95									
Prem League	2nd	42	26	10	6	77	28	88 (62)	73.8%
FA Cup	F	7	5	1	1	16	6		
League Cup	R3	3	2	0	1	4	3		
European Cup	Gp	6	2	2	2	11	11		
Charity Shield	W	1	1	0	0	2	0		
1995–96									
Prem League	1st	38	25	7	6	73	35	82 (57)	75.0%
FA Cup	W	7	6	1	0	14	5		
League Cup	R2	2	1	0	1	3	4		
UEFA Cup	R1	2	0	2	0	2	2		
1996–97									
Prem League	1st	38	21	12	5	76	44	75 (54)	71.1%
FA Cup	R4	3	1	1	1	3	2		
League Cup	R4	2	1	0	1	2	3		
European Cup	SF	10	4	1	5	10	5		
Charity Shield	W	1	1	0	0	4	0		

Season	Outcome	Played	Won	Drawn	Lost	Goals For	Goals Against	Points	%age
1997–98									
Prem League	2nd	38	23	8	7	73	26	77 (54)	71.1%
FA Cup	R5	4	2	1	1	13	8		
League Cup	R3	1	0	0	1	0	2		
European Cup	QF	8	5	2	1	15	6		
Charity Shield	W (p)	1	0	1	0	1	1		
1998–99									
Prem League	1st	38	22	13	3	80	37	79 (57)	75.0%
FA Cup	W	8	6	2	0	12	3		
League Cup	R5	3	2	0	1	5	4		
European Cup	W	13	6	7	0	31	16		
Charity Shield	F	1	0	0	1	0	3		
1999–2000									
Prem League	1st	38	28	7	3	97	45	91 (63)	82.9%
FA Cup	–	–	–	–	–	–	–		
League Cup	R3	1	0	0	1	0	3		
European Cup	QF	14	8	3	3	21	11		
Euro Super Cp	F	1	0	0	1	0	1		
Inter-Cont	W	1	1	0	0	1	0		
World CC	R1	3	1	1	1	4	4		
Charity Shield	F	1	0	0	1	1	2		

Appendix II

Season	Outcome	Played	Won	Drawn	Lost	Goals For	Goals Against	Points	%age
2000–01									
Prem League	1st	38	24	8	6	79	31	80 (56)	73.7%
FA Cup	R4	2	1	0	1	2	2		
League Cup	R4	2	1	0	1	4	2		
European Cup	QF	14	6	4	4	22	13		
Charity Shield	F	1	0	0	1	0	2		
2001–02									
Prem League		34	22	4	8	83	44	70 (48)*	
FA Cup	R4	2	1	0	1	3	4		
League Cup	R3	1	0	0	1	0	4		
European Cup		13	7	4	2	25	9*		
Charity Shield	F	1	0	0	1	1	2		

* 2001–02 Premier League and European Cup statistics to 8 April 2002.

CAREER TOTALS

	Outcome	Played	Won	Drawn	Lost	Goals For	Goals Against	Points	%age
Manchester United		851	471	219	161	1505	808	1167 (845)	
All Clubs		1474	813	367	294	2693	1406	1759 (1437)	

575

Notes

Key to interviewers
AEM – Alex Millar
APD – Angus Dixon
CPG – Chris Green
MLC – Michael Crick
RML – Rochelle Libson

Preface
1. *Sun*, 21 July 1999.

Chapter 1: The Boy Out of Govan
1. *Daily Mail*, 12 January 1995.
2. Patrick Donnelly, *Govan on the Clyde*, Glasgow City Libraries, 1994, p.10.
3. *Sun*, 10 May 1983.
4. Alex Ferguson, *Six Years at United*, Mainstream, 1992, p.155.
5. Alex Ferguson, *Managing My Life*, Coronet, 2000, p.5.
6. E-mail to author from Glentoran historian Roy France.
7. Martin Ferguson, interview with APD.
8. Ibid.
9. Ferguson, *Managing My Life*, p.1.
10. *A Decade of Glory* video, Paul Doherty International/VCI, 1996.
11. M. Ferguson interview.
12. Ibid.
13. Sam Gilmour, interview with APD.
14. Ibid.
15. *Today*, 14 May 1994.
16. *Daily Mail*, 12 January 1995.
17. *Guardian*, 5 August 1995.
18. *Daily Star*, 11 May 1983.
19. M. Ferguson interview.
20. *Evening Standard*, 11 September 1995.
21. *Mirror*, 29 May 1999.
22. Ferguson, *Six Years at United*, p.155.
23. *Sunday Times*, 26 March 2000.
24. M. Ferguson interview.
25. *A Decade of Glory*.
26. M. Ferguson interview.
27. *Glasgow Herald*, 11 April 1983.
28. M. Ferguson interview.
29. Ibid.
30. *Independent*, 26 July 1999.
31. *Mirror*, 29 May 1999.
32. *Telegraph Magazine*, 25 April 1998.
33. *Daily Record*, 10 May 1983.
34. M. Ferguson interview.
35. Ibid.
36. *The Alex Ferguson Story*, Granada TV/Patience Productions, ITV, 14 and 21 September 1998.
37. Tommy Hendry, interview with APD.
38. *The Alex Ferguson Story*.
39. Programme, Manchester United v. Rest of the World XI, Alex Ferguson Testimonial, 11 October 1999.
40. *The Alex Ferguson Story*.
41. *Sun* (Scottish edn), 6 August 1999.
42. Ibid.
43. Elizabeth Thomson, interview with APD.

44. *Sun* (Scottish edn), 6 August 1999.
45. *Red News*, vol. 7, no. 1.

Chapter 2: Left Foot Forward
1. *Celebrity*, 15 May 1986.
2. Patrick Prior, *Could This Be Thistle's Year?*, ScotsRun, 1989.
3. *A Decade of Glory* video, Paul Doherty International/VCI, 1996.
4. Alex Ferguson, *Just Champion!*, MUFC, 1993, p.150.
5. Martin Ferguson, interview with APD.
6. Ferguson, *Just Champion!*, p.150.
7. M. Ferguson interview.
8. Stephen F. Kelly, *Fergie*, Headline, 1997, p.19.
9. Duncan Petersen, interview with APD.
10. Tommy Hendry, interview with APD.
11. M. Ferguson interview.
12. *Scotsman*, 29 April 1988.
13. M. Ferguson interview.
14. Petersen interview.
15. *Mirror*, 29 May 1999.
16. M. Ferguson interview.
17. *The Alex Ferguson Story*, Granada TV/Patience Productions, ITV, 14 and 21 September 1998.
18. *Mirror*, 29 May 1999.
19. Ibid.
20. *The Alex Ferguson Story*.
21. *Sun* (Scottish edn), 6 August 1999.
22. M. Ferguson interview.
23. Boys' Brigade website: www.boys-brigade.org.uk.
24. John Boreland, interview with APD.
25. Ibid.
26. Ibid.
27. Alex Ferguson, *A Light in the North*, Mainstream, 1985, p.168.
28. Boreland interview.
29. Alex Ferguson, *Managing My Life*, Coronet, 2000, p.16.
30. Boreland interview.
31. Ferguson, *Managing My Life*, p.14.
32. Bill Dobie, interview with APD.

33. Ibid.
34. Ibid.
35. *Guardian*, 20 August 1994.
36. *Daily Star*, 11 May 1983.
37. M. Ferguson interview.
38. Hendry interview.
39. Ibid.
40. *Sunday Times*, 24 January 1993.
41. Petersen interview.
42. Hendry interview.
43. Douglas Smith, interview with APD.
44. Ibid.
45. Ibid.
46. Ibid.
47. M. Ferguson interview.
48. Craig Brown, interview with APD.
49. *Manchester United* magazine, November 1996.
50. Ibid.
51. Ibid.
52. Ibid.
53. *Glasgow Evening Citizen*, 23 December 1963.

Chapter 3: Apprentice Striker
1. *Independent*, 16 November 1991.
2. *Glasgow Evening Times*, 15 November 1958.
3. Alex Ferguson, *Managing My Life*, Coronet, 2000, pp.33–4.
4. *Scottish Sunday Express*, 16 November 1958.
5. Ibid., 23 November 1958.
6. Stephen F. Kelly, *Fergie*, Headline, 1997, p.24.
7. *A Decade of Glory* video, Paul Doherty International/VCI, 1996.
8. Hugh McDonald, interview with APD.
9. Willie Omand, interview with RML.
10. Ferguson, *Managing My Life*, p.28.
11. Duncan Petersen, interview with APD.
12. Ferguson, *Managing My Life*, p.28.
13. Bert Cromar, interview with APD.
14. Petersen interview.
15. Ibid.

16. Cromar interview.
17. Alex Willoughby, interview with APD.
18. Gavin Keown, interview with APD.
19. I am indebted for the following passages on Alex Ferguson's trade-union career to research carried out for me by Alan McKinlay of the University of St Andrews.
20. Kelly, *Fergie*, p.21.
21. Ibid.
22. Alan McKinlay, interview with APD.
23. *Independent*, 16 November 1991.
24. Kelly, *Fergie*, p.21.
25. 'Token Strike', hand-written note delivered to SEEA, 24 February 1960, Glasgow City Archive, TD1059/9/60/81.
26. *Independent*, 16 November 1991.
27. *A Decade of Glory*.
28. *Independent*, 16 November 1991.
29. Open letter, Clydeside Apprentices' Campaign Committee, March 1960.
30. Stephen Shanahan, interview with APD.
31. Jimmy Wilson, interview with APD.
32. *The Alex Ferguson Story*, Granada TV/Patience Productions, ITV, 14 and 21 September 1998.
33. Scottish Engineering Employers' Association report, April 1964.
34. Tool Makers' Analysis Form, Remington Rand, March 1964, Glasgow City Archive.
35. Scottish Engineering Employers' Association report, April 1964.
36. Wilson interview.
37. Ferguson, *Managing My Life*, p.58.
38. Ellison Mackay, interview with APD.
39. For Stephen F. Kelly's book, *Fergie*, and *The Alex Ferguson Story*.
40. Alan McKinlay, e-mail to author.
41. *Daily Record*, 29 August 1964.
42. Ferguson, *Managing My Life*, p.59.
43. *Knowing the Score* video, Executive Business Channel/Nottingham Business School, 2000.
44. *The Times*, 31 July 1999.
45. *Daily Record*, 23 December 1963.
46. Ferguson, *Managing My Life*, p.39.
47. Doug Newlands, interview with APD.
48. Bobby Brown, interview with APD.
49. Willie Coburn, interview with APD.
50. Newlands interview.
51. *Manchester United* magazine, November 1996.
52. Brown interview.
53. Ibid.
54. *Daily Record*, 23 December 1963.
55. *Sunday Mail*, 22 December 1963.
56. Ferguson, *Managing My Life*, p.52.
57. Ibid., pp.52–3.
58. *Sunday Mail*, 22 December 1963.
59. *Glasgow Evening Citizen*, 23 December 1963.
60. *Scottish Daily Express*, 23 December 1963.
61. *Sunday Mail*, 22 December 1963.
62. *People's Journal* (Perthshire edn), 4 January 1964.
63. *Perthshire Advertiser*, 5 February 1964.
64. Petersen interview.
65. *The Alex Ferguson Story*.
66. Ibid.
67. McDonald interview.
68. *The Alex Ferguson Story*.
69. *A Decade of Glory*.
70. *The Alex Ferguson Story*.

Chapter 4: Razor Elbows
1. *Telegraph Magazine*, 25 April 1998.
2. *A Decade of Glory* video, Paul Doherty International/VCI, 1996.
3. Duncan Simpson, interview with RML.
4. Harry Melrose, interview with APD.
5. Alex Totten, interview with MLC.
6. *Manchester United* magazine, November 1996.
7. Ibid.

8. Ibid.
9. Alex Ferguson, *A Year in the Life*, MUFC/Virgin, 1995, p.252.
10. *News of the World*, 19 May 1997.
11. *Daily Express*, 12 May 1990.
12. Melrose interview.
13. *Daily Express*, 12 May 1980.
14. *Manchester United* magazine, November 1996.
15. *The Alex Ferguson Story*, Granada TV/Patience Productions, ITV, 14 and 21 September 1998.
16. *United Review*, v. Portsmouth, 12 January 1994.
17. *Daily Star*, 11 May 1983.
18. *Observer*, 27 March 1994.
19. *Manchester United* magazine, November 1996.
20. George Miller, interview with RML.
21. Alex Smith, interview with APD.
22. Bert Paton, interview with RML.
23. *Daily Express*, 12 May 1990.
24. Totten interview.
25. Alex Ferguson, *Managing My Life*, Coronet, 2000, p.63.
26. Melrose interview.
27. Ibid.
28. Simpson interview.
29. *Daily Record*, 23 April 1965.
30. Ferguson, *Managing My Life*, p.68.
31. *Knowing the Score* video, Executive Business Channel/Nottingham Business School, 2000.
32. Ibid.
33. *Glasgow Herald*, 11 April 1983.
34. Willie Cunningham, interview with APD.
35. *Daily Record*, 20 January 1966.
36. *The Alex Ferguson Story*.
37. *Daily Record*, 8 March, 9 March, 1 April 1967.
38. Programme, Scottish League v. English League, 15 March 1967.
39. Stephen F. Kelly, *Fergie*, Headline, 1997, p.30.
40. Programme, Auckland v. Scotland XI, 8 June 1967.
41. Bobby Brown, interview with APD.
42. *Glasgow Herald*, 7 September 1967.

Chapter 5: Lone Ranger
1. Alex Ferguson, *Managing My Life*, Coronet, 2000, p.87.
2. *Daily Record*, 1 August 1967.
3. *Glasgow Herald*, 11 April 1983.
4. *Daily Record*, 1 August 1967.
5. *Aberdeen Evening Express*, 5 February 1979.
6. Ibid., 5 August 1978.
7. *News of the World*, 26 September 1965.
8. *Telegraph Magazine*, 25 April 1998.
9. *Daily Mail*, 15 September 1998.
10. *Aberdeen Evening Express*, 5 August 1978.
11. *Independent*, 16 November 1991.
12. Ferguson, *Managing My Life*, p.95.
13. *Guardian*, 12 August 1999.
14. Alex Ferguson, *A Year in the Life*, MUFC/Virgin, 1995, p.171.
15. *Glasgow Evening Citizen*, 10 August 1967.
16. *Independent*, 16 November 1991.
17. Alex Ferguson, *A Light in the North*, Mainstream, 1985, p.166.
18. *Independent*, 16 November 1991.
19. Harry Harris, *The Ferguson Effect*, Orion, 2000, p.73.
20. David Mason, interview with APD.
21. Harris, *The Ferguson Effect*, p.73.
22. Ferguson, *Managing My Life*, p.99.
23. John Greig, interview with APD.
24. Ferguson, *Managing My Life*, p.87.
25. Davie Provan, interview with APD.
26. Ferguson, *Managing My Life*, p.105.
27. Ibid., p.99.
28. Harris, *The Ferguson Effect*, p.75.
29. *Glasgow Herald*, 10 March 1969.
30. *Daily Record*, 10 April 1969.
31. Ibid., 25 April 1969.
32. Ibid.
33. *Glasgow Herald*, 28 April 1969.
34. *The Alex Ferguson Story*, Granada TV/Patience Productions, ITV, 14 and 21 September 1998.
35. *Daily Mail*, 2 August 1999.

36. Billy McNeill, interview with APD.
37. Greig interview.
38. *Glasgow Evening Citizen*, 28 April 1969.
39. Alfie Conn, interview with APD.
40. Alan Rough, *Rough at the Top*, John Donald, 1988, p.97.
41. Kenny Dalglish, *My Autobiography*, Hodder & Stoughton, 1996, p.240.
42. Tom Donnelly, interview with APD.
43. *The Glory Game: Football and the New Celts*, Grampian TV, 2000.
44. Ferguson, *Managing My Life*, p.106.
45. Alex Willoughby, interview with APD.
46. *The Alex Ferguson Story*.
47. William Murray, *The Old Firm: Sectarianism, Sport and Society in Scotland*, John Donald, 1984, p.252.
48. Willie Johnston, interview with APD.
49. Ibid.
50. Ferguson, *Managing My Life*, p.100.
51. Alex Ferguson, *A Will to Win*, André Deutsch, 1997, p.270.
52. *Sun*, 31 July 1999.

Chapter 6: Fighting on All Fronts
1. Gregor Abel, interview with APD.
2. *Falkirk Herald*, 1 August 1970.
3. Alex Ferguson, *Managing My Life*, Coronet, 2000, pp.107, 109.
4. Programme, Falkirk v. Stenhousemuir, 20 December 1969.
5. Willie Cunningham, interview with APD.
6. Michael White, interview with APD.
7. Jim Shirra, interview with APD.
8. *Falkirk Herald*, 15 August 1970.
9. Ibid., 12 September 1970.
10. John Greig, interview with APD.
11. *Falkirk Herald*, 26 February 1972.

12. *Celebrity*, 15 May 1986.
13. Ibid.
14. Abel interview.
15. Unknown publication, 23 August 1972.
16. *Falkirk Herald*, 26 August 1972.
17. Ferguson, *Managing My Life*, pp.116–17.
18. Shirra interview.
19. Cunningham interview.
20. Ibid.
21. *Falkirk Herald*, 3 March 1973.
22. Ibid., 14 April 1973.
23. Ibid., 16 June 1973.
24. Programme, Ayr United v. Clyde, 22 September 1973.
25. Johnny Graham, interview with MLC.
26. Alec Ingram, interview with RML.
27. Graham interview.
28. Sunday Post, 9 December 1973.
29. Graham interview with MLC.
30. Ibid.
31. Pat Harkins, interview with APD.
32. Ibid.
33. John Telfer, interview with APD.
34. *Sun*, 6 August 1999.
35. Ferguson, *Managing My Life*, p.132.
36. Ibid., p.131.
37. Davie Provan, interview with APD.
38. Telfer interview.
39. Jim Martin, interview with APD.
40. Telfer interview.

Chapter 7: 'A Big Job on My Hands'
1. *Sun*, 31 December 1991.
2. Simon Inglis, *Football Grounds of Britain*, HarperCollins, 1996, p.312.
3. Alex Ferguson, *Managing My Life*, Coronet, 2000, p.138.
4. Bob Shaw, interview with APD.
5. Ibid.
6. Stephen F. Kelly, *Fergie*, Headline, 1997, p.40.
7. *Aberdeen Evening Express*, 5 August 1978.
8. *Falkirk Herald*, 29 June 1974.

9. Mel Henderson, interview with APD.
10. *Daily Mirror*, 29 October 1995.
11. *Falkirk Herald*, 29 June 1974.
12. Henderson interview.
13. *Sunday Times*, 30 May 1999.
14. Jim Mullin, interview with APD.
15. *Sunday Times*, 30 May 1999.
16. Jim Meakin, interview with APD.
17. *Independent*, 5 April 1990.
18. *Daily Mail*, 22 May 1999.
19. Meakin interview.
20. *Sunday Times*, 30 May 1999.
21. *Daily Mail*, 31 December 1991.
22. *Daily Mirror*, 31 December 1991.
23. *Daily Mail*, 31 December 1991.
24. Ibid., 22 May 1999.
25. Tom Donnelly, interview with APD.
26. *Sunday Times*, 30 May 1999.
27. Ibid.
28. Donnelly interview.
29. *Scotland on Sunday*, 25 April 1999.
30. *Sunday Times*, 30 May 1999.
31. *Falkirk Herald*, 5 October 1974.
32. *Sunday Times*, 30 May 1999.
33. Meakin interview.
34. Harold Currie, interview with APD.
35. *Falkirk Herald*, 19 October 1974.
36. Alan McMillan, *Showing in Black and White Only*, Garrell, 1981, p.31.
37. *Glasgow Herald*, 11 April 1983.
38. Kelly, *Fergie*, p.42.

Chapter 8: The Paisley Pattern
1. *Daily Telegraph*, 6 December 1997.
2. Alex Ferguson, *Managing My Life*, Coronet, 2000, p.viii.
3. *Paisley Daily Express*, 21 October 1974.
4. *Telegraph Magazine*, 25 April 1998.
5. *Sun*, 20 July 1984.
6. Fred Douglas, interview with APD.
7. *Aberdeen Evening Express*, 5 February 1979.
8. Alex Ferguson, *A Light in the North*, Mainstream, 1985, p.53.

9. Alex Ferguson, *Six Years at United*, Mainstream, 1992, p.155.
10. Harold Currie, interview with APD.
11. Tony Fitzpatrick, interview with APD.
12. *A Decade of Glory* video, Paul Doherty International/VCI, 1996.
13. Fitzpatrick interview.
14. Currie interview.
15. Douglas interview.
16. Ferguson, *Managing My Life*, p.150.
17. Jimmy Bone, interview with APD.
18. *Independent*, 16 November 1991.
19. Alex Ferguson, *Just Champion!*, MUFC, 1993, p.137.
20. Currie interview.
21. Ferguson, *Managing My Life*, pp.154–5.
22. Ibid., p.152.
23. Bone interview.
24. Fitzpatrick interview.
25. SFA Referee Committee minutes, January 1975.
26. *Sun*, 14 January 1976.
27. *Paisley Daily Express*, 14 January 1976.
28. SFA Referee Committee minutes, January 1975.
29. Ibid., April 1975.
30. *Daily Record*, 31 July 1977.
31. *Paisley Daily Express*, 1 February 1977.
32. St Mirren Travel Association brochure, 1977.
33. *The Alex Ferguson Story*, Granada TV/Patience Productions, ITV, 14 and 21 September 1998.
34. *FourFourTwo*, September 1998.
35. *Paisley Daily Express*, 18 February 1977.
36. *The Saint*, 21 March 1977.
37. Programme, St Mirren v. Queen of the South, 7 February 1976.
38. *News of the World*, 19 May 1996.
39. *Glasgow Herald*, 11 April 1983.
40. Programme, St Mirren v. Kilmarnock, 28 August 1976.

41. Douglas interview.
42. Tom Moran, interview with APD.
43. Ferguson, *Managing My Life*, p.153.
44. Ibid., pp.153–4.
45. Campbell Scouler, interview with APD.
46. Moran interview.
47. Ferguson, *Managing My Life*, p.155; Alex Ferguson, *A Will to Win*, André Deutsch, 1997, p.5.
48. *Glasgow Herald*, 1 June 1978.
49. Fitzpatrick interview.
50. Bill Waters, interview with APD.
51. Jim Crawford, interview with APD.
52. Iain Munro, interview with APD.
53. Ibid.
54. Bone interview.
55. Davie Provan, interview with APD.
56. Bone interview.

Chapter 9: When Fergie Was Fired
1. *Sun*, 20 July 1984.
2. *Paisley Daily Express*, 1 May 1978.
3. Alex Ferguson, *Managing My Life*, Coronet, 2000, p.158.
4. *Paisley Daily Express*, 1 May 1978.
5. *Daily Star*, 11 May 1983.
6. *Aberdeen Evening Express*, 5 February 1979.
7. *Scotsman*, 1 December 1978.
8. *Paisley Daily Express*, 1 December 1978.
9. *Glasgow Herald*, 1 December 1978.
10. Jimmy Bone, interview with APD.
11. Tom Moran, interview with APD.
12. Ferguson, *Managing My Life*, p.155.
13. Alex Ferguson, *A Light in the North*, Mainstream, 1985, p.13.
14. Ferguson, *Managing My Life*, pp.156–7.
15. Industrial-tribunal report, 21 December 1978, p.2.
16. Ibid., p.3.
17. *Scotsman*, 30 November 1978.
18. Industrial-tribunal report, 21 December 1978, p.12.
19. *Glasgow Herald*, 8 December 1978.

20. Industrial-tribunal report, 21 December 1978, p.5.
21. *Glasgow Herald*, 8 December 1978.
22. *Scotsman*, 1 December 1978.
23. *Yorkshire Post*, 8 December 1978.
24. Ferguson, *Managing My Life*, p.157.
25. Industrial-tribunal report, 21 December 1978, p.13.
26. Ibid., p.9.
27. Ibid., p.14.
28. Ferguson, *Managing My Life*, p.157.
29. Industrial-tribunal report, 21 December 1978, p.8.
30. *Sun*, 20 July 1984.
31. Industrial-tribunal report, 21 December 1978, p.8.
32. Ibid., p.14.
33. *Scotsman*, 30 November 1978.
34. Industrial-tribunal report, 21 December 1978, p.8.
35. *Scotsman*, 30 November 1978.
36. Industrial-tribunal report, 21 December 1978, p.9.
37. *Paisley Daily Express*, 8 December 1978.
38. Industrial-tribunal report, 21 December 1978, p.10.
39. Ibid.
40. *Yorkshire Post*, 8 December 1978.
41. *Daily Record*, 30 November 1978.
42. Industrial-tribunal report, 21 December 1978, p.11.
43. Ibid., pp.15–16.
44. Ferguson, *Managing My Life*, p.164.
45. *Glasgow Herald*, 23 December 1978.
46. *Aberdeen Evening Express*, 5 February 1979.
47. Ralph Auchincloss, interview with APD.
48. *The Alex Ferguson Story*, Granada TV/Patience Productions, ITV, 14 and 21 September 1998.
49. Ferguson, *Managing My Life*, p.164.
50. *Daily Star*, 11 May 1983.

51. *Telegraph Magazine*, 25 April 1998.
52. Ferguson, *Managing My Life*, p.164.

Chapter 10: Aberdeen Fairy Tale
1. *Red News*, no. 78 (Fergie Special), summer 2001.
2. Alex Ferguson, *Managing My Life*, Coronet, 2000, pp.191–2.
3. Billy McNeill, interview with APD.
4. Alex Ferguson, *A Light in the North*, Mainstream, 1985, p.182.
5. Ferguson, *Managing My Life*, p.161.
6. Ferguson, *A Light in the North*, p.144.
7. Harry Harris, *The Ferguson Effect*, Orion, 1999, pp.56–7.
8. Ibid., p.58.
9. Gordon Strachan, *Strachan Style*, Mainstream, 1991, p.73.
10. Ferguson, *Managing My Life*, p.236.
11. Ferguson, *A Light in the North*, p.142.
12. Jack Webster, *The Dons*, Stanley Paul, 1990, p.242.
13. Ian Donald, interview with MLC.
14. Webster, *The Dons*, p.242.
15. Ferguson, *A Light in the North*, p.142.
16. *Glasgow Herald*, 11 April 1983.
17. Strachan, *Strachan Style*, p.73.
18. Harris, *The Ferguson Effect*, p.56.
19. Willie Garner, interview with APD.
20. Programme, Aberdeen v. Manchester United, Teddy Scott Testimonial, 18 January 1999.
21. Ferguson, *Managing My Life*, pp.161–2.
22. Pat Stanton, *The Quiet Man*, Sportsprint, 1989, p.88.
23. Alex McLeish, *The Don of an Era*, John Donald, 1988, p.72.
24. Joe Harper, interview with APD.
25. *Daily Telegraph*, 15 May 2000.
26. *Glasgow Herald*, 11 April 1983.
27. Len Taylor, interview with MLC.
28. *Aberdeen Evening Express*, 15 August 1978.
29. *Sun*, 10 May 1983.
30. Ferguson, *A Light in the North*, p.17.
31. Gordon Strachan, *An Autobiography*, Stanley Paul, 1984, p.49.
32. Pat Stanton, interview with APD.
33. Ian Taggart, interview with MLC.
34. Webster, *The Dons*, p.241.
35. *Aberdeen Evening Express*, 1 November 1978.
36. Ferguson, *A Light in the North*, p.26.
37. Programme, Manchester United v. Rest of the World XI, Alex Ferguson Testimonial, 11 October 1999.
38. Willie Miller, interview with APD.
39. Webster, *The Dons*, p.242.
40. Harper interview.
41. *Daily Mirror*, 26 September 1989.
42. *Aberdeen Evening Express*, 1 March 1979.
43. Ferguson, *Managing My Life*, p.164.
44. SFA Disciplinary and Referee Committee minutes, 19 April 1979; *Aberdeen Evening Express*, 7 March 1979.
45. Ferguson, *A Light in the North*, p.174.
46. Ferguson, *Managing My Life*, p.164.
47. Fred Douglas, interview with APD.
48. Willie Miller, *The Miller's Tale*, Mainstream, 1989, p.42.
49. Harper interview.
50. Taggart interview.
51. Harper interview.
52. *Daily Mirror*, 26 September 1989.
53. Harper interview.
54. Ferguson, *Managing My Life*, p.163; Ferguson, *A Light in the North*, p.48.
55. *Guardian*, 12 May 1980.
56. *Sunday Times*, 8 May 1983.

57. Ferguson, *Managing My Life*, p.162.
58. Strachan, *Strachan Style*, p.140.
59. Ferguson, *A Light in the North*, p.32.
60. Miller, *The Miller's Tale*, p.68.
61. Ferguson, *A Light in the North*, p.32.
62. Alex Ferguson, *Six Years at United*, Mainstream, 1992, p.154.
63. *Sun*, 10 May 1983.
64. Ferguson, *A Light in the North*, p.37.
65. *Sun*, 10 May 1983.
66. Ferguson, *A Light in the North*, p.45.
67. Jim Leighton, *In the Firing Line*, Mainstream, 2000, p.19.
68. Ferguson, *A Light in the North*, p.43.

Chapter 11: Furious Fergie
1. *Mail on Sunday*, 31 December 1989.
2. Alex Ferguson, *A Light in the North*, Mainstream, 1985, p.48.
3. Joe Harper, interview with APD.
4. Len Taylor, interview with MLC.
5. *Daily Express*, 28 January 1995.
6. Alex McLeish, *The Don of an Era*, John Donald, 1988, p.70.
7. *Daily Express*, 12 May 1990.
8. John Hewitt, interview with MLC.
9. Willie Garner, interview with APD.
10. Ian Taggart, interview with MLC.
11. McLeish, *The Don of an Era*, p.70.
12. *FourFourTwo*, September 1998.
13. Gordon Strachan, *An Autobiography*, Stanley Paul, 1984, p.51.
14. *A Decade of Glory* video, Paul Doherty International/VCI, 1996.
15. Ferguson, *A Light in the North*, p.70.
16. *Radio Times*, 12 August 1995.
17. *Red News*, no. 78 (Fergie Special), summer 2001.
18. *Sunday Times*, 21 April 1991.
19. *Sun*, 13 March 1993.
20. McLeish, *The Don of an Era*, p.71.
21. Stewart McKimmie, interview with MLC.
22. *Sun*, 30 January 1987.
23. *The Alex Ferguson Story*, Granada TV/Patience Productions, ITV, 14 and 21 September 1998.
24. McKimmie interview.
25. *Daily Star*, 22 September 1984.
26. George Welsh, interview with APD.
27. *FourFourTwo*, September 1998.
28. *Sunday Times*, 8 May 1983.
29. Pat Stanton, interview with APD.
30. Taylor interview.
31. Ibid.
32. Ibid.
33. Eric Black, interview with APD.
34. Ian Donald, interview with MLC.
35. Alex McLeish, interview with APD.
36. Ferguson, *A Light in the North*, p.146.
37. Barbara Cook, interview with MLC.
38. Taylor interview.
39. *The Alex Ferguson Story*.
40. Ibid.
41. Garner interview.
42. Harry Laurie, interview with APD.
43. Donald interview.
44. Stanton interview.
45. Jack Sim, interview with APD.
46. Ibid.
47. *Guardian*, 12 May 1990.
48. Ibid., 5 August 1995.
49. Black interview.
50. McLeish, *The Don of an Era*, p.72.
51. Black interview.
52. Alex Ferguson, *Managing My Life*, Coronet, 2000, p.161.
53. *Aberdeen Evening Express*, 7 March 1979.
54. *Guardian*, 6 April 1988.
55. Stanton interview.
56. *Sunday Telegraph*, 20 April 1997.
57. Ferguson, *A Light in the North*, p.41.
58. *The Alex Ferguson Story*.
59. Ian Paul, interview with APD.

60. *Sunday Times*, 8 May 1983.
61. Gordon Strachan, *Strachan Style*, Mainstream, 1991, p.79.
62. Ibid., p.80.
63. *FourFourTwo*, September 1998.
64. Charlie Nicholas, *Charlie: An Autobiography*, Stanley Paul, 1986, pp.75, 77.
65. McLeish interview.
66. Ferguson, *A Light in the North*, pp.164–5.
67. *Sun*, 21 January 1982.

Chapter 12: Glory in Gothenburg

1. Keith Anderson, *Here We Go!*, Sports Projects, 1983, p.37.
2. Alan Hansen, *A Matter of Opinion*, Bantam, 2000, p.101.
3. Stewart McKimmie, interview with MLC.
4. Pat Stanton, interview with APD.
5. Anderson, *Here We Go!*, p.37.
6. Gordon Strachan, *An Autobiography*, Stanley Paul, 1984, pp.111–12.
7. Anderson, *Here We Go!*, p.37.
8. Willie Miller, interview with APD.
9. *The Alex Ferguson Story*, Granada TV/Patience Productions, ITV, 14 and 21 September 1998.
10. Willie Miller, *The Miller's Tale*, Mainstream, 1989, p.90.
11. Miller interview.
12. Alex Ferguson, *A Light in the North*, Mainstream, 1985, p.91.
13. Alex Ferguson, *Managing My Life*, Coronet, 2000, p.178.
14. Strachan, *An Autobiography*, pp.127–8.
15. Anderson, *Here We Go!*, p.95.
16. Jim Leighton, *In the Firing Line*, Mainstream, 2000, p.24.
17. *A Knight to Remember* video, Paul Doherty International/VCI, 1999.
18. Strachan, *An Autobiography*, p.139.
19. Leighton, *In the Firing Line*, p.24.
20. Strachan, *An Autobiography*, p.136.

21. *Sun*, 23 May 1983.
22. Leighton, *In the Firing Line*, p.24.
23. Alex McLeish, *The Don of an Era*, John Donald, 1988, p.34.
24. Programme, Aberdeen v. Celtic, 22 October 1983.
25. Graeme Souness, *No Half Measures*, Willow Books, 1985, p.16.
26. McLeish, *The Don of an Era*, p.2.
27. Ferguson, *A Light in the North*, p.158.
28. Gordon Strachan, *Strachan Style*, Mainstream, 1991, pp.64, 77.
29. Ferguson, *A Light in the North*, p.154.
30. Strachan, *An Autobiography*, p.52.
31. Ferguson, *A Light in the North*, p.156.
32. Strachan, *Strachan Style*, pp.65, 67.
33. Jack Webster, *The Dons*, Stanley Paul, 1990, p.244.
34. Strachan, *Strachan Style*, p.68.
35. Ferguson, *A Light in the North*, p.160.
36. Webster, *The Dons*, p.249.
37. *Glasgow Herald*, 7 September 1984.
38. Ferguson, *Managing My Life*, p.225.
39. *Glasgow Herald*, 7 September 1984.

Chapter 13: Restless Ambition

1. *Sports Personality of the Year*, BBC1, 9 December 2001.
2. Alex Ferguson, *A Light in the North*, Mainstream, 1985, p.65.
3. Ibid., p.166.
4. *Sun*, 3 November 1983.
5. *Glasgow Herald*, 9 November 1983.
6. Ferguson, *A Light in the North*, pp.166–7.
7. Stephen F. Kelly, *Fergie*, Headline, 1997, pp.73–4.
8. George Ramsay, interview with MLC.
9. Alex Ferguson, *Managing My Life*, Coronet, 2000, p.230.
10. *Sun*, 22 December 1983.

11. *Daily Mirror*, 25 January 1989.
12. Ferguson, *A Light in the North*, p.168.
13. Harry Harris, *The Ferguson Effect*, Orion, 2000, p.127.
14. Ferguson, *A Light in the North*, pp.168–9.
15. Irving Scholar and Mihir Bose, *Behind Closed Doors*, André Deutsch, 1992, p.98.
16. Harris, *The Ferguson Effect*, p.128.
17. Mihir Bose, *Manchester Unlimited*, Orion, 1999, p.242.
18. *Daily Mirror*, 23 May 1984.
19. Ibid., 25 January 1989.
20. Alex Ferguson, *Just Champion!*, MUFC, 1993, p.133.
21. Jimmy Burns, *Barça: A People's Passion*, Bloomsbury, 1999, p.287.
22. *Glasgow Herald*, 7 September 1984.
23. Ferguson, *A Light in the North*, p.11.
24. Teddy Scott, interview with MLC.
25. Ferguson, *Managing My Life*, p.231.
26. Ferguson, *A Light in the North*, p.12.
27. Bill Campbell, interview with MLC.
28. Ibid.
29. Ferguson, *A Light in the North*, p.186.
30. Ferguson, *Managing My Life*, p.230.
31. Programme, Aberdeen v. Clyde, 27 August 1986.
32. Ferguson, *Managing My Life*, p.229.
33. Willie Garner, interview with APD.
34. *Scotland on Sunday*, 17 January 1999.
35. Alex McLeish, *The Don of an Era*, John Gordon, 1988, p.40.
36. *Sunday Times*, 21 April 1991.
37. *Mail on Sunday*, 17 August 1997.
38. Ibid.
39. *Daily Star*, 20 December 1983.
40. Alex McLeish, interview with APD.
41. Ferguson, *A Light in the North*, pp.151–2.
42. Billy McNeill, interview with APD.
43. Eric Black, interview with APD.
44. Ian Donald, interview with MLC.
45. Willie Miller, interview with APD.
46. Frank Gilfeather, interview with APD.
47. Ramsay interview.
48. Christine Anderson, interview with MLC.
49. *Observer*, 1 October 1989.
50. *Guardian*, 31 March 1999.

Chapter 14: Keeping Scotland's Dignity

1. *Aberdeen Evening Express*, 6 September 1980.
2. Alex Ferguson, *A Light in the North*, Mainstream, 1985, p.172.
3. Alex McLeish, *The Don of an Era*, John Donald, 1988, p.77.
4. Gordon Strachan, *Strachan Style*, Mainstream, 1991, p.132.
5. Ken Gallacher, *Jock Stein: The Authorised Biography*, Stanley Paul, 1988, p.145.
6. Ibid., p.150.
7. Ibid., p.139.
8. *Sun*, 21 August 1984.
9. Alex Ferguson, *Managing My Life*, Coronet, 2000, p.196.
10. *The Times*, 24 January 1986.
11. Willie Miller, interview with APD.
12. Kenny Dalglish, interview with AEM.
13. Ferguson, *Managing My Life*, p.197.
14. Mo Johnston, *Mo: The Maurice Johnston Story*, Mainstream, 1988, p.65.
15. Ibid., p.70.
16. Ibid., p.66.
17. Charlie Nicholas, *Charlie: An Autobiography*, Stanley Paul, 1986, pp.83–4.
18. *A Decade of Glory* video, Paul Doherty International/VCI, 1996.
19. Alan Hansen, *Tall, Dark and*

Hansen, Mainstream, 1988, pp.86, 84.

20. Ferguson, *Managing My Life*, p.213.
21. *Express*, 7 August 1999.
22. Ferguson, *Managing My Life*, p.194.
23. Dalglish interview.
24. Harry Harris, *The Ferguson Effect*, Orion, 2000, p.65.
25. Programme, Aberdeen v. Dundee, 9 November 1985.
26. Strachan, *Strachan Style*, p.98.
27. Roy Aitken, *Feed the Bear*, Mainstream, 1987, p.78.
28. *Observer*, 9 November 1986.
29. Alan Rough, *Rough at the Top*, John Donald, 1988, p.65.
30. Craig Brown, interview with APD.
31. Strachan, *Strachan Style*, p.111.
32. Rough, *Rough at the Top*, p.68.
33. Strachan, *Strachan Style*, p.115.
34. *A Decade of Glory*.
35. *Sun*, 7 August 1993.
36. Ferguson, *Managing My Life*, p.219.
37. Ibid., p.218.
38. Ibid., p.220.
39. Rough, *Rough at the Top*, p.28.
40. *Manchester United* magazine, June 1994.

Chapter 15: Manchester Mission
1. *Daily Telegraph*, c. 6 November 1991.
2. Tom Tyrrell and David Meek, *Manchester United: The Official History*, Hamlyn, 1988, p.187.
3. Ibid., pp.185–6.
4. *Sun* (Scottish edn), 8 November 1986.
5. Harry Harris, *The Ferguson Effect*, Orion, 1999, p.79.
6. Bryan Robson, *Glory, Glory Man United!*, CollinsWillow, 1992, p.43.
7. Ron Atkinson, *Big Ron*, André Deutsch, 1998, pp.4–5.
8. Ibid., p.9.

9. Ibid., p.6.
10. Alex Ferguson, *Managing My Life*, Coronet, 2000, p.233.
11. Ibid., p.233.
12. Ibid., p.231.
13. Harris, *The Ferguson Effect*, p.59.
14. Archie Knox, interview with MLC.
15. Ibid.
16. Ferguson, *Managing My Life*, p.233.
17. Gordon Strachan, *Strachan Style*, Mainstream, 1991, p.140.
18. *Daily Telegraph*, 8 November 1986.
19. Mark Hughes, *Sparky*, Mainstream, 1989, p.48.
20. Alex Ferguson, *Just Champion!*, MUFC, 1993, p.17.
21. Stephen F. Kelly, *Fergie*, Headline, 1997, p.114.
22. *Independent*, 8 November 1986.
23. *Manchester Evening News*, 2 February 1987.
24. *Daily Star*, 14 May 1987.
25. Ibid.
26. *Manchester Evening News*, 14 May 1987.
27. Ibid., 18 April 1987.
28. *Daily Mail*, 8 November 1986.
29. Ferguson, *Just Champion!*, p.22.
30. *News of the World*, 25 January 1987.
31. Alex Ferguson, *Six Years at United*, Mainstream, 1992, p.17.
32. *News of the World*, 9 November 1986.
33. *Manchester Evening News*, 15 November 1986.
34. Ferguson, *Six Years at United*, p.17.
35. *Independent*, 16 November 1991.
36. *The United Family Tree*, BBC2, 19 May 1996.
37. *Manchester Evening News*, 28 November 1986; *Daily Mirror*, 27 November 1986.
38. *Manchester Evening News*, 28 November 1986.
39. Colin Gibson, interview with AEM.

40. Frank Stapleton, interview with AEM.
41. Knox interview.
42. *Daily Mirror*, 27 November 1986.
43. *Sun*, 18 January 1987.
44. Stapleton interview.
45. Gibson interview.
46. Ibid.
47. *Manchester Evening News*, 27 December 1986.
48. Knox interview.
49. *Sunday Express*, 8 March 1987.
50. *Sunday Times*, 27 October 1996.
51. *Independent*, 21 November 1986.
52. Ferguson, *Just Champion!*, p.129.
53. Ferguson, *Six Years at United*, p.21.
54. Ferguson, *Just Champion!*, p.19.
55. Ferguson, *Six Years at United*, p.21.
56. Frank Stapleton, *Frankly Speaking*, Blackwater Press, 1991, p.86.
57. *Daily Mirror*, 30 October 1987.
58. *Sunday Telegraph*, 3 November 1996.
59. Ferguson, *Managing My Life*, p.264.
60. *News of the World*, 29 November 1992.
61. *Sun*, 6 November 1987.
62. Michael Crick and David Smith, *Manchester United: The Betrayal of a Legend*, Pelham, 1989, p.243.
63. *Sun*, 15 August 1987.
64. *Manchester Evening News*, 23 January 1988.
65. *Manchester Evening News Football Pink*, 23 January 1988.
66. *Guardian*, 5 April 1988.
67. *Daily Express*, 5 April 1988.
68. Robson, *Glory, Glory Man United!*, p.54.
69. *Sun*, 29 August 1988.

Chapter 16: Chucking-Out Time
1. *Sunday Times*, 27 October 1996.
2. *Sun*, 18 January 1987.
3. *Today*, 27 June 1987.
4. *Guardian*, 30 March 1988.
5. *Manchester Evening News*, 8 April 1988.
6. Ibid.
7. Ibid., 6 April 1988.
8. Alex Ferguson, *Six Years at United*, Mainstream, 1992, p.33.
9. Tom Tyrrell and David Meek, *Manchester United: The Official History*, Hamlyn, 1988, p.192.
10. Paul McGrath, *Ooh, Aah, Paul McGrath*, Mainstream, 1994, pp.91, 127.
11. Alex Ferguson, *A Year in the Life*, MUFC/Virgin, 1995, p.35.
12. Alex Ferguson, *Managing My Life*, Coronet, 2000, p.240.
13. *Telegraph Magazine*, 25 April 1998.
14. Colin Gibson, interview with AEM.
15. Gordon Strachan, *Strachan Style*, Mainstream, 1991, pp.16–17.
16. *Sun*, 13 March 1993.
17. Strachan, *Strachan Style*, p.15.
18. Ferguson, *Managing My Life*, p.253.
19. Strachan, *Strachan Style*, p.17.
20. Ferguson, *Six Years at United*, pp.26, 44.
21. *News of the World*, 9 October 1988.
22. *The United Family Tree*, BBC2, 19 May 1996.
23. Gibson interview.
24. Ibid.
25. Ibid.
26. McGrath, *Ooh, Aah, Paul McGrath*, p.128.
27. Ibid., p.116.
28. Ibid., p.118.
29. Ibid., p.121.
30. Ibid.
31. *News of the World*, 15 October 1989.
32. Gibson interview.
33. Mel Stein, *Gazza*, Bantam, 1996, pp.80–1.
34. Ibid., p.83.
35. Ferguson, *Managing My Life*, p.265.
36. Stein, *Gazza*, p.90.

37. Ibid., p.91.
38. Ibid., p.93.
39. Ibid.
40. Ferguson, *Managing My Life*, p.264.
41. Bryan Robson, *Glory, Glory Man United!*, CollinsWillow, 1992, p.55.
42. *Sun*, 26 January 1996, 26 June 1996.
43. Ibid., 26 June 1996.
44. *Daily Express*, 14 November 1987.
45. *The Times*, 12 May 1988.
46. Jim Leighton, *In the Firing Line*, Mainstream, 2000, pp.46–7.
47. Mark Hughes, *Sparky*, Mainstream, 1989, p.53.
48. Ibid., p.10.
49. *Manchester United* magazine, March 2001.
50. *Red Issue*, vol. 1, no. 4, May 1989.
51. Ferguson, *Six Years at United*, p.58.
52. Ferguson, *Managing My Life*, p.255.

Chapter 17: Orange-Juice Heroes
1. Jim Drewett and Alex Leith, *Alex Ferguson: Ten Glorious Years, 1986–1996*, André Deutsch, 1996, p.24.
2. *Class of '92* video, Paul Doherty International/VCI, 2000.
3. *Manchester Evening News*, 7 May 1988.
4. Drewett and Leith, *Alex Ferguson: Ten Glorious Years*, p.24.
5. *Manchester Evening News*, 7 January 1987.
6. *Class of '92*.
7. Alex Ferguson, *Six Years at United*, Mainstream, 1992, p.24.
8. *Class of '92*.
9. Drewett and Leith, *Alex Ferguson: Ten Glorious Years*, p.24.
10. *Independent*, 27 August 1988.
11. *Manchester Evening News*, 21 March 1987.
12. *World in Action*, Granada TV, 28

January 1980, and background notes.
13. Alex Ferguson, *A Year in the Life*, MUFC/Virgin, 1995, p.84.
14. Ryan Giggs, *My Story*, MUFC/Virgin, 1994, pp.11, 19.
15. Eric Harrison, *The View from the Dugout*, Parrs Wood Press, 2001, p.127.
16. *Class of '92*.
17. Ibid.
18. Simon Davies, interview with AEM.
19. Deiniol Graham, interview with AEM.
20. Russell Beardsmore, interview with AEM.
21. Kevin Pilkington, interview with AEM.
22. Harrison, *The View from the Dugout*, pp.127, 126.
23. Pilkington interview.
24. *News of the World*, 9 October 1988.
25. *Sun*, 27 January 1989.
26. *Daily Mirror*, 25 January 1989.
27. *Sunday Times*, 14 April 1996.

Chapter 18: 'Fergie, Fergie, on the Dole!'
1. *Sun* (Scottish edn), 19 May 1990.
2. Michael Crick and David Smith, *Manchester United: The Betrayal of a Legend*, Pan, 1990, p.283.
3. Michael Edelson, interview with MLC.
4. *Sun*, 10 August 1989.
5. Alex Ferguson, *Six Years at United*, Mainstream, 1992, p.28.
6. *Evening Standard*, 15 September 1989.
7. *Sun*, 29 January 1994.
8. Ibid., 25 September 1989.
9. Ibid., 3 February 1990.
10. *United Review*, v. Manchester City, 3 February 1990.
11. *Daily Mirror*, 26 September 1989.
12. Ibid., 16 August 1989.
13. Alex Ferguson, *Just Champion!*, MUFC, 1993, pp.28–9.

14. *Sunday Telegraph*, 3 November 1996.
15. *Observer*, 1 October 1989.
16. *Red News*, no. 78 (Fergie Special), summer 2001.
17. Ibid., vol. 3, no. 2, November 1989.
18. Ibid.
19. *The Alex Ferguson Story*, Granada TV/Patience Productions, ITV, 14 and 21 September 1998.
20. *Red Issue*, vol. 2, no. 6.
21. Jim Leighton, *In the Firing Line*, Mainstream, 2000, p.53.
22. *A Knight to Remember* video, Paul Doherty International/VCI, 1999.
23. *A Decade of Glory* video, Paul Doherty International/VCI, 1996.
24. *News of the World*, 7 January 1990.
25. Ferguson, *Just Champion!*, p.27.
26. *A Decade of Glory*.
27. *Manchester United* magazine, February 2000.
28. *Independent*, 6 November 1996.
29. *Daily Mirror*, 18 December 1989.
30. *Sun*, 6 January 1990.
31. Ibid., 28 December 1989.
32. *Manchester Evening News*, 2 January 1990.
33. *Today*, 6 January 1990.
34. Ferguson, *Just Champion!*, pp.30–1.
35. Stephen F. Kelly, *Fergie*, Headline, 1997, p.9.
36. *Sun*, 28 December 1989.
37. *A Decade of Glory*.
38. *Independent on Sunday*, 14 May 1995.
39. *Daily Telegraph*, 8 January 1990.
40. *Fergie's Dream Team* video, Paul Doherty Productions, 1994/95.
41. *Sun*, 7 April 1990.
42. *The Times*, 13 April 1990.
43. Ferguson, *Six Years at United*, p.77.
44. *A Decade of Glory*.
45. Leighton, *In the Firing Line*, pp.54, 51.
46. *Sun* (Scottish edn), 19 May 1990.

47. Ferguson, *Just Champion!*, p.45.
48. Leighton, *In the Firing Line*, p.51.
49. Ibid., p.52.
50. Ferguson, *Six Years at United*, p.69.
51. Alex Ferguson, *Managing My Life*, Coronet, 2000, p.287.
52. Alex Ferguson, *A Year in the Life*, MUFC/Virgin, 1995, p.253.
53. Archie Knox, interview with MLC.
54. *Daily Mirror*, 21 January 1993.
55. *Sun*, 1 December 1990.
56. *The United Family Tree*, BBC2, 19 May 1996.
57. *Daily Mirror*, 21 January 1993.
58. Ferguson, *Managing My Life*, p.243.
59. Clayton Blackmore, interview with AEM.
60. *Mail on Sunday*, 6 May 1990.
61. *Evening Standard*, 11 May 1990.

Chapter 19: Twenty-Five Years and Counting

1. *Today*, 17 August 1991.
2. *Red News*, no. 78 (Fergie Special), summer 2001.
3. *Sun*, 12 February 1991.
4. *Daily Mail*, 12 February 1991.
5. *Independent*, 11 April 1992.
6. *Sun*, 16 May 1991.
7. Alex Ferguson, *Just Champion!*, MUFC, 1993, pp.64, 68.
8. *Sun*, 19 October 1991.
9. *Aberdeen Evening Express*, 5 February 1979.
10. *Manchester United* magazine, February 2000.
11. Alex Ferguson, *Six Years at United*, Mainstream, 1992, p.93.
12. Ibid.
13. *Manchester United* magazine, July 1994.
14. *Daily Star*, 21 April 1992.
15. *Daily Express*, 21 April 1992.
16. Ferguson, *Six Years at United*, p.111.
17. Ferguson, *Just Champion!*, pp.51, 54.

18. *Daily Express*, 12 August 1992.
19. Ferguson, *Six Years at United*, p.109.
20. *Daily Mirror*, 19 December 1992.
21. Alex Ferguson, *Managing My Life*, Coronet, 2000, p.313.
22. Ibid., p.319.
23. *News of the World*, 15 November 1998.
24. *The Alex Ferguson Story*, Granada TV/Patience Productions, ITV, 14 and 21 September 1998.
25. *News of the World*, 15 November 1998.
26. *Manchester United* magazine, February 2000.
27. Shelley Webb, *Footballers' Wives Tell Their Tales*, Yellow Jersey Press, 1998, pp.40–1.
28. Ibid., p.41.
29. Ferguson, *Six Years at United*, pp.122–3.
30. Webb, *Footballers' Wives Tell Their Tales*, pp.42, 43.
31. *Sunday Times*, 24 January 1993.

Chapter 20: The Can-Opener
1. *Sunday Times*, 27 October 1996.
2. Alex Ferguson, *Just Champion!*, MUFC, 1993, p.82.
3. Ibid.
4. Ibid.
5. Ian Ridley, *Cantona*, Victor Gollancz, 1995, p.65.
6. Ibid., p.85.
7. *Red News*, no. 78 (Fergie Special), summer 2001.
8. *A Decade of Glory* video, Paul Doherty International/VCI, 1996.
9. Alex Ferguson, *A Year in the Life*, MUFC/Virgin, 1995, p.117.
10. Howard Kendall, interview with AEM.
11. Ferguson, *A Year in the Life*, p.38.
12. Ferguson, *Just Champion!*, p.72.
13. Ibid., pp.84, 72.
14. Alex Ferguson, *Six Years at United*, Mainstream, 1992, p.141.
15. Ibid., pp.141–2.

16. Ferguson, *Six Years at United*, p.146.
17. Ferguson, *Just Champion!*, pp.8–9.
18. Ibid., p.7.
19. Garth Dykes, *The United Alphabet*, ACL & Polar, 1994, p.67.
20. *Mail on Sunday*, 9 May 1993.
21. Alex Ferguson, *Managing My Life*, Coronet, 2000, p.338.
22. Ferguson, *Just Champion!*, pp.133, 129.
23. Ibid., p.128.
24. Jack Charlton, interview with AEM.
25. *Guardian*, 6 December 1994.
26. *Daily Mirror*, 31 December 1993.
27. Peter Schmeichel, *The Autobiography*, Virgin, 1999, pp.108, 110.
28. Ibid., p.111.
29. Ibid.
30. Andrei Kanchelskis, *Kanchelskis*, MUFC/Virgin, 1995, p.104.
31. *Manchester United* magazine, February 2000.
32. Ibid.
33. David Emery, *Double Winners*, Simon & Schuster, 1994, p.94.
34. *Sunday Times*, 27 March 1994.
35. Ibid.
36. Ferguson, *Managing My Life*, p.340.
37. *Independent*, 26 March 1994.
38. Ferguson, *Managing My Life*, pp.341–2, 341.
39. Eric Cantona, interview with MLC.
40. *Daily Telegraph*, 9 May 1994.

Chapter 21: Losing the Plot
1. *Daily Express*, 3 November 1994.
2. Kevin Pilkington, interview with AEM.
3. *Guardian*, 6 December 1994.
4. Alex Ferguson, *Just Champion!*, MUFC, 1993, p.45.
5. *A Decade of Glory* video, Paul Doherty International/VCI, 1996.
6. Joe Royle, interview with AEM.
7. Frank Clark, interview with AEM.

8. Royle interview.
9. Alex Ferguson, *A Year in the Life*, MUFC/Virgin, 1995, p.140.
10. Clark interview.
11. Ferguson, *A Year in the Life*, p.167.
12. Keith Gillespie, interview with AEM.
13. Alex Ferguson, *Six Years at United*, Mainstream, 1992, p.147.
14. Colin Gibson, interview with AEM.
15. Gillespie interview.
16. Ibid.
17. Gary Twynham, interview with AEM.
18. Ian Ridley, *Cantona*, Victor Gollancz, 1995, p.27.
19. Ibid., p.28.
20. *News of the World*, 29 January 1995.
21. Ferguson, *A Year in the Life*, p.188.
22. Sir Richard Greenbury, interview with MLC.
23. Ridley, *Cantona*, p.125.
24. *Daily Express*, 3 April 1995.
25. *Sunday Telegraph*, 9 April 1995.
26. *A Decade of Glory* video.
27. Kenny Dalglish, interview with AEM.
28. Ferguson, *A Year in the Life*, p.277.
29. Royle interview.
30. Alex Ferguson, *Managing My Life*, Coronet, 2000, p.360.
31. Joe Royle, interview with AEM.
32. *Daily Express*, 7 August 1995.
33. Mick Hucknall, interview with MLC.
34. *Daily Mail*, 6 June 1995.
35. *Manchester Evening News*, 23 June 1995.
36. Richard Kurt, interview with MLC.
37. IMUSA newsletter, July 1995.
38. Kurt interview.
39. *Sunday Mirror*, 16 July 1995.
40. *News of the World*, 23 July 1995.
41. Kurt interview.
42. *People*, 19 November 1995.
43. Ferguson, *Managing My Life*, p.362.
44. *A Decade of Glory*.
45. Andrei Kanchelskis, *Kanchelskis*, MUFC/Virgin, 1995, p.129.
46. *Daily Mirror*, 10 November 1995.
47. *Daily Star*, 24 June 1995.
48. *Guardian*, 12 July 1995.
49. Ferguson, *Managing My Life*, pp.308–9.
50. *Express*, 3 August 1999.
51. Ferguson, *Managing My Life*, p.364.
52. *Evening Standard*, 11 September 1995.
53. *Daily Express*, 23 December 1994.
54. Ferguson, *Managing My Life*, p.304.
55. Russell Beardsmore, interview with AEM.
56. FA Premier League Inquiry, Kanchelskis report, 1997, pp.2–3.
57. Ibid.
58. *Sunday Telegraph*, 13 August 1995.
59. Ferguson, *Managing My Life*, p.371.
60. Ibid., p.366.
61. *Evening Standard*, 11 September 1995.

Chapter 22: Nothing With Kids

1. *Match of the Day*, BBC1, 19 August 1995.
2. Keith Gillespie, interview with AEM.
3. Ibid.
4. *Match of the Day*, BBC1, 19 August 1995.
5. Alex Ferguson, *Just Champion!*, MUFC, 1993, p.147.
6. *United Review*, v. Port Vale, 5 October 1994.
7. Alex Ferguson, *A Year in the Life*, MUFC/Virgin, 1995, p.41.
8. Ibid., p.44.
9. Edward Freedman, interview with MLC.
10. *Daily Telegraph*, 18 April 1996.
11. *Daily Mail*, 19 April 1996.
12. *The Times*, 30 April 1996.
13. *Daily Star*, 3 February 1996.

14. Alex Ferguson, *Managing My Life*, Coronet, 2000, p.378.
15. Graham Kelly, *Sweet FA*, CollinsWillow, 1999, p.235.
16. Ibid., p.236.
17. Mihir Bose, *Manchester Unlimited*, Orion, 1999, p.248.
18. *United Review*, v. Wimbledon, 26 August 1995.
19. Ferguson, *Managing My Life*, p.378.
20. *Daily Mail*, 17 May 1996.
21. *Daily Telegraph*, 30 January 1996.
22. *Independent*, 19 May 1996.
23. *Daily Mirror*, 4 May 1995.
24. Alex Ferguson, *A Will to Win*, André Deutsch, 1997, p.164.
25. *Birmingham Post*, 22 July 2000.
26. Chris Evans, interview with CPG.
27. Ferguson, *A Will to Win*, p.19.
28. *Sunday Telegraph*, 11 August 1996.
29. Ferguson, *A Will to Win*, p.26.
30. *Mail on Sunday*, 3 November 1996.
31. Ferguson, *A Will to Win*, pp.41–2.
32. Ibid., p.263.
33. *The Alex Ferguson Story*, Granada TV/Patience Productions, ITV, 14 and 21 September 1998.
34. Kevin Pilkington, interview with AEM.

Chapter 23: 'Football, eh? Bloody Hell!'

1. Alex Ferguson, *A Will to Win*, André Deutsch, 1997, p.206.
2. Alex Ferguson, *Managing My Life*, Coronet, 2000, p.395.
3. Ibid., p.396.
4. Alex Fynn and Lynton Guest, *For Love or Money*, Boxtree, 1998, pp.30–1.
5. Ferguson, *A Will to Win*, p.139.
6. Ferguson, *Managing My Life*, p.389.
7. Ibid., p.390.
8. *The Times*, 17 April 1998.
9. *Red News*, no. 55.
10. Ferguson, *Managing My Life*, p.441.
11. Mihir Bose, *Manchester Unlimited*, Orion, 1999, pp.68, 70–1.
12. Ferguson, *Managing My Life*, pp.469–70.
13. *Manchester United* magazine, March 1999.
14. *The Times*, 10 September 1998.
15. Ferguson, *Managing My Life*, p.441.
16. *Guardian*, 12 August 1999.
17. Keith Harris, interview with MLC.
18. Alex Ferguson, *The Unique Treble*, Hodder & Stoughton, 2000, p.12.
19. *Guardian*, 17 February 1999.
20. *A Knight to Remember* video, Paul Doherty International/VCI, 1999.
21. *Manchester United* magazine, February 1999.
22. *Sun*, 5 December 1998.
23. Andy Cole, *The Autobiography*, André Deutsch, 1999, pp.134–8.
24. Dave Fevre, interview with AEM.
25. Ibid.
26. Ferguson, *The Unique Treble*, pp.134–5.
27. Ken Ferris, *Manchester United: Tragedy, Destiny, History*, Mainstream, 2001, p.324.
28. *The Alex Ferguson Story*, Granada TV/Patience Productions, ITV, 14 and 21 September 1998.
29. Ferguson, *The Unique Treble*, p.10.
30. Ibid.
31. Ibid., p.157.
32. Cole, *The Autobiography*, p.203.
33. Fevre interview.
34. Jaap Stam, *Head to Head*, CollinsWillow, 2001, p.74.
35. Ferguson, *Managing My Life*, p.439.
36. *The Alex Ferguson Story*.
37. Programme, Manchester United v. Rest of the World XI, Alex Ferguson Testimonial, 11 October 1999.
38. Ferris, *Manchester United: Tragedy, Destiny, History*, pp.368–9.
39. Stam, *Head to Head*, p.74.

40. Programme, Manchester United v. Rest of the World XI, Alex Ferguson Testimonial, 11 October 1999.
41. Ferris, *Manchester United: Tragedy, Destiny, History*, p.369.
42. *The Treble* video, Paul Doherty International, 1999.

Chapter 24: Taking on the World
1. *Knowing the Score* video, Executive Business Channel/Nottingham Business School, 2000.
2. Alastair Campbell, conversation with MLC.
3. *Manchester United* magazine, December 2000.
4. Bill Campbell, interview with MLC.
5. Alex Ferguson, *Managing My Life*, Hodder & Stoughton, 1999, p.442.
6. Ibid., pp.394, 415.
7. *Mail on Sunday*, 6 December 1998.
8. Alex Ferguson, *Managing My Life*, Coronet, 2000, p.414.
9. *Match of the Day*, BBC1, 14 May 1994.
10. *Sun*, 13 March 1995.
11. Alex Ferguson, *A Year in the Life*, MUFC/Virgin, 1995, p.239.
12. *Manchester United* magazine, October 1999.
13. David O'Leary, *Leeds United on Trial*, Little, Brown, 2002, p.133.
14. Howard Kendall, interview with AEM.
15. *Mirror*, 7 August 1999.
16. Dave Fevre, interview with AEM.
17. Ibid.
18. *Mirror*, 23 February 2000.
19. O'Leary, *Leeds United on Trial*, p.133.
20. Fevre interview.
21. *Mirror*, 5 August 1999.
22. Ferguson, *Managing My Life*, p.462.
23. *Guardian*, 8 October 2001.

24. *Mirror*, 29 April 1997.
25. Ibid.
26. *Chiles on Saturday*, BBC Radio 5, 4 March 2000.
27. *Sunday Mirror*, 14 May 1995.
28. *Independent*, 16 November 1991.
29. *New Labour New Britain*, summer 1996.
30. *Independent on Sunday*, 14 May 1995.
31. Martin Stephen, interview with MLC.
32. Victoria Beckham, *Learning to Fly*, Michael Joseph, 2001, p.283.
33. Ferguson, *Managing My Life*, p.473.
34. Beckham, *Learning to Fly*, pp.248–9, 284.
35. Ferguson, *Managing My Life*, p.452.
36. Ibid., p.447.
37. *Independent*, 28 April 2001.
38. *Express*, 22 August 2000.
39. *Daily Express*, 3 May 2001.
40. *Daily Telegraph*, 25 April 2001.
41. *The World at Their Feet*, Channel 4, 3 December 2001.
42. Mick Hucknall, interview with MLC.
43. Sean Hamil (ed.), *The Changing Face of the Football Business*, Frank Cass, 2001, p.viii.
44. *United Shareholder*, October 2000.
45. *Evening Standard*, 11 September 1995.
46. Sir Richard Greenbury, interview with MLC.
47. *Chiles on Saturday*, BBC Radio 5, 4 March 2000.
48. Hucknall interview.
49. Press Association, 31 May 2001.

Chapter 25: Jason and the Larger Noughts
1. *Manchester United* magazine, February 2000.
2. *Sun*, 26 July 1987.
3. Alex Ferguson, *A Year in the Life*, MUFC/Virgin, 1995, p.116.

4. *Manchester United* magazine, December 1995.
5. Mike Williams, interview with AEM.
6. Howard Kendall, interview with AEM.
7. Paul Doherty, e-mail to author.
8. Ibid.
9. Alex Ferguson, *A Will to Win*, André Deutsch, 1997, p.227.
10. Paul Stretford, interview with AEM.
11. *Daily Mail*, 6 November 2001.
12. www.ananova.com, 6 November 2001.
13. *News of the World*, 15 August 1999.
14. Josh Howard, interview with AEM.
15. Ibid.
16. Beverley Howard, interview with AEM.
17. Paul Wheatcroft, interview with AEM.
18. Dominic Studley, interview with AEM.
19. Ibid.
20. J. Howard interview.
21. Steve Lock, interview with AEM.
22. *United We Stand*, October 1999.
23. *Manchester Evening News*, 3 April 2000.
24. Lock interview.
25. Bryan Flynn, interview with AEM.
26. *Manchester United* magazine, February 2000.
27. Stretford interview.
28. David Beckham, *My World*, Hodder & Stoughton, 2000, p.88.
29. Francis Martin, interview with AEM.
30. Peter Kenyon, interview with MLC.
31. *Mail on Sunday*, 2 September 2001.
32. Martin interview.
33. Ibid.
34. Williams interview.
35. Jaap Stam, *Head to Head*, CollinsWillow, 2001, p.18.
36. *Mirror*, 5 December 2001.
37. Williams interview.
38. *Daily Telegraph*, 30 August 2001.
39. *Mail on Sunday*, 2 September 2001.
40. Manchester United PLC annual report, 2001, p.2.
41. www.soccernet.com, 22 November 2001.
42. *Manchester Evening News*, 16 November 2001.
43. Williams interview.
44. David Healy, interview with AEM.
45. John Curtis, interview with AEM.
46. Jonathan Barnett, interview with AEM.
47. *Sunday Times*, 10 February 2002.
48. *Daily Express*, 20 March 2002.
49. *Observer*, 3 March 2002.

Chapter 26: 'You Know the Rules Here'
1. *Daily Express*, 7 May 1996.
2. David Thomas, conversation with MLC.
3. Andy Melvin, e-mail to author.
4. Monte Fresco, letter to Simon & Schuster, 16 January 2002.
5. Alex Ferguson, *A Will to Win*, André Deutsch, 1997, p.77.
6. *Radio Times*, 12 August 1995.
7. *Sunday People*, 20 March 1994.
8. Russell Beardsmore, interview with AEM.
9. David Anderson, interview with MLC.
10. Bob Cass, interview with MLC.
11. Alex Ferguson, *Managing My Life*, Coronet, 2000, pp.383–4.
12. *The Times*, 29 December 2001.
13. Alex Ferguson, *A Year in the Life*, MUFC/Virgin, 1995, p.6.
14. Frank Clark, interview with AEM.
15. *Match of the Day* magazine, September 2000.
16. *News of the World*, 10 April 1994.
17. Anderson interview.
18. Ken Lawrence, interview with MLC.
19. Anderson interview.
20. Frank Gilfeather, interview with APD.

21. Ibid.
22. Joe Harper, interview with APD.
23. Anderson interview.
24. Ibid.
25. www.ananova.com, 28 February 2002.
26. *Sun*, 19 January 1993.
27. *Guardian*, 24 November 2001.
28. Tommy Docherty, interview with MLC.
29. *Match of the Day* magazine, September 2000.
30. Tim Glynne-Jones, interview with MLC.
31. Alan Green, *The Green Line*, Headline, 2000, p.30.
32. Untransmitted *Match of the Day* recording, 28 October 1995.
33. Green, *The Green Line*, p.21.
34. Alan Green, interview with MLC.
35. Ken Barnes, interview with AEM.
36. Cass interview.
37. Harry Harris, *The Ferguson Effect*, Orion, 1999, p.139.
38. Ferguson, *A Will to Win*, p.182.
39. *Sunday Times*, 21 June 1998.
40. Gilfeather interview.
41. Ferguson, *A Will to Win*, p.170.
42. *News of the World*, 30 December 2001.
43. Ibid.
44. *Scotsman*, 1 January 2002.

Chapter 27: Extra Time
1. *Sun*, 12 February 2002.
2. *Daily Mail*, 15 May 2001.
3. *Guardian*, 19 May 2001.
4. George Ramsay, interview with MLC.
5. *Sun*, 6 February 1993.
6. *Sun* (Scottish edn), 4 May 1994.
7. *The Times*, 18 July 2000.
8. *Observer Sport Monthly*, December 2001.

9. *Guardian*, 21 July 2001.
10. *Daily Express*, 21 May 2001.
11. *Guardian*, 21 July 2001.
12. *Observer Sport Monthly*, December 2001.
13. *Daily Telegraph*, 15 May 2000.
14. *Racing Post*, 31 August 2001.
15. Ibid.
16. *The Times*, 23 February 2002.
17. *Mirror*, 13 August 2001.
18. Jaap Stam, *Head to Head*, CollinsWillow, 2001, pp.15–16.
19. *Mirror*, 21 August 2001.
20. Stam, *Head to Head*, p.115.
21. Ibid., pp.115–16.
22. Ibid., p.159.
23. Mike Williams, interview with AEM.
24. www.ananova.com, 27 August 2001.
25. *The Times*, 28 August 2001.
26. *Sun*, 27 August 2001.
27. Williams interview.
28. *Daily Express*, 8 November 2001.
29. *The Times*, 7 November 2001.
30. www.ananova.com, 24 February 2002.
31. *Sunday Times*, 10 February 2002.
32. BBC Ceefax, 30 January 2002.
33. *Mail on Sunday*, 10 February 2002.
34. *Scotsman*, 6 February 2002.
35. *Mail on Sunday*, 10 February 2002.
36. Ibid.
37. *Sunday Times*, 10 February 2002.
38. *The Times*, 6 February 2002.
39. *Mail on Sunday*, 10 February 2002.

Epilogue
1. Gary Twynham, interview with AEM.
2. *Guardian*, 23 February 2002.

Index

AF denotes Alex Ferguson
MUFC denotes Manchester United

McGibbon, Pat, 403
McGowan, Mick, 25–6
McGrain, Danny, 77
McGrath, Paul, 258, 275, 276–7, 283,
   283–7, 346, 448; at Aston Villa, 357;
   disciplinary hearing, 284–5; and
   drinking, 277–8, 283, 284; leaves
   MUFC, 286
McGregor, Jim, 284, 344
McGuinness, Wilf, 248, 267, 332,
   533
McHardy, Deirdrie, 260, 517
Machin, Mel, 313
McIlvanney, Hugh, 8, 229, 368, 369,
   446, 447, 506, 523
Mackay, Calum, 38, 41, 42–5
Mackay, Malcolm, 33
McKimmie, Stewart, 181–2, 198
McKinlay, Alan, 38, 44
McKinnon, Ronnie, 24, 80, 85, 86
McLaughlin, John, 61, 62, 63, 64
McLean, George 'Dandy', 70, 71, 97–8,
   99
McLean, Jim, 165, 173
McLeish, Alex, 165–6, 197, 226, 469; at
   Aberdeen, 167, 178, 179, 181, 185,
   186, 189, 194, 200, 204, 224–5;
   plays for Scotland, 166, 205, 225,
   231; relationship with AF, 206,
   223–4; and World Cup, 245
MacLeod, Ally, 97, 108, 142–3, 157,
   158, 159–60, 241
McLindon, Dan, 55
McManaman, Steve, 506
McManus, J. P., 538, 539, 540
McMaster, John, 166, 200
McMenemy, Lawrie, 251, 252
McNee, Gerry, 523, 525, 535
McNeill, Billy, 63, 66, 80, 81, 101, 114,
   157–8, 160, 192, 225, 256
MacPherson, Archie, 213
McRae, Alan, 227
Magnier, John, 538, 539–40
Magnier, Sue, 539
Mail on Sunday, 511, 523, 524, 528
Maiorana, Jules, 303, 305
Managing My Life (Ferguson), 142, 369,
   446–50, 453, 461
Manchester City: v MUFC, 309–10;
   youth programme, 297
Manchester Evening News, 315, 396,
   508–9, 523–4

Manchester Grammar School (MGS),
   459–60
Manchester United: (1987–88) season,
   271–4; (1988–89), 294–5;
   (1989–90), 309–10, 316, 325;
   (1990–91), 328–9, 331; (1991–92),
   335–9, 342, 346–7; (1992–93),
   353–4, 355–6, 357–9; (1993–94),
   363–4, 367, 369–72; (1994–95),
   373, 383–6, 398; (1995–96), 401–6,
   408; (1996–97), 414–15; (1997–98),
   417–18; (1998–99), 431–2, 435–6;
   (1999–2000), 462–5; (2000–01),
   531–2; (2001–02), 541, 545–9; AF
   and supporters/fans, 357; AF's
   approach and style of management,
   266–7; AF's contract/pay and
   disagreements over, 255–6, 335, 361,
   398–9, 406–7, 408, 425; AF's
   dealings with Rune Hauge, 394–5,
   517; AF's decision not to retire and
   three-year contract with, 551–4; AF's
   devotion to, 469; AF's handling of
   media, 508–29; AF's outbursts, 275,
   281, 374–5; AF's post-retirement role
   and contract issue, 532–6; AF's pre-
   match press conferences, 511–12;
   AF's stance towards players'
   international careers and response to
   international call-ups, 343–5; AF's
   testimonial year, 487–92;
   appointment of AF as manager,
   249–56; Atkinson and AF
   contrasted, 265–6; attempt to buy
   Gascoigne, 288–91; attempt to buy
   Shearer, 412–13; attendances, 271,
   273–4, 295, 325; bad state of pitch,
   259–60; becomes full public
   company and floating of on stock
   exchange, 335; BSkyB takeover bid,
   424, 427–30; buying of players by
   Atkinson, 261–2; buying of players
   and transfers by AF, 269–71, 273,
   276, 280–1, 293–4, 308–9, 352–3,
   361–2, 377, 413–14, 417, 421–2,
   464–5, 465–6, 467, 540–41, 549;
   Cantona's attack on fan, 380–3;
   constraints on being a PLC, 421,
   422; criticism of AF after bad results,
   309–15; dealing with youngsters by
   AF, 301–3; disappointments on
   transfer front and financial